THE ULTIMATE
ENCYCLOPEDIA OF
*W*INE

Project Editor: Martin Corteel
Project art direction: Paul Messam
Production: Sarah Schuman
Picture research: Charlotte Bush
Designer: Lisa Pettibone

Printed and bound in Dubai

Author's acknowledgements
Writing this book would not have been
possible without the help and hospitality
of countless wine-makers around the world
who at various times have been
extraordinarily generous with their time
and expertise. I should also like to give
specific thanks to Michael Stevenson,
Louise Abbott, Simon Woods, Simon
Clarke, Justin Howard-Sneyd, Philippa
Rome, Piers Russell-Cobb, Margaret Rand,
Martin Corteel and Charlotte Bush, all of
whom, in their individual ways were
crucial to the production of the book. They
all deserve to share the praise for the book;
all the failings are my responsibility alone.

(Previous page) Window at Silver Oak Winery,
Napa Valley, California

(Opposite) Grape picking at Martilly les
Brancion, France

(Contents pages) (Clockwise from top left)
Barrels at Bodegas Torres, Spain; Yvorne,
Switzerland; Lindemans Winery, Hunter Valley,
Australia; Station Hills, Washington State, USA;
Douro Valley, Portugal; Château Cos d'Estournel,
Médoc, France; Côtes de Buzet, France

THE ULTIMATE
ENCYCLOPEDIA OF
*W*INE

ROBERT JOSEPH

CARLTON

CONTENTS

$\mathcal{I}$NTRODUCTION

$\mathcal{I}$F YOU drink wine anywhere in the world today, you are in luck – this is the best time there has ever been to do so. We are living in the middle of a revolution, with better wines and a wider range of wines than ever before. The only problem is that, as the number and the variety of wines has grown, and as Australia, Canada, Uruguay and Zimbabwe have all lined up to compete with France, Italy and Germany, choosing a bottle has become a lot more confusing. It was bad enough when you had to decide between such very different French wines as Pouilly-Fuissé, Pouilly-Fumé and Pouilly-sur-Loire, but nowadays you are as likely to be offered a dozen Chardonnays from half a dozen different countries. How does anyone know where to start?

Wine was one of the subjects that somehow I never got round to learning at school. Like how to dance without stepping on your partner's toes, to tell a weed from a baby geranium and how to match the right shoes to the right trousers, the trick of how to choose a bottle of wine was just one of those adult skills I was supposed to pick up as I went along. At first, wine seemed rather easier to bluff my way around than the dance floor; like most other people, I simply found a few styles I liked – Burgundy, Rioja, Muscadet, Côtes du Rhône – and stuck to them.

Somehow, though, I couldn't prevent my attention wandering across to all those other names on the wine list, to that bewildering parade of labels and bottle shapes on the off-licence shelf. What was I missing by playing safe?

So, I decided to learn about wine. And then almost gave up before I even began. The people who "knew" about it all seemed the same to me – men (very few women were then acknowledged to be experts) who had all been to the right school, where they had presumably learned all about such impenetrable wine expressions as "bouquet", "elegant" and "austere", and who knew without thinking whether a Bordeaux château was a third or fifth "growth".

What I wanted to know was *why* the wines I liked tasted the way they did, why they all had such deliciously individual flavours, and why their prices varied so widely. And when I went looking for the answers to these kinds of question, the pinstriped experts, "elegant" and "austere" as they were themselves, didn't seem able to help me very much.

Then I met my first wine-maker – a whiskery old Frenchman in Burgundy, with more chins than fingers. He spoke no English, and my schoolbook French was no match for the situation. But he was an enthusiast. As he drew a glassful of his wine from a barrel, sniffed it as though it were some new kind of flower and took a copious mouthful, licking his lips thoughtfully to savour every drop, he came alive. Eagerly, he led me out into the vineyard behind his house, trying to make me understand what it was that made his wine taste the way it did, and why he thought that the Chardonnay grape was the best variety in the world. Our communication difficulties seemed to melt away – here, at last, was someone who spoke my language.

That old Frenchman had probably rarely tasted a wine produced more than a few kilometres from his cellar door; the idea that wine-makers in Australia might be making good wine from the Chardonnay using the same methods as he was, ageing it in the same kinds of barrels, made out of oak from the same French forests, would almost certainly have made him break out into one of his rare, disbelieving smiles.

Today, the Burgundy from his estate – now made by his son – is sold all over the world alongside Chardonnays from Australia, California, Chile, Bulgaria, Italy and apparently almost everywhere else on earth.

But wherever it comes from and whatever grape it is made from, wine is all manner of things at once. It can be the most basic of drinks, served in French cafés from a cracked jug or, as in South America, from the waxed cartons we more often expect to contain milk. But then again, in a dust-caked bottle with a scarcely legible label, it can also be the liquid equivalent of an old master, an object of mystery, a work of art to be treated with reverence or an investment to be hoarded behind lock and key.

Wine has a weird and unique relationship with time. If you can afford the few hundred thousand dollars it would cost, you could buy yourself a bottle of the wine Thomas Jefferson bought by the barrel two centuries ago as a young diplomat in France. For a thousand dollars, you could probably still pick up a pre-Revolutionary Russian wine from the Czar's own cellars. For the price of a dinner for two in a reasonable restaurant, you can still buy a bottle of 1963 port, made when the world was still reeling from the news of Kennedy's assassination. And even when you spend a modest few pounds on a 1989 Reserve Cabernet Sauvignon from Bulgaria or Hungary, you're buying wine made from grapes picked by men and women whose harvest songs celebrated the taste of freedom.

Old wine buffs reminisce about the "good old days" when 2 or 3 old pence would buy a pint of vintage port and still leave change for a glass or two of Lafite, but it is the wine drinkers of the end of the twentieth century who can have the greater fun – and the greater value for money.

In the pages that follow, we will travel around the world of wine, from grape to glass, from Albania to Zimbabwe, from the grandest of Bordeaux châteaux to the tiniest, most traditional estate in Chianti and the most high-tech of million-dollar wineries in California's Napa Valley. I can't say that the journey will turn you into an instant wine expert, but it will, I hope, give you confidence when buying your wine and more enjoyment in drinking it, as well as introducing you to thousands of different wines, producers and, most importantly, flavours.

Robert Joseph
LONDON,
JULY 1996

Honeycomb effect: Bottles of vintage port

$\mathscr{F}$ROM OLD TO NEW

$\mathscr{W}$INE-MAKING is probably the world's second oldest profession. Since long before an unknown Babylonian attached a cylindrical seal to an *amphora* 6,000 years ago, wine of one kind or another has made people throughout most of the civilized world uproariously drunk, gloriously poetic and thoroughly romantic. More often than not, though, it has quite simply slaked their thirst and made them rather happy.

An essential thing to remember about wine is that, despite the eager efforts of the anti-alcohol campaigners to associate wine with tobacco and almost every other kind of health-endangering drug, it is – or at least it should be – one of the most natural and, when drunk in moderation, healthiest substances man consumes.

Unlike cigarettes, which are a relatively sophisticated human invention, wine more or less created itself. No one knows quite when man – or more probably woman – first discovered this phenomenon, but it could have been at any time since humans became capable of picking and appreciating fruit. According to one legend, it was Noah who, soon after grounding his ark in what we would now call Turkey, noticed that one of his goats was getting its kicks by nibbling at grapes that had begun to ferment in the sun. Noah became not only the first wine-maker, but also the first wine-drinker; as the Bible says, he "planted a vineyard: and he drank of the wine, and was drunken; and he was uncovered within his tent…". A state with which many a more modern wine-drinker will have ample sympathy.

The Persians agree that the joys of wine were discovered by accident, but disagree on the sex of the discoverer. King Jamshid apparently used to store grapes in jars where they were supposed to turn into raisins that could be eaten during the winter. One jar was set aside as poisonous because its contents were frothy, and it was from this unprepossessing liquid that a young girl, bent on suicide, drew what she thought would be her last drink. Needless to say, a few sips were enough to give her a taste for both life and wine.

From those earliest vintages in what we now call the Middle East, and the first

How it began: The Ancient World, as seen by Hendrick van Borlen and Jan Brueghel in "Bacchanal", 1620

attempts at wine-making in the Caucasian republic of Georgia – where vines are thought to have been cultivated by man in 5,000 BC – the story of wine has unfolded alongside the history of most of the civilized world.

Egypt has never enjoyed a dazzling international reputation for its wines, though archaeologists know they have been made for at least 3,000 years. Nor, despite the current renaissance of the viticulture there, has China. Vines were imported from Persia in 128 BC and some 1,300 years later Marco Polo claimed to have enjoyed drinking the wine they produced. However, many of the other regions we know today, such as Bordeaux, the Rhine and Mosel, had already been established by the time the Romans arrived in Britain in 55 AD.

The Romans took their wines seriously, separating *amphorae* of different quality and laying down the best vintages for as long as a century. They made sure to have wine to drink wherever they went, even planting vines in England – in Wiltshire,

Gloucestershire and London – to save the trouble of importing wine from other parts of the empire. (Unfortunately for those who claim a Roman heritage for English wine, archaeological remains suggest that, then as now, imported wine – principally from Italy, Spain and Germany, and possibly Bordeaux – was far more popular than the stuff made in the vineyards of the chilly new colony.)

A thousand years later, in 1154, King Henry II married Eleanor of Aquitaine and took control of Bordeaux. Although that region fell out of English hands 300 years later, the relationship was established and "claret" became the "Englishman's drink" it has always remained. Indeed, in the mid-thirteenth century, imports of Bordeaux wine reached the heady figure of over 30 million bottles per year.

As countries and regions quarrelled, made treaties and expelled their religious minorities, over the centuries wine travelled throughout the continent. During this time, most vineyards were in the hands of the church – which explains why English wine-making came to such an abrupt halt in the sixteenth century when Henry VIII dissolved the monasteries, and why, 200 years later, many of France's wine regions were thrown into such turmoil by the anti-clerical decrees of the Revolution.

Politics of another kind helped to create a wholly new style of wine when, following a falling-out between Britain and France in the seventeenth century, British merchants had to look elsewhere for their red wine. The country they turned to was Portugal, and the wine they found and fortified, to make it more stable for the long sea journey home, was port.

Port was thus essentially a British invention – hence the survival today of British-owned port houses such as Cockburn, Dow's and Taylor's. But this was not the only fortified wine into which the British were dipping their toes. In Jerez, merchants named Williams, Humbert and Harvey created the market for sherry; in Madeira, it was a soldier called Blandy; in Marsala, a Liverpudlian called Woodhouse.

It was also the English who – with the help of the Irish – built up some of the best estates in Bordeaux, as is clear from the names of such illustrious châteaux as Lynch-Bages, Léoville-Barton, Smith-Haut-Lafitte and Cantenac-Brown.

Elsewhere, immigrants from a wide range of countries introduced wine to the New World: the Dutch in South Africa, Spanish missionaries in Chile and California. Sometimes traces of the pioneers' roots are to be found in the wines. In Australia's Barossa Valley, some of the wine-makers still speak a dialect of German – and make top-class Riesling. Familiar names such as Heitz, Mondavi and Paul Masson reveal the diverse set of European influences which have helped to create the wine industry in California.

By the late nineteenth century, political disputes notwithstanding, it appeared as though nothing could stop the progress of wine-making and the trading of wine throughout the western world. Then disaster struck – in the shape of a tiny louse, *phylloxera vastatrix*, whose ideal diet consisted of fresh vine roots.

In its native North America, *phylloxera* caused little damage; there was almost no wine being produced and much of what was made came from a species of vine that was naturally resistant to the louse. The moment it arrived in Europe, however, the louse started behaving like a cake addict in a patisserie. Gradually, but inexorably, it munched its way across the continent.

The Europeans finally admitted defeat and accepted that the only way they could protect their livelihood was by grafting the types of vine they had traditionally grown onto the same kind of resistant stock that flourished naturally in North America. Since the beginning of this century, almost every wine vine in the world – with the exception of those planted in a few areas that are geographically isolated or enjoy some kind of natural protection (the *phylloxera* louse hates sand, for example) – has been grafted onto American rootstock.

The provision of resistant rootstock was the Americans' first contribution to the way wine was made around the world. During this century, since the repeal of Prohibition in 1933, the influence of America – to be more precise, California – has been felt almost everywhere; it is the Californians, more than anyone else, who have developed grape-growing and wine-making from a blend of tradition-bound agriculture and cooking into a highly sophisticated science. And, ironically, in the 1980s it was the Californians who, overestimating the resistance of the rootstocks they had chosen to plant, saw many of their best vineyards devastated by the return of the *phylloxera* louse which had been effectively overcome elsewhere.

Although the number of places where wine is produced has increased enormously, and scientific knowledge and equipment have enabled modern wineries to make more and better wine more consistently than in the past, the fundamental principles are still the same as they were 3,400 years ago, when a man called Kha'y was producing wine for Tutankhamun.

To make good wine, you need the right kind of grapes, the right piece of land, the right climate and the right skills. Today, for example, an Australian wine-maker who talks proudly about his new French oak barrels is, in fact, using pretty much the same kind of casks as the Romans.

And to appreciate wine, all you have to do is to take the trouble to notice how it can differ in flavour and quality – though you might decide not to go as far as the host who, Pliny the Younger wrote, "had apportioned in small flagons three different sorts of wine… . One was for himself and me; the next for his friends of a lower order … and the third for his own freed-men and mine". Nor as far as Richard Nixon who, 2,000 years later, according to Bob Woodward and Carl Bernstein in *All the President's Men*, served visiting congress-men "a rather good six-dollar wine" while he enjoyed "his favourite, a 1966 Château Margaux which sold for about $30 a bottle". Some things never change.

*The **modern world**: Industrial-scale processing of skins and pips at Lindemans winery in Australia*

$\mathcal{T}$HE GRAPES

$\mathcal{J}$N A WORLD where Chardonnay has almost become just another word for dryish white wine, it is chastening to think that, as recently as the early 1980s, the idea of asking for a wine by the name of the grape rather than the region was still quite novel. Even today wine-drinkers in countries like France, Italy, Portugal and Spain are generally blissfully ignorant of the grapes used to produce their favourite wines. Just stop any middle-aged Frenchman with a supermarket trolley full of bargain bottles of Bordeaux Rouge and Bourgogne Blanc and ask him to name the types of grape from which those wines were made. I'll bet that he will be no more able to provide a correct reply than if you had wanted him to identify one of the more obscure components of the engine of his car.

And that, with few exceptions, is pretty much the way traditional Europeans view grapes – as component parts, of secondary importance to the region in which a wine is made. A Burgundian wine-maker might admit that his Chablis is made solely from Chardonnay grapes, but would never allow it to be sold in a line-up of non-French wines bearing the name of that grape on their label, any more than a caviar merchant would wish his beluga to be stacked among the free-range eggs. Besides, he might say, his wine is an exception to the rule: most of the classics are blends of different varieties.

In the New World, it is often the other way round. Ask an Australian to point out on a map where the Chardonnay he has just bought was made and he'll most probably admit his ignorance. And you can't really blame him: some of Australia's best-selling Chardonnays simply declare themselves to be the produce of south-eastern Australia, a designation covering all three of Australia's principal wine-making states and some 90 per cent of the nation's vineyards.

The two views appear to be incompatible, but there is a gradual and inexorable coming-together. In France, despite official efforts to ban grape names from the labels of all but a few traditional wines, it is now common to see white Bordeaux describing itself as Sauvignon Blanc. Meanwhile, throughout the New World, there is a growing trend toward creating regional appellations; the wine-makers of Margaret River and Marlborough, for example, take pains to ensure that their customers are left in no doubt where their respective Sauvignon Blancs are made.

Similarly, while the Chardonnay, Cabernet Sauvignon and Merlot are still the grapes most New-World producers are rushing to plant, they are increasingly being blended with other varieties – often in delicious, but previously unimagined, cocktails.

How it all starts: *Taking the grapes to the winery in the time-honoured fashion*

57 VARIETIES?

There are about 20 different species of grapevine in the world, but only one, *vitis vinifera*, seems to be any good for making wine. There is another, wilder species called *vitis labrusca* which makes occasionally unexceptional wine in the eastern states of North America, and a number of hybrids – crosses between *labrusca* and *vinifera* – are grown there and in the UK, but nothing of really fine quality. Other species grow in all sorts of climates, ranging from sub-tropical to Siberian, but *vitus vinifera* flourishes in temperate Mediterranean conditions.

Even within the one species of *vitis vinifera* there are some 5,000 varieties. So, you might suppose, wine could have 5,000 different flavours. But you'd be wrong. Although scientists have isolated thousands of different flavour traces present in wine, there are probably only 50 or 60 grape varieties which can really give a recognizable flavour to the stuff in your glass.

The names of most of these varieties, however, would have been quite unfamiliar to the wine-makers of a century ago, who, accustomed to growing the same grape varieties as their ancestors, viewed imports from other countries and regions with as much suspicion as they might visitors from another galaxy. But just as twentieth-century man has mastered the way in which the most successful apples are grown, so he has not only selected the best examples of the most successful types of grape variety for any given set of conditions and propagated them as "clones", but also, by marrying previously separate varieties, developed completely new vines.

A few of these crosses, such as the brilliant grapefruity Scheurebe, are welcome additions to the wine world; others – heavy-cropping and dull-tasting – are about as welcome a creation as the Golden Delicious apple.

Properly used, and in well-judged blends, grapes like the Müller-Thurgau (which was created by crossing the Riesling and Sylvaner) have permitted wine-makers to produce a regular stream of reliable, if sometimes unexciting, wine in regions – such as the British Isles – where neither parent grape naturally flourishes. That's the good news. Unfortunately, this is precisely the same variety with which lazy, greedy producers in northern Germany have replaced their Riesling – the grape on which their nation's vinous reputation had been built.

RED GRAPE VARIETIES

Baga

The berryish grape of Bairrada in Portugal. Probably that country's best indigenous variety.

Barbera

A grape native to Piedmont, but probably now the most prolifically grown grape throughout Italy, and second in importance there only to the Nebbiolo. However, it has in recent years suffered a slump in popularity and prestige, and many growers are replanting – a pity, because the grape can make good, fruity, chewy wines, with firm acidity, which need far less ageing than many quality Italian reds to show at their best. It's also very versatile, lending itself to a myriad of styles; light or full, dry or sweet, rosé and *frizzante* – even *spumante* – wine.

Some Californian producers, tired of the French grape bandwagon that grinds remorselessly through that state, are growing the Barbera with success; it is also found in Australia – at Brown Bros – in South America and Yugoslavia.

Blaufränkisch

Spicy grape used with increasing success in Austria, especially in blends with Cabernet.

Cabernet Franc

A lesser grape than its "noble" brother, the Cabernet Sauvignon, the Franc usually makes "greener", "grassier" wine with lighter colour and less obvious tannin. Imagine the smell of blackcurrant leaves, or the taste of barely ripe blackcurrant fruit, and you're well on the way to recognizing Cabernet Franc; or possibly Cabernet Sauvignon grown in a cool climate or picked prematurely in a country like South Africa.

It is grown throughout Bordeaux, to be used in blends with the Cabernet Sauvignon, Merlot, small quantities of Petit Verdot and – though rarely nowadays – the Malbec. It is particularly important in the Merlot-dominated vineyards of Pomerol and St Emilion, where some properties (most notably Château Cheval Blanc) make superb Merlot-Cabernet Franc blends from vineyards whose soil is unsuited to the Cabernet Sauvignon.

In the Loire, both Cabernets are grown and often blended to make red and rosé wines labelled simply as "Cabernet". These blends can be delicious, but the big names in Loire reds, Chinon and Bourgueil, are pure Cabernet Franc – as are, the locals say, the best wines of the Touraine region. Here the grape can take on notes of raspberry and strawberry, particularly when it is used in the region's sparkling rosés, most notably Saumur.

In Italy, the Cabernet Franc is grown throughout the north, making wines which are dry and light but seem almost sweet in their ripeness. Look out for Grave del Friuli.

New-World examples are rare, but there have been successful efforts at pure, unblended styles in Australia (at the Heritage winery) and California (at Carmenet). There is a growing trend toward using it in Bordeaux-style blends – by Australians in Piper's Brook's Tasmanian Ninth Island reds and Lindemans' Pyrus from Coonawarra, and by Californians in a growing range of so-called "Meritage" wines.

Cabernet Sauvignon: *This is the world's best-known red grape*

Cabernet Sauvignon

The king of red grapes. In the Médoc, in Bordeaux, it is blended with the softer Merlot to produce some of the world's finest, most complex, longest-lived (and most expensive) wines; elsewhere it is similarly successful, used neat or blended with a variety of other grapes.

Rich yet dry, with the smell and flavour of blackcurrants, cedarwood, green peppers and, occasionally, mint and eucalyptus, its thickish skins help to give it the tannic backbone necessary for long life. Perhaps surprisingly, it is little seen in France outside

Bordeaux, except for the Loire, where the cooler climate gives it a grassier tang and, many tasters claim, a characteristic note of green pepper. In Italy it is increasingly used, and increasingly successful, although Italian wine laws have until recently often precluded its wines, and the blends in which it is used, from carrying any designation other than *vino da tavola*. Progressive producers in Spain and Portugal, and even Greece, are using the grape to great effect too, but the most remarkable European Cabernet Sauvignon success story of recent years has been Bulgaria, both in its inexpensive, simple, jammy form and in some rather more serious examples from, for example, Suhindol.

New-World Cabernets range from the ultra-classy to the jammily simple, depending on the prevailing climate and style of wine-making. As a rule, however, Chile produces some of the purest, most blackcurranty examples, Australia makes big, approachable Cabernet (though cooler regions in Victoria and Western Australia are known for lighter, mintier, more berryish versions), California a more tannic style (though in the 1990s there has been a trend toward greater softness), while New Zealand and, to an even greater extent, South Africa make light, green, grassy wines.

Cannonau

See Grenache.

Carignan

A black grape widely used for table and dessert wines, mainly in the south of France. Though lacking any precise flavour, it is used in Provençal rosés and in red and rosé Languedoc wines such as Fitou – one of the best wines of the region – Minervois and Corbières. It is also grown in South America, North Africa, Israel and southern Spain – more particularly, in the Cariñena area of Aragon, where it is said to have originated.

Cencibel

One of the many Spanish names for the Tempranillo.

Charbono

Rare, spicily intense variety grown in California by brilliant eccentrics like Duxoup.

Cinsault/Cinsaut

Grown in almost exactly the same countries as the Carignan, this is a similarly useful grape, imparting a spicy, attractive warmth to blends. It is one of the parents of the Pinotage cross grown in New Zealand and South Africa, where the Cinsault is also widely grown, though here it is confusingly known as the Hermitage. A blend of Cabernet, Syrah and Cinsault is proving successful for Australian and southern French producers, and for Serge Hochar of Château Musar in the Lebanon.

Cot

See Malbec.

Dolcetto

Piedmont's answer to fuller-flavoured Gamay, Beaujolais, this makes full, plum-and-cherryish reds which can be drunk young or after a little wood-ageing. Wines – like Dolcetto d'Alba – are often named after the grape.

Dornfelder

Recently developed grape, used to make some of Germany's most attractive, plummiest reds. Dwrink young.

Freisa

Unusual floral, mulberryish variety making a comeback in Piedmont, thanks to producers like Bava. Drink this young too.

Gamay

Gamay is Beaujolais. How it is that it can be delicious when grown in a hilly region south of Burgundy, but flat and soupy virtually everywhere else, is a mystery. The colour ranges from darkest pink to medium red, and an unusually blue pigment in the grapes' skins gives young Beaujolais a characteristic violet hue. Its acidity is high, and its taste a mouthful of almost any fresh, ripe red fruit, though cherry is a frequently found flavour. Gamay is best drunk young, though some of the Beaujolais *crus* age well; with maturity, the Gamay takes on chocolatey-raspberry flavours not dissimilar to the Pinot Noir, to which it is thought to be related.

Passable Gamay can also be found in the Loire, most successfully as Gamay de Touraine, though rarely elsewhere.

Grenache

Widely planted in the Rhône, it contributes, on average, a full-flavoured, ripely alcoholic 60 per cent of any Châteauneuf-du-Pape and, with the Syrah, is the chief component of Côtes du Rhône. Elsewhere in this region, it is used to make the often disappointing rosés of Provence, Lirac and Tavel, where its essentially peppery tang occasionally shows through, and in the extraordinary red dessert wines of Banyuls in Roussillon.

In Spain, it is known as the Garnacha and, together with the Tempranillo, is one of Rioja's major grapes. It is used to make Cannonau in Sardinia where it may have begun life. California also uses the variety to make mostly forgettable "blush" rosés while "bush" Grenache from the warm Barossa Valley is among the most impressive wines to come out of Australia.

Grignolino

Bright cherryish variety grown in Piedmont and (rarely) in California. Best drunk young.

Kadarka

Earthily tough variety common in Hungary, Bulgaria (where it's called Gamza) and Romania.

Malbec

Spicy variety, now almost expelled from the best vineyards of Bordeaux where it was once part of the standard recipe. Grown in Cahors, (less successfully) as "Cot" in the Loire and (often very tastily) in Argentina and Chile.

Mataro

See Mourvèdre.

Mavrodaphne

Variety used to make plummy, grapey wine in Greece.

Mavrud

Spicy grape used to some effect in Bulgaria.

Merlot

Merlot wines are buttery, plummy, toffeed and sometimes slightly minty too. Almost always soft, they can be dull or delicious. Used throughout Bordeaux – and now elsewhere – to temper the tough Cabernet Sauvignon, the Merlot dominates the St Emilion and Pomerol regions with, in good wine-making hands, its intense, supple, velvety fruit. Outside France, any country growing Cabernet Sauvignon will usually grow Merlot too. The Italians have been doing so for longer than most, vinifying it

Merlot: Usually, but not always, blended with other grapes

notably, Bandol, whose fresh, spicy reds are best drunk young. It has been introduced to the Languedoc to improve more basic *vins de pays* and can now be found in California and Australia under the pseudonym of Mataro.

Nebbiolo

Italy's answer to the Syrah, traditionally making black, dry, tannic Barolo and Barbaresco in the Piedmont hills. More modern-style wines are far fruitier and benefit from the sweetness of new oak barrels. Both can develop surprisingly complex flavour with a unique, chocolatey, pruney sweetness – rather like long-forgotten home-made jam. More approachable versions are labelled as Spanna, and Nebbiolo d'Alba, for example. Elsewhere in Italy, the Nebbiolo swaggers under tough, provocative names like Grumello and Inferno.

Periquita

Characterful grape used in Portugal.

Petit Verdot

Hard-to-ripen, spicy, herby variety, used in small (under 10 per cent) doses in Bordeaux blends.

Pinot Noir

Probably the world's most sulky and infuriating variety, this home-loving grape has only recently begun to stray successfully beyond its base in Burgundy. Fine (though sadly rare) examples of Burgundian Pinot Noir display extraordinary delicacy and elegance, with characteristic flavours of wild raspberry, strawberry and, occasionally, black cherry when young. With age, they take on chocolatey, gamey, "farmyard" overtones.

If a Champagne has raspberry-chocolatey flavours there's a good chance that it contains a fair proportion of Pinot Noir. In this northerly region of France, most producers don't – thank goodness – even begin to try to turn the grape into a red wine, but blend its clear juice with that of the Chardonnay.

In all but the very warmest years, Alsace and the Loire make thin but passable Pinots but vinify them far more successfully as rosé, particularly in Sancerre. In Oltrepó Pavese the Italians coax it into giving light, smoky, Burgundian-style reds, and Spain is beginning to produce some more creditable

singly to make light, juicy wines (as do Eastern European wine-makers) and, more recently, blending it with Cabernet to make wines with more depth and complexity.

New-World wine-makers, having triumphed with the Cabernet, are also cottoning on to the idea of blending it with the Merlot, particularly in California. The greatest potential so far, though, has been seen in Washington and New York states and Chile. New Zealand and South Africa should do well with it, as should Australia, but successes are rare.

Morellino

See Sangiovese.

Mourvèdre

Originally from Spain – where it is called Monastrell – this black grape is now most commonly found in the south of France, contributing colour and spice to Châteauneuf-du-Pape, and making solid, fruity, "café" wines in many other Rhône *Appellations*. In Provence, it provides the fruit in the wines of Cassis, Palette and,

efforts. In Germany and Switzerland it also makes light, often almost rosé, wines and in Eastern Europe the Pinot Noir is used to make sweet reds, though Romania has proved capable of good dry examples.

The New-Worlders have been increasingly successful with the Pinot Noir in Oregon, California, the cool regions of Australia and Chile and – though the stars can be numbered on one hand – South Africa and New Zealand.

Ruby Cabernet

A cross between Cabernet Sauvignon and Carignan, used in California and Australia to produce wine like jam made from unripe blackcurrants.

Sangiovese

Chianti, Brunello di Montalcino and Vino Nobile di Montepulciano would be lost without this Tuscan grape, which proliferates throughout Italy yet only achieves greatness in these wines. Its quality and complexity vary enormously, largely because of the number of different clones which exist. At its best, the Sangiovese – or Sangioveto or Morellino, as two of its clones are known – can be the most exciting, herby-spicy grape in Italy – either pure, or in blends with the Cabernet and/or Merlot in so-called "Super-Tuscan" reds. Only the best of its wines can take being aged, though this has not deterred Californians from treating it as a potential flavour of the month in their vineyards. Argentina has some too: we'll see.

Spanna

See Nebbiolo.

Syrah/Shiraz

Within the forbidding frame of smoke, tar and creosote often encountered in the Syrah, there can lurk a deep, sweet, blackberry richness, needing age to show itself. Traditionally used in France to give colour and body to feebler fare (a role it once performed in Bordeaux), it is vinified singly for northern Rhône wines such as Hermitage and Côte-Rôtie and both neat and in blends in Languedoc-Roussillon. In Australia, it produces Penfolds' great Grange but also does well in blends with the Cabernet Sauvignon. More recently a number of wineries in California have successfully introduced the Syrah; examples in South Africa, however, are light and

disappointing. Watch out for new plantings in Chile, Spain and Italy.

Tannat

Tough, rustic variety used to make Madiran in France and some fair-quality reds in Uruguay.

Tarrango

Recent cross used by Brown Bros and others in Australia to make Beaujolais-style reds.

Teroldego

Juicy grape used to make good-value wines in Italy.

Tempranillo

Found all over Spain under a variety of names (such as Cencibel, Tinto Fino, etc.) and responsible for the strawberryish, soft, relatively light, toffeeish taste of Rioja and much Spanish red. Modern producers like Berberana are proving that, bottled young, the Tempranillo can make lively refreshing wine to compete with Beaujolais, while

Miguel Torres marries it successfully to Cabernet Sauvignon. In Argentina, it changes character to produce rather hefty, rustic wine. Plantations of it in France are on the increase.

Zinfandel

Thank goodness California has something to call its own – this is it. A black grape, which some – myself included – think could be the Italian Primitivo, though others say what was Yugoslavia may have been its homeland. In California, it performs the great vinous feat of being all things to all men. It makes jug wine, fine wine and "port", not to mention its main role these days – in blends with the Muscat – semi-sweet "white" and "blush" rosé. This last style has become so successful that wine waiters find it hard to persuade some customers that Zinfandel can be red as well as pink. Dry rosé, for which it is ideal, is even trickier to sell. It is also found in small pockets in Australia, South America and South Africa.

Pinot Noir: In Alsace, as here, Pinot seldom gets as ripe as it does further south in Burgundy

WHITE GRAPE VARIETIES

Airén

The world's number-one grape – in terms of hectares planted – grown throughout Spain and, when it is not being distilled into brandy, used to make impressively flavourless wine.

Aligoté

A Burgundy grape which makes freshly acidic white wines that are generally named after the grape and are best drunk young. The most traditional way to drink Aligoté is with cassis (blackcurrant liqueur) in the form of "Kir", a drink which was invented to improve the palatability of the often aggressively acidic wine. It is also grown for still whites in Romania and Russia.

Alvarinho/Albariño

A Vinho Verde bearing the name of this grape is likely to have a fresher, spicier flavour than the rest. In Spain it is known as the Albariño in Galicia and produces small quantities of lovely flowery-spicy wines.

Arneis

Distinctive, spicy-floral variety grown in Piedmont in Italy.

Bacchus

A cross derived from the Riesling, Sylvaner and Müller-Thurgau, displaying many of the characteristics of the last of these, but with a more pronounced, almost Muscatty grapiness. Grown throughout Germany, it is also proving successful in England.

Bouvier

Dull modern grape used in Austria to make late-harvest wines.

Chardonnay

By a whisker, the greatest of white wine grapes – and certainly currently the most

Chardonnay: These grapes are about to be turned into Mâcon-Viré at the local co-op

fashionable. Now grown throughout the world, it is thought to have originated in the Lebanon; but it is in Burgundy that it has traditionally, and indisputably, achieved its finest potential. Even in this region, its flavours can vary enormously from village to village: butter and hazelnut in Meursault, the buttered-digestive-biscuit and ripe fruit of Chassagne-Montrachet, pineappley-fresh in the Mâconnais, flinty and steely in Chablis. When mature, fine Burgundian Chardonnay can also take on a not unpleasant rotty, vegetal richness. The grape also has a natural affinity with oak, which can lend a delicious, toasty complexity to the wine.

Elsewhere in France, the Chardonnay also achieves greatness in Champagne, especially when used "neat" for creamy *blanc de blancs*. It is grown in the Loire for still and sparkling wines, in the Ardèche and the Jura, and in the rapidly growing vineyards of Languedoc-Roussillon.

Ready to pick: *Chardonnay on the vine*

In Eastern Europe, the grape has yet to fulfil its promise; in Germany, it can be found in various blends, but is often confused with the *Weissburgunder* – the Pinot Blanc. The same is true in Italy, where the muddling of the two grapes often obscures the fact that some fine if high-priced Chardonnay is produced. Switzerland and Austria also make passable Chardonnay.

There are good Chardonnays being made in Spain, South America and South Africa, and even India is growing the variety for *méthode champenoise* wines, but it is in California and the Antipodes that world-class non-Burgundian Chardonnay is to be found. Thus far, the Californians have been closest to the Burgundian bull's-eye, though New Zealand efforts and Australian examples from cooler regions are now chasing them hard. Oregon's Chardonnays are rarely impressive, but Washington state is making progress, as is Canada.

Chasan

A cross between the Chardonnay and Palomino, used in southern France to make pleasant, commercial sub-Chardonnay wine.

Chasselas

The widely grown Chasselas produces pleasant, ordinary white wines. It seems to do best in Switzerland, where it is known as the Dorin or Fendant, and in the Vaud region makes some dry, sturdy whites. In the Loire (where it was supplanted by the Sauvignon Blanc) it is still used for the tiny annual production of Pouilly-sur-Loire. It is also responsible for sparkling Seyssel in the northern Rhône and is found dotted throughout the north and centre of France. It is known as the Gutedel in Germany and grown chiefly in Baden; it is also found in California, under the name Chasselas Doré, and in Algeria and Hungary.

Chenin Blanc

One of the world's trickier grapes, but very widely planted. It ripens late and has a great deal of acidity, with a propensity to bring out the worst in the sulphur dioxide which the wine-makers in its Loire homeland are, in any case, prone to over-use. Good dry examples are rare but can be found in good vintages in Vouvray, occasionally in South Africa (where it is called the Steen), New Zealand and Australia – in all of which it is given the benefit of new oak barrels, which are rarely used in the Loire.

Otherwise, the Chenin's acidity and its vulnerability to *botrytis* – noble rot – provide the essential components for ageing and complexity in the great, sweet wines of the Loire in which the grape reveals honeyed, apple and apricot flavours, and occasion-ally a smell and taste of wet straw. It also makes an ideal, high-acid base for the Loire's sparkling wines.

Colombard

Originally from the Charentais in France, where it is still used in Cognac and Armagnac production, the Colombard is now grown in south-west France and Provence to make simple, fresh, fruity wines like Vin de Pays des Côtes de Gascogne which can be good value. It has also been widely adopted for blending in Australia and in California, where it is – to the annoyance of the authorities in France – known as "French Colombard" and – to their further annoyance – used to make "Chablis".

Fendant

Swiss name for – occasionally better than average – Chasselas.

Furmint

Limey grape used to make Tokay in Hungary and, more recently, tangily light dry table wine.

Gewürztraminer/Traminer

One of the most difficult wines to sell, because of its unpronounceability, but one of the easiest grapes of all to recognize "blind", with its perfumed (Parma violets), spicy, exotic fruit (lychee) smells and flavours and oily richness. Supposedly it is a spicy – hence the addition of the German word *Gewürz*, or "spice" – variant of the Italian Traminer grape. There is now some confusion over the two names, both of which may be applied to the same grape. Some Italian and New-World labels opt for the more easily pronounced Traminer.

The Gewürztraminer is successfully grown in Germany, but is without doubt at its greatest in Alsace, particularly in the *vendange tardive* – late-picked – style. Outside France, in Australia and more particularly in New Zealand, some good "Gewürz" is being made in cooler areas. Experimentation with the grape is promising in North America and Chile, and in Spain it is a key component of Torres' Vina Esmeralda.

Macabeo

Potentially fragrant but more usually dull grape grown in southern France and in Spain where it is also known as the Viura, some examples of which are increasingly successful.

Malvasia

The grape that produced the vat of Malmsey in which the Duke of Clarence drowned, the Malvasia still makes rich, sweet fortified wine on Madeira, but this originally Greek variety has also for centuries been grown in Rioja, where it not only makes white wine but is also traditionally blended into some reds; the Malvasia is used in this way in France and Italy (where it is an ingredient of DOC Chianti) and now California.

It also makes a wide range of white wines in Italy, Spain and the south of France – dry and sweet, still and frothing – and is used in Portugal for white port. There are plantings, too, in South Africa, South America and California. Good examples can be marmaladey but "stale and nutty" is more often the accurate description.

Marsanne

Chiefly found in the Rhône valley, where it is used with the Roussanne for wines like Hermitage and Côtes du Rhône Blanc. It makes strong, fleshy whites in Cassis in

Provence, and dry and sweet, still and sparkling St Péray. Rare but good Australian Marsanne can also be found, and it is widely planted (though to little effect) in Algeria. Frustratingly, especially in the Rhône, the Marsanne can make wines which are wonderfully flowery in their youth, and nutty, lemony and rich after a decade or so – but very dull in between.

Melon de Bourgogne

The unexceptional variety used to make Muscadet – and so-called Pinot Blanc in California.

Moscatel

The Muscat's more workaday brother, with a wide variety of synonyms including Muscat of Alexandria, Gordo Blanco ("the big fat white one") and South Africa's Hanepoot ("honeypot"). It is best used to produce sweet wines, often high in natural alcohol or fortified; some Australian late-harvest Muscats are made from this variety, as is the Portuguese Moscatel de Setúbal, Spain's Málaga, the dessert wines of North Africa and the French *vins doux naturels* of Lunel and Rivesaltes. The latter rarely compare with those of Beaumes de Venise and Frontignan, made from the "true" Muscat, but can be powerful, if rather heavy-handed, good-value alternatives.

Müller-Thurgau

"Invented" in 1872 by a Dr Müller of Thurgau in Switzerland, who crossed Riesling and Sylvaner vines, this is now shamefully Germany's most widely planted grape and gives that soft, flowery gulpability to the great mass of ordinary Liebfraumilch and Niersteiner. It can be capable of more, sometimes managing a passable thumbnail sketch of the Riesling it would like to be, though with a touch of the "cat's pee" smell more usually associated with Sauvignon Blanc.

Perversely, the better examples often come not from the variety's native land but from England and north-east Italy, where producers treat it with more care, though under its alias of Rivaner there are occasional successes in Germany too.

Muscadelle

An obscure, spicy grape used in white Bordeaux blends and by Australians in its pure state to make Liqueur Tokay in north-east Victoria. Good examples of this smell of fish oil or – more pleasantly – of tea leaves.

Muscat

More accurately called the Muscat Blanc à Petits Grains, this goes under a huge variety

Moscatel: For showy, aromatic sweet wines

of names and is grown all over the world, though the wine it makes tends to share one overriding characteristic – it actually tastes of grapes.

In Alsace, where examples are sadly rare, it is very dry, but as perfumed and crunchy-fresh as a bunch of the best from the hothouse in autumn. Rosenmuskateller wines from Italy's Alto Adige are less fat, but equally delicious, and some pleasant dry Muscats have been made in the New World, most particularly in Australia which is also the place to find the lusciously powerful, Christmas-puddingy liqueur Muscats of north-east Victoria.

Back in Europe, however, the Muscat is best known in its fortified state as Beaumes de Venise and Frontignan in France or as the golden, liquorous Greek Muscats of Samos and Patras.

The Muscat is also used to make the mouthwateringly grapey French fizz, Clairette de Die. In Italy, as the Moscato, it produces deliciously sweet, much-underrated "playpen" sparkling wines, Asti and Moscato Spumante.

Muscat Ottonel

Just as Eastern and Middle Europe have an inferior alternative to the Riesling, the Welschriesling, so they make wine from this lesser version of the Muscat, the Ottonel. However, in Austria, where it is a particularly important variety, it can make fresh, pleasant wine, and it can also produce very acceptable dessert wines in Romania.

Palomino

A Spanish grape which is enormously import-ant in Jerez, where it is the principal variety for sherry, but grown there and all around the country for dull, dry white table wine.

Parellada

Dull Spanish variety whose use handicaps Cava sparkling wine.

Pedro Ximénez/PX

A very sweet Spanish grape, grown mainly in Andalusia. It makes strong, rich, dark dessert wines – often reaching 16 per cent in alcohol – in Málaga and, sun-dried and concentrated, produces a sweetening wine for sherry which is sometimes bottled and sold under its own name. In Moriles, Córdoba and other areas of Spain it can be completely fermented to give dry, powerful aperitifs and table wines.

Petit Manseng

Characterful lemony, herby grape used (with the less fine Gros Manseng) for Jurançon and Pacherenc du Vic-Bilh in France.

Pinot Blanc/Pinot Bianco

A grape found in almost every wine-growing region of the world, nearly everywhere producing different flavours and textures, almost none of which inspires real excitement. In France, it is occasionally found in white Burgundies, but is at its rich, slightly nutty best in Alsace and in the Jura, where it makes the unusual *vin de paille*. It is becoming increasingly popular – as the *Weissburgunder* – in Germany, where it is used both for dry whites and for the more traditional Germanic styles, and over the border almost throughout Italy. In the Alto Adige it makes some sparkling – *spumante* – and good, fragrant, dry wines, though these are often mislabelled as Chardonnay. California, too, claims some examples, though these are probably made from Melon de Bourgogne. It is also grown, though rarely impressively, in Luxembourg, Austria, Chile, Hungary, Uruguay and the former Yugoslavia.

Pinot Gris/Pinot Grigio/ Tokay-Pinot Gris

In Italy and Alsace this pink-skinned grape is rapidly becoming a new superstar. As the Pinot Gris it makes pleasant rosés in Touraine, but as Tokay-Pinot Gris in Alsace, it produces lovely, smokily spicy, golden wines, dry or slightly sweet and excellent with food. In Germany it makes good juicy wines in Württemberg, the Pfalz and Baden, and is important, too, for the dry whites from Geneva and the soft dessert wines of the Valais in Switzerland. In Italy, "neat" Pinot Grigios can be deliciously fresh and, blended with Pinot Nero (Pinot Noir), it makes a lovely white from Oltrepó Pavese. It is also found in Abruzzi, and is creeping into the central west area. In Mexico, it makes the "Hidalgo" wines, and it is also grown in the Crimea and for dessert wines in the Murfatlar vineyards of Romania. Occasionally it occurs in Burgundy and it is expected to become popular in California.

Riesling

Chardonnay's only rival as the world's top white grape and probably the most wrongly pronounced variety of them all (the first syllable rhymes with Nice the place, not nice the adjective). It is far more versatile than the Chardonnay because it is used to make some of the world's greatest sweet wines as well as some of the steeliest and driest. However, its very versatility makes it far trickier to handle well. In Germany, where it is thought to have originated in the Rhine Valley (hence its often-used pseudonyms, "Rhine" and "Johannisberg" Riesling), it was once almost solely responsible for all of the best dry and sweet wines, but it has recently had to fend off competition from newer varieties such as the Müller-Thurgau.

At their best the Riesling's flavours can combine lime, grape, apple and spice – sometimes baked apple (complete with brown sugar and cloves) can be a very apt description. The variety's great quality is its ability to preserve acidity while building up grapey, honeyed ripeness, enabling fine German wine to age and develop stunningly well. On the other hand, that acidity can be raspingly unwelcome when the grapes are picked unripe, as in some of the *Trocken* wines from the Rhine. When mature and ripe, really good Riesling can take on a spicy-oily character most usually, and accurately, described as "petrolly" – and delicious.

The Riesling occasionally makes lovely, steely, lemon-fresh wine in Italy's Trentino-Alto Adige region – as it does, more rarely still, in Austria and Switzerland. The "Riesling" grown in Eastern Europe, however, is almost invariably not this noble grape but the inferior Welschriesling (q.v.). Its French home is Alsace, where growers

Riesling: Most fascinating of all white grapes, here seen growing in Germany's Mosel valley

consider it their finest variety. Here it can make wine with all the freshness, fruit and complexity of German Riesling, but with added weight and dry, fatty fullness.

Australia has by far the most successful dry, off-dry and late-harvest New-World Rieslings – particularly from the Clare Valley and cooler parts of Barossa – but New Zealand is hot on its heels. In the US, Oregon, Washington state and New York state have all done better with it than California, where it has received little in the way of loving attention.

Rivaner

Another name for the Müller-Thurgau – and the one by which pioneers in Germany are labelling some surprisingly good, late-harvest examples of this grape.

Roussanne

More interesting partner to the Marsanne in the Rhône, with a more immediately spicy (though possibly less floral) character.

Sauvignon Blanc

One of the most easily recognized white varieties – just look for cat's pee, gooseberries, blackcurrant leaf, asparagus or mushy peas – and one of the most popular, to judge by the ubiquity in restaurants of French wines made from it, such as Sancerre and Pouilly-Fumé, and in supermarkets of pure examples from Bordeaux. New Zealand has, since the early 1980s, proved especially adept at bringing out its most pungent flavours, though there is also a growing number of good Sauvignons being made in Chile, South Africa and the cooler regions of Australia.

However, despite this instant success, I wonder just how much further the Sauvignon can really go. In the US, for example, though producers in Washington state have released good versions, critics write it off and most wineries do their best to hide the Sauvignon's true grassy, herbaceous character by using lots of oak (and labelling the wine as Fumé Blanc) or by making it very sweet. Unlike the Sémillon, the Sauvignon rarely ages well – unless you like the flavour of tinned asparagus – and is remarkably vulnerable to poor wine-making (in Sancerre for instance). All of which is a great pity, because, at its best, no variety is better suited to partner spicy oriental food, not to mention the new east-meets-west cuisine of California and the Antipodes.

Scheurebe

A Riesling/Sylvaner cross invented in 1916 by George Scheu, this German grape – by far the most interesting modern variety – makes wonderfully and extraordinarily grapefruity white wine. It is used in blends, but is more often made into a varietal wine, particularly in the *Auslese* style, and in later-harvest versions by the Austrians who call it Sämling 88. The Scheurebe is also one of the most successful grapes to be grown in England.

Sémillon

A split-personality white grape. In Bordeaux, it is used (in blends with the Sauvignon) to make huge quantities of flabby, unrefreshing basic dry white. But it also produces elegant, golden savoury stuff in Pessac-Léognan and wines of exquisite, complex sweetness in Sauternes and Barsac. In Australia, where it is widely planted, it helps to make the (more expensive) Chardonnay go further – and produces wonderful, long-lived peachy-lemony wines in the Hunter and Barossa Valleys, plus luscious late-harvest dessert wine from the otherwise unimpressive region of Riverina. In cool New Zealand it mimics the Sauvignon, as it tends to in both Chile and California; good examples are, so far, rare in South Africa. Watch this space.

Sylvaner

An important white grape in terms of planting and production, but a minor variety as regards quality. Its flavour can be rather bland and earthy, and its chief virtue is its ability to provide body and firmness in blends, for which purpose it is widely used in Eastern Europe. Its best wines are made in Alsace (where it is increasingly rare); Germany (particularly in Franken); Italy's Alto Adige, Switzerland and Austria, thought to be its country of origin.

Torrontes

Muscat-like grape used almost exclusively in Argentina, though also encountered in Spain. Attractive wines which smell sweet and taste dry.

Tokay

Australian name for the Muscadelle when it is produced as a fortified wine in north-east Victoria.

Trebbiano/Ugni Blanc

Italy and southern France (where it is called

Sylvaner: Not one of the world's most thrilling varieties, though it comes into its own in Franken

the Ugni Blanc) are heavily planted with this grape, which is one of the most important in Europe in terms of production figures, though not, alas, in quality. It may make superlative Cognac in the Charentais, but, without skilled wine-making and/or unusual clones, it tends to make neutral-tasting, inoffensive white table wine – which is why the vine is the mainstay of basic southern French plonk, pleasantly inoffensive Vin de Pays des Côtes de Gascogne and Italian whites like Orvieto, Soave and Frascati. A good wine from any of these appellations will owe very little to the Trebbiano, and much to a skilful wine-maker who has fermented it as cool as possible to bring out what little flavour it has – or blended it with more flavoursome varieties: look also for Tuscany's Galestro, or the superior French dry whites of Bandol and Palette.

Verdejo

A little-known Spanish white grape grown in Rueda where it is contributing to a new wave of fresh, dry wines.

Verdelho

A Portuguese white grape which lends its name to a delicious, dry style of Madeira, the variety is also used in its native country for dry table wine and white port. In Australia, it produces some good, dry, lime-flavoured wines.

Viognier

A rapidly rising star, this white French grape was, until recently, only planted in the Rhône at Château Grillet and Condrieu. Today, however, it is rapidly being introduced to southern France, Australia, Tuscany and, most notably, California. At its best, it produces wonderfully perfumed wines with a smell of peaches and apricots, but it is far from easy to produce good and inexpensive examples. Beware of over-production and of wines which have aged poorly.

Viura

More common name for Macabeo – and the one used for successful new-wave whites in Rueda.

Welschriesling

In Hungary, where it is called the Olasz Rizling, and in north-east Italy, as the Riesling Italico, this grape can produce some sprightly, floral whites; in Austria, it is used not only for light, perfumed dry wines but, when attacked by noble rot, for often impressive versions of Germany's rich, sweet, late-picked styles. But it should never be mistaken for true Rhine Riesling, though its wealth of pseudonyms do their best to encourage confusion. Most Welschriesling rarely rises above acceptable, quaffing "party wine" while Yugoslavia's Laski Rizling is more usually a flabby, sugary disgrace.

HOW WINE IS MADE

GOD, THEY SAY, helps those who help themselves. Well, help yourself to a handful of grapes, crush them, and leave them be for a few days in a reasonably warm place, remove the skins and pips and, hey presto, you'll have made an alcoholic liquid which could legally describe itself as wine. It makes life hard for all those religious anti-alcohol nuts: if God *really* didn't want us to drink wine, why did He create a self-contained wine-making kit in every grape?

The stuff you've made will probably taste quite foul, of course, but it's only your first attempt, after all, and you've not used much in the way of skill or equipment. All you've done is allow the liquid and the natural sugar within the grape to combine with the millions of yeast cells on the fruit surface which kicked off the natural process of fermentation.

There are all sorts of ways of managing this process to achieve a particular style of wine, but nothing the wine-maker does can ever influence the ultimate flavour of the stuff in the bottle as much as the raw materials: the type of grapes used, where and how they were grown and harvested, and, of course, the climate.

GRAPE EXPECTATIONS

The grape variety (or varieties – wines are often blends of more than one) used for making any wine is as fundamental to its taste as the type of meat or fish will be to a particular dish. The differences in the flavour of freshly picked Riesling and Gewürztraminer grapes are even more apparent in the wines they are used to make.

Some varieties, such as Burgundy's Pinot Noir and Chardonnay, traditionally perform best as soloists; most, however, are ensemble players, and are more usually found in blends. Claret, for example, is almost always a mixture of two or more varieties, principally the Cabernet Sauvignon, Merlot and Cabernet Franc.

Old World countries' wine laws (Germany being a notable exception) prescribe and proscribe certain varieties for each of their designated quality wine areas, based on experience of what grows best there. Only certain grapes – or blends of grapes – may be used to produce a wine labelled with that appellation.

In the New World, rules like these are almost non-existent; producers are free to experiment with as many varieties as they like. The advantage of this approach lies in the way it allows the wine industry to develop new styles without the constraints of potentially irrelevant laws. On the other hand, as consumers have discovered in their high streets throughout the world, a wholly free market rarely favours the demanding, the small and the unfashionable.

Without some kind of appellation system, traditional but little-known grapes like the Gros and Petit Manseng, which are used to make the equally traditional and little-known wine of Jurançon in France, could disappear in the same way as the local butcher and fishmonger.

SOME LIKE IT HOT

Whatever the flavour or fashionability of the grape variety, it will never make decent wine unless it has enough sun to ripen properly. The climatic conditions demanded by wine-making vines are pretty precise.

Ideally, winters should be cold – cold enough for the vine to lie dormant and conserve all its growing energy until the spring when the vine flowers. From this moment until the harvest, the most important element is timely, well measured doses of sun. The all-important final ripening of the grapes should happen in the cooler months of autumn, not all in a rush in the blazing heat of high summer. Too long or hot a blast encourages growth to be too prolific and too rapid to concentrate the subtleties of flavour which can develop naturally through a slower ripening.

The wine-producing regions of the world lie in two quite sharply defined bands: the moderate, temperate zones between 50° and 30° latitude in the northern hemisphere, and 30° and 50° in the southern hemisphere. Within these bands, in general, fine wines are made in the cooler areas furthest removed from the equator.

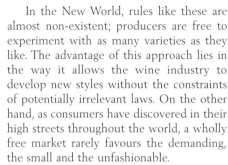

Palm-reading: *Portugal's Douro Valley is hot enough for olives and almonds – and vines*

Unless they are carefully handled, grapes from truly warm regions tend to produce large quantities of soft, jammy wine.

However, even within the same latitudes, the climate can vary widely, depending on altitude, distance from the sea and mountains and the influence of such phenomena as the Gulf Stream. To help to define particular local conditions, a Californian scale of "heat units" was devised, based on the average daily temperature during the growing season. This kind of scale tends to underestimate factors such as the difference in day and night-time temperatures – and just how hot and cold the weather tends to get. Grapes simply do not mature when it is too hot or cool, so high-altitude Idaho, which according to its average temperatures ought to ripen grapes well, cannot usually do so: after a chilly night, they get an hour or so of moderate warmth mid-morning before the noonday heat becomes intense enough to send the fruit off for a self-protective siesta. Elsewhere, on the other hand, in parts of Chile, and the Barossa Valley in Australia, for example, cool nights help to prevent the grapes from becoming over-ripe.

HANDLING THE RAINS

Like any other plant, vines need water to grow properly. If they don't get it, however ideal the rest of the weather, the grapes will be parched and their tough skins will make for hard, tannic red wine. Worse still, a vine which gets no water during crucial periods of its growing season will simply stop growing. On the other hand, what the vines don't need is an untimely storm just before or during the harvest, when the rain will simply dilute the juice of the grapes.

Sometimes these late storms spoil what might have been a fine vintage; sometimes, on the other hand, as in the early 1990s in Bordeaux, nature meanly subjects the vines to both drought and storms so that the end result is both watery and unripe.

In the New World, Southern France and – more recently – Spain, growers will irrigate the plants to avoid the effects of drought or "stress". French traditionalists in particular, however, dismiss even the most carefully measured irrigation as "industrialized" wine-making and ban it outright. Oddly, they take a more tolerant view when richer château owners hover over their vineyards in helicopters in an elaborate ploy to protect the vines from the ravages of the rain.

The French fear of irrigation *per se* is unreasonable, as the Bordelais who have gone to make wine in Chile where grapes cannot be grown without additional water would have to admit. But Chile, like Argentina and the more basic vineyards of Australia and California, does offer an object lesson in the dangers of *over*-irrigation. If your Bordeaux tastes dilute, it's God's fault; if your South American Cabernet Sauvignon is watery, blame the grape-grower.

SITING THE VINEYARD

The way in which the vines are selected, planted and looked after dictates the quality of the fruit they will yield. If the best vineyards are sited in relatively cool areas, to prevent the vine from over-stretching itself, maximum use must be made of the precious – sometimes elusive – summer sun. So the best location for a vineyard in the northern hemisphere is normally on a south-facing slope which, from dawn until dusk, catches as many of the sun's rays as possible.

Vines planted in flat land receive less sunshine, are badly drained, and are prone to frost. The lowest part of the slope is better off, but will suffer from any damp conditions prevailing on the flat land, particularly if there happens to be a stream or river running through it. Vines half-way up the hill receive the most direct sunlight and are well-drained. Higher up, altitude causes cooler temperatures which inhibit ripening. The top of the hill is thus no better than the bottom, suffering from cool temperatures, wind and reduced direct sunlight. In the best wine-growing areas of France, the hilltops are covered by trees.

You do not have to travel far to realize, though, that this recipe can vary enormously from one quality wine region to another. The vineyards on the banks of the Rhône, Rhine and Douro rivers, for example, often appear steep enough to call for the skills of an amateur mountaineer. The slopes in Beaujolais and Chianti are gentler while those in the Médoc are often hardly noticeable at all, and parts of the valley floors of the Napa and Marlborough Valleys, in California and New Zealand respectively, have a billiard-table flatness.

If a vineyard is particularly prone to frost – as is the case in Chablis, Champagne and the Napa Valley – there are ways to

Water, water everywhere: But only if you bring it in. Irrigation is permitted here in Argentina.

combat it: water sprinklers, oil burners or wind machines to mix in warm air and dispel the cold air lying close to the vines. Over the years, however, man has ingeniously devised non-mechanical methods to improve the environment in which he wants to grow his grapes, draining the soil in Bordeaux and Ontario for example, planting trees as a wind-break in Tasmania and chopping a few of them down in California to allow air to pass through and blow away the pools of cool air which can cause frost. The most dramatic example of this Godlike remodelling of the earth is the E & J Gallo estate in Sonoma where 800 hectares (2,000 acres) were totally re-landscaped before the vines were planted.

The Language of the Vineyard

Botrytis cinerea Often called noble rot; in France, *pourriture noble*, and in Germany, *Edelfäule*. Fungus which dehydrates grapes, not only concentrating sugars and acids, but imparting its own characteristic flavour to sweet wines.

Black rot Fungal disease of both grape and vine due to humid weather conditions.

Bordeaux mixture Copper sulphate and lime compound used against vine disease.

Canopy management Modern vine-training methods devised to maximize the quality of the grape.

Chlorosis Yellowing of the vine leaves through mineral deficiency.

Clone A selection within a variety of vine taken from one plant exhibiting desirable characteristics.

Coulure The shedding of flowers or berries, caused by over-vigorous growth, disease or rainstorms at flowering.

Cross Vine whose parents are two or more varieties within the same species.

Débourrement The budding of the vines after leaf formation.

Downy mildew *Peronospera*, a fungal disease. Treated with *Bordeaux mixture*.

Drip irrigation New-World method (sometimes computerized) of watering.

Espalier A method of training vines. Vertical shoots lead off a central trunk of two horizontal stems.

Eutypiose A fungal infection which withers the vine. Threatens to destroy the world's vineyards as *phylloxera* did in the late nineteenth century.

Floraison Flowering of the vine.

Geneva Double Curtain Method involving training vines along high trellises to maximize sunshine.

Gobelet Training and pruning of the vine into a bush-like form.

Grafting The near-universal process of attaching young vines to (*phylloxera*-resistant) rootstock.

Grey rot or *pourriture gris* Unwanted *botrytis* infection.

Guyot (Single or Double) Common vine-training systems; growth is concentrated into one or two stems.

Hectare Metric measure equivalent to 10,000 square metres or 2.47 acres.

Herbaceous The taste of wines made from unripe grapes.

Hybrid A *cross* between a *vinifera* and a *labrusca* vine.

Leaf-plucking Process of stripping surplus leaves away to allow more sunlight in to ripen the fruit.

Micro-climate The precise climate of a vineyard or set of vineyards which will influence the way grapes grow there. Some vineyards, for example, are protected from storms by "rain shadows" created by nearby hills.

Millerandage Uneven development of grapes within a bunch as a result of cold or wet weather at flowering. Can reduce the size of the crop per vine and thus – sometimes – lead to wine with more concentrated flavours.

Oidium (Powdery mildew) A fungal disease controlled by sulphur spraying.

Phylloxera vastatrix Parasitic louse that attacks the roots of the *vitis vinifera* grapevine. It devastated the world's vineyards in the late nineteenth century, since most vines are *grafted* onto *phylloxera*-resistant *labrusca* rootstock. Unfortunately, in California, one of the rootstocks used has proved vulnerable to the louse and, in the late 1980s and 1990s, large proportions of the vineyards in the Napa Valley have had to be replanted.

Pruning The selective trimming of a vine to control its shape and the quantity and quality of its produce.

Rootstock The rooted part of the vine on to which the scion is grafted.

T-budding The *grafting* of one type of vine on to another. A less than ideal means of switching from a commercially unpopular variety to a more saleable one without having to wait the three or four years it takes for new plants to yield their first crop.

Training The way in which a vine is forced to grow to optimize yield, ripening, ease of harvest etc.

Trie/Triage Selective harvesting of grapes to pick them at their optimum condition.

Véraison Final stage in the ripening of the grapes.

Vitis labrusca US vine species far better for eating and drinking as juice than for wine-making. Never used for quality wine-making.

Vitis riparia Vine species native to the US and Canada. The wine it produces smells weirdly "foxy". Important for its *phylloxera*-resistant rootstock and thus used around the world.

Vitis vinifera The botanical name of the wine-making vine; European varieties are nearly always members of this species.

Yeasts The "bloom" on grapes is an accumulation of wild yeasts which, left to their own devices, will naturally but unpredictably begin fermentation. New-World wine-makers generally prefer to use cultured yeasts, though some are rediscovering the benefits of allowing natural yeasts to do the job.

THE ANSWER LIES IN THE SOIL

Vine-growing is not unlike gardening: just as you can't grow roses in a garden with unsuitable soil, most varieties of vine have been historically proven to have strong preferences as to where they like growing. These preferences have led French traditionalists to build up a mystique surrounding what they call the *goût de terroir* of their better wines. Translated literally, this refers to the taste of the earth in which the grapes are grown; in fact the term includes other factors such as the physical situation of the vineyard and the climate.

Like most living things (ourselves included), grapes consist largely of water, and so, in turn, does wine. The water content of a grape will inevitably have passed through the soil in which the vine has planted its roots. Different soil types therefore affect the taste of wine as well. Around the world, the structure of the earth varies considerably. Conditions may repeat themselves, but often a particular region's geology is unique and accounts for the individuality of its wine

The idea, however, that it is the specific minerals in the soil of a given plot of land, which actually contribute to the flavour of a wine made from vines grown there, has come in for increasingly sceptical treatment. Today, the general consensus is that the influence of the soil has far more to do with its natural acidity or alkalinity and its physical structure: the way it holds and reflects heat and its capacity for draining water. Vines, for example, as their growers say, have just as great a dislike of standing around with wet feet as they do of being thirsty.

TENDING THE VINES

Growing vines is farming, just as much as growing barley or rearing pigs, and demands long hours and dedicated attention if the harvest of grapes is to be worth waiting for. Before a vineyard can be planted, it must be prepared and the soil properly turned over and aired. In some instances, it may need to be fumigated; in others growers may decide to correct its acidity or alkalinity.

Next, it is time to plant the vines – a less straightforward business than one might suppose. Unless your chosen site is in a place like Chile, Argentina or parts of the Antipodes which have yet to fall prey to the otherwise ubiquitous *phylloxera* louse, you are almost bound to have to graft your baby plants onto some kind of rootstock that is resistant to the louse.

Rootstock comes in a number of forms, most of which are distinguished by sets of letters or numbers. Until the mid-1980s, the identity of individual types of rootstock was of little interest to growers who merely noted that some were more productive than others. Then came the discovery that AXR, the particular rootstock recommended by the University of California to vine-growers

throughout that state, proved – as French experts had predicted in vain – to be less than wholly resistant to new biotypes of *phylloxera*. During the late 1980s and early 1990s, the louse attacked well over three-quarters of the vineyards of the Napa Valley, allowing those who had disregarded the University's advice by planting other (reliably resistant) rootstocks to continue to harvest their crops while their neighbours had to replant their entire estates.

Having selected the rootstock, the next task is to choose a clone of the variety you want to grow (see p. 29), the number of vines you are going to plant per hectare and the way you are going to train and prune them.

In the Old World, the density of your vineyard and the method of training will often be pre-ordained by tradition and law. Elsewhere, your decision will depend on the grape variety, the climate – in warm regions you can have fewer vines per hectare – and the style, quality and quantity of wine you want to make.

Methods of training are traditionally adapted to the climates of the countries where the vines are grown. In the late 1980s, though, vine-growers throughout the world

began to acknowledge that they might have something to learn from systems of vine "canopy management" developed in New Zealand and Australia by a man called Richard Smart.

In hot countries with limited rainfall, vines are likely to be trained to grow relatively close to the ground, so that the limited moisture available does not have to waste itself on producing too many shoots and leaves, but can be directed into the grapes. In cooler climates, with more rainfall and less sun, priorities are different. Here grapes are usually trained higher, to catch the limited sun more effectively, and reduce the risks of mildew and rot by permitting a free flow of air around the bunches of grapes.

Inevitably, this all paints a very simple picture of what is an extremely complicated subject, with innumerable methods of training and pruning vines. Among those frequently encountered are the Single and Double Guyot, Gobelet, Lenz Moser and the exotically named Geneva Double Curtain, which, needless to say, has nothing to do with Switzerland, but originated in New York State.

First stake your vine: High-density planting typical of Europe (left)
Canopy management in New Zealand: Innovative systems for better quality (below left)
Burning the prunings in Burgundy: In much of Europe, everything must be done by hand (below)

FROM VINEYARD TO WINERY

Until quite recently, in the Old World at least, the emphasis has been on the vineyard rather than the winery or cellar. French wine-producers, for example, routinely describe themselves as *viticulteurs* and *vignerons* – both terms which refer to vine-growing – and rarely, if ever, as *vinificateurs*, the word which most accurately covers the job of converting the grapes into wine.

For many, in both the Old and New Worlds, the task does indeed stop with the harvest; they simply deliver their crop to the local co-operative or bigger winery. But for tens of thousands of smaller estates, picking the grapes only marks the end of a chapter. There's many a slip between the snip of the secateurs and the sip of the wine.

In the 1970s and 1980s, the traditionally conservative world of wine was shaken to its roots by the arrival of technology in the shape of stainless steel tanks to replace the old wooden vats, cooling and heating equipment for the fermentation vats and all manner of high-tech presses and filters – not to mention computers to save human beings from having to watch the gauges and flick the switches.

The wine chemists – the oenologists – and biologists were playing their part too, developing special enzymes and yeast strains to replace the unpredictable stuff found on the skins of the grapes or in the cellars. Taken together, these innovations removed much of the guess-work from the wine-making process, turning, as one Australian gleefully admitted, what was an art or a craft into a science.

If wine-making is a natural process, certain refinements are necessary to make sure that the wine you make tastes good. Present in the white bloom on the skin of grapes are not only good wine yeasts, but tricky wild yeasts and bacteria as well. These are brought to the grapes by insects, or just carried in the air, and are fashionably aerobic – meaning they need plenty of oxygen to work.

If you were to leave fermentation to take place unaided in the open air, the wild yeasts would set to work in a furious rush until they were overcome by alcohol (at a strength of about 4 per cent). The slower-working, but more persistent, wine yeasts would then take over until they had completed the job, leaving the fruits of their labours exposed to the bacteria which feed on alcohol, turning it into vinegar.

Obviously, the bacteria must be prevented from getting a hold, along with the wild yeasts, which work too quickly for the good of the wine. There are two ways of doing this; one is to seal the tanks and starve them of oxygen, and the other is to add sulphur dioxide to the wine juice (or *must*), which feeds on oxygen and forms an oxygen-exclusive coating on top of the must. These precautions taken, vinification is quite straightforward.

Wine-making is rather like cooking. If the ingredients are fresh and of good quality, and if the basic rules are followed, the final result should be good wine. But just as each cook may have an individual touch, every quality wine-maker will aim to produce wines which bear his own stamp. This he can do by following the rules in his own way.

The temperature of the fermentation, the length of time it is allowed to carry on, the choice of wooden barrels or stainless steel tanks, the age and size of the casks, the period before bottling: all these are factors over which the wine-maker has complete control and which will influence the character of the finished wine.

Much of the fascination of wine-tasting lies in guessing exactly how each particular wine was made. Every glass of wine you drink will have gone through one of the processes described on these pages.

Cold steel: *Temperature-controlled fermentation tanks like these have revolutionized wine making*
Backache: *Most of the world's finest wines (this is Château Cos d'Estournel) are picked by hand*

HOW DRY WHITE WINE IS MADE

1. Grapes are picked, possibly by mechanical harvesters which shake them from the vines. They may be sorted; rotten ones are removed. The rest are taken quickly back to the winery. The longer the journey, the greater the risk of oxidation by heat and air.

2. For heavier-bodied wines, grapes may be crushed and allowed to macerate for 24 hours in a cool tank. This "skin-contact" is particularly popular in the New World.

3. For crisp, fruity wines, grapes are lightly crushed and the solid matter passed straight into the press. Wine-makers may control the temperature, keeping it cool for enhanced crispness.

4. The more you press, the more bitter the result. Some pressed juice is generally added to the "free-run" juice drawn off from the crusher, and the mixture passed into vats. Sulphur is added to kill off bacteria and prevent oxidation.

5. In the vat, suspended matter will drop out of the juice, which can then be allowed to ferment – in vats or in wooden barrels. Modern wineries may use vacuum pumps or centrifuges to separate solids from liquid.

The parting of the ways: White grapes arriving at the winery

6. In Old-World wineries, the natural yeasts found in the cellars will be responsible for fermentation. New-World and Flying Wine-makers generally prefer to use enzymes and selected cultured yeasts which are more predictable and can, between them, help to give potentially dull wine more flavour though in California there is a trend towards using "natural yeasts" as in Europe.

7. Fermentation may be fast or slow, warm or cool. "Warm" means between 18°C and 25°C; "cool", 18°C. The cooler the fermentation, the fruitier, but possibly less complex, the wine.

8. Barrel fermentation – particularly in small, new oak barrels, as in Burgundy – will give the wine an oaky, vanilla character and some longevity-bearing tannin. This is only appropriate for certain grapes, notably the Chardonnay and Sémillon, and not for more aromatic ones like Muscat and Gewürztraminer. Tank-fermented wine may then go into barrel, or stay in tank.

9. If there is insufficient grape sugar, (powdered) sugar or concentrated grape juice may be added to increase the final alcohol level in a process known as chap-talization. This procedure is banned in most warm regions and supposedly closely controlled in the cool ones. If there's too little acidity (as is often the case in warm regions), tartaric or citric acid can correct the balance; if there's too much, chalk will remove it.

10. Malolactic fermentation – the natural conversion of (appley) malic acid to (yoghurty) lactic – may take place partially or fully, either of its own accord or with the help of a specially developed innoculum, except where producers want to retain that acidity – as in some New-World styles and Vinho Verde.

11. The wine will then be fined, probably with bentonite, a powdery clay which drags any remaining solid matter, or "lees", to the bottom of the vat or barrel. It will then be "racked" – passed into another vat – before (usually but not invariably) filtering and bottling months or, in some cases, years after the harvest.

12. Some wines, notably Muscadet, are left *"sur lie"* – on their lees – and so taste slightly yeasty.

13. Inexpensive white wine is often "cold stabilized": chilled so that its tartaric acid forms harmless crystals which can be filtered out rather than be allowed to form in the bottle.

14. If barrels are used, there is the choice of how long the wine remains in them, and what kind and size of barrel to use. Chardonnay gains from being matured in small new oak barrels. Old-fashioned white Dão tends to remain for a long time in large old ones which remove the little fruit flavour with which it was born.

15. Sulphur dioxide is added before bottling to protect the wine. The dose must be carefully judged, otherwise the wine will suffer from a "bad egg" smell.

HOW RED WINE IS MADE

Red wine is made almost exclusively from black grapes, the colour coming from the skins.

1. In some regions – Burgundy for example – grapes are left to macerate in a cool-room or beneath a coating of sulphur for 24 hours or longer before fermentation is allowed/encouraged to begin.

2. All or most of the freshly picked bunches of grapes are first put through a crusher (unless *macération carbonique* is being used – see 4), which just breaks the skins. Depending on the sort of wine to be made, and the amount of tannin required, the stalks may or may not be discarded at this stage.

3. From the crusher, the grapes go straight into the fermentation vats, skins and

*I*magine calling up your favourite Italian restaurant and asking if the chef would mind your sending a young friend into his kitchen to cook dinner for you on your next visit, and every time thereafter. Your friend – an Australian who doesn't even speak Italian – would use the restaurant's ingredients and equipment to prepare precisely the same dishes the chef has been making for years. But he's going to make them the way you want.

Well, hard though it may be to believe, that's the precise equivalent of the proposal Britain's biggest wine-retailers successfully made during the 1990s to dozens of wineries in France (including such classic regions as Bordeaux and Burgundy), Spain, Portugal, Italy, Germany and Eastern Europe, as well, more surprisingly, as such New-World countries as South Africa, Chile and California. Could they send in their own Antipodean "Flying Wine-makers" – young men and women, most of whom arrived shortly before the harvest and left shortly afterward?

What was the secret of these mercenaries of the wine world? And why were they almost all Antipodean? The answer is one of philosophy: unlike many of their Old-World counterparts who tend to let nature and the climate decide on the style of wine produced in any given year, the New-World wine-makers start out with a pretty clear idea of the kind of wine they want to make.

Outsiders also acknowledge that the Flying Wine-makers are readier to work longer hours – no long lunches and week-ends off – and to pay greater attention to cleanliness and hygiene than the bosses of the Old-World co-operatives and larger commercial wineries in which they work.

Critics complain that Flying Wine-makers' wines all taste the same; supporters point out that, in blind tastings, and when British and Dutch consumers are allowed to vote with their wallets, it is the interlopers whose bottles regularly win the greatest favour. In 1995, there were over 100 Flying Wine-makers working in Europe – and few signs that their temporary hosts were learning enough from them to make their presence unnecessary.

all. Fermentation can take a few days or up to four weeks or longer to complete, some wine-makers relying on natural yeasts while others prefer cultured ones. The higher the temperature, the more colour and tannin is extracted.

4. To produce youthful, soft, lighter reds, whole grapes are fermented in sealed vats in a process known as carbonic maceration or "whole berry" fermentation. Carbon dioxide trapped in the vat forces the grapes to ferment quickly – sometimes inside their skins – under pressure, and the whole process can be completed in as few as five days. Quite often, modern producers use a "semi-carbonic" system in which some of the grapes are crushed.

5. A wine's colour and tannin content are dictated partly by the length of time the fermenting must remains in contact with the skins and pips. Unless these are restrained under the surface of the must, by a mesh or other device, they will be carried to the surface of the vat by the carbon dioxide formed during fermentation, and form a "cap" there. If there is no such device, the must is pumped up and over the cap from time to time or dripped through a sprinkler, to break it up and extract colour.

6 To produce bigger, richer reds, the skins may be left in contact with the juice for days or even weeks once fermentation is complete. Paradoxically, this prolonged contact with the tannin-bearing solids can make for softer-tasting wine.

7. If necessary, the must will be chaptalized (see How White Wine is Made).

8. Some Australian wine-makers – unusually – transfer the liquid into barrel before fermentation is complete. This process, which maximizes the effect of new oak on the still-fermenting wine, seems to suit big red styles, though there have been successful, lighter Pinot Noirs made in this way too.

9. The weight of the mass of grapes is sufficient to squeeze the fermented juice out of the grapes, which is then allowed to run into a cask as free-run wine.

10. The rest of the bulk goes into a press and is crushed to produce a highly tannic, dark wine. This "press wine" may be added to the free-run wine to add structure to the blend. The wine from both vat and press are transferred to tanks or barrels where the malolactic fermentation (see p. 25) will occur.

11. Red wine generally needs more time to mature than white. The tannin mellows in time, while the other components of the wine have time to blend together harmoniously. Wood barrels are often used for the maturation of red wines and the oak contributes not only additional flavour and complexity but also greater staying power to the wine.

12. In the case of Bordeaux and other blended wines, the "assemblage" will probably take place within a few months of the harvest. It is at this stage that particularly good or disappointing vats or barrels can be set aside for sale separately.

13. "Fine" wine almost always spends at least a year in barrels, large or small, new or old. During this time it must be "racked" (passed from one container to another, leaving the solids behind) to avoid growing stale and almost certainly "fined" with egg-white, which drags suspended yeasts and other solids in the wine downwards. Many quality-conscious producers now choose not to filter their wines to avoid removing flavour, but most commercial reds will pass through a filter before bottling.

14. Finally, time spent in bottle is important, but not every wine needs it. A complex (and expensive) bottle of red will almost certainly benefit from bottle ageing, as will whites with both body and high enough acidity. Simple wines, intended for prompt drinking, will lose colour, freshness and just about everything that makes wine enjoyable, if left for too long.

HOW WINE IS MADE TO SPARKLE

Sparkling wines are made by every wine-producing country in the world. The carbon dioxide which creates the bubbles in the wine is a natural by-product of fermentation.

If the wine-maker intends his product to be sparkling, he traps the gas in the wine. There it remains dissolved until the pressure is released, when it rapidly makes its way to the surface in the form of tiny bubbles.

There are various ways of capturing fizz in a wine. The best is the *méthode champenoise*, used not only in Champagne but throughout the wine-making world. The way in which the gas is trapped can vary, from a highly skilled, labour-intensive science to a heavy-handed, mass-produced routine, as can the quality of the base wine itself. The best base wines for sparkling wine are those with high acidity and little character. That the soil (chalk) and climate (cool) of Champagne are ideally suited to producing wines of this type is a major factor in explaining Champagne's pre-eminence among sparkling wines.

The Champagne Method (AKA méthode classique or traditionelle)
Used for: Champagne; Cava; Crémant de Loire, de Bourgogne and d'Alsace; Blanquette de Limoux; quality New-World sparkling wines; Italian "Metodo Classico"; quality German Sekt.

After the blending of the base wines, a solution of wine and sugar is added, along with specially cultured yeasts, to provoke a secondary fermentation. The bottles are then stacked on their sides in a cool cellar and left for the second fermentation slowly to run its course.

Traditionally, the bottles were then placed, neck first, into specially designed sloping racks, called *pupitres*, where skilled *rémueurs* would, over the course of a few weeks, daily shake, rotate and tilt the bottle slightly to shift the sediment down so that it rested on the cork. Nowadays this job is generally done – many say – just as effectively by machines called *giropalettes*.

Finally the necks of the bottles are chilled, freezing the sediment into a solid plug. When the corks are removed, the plug pops out under the pressure of the carbon dioxide in the bottle. The wine remaining in the bottle is then topped up with more of the same wine and a little liquid sugar, known as the *dosage*, before being corked with the traditional Champagne cork tied down with wire.

The Transfer Method
Used for: more run-of-the-mill European wines such as Kriter from France; some New-World fizz.

This is essentially a "second-best" cross between the Champagne and *cuve close* (see below) methods. The second fermentation takes place in the bottle and the wine is transferred under pressure to tanks for dosage, filtering and re-bottling.

The Cuve Close, Charmat or Tank Method
Used for: basic French sparklers; all but the best German Sekt; most Asti; Spanish "Granvas" fizz.

Invented by the Frenchman Charmat, this method can make tolerable sparkling wine – ideal, perhaps, for mixing a Buck's Fizz. The base wine is run into huge stainless steel tanks where secondary fermentation takes place at a controlled temperature, followed by *dosage*, filtering and bottling.

Taking the temperature: Keeping the fermentation cool is vital for freshness

HOW ROSE IS MADE

The classic way of making pink wines is to follow the red wine process until about 24 hours into step two. The wine is thus in contact with the black skins for just long enough to become delicately coloured. It is then racked off to complete fermentation on its own. Alternatively, the grapes may be allowed to macerate on the skins for a few hours before they are pressed and vinified like a white wine. The simple addition of red wine to white is illegal for quality still wines in Europe – but permitted for rosé Champagne, and customary for "white" or "blush" Zinfandel which is, in fact, often a blend of red Zinfandel and white Muscat.

SWEET AND FORTIFIED WINES

Sweet wines are the most difficult of wines to make and yet can be the best value of any wines in the world. Out of fashion for many years, and still frowned upon by health fascists who would prefer us to consume neither alcohol nor sweetness, good, rich, honeyed white wine is beginning to enjoy a comeback. Quality sweet wine depends on using grape varieties which naturally contain a lot of sugar, picking them late to

Methods of Fortification

The other way to make sweet wines is to add alcohol to the fermenting juice. Those who fortify wine in this way can produce wines – varying in strength from under 16 per cent to as much as 25 per cent – such as port, Marsala, Madeira, the delicious fortified Muscats of Australia and the *vins doux naturels* of France: Muscat de Beaumes de Venise and Rivesaltes.

With a few exceptions, fortified wines tend to be sweet. This is either because the addition of alcohol was made whilst there was still sugar in the grapes, or because in a few cases – most notably certain sherries – the final result is sweetened.

The French distinguish between *vins de liqueur*, which are made by alcohol being added to the grape juice before it has begun to ferment, and *vins doux naturels*, in which it is added during the fermentation process. Least prestigious of the *vins de liqueur* are the *mistelles*. The best-known are Pineau des Charentes, made in Cognac, Ratafia de Champagne and Floc de Gascogne. Others are used as the base for branded aperitifs.

Of the *vins doux naturels*, the most popular are the Muscats from the Rhône, Roussillon and Languedoc regions, such as Beaumes de Venise, Rivesaltes and most notably Banyuls, made in Roussillon from the Grenache grape.

Of the other fortified wines, port and Madeira are made by the *vin doux naturel* method. Sherry is fermented to dryness, then fortified before oxygen and yeasts start to act on the wine.

THE VARIETIES OF SOIL

Gravel
A great number of vineyards are perched on the side of river valleys, in well-drained gravel deposits. Vines do better in poor, well-drained soils which make them plunge their roots deeper to find water and goodness. The great wines of Bordeaux come from gravel soils *(Graves* means gravel) which particularly suit the Cabernet Sauvignon. Much depends, however, on the other kinds of soil with which the gravel is combined. If it is over clay, the wine will have less acidity than if it is over limestone.

Granite
The granite vineyards of the southern Rhône, home of Châteauneuf-du-Pape and Tavel rosé, are littered with huge "pudding stones", making the cultivation of anything seem virtually impossible. Once vines are established, however, the stones act as reflectors, bouncing the heat from the sun back on to the grapes. The end result is that they produce big, high-in-alcohol reds and France's most famous dry rosé. In the Beaujolais, granite suits the Gamay; its chemical properties reduce the wine's natural acidity.

Chalk
Chalk, too, makes for very good drainage and forces the vines to work hard for a living. Not all vine varieties like predominantly alkaline soil. Those that do best on chalky hillsides produce white wines of unique character such as the Chardonnay, which forms part of the inimitable blend for Champagne. The keynote of wines made from grapes grown on chalky – limestone – soil is their acidity, a characteristic that links Champagne, Chablis and Sancerre.

Slate
The richer minerals found in slatey soils suit some vines admirably. The alluvial deposits on the banks beside the Rhine and Mosel rivers in Germany are responsible for the delicate fragrance of the gently fruity local wines, produced on the precipitous, barren-looking slopes. The locals say: "Where the plough may go, no great wines grow." The main advantage of slate in regions like the Mosel is its heat retention, which compensates for the low temperatures in which the grapes have to ripen. Slate is also credited with the quality of Rieslings from the far warmer region of Clare in South Australia.

get all the sweetness of really ripe fruit.

The sugar contained in any grape will, given half a chance and a bit of yeast, ferment into alcohol. The sweeter the grape, the stronger the wine – in theory. In practice, once the strength rises to 15–16 per cent, the alcohol itself will kill off the yeast, leaving you with rather sweet, very alcoholic wine.

So, the key is to stop the fermentation before it gets to this stage. This can be achieved in one of two tricky ways. One method inevitably involves the use of the wine-maker's friend and, occasionally, wine-drinker's enemy – sulphur. Sulphur is needed for almost all white wines, but the sweeter examples need larger doses which,

The Language of the Winery

Acid Essential component – in malic (appley) and tartaric form – of wine, giving freshness and bite. Malic acid is naturally converted to the softer (yoghurty) lactic acid via *malolactic fermentation*, which naturally tends to follow the alcoholic fermentation which has turned the sugar into alcohol. Tartaric acid is often added in warm regions.

Alcohol The by-product of fermentation, created by yeasts working on sugar. It is also added in neutral form during or after fermentation to produce fortified wines. Measured as a percentage of volume.

Anthocyanin Grape-skin tannin responsible for colour and flavour in red wines.

Autolysis Interaction between wine and solid yeast matter giving a distinctive flavour, encouraged by ageing wine on its *lees* in Muscadet and Champagne.

Back-blending See *süssreserve*.

Barrel-ageing Maturing of wine in (usually new or newish) oak casks.

Barrel-fermented Fermented in barrel in order to intensify oak and vanilla flavours.

Barrique The traditional Bordelais oak barrel, now widely adopted elsewhere, with a capacity of 225 litres (50 gallons). Term used by Italian wine-makers to indicate the use of new oak barrels.

Baumé See *sugar*.

Bentonite Clay used for *fining*.

Blending The mixing of several wines to create a balanced *cuvée*. Also called *assemblage*.

Brix See *sugar*.

Cap The floating skins in a red wine must.

Capsule Once lead – now foil or plastic – film which covers and protects cork and bottle neck. Wax is also sometimes used – particularly for vintage port.

Carbon dioxide (CO$_2$) By-product of fermentation, trapped in wine as bubbles by sparkling wine-makers using the Champagne method, and otherwise induced in or injected into all sparkling wines.

Carbonic maceration Uncrushed grapes ferment under a blanket of CO_2, intensifying fruit flavours. Also known as "whole-berry fermentation".

Centrifuge Machine used to separate wine from the lees after fermentation. Also used in production of low-alcohol wines.

Champagne method See *méthode classique*.

Chaptalization See *sugar*.

Concentrated grape must Grape juice that has been reduced by heating to 20 per cent of its volume. If "rectified", it has also had its acidity neutralized. An alternative to using sugar in *chaptalization*.

Congeners The colouring and flavouring matter in wines.

Cool fermentation Temperatures are kept below 18°C (64°F).

Crushing The gentle breaking of berries before fermentation.

Cryoextraction A recently developed technique which involves partially freezing grapes before crushing them in order to separate the sweet, flavoursome juice from the water (which freezes more easily). Used in rainy vintages.

Cuvaison Period of time a red wine spends in contact with its skins.

Cuve A vat traditionally made of wood used for storage or fermentation.

Cuvée A specific blend.

Débourbage Period during which the sediments drop to the bottom of the tank allowing them to be separated from the fresh must.

Egrappoir Machine which removes stalks from grapes before they are crushed.

Elevage The "rearing" or maturing of wines before bottling.

Fermentation The conversion of sugars into alcohol through the action of yeasts.

Filtration Passing the wine through a medium to remove bacteria and solids (and possibly flavour – which is why some producers prefer not to filter).

Fining The clarification of must or wine, usually using natural agents such as egg white, gelatine, isinglass or bentonite which, as they sink, attract and drag down impurities (and possibly desirable flavours) with them.

Fortification The addition of alcohol to certain wines (e.g. sherry and port) either before or after fermentation is complete.

Free-run juice The clear juice which runs from the crushed grapes before they are pressed. The best-quality juice.

Hectolitre 100 litres.

Isinglass Fining agent derived from fish.

Lees Dead yeasts left after fermentation.

Maceration Period of contact between wine and skins in red wines.

Maderization Term for heat-induced oxidation, e.g. in Madeira.

Made wine Wine made from concentrated must – not fresh grapes.

Malolactic fermentation Natural or induced conversion of malic acid to the softer lactic acid.

Marc Skins, stalks and pips left after pressing. May be distilled into brandy.

Méthode champenoise Now-defunct term replaced by *méthode classique*.

Méthode classique The method used in Champagne of inducing secondary fermentation within the bottle in which the wine is sold.

Must Unfermented grape juice.

Must concentrators Ingenious machines used to remove water from the juice of grapes picked in the rain. See *cryoextraction*.

Must weight Amount of sugar in the must.

Mûtage The addition of alcohol to stop fermentation – used to make sweet fortified wines.

Oak Preferred type of wood in which to mature wine. Provides character and imparts flavour. Also used in chip form.

Oechsle See *sugar*.

Oenology The science of wine-making.

Oxidation Result of air contact with wine. Controlled in the maturation process; destructive in excess.

Pasteurization Sterilizing (usually cheap) wine by heating.

pH (number) Measure of acidity (low) or alkalinity (high).

Press Machine used gently to squeeze out juice remaining in skins.

Press wine Blending wine obtained by pressing the grape skins after *maceration*.

Pumping over The process of pumping the must over the floating cap of skins to obtain more colour and flavour.

Racking Decanting from one vessel to another leaving the lees behind.

Skin contact See *maceration*.

Sugar The sugar in fresh grape juice is measured prior to fermentation as this will determine the alcohol content and style of wine. Scales of sugar measurement are: in France, Baumé; in the New World, Brix; in Germany, Oechsle. In some regions, sugar may be added to *chaptalize* the must – to raise its potential alcoholic strength, but not to sweeten it.

Sulphur dioxide (SO$_2$) Invaluable antiseptic, antioxidant and preservative. Used sparingly by wise wine-makers.

Süssreserve In Germany, England and a few other regions, wines can be sweetened by the addition – back-blending – of sweet, unfermented grape juice.

Tannins Extracts from red grape skins and oak which give a red wine backbone. The mouth-drying quality of cold black tea is due to tannin.

Tartaric acid See *acid*.

Tartrates Potassium bitartrate is naturally present in all wine. Most is removed before bottling but some may linger in the form of harmless tartrate crystals.

Ullage The air space between the wine and roof of cask or, in bottle, cork.

Varietal Wine made and named after one or more grape varieties.

Yeast Naturally present on grapes, or added in cultured form, this is what makes grape juice ferment.

unless they are handled very carefully, give the wines an irritating throat-tickling character. Sadly, while wine-making skills have improved elsewhere, producers of sweet wines are often set in their sulphurous ways. Which is why cheap Sauternes and German late-harvest wines are often so poor – and why Austrian, New Zealand, South African, Australian and US wines, though rarely as complex as the best classic examples, are rapidly gaining in popularity.

Wherever a sweet wine is made, ideally it should be produced from grapes affected by "noble rot" – a fungus correctly known as *botrytis cinerea*. Mysteriously, and despite its name, the fungus doesn't actually rot the grapes as much as dehydrate them, breaking through their skins, allowing the water content to evaporate and thus concentrating the richness of the sugar which remains.

In California, where wine-makers have already learnt to master the yeasts which make wine ferment, the aim now is to create great sweet wine every year by *spraying* rot onto the grapes. Scientists are eagerly devising methods of duplicating exactly the effect of the mould as it creeps over the vines of Bordeaux, the Loire and the Rhine. Purists believe that such pre-empting of nature is cheating, but there are

plenty of producers in Sauternes who, in the all-too-frequent years when the *botrytis* fails to form, must feel very tempted to pre-empt nature too.

Rotten luck: An attack of "botrytis" on ripe grapes in Sauternes is cause for celebration

Send in the Clones

Anyone who read or saw *The Boys from Brazil* will recall the idea of propagating human beings from cells taken from a particular individual. The ability to create clones of Adolf Hitler may still be the subject of fiction, but vine-growers throughout the world have, since the 1980s, been able to plant identical copies of, say, one of the healthiest, most reliable Chardonnay vines in the Le Montrachet vineyard of Burgundy.

The clone sold by their local nursery will have been reproduced by a process of taking cuttings of successive generations and rejecting any that do not have precisely the same characteristics as the original, until "dissident" examples simply cease to occur. Cuttings taken from the successful strain will always have the desirable features of that original Le Montrachet vine.

Critics of clones complain that planting an entire vineyard with the same clone makes for wines lacking in complexity; most quality-conscious growers recognize this and now opt for a "cocktail" of different clones.

ROLL OUT THE BARREL

Wine-makers have been using oak barrels since the Romans became frustrated with the tendency of *amphorae* to break. The difference between then and now, however, is that, until the 1970s, the only time they brought in *new* oak barrels was when the old ones fell apart. This is not to say that no-one had realized that in the first three years of their working life, oak casks could add an extra note of sweet vanilla spice to the wines they contained – nor that certain forests produced wood with distinctive and attractive flavours. But the systematic use of oak as an ingredient did not begin until the best châteaux of Bordeaux used the newly acquired funds from the post-war vintages to replace tired casks and New-World wine-makers, eager not to miss a trick, followed in their footsteps...

There is no question that the flavour of oak can improve and add complexity to a wine – and that particular styles of wine work better with particular styles of oak (Rioja and Australian Shiraz do well in American oak while fine Chardonnay prefers wood from the forests of

Nevers, Allier or Vosges in France). New barrels are expensive however and, even if "scraped" and re-fired, have a relatively short life. Flying Wine-makers (see p. 25) and others achieve something of the same effect by putting the oak – in the form of chips – in the wine rather than vice versa. For some odd reason, this practice is frowned on by Old-World authorities.

Traditionalists frequently complain about wines being "over-oaked" and even Professor Emile Peynaud, the so-called "father of modern Bordeaux" and the man often credited with and blamed for creating the fashion for new oak, believed that few wines are concentrated and complex enough to support the 100 per cent new oak they are often given.

Thirty years on, Professor Peynaud's suspicion of oak abuse is beginning to strike a chord with wine-makers. In 1995, Andrew Pirie's Pipers Brook winery in Tasmania won "White Wine of the Year" at the International Wine Challenge with an unoaked Chardonnay, while the first reds made in Chile by Paul Pontallier and Bruno Pratts of Bordeaux were bravely almost devoid of obvious oak flavour.

VINTAGES

ONE OF the greatest areas of wine mystery and mystique is the difference between vintages. Was 1990 a good year for Châteauneuf-du-Pape? When ought I to drink my 1989 claret? Which was better for red Burgundy – 1990 or 1993?

Unfortunately, the closer you look at vintages, the more confusing the subject tends to become; if you want a simple, reliable, easy-to-follow vintage chart that will fit on the back of a credit card, I'm afraid that you are out of luck. If, on the other hand, what you are looking for is good flavour and good value, you've come to the right place – because it's surprising how often the best buys are to be found in years that get the cold shoulder from most vintage charts. The chart on the following pages is different because it looks at drinkability – the readiness of the wine to be enjoyed – as well as quality.

When thinking about vintages, it is worth bearing the following points in mind:

- "Great" vintages aren't always the ones you want to buy – particularly if the wines are young and you are going to open them soon. Many "lesser" vintages – such as 1987, 1992 and 1993 for red Bordeaux – are much more enjoyable when they are only a few years old, at an age at which "better" ones – such as 1986, 1988 or 1990 – are not yet ready to drink.
- The quality of a vintage – or lack of it – is only partly dependent on the weather during the summer. The clock begins ticking in the spring when the first leaves appear on the vines, and continues right up until the moment when the last grapes are safely picked and carried into the winery. A spring frost can harm the vines; bad weather at the flowering in the early summer can cut down the size of the crop; rain coupled with warm weather in the summer may lead to rot developing on the fruit; cold temperatures at summer's end may prevent the grapes from ripening properly; storms during the harvest may dilute the wine; hail can tear the bunches from the vines.
- Weather conditions can vary widely within the same country and even region. So, a great year for Burgundy in the east of

No Cinderella: A fine wine rests beneath nearly three-quarters of a century of cobwebs and dust

France may be a rotten one for Bordeaux, down in the south-west. Chablis can have markedly better weather than Chassagne-Montrachet, 100 miles further south – despite the fact that both are usually given the same "White Burgundy" rating on most vintage charts.

- Different grape varieties react in different ways. In Bordeaux, for example, the Merlot – which is the predominant grape in St Emilion and Pomerol – ripens earlier than the Cabernet Sauvignon, which is the main variety in the Médoc. So, in years like 1964, when rainstorms ruined the harvest in the Médoc, the Merlot grapes of the former areas had already been picked in perfectly dry weather.

Similarly, the varieties used to make Sauternes and Barsac need damp weather to develop noble rot – the very same damp weather that can cause havoc in neighbouring vineyards where the grapes for dry red wine are grown. Both 1967 and 1965, which were disastrous years for claret, produced stunning Château d'Yquem. Great years for white Burgundy – 1973, 1979, 1982 and 1986 – are often less impressive for red, partly because the Chardonnay is happier than the Pinot Noir in cooler weather, and partly because, unlike that variety, it has the capacity to produce good wine in heavily productive vintages.

- Wine-makers can get it right in bad years – and wrong in good ones. A week's

holiday taken during the crucial week when neighbouring growers discover they have to spray against rot can make all the difference between making great wine and poor, rotty stuff. Similarly, growers who do not prune tightly enough can allow their vines to over-produce in potentially good vintages and will make thin, dilute wine. If the weather during the harvest is too hot, wine-makers who do not have cooling equipment can see their fermenting vats overheat and their wine irredeemably spoiled.

On the other hand, in rainy years, richer wine-makers can use sophisticated cryoextraction systems to freeze grapes and remove water from the juice and consequently to produce more concentrated wines. Even when not using such new-fangled methods, producers such as the owners of the smarter châteaux in Bordeaux can, in any case, afford to omit all but their best wine from the bottles which will carry the château name. Which helps to explain why, say, in the rainy years of 1992 and 1993 big-name clarets were comparable to those from better, drier vintages while smaller producers made stuff which was downright unacceptable.

KEY

Still needs keeping	△
Can be drunk but will improve	▲
Ready now but no hurry	●
Should be drunk now	▼
Possibly over the hill	▽

FRANCE

Bordeaux (Red) Bear in mind the differences between the various regions of Bordeaux – and the differences between what particular wine-makers are trying to produce. A wine simply labelled as Bordeaux Rouge is made for fairly immediate consumption, however good the vintage. At the other end of the scale, a top-class château will normally be aiming to make long-lived wines in good vintages; their "second label" wines (like Château Margaux's "Pavillon Rouge du Château Margaux" and Château Léoville Lascases's "Clos du Marquis") are usually made to be drunk younger than the "first label" wines from the same property and the same vintage.

Type/Region	95	94	93	92	91	90	89	88	87	86	85	84	83	82	81	80	79	78	77	76	75	74	73	72	71	70	69	68	67	66
Northern Haut-Médoc (Pauillac, St-Estèphe, St-Julien)	8△	7△	5△	4●	4●	9△	9▲	8△	4●	8▲	8▲	3▼	8●	9▲	6●	5▼	6▼	8▲	4▼	6▼	6▲	2▼	2▼	2▽	5▼	7●				
Southern Haut-Médoc (Margaux)	8△	7△	5△	5△	4▲	8△	8△	8△	5△	8▲	8▲	4●	9△	8△	7▲	5●	6●	8▲	4▼	5▼	7●	2▼	2▼	2▽	5▼	7▼				
Graves	8△	7△	6△	5△	4△	8△	8△	8△	6△	8△	8▲	5●	9▲	9▲	7▲	6●	7▲	8▲	4●	6●	7▲	3▼	3▼	3▽	6●	8●				
St Emilion/Pomerol	8△	7△	6△	6△	4△	9△	8△	9△	6△	7▲	8▲	3▲	8▲	9▲	7●	4●	7●	7●	4▼	6●	8●	3▼	3▼	3▼	6●	8●				

Bordeaux (White) Until recently, there was very little dry white Bordeaux worth drinking at all – let alone cellaring. Sweet wines from Sauternes and Barsac can, however, last for an extraordinarily long time when they are from top-class châteaux.

Type/Region	95	94	93	92	91	90	89	88	87	86	85	84	83	82	81	80	79	78	77	76	75	74	73	72	71	70	69	68	67	66
Graves	8△	8△	7▲	6●	6●	8●	7●	9▲	8▲	8●	8●	6●	8●	7▲	6▲	5▲	8▲	7●	4●	8▲	8●	4▼	4▼	4▽	8●	8●				
Sauternes/Barsac	7△	6△	3△	3△	5△	8△	9△	9△	5△	8△	7△	3△	9△	5▲	6▲	5●	6●	5●	2●	8●	8●								8●	7●

Burgundy (Red) Burgundy is possibly the most varied (in quality terms) region in France. As a general rule, the reds of the Côte de Nuits live longer than those of the Côte de Beaune, while the Côte Chalonnaise and the Mâconnais tend to produce wines for younger drinking.

Type/Region	95	94	93	92	91	90	89	88	87	86	85	84	83	82	81	80	79	78	77	76	75	74	73	72	71	70	69	68	67	66
Côte de Nuits	8△	5△	6△	7△	6▲	9▲	8▲	9△	7▲	7△	9△	6●	7△	7●	4▼	8●	7●	8●	4▽	7▼					4▼	4▼	8●	9●	6▼	8▼
Côte de Beaune	8△	5△	6△	7△	6▲	9△	8▲	9△	7▲	7△	9△	5●	7△	6●	4▼	7●	6●	8●	3▽	6▼					3▼	3▽	8▼	9▼	6▼	8▼
Côte Chalonnaise/Mâconnais	8△	5△	6△	7△	6▲	9△	8▲	8▲	7▲	7△	8▲	5●	6△	6●	3▼	7●	6●	8●	3▽	6▼					3▼	3▽	8▼	8▼	5▽	8▼

Burgundy (White) Top-class white Burgundy can last supremely well – but don't push your luck by trying to cellar most basic examples for longer than four or five years. In Burgundy, a good vintage for reds can, confusingly, be a poor one for whites – and vice versa.

Type/Region	95	94	93	92	91	90	89	88	87	86	85	84	83	82	81	80	79	78	77	76	75	74	73	72	71	70	69	68	67	66
Chablis	9△	7▲	6▲	7●	5●	8●	8▲	8△	7●	9▲	8▲	7▲	6●	8▼	7●	5▼	8●	8●	6▼	6▼					5▼	5▽	8▼	9▼	6▼	8▼
Côte d'Or	9△	6△	6△	9△	5▲	9▲	7△	8△	7▲	9△	8▲	7▲	6●	5●	7●	5▼	9●	8●	6●	6▼					4▽	6▽	8▼	8▼	6▼	8▼
Côte Chalonnaise/Mâconnais	8△	6△	6▲	8▲	6●	8●	7△	8△	7●	9●	●	8●	7●	5●	6▼	7▼	5▽	8▼	8▼	5▽	5▽									

Alsace Good examples of Alsace can be extraordinarily long-lived – particularly the late-picked Vendange Tardive and Sélection de Grains Nobles wines. However, the region's reds, relatively delicate wines from the Pinot Noir, are for early consumption.

Type/Region	95	94	93	92	91	90	89	88	87	86	85	84	83	82	81	80	79	78	77	76	75	74	73	72	71	70	69	68	67	66
Gewürztraminer	7△	7△	7△	8△	6▲	9▲	9△	7△	5△	8△	9△	3▲	8▲	4▼	6●	4▼	6▼	4▼	2▽	8●	7▼	5▼	5▼		8●	5▼	5▼			
Riesling	7△	6△	7△	6△	5▲	8▲	9△	8△	6△	8△	9△	4▲	6▲	5●	7▲	5●	7●	5●	5●	9▲	8●	6●	6●		9▲	6●	6●			
Tokay-Pinot Gris	7△	6△	7△	7△	6▲	8▲	9△	8△	5△	7△	9△	3▲	9▲	4●	7▲	4●	6▼	5●	3▼	8●	7▼	5▼	5▼		8●	6●	6●			

Rhône (Red) Basic Côtes du Rhône, like Beaujolais, is made to be drunk young. Châteauneuf and Gigondas will age better, but for real keeping potential you have to head north to Hermitage, Côte Rôtie and Cornas, some of whose wines are almost undrinkably tough when they are less than five or even 10 years old. These wines, however, are very vintage-dependent, and from lesser years will drink younger.

Type/Region	95	94	93	92	91	90	89	88	87	86	85	84	83	82	81	80	79	78	77	76	75	74	73	72	71	70	69	68	67	66
Hermitage	8△	6△	5△	6△	7△	9△	7▲	8▲	5▼	6●	9▲	6●	9●	8▼	6▼	6▼	6▼	9●	4▼	8▼			6●	6●	9●	8●	8●		7●	8●
Côte Rôtie	8△	6△	5△	6△	7△	8△	8▲	8▲	7●	6●	9▲	6●	9●	8▼	7●	6▼	6▼	9●	4▼	8▼			5▼	5▼	9●	7●	9●		6▼	8▼
Cornas	8△	6△	5△	6△	7△	9△	7▲	8●	6▼	6●	9●	5▼	9●	8▼	6▼	6▼	6▼	9●	4▼	8▼			5▽	5▼	8▼	7▼				
Châteauneuf-du-Pape	8△	6△	6△	5▲	4▼	9△	7●	8●	6▼	6●	8●	5▼	9▼	8▼	7●	6▼	7▼	9▼	5▼	5▽			5●	5●	7▽	8▼	8▼		9▼	8▼

Rhône (White) White Rhônes can be gloriously fragrant when they are young and richly exotic when they are at least a decade old. Between the two stages, although perfectly drinkable, they are for some reason far less attractive than when at either extreme.

Type/Region	95	94	93	92	91	90	89	88	87	86	85	84	83	82	81	80	79	78	77	76	75	74	73	72	71	70	69	68	67	66
Hermitage/Condrieu	8△	7△	6▲	6▲	7●	8●	9●	8●	7●	6▼	8▼	4▽	7▼	8▼	5▽	5▽	6▽	9▼	4▽	6▽										

Champagne Until the 1970s, Champagne vintages were rare; they were only "declared" by producers in what they believed to be exceptional years. Today, thanks to better weather and a keen market, at least a few examples of vintage Champagnes are available almost every year.

Type/Region	95	94	93	92	91	90	89	88	87	86	85	84	83	82	81	80	79	78	77	76	75	74	73	72	71	70	69	68	67	66
Champagne				7△	6△	10△	9△	8▲		6▲	9△		7▲	8▲	7●	5▼	8▼	5▼	4▼	8▼	7▼	4▽	6▼		9▼	8▽	6▽			8▼

Loire (Red) Although they can have an attractive youthful fruitiness when they are young, good-quality red Loires really do repay keeping.

Type/Region	95	94	93	92	91	90	89	88	87	86	85	84	83	82	81	80	79	78	77	76	75	74	73	72	71	70	69	68	67	66
Loire Red	9△	6△	6△	5●	4●	9▲	9▲	8●	6▼	8▼	9▼	4▽	7▼	6▼	5●	5▼	6▼	8▼	2▽	9●	6▽	3▼	4▽	3▽	6▽	5▽				

Loire (White) Good examples of dry white Loires (Muscadet, Sancerre, Savennières, etc.) can last well, but they rarely improve beyond the first few years. Sweet Loires often need to age to tame their acidity. Many appear to last indefinitely.

Type/Region	95	94	93	92	91	90	89	88	87	86	85	84	83	82	81	80	79	78	77	76	75	74	73	72	71	70	69	68	67	66
Coteaux de Layon	9△	8△	4△	4●	5▲	8△	9●	8●	4▼	7▼	8●	3▼	7●	5▼	6●	5▼	6▼	6▼	2▽	9●	7▼	3▽	4▽	3▽	6▼	3▽				
Vouvray	7△	8△	4△	4●	5▲	8△	9●	8●	5▼	9▼	8●	6▲	7●	5▼	6●	5▼	6▼	6▼	2▽	9●	7▼	3▽	4▽	3▽	6▼	3▽				

Beaujolais (Crus) Basic Beaujolais and Beaujolais Nouveau should usually be drunk in the year or so after the harvest (nothing awful happens to Nouveau if you don't drink it before Christmas following the harvest). Of the 10 Beaujolais *cru* villages, the ones to keep the longest are Moulin-à-Vent and Morgon, followed by Juliénas and Chénas. Regnié, Chiroubles and Brouilly need drinking up first.

Type/Region	95	94	93	92	91	90	89	88	87	86	85	84	83	82	81	80	79	78	77	76	75	74	73	72	71	70	69	68	67	66
Cru Beaujolais	7●	7●	7●	5●	9●	7●	8▼	8▼	8▼	5▼	9▼	4▼	7▼	6▼	6▼	5▼														

ITALY

Piedmont Most Barolo needs at least five, if not 10, years to soften enough to be enjoyable. Barbaresco is usually approachable younger.

Type/Region	95	94	93	92	91	90	89	88	87	86	85	84	83	82	81	80	79	78	77	76	75	74	73	72	71	70	69	68	67	66
Barolo/Piedmont	9△	8△	7△	5△	6▲	9△	9△	8●	5▼	7▼	8●	4▼	6▼	9▲	6▼	4▼	8▲	8▲	5▽	5▼	5▼	8▼	6▼		9▼					

Veneto Valpolicella and Bardolino are generally made to be drunk young (though a few exceptions are breaking that rule). *Amarone* and *recioto* keep well, and this applies to white Recioto di Soave as well.

Type/Region	95	94	93	92	91	90	89	88	87	86	85	84	83	82	81	80	79	78	77	76	75	74	73	72	71	70	69	68	67	66
Amarone/Recioto Veneto	8△	8△	7△	5△	9▲	9△	6▲	9△	3●	8▼	9▲	5●	8●	7●	8▲	5●	8●	8●	8●											

Tuscany While Tuscany is usually thought to be the land of Chianti, it is increasingly the place to find exciting wines made from the same varieties as red Bordeaux. These (Sassicaia is a good example) often continue to mature for longer than all but the very best Chianti, most of which is made to be drunk quite young. Many are labelled merely *vino da tavola*, so the name of the wine and producer are important.

Type/Region	95	94	93	92	91	90	89	88	87	86	85	84	83	82	81	80	79	78	77	76	75	74	73	72	71	70	69	68	67	66
Chianti/Tuscany	8△	9△	6△	5△	6▲	9△	5●	9▲	5▼	7▼	8▲	4▼	7▼	8●	7▼	4▼	8▼	9●	7▼	3▽	6▼	4▼	6▼		8▼					

SPAIN

In general Spanish producers indicate their best and better vintages by calling them "*Gran Reserva*" and "*Reserva*" respectively. Both these terms will indicate longer oak-ageing and – in theory – greater potential longevity. Spain produces very few white wines that are built to last.

Type/Region	95	94	93	92	91	90	89	88	87	86	85	84	83	82	81	80	79	78	77	76	75	74	73	72	71	70	69	68	67	66
Rioja Reserva/Gran Reserva	8△	9△	5△	7▲	8△	7▲	7▲	5▲	8●	6●	7●	5▼	7●	9▲	8●	7●	6●													
Penedés (Red)	8△	8△	7△	6▲	9▲	7△	7△	7△	9▲	6●	8△	5▽	7●	7▽																
Ribera del Duero	8△	9△	5△	6▲	8△	9△	6△	6△	9●	8●	7●	3▽	7▲	9●																
Penedés (White)	8△	7△	6△	6▲	9▲	6●	6▲	8▲	7▲	6●	7●	8▼	7▼	7▼																

PORTUGAL

Like Spain, Portugal makes few long-lived whites. Its reds last better – and are often sold when they are already mature. The term "*garrafeira*" indicates a reserve wine that ought to last well. Vintage port, though always supposedly intended for cellaring, does vary in its likely longevity. Curiously, top-class houses never "declare" a vintage two years running. Most late-bottled vintage port does not develop or improve with age.

Type/Region	95	94	93	92	91	90	89	88	87	86	85	84	83	82	81	80	79	78	77	76	75	74	73	72	71	70	69	68	67	66
Bairrada	9△	8●	8●	8●	8●	9●	5▼	8●	4▼	4▼	7●	4▼	8▼	8▼	4▼	8●	5▼	8▼	5▼	5▼	8▼									
Dão	9△	8●	8●	8●	8●	9●	6▼	8●	4▼	4▼	7●	4▼	8▼	8▼	4▼	8●	5▼	5▼	5▼	7▼	8▼									
Vintage port		9△		7△	9△				8△		7△	6△		7△			10△	5▼				9▲				6●				

GERMANY

The new trend toward "dry", "*Trocken*", wines in Germany complicates the life of anyone trying to draw up a chart like this. These wines – particularly the Rieslings – often take longer to be pleasurably drinkable than their sweeter equivalents, but they don't live as long. Germany's sweetest whites – *Beerenauslesen* and *Trockenbeerenauslesen*, which are mostly made only in the best vintages – can last almost indefinitely.

QbA, Kabinett, Spätlese

Type/Region	95	94	93	92	91	90	89	88	87	86	85	84	83	82	81	80	79	78	77	76	75	74	73	72	71	70	69	68	67	66
Mosel	8△	8△	9△	8△	7●	9▲	8●	9●	6●	7●	9●	6▼	8▼	6▼	6▼	4▽														
Rhine	8△	7△	8△	8△	6●	9▲	8●	8●	6●	7●	8●	5▼	8▼	5▽	5▽	6▽														

Auslese, Beerenauslese, Trockenbeerenauslese

Type/Region	95	94	93	92	91	90	89	88	87	86	85	84	83	82	81	80	79	78	77	76	75	74	73	72	71	70	69	68	67	66
Mosel	8△	8△	9△	8△	7△	9△	8△	9△	5▲	6▲	9▲		9●																	
Rhine	7△	8△	8△	8△	7△	9△	8△	8△	5▲	6▲	9▲		9●																	

AUSTRALIA

As in the USA, styles and regions can vary enormously. However, it is fair to say that, while few Australian Chardonnays have been built to last, old Sémillons, Cabernet Sauvignons and Shirazes (and blends of the latter two) can be the longest-lived of all New-World wines.

Type/Region Red	95	94	93	92	91	90	89	88	87	86	85	84	83	82	81	80	79	78	77	76	75	74	73	72	71	70	69	68	67	66
New South Wales Red	9△	7▲	8▲	5●	7●	7●	4▼	8●	8▲	9▲	8●	6▼	7▼	9●	5▼	8▼														
South Australia Red	9△	8▲	8▲	6●	8▲	8●	5▼	7▼	8●	8▲	8●	9●	6▼	9●	6▼	8●														
Victoria Red	9△	8▲	6●	8●	8▲	8●	6▼	8●	8●	9▲	8●	7●	6▼	9●	6▼	8▼														
Western Australia Red	9△	9▲	7●	7●	7▲	8●	6▼	7▼	8▲	8▲	9●	8●	8▼	8●	6▼	8▼														

Type/Region White	95	94	93	92	91	90	89	88	87	86	85	84	83	82	81	80	79	78	77	76	75	74	73	72	71	70	69	68	67	66
New South Wales White	9●	7●	8●	5●	8▼	6▼	5▼	8▼	8▼	9●	8●	6▼	7▼	9▼	5▽	8▽														
South Australia White	9●	8▲	8●	6●	8●	8●	6▼	7▼	8▼	9●	8▼	8▼	6▼	9▼	6▼	8▽														
Victoria White	9●	8▲	6●	8●	8●	8▼	6▼	8▼	8▼	9●	8▼	8▼	6▼	9▼	5▼	8▼														
Western Australia White	9●	9▲	7●	5●	7●	7▼	6▼	7▼	8▼	8●	9▼	8▼	8▼	8▼	6▼	8▽														

UNITED STATES

The variation between producers' styles and between grape varieties makes it very difficult to generalize in the USA. And, of course, it is a huge country – California is large and varied enough in itself to warrant an extensive vintage chart of its own. Even so, the following should provide useful guidelines for the more commonly seen wines. The ageability of all but a very few US wines is, as yet, unproven.

Type/Region	95	94	93	92	91	90	89	88	87	86	85	84	83	82	81	80	79	78	77	76	75	74	73	72	71	70	69	68	67	66
California Red	8△	7△	6△	8▲	9▲	9●	7▲	7●	8●	8●	9▲	8●	5▼	7▼	6▼	7▼	6▼	7▼	6▼	7▼	7▼	9▼								
California White	8△	7▲	6▲	8●	9●	8▼	6▼	7▼	7▼	8●	9▼	7▼	5▼	7▼	8●															
Pacific North-West Red	7△	7▲	6●	8▲	8▲	8●	8●	9▲	8▼	7▼	9●	5▼	9▼	6▼	7▼	8▼	7▼	8▽	7▽	8▽	9▽									
Pacific North-West White	8△	7●	6●	8●	8●	8●	8●	8●	8▼	7▼	9●	5▼	9▽	6▼																

NEW ZEALAND

Reds here are still rarely built to keep successfully, but Chardonnays are already top-class and worth cellaring and Sauvignons last surprisingly well.

Type/Region	95	94	93	92	91	90	89	88	87	86	85	84	83	82	81	80	79	78	77	76	75	74	73	72	71	70	69	68	67	66
Red	7●	8●	7▲	8▲	8▲	7▲	9●	7●	8▼	7▼	8▼		9▼																	
White	6●	8●	6●	8●	8●	6▼	9▼	7▼	7▽	8▼	8▼		8●																	

SOUTH AFRICA

Styles here are evolving so fast, and vary so much from producer to producer, that generalization is hard. The best reds seem able to age for a few years.

Type/Region	95	94	93	92	91	90	89	88	87	86	85	84	83	82	81	80	79	78	77	76	75	74	73	72	71	70	69	68	67	66
Red	8▲	7▲	7●	8▲	9▲	7●	8●	7▲	9●	8●	5▼	6●																		
White	7●	7●	7●	7●	8▼	6▼	4▼	4▽	8▼	6▽	5▽																			

READING THE LABEL

*W*ine labels are a cross between a passport, with all its legally required information, a visiting card, and a full-scale advertisement for the contents of the bottle. Some are so overloaded with techno-speak that they seem to be aimed at people whose main interest in wine is scientific; others are coy; and some seem to aspire to be thought works of art. But even a label that appears to tell you the bare minimum can be quite revealing: read it carefully and you should know the name of the wine, where and possibly when it was made, the identity of the

person or company that produced and/or bottled it, its alcoholic strength and the amount you are getting for your money. And, if you live in an EU country, you will be protected from the kind of labelling featured in our African example below.

Other labels, more helpfully, may reveal a whole lot more. In the traditional countries of Europe, they might indicate the officially designated quality of the wine (such as *Appellation Contrôlée*, *Premier* or *Grand Cru*) and the style in which it has been made (its sweetness or

dryness, and the fact that it is aged in oak barrels, for instance). "New-World" wines from the USA, Australia or elsewhere are more likely to tell you the name of the grape variety from which they are made.

Whatever the wine, and however many helpful or baffling words appear on the label, don't forget that once you know its style, the most important fact about any wine is the name of its producer. Over 1,000 different people make wine labelled as Beaujolais. And they make it to very different standards.

The merchant

High-status French terms, used here to "add" quality by association. Zimbabwe has no quality control system; nor would the EU allow this wine to be sold under this label in Europe

"Description" of the wine (you may or may not believe everything said here)

The merchant has neither produced nor, apparently, blended or bottled the wine

Further misleading suggestions of quality, this time garnered from Germany. Cabinet/ Kabinett has no recognized association with quality unless it appears on a bottle of German wine

This is no guarantee that the wine was grown in Zimbabwe, though there seems little reason to lie

The domaine

The village name

Vintage

Name and address of bottler (obligatory)

Produce of France, mandatory for all wines that are or may be exported

Alcoholic strength

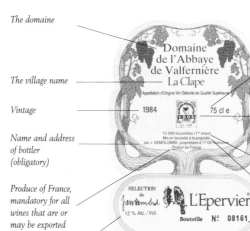

The contents by volume. 75 cl is a standard size for EC wines, indicated by the letter "e"

These numbered stamps guarantee the wine's VDQS quality

The number of bottles produced of this particular cuvée

Estate-bottled

Bottle number

Though officially a vin de pays, this is one of the finest wines in the South of France

Bottled at the domaine

Produce of France

"Country wine" from the Hérault département

Contents by volume (mandatory in the EU)

Owner and grower based at Aniane, France

It is quite common for the "Appellation" to be writ large as the wine's name, then repeated in the standard AC format below

Contents by volume (mandatory)

A spot of culture: this cuvée takes its name from a Victor Hugo poem, rather than an individual vineyard. Jaboulet has registered both "Le Grand Pompée" and the crest below as trademarks ("marques deposées")

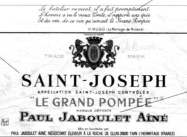

Paul Jaboulet is one of the biggest and best "négociants" in the Rhône; his name is thus printed large as a selling point, as well as appearing with the legally required bottling address below

Morgon is one of the 10 Beaujolais "crus": since each has an "Appellation Contrôlée" in its own right, there is no need to mention Beaujolais at all on the label.

The "old parchment" look is characteristic of labels from Burgundy

Like all Beaujolais Nouveau or Primeur this is in fact merely Beaujolais that is sold soon after the harvest.

Wine from the first pressing of the grapes, as youthful and lively as the hard-working babes pictured, and as full of fruit as their baskets.

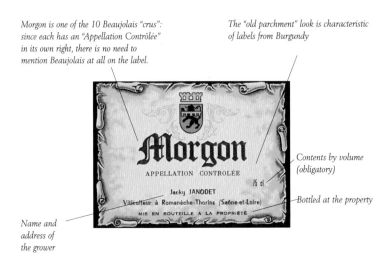

Contents by volume (obligatory)

Bottled at the property

Name and address of the grower

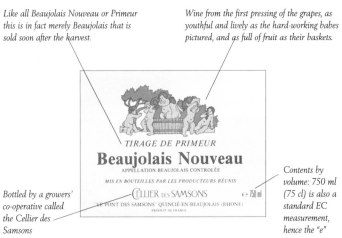

Bottled by a growers' co-operative called the Cellier des Samsons

Contents by volume: 750 ml (75 cl) is also a standard EC measurement, hence the "e"

The brand name. This is a "Prestige Cuvée"

The town where it was made

The wine is solely from this Premier Cru vineyard, one of only 14 sites so designated. A blend of wine from two or more of them may still be labelled "Premier Cru"

High-quality, though not the very best (Grand Cru) Chablis; however, Premier Cru is prestigious enough to warrant mentioning here as well as within the standard AC format below

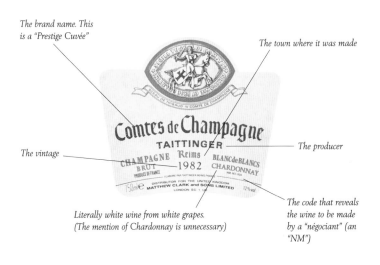

The vintage

The producer

Literally white wine from white grapes. (The mention of Chardonnay is unnecessary)

The code that reveals the wine to be made by a "négociant" (an "NM")

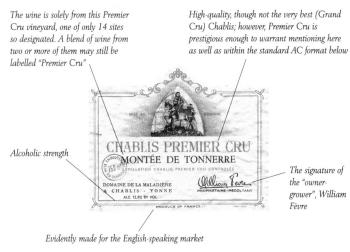

Alcoholic strength

The signature of the "owner-grower", William Fèvre

Evidently made for the English-speaking market

The wine was selected in 1986 by the tasting jury of the Confrérie des Chevaliers de Tastevin, a Burgundian brotherhood that seeks to maintain quality standards

The name of the wine, a basic "Appellation" which can promote some good wines

"Crémant" means sparkling usually – "Appellation Contrôlée" – "Méthode Champenoise"

Produced by the Champagne method. Since 1992, only wines from Champagne are allowed to use this term

Wines given the taste vintage label are individually numbered

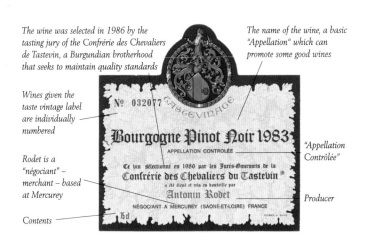

"Appellation Contrôlée"

Rodet is a "négociant" – merchant – based at Mercurey

Producer

Contents

Dry

Alcohol by volume

The producer: the Saumur Co-operative

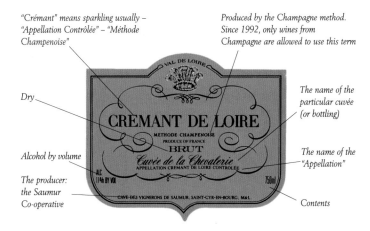

The name of the particular cuvée (or bottling)

The name of the "Appellation"

Contents

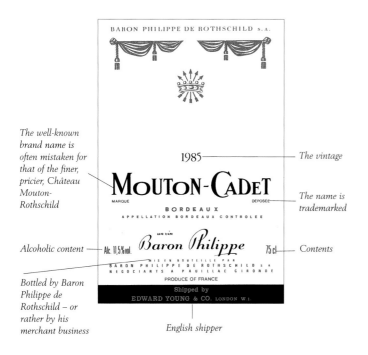

The well-known brand name is often mistaken for that of the finer, pricier, Château Mouton-Rothschild

The vintage

The name is trademarked

Alcoholic content

Contents

Bottled by Baron Philippe de Rothschild – or rather by his merchant business

English shipper

A "Cru Bourgeois" – not included in the 1855 classification, but potentially good value

The name of the château

From the fairly basic Médoc "Appellation"

The vintage

The owners (Gilbeys) are based at St Yzans

Contents

Bottled at the château

Appellation and name of commune

Pauillac is a commune – like an English parish

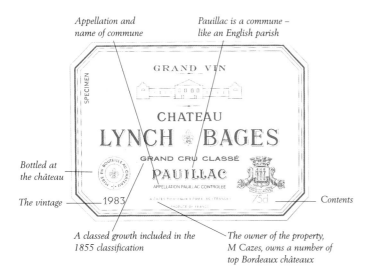

Bottled at the château

The vintage

A classed growth included in the 1855 classification

The owner of the property, M Cazes, owns a number of top Bordeaux châteaux

Contents

The domaine

The name of the château

French note for the English-speaking drinkers

The Muscadet "Appellation"

Contents

Village

Bottled on its "lees", the wine has gained extra weight and flavour

Bottled at the château

The "Appellation"

Vintage

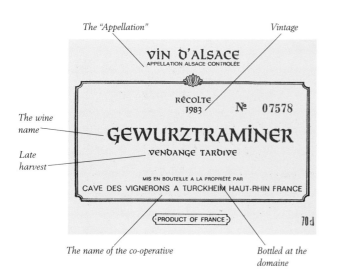

The wine name

Late harvest

The name of the co-operative

Bottled at the domaine

Literally "half-dry". These wines can be quite sweet and rich, especially given bottle age. May also say "sec" – dry – or "moëlleux" – soft, sweet

The name of the domaine

"Appellation"

Contents

Alcoholic strength

The main area of production

A "quality wine" – a QbA

The quality control number

RHEINPFALZ

Dornfelder
Dry Red Wine
QUALITÄTSWEIN
A.P.Nr. 5042092 24589
SELECTED FOR TESCO
ERZEUGERABFÜLLUNG
GEBIETS-WINZERGENOSSENSCHAFT
DEUTSCHES WEINTOR eG
D 6741 ILBESHEIM/SÜDL.WEINSTRASSE
Alc. 12% vol   PRODUCE OF GERMANY   e 75 cl

The grape from which this is made

A description for the English market

The UK retailer

The contents

The name of the wine, spelt the German way here but the Italian way elsewhere on the label. Wines from the Alto Adige are peculiar in that they are frequently written in both languages

Quality control for the region, in both German (QbA) and Italian (DOC)

Province

Stamp of local co-op (in Italian)

Winery or co-op

Alcoholic strength by volume

Estate-bottled

Contents

KLASSISCHER
St. Magdalener
Denominazione di origine controllata

St. Magdalena
St. Justina
Leitach

Qualitätswein b.A.
Erzeugerabfüllung · Imbottigliato all'origine
KELLEREIGENOSSENSCHAFT
ST. MAGDALENA
BOZEN   ITALIEN
ESTATE BOTTLED
12,5 % Vol.   PRODUCT OF ITALY   0,75ℓ e
76/BZ

Name of the producer. Many German labels are addicted to Gothic lettering which makes few concessions to readability for non-Germans

Vintage

The grapes came from the Burgergarten vineyard, in the village of Haardt

Region of production

Alcohol content

Quality category: "Kabinett" is a level within QmP category

Weingut

seit 1744
Müller-Catoir
Gutsabfüllung · D-67433 Neustadt/Weinstrasse-Haardt

1994er Riesling
Haardter Bürgergarten Kabinett
alc.10,5%vol · Pfalz · 750 mle
Qualitätswein mit Prädikat · Amtl.Prüf.Nr. 5 174 079 1195

Official bottling number given to every German wine

Volume

Year the winery started making wine

Address of the bottler: in this case the same as the producer

Grape variety: Germany's best, so given prominence

Wine's official quality level

The "brand name" of the producers' Valpolicella, written larger to distance it from lesser examples

Better-quality Valpolicella conforming to higher standards

"Bottled in the zone of production"

Contents

Vendemmia 1985 FAC = SIMILE   № 22964

VIGNETI DI
Marano

VALPOLICELLA CLASSICO SUPERIORE
Denominazione di origine controllata
Imbottigliato in zona di produzione da
Paolo Boscaini e figli
in Valgatara di Marano / Italia
CONT. 750 ml   BOSCAINI   Alc. 12% by Vol.

PRODUCE OF ITALY

Individually numbered bottle

Guarantee of origin

Producer and merchant

The alcoholic strength-percentage of alcohol

By volume: many Barolos are notable for their high strength of alcohol

The number of bottles, magnums and double magnums produced in this vintage

The abbreviation for the official EU term, "Vin de Qualité Produit Dans une Région Delimitée"

MONPRIVATO®
IN CASTIGLIONE FALLETTO
ALC. 14% BY VOL. 1982   750 ML
13148 ALBEISE - 66 MAGNUM - 30 GRANDI ALBEISE
ALBEISA   № 11553

BAROLO
DENOMINAZIONE D'ORIGINE CONTROLLATA E GARANTITA
VQPRD - IMBOTTIGLIATO ALL'ORIGINE DAL VITICOLTORE
MAURO MASCARELLO A MONCHIERO - ITALIA - R.I. 555/CN
NELLA CANTINA
MASCARELLO
GIUSEPPE E FIGLIO
PROPRIETARI PRODUTTORI DAL 1881

The name of the wine, registered as a trademark

Contents

Individual bottle number

Estate-bottled by grower

Denominazione de Origine Controllata e Garantita; the highest Italian quality designation

Semi-sweet

DOC quality. Semi-sparkling "natural fermentation"

Brand name (registered)

Co-op bottled

Town of co-op

AMABILE
CAVICCHIOLI®
LAMBRUSCO DI SORBARA
VINO DI QUALITA PRODOTTO IN REGIONE DETERMINATA
DENOMINAZIONE DI ORIGINE CONTROLLATA
VINO FRIZZANTE A FERMENTAZIONE NATURALE
IMBOTTIGLIATO NELLE CANTINE
CAVICCHIOLI U.&F.
SAN PROSPERO (MO)
PRODOTTO IN ITALIA   8+3% VOL.

75 CL e

Contents

Alcohol content: 8 per cent. The 3 per cent refers to the potential alcohol of the wine's residual sugar

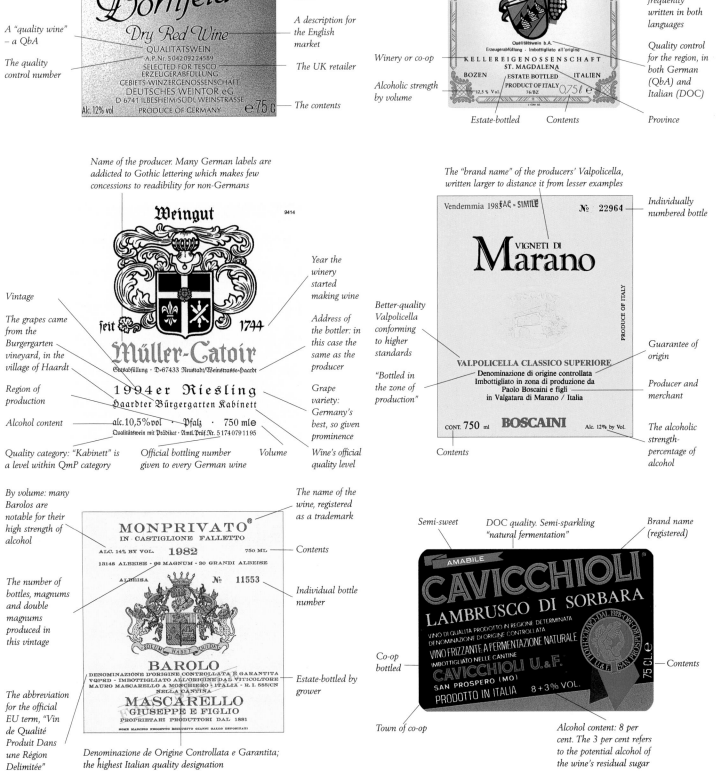

37

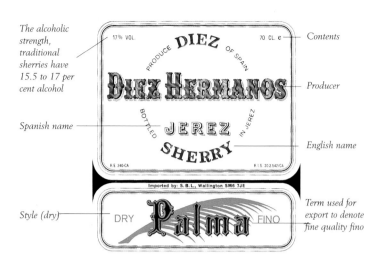

The alcoholic strength, traditional sherries have 15.5 to 17 per cent alcohol

Contents

Producer

Spanish name

English name

Style (dry)

Term used for export to denote fine quality fino

Shipper and bottler

Name of the wine, made on the island of Madeira

Brand name

Producer

Style (grape variety)

Contents

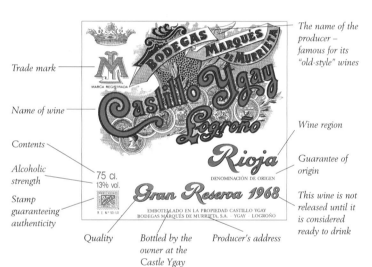

Trade mark

Name of wine

Contents

Alcoholic strength

Stamp guaranteeing authenticity

Quality

Bottled by the owner at the Castle Ygay

Producer's address

The name of the producer – famous for its "old-style" wines

Wine region

Guarantee of origin

This wine is not released until it is considered ready to drink

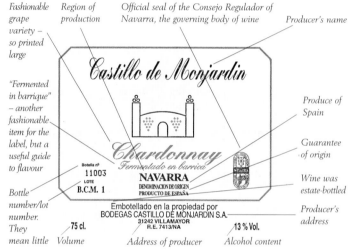

Fashionable grape variety – so printed large

Region of production

Official seal of the Consejo Regulador of Navarra, the governing body of wine

Producer's name

"Fermented in barrique" – another fashionable item for the label, but a useful guide to flavour

Bottle number/lot number. They mean little

Volume

Produce of Spain

Guarantee of origin

Wine was estate-bottled

Producer's address

Address of producer

Alcohol content

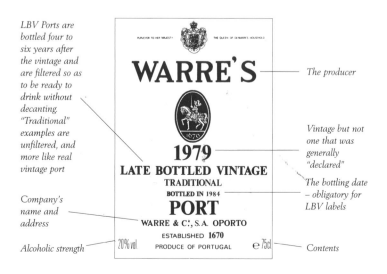

LBV Ports are bottled four to six years after the vintage and are filtered so as to be ready to drink without decanting. "Traditional" examples are unfiltered, and more like real vintage port

Company's name and address

Alcoholic strength

The producer

Vintage but not one that was generally "declared"

The bottling date – obligatory for LBV labels

Contents

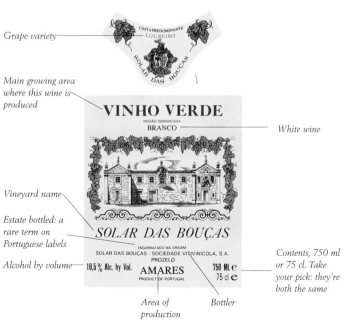

Grape variety

Main growing area where this wine is produced

Vineyard name

Estate bottled: a rare term on Portuguese labels

Alcohol by volume

White wine

Contents, 750 ml or 75 cl. Take your pick: they're both the same

Area of production

Bottler

38

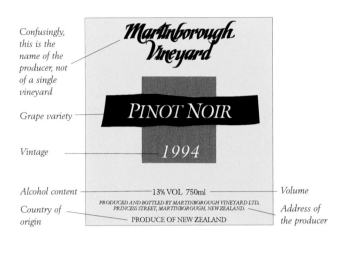

Confusingly, this is the name of the producer, not of a single vineyard

Grape variety

Vintage

Alcohol content

Country of origin

Volume

Address of the producer

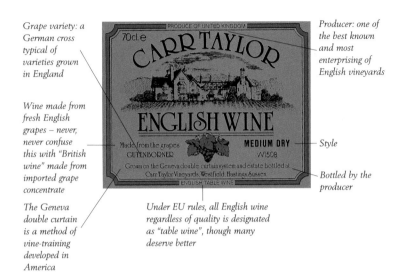

Grape variety: a German cross typical of varieties grown in England

Wine made from fresh English grapes – never, never confuse this with "British wine" made from imported grape concentrate

The Geneva double curtain is a method of vine-training developed in America

Producer: one of the best known and most enterprising of English vineyards

Style

Bottled by the producer

Under EU rules, all English wine regardless of quality is designated as "table wine", though many deserve better

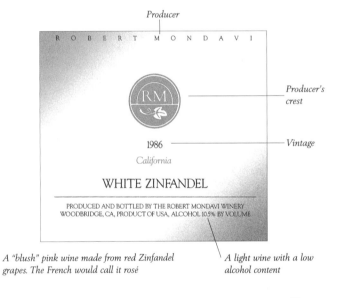

Producer

Producer's crest

Vintage

A "blush" pink wine made from red Zinfandel grapes. The French would call it rosé

A light wine with a low alcohol content

Name of the producer. Coonawara is is one the finest vineyard areas in Australia, but here it forms part of a company name

Added to Wynn's labels to mark their centenary in 1991

Vintage

Address

Alcohol content

Grape variety

Volume

Address of the British importer

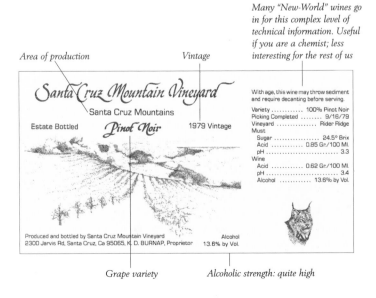

Area of production

Vintage

Many "New-World" wines go in for this complex level of technical information. Useful if you are a chemist; less interesting for the rest of us

Grape variety

Alcoholic strength: quite high

Producer

This is a single-estate wine bottled by a "negociant" company called The Bergkelder

Grape variety

Volume

Alcoholic content

Region of origin

Seal of the "negociant" company

CHOOSING A STYLE

Life was easy for Jack Spratt and his wife; each was able to choose the part of the meat he or she liked. Buying a bottle of wine for two can be trickier – especially if one likes red and the other white, or if one has a sweet tooth and the other doesn't. Compromises are not always obviously available. On the other hand, there are now so many different wines on offer – especially in countries like Britain, the USA and Australia, where a semi-ambitious merchant may sell up to 600 styles compared to the dozen or so available in the 1960s – that there is, quite literally, usually something for everybody. The trick lies in deciding on the styles you enjoy, and knowing where to look for them.

Unfortunately, though, many people forget that this is only the first stage. They simply find a wine they like, and stick to it, picking up the same Rioja, Côtes du Rhône or California Chardonnay every time, confident in the knowledge that they know what they are getting – just as there are people who invariably go to the same restaurant and order the same dishes.

Of course, playing safe does have its

advantages, but for every occasion when it protects you from disappointment, there are probably at least a couple of times when it'll stop you from discovering a delicious wine – and, quite probably, a bargain.

It's true that the array of wines on offer can be bewildering, but it is possible to group them simplistically by colour, sweet-ness and body. Indeed this was precisely what British wine-retailers attempted to achieve with a widely adopted coding system for white wines in the 1980s which graded them according to their sweetness – from "1" for a bone-dry Muscadet to "9" for an ultra-sweet Muscat de Beaumes de Venise. At first, traditionalists mumbled and grumbled that one really oughtn't to be categorizing – and thus "demystifying" – wine in this way but, within a very short while, the code became commonplace on bottle labels and shelves.

The success of the white-wine scale, and its popularity among the general public, led inevitably to calls for a similar guide to reds. This proved to be rather more contentious at first, partly because it was suggested that any such innovation might contravene one of the European Union's more arcane regulations. Eventually, however, an A–E scale was widely introduced that now gives wine-buyers a good idea of whether the wine they are looking at is as lightweight as a Beaujolais or as much of a bruiser as a Barolo. By the mid-1990s, the two scales were thought useful enough for one supermarket to decide to group its wines, irrespective of nationality, strictly according to sweetness and price.

Clearly, however, any such codes, by their very nature, inevitably tend both to simplify and to generalize. Some Beaujolais may be a great deal more muscular than others – and there are some middleweight modern Barolos. Although most wines of a particular style or *Appellation* can be fitted into the niche of a single number or letter, there will always be exceptions to prove the rule. Most wine-retailers handle these anomalies by allocating codes to specific wines rather than styles, describing one red Burgundy, for example, as a "B" and another, bigger, one as a "C".

Even so, codes like these can make for odd bedfellows. A New Zealand Sauvignon and a Soave may both be white and similarly dry, but one tastes like over-ripe gooseberries while the other is light, creamy and almondy. A Tavel rosé and a *Trocken* wine from Germany may, by the same token, taste equally dry, but their flavour is as different as their colour.

Supermarket sweep: The choice can be baffling

Double bubbles: *Brut Champagne like this is dry, whereas Gancia is sweeter*

Another, more useful, means of grouping wines adopted by merchants is by the grape or grape varieties from which they are made. Cabernet Sauvignons and Merlots from coolish vineyards in Bulgaria may indeed be comparable to Bordeaux made from the same varieties. Climate, soil and wine-making styles, however, play such a major part in the flavour of a wine that it can be dangerously misleading to suggest that a trio of Chardonnays – a tropical Australian, semi-sweet Californian and grassy South African, for example – bear any more resemblance than cousins brought up on three different continents.

If you like traditional Bordeaux, the flavour you really enjoy is of a blend of Cabernet Sauvignon, Merlot and Cabernet Franc grapes, coupled with the leanness imposed by a fairly cool climate and made by wine-makers for whom "fruitiness" is not, in any case, a prime consideration. A jammy, blackcurranty Australian Cabernet Sauvignon from, say, the warm Barossa Valley, aged in vanilla-packed, new oak barrels will, on the other hand, probably have more in common with some New-Wave Rioja and Rhônes than with most offerings from the Médoc and St Emilion.

And just to complicate matters a little further, there can be a huge variation in the style and quality of wine-making within

even quite small regions: some Australians are making surprisingly lean red wines, while some Bordeaux châteaux are producing wines which taste as though they could have come from the heart of the Napa Valley in California.

To help you through this jungle, I have listed below wines whose flavours are likely to share at least a few discernible characteristics, including them, where appropriate, in more than one group. For recommended producers, see *The Essentials* boxes for each region, where relevant, in the main section of the book.

Oaky whites

Traditional white Rioja (rare these days)
Graves or Pessac Léognan – new style Bordeaux *(France)*
Chardonnay – from just about everywhere (though some will be lightly or un-oaked)
Fumé Blanc *(California, South Africa, Chile, New Zealand, Australia)*
Classy white Burgundy, though how much oak to expect nowadays is impossible to guess *(France)*
Italian wines with "Barrique" on their labels.

Fresh/grassy whites

Most inexpensive Bordeaux Blanc and young south-west French whites *(France)*
Sancerre, Pouilly Blanc Fumé *(France)*
New Zealand Sauvignon Blanc
North German (Mosel, Rheingau) *Trocken*
South German (Scheurebe) *Trocken*
Sauvignon de Touraine *(France)*
English dry Müller-Thurgau.

Aromatic/spicy whites

Alsace Gewürztraminer *(France)*
Alsace Tokay-Pinot Gris *(France)*
Condrieu *(France)*
Viognier *(France, California, Australia)*
Arneis *(Italy)*
Albariño *(Spain)*
Pinot Grigio *(Italy)*
Grüner Veltliner *(Austria)*
Viña Esmeralda *(Spain)*.

Rich, unoaked whites

Alsace Pinot Blanc *(France)*
New Zealand Riesling
Most Mâcon Villages *(France)*
Trocken Riesling
Alsace Muscat *(France)*
English dry
Hermitage *(France)*

Australian Riesling
Graves (old-style) *(France)*
Gavi *(Italy)*
Australian Hunter Valley Sémillon
Frascati *(Italy)*.

Dry and off-dry grapey whites

Alsace Riesling *(France)*
German Kabinett
English medium
German Halbtrocken
Australian dry Muscat
French dry Muscat
Argentinian Torrontes
Portuguese dry Muscat.

Sweet grapey whites
(still and sparkling)

Clairette de Die *(France)*
Auslese Riesling *(Germany, Austria)*
Muscat de Beaumes de Venise, Rivesaltes etc. *(France)*
Moscato d'Asti *(Italy)*
Moscatel de Setúbal *(Portugal)*
Alsace Riesling Sélection de Grains Nobles *(France)*
Moscatel de Valencia *(Spain)*
Samos Muscat *(Greece)*
Alsace Muscat Vendange Tardive *(France)*
Australian Fruity Gordo
Muscat Canelli *(California)*.

Sweet honeyed whites

Sauternes *(France)*
Moëlleux Vouvray, Quarts de Chaume etc. *(France)*
Vouvray *demi-sec (France)*
Jurançon *(France)*
Ste-Croix-du-Mont *(France)*
Monbazillac *(France)*
Orvieto Amabile *(Italy)*
Late-harvest Sémillon *(Australia)*
Late-harvest Riesling *(Australia, New Zealand, California, South Africa)*.

Botrytized whites

Alsace Vendange Tardive or Sélection de Grains Nobles *(France)*
Bonnezeaux *(France)*
Vouvray *Moëlleux*/Quarts de Chaume *(France)*
Barsac or Sauternes *(France)*
Any "Bunch Select" wine
German Auslese or Beerenauslese or Trockenbeerenauslese
Edelbeerenlese *(Romania)*
Hungarian "5 puttonyos" Tokay
Austrian Ausbruch.

Dry sparkling whites

Brut Champagne *(France)*
Prosecco *(Italy)*
Crémant de Bourgogne *(France)*
Cava *(Spain)*
Blanquette de Limoux *(France)*
Crémant d'Alsace/Loire *(France)*
Californian sparkling wine
Australian sparkling wine
New Zealand sparkling wine
South African sparkling wine.

Medium and sweet sparkling wines

(Only if you must; few outside Champagne, Asti and Clairette de Die are good; most are filthy)
Moscato Spumante and Asti *(Italy)*
Demi-sec Cava *(Spain)*
Demi-sec and *doux* or rich Champagne
Demi-sec from just about anywhere
White Lambrusco *(Italy)*
Sekt *(Germany)*
Clairette de Die *(France)*.

Dry rosé

Clairet de Bordeaux *(France)*
Burgundy *(France)*
Provence *(France)*
Côtes du Rhône *(France)*
Rioja *(Spain)*
Lirac, Tavel *(France)*
Chiaretto di Bardolino *(Italy)*
Grenache rosé from California and Australia.

Medium rosé

(Mostly dire)
"Blush" wine from California or just about anywhere else
Portuguese rosé
Rose d'Anjou *(France)*.

Beaujolais-style/light reds

Alsace Pinot Noir *(France)*
Sancerre Rouge (light example) *(France)*
Bourgogne Passetoutgrains *(France)*
Teroldego Rotaliano *(Italy)*.

Compare and contrast:
Cabernet Sauvignons from Vin de Pays d'Oc, France (left) and Bulgaria

Côtes du Rhône Nouveau/Primeur
(France)
Dornfelder *(Germany)*
German Spätburgunder
Gamay from Gaillac, Anjou and Touraine
(France)
Lemberger *(Washington State)*
Gamay and Pinot Noir *(Switzerland)*
Bardolino (young) *(Italy)*
Tarango *(Australia)*
"Joven" (young) reds from Spain.

Bordeaux-style

Buzet, Chinon, St-Nicolas-de-Bourgueil,
Pécharmant *(France)*
Italian "Super-Tuscans" (such as Ornellaia,
Tignanello, etc.)
Californian Cabernet Sauvignon
Château Musar *(Lebanon)*
Bergerac *(France)*
Chilean Cabernet Sauvignon
Australian Cabernet Sauvignon from the
cooler regions of Victoria and Western
Australia (Margaret River)
New Zealand Cabernet Sauvignon
Bulgarian Cabernet Sauvignon/Merlot
Washington State Merlot/Cabernet
Sauvignon
Spanish Cabernet Sauvignon
Slovenian Merlot and Cabernet

Italian Merlot/Cabernet
Hungarian Merlot
Vin de Pays d'Oc Merlot and Cabernet
Sauvignon *(France)*.

Tough, tannic reds

Traditional Barolo, Barbaresco *(Italy)*
Cahors (France) – though only old-
fashioned examples
Traditional Hermitage and Cornas *(France)*
St-Estèphe *(France)*
Douro *(Portugal)*
Priorato *(Spain)*
Bigger Californian Zinfandel
Some Australian Shiraz
South African Merlot, Cabernet, Pinotage.

Rustic reds

Corvo, Taurasi, Montepulciano d'Abruzzo
(Italy)
Cahors, Corbières/Fitou/Minervois *(France)*
Dão *(Portugal)*
Bulgarian "Country Reds"
Valdepeñas, La Mancha *(Spain)*
South African Pinotage.

Sweet and off-dry reds

Piat d'Or *(France)*

Recioto di Valpolicella *(Italy)*
Lambrusco *(Italy)*
Some Crimean reds
Romanian Pinot Noir.

Burgundy-style

Older *cru* Beaujolais *(France)*
Oregon and Californian Pinot Noir
Bouzy Rouge *(France)*
Antipodean Pinot Noir
Chilean Pinot Noir
South African Pinot Noir
St Laurent *(Austria)*
Dry Romanian Pinot Noir.

Rich and raisiny

Málaga *(Spain)*
Recioto di Valpolicella *(Italy)*
Malmsey Madeira *(Portugal)*
Mavrodaphne *(Greece)*
Marsala *(Italy)*
Australian Liqueur Muscat and Tokay
Commandaria *(Cyprus)*
Pedro Ximénez sherry *(Spain)*.

Medium-bodied spicy reds

Côtes du Rhône, Crozes Hermitage, St-
Joseph, Vin de Pays d'Oc Syrah *(France)*
Nebbiolo d'Alba *(Italy)*
Lighter-bodied Zinfandel *(California)*
Medium-bodied South African Pinotage
Chilean or Argentinan Malbec
Château Musar *(Lebanon)*
South African Pinotage.

Fuller-bodied spicy reds

Côte Rôtie, Cornas, Hermitage *(France)*
Fuller-bodied South African Pinotage
Australian Shiraz/Cabernet, Shiraz,
Grenache, and warmer-climate Cabernet
(e.g. Barossa)
Californian Syrah, Grenache, Zinfandel
Barolo *(Italy)*
Priorato *(Spain)*.

Sherry-like wines

Vin Santo *(Italy)*
Sercial Madeira *(Portugal)*
Montilla *(Spain)*
Vin jaune (France).

Port-like wines

Banyuls *(France)*
Recioto della Valpolicella, Anghelu Ruju
(Italy)
Commandaria *(Cyprus)*
New-World "Port".

NEW WORLD OR NEW WAVE

*I*n the late 1980s, as they became increasingly and uncomfortably aware of growing competition from wines made on the other side of the world, producers in France in particular began to distinguish between what they considered the "simple" wines of the New World – which, as they saw it, were merely the produce of single grape varieties grown in warm regions – and the more complex, finer fare from Old-World vineyards with the classic "*terroir*" qualities of soil and climate.

At first, these traditionalists had a point; quite soon, however, their apartheid-like division of the world between the New and the Old lost its relevance as Frenchmen increasingly took to making wine in countries like Chile, New Zealand and California, while pioneering, native-born wine-makers of these and other New-World countries themselves developed new cooler regions and styles which were completely different from the fruit-and-oak cocktails with which they had been associated a few years earlier.

By 1995, New-World producers had developed wines with such Old-World-style complexity that a chagrined team of France's top tasters were unable to tell several of them from examples hailing from some of the most distinguished vineyards in Bordeaux and Burgundy.

More to the point, though, than what one might call the "Europeanization" of New-World wines, was the "Californianization" of some of the Old-World classics. Just as hamburgers and shopping malls made their inexorable way into Florence, Bordeaux and Barcelona, wine-makers consciously or unconsciously adapted their wine-making to suit Anglo-Saxon wine critics and the more "international" palate over which they held sway. New oak barrels, ripe fruit flavours and "soft tannins" became the order of the day on a number of Old-World estates which, unsurprisingly perhaps, were swiftly rewarded by acclaim and orders.

Meanwhile, increasing numbers of dynamic producers in previously overlooked regions of the Old World such as Languedoc Roussillon in France, Navarra in Spain and – to a lesser extent – areas in southern Italy, also turned their hands successfully, with or without the help of New-World wine-makers and consultants, to competing with the oaky varietal wines of Australia and California.

STORING

TO JUDGE by some of the so-called "wine collectors" about whom one can regularly read in the glossier American wine magazines, it is not enough to have laid out a few million dollars on examples of every vintage of Château Latour since the French Revolution – you also have to create a Bluebeard's palace in which to hide it all away.

Even the owners of more modest collections sometimes fall into the trap of imagining that the flashiness of the storing system somehow reflects the seriousness of the wines. Expensive, glass-fronted, refrigerated cabinets or shelving with mahogany doors often have more to do with impressing visitors than appropriate storage.

Of course, people lucky enough to have several thousand bottles of priceless old claret would be foolish if they did not make the effort to keep them in the best conditions possible, but that's not to say that they – or anyone else – have to throw unlimited amounts of money at the problem.

Storing wine doesn't have to be complicated – indeed, it is astonishing how well even fine wine will put up with less than ideal conditions. Provided your bottles are left lying horizontally in a draught-free (but not airless), reasonably cool, dampish, rather dark place, the wine in them should develop and survive as its makers originally intended.

All that is necessary is to decide how many bottles you are likely to want to store, then find a suitable space which you can assign to them. There are then any number of simple ways to give your wine the necessary protection from the effects of

CREATING A CELLAR

When you create and maintain a wine store, you're aiming for not only an environment in which your wine will be happy, but one which, by being well kept, will never have you searching frantically for a wine you think you still have a bottle of ... somewhere.

If you aren't fortunate enough to have an actual cellar, similar conditions can be obtained either by building one of the kit versions now available into the floor of your house, or by buying a thermostatically controlled cabinet such as the French Eurocave. But if, like the majority of us, you are converting a spare box-room or cupboard into your wine store, you'll need to start with the basics.

Light is easy to keep out; insulation can help to maintain a steady temperature; and a damp sponge left on a saucer will provide essential humidity. Don't make it too airtight – you should avoid your store smelling musty – but draughts are to be prevented too.

In general terms, and over a period of several years, the warmer the cellar, the faster your wine will develop or – possibly – decay.

The temperature to aim for is 7–10°C – about as cool as you will normally want to drink your white wines. Below 5°C is risky as light wines can freeze at temperatures close to that and corks can be forced out of the bottles. At over 20–25° you risk cooking off some of the more delicate characteristics, particularly of older and more delicate wines. Whatever the average temperature of your storage area, the crucial thing is to keep it as constant as possible: a wine will suffer more from a daily switchback ride from 15° to 20° than from a steady level of 20–22°. Which is why the average kitchen with its violent changes in temperature is just about the worst

place you could choose to keep your most treasured bottles.

Racks
Wooden self-assembly and folding racks are inexpensive and readily obtainable. Avoid models which have sharp metal edges – these tend to tear labels as bottles are being inserted or removed. Handier folk can, given the space, build bin-units using wooden shelving, chimney pipe or breeze blocks in which several bottles of the same wine can be kept in a pile. It is useful to be able to attach cards with numbers or wine names to the rack so that unnecessary searching is reduced to a minimum. If you buy purpose-made racks, remember that they are not generally suited to half-bottles, magnums and larger bottles. Leave space for these. Save rack space by not unpacking any wine or port which has arrived in wooden cases (important in any event if you subsequently decide to resell the wine). By the same token, cheap daily-drinking wine can be left in stout cardboard cartons – but only provided the store is not too damp.

Cellar book
This is essential, as is a well kept plan showing exactly where all the wines have been placed. A good cellar book will remind you of when you bought particular wines and how they tasted last time you opened a bottle. If you do have a real cellar, or a reasonably damp store, avoid leaving the book in it – otherwise the paper can disintegrate and the ink run. A chinagraph pencil or laundry marker and white plastic cards can be useful for this reason. Similarly, Hugh Johnson suggests spraying wine labels with scentless hair lacquer to protect them from the damp. As a

more versatile alternative to a cellar book, you could, of course, use a spreadsheet or database program on your personal computer – which would also permit you to sort the information by region, price, vintage and even, if you so wish, by the score you have given each wine out of 20 or 100.

Order
Try to establish a pattern for where you store each wine type, but don't be too rigid in your planning, otherwise you will forever be trying to squeeze 60 bottles into the space you allowed for 48. One way to avoid this problem is to use a system you may recall from the game of *Battleships* – code the wine racks vertically and horizontally, alphabetically and numerically, so that each "hole" has a code – A56, G12, X78 and so on – that you can assign to the bottle it contains when entering it in your cellar book or database.

Insurance
One final point. Your cellar will be worth a certain amount when you start to fill it. With luck, that value will rise – perhaps considerably so – over the years. Forgetting to be properly insured would be a pity.

What to buy
It may seem obvious, but if you're buying wine to drink, then stick to what you like. In other words, if your passion is Burgundy, then don't be pressurized into buying lots of Bordeaux just because everybody says it's a must-have vintage. If you never eat fish, then you won't need so much white; if port gives you a headache, then it's not a bargain, no matter how low the price.

light, heat and dehydrated air. An old fireplace, a wall in the spare room, beneath the staircase, a box-room, an unused cupboard ... all kinds of places can be turned into useful wine stores with a little imagination and, on occasion, a touch of do-it-yourself.

Then comes the fun part – deciding what you're going to put into it, and how much you're going to spend. I've given suggestions for some well balanced selections here, but you'll have your own tastes and needs to accommodate. Any good wine merchant should be pleased to advise you if you want to splash out on a "ready-made" cellar – or you may want to build up

Perfectly stored: You might have to go to the Loire Valley, though, to have a cellar like this

your selection slowly. With suitable storage space to hand, you'll be able to stock up on good buys as and when you come across them – and store up a great deal of future drinking pleasure.

BEST CELLARS
It is as impossible to recommend an ideal cellar for a complete stranger as it is to advise them on the ideal contents of their wardrobe. However, this is my personal selection.

Bordeaux
Médoc: Châteaux Léoville Lascases, Palmer, Léoville-Barton, Pichon-Longueville-Lalande, Pichon-Longueville, Lynch-Bages, Ducru-Beaucaillou, Cos d'Estournel, Palmer, La Gurgue, Haut-Bages-Libéral, Chasse-Spleen; *Graves*: Domaine de Chevalier, Châteaux la Louvière, Fieuzal, Haut-Bailly (red); *Pomerol* and *St Emilion*, and satellites: Châteaux Pavie, Figeac, Lafleur, Le Bon Pasteur, Certan-de-May, Vieux-Château-Certan, Haut Bertinerie, Puygeraud, Canon (Canon-Fronsac); *Sauternes and Barsac*: Châteaux Rieussec, Gilette, Bastor-Lamontagne, Doisy-Daëne.

Burgundy
Nuits St Georges: Gouges, A Michelot, Faiveley; *Vosne Romanée*: D Rion, Méo-Camuzet; *Volnay*: M Lafarge, Pousse d'Or; *Meursault*: Michelot-Buisson, Lafon; *Puligny-Montrachet*: Carillon, Leflaive, Chartron et Trébuchet; *Chassagne-Montrachet*: Carillon, Sauzet.

Rhône
Hermitage: Chave, Guigal; *Crozes-Hermitage*: Graillot; *Côte Rôtie*: Guigal, Jaboulet Ainé; *Châteauneuf-du-Pape*: Château Beaucastel.

Southern France
Mas de Daumas Gassac, Domaine de Trevallon,

Domaine Hortus, Château Vignelaure.

Barolo
Elio Altari, G Mascarello, Aldo Conterno.

Italian superstars
Gaja Chardonnay, Sassicaia, Tignanello, Solaia, Cepparello.

Rioja
Campillo, Contino, Remelluri.

Navarra
Chivite.

Spanish superstars
Pesquera, Vega Sicilia, Jean Leon Cabernet, Marques de Griñon, Torres Mas la Plana and Milmanda Chardonnay.

Germany
Mosel: Dr Loosen, Egon Müller, Deinhard, F W Gymnasium; *Rhine/Nahe*: Balthasar Ress, Burklin-Wolf, Bassermann-Jordan, Müller Cattoir, Tony Jost, Kurt Darting.

Champagne
Pol Roger, Bollinger, Billecart-Salmon, Gosset, Boizel, Deutz, Krug.

Vintage and tawny port
Dow's, Graham's, Taylor's, Niepoort, Fonseca-Guimaraens, Noval, Quinta de la Rosa, Quinta do Crasto.

Top-quality sherry Barbadillo, Gonzalez Byass, Lustau.

Other sparkling wine
"J" by Jordan, J Schram, Scharffenberger, Croser, Iron Horse, Green Point.

NEW WORLD
Cabernet Sauvignon
Penfolds Bin 707 (Aus.), Coleraine (NZ), Mondavi Reserve (Cal.).

Chardonnay
Kumeu River (NZ), Leeuwin Estate, Petaluma (Aus.), Inniskillin (Canada), Hargrave (Long Island), Sonoma Cutrer, Simi, Kistler (Cal.).

Sauvignon Blanc
Cloudy Bay (NZ), Cullens (Aus.), Thelema (SA), Casablanca Vineyards (Chile).

Sémillon
McWilliams (Aus.).

Riesling
Hardy's Siegersdorf (Aus.), Kiona (Washington), Knappstein (Aus.), Renaissance (Cal.).

Pinot Noir
Martinborough (NZ), Dom Drouhin (Oregon), Hamilton Russell (SA), Saintsbury, Au Bon Climat (Cal.), Coldstream Hills, Wignalls (Aus.).

Merlot
Matanzas Creek, Newton (Cal.), Casa Lapostolle (Chile).

Syrah/Shiraz
Grange, Yarra Yering, Henschke, Peter Lehman (Aus.), Phelps, Bonny Doon (Cal.).

Zinfandel
Ridge, Ravenswood (Cal.), Cape Mentelle (Aus.).

Late-harvest and fortified, Petaluma, Brown Bros Orange Muscat and Flora, Morris Liqueur Muscat (Aus.), Phelps, Renaissance (Cal.).

SERVING

Wine can be an etiquette minefield, in which otherwise confident adults seem to imagine that if the port were to be passed the wrong way, or a red opened before a white, or poured into the wrong kind of glass, the sky would fall in on their guests.

Well, I'll leave this and just about every other social dilemma to Debrett's and concentrate instead on offering a set of simple (and by no means hard and fast) rules which should allow you to relax and relish each and every bottle of wine you open at its best.

UNCORKING

The best corkscrew by far is the American Screwpull. Any other types should be formed like a spiral, rather than the screw after which they are named. The device with two flat prongs rather than a screw or spiral is either called an "Ah So" because of its purported ease of use, or "Butler's Friend", because it supposedly allowed deceitful servants to appropriate a glass or two of wine, top the bottle up with water and replace the undamaged cork without detection. The trick of using it – sliding the prongs down between cork and bottle, then pressing them together as you draw the cork – takes a bit of mastering: practise on an already-opened and recorked bottle.

Ironically, the tool which no traditional cellar or *sommelier* once lacked, a knife to cut the foil, or a "foil cutter", is much more necessary today than it ever was in the past, now that tinfoil and infuriatingly shrink-fitted plastic have replaced the easily peelable – but medically suspect – lead capsule.

DECANTING

There's a great deal of nonsense talked about the importance of letting a wine "breathe" – and a fair bit of sense too. In fact, the principal reason for decanting wine, or port, should be to remove sediment, which

The perfect pour: Decanting is seldom essential, but can often help wine to breathe

many wines – Rioja and red Burgundy, for example – do not have. So why decant a wine with no sediment? Well, what you are doing is, in effect, letting it get its act together before it hits your and your guests' glasses. Wines which appear "dumb" or "closed" may open up with a little time in the decanter; others with a lot of tannin (for example, claret, Barolo, many Californian

Cabernets and most Portuguese reds) can certainly benefit from being decanted – or at least uncorked and simply left open for a while before they are drunk. Rather astringent cheaper wines may soften up too.

On the other hand, some wines are somewhat short of an act to get together; young flavourless reds and venerable bottles which have lost their fruit over the years in the rack are going to gain no more from a period of enforced breathing than an eight-stone weakling or an ailing 70-year-old might benefit from an enforced cross-country run. Remember that decanting can be an unsettling procedure. Some more delicate wines, such as mature red Burgundy, can be quite spoiled by decanting.

But assuming the wine is worth decanting, how do you do it? For the nervous, muslin or a coffee filter paper will effectively separate sediment from liquid; for the steadier of hand, a candle flame, a torch or a piece of white card held just behind the neck of the bottle should enable you to see when the trickle of transparent wine begins to become thicker sludge. Be certain not to shake up the bottle before decanting and pour slowly, keeping the flow constant.

GLASSES

There's no doubt that a beautifully made and shaped glass can make the drinking of a finer wine seem just that bit more special than simply slugging it down from a beaker – even Keats's "beaker full of the warm South".

Certain glass shapes are by tradition associated with certain types of wine – but remember that this, again, is only tradition, not law. Moreover, some of these traditions are actually bad for the wine. The saucer-shaped Champagne glass will make your fizz as flat as a pancake, while a Jerezano

A glass for every wine: You don't have to go this far, but certain shapes are suited to certain wines, like flutes for Champagne

would be appalled by the thought that the delicate aromas of his elegant *fino* sherry were destined to evaporate from the brimming surface of a tiny, overfilled "schooner".

If you haven't got the "right" shape of glass, make sure the one you have got is smaller at the rim than across the bowl, which will prevent the bouquet of the wine from escaping. Whatever the wine and whatever the glass, don't over-pour. A third to half full is just about right.

ORDER

There exists a set of principles which dictate the most sensible order in which wines should be served during the course of a meal. Basically they are: white before red; dry before sweet; light before heavy; young before old; ordinary before fine. The underlying aim is to lead your palate gently up the scale of increasing fullness, "flavoursomeness" and quality, rather than swinging wildly between styles.

But it's sometimes impossible to observe one of these rules without breaking another – so check against the rest of the list. The more that "agree", the better; a mature, full California Chardonnay can safely follow a young, light Beaujolais, for example, even though this breaks the white/red rule.

It's a good idea anyway to make sure there is a jug or bottle of water on the table, so that palates can be cleansed and refreshed between wines.

TEMPERATURE

For reds, the word *chambré* – meaning at room temperature – is rather misleading. Which room? What temperature? Supposedly "standard" conditions can vary a great deal. Remember that a century ago, when the French coined the term *chambré*, even the wealthiest of wine-drinkers lived in homes that were far less warm than our centrally heated cocoons. To them "room temperature" often meant only a few degrees warmer than the cellar from which the wine was brought.

But not all reds are the same. Served too warm, even the finest red wine can seem heavy and rather dull. In fact, some red wines are best drunk slightly chilled – fresh, fruity Beaujolais and light red Loires desperately need to be served at temperatures only slightly higher than

Serving Temperatures

The figures given for the following wine styles are approximate, but if you really want to be precise, you could use one of the floppy plastic thermometers which, though intended for recalcitrant children's foreheads, will wrap round and adhere to the neck of a bottle very satisfactorily.

Red Wine
The tougher and more tannic a wine, the more it will benefit from being served a little warmer, while younger, fruitier reds will be best at a lower temperature

- Chill lightly (10–13°C, or no more than an hour in the door of the fridge): *Beaujolais – but not the crus (Fleurie, Morgon etc.); red Loire (Gamay, Pinot Noir and Cabernet); young French vins de pays; young Bardolino and Valpolicella and Vino Joven – young, unoaked – reds from Spain.*
- "Room temperature" (14–16°C, which is actually rather cooler than most living rooms; your wine should certainly not be stored anywhere warmer than this, and if you are bringing it up from a chilly cellar it may need a little standing time): *Most other reds, particularly younger red Burgundy and Rhônes and older Bordeaux, Pinot Noirs from the New World, Chianti, younger Rioja, New-World Grenache and Pinotage from South Africa.*
- Open at least an hour before serving and serve a little warmer (16–18°C): *Older Burgundy; younger, more tannic Bordeaux and Rhônes; Californian Zinfandel, bigger New-World Cabernet Sauvignon, Merlot and Shiraz; Barolo, and other bigger Italian reds, older Rioja and wines from Ribera del Duero.*
- Decant an hour or so before serving:

Young claret; heavy Portuguese reds; bigger Italians such as Barolo and Barbaresco (though older ones should be decanted just before the meal); Australian Shiraz.

Rosé
- Chill, but don't over-chill, particularly if the wine is dry; two hours in the door of the fridge or 5–10 minutes in a bucket of ice and water is ample.

White Wine
The rule here is to weigh up the concentration of aroma and flavour of the wine, its age and the richness of its texture. The lower the temperature, the less a wine will smell and the less evident any richness it may have.

- Serve coldest – around 4–8°C – a good two or three hours in the fridge or 10–15 minutes in a bucket of ice and water: *Lighter sweeter wines such as Rieslings from Germany, dessert and the more everyday sparkling wines..*
- A little less cool (8–11°C): *Most fuller-bodied, drier and semi-dry whites and Champagne, along with bigger, more complex dessert wines such as Sauternes and Beerenauslese wines from Germany; aromatic wines such as Arneis from Italy, Viognier from the Rhône and the New World and Gewürztraminer; younger simpler Sauvignons and Chardonnays from just about everywhere.*
- Around 12–13°C – about an hour in the fridge door. Or 5–10 minutes in a bucket of ice and water: *Richer dry wines such as Burgundy, Alsace, traditional white Rioja; bigger, more complex Sauvignons, Sémillons and New-World Chardonnays.*

that at which you would serve a white Burgundy.

What about chilling wine? If you are unfortunate enough to have to give your guests a truly unpalatable red, white or pink wine, bear in mind that the colder any food or drink, the less one can taste it. Chilled heavily enough, Coca-Cola would be almost indistinguishable from sweet Champagne.

Sweet wines such as Sauternes and Muscat de Beaumes de Venise can just about take being served almost vodka-cold, though they deserve rather gentler treatment; dry ones, particularly richer

wines like white Burgundy and older New-World Sémillon, need far gentler handling. Indeed, the best of these are at their best a degree or two *warmer* than some lighter-bodied reds.

If you're chilling in a hurry, an ice bucket filled with cold water and generous handfuls of ice cubes is far more successful than ice alone – and so much easier to get the bottle back into. Serve only small portions at first to allow the rest of the wine to cool down further. If you need to warm a wine up, stand it in a bucket of tepid water for 10 minutes.

TASTING

There are few more pretentious sights than a restaurant diner taking his time pompously sniffing, sipping and considering a wine while his embarrassed guests pause in their conversation so as not to jeopardize his (yes, it is almost always a man) concentration. Especially when it transpires that the object of all this attention is the house red. There are, of course, occasions when it is appropriate to examine a wine as if it were a rare manuscript, but these are rare. The best way to spot the real wine expert is to look for the person who simply takes a brief sniff of the glass he is offered before nodding his approval.

But why go through the rigmarole of tasting in the first place? Well, there are four basic reasons for doing so:

• to see if there is anything wrong with it;
• to decide whether or not you like it;
• to judge whether it is a good example of its type;
• to guess its identity and vintage in a "blind" tasting.

Most people are only usually concerned with the first two of these. But the third can be as important to the wine-drinker as it is, say, to a wine-merchant or restaurateur. Is the wine a "good buy"? And does it taste as it should? Of course, wines that are atypical of their style or region can be delicious, too, but if that glass of pleasant "Sancerre" is actually filled with a blend of heaven-knows-what from heaven-knows-where, it should have cost you a lot less money. A little knowledge and practice will enable you to recognize and memorize styles and flavours.

Being able to tell a Rioja from a claret when you have both in front of you, however, is far easier than guessing the precise identity and age of a single glass of wine "blind". This is the skill professional tasters develop – not as a glorified party trick, but to help them assess each wine they encounter quite simply on its own merits.

The key to identifying a wine lies in its combination of visual, smell and taste "triggers" – the ones you remember from the last time you tasted it. You are using your memory just as you would to recognize a Rolling Stones song from the first Keith Richards guitar chord or a Strauss waltz by its distinctive lilt, orchestration and harmonies.

These triggers often work unconsciously – but they do rely on the information having been stored in the first place. So concentrate for a moment or two on every glass of wine you drink. Will you recognize it next time you taste it?

COLOUR

First of all, scrutinize the colour, holding the wine, if possible, against a well-lit white surface. Since white wines tend to darken as they age, paleness will suggest youthfulness. A pale wine, perhaps with greenish glints, will be light in body and may well be from a cool climate – grapes grown in hot climates such as Australia or California have deeper pigmentation and so impart more colour to the fermenting juice. A wine with lots of yellow-tinged colour could be a recent vintage from a warm climate, or it might be a moderately mature wine with long barrel-ageing such as an old-style Rioja. Alternatively, fine old Chardonnays darken when in an advanced state of maturity, while dessert wines often look golden.

With red wines, the general colour depends on where the grapes are from, regardless of age. So look at the rim: an intense

purple is indicative of a young full-bodied wine, perhaps from the very warm Rhône, while a fresh, ruby colour is characteristic of a lighter wine and might suggest, for example, a Beaujolais. A chestnut rim suggests a more mature wine but beware – wines mature at different rates. It could be a relatively young Rioja that has had long barrel-ageing, or a young wine from a poor vintage near the end of its foreshortened life. Or it could be a very mellow Burgundy or claret.

Then, swirl the wine in the glass (the increased air contact makes the wine release more of its aromas), and take a big sniff.

SMELL

The smell of a wine is its taste. Just as you can tell that a piece of meat is "off" by sniffing it, you can also use your nose to tell you whether there is anything wrong with a wine. On the other hand, there are some perfectly normal wine smells which you simply may not like. Sancerre is often said to smell of cat's pee; Australian Shiraz of "sweaty saddle"; and old red Burgundy, "farmyardy". None of these are odours many people find pleasant as such, but they can be likened (hopefully not too exactly) to characteristic traits of an old friend: essential facets of his or her personality.

The majority of good wines, however, display a wonderfully diverse collection of pleasant smells. Few of these appear to have any direct relation to grapes – indeed, it's astonishing how this single fruit, grown and vinified in different ways, manages to produce not only so many aromas, but in blends of a complexity and success a perfumier would be hard-pressed to match.

And just as a perfumier divides scents into groups, so wine-smells fall into categories – fruity, floral, spicy, vegetal, earthy and woody. So when you sniff a wine and find apricot where someone else finds plum, don't worry, neither of you is wrong; you're both choosing nuances you recognize from the same "fruity" group. And if you think that a wine smells of something truly

Getting a nose for it: The sniff–sloosh–slurp brigade get down to business

bizarre – Chablis of wet wool, for instance – take note of it; it's your personal key to picking out Chablis "blind" next time.

The glossary of tasting terms here will give you an indication of smells often associated with particular wines.

For some reason, women are often better at this aspect of wine-tasting than men. The female nostril may well naturally be more sensitive than the male – after all, women choose perfume much more carefully than most men select their aftershave – or it may be that they are simply more used to paying attention to the way things smell.

The key to being able to identify wines by their smell lies in constructing your own smell vocabulary, which can be built up by practising on the aromas you encounter every day. Do Golden Delicious apples smell the same as Cox's? Compare the smell of new and old leather…

A final point: what if a wine doesn't appear to smell of anything at all? Well, it's either a very boring wine, or one that is very reluctant to release its bouquet; professional tasters will simply describe it as a "dumb nose" and move on to the taste in order to find out why.

TASTE

Take a generous sip – and roll it around in your mouth. When wine-tasters suck in air through their teeth and make slurping noses, they're aerating the wine in their mouth just as they swirl it in the glass before sniffing.

What your mouth (your "palate") is going to tell you about the wine is not its flavour – the flavours you "taste" in your mouth are actually being "smelt" in your nasal cavity above – but its structure; that is, its texture (rough or smooth), its "body" (light or full), and its "balance" – the happy or unhappy combination of elements such as sweetness, acidity, fruit, alcohol and, in red wine, tannin.

The first question to ask yourself when tasting any wine is "does it taste good?" If it does, it's a fairly good indication that it has been well made. Of course, if you absolutely detest sweet wine, the finest Sauternes or Trockenbeerenauslese isn't going to give you much pleasure. Even so, most people can give a fair judgement on whether a piece of music is played well or not, even if it isn't to their taste.

But just as the trio can drown the singer's voice, the essential quality of any good wine – cheap or expensive – is its balance. A young wine can appear to be unbalanced, most commonly because high acidity or tannin are

---

TRAINING YOUR TASTEBUDS

*T*aste buds are like muscles; so I've devised a few exercises – comparative tastings – with which to keep them in trim.

- **Fruity reds** Taste a range of blackcurranty Cabernet Sauvignons and Cabernet Francs, such as Bordeaux from the Médoc, red Loires such as Chinon or Bourgueil, and examples from Bulgaria, California and Australia. Then move onto the more cherry-like flavours of Beaujolais and good young Bardolino, and the raspberry taste of the Pinot Noir (from Burgundy, Sancerre, Alsace, Australia, Chile, California or Oregon).
- **Oaky wines** For this, you'll need a bottle or two of red Rioja con Crianza, a traditional white Rioja such as Monopole by CVNE, a Chardonnay from Australia (such as Rosemount's "Show Reserve") and a classy young Bordeaux (such as Château Lynch-Bages).
- **Spicy wines** The pepper of any Grenache from the southern Rhône (ideally Gigondas or Châteauneuf-du-Pape) can be compared with the deeper spice of the Syrah from further north (in Côte Rôtie or Hermitage) or Australia (where it's called the Shiraz), and with the tobaccoey flavours of good Nebbiolo from Barolo or Barbaresco.
- **Botrytis** Take a good Sauternes, a Beerenauslese from Germany or Austria and a "late-picked" Riesling from California or Australia – and look for that flavour of dried apricots.

---

obscuring the flavour of the fruit. When they are first made, red wines which have been built to last can be very tannic. Experienced tasters should be able to discern future quality nevertheless, but even they can get it wrong sometimes. A very tannic, apparently fruitless, young wine can develop into a rich and complex mature one, but the fruit has to be in there somewhere.

Young white wines can taste very acidic but, similarly, it is this acidity which will enable them to age – provided they are of a style which needs maturity. White wines intended to be drunk young – Muscadet, Frascati, Vinho Verde – need acidity to give them freshness, but in these cases that tang must be balanced by fruit. If your bottle tastes tart and fruitless, you simply have an inferior example which is unlikely to improve.

No wine should ever taste sharp or bitter – although some Italian whites seem to be resolutely sour. If you think a wine tastes of vinegar, it may well have been got at by "acetobacters" – vinegar bacteria. On the other hand, wines which seem flabby

---

are probably suffering from too little acidity, often the result of the grapes having been carelessly handled in a warm climate.

Inexperienced tasters often imagine that poor wine tends to be acidic and vinegary; generally though, far too many poor wines are simply dull and inoffensive, tasting of nothing at all. These should not, however, be confused with some good wines which are reticent with their flavours, just as they were "dumb" on the nose – these are described as "closed", needing more time in bottle, or a little contact with oxygen to "bring them out". How do you tell the difference? It's like guessing whether a shy person has anything to say. Does there seem to be something worth digging out? If so, leave the wine in the glass for a while and come back to it.

Finally, the "finish". Tasters often describe wines as "long" or "short" – meaning that the wine's flavour either lingers pleasantly in the mouth after the wine is swallowed, or seems rapidly to melt away. If a wine is slightly faulty or off-balance, you may find that it is the flawed or excessive element that comes out most strongly on the finish – the dry-mouthed sensation created by high tannins or too much oak, for example.

So, your tasting armoury is complete. Your smell and taste "triggers" will have helped you to make a guess at the wine's origin and grape variety; the colour, its age; qualities of its structure may help to verify both, and tell you whether the wine is too young, too old, or ready to drink. If all (or nearly all) of these elements are pleasing and, essentially, they come together to give balance, you have a good wine.

But what makes a good wine "great"? Well, everything that makes it good must be there in spades – but then one moves on into less easily definable territory. Tasters may use words like "classy" or "elegant" to describe a fine wine. A great wine's key characteristic is complexity – the perception of a host of nuances and flavours, perfectly interwoven, to which one wants to return again and again. Many people scoff at the artistic analogies tasters use – indeed, the whole concept of the "art of the wine-maker" – as pretentious nonsense. But they can be useful when you are trying to place a wine on the quality scale, and if you remember that one doesn't necessarily want "greatness" and complexity every time one has a glass of wine. A country church can be just as pleasing, in its own way, as St Peter's in Rome – perhaps even more so on a beautiful summer afternoon; musically, many of us would prefer, after a hard day, to unwind with Sondheim, not Stravinsky.

The Language of Wine-Tasting

Acetic Vinegary – the wine has been "got at" by bacteria.

Acidity The essential natural component which gives wine freshness and zing and prevents it from cloying.

Aggressive Over-tannic or over-acidic.

Alcoholic Over-alcoholic wine tastes "hot", burns the palate.

Almond Bitter almond can denote Tocai from Italy.

Aniseed Found in red Burgundy and – to a lesser extent – Bordeaux and some Northern Italian whites.

Apple A smell often found in young white wines, from the Bramley freshness of Vinho Verde, young Loire, Chardonnay and English wines, through to the ripe Cox's of more mature white Burgundies, Champagne and some white Bordeaux. Stewed or baked apple can be a sure sign of Riesling. Unripe apple is often a sign that a wine has not undergone its malolactic fermentation.

Apricot Common in the white Rhônes of Condrieu and Château-Grillet and other examples of the Viognier grape, and in wine from *botrytis*-affected grapes.

Aromatic Often associated with wines made from grapes such as the Gewürztraminer and Muscat.

Artificial *also* **Contrived, Confected** Used to describe wines whose taste appears to have been created chemically.

Attack The quality in a wine which makes you sit up and take notice.

Austere A wine difficult to approach, with fruit not obvious. Wait for the flavour to open out in the mouth.

Backward Not as developed as its age would lead you to expect.

Bad eggs Presence of hydrogen sulphide, usually a result of faulty cellaring or wine-making.

Baked Like stewed fruits, probably from an over-warm vintage.

Balance A balanced wine has its fruitiness, acidity, alcohol and tannin (for reds) in pleasant harmony.

Banana A smell usually associated with young wine, fermented at low temperatures and – in the case of reds – in an oxygen-free environment. A sign of *macération carbonique*.

Beefy Big, hearty, meaty wine.

Beeswing A skin which forms on certain old ports, leaving a characteristic residue in the glass.

Big Mouth-filling, full-flavoured, possibly strongly alcoholic.

Biscuity Often used to describe the bouquet of Champagne.

Bite High acidity, good in young wine.

Blackcurrant Found in Cabernet Sauvignon and Pinot Noir wines. *See also* **Cassis**.

Blowsy Exaggeratedly fruity, lacking bite.

Body A full-bodied wine fills the mouth with flavour.

Bottle-sick Newly bottled wines may take some time (sometimes months) to recover from the shock of air-contact and sulphuring at bottling.

Bottle stink Wines which have just been opened may have a musty smell – bottle stink – which disappears in the glass.

Bouquet Smell.

Brettanomyces/"Brett" A "mousey" bacterial fault about which Californians are often fanatical, finding it almost everywhere they taste, from Bordeaux to the Barossa Valley. Tasters from other countries seem far less sensitive to it.

Butter A richness of aroma and texture found in mature Chardonnay, and/or evidence of malolactic fermentation.

Caramel A buttery toffee smell in wines like Madeira.

Cassis Literally, blackcurrant; used when the sensation is of an intense, heady syrup rather than the fresh fruit.

Cat's pee The pungent smell of Sauvignon Blanc and Müller-Thurgau.

Cedar An aroma of maturing claret.

Chaptalized Chaptalization is the process of adding sugar to fermenting must to increase the alcoholic strength. If overdone, a wine tastes "hot".

Cherry A characteristic of Beaujolais – particularly Morgon.

Chocolate For some people, a sure sign of the Pinot Noir grape.

Cigar-box *See* cedar.

Closed Has yet to show its quality.

Cloudy A sign of a faulty wine.

Cloying A sickly taste, sweetness without acidity.

Clumsy An unbalanced wine.

Coffee Special characteristic of old, great Burgundy, though I also find it in some great claret such as Mouton Rothschild.

Commercial Light, drinkable, undemanding wine.

Complex Having a diverse, well-blended mixture of smells and flavours.

Cooked A "warm", stewed-fruit flavour – may suggest over-warm fermentation or the use of grape concentrate.

Corked A wine spoiled by a bad cork has a musty smell and flavour.

Crisp Fresh, lively, with good acidity.

Crust Deposit thrown by a mature port.

Depth Wine with depth fills the mouth with lingering flavour.

Dirty Badly made wine can taste unclean.

Dirty socks Cheesy sourness accompanying badly made white wine.

Dry Having no obvious sweetness.

Dried out A wine which has lost its fruit as it has aged.

Dumb No apparent smell.

Dusty Sometimes used to describe tannic Bordeaux – literally the "dusty" smell of an attic.

Earthy Not as unpleasant as it sounds – an "earthy" flavour can characterize certain fine Burgundy.

Eggy Carelessly handled sulphur can produce an eggy smell.

Elegant Restrained, classy.

Esters Sweet-smelling, often fruity compounds.

Eucalyptus A flavour and smell often found in Cabernet Sauvignon from Australia, Californian Cabernet Sauvignon (Martha's Vineyard) and, though more rarely, in Bordeaux (e.g. Château Latour).

Extract The concentration of the grape's flavours in a wine.

Farmyard A characteristic of Burgundian Pinot Noir.

Fat Used to describe mouth-filling wines, especially Chardonnay and white wines from the Rhône and Alsace.

Finesse Understated, classy.

Finish How a wine's flavour ends in the mouth. Can be "long" or "short".

Flabby Lacking balancing acidity.

Flat Short of acidity and fruit.

Flinty/gunflint "Stonily" crisp, used of whites; Pouilly-Fumé, for example.

Flor A yeast film which grows on top of the fermenting must of *fino* sherry.

Forward A precocious wine showing its qualities earlier than expected.

Foxy A peculiar "wild" smell found in *labrusca* grapes and wine in the USA.

Gamey Used of mature Burgundy, Rhône Syrah and Australian Shiraz. It's a smell that combines meat and spice.

Generous Big, mouth-filling, round.

Geraniums The smell of the leaves of this flower indicates the presence of an unwelcome micro-organism formed during fermentation.

Glycerine The "fatty" constituent in some wines, making them taste richer – the "legs" which flow down the inside of the glass.

Gooseberry The smell of Sauvignon, especially Loire and New Zealand.

Grapey It's surprising how rare this flavour is: Muscat and Riesling are often grapey; so is good Beaujolais.

Grassy "Green" smell of young wine,

especially Sauvignon Blanc and Cabernet Franc.

Green pepper Can be the sign of Cabernet Sauvignon – in Bordeaux, or indeed anywhere else.

Grip Firm wine has "grip". Essential to some styles.

Gris Very pale pink.

Hazelnut Along with toasted almonds, can indicate rich maturing Chardonnay.

Herbaceous Think of a cross between grass and flowers – "planty".

Herby Some wines from the south-west of France, as well as from Italy, can smell positively herby – almost like a pizza, fresh from the grill.

Hollow Lacking depth and roundness.

Honey An obvious description for most of the great sweet white wines of the world, but also a characteristic – in its richness rather than its sweetness – of some mature white Burgundy and much Chenin Blanc from the Loire.

Hot Used to describe over-chaptalized, over-alcoholic wine.

Iodine A smell and taste sometimes encountered in wines made from grapes grown close to the sea.

Jammy A jammy fruit smell often signifies red wines from hot countries.

Lanolin Some white wines have an oily softness reminiscent of lanolin.

Legs The visible evidence of glycerine in a wine, these are the "tears" that run down the glass's side after swirling.

Lemon Young whites may display a lemony freshness.

Length The time the flavour stays in the mouth.

Liquorice Encountered in all sorts of wine – from claret and port to Burgundy.

Lychees Common in wines made from the Gewürztraminer grape.

Maderized The *rancio* character of heat-induced oxidation.

Malic acid The component of wine converted by malolactic fermentation into softer lactic acid. Smells like green apples in young white wines.

Meaty A wine to get your teeth into.

Mellow Soft and mature.

Mercaptans A smell of rotten eggs or burnt rubber, stemming from the mishandling of sulphur dioxide.

Metallic Taste/smell arising from the use of poor equipment.

Mint Often found in Cabernet Sauvignons.

Mouldy Taste/smell arising from rotten grapes, poor wine-making or a bad cork.

Mouth-puckering Young, tannic or over-acidic wine has this effect.

Mulberry The ripe berry flavour of some Pomerol.
Mushroom Can indicate quality reds but also a wine past its prime.
Nose The smell of a wine.
Nutty Especially of Chardonnay and sherry.
Oaky In moderation, pleasant, like vanilla. Especially New-World wines and Rioja.
Old socks (clean) A promising sign of young white Burgundy, particularly Chablis.
Oxidized If a table wine looks and smells of sherry, it's oxidized – a diagnosis confirmed by its colour: brown for red wines, deep yellow for whites.
Palate The flavour, and what you taste it with.
Pear drops Smell which is usually the mark of a very young wine.
Pepper Black, not green: the sign of the Grenache or Syrah in the Rhône.
Pétillant Slight sparkle or spritz.
Petrol A desirable aroma of mature Riesling.
Pine Aroma found in Retsina.

Plum Especially clarets, Rioja and Burgundy.
Quaffing, quaffable Everyday wine, usually soft, fruity and undemanding.
Rancio Rich, distinctive flavour of certain wines, particularly southern French *vins doux naturels* stored in barrels exposed to heat.
Raspberry Aroma associated with Syrah, Gamay and much Pinot Noir.
Residual sugar The natural grape sugar left in a wine which has not been fermented into alcohol.
Ripe Grapes were fully ripe when picked.
Robust Solid, full-bodied.
Rose Often the choicest clarets, some *cru* Beaujolais and Côte de Beaune.
Rough Unbalanced and coarse.
Round Smooth and harmonious.
Rubber Some wines can smell rubbery, though not unpleasant. This is an aroma often associated with red wines from South Africa, Beaujolais, Californian Zinfandel and American Pinot Noir.
Salt A salty tang, almost like iodine, associated with *Manzanilla* sherry.
Sediment Precipitation of tannins in

red wine due to ageing.
Short Wine with a short finish.
Silky Exceptionally smooth.
Smoke The most famous smoky wine is Pouilly Blanc Fumé, made from the Sauvignon Blanc. Alsace Tokay-Pinot Gris, Corsican rosés, some Bordeaux, and Syrah from the Rhône may also be smoky.
Spicy Wines made from grapes such as the Syrah, Grenache and Zinfandel can be positively spicy. Also whites from the Gewürztraminer, Albariño, Arneis, Viognier.
Spritz Slight sparkle. Or faint fizz. Similar to *pétillant*.
Stalky or **Stemmy** The flavour of the grape stem rather than of the juice.
Steely Attractively crisp, with a firm backbone of acidity.
Strawberry The taste of some Gamay, Pinot Noir and Rioja.
Structure Wine with good structure has, or will have, all its elements in harmony.
Sulphur The antiseptic used to protect wine from bacteria. Its throat-tickling aroma should disappear after the wine has been

swirled in the glass for a moment, or left in the open bottle for a while. Often, however, it is "locked in" and prevents the wine from ever being pleasant.
Tannin The mouth-puckering ingredient in red wine. Softens with age.
Tobacco Like cigar-box, found in oak-aged reds, especially clarets.
Toffee Often indicates the presence of the Merlot grape in red Bordeaux.
Truffles Mushroom and vegetal aromas, especially in red wines.
Vanilla Aroma of wines matured in American oak casks; also white Burgundy and oak-aged Rioja.
Vegetal Earthy, wet-leaf smell; cabbagey, often of big Italian red wines.
Violets Floral red Burgundies and Chiantis can smell intensely of violets.
Volatile In an unstable – volatile – wine, acids evaporate from the surface giving vinegary, sometimes "greasy" smells.
Yeast Like newly baked bread; smell found in Champagne, Muscadet *sur lie* and some nuttily rich white wines.

FAULTS

*O*ne of the greatest areas of confusion when tasting and drinking wine is whether "it's supposed to taste like this". In other words, is it worth sending the bottle back and requesting another?

There are two kinds of faulty wine: the ones which have been badly made – in which case the whole vat or barrel will be equally unpleasant – and the odd bottle which has been mistreated or "got at" by bacteria. When in doubt, wine experts generally give the wine-maker the benefit of the doubt by calling for a replacement; sometimes it is perfect and sometimes it as nasty or nastier than the stuff it is replacing.

To help you discern faults for yourself, though, the following are some you might find.

Appearance

A wine which looks cloudy when carefully poured from a bottle which has been allowed to stand for a few hours is probably faulty, though it may taste fine. Carelessly decanted wines and ones which have been shaken up before serving may also look cloudy of course.

Do not worry about the fine, dark film which is sometimes found within bottles of Australian red – it is simply the deposit – nor about the white crystals encountered at the bottom of some whites. Known as "wine diamonds" in Germany, these are a natural tartrate deposit which would be far more commonplace if producers did not generally chill

their white wines to precipitate them before bottling.

Any wine which looks brown, unless you know it to be of an advanced age, is probably past its sell-by date or has been oxidized by poor handling.

Smell

If the stuff in your glass smells like sherry and does not describe itself as sherry or one of the rare sherry-like wines described on p. 43, it is oxidized. This could be caused by age, a leaky cork or storage in a warm place. Unless you suspect age to be the culprit, ask for a replacement. If it smells vinegary, this again could be a case of a poor bottle, though there's a significant chance that careless wine-making could be responsible. Mustiness is another frequent problem. But before complaining, give the wine a chance to breathe; sometimes what older wine buffs used to call "bottle stink" will disappear after a few minutes' exposure to the air. If the symptoms persist, you may have a wine which was matured in dirty wooden casks or one which is "corked".

This last condition, often wrongly diagnosed on the basis of a few harmless crumbs of cork floating on the surface of the wine – the result of the cork breaking apart as it is pulled from the bottle – is caused by generally invisible, but sadly quite prevalent, types of mould. Corked bottles are recognizable from a smell which resembles a

combination of stale dried mushrooms and damp cellars which tends to intensify the longer the bottle is open. Cork wholesalers themselves admit that between one in 20 and as many as one in 12 corks may be more or less affected by this mould. Buying a pricey wine does little to lengthen the odds against getting a bad bottle – though there is little question that "agglomerate" corks, made from tiny chips glued together and used almost exclusively for cheap wines, seem particularly subject to mouldy smells and flavours. Ironically, research has shown that the most efficient way to seal a wine bottle would be with a screwcap, but since few wine buffs are ready to unscrew a bottle of Mouton Rothschild, go-ahead producers in California and Chile and supermarkets in Britain have instead switched to recently developed polypropylene corks.

Another fault you may encounter is the presence of some form of sulphur. Cough-inducing sulphur dioxide is common in recently bottled wines and most particularly sweet ones from the traditional areas of Europe (New-World wine-makers are less tolerant of it), while a gluey or a manure-like smell reveals unwelcome sulphur compounds in the wine. One way to check your diagnosis of these is to drop a copper coin into the glass and leave it in contact with the wine for a few minutes. Often, the copper will clean up the problem. Unfortunately, a bottle with one of these sulphur-related conditions is probably typical of a whole batch.

COOKING WITH WINE

"GO ON – slosh in a bit more wine. Can't do any harm." Or can it? All sorts of nonsense has been spoken and written about cooking with wine. On the one hand, there are those wonderful old cookery books that recommend you use a priceless bottle of Chambertin for your *coq au vin* or *boeuf bourguignon* – because that's what the Duke of Burgundy's cook (who didn't have to pay for the stuff) would have used 600 years ago. On the other, there are the people who maintain that any wine that's too caustic to drink will be perfect for a sauce to serve with fillet steak.

Easy does it: *Applying the finishing touches*

Neither attitude makes sense. There is no point in boiling up a top-class red or white wine; nor, though, can you hope to get away with using just any old wine – any more than you can make a decent dish by casseroling any tough old chicken. First, ask yourself why (and how) you are going to use wine to prepare this dish. The answer is not as straight-forward as you might imagine. There are some dishes in which the wine's essential role is as part of a marinade that will make tough meat tender; in others, such as *coq au vin* and that *boeuf bourguignon*, it will be the liquid in which the food is cooked. Often the wine will be added at the last minute to turn the juices and fats at the bottom of a roasting pan into a sauce; in a few cases, as in sherry trifle, it will simply taste of itself.

Give a thought, too, to the bottle you are going to serve with the meal. French traditionalists recommend that the two should be the same, or at least come from the same region; a more pragmatic approach would be to aim for wines of a similar style.

Be adventurous. After all, you could end up inventing a dish – in the way a long-forgotten Burgundian did when he or she first made the now-classic *oeufs en meurette*, by poaching eggs in the region's red wine.

Rules and hints

- Try to choose a style of wine that suits the particular dish you are cooking with as much care as you choose the food. A chicken does not taste like a duckling; a Beaujolais will not make the same kind of sauce as a Barolo.
- Don't cook with any wine you could not imagine drinking.
- Unless you are making a dish such as sherry trifle, in which you want the flavour of the alcohol to be apparent, don't pour in the wine right at the end of the cooking; cook the liquid for long enough for the alcohol to evaporate.
- Don't overdo it; adding another glassful of wine "for luck" can be too much of a good thing.
- You can make use of left-over wine and ensure that you always have some cooking wine to hand by preparing for yourself a "wine concentrate". All you have to do is simmer the wine (white or red) in a pan until its volume has been reduced by half. Prepared in this way, and frozen in ice-cube trays or stored in sterilized jam jars, the concentrate should keep almost indefinitely.

THE RIGHT WINE FOR THE RIGHT DISH

Champagne

When making dishes whose recipes call for Champagne (such as Champagne sorbet), don't make the mistake of substituting a cheap, basic sparkling wine. It wasn't the bubbles that the original cook was after, but the nutty, yeasty flavour. If you are not going to use Champagne, either go for a better-quality fizz from France, Australia, California or New Zealand or, perversely, you could try a high-quality Muscadet de Sèvre-et-Maine *sur lie* – these two words indicate that the wine has enjoyed the same yeasty contact as Champagne.

Dry white wine

Muscadet, Gros Plant and good dry, fairly neutral wines, such as young southern French *vins de pays* whose labels do not declare them to be Chardonnay, Sauvignon or whatever, basic Italian whites and modern-style white Rioja can be ideal for sauces to accompany shellfish. Richer wines, such as young white Burgundy and Bordeaux, Australian Sémillon (though only the lighter examples) and Alsace Pinot Blanc, can be better suited to white-meat dishes such as veal and pork. Sauvignon Blanc from New Zealand or the Loire can be used for these dishes or for poultry, as can dry Rieslings from Alsace or Germany and dry English wines. Another original idea is to sprinkle fruit salad with dry Riesling or Sauvignon just before serving.

Madeira

The sweeter styles of Madeira – Bual and Malmsey – are the ones to use for the classic *sauce Madère*, while the drier Sercial and Verdelho can be added to *consommé*. Sweet Madeira can also be poured over sorbet, substituted for Marsala in *zabaglione* or added to an apricot sauce for a fruit pie.

Marsala

When Marsala is specified in a recipe, as for example in *zabaglione*, it is almost always the sweet *dolce* style that is meant.

Medium white wine

Any recipe that simply calls for "medium white wine" is being very unhelpful; there is a huge difference in flavour between a cheap-and-nasty, semi-sweet "Rizling" from Eastern Europe and a *demi-sec* Vouvray, though both can fairly be described as "medium white". As a rule, go for the grapier (German *Spätlese* and *QbA*; Australian Rieslings) styles with any dish that includes grapes, and use *demi-sec* Loire Chenin Blancs and most examples of that grape from California for dishes with apple.

Muscat

Recipes that simply list Muscat probably mean a sweet, fortified version, such as Muscat de Frontignan or Beaumes de Venise.

Port

When French recipes require port, they can mean either cheap, basic tawny, or ruby – the two styles with which Gallic wine-drinkers are most familiar. Both can be used in variations of *zabaglione*.

Red wine

If the wine is going to be used as a marinade, choose one that has plenty of colour, flavour and tannin. Red Burgundy (with a few exceptions, such as Fixin) or Rioja are far less ideal for this purpose than more hard-edged, full-bodied wines, such as Barbera from Italy, Shiraz from Australia, Zinfandel from California, Douro from Portugal, or Corbières, Minervois or Cahors from France.

Similar styles of wine can be used when you are making sauces from the fat and juices that remain in the pan after you have roasted or sautéed almost any kind of meat.

On the other hand, finer-flavoured wines such as Burgundies and Bordeaux are perfect for dishes that require the meat to be gently cooked in the wine.

Don't limit yourself to meat dishes with red wine; it can also be used with fruit to make all sorts of simple puddings. Fruit juice, sugar and wine can make a delicious sweet sauce, and various kinds of fruit can be poached in wine (pears in red wine is perhaps the best-known combination). If you find that you have a little faded (but not vinegary) Bordeaux or Burgundy, you could follow the example of cooks in both these regions by pouring the wine over fresh strawberries.

Riesling

As a general rule, Riesling can be used for almost any recipe that calls for white wine and grapes. It can also make a tasty difference to fresh fruit salad. Sweeter (*Kabinett* and *Spätlese*) Rieslings are widely used in Germany when cooking the veal and pork dishes that are so popular in that country, and chicken in a Riesling sauce is a delicious speciality of Alsace.

Sauternes

Like Champagne, Sauternes is often wrongly thought by cooks to be a catch-all term – in this case covering almost any kind of sweet white wine. In fact, however, the flavour you are looking for here is that of *botrytis*, the "noble rot" that gives almost any wine a peachy, dried-apricot flavour that, once tasted, is instantly recognizable.

Unfortunately, this is one area where you may find that you do have to spend a little extra on buying the right kind of wine because, unless it's a good example of Sauternes from a good vintage, it way well not have any of that flavour. You would do better to substitute a French alternative from Monbazillac, Loupiac or Ste-Croix-du-Mont or, more reliably, a German or Austrian Beerenauslese, an Alsatian Sélection de Grains Nobles or a "late-harvest" wine from Australia or California. Any such wine could be used to pour over peaches – or, inventively, to make a *sauce Sauternes* to serve with chicken, which gives it a wonderfully rich flavour.

Sherry

Some of the most unhelpful recipes of all are the ones that simply tell you to add sherry, without indicating what kind of sherry they mean, Sherry can be bone-dry, almost savoury – or Christmas-puddingy sweet. Bristol Cream will do your *consommé* no good at all, while the salty tang of *manzanilla* is not a flavour most people associate with sherry trifle. Swap the two styles and both dishes will be delicious. And bear in mind that dry sherry can be a handy substitute for the rice wine called for in Chinese recipes.

Glazed expression: A tempting dessert

WINE AND FOOD

"YOU CAN'T possibly wear that shirt with that jacket!" "How could you even dream of drinking a white wine with meat?" The business of putting together foods and wines, like that of choosing clothes or furnishing fabrics, is full of rules and traps for the unwary which can be so daunting that one could be forgiven for dismissing them all and eating and drinking what you like. After all, a full-flavoured New-World Chardonnay could be perfect with all sorts of meat dishes and Burgundians traditionally poach trout in red wine. Some of the traps are real though – like orange ties against green shirts, sardines and claret taken together taste downright nasty – and some of the rules, provided they are not taken too seriously, can be quite handy.

It is worth bearing in mind the style of food a wine was originally intended to partner – usually the dishes enjoyed in the region where the wine was made. A wine like Barolo, for example, was never made to be drunk with a plateful (or rather half-full) of dainty *nouvelle cuisine* morsels – any more than Sauternes was intended to be served with grilled sole.

But today, people, dishes and wines travel far more widely than ever before. A London or New York dinner party might easily include dishes from three different countries – and wines from three more. And some unexpected partnerships of flavour and style can be the most successful of all.

There are three kinds of relationship between food and wine. There are the personality clashes, in which each brings out the worst in the other. Try drinking red Burgundy with a plateful of oily sardines, or with a grapefruit, and you will know exactly what I mean. At the other end of the scale, there is the love-at-first-sight relationship which, like a bowlful of strawberries and cream, tastes magically better and somehow quite different to either ingredient taken by itself.

Between the two, there is the great mass of food and wine pairings in which the two rub along well enough, never actively clashing, but not doing an awful lot for each other either.

And, finally, there are the handy "bridges", the components which can bring otherwise incompatible flavours together. Try a tannic claret with a rare piece of beef and you will probably find that the meat makes the wine taste tougher. Now add a touch of mustard and have another taste. Astonishingly, the combination of the three flavours disarms that toughness completely.

The key to discovering partnerships that work lies in understanding the *weight* as well as the *type* of flavours you are dealing with – plus a helping of courage. Brave were the souls who first discovered how delicious game with chocolate, or a little pepper sprinkled over fresh strawberries could be.

DESSERT WINES

According to some rule books all desserts deserve Sauternes – except those which involve chocolate or ginger, both of which are believed to be incompatible with any wine. But while, at its most spicy, ginger overpowers almost any other flavour, at its mildest, it can match late-harvest Gewürztraminer.

Rich food, rich wine: *A combination that sings*

Chocolate can be lovely with Australian or Californian Orange Muscats or, surprisingly, with rich, fruity Cabernet Sauvignon from California. Fresh fruit tarts and mousses need fruity wines. A sweet Riesling (such as German *Auslese*) or Muscat (a late-harvest Alsace, a Beaumes de Venise from the Rhône, or a Moscatel de Setúbal from Portugal) can be perfect.

Creamy desserts such as syllabub and *crème brulée* are better served by sweet wines from the Loire, like Vouvray Moelleux, or by Sauternes.

Very sweet desserts such as baked or steamed sponge puddings will overpower all but the most intense of wines. You could try Hungarian Tokay, Malmsey or Bual Madeira, or my favourite: Liqueur Muscat or Tokay from Australia.

Wine for cheese

Red wine is not as perfect a partner for cheese as most people imagine; in fact, white wine can be far better – especially with high-fat cheeses.

Dutch cheeses and goat's cheese are delicious with Sancerre or Pouilly Blanc Fumé, though New Zealand Sauvignon Blanc and Chablis can be successful too.

One of the great wine-and-cheese partnerships is Roquefort and Sauternes. The combination of honeyed sweetness and salty tang is perfect, but you can swap the Roquefort for any similar blue cheese and replace the Sauternes with a late-harvest Riesling or even a *moëlleux* wine from the Loire.

Soft French cheeses are made for gentle, fruity red Burgundy. Cheddar can go with Bordeaux – in particular, examples made primarily from the rich-flavoured Merlot grape – but I would opt for port (vintage or tawny) or Madeira. And don't forget Stilton and port.

Matching Wine with Food

Wine for fish
To avoid the nasty metallic taste that you get when you drink red wine with fish, the trick is to choose the right wine for the right fish. Oily ones like sardines need crisp dry whites – such as Vinho Verde or Muscadet.

Salmon
Subtle poached salmon needs white wine without too much acidity. Lighter-bodied Chardonnay such as Mâcon-Villages can be ideal – as can good Soave, Frascati or white Châteauneuf-du-Pape. Smoked salmon is said to go well with Alsace Gewürztraminer; I prefer another Alsace – Tokay-Pinot Gris – or white Hermitage.

Seafood
Oysters call for bone-dry whites – Muscadet, Sancerre, Chablis or Verdicchio. For scallops, try slightly richer wines such as lighter Italian Chardonnays or Pinot Bianco – and lobster can be perfect with, again, Tokay-Pinot Gris from Alsace.

Grilled fish
Sea bass and river fish such as trout go well with Chardonnay – particularly southern Burgundies such as St-Véran, as well as oaky white Rioja (particularly Monopole) or top-class Soave (try Pieropan's version). Dry German or Australian Riesling is perfect with turbot.

Wine for poultry & game
Chicken and turkey
Avoid too strong or too subtle a wine with these; simply cooked dishes go well with light reds (Beaujolais or red Loire, for example). For a white to accompany plainly roasted poultry, try a Chardonnay or an Alsace or German Riesling.

Creamy chicken dishes need the acid bite of dry, fruity Sauvignon (from New Zealand), good dry Vouvray or Alsace Riesling.

Duck
Roast duck can be as delicious with fruity wines as with fruity sauces. Try Beaujolais, blackcurranty Cabernet Sauvignon from Chile, a red Loire or a light claret.

Game birds
The gamier the meat, the spicier the wine must be. So, for subtler game birds, try Bordeaux from St Emilion and Pomerol or a red Burgundy. For stronger-flavoured meat, go for northern Rhône reds such as Crozes Hermitage, St-Joseph, Hermitage or Côte Rôtie, Australian Shiraz or Californian Zinfandel.

Venison and rabbit
The strong flavours of venison are best matched by spicy French wines such as Cahors, Madiran, Hermitage and Châteauneuf, Barolo from Italy, Australian Shiraz-Cabernet and Californian Zinfandel and Cabernet. With rabbit or hare, serve old-fashioned, country-style wines such as Italian Barbera and Chianti, or Bairrada and Douro from Portugal.

Wine for meat
Tradition dictates that red meat calls for red wine, but the kind of red wine depends on the type of meat and the sauce in which it has been prepared. If the sauce has been made with a wine from a particular region, there is an argument for serving it with a wine from the same region. A creamy sauce, however, needs a soft wine with plenty of fresh, fruity acidity to cut through the richness – say, a good Beaujolais or a Bardolino from Italy. A rich, meaty casserole requires heartier wines such as Châteauneuf-du-Pape, Californian Zinfandel, Australian Shiraz or Grenache, Barolo, a rich Burgundy such as Gevrey Chambertin or a Bordeaux from St Emilion. Roast beef and steaks prepared without sauce go well with full-flavoured but not overly tannic Bordeaux, Burgundy, Rioja, richer *cru* Beaujolais, Chianti, Douro or lighter Zinfandels from California. Lamb teams well with a rich Rioja or a red wine from Provence or a Cabernet from Chile, though French traditionalists would suggest Bordeaux from Pauillac. Pork can be paired equally well with red or white wines. For white, try a rich Chardonnay, a traditional Rioja, a Tokay-Pinot Gris or a Pinot Blanc from Alsace, or a drier Riesling from Germany. If you prefer red, then go for a medium-bodied wine such as a Dolcetto, a Valpolicella or Chianti, a red Loire or a Beaujolais.

Foreign flavours
In some parts of the world, such as India and China, wine has no traditional place at all. Consequently, their cuisine can offer something of a challenge when it comes to selecting wine.

Some curries are so dominated by the flavour of peppers and spice that it is certainly not worth choosing a top-quality wine. But if you must have wine, try fresh fruity or warm spicy styles, such as chilled young Beaujolais, red Loire, young Rhône or Australian Shiraz, dry German Riesling – or a fruity, off-dry rosé such as Mateus. For milder curries try Dolcetto, Valpolicella or Bairrada, while creamy dishes are well-matched with Sauvignon.

Creole, Chinese and Thai food often combine so many sweet, sour and savoury flavours that it is best to go for a very tasty wine. My favourite is New Zealand Sauvignon Blanc, but Alsace Gewürztraminer and southern French rosés are lovely – as is chilled Asti. The same rules apply to Japanese food, though *sake* – rice wine, which is usually drunk warm – is more traditional.

55

WINE IN RESTAURANTS

AS RECENTLY as a decade ago, the cellars of better restaurants were piled high with well-chosen bottles of wine, laid down over the years so as to be precisely ready to drink on the evening when you or I ordered them from the list. Today, all that has changed; stocks of ready-to-drink old wine have evaporated under the heat of the accountants' and bankers' scrutiny. Some restaurateurs still cellar their wines, or buy at auction, but far too few bother – which explains why, traditional claret-drinkers who would ideally like to be drinking 20- and 25-year-old wines from the 1970s are offered examples which often have yet to celebrate their first decade. Fortunately, modern wine-making has given these bottles a youthful accessibility rarely found in the clarets of the past. Even so, paying a restaurant mark-up for a Bordeaux of the same age as the one in the local off-licence hardly adds to the magic of a special occasion.

Wine-waiters, too – in restaurants sufficiently ambitious to keep such a beast – are rarely the fine, mature specimens they once were. Some are young and enthusiastic; too many, however, persevere in trying to make the customer feel uncomfortable. This is, perhaps, a defensive measure against wine-literate diners, who have only to wander around the wine section of any good supermarket to know as much as – and maybe more than – their waiter about sparkling wines from the Penedés in Spain, Pinot Grigios from north-east Italy, the Rieslings of Washington State, Chardonnay from Australia's Hunter Valley, Cabernets from California and Sauvignons from New Zealand.

So, if you want to stay one step ahead of a sniffy *sommelier*, here's how to avoid the pitfalls of the restaurant wine list.

The right stuff: *The wine waiter should know his wines in detail*

THE CHOICE

If your eye is immediately caught by wines of the kind listed on the left, you're off to a good start. A restaurateur with the confidence to choose and offer something a little different from the "standard" styles obviously takes an interest in what his customers are drinking, and may well ensure that his staff are informed and ready to offer advice on unfamiliar wines. If you're still not quite confident about his powers of discrimination, order a glass of house red or white as an aperitif. If that's good, you can be pretty confident that somebody cares about the contents of the cellar; buying the kind of wine that is served by the glass calls for far more skill than listing a well known claret from a good vintage.

THE VINTAGE

Any wine list that neglects to mention the vintages of the wines it lists clearly doesn't care about them or the drinker – but ones that print "1988/9" are no better. After all,

---

WHAT TO ORDER

There are thousands of wines from which a restaurateur might choose for his list, but some do crop up frequently. I myself would confidently order wines from the following producers – and feel happy about opting for an unfamiliar maker if several of these names featured on the list:

Red and white Bordeaux Michel Lynch; Châteaux Bonnet; Léoville Barton; Lynch-Bages; Haut-Marbuzet; d'Angludet; Chasse-Spleen; La Gurgue; Haut-Bailly; La Louvière; La Rivière; Potensac; Dourthe No 1 (white). Listing Mouton Cadet, unless accompanied by more interesting alternatives, shows a lack of interest and taste.
Red and white Burgundy Laroche; Louis Latour (whites); Joseph Drouhin; Louis Jadot; Olivier Leflaive; Chartron et Trebuchet; Jaffelin; Leroy; Vallet Frères. Wine-wise restaurants tend to offer Louis Latour white Burgundies rather than reds, revealing that they know that this merchant is better at making the former than the latter.
Beaujolais Georges Duboeuf; Joseph Drouhin; Loron; Louis Jadot.
Alsace Kuentz-Bas; Trimbach; Hugel; Zind-Humbrecht; Schlumberger; Rolly Gassman.
Loire Vacheron; de Ladoucette; Dézat; Huet; Poniatowski.

Rhône Guigal; Delas; Jaboulet Aîné; Chave; Graillot.
Chianti Castello di Volpaia; Antinori; Badia a Coltibuono; Frescobaldi; Isole e Olena.
Barolo Aldo Conterno; Fontanafredda; Borgogno.
Barbaresco Gaja.
Other Italian Lungarotti; Tignanello; Tiefenbrunner; Avignonesi; Pomino; Sassicaia.
Rioja Marqués de Murrieta; Marqués de Riscal (recent vintages); La Rioja Alta; CVNE; Montecillo; Faustino; López de Heredia; Contino; Martinez-Bujanda; Remelluri.
Catalonia Torres; Jean León; Raimat.
Germany Deinhard; Lingenfelder; Sichel; Egon Müller; F W Gymnasium; Müller Cattoir; Tony Jost; Kurt Darting; J J Prum; Bassermann-Jordan; Bürklin-Wolf.
California Mondavi (though *not* the Woodbridge wines); Fetzer; Stag's Leap; Saintsbury; Calera; Bonny Doon; Frogs Leap; Simi; Ridge; Trefethen; Firestone; Château St Jean; Iron Horse.
Australia Petaluma; Penfolds; Lindemans; Hardy's; Rothbury; Rosemount; Brown Brothers.
New Zealand Montana (especially Church Road); Jackson Estate, Neudorf; Kumeu Estate; Collards; Corbans; Selaks; Cloudy Bay; Nobilos; Hunters.
Chile Casablanca; Casa Apostolle; Caliterra.

they'd never dream of trying to sell you "Beef/Pork Casserole". Even when a vintage is named, beware of the switch 'twixt list and table. You order the 1990 and the stuff that is poured for you to taste is the 1992: be as firm as you would be if your avocado came with prawns when you ordered vinaigrette.

THE PRODUCER

Beware of lists that do not include the name of the producer alongside or beneath that of *every* wine. The omission does not necessarily mean that there will be no good wines on offer – just that their presence will be something of a fluke. And, like vintages, producers get switched too. You order the Sancerre produced by M. Dupont; the one with which you are presented is made by M. Chevalier, who might be a perfectly delightful man and a great trumpet-player in the village band – but a far worse wine-maker than his next-door neighbour Dupont.

THE PRICE

The price you pay for your meal and wine is up to the restaurateur and yourself; just remember, your readiness to hand over four times what he or she paid for an indifferent young Chablis merely helps to perpetuate a scandal. As a general rule, unless the restaurant is so luxurious that everything carries an in-built surcharge to cover the cost of the designer crockery, anything beyond two and a half times the retail price is completely out of court. A restaurateur's mark-up ought generally to be between 100 per cent and 200 per cent on the price he paid, which – to put this in perspective – is usually around 25 per cent less than the retail, by-the-bottle, price you would have to pay in most wine-merchants.

THE SERVING

If you don't want to appear pretentious and silly, keep the sniffing and tasting ritual to a minimum. Some wine buffs seem to imagine that a protracted session of examining the cork, inhaling the wine and gargling with it are all some form of essential foreplay that mark the expert from the novice.

Not a bit of it. The real expert rarely

pays much attention to the cork – provided that he or she has seen it being drawn from the bottle – but will usually satisfy him or herself with giving the wine the briefest of sniffs (just like the one you might give a carton of milk that's been in the fridge for a few days). If the wine smells fresh, clean and fruity, don't bother to taste it – just ask the waiter to serve.

THE TASTE

If you are not certain about the smell, take a sip. What if you then don't like it? Well, first things first. What don't you like? If it's just a matter of the wine being too sweet or too dry for your taste, your right to send the wine back may be no greater than your right to complain that you don't like the tarragon in the sauce on the chicken. On the other hand, just as you would have every justification in returning a *crème brulée* served with cream that had gone sour, you have every reason to send back a wine that has something wrong with it. (For specific faults, see *Tasting* on p. 48.)

THE TEMPERATURE

If your wine is too warm, ask for an ice bucket. Your wine-waiter will look down his nose when he realizes it's for the light red Loire or Beaujolais that he zealously parked in hot water in the kitchen for 10 minutes to bring it to the tepid state you find so unappealing, but don't be deterred – at least you will be able to drink and enjoy the wine

in the way its maker intended. While it's chilling, sip slowly at a mean portion until the rest of the wine has cooled down – don't let the waiter hover over you carefully refilling your glass after every mouthful.

If the temperature of a white is too low, simply deter the waiter from replacing the bottle in the bucket. Let him top up your glass to his heart's content, cupping it meanwhile in your hands to warm the wine within.

THE SECOND BOTTLE

Half-way through the meal you absent-mindedly order another bottle of the Sancerre. What arrives could well be of a different vintage or by a different producer – or it could be a duff bottle of the same wine. So, make sure you get a look at the label and a taste of the wine before it's served – otherwise several half-full glasses of good wine from the first bottle could be spoiled by bad wine from the second.

THE TIP

Very few wine-waiters get the chance to taste many of the wines they serve. If you have ordered one of the more interesting bottles from the list and the person who has served you has seemed enthusiastic and interested, invite him or her to taste it – or leave a little in the bottle.

Final check: *Is it the vintage you ordered?*

WINE AND HEALTH

NOTHING IS QUITE clear in the alcohol-and-health debate, and matters are certainly not simplified when, on the one hand, dignified Frenchmen straightfacedly publish books suggesting that the wine from the village of Morgon in Beaujolais cures influenza while, on the other, anti-alcohol lobbyists refuse to discuss wine without bringing up references to motor accidents and the effects of violence committed by drunks.

Wine, like every other kind of alcohol, is of course a potentially dangerous substance – if it is abused and taken in excess. But this is no reason to treat it as a poison. After all, an overdose of nutmeg can be deadly, and no one has so far advocated posting health warnings on spice racks.

Besides, wine does have an extra-ordinarily honourable heritage in the annals of western civilization – as any book of quotations makes immediately clear. Excise it from the works of Chaucer, Shakespeare or Dickens – or the Bible for that matter – and you have to rewrite a large chunk of great literature. The "anti" lobby would argue that art and literature contain as many references to the damaging effects of drink. Where these occur, however, wine is rarely the culprit; what is more, the alcoholic drinks we consume today are very different to those of the past. The "gin" of Gin Lane was a rough, almost industrial spirit; Bill Sykes's violent outbursts were not the result of an excess of Muscadet.

And, as a growing number of reports from around the world confirm, there is in any case now plenty of evidence that, far from being harmful, sensible levels of wine- drinking actually do contribute to good health.

First, there is the so-called French Paradox which became a catch-phrase in America when it was revealed by CBS in its popular *60 Minutes* television programme that, despite their rich diet, wine-drinking Frenchmen had fewer heart attacks than health-conscious, non-drinking Americans. The research by French scientist Serge Renaud, which was the basis of that pro-gramme, was supported by a Danish study of 13,000 people, the results of which were published in 1995. Over 10 years, tee-totallers had twice as much risk of dying as wine-drinkers with a daily intake of three to five glasses of wine. Reviewing these and other results, Dr Curt Ellison of Boston University was prepared to say that drinking one or two glasses of red wine with a daily meal will "most likely reduce the risk of heart disease". Taking the subject a little further, in 1995 Canadian writer Frank Jones published the *Save Your Heart Guide*, which provided credible scientific evidence for specifically recommending red Burgundy and other wines made from the Pinot Noir grape as being especially effective against heart disease.

Other research has suggested that tannic red wine may even help to cure herpes, while a study by the American Cancer Society, focusing on 250,000 subjects, suggested that a drink a day (though not necessarily of wine) reduced their chances of getting cancer by 10 per cent.

Wine and other kinds of alcohol

There have been various research projects devoted to the question of whether wine is a healthier form of alcohol than beer or spirits. Though none has reached a satisfactory conclusion, most suggest that wine in general, and red wine in particular, does seem to have the edge over other drinks.

Wine strength

Wines can vary in strength from the non-alcohol and low-alcohol styles, which range from zero to 5 per cent, to fortified wines that can weigh in at as much as 27 per cent (nearly three-quarters the strength of whisky, and usually served in rather larger measures). In general, however, most table wines and fizz have strengths of between 9 per cent and 13 per cent, and most

Calories in Wine by Strength and Sweetness

This chart shows the variation in calorie content between different styles of wine – and whether the calories (kcal) come from the alcohol or the sugar. Figures are per 12.5 cl glass (approximately six measures per bottle) for table wines, and per 7 cl glass (16 measures per bottle) for fortified wines. 1 gm/litre sugar provides 3.75 kcal: 1 gm/litre alcohol (= 1% strength) provides 7 kcal.

TABLE WINE

	Strength	kcal	Sweetness	kcal	Total kcal
Low-alcohol	3.0%	26	40 gm/litre	2	28
Trocken (dry)	9.0%	79	0 gm/litre	0	79
Kabinett	9.0%	79	10 gm/litre	5	84
Moscato	6.5%	57.5	57 gm/litre	25.5	84
Vinho Verde	9.0%	79	10 gm/litre	5	84
Liebfraumilch	9.0%	79	15 gm/litre	7	86
Muscadet	11.5%	100	0 gm/litre	0	100
Claret	12.0%	105	0 gm/litre	0	105
Australian Chardonnay	13.0%	114	5 gm/litre	2	116
Châteauneuf-du-Pape/					
Australian Red	14.0%	123	0 gm/litre	0	123

FORTIFIED WINE

	Strength	kcal	Sweetness	kcal	Total kcal
Dry sherry	17.0%	83	0 gm/litre	0	83
Sweet sherry	19.0%	94	130 gm/litre	34	127
Port	22.0%	108	100 gm/litre	27	135

fortified wines – such as sherry or port – average 15–20 per cent.

To help people to drink sensibly, the system of "units" used in the table opposite illustrates how strengths can vary. A 12.5 cl glass of German wine at 8 per cent is most convenient, containing just one unit of alcohol. But if you fancy a change – a big Châteauneuf, for example – that figure could virtually double.

It is generally considered that the maximum advisable number of units of alcohol for any man to consume in a week is 21–35. For women the figure is lower – 14–21 – which may seem unfair, but in fact there is a wealth of evidence to prove that, because of their lower body mass but relatively higher proportion of body fat, women metabolize alcohol less efficiently than men. Some doctors also recommend an alcohol-free day or two per week, while the Danish study contradictorily suggests that the most beneficial effects are felt if the wine is taken in moderate daily doses rather than weekend binges.

Wine and weight

Wine is fattening – like almost everything else we enjoy eating and drinking. Alcohol is actually more fattening than sugar; drinking a strong dry white wine like a 14 per cent Meursault will put more weight on you than than a hock which is sweeter but has less alcohol – or a light-bodied red, such as a 12.5 per cent claret.

Wine and pregnancy

Less than 50 years after doctors routinely recommended mothers-to-be to build themselves up with Guinness, barmen in the US now treat pregnant customers like prospective murderers. Today, women are not only officially told to lay off alcohol while expecting but, according to some research, would be wise to stick to soft drinks prior to conception – though if too many took this advice a great deal of conception would probably never occur in the first place! Curiously, in European wine-producing countries, where the Foetal Alcohol Syndrome which so worries North Americans is almost unknown, pregnant women often do continue drinking before, during and after pregnancy – but in far greater moderation.

Wine and driving

Sorry, but if you want to drive safely – never mind legally – there are no get-out clauses

or loopholes. Tests have proved that while it tends to promote feelings of confidence, even the smallest amount of alcohol in the bloodstream can impair judgement – especially in people who are tired or in any other way under the weather. To be safe at the wheel, the only answer is to drink no wine at all – or, for those extraordinarily self-conscious individuals who claim to "feel silly" holding an orange juice, one that has been de-alcoholized.

Wine and food

To most southern Europeans, food and wine are two halves of a whole; they rarely consume one without the other. Just as their lunch or dinner almost always includes wine, the glass of red they order in a pavement café is usually accompanied by savoury titbits. It's a habit worth adopting; and it may help the wine perform the medical miracles described above.

Wine and time

The average human body takes around an hour to deal with a single glass of average-strength wine. Heavily built men may find that they can cope with more than this; lighter men and most women, however, may equally discover this to be too rapid a rate of input for their bodies.

Although it is advisable to accompany any alcohol with food, and to punctuate it with the occasional glass of water or other

A glass a day may help to keep the doctor away. *There are few more enjoyable methods.*

non-alcoholic drink (to counteract the alcohol's dehydrating effects), it has to be said that there is no effective way to speed up the process of metabolizing the alcohol. The supposed capacity of black coffee to achieve this is a myth. Similarly, excessive drinking with dinner can leave you with alcohol in your bloodstream the following morning.

Hangovers

Even the most sensible drinkers sometimes suffer the consequences of swallowing too much of a good thing – especially if they forget to down a pint or so of water (more if possible) to ward off the effects of alcohol-induced dehydration.

If it's too late for prevention, is there a cure? Ignore any advice to indulge in the hair of any species of dog – that's an anaesthetic, not a remedy – and stick to easily digestible protein, and plenty of liquids such as orange or tomato juice with which to rehydrate the body. Vitamin B tablets are another lifesaver on the morning after the night before, partly because alcohol reduces the ability of the body to assimilate the vitamin.

As a final hint, beware particularly of over-indulging in vintage port, whose reputation as hangover-fare is wholly earned. Tawny will leave you feeling fitter.

ORGANIC WINE

UNTIL MAN LEARNED how to manufacture chemical herbicides, fungicides, insecticides and fertilizers, grape-growing and wine-making were tricky, unpredictable tasks, at the annual mercy of all manner of hazards. On the other hand, there was one way in which life in the vineyard was actually better then: everything was in some kind of balance.

Today, even some of the most vociferous of "non-organic" grape growers would agree that the growing immunity of the pests and the deficiencies in the overworked, over-treated soil are creating a vicious circle in which scientists are driven to develop ever more sophisticated treatments.

"Organic" producers want to break that cycle by giving nature more of a chance to manage its own affairs, allowing "good" bugs to kill "bad" ones and encouraging the natural organisms – up to a billion per gram – within the soil to recreate its essential balance. Some of these vinous reactionaries – or should we call them revolutionaries? – follow "biodynamic" practices which can seem downright eccentric, including sprinkling the earth with herbs on days chosen according to the phases of the moon. But before you mock these activities, pull the cork on a bottle from the Domaine Leroy in Burgundy or from Didier Dagueneau, or Nicolas Joly's Roche aux Moines vineyard in the Loire – and think again. These wines, made in some of the most climatically hazardous vineyards in the world, are leagues ahead of the stuff made by their more conventional neighbours.

Organic viticulture, like the political movement it often resembles, comes in many different flavours. While those small producers are out scattering powdered quartz and infusions of nettles and cam-omile on their vines, huge companies like Fetzer and Mondavi in California and Penfolds and BRL Hardy in Australia are now making large quantities of organic wine. It is no accident that these bigger producers are all in the New World, where climatic conditions are relatively predictable. But with firms like these already

Fetzer Vineyards: This Californian producer is committed to organic viticulture

on board, the organic bandwagon is sure to attract more passengers.

Beware though of wine-makers whose organic credentials can sometimes prove to be very questionable – and pay equal heed to producers who quietly suggest that, without making a fuss about it, they might be making wines that were more authentically organic than the ones on offer from some of their supposedly "green"-fingered competitors.

ORGANIC WINE-MAKING: HOW IT DIFFERS

In theory, it is quite possible to produce wine simply by crushing grapes, allowing them to ferment and bottling the resulting liquid. Unfortunately, as most home wine-makers will have discovered, wines made in this way often stop tasting good within a very, very short time.

Vines and grapes are subject to all kinds of pests, fungi and diseases that can either prevent growers from making any wine at all, or leave them with a drink that has the

unpleasant musty smell and taste of rotten grapes. Once it has been made, wine is similarly subject to the attentions of various kinds of bacteria that are eager to convert it into vinegar.

In the vineyard, there are a number of chemical sprays that can be used to protect the vines from rot and insects; in the winery, producers almost always have to use sulphur dioxide as an antiseptic to ward off bacterial infection. In addition, wine-growers can, for example, use fertilizers to increase the yields of their vines.

When fining their wine, European wine-makers can (though rarely, and only under supervision) legally use potassium ferrocyanide instead of such traditional agents as powdered clay, milk protein, beaten egg white, fish scales or even ox blood. In principle, the fining agent does not combine with the wine, merely passing through it – dragging, as it sinks, any solid matter with it – but very few conscientious producers, organic or otherwise, believe this sufficiently to use potassium ferrocyanide. Indeed, the substance is banned from use in this way in the USA.

Organic wine-makers aim to avoid all unnecessary use of chemicals and accept the lower yields of non-fertilized vines. (In

Les Baux de Provence: The dry climate in this part of France makes organic winegrowing easier

warm, dry climates, this involves rather fewer sacrifices than in the cooler, wetter regions of northern Europe, where growers who do not spray their vines can sometimes lose an entire crop.) In the winery, organic producers use as little sulphur dioxide as possible, and fine with natural materials such as egg white.

So far, so good – and very laudable too. Unfortunately, the problem for anyone who would rather drink wine made by these producers is that it is often difficult to know how to differentiate it from other, less "organic" wines. Some labels carry the symbols of various associations – but some top-class organic wine-makers neglect to pin their colours to the mast.

The avowedly organic wine-makers form an incredibly loose-knit band of separate associations around the world, each of which has its own insignia and rules and – in some cases – petty jealousies. To compound the confusion, at least one such organic association in France is actually funded by the manufacturers of organic products for use by the growers: use our products, and you're a member of the club.

CRIME AND PUNISHMENT

IN 1984, the news broke that samples of Austrian wine had been found to contain substantial doses of DEG – diethylene glycol – a chemical most easily described as first cousin to anti-freeze, and harmful if drunk in large quantities. As laboratories in several countries analysed thousands of samples of wine, it was discovered that wines from Germany and Italy contained the chemical too – though in far smaller proportions.

Despite initial claims that DEG was just another of the naturally occurring chemicals found in all food and drink, it rapidly became apparent that the only way that the chemical could have got into the wine was for someone to have put it there – to "enrich" its flavour. The reason the German and Italian wines contained such small amounts was that their producers had almost certainly not added it to their vats themselves, but had beefed up their wine with bought-in wine or grape concentrate which had – unknown to them – been adulterated.

What became known as the "Anti-Freeze Scandal" was followed by a far more serious – indeed fatal – case of fakery in Italy, in which, it was said, only Italian bureaucracy saved those responsible for adding a dangerous industrial alcohol to wine from standing trial for manslaughter.

The Austrian and Italian scandals of the 1980s have made the authorities throughout the world so sensitive to how wine ought and ought not to be made that, in 1990, a number of Chilean wines were removed from the shelves in Britain because they had been found to contain sorbitol, a harmless and natural ingredient that is legitimately added in the making of all sorts of foods and drinks, yet is illegal in wine.

The wine-drinkers of the past were far less well protected, for wine has been faked and adulterated in one way or another for almost as long as it has been drunk. Virgil, predicting that "The ripening grape shall hang on every thorn", had no doubt that crooks in cold countries where vines could not be grown would pass off as "wine" the fermented juice of whatever fruit they found in the hedgerow.

In the nineteenth century, the French author Stendhal recorded visiting a factory in France where, "Out of wine, sugar, iron filings, and some flower essences they make the wines of every country." Far more often, though, wine merchants merely blended in wines from other regions. Pale burgundy would be enriched with a dollop of thick, dark wine from North Africa; claret was quite openly "improved" by the addition of a little wine from Hermitage, on the other side of France.

In the 1970s, Bordeaux was rocked by the revelation that Cruse, one of the city's best-known and most respected merchants, was selling fake wines and illegal blends under the names of popular appellations. That scandal led to a tightening-up of the regulations in France and elsewhere in Europe, but wine crime has proved as impossible to eradicate as any other. In the 1980s, batches of false Moët et Chandon found in the USA were traced back to South Africa, while an Italian gang were found to have created false bottles of Mumm Champagne. It was only by chance, in late 1994, that the highly regarded Domaine de Malandes in Chablis discovered that crooks in Germany were using a forgery of its labels to sell a blend of cheap *vin de pays* and German wine as *Grand Cru* Chablis. If the Saarbrucken discount store in which the wine was on offer had not advertised it at a ludicrously low price, no one might have noticed until the fake wine had all been sold. The best insurance for a consumer against this kind of fraud is to buy your wine from a company that cares about the quality and authenticity of what it is selling.

FACTS AND FALLACIES

THERE ARE all kinds of misconceptions about wine – many of them wilfully promoted by the people who make the stuff, and by lazy wine-writers who merely copy what they have read elsewhere. Which is why I thought it might he a good idea to dispel some of these illusions. And to reveal a few hard-to-believe facts about wine that are guaranteed to be authentic.

Sherry lasts indefinitely
The sweeter styles will keep but, even before you pull the cork, dry *fino* and *manzanilla* sherries may have lost their original, tangy freshness. So avoid leaving the bottle hanging around before you open it – and drink it up within the week. If you are likely to take longer than that, either pour half the sherry into a half-bottle when you first open it – or, wiser still, buy it in a half-bottle in the first place.

Sherry, port and Champagne can be made anywhere
In the USA, though not in Oregon where stricter rules apply, all sorts of cheap fizzy wine can call itself Champagne. In Europe, however, reasonable EC regulations forbid the sale of "Champagne" made anywhere outside the French region of that name. Likewise, genuine sherry only comes from Spain and port from the Douro in Portugal.

Canadian, Japanese and British wine is made from grapes grown respectively in Canada, Japan and Britain
Canada and Japan traditionally make wine from their own grapes but also import grape concentrate from South America and bottle it as local produce (Ontario and British Columbia both grow wine grapes but "Quebec wine" will almost certainly come from a long way further south).

"British" wine – unlike English wine (which confusingly includes Welsh wine) is actually produced by a British technique of diluting and fermenting the grape concentrate which, in this instance, tends to come from Cyprus.

In fact, under European law, none of these reconstituted drinks is defined as "wine" which, by the EC definition, has to be made from freshly picked grapes. English wine is the real stuff – though even this is allowed to contain a little sweetening juice from Germany.

Red Bordeaux is made from the Cabernet Sauvignon
Well, quite a lot of it is – but actually, the Merlot is the most widely planted grape in Bordeaux. And in the communes of St Emilion and Pomerol, the blend is often just Merlot and Cabernet Franc.

All wines improve with age
This is a belief still common in the countries of southern and eastern Europe and South America, where older wines are thought to be better by definition and people have become used to drinking wine with the taste of oxidation – the sherry-like character of wines that are past their best. Most modern wine-drinkers now prefer wines with fresher, fruitier flavours. Almost all inexpensive white wines should be drunk within a couple of years (at most) of the harvest, and even Bordeaux may need drinking young in vintage.

Cheap wines don't travel
Some don't – but then again, nor do some frail, old, expensive ones. In the case of young, cheap wine, everything depends on the way it has been produced. Well-made wine, whatever its price, should have no difficulty in being carried from one side of the world to the other. When a wine you enjoyed on holiday and brought back with you doesn't taste quite the same at home, it's very likely to be because the circumstances have changed, not the wine.

Great wine can never be made in stainless steel tanks
Some of the best châteaux in Bordeaux ferment their wine in stainless steel nowadays – and make better wine than ever.

The word "château" indicates quality
It certainly does no such thing – however smart the label. Any wine estate in France can call its building a château (even if it is little smarter than a garden hut) and, in Bordeaux, almost every estate will do so. To complicate matters still further, some co-operatives use a loophole in the rules to put "château" labels on wines they make.

Great wines are never blends; they always come from specific vineyards
What about Champagne like Krug and vintage port, both of which are almost always blends? And what about Grange, the Australian red which has, since its creation in the 1950s, always been a blend from several regions of South Australia?

"Legs" are the sign of a better wine
What the French call the "legs" – and what the Germans call "cathedral windows" – are the streams that flow down the glass once you have swirled the wine around. These are often thought to mean that the wine is especially good. All they really indicate is that the wine is rich in glycerine and was thus made from ripe grapes. Even ripe grapes can be turned into bad wine.

All Rieslings are basically the same grape
The grape of this name grown in Germany and Alsace is the only one of any real quality. When it's grown elsewhere, it is often called the Johannisberg Riesling or the Rhine Riesling to avoid confusion with the completely unrelated and inferior Laski, Welsh and Italico Rizlings. And the grape the Australians used to call the "Hunter Valley Riesling" is actually the Sémillon.

Beaujolais Nouveau has to be drunk by Christmas
There is technically no difference between Beaujolais Nouveau and the kind of Beaujolais we all drink during the rest of the year – except that it is sold earlier. It is usually best drunk quite young, but good Nouveau from one of the region's better producers and vintages can be delicious – and sometimes even better – a year after the harvest.

Screw-top bottles are not as "good" as corked bottles
They are certainly less romantic, but numerous tests have proved that they are far more effective and eliminate the risk of corkiness.

INCREDIBLE – BUT TRUE

According to the *Guinness Book of Records*, the longest distance a cork has flown from an untreated, unheated Champagne bottle is 54.18 metres. The previous record was beaten at Woodbury Winery and Cellars, in New York state, on June 5 1988, by Professor Emeritus Heinrich Medicus.

The tallest Champagne fountain was built – where else? – in Las Vegas at Caesar's Palace, required 23,642 traditional long-stemmed glasses and rose 47 glass storeys – 7.85 m/25 ft 9 in. And the Champagne? That was Moët & Chandon.

The highest price ever paid for a wine at auction was the £105,000 paid at Christie's in London for a 1787 "Jefferson" Château Lafite whose bottle was engraved with the US President's initials and is supposed to have been bought by him while he was serving as a diplomat in France. In November 1986, 11 months after the sale, the cork, dried out by the exhibition lights, slipped into the bottle, allowing its contents to become, in their turn, the world's most expensive bottle of old vinegar.

A similarly impressive sum – Fr8,600 – was paid for another Guinness record-holder, a glass of 1993 Beaujolais Nouveau which was auctioned for charity in the cellar of Pickwick's pub in Beaune within hours of its first release to the market.

A wine whose label declares its vintage to be 1985 could have been made from grapes which were picked in 1986. "Eiswein" is a German and Austrian style made from grapes that have been left to freeze on the vine. Sometimes, the wine-growers have to wait so long for the necessary severe frost that they do not harvest the grapes until January, three or four months after the grapes for more conventional wines have been picked.

A teaspoon suspended in an opened bottle of Champagne will help it to keep its fizz. Even the experts at Moët & Chandon admit that they are foxed as to why this works – but it does.

Mikhail Gorbachev was an enemy of wine who introduced a scheme to uproot vineyards in several regions of the former Soviet Union, as part of a campaign to combat the alcoholism that costs tens of thousands of lives per year. During the heyday of the Communist regime, however, wine was shipped from one republic to another, sometimes swapped litre-for-litre for petrol.

In the US, the label of every wine sold has to be approved by the authorities – which explains why, on occasion, wines from such illustrious producers as Château Mouton Rothschild have been outlawed because their labels were thought to be too sexy.

Spain has the largest area of vineyards in the world – but ranks only third in terms of production; low rainfall makes for low yields per vine. Similarly, Spain's Airén, one of the most unmemorable grape varieties, is still the most widely planted, though again production is, thank goodness, relatively small.

The international success of Australia's wines in the 1980s and 1990s was so great that exports rose in the decade or so up to 1994 from around 10 million bottles to nearly 150 million.

China and Taiwan increased their vineyards from 34,000 ha (84,000 acres) in the early 1980s to 168,000 ha (415,000 acres) in 1993. With an annual production of around 500 million bottles, they now account for over 1per cent of the world's wine harvest.

One American wine company – E & J Gallo – produces more wine each year than the whole of Champagne.

White grapes have to be used in red Chianti. Not because they improve its flavour, but because this bit of Tuscany has a surplus of white grapevines. The obligatory dose in Chianti Classico is so small, however, at 2–5 per cent, that the law cannot be enforced. Wine-growers in Hermitage in the Rhône and in Rioja in Spain, however, can voluntarily choose to put some white grapes in their red wine.

A copper coin can remove a nasty smell from a wine. If the wine smells like rotten eggs, the chances are that some of the sulphur dioxide used in its preparation has turned into hydrogen sulphide. Immersing a copper coin will convert it into copper sulphate, leaving the wine smelling fine.

Salt and white wine can both stop red wine from staining. Even a deeply coloured wine, such as Barolo, should leave no stain if you dollop on a generous pile of salt, or a splash of white wine, as soon as the wine is spilled.

A peach immersed in Champagne (actually, in any sparkling wine) will soon begin to spin round and round of its own accord. The trick requires rather a large glass – but a smaller downy or hairy fruit (the hairs trap the bubbles), such as a kiwi or gooseberry, will perform to equally entertaining effect. Similarly, a raisin will "swim" up and down the bubble stream of sparkling wine.

You can always tell a corked wine by smelling the cork
Sometimes a musty-smelling cork will warn you that a wine is faulty; quite often, however, the cork may show no signs of deterioration at all. The sure way to tell a corked wine from a dirty, or otherwise faulty, one is that it will actually smell and taste worse the longer it is in the glass.

All red wines improve with decanting
Some do benefit from the airing they get by being poured from a bottle into a decanter, but less full-bodied wines – such as red Burgundy – can lose some of their fruit by being manhandled in this way.

As a general rule, the only wines that need to be decanted are the ones that have a heavy deposit – all vintage port, most mature red Bordeaux, old Rhônes, Barolos, Australian and Californian reds, for example.

Brut Champagne is bone-dry
It tastes dry; in fact, all Brut Champagnes are slightly sweetened. If you want a bone-dry fizz, go for Brut Zero or Brut Sauvage, which have "zero dosage" – no sweetening at all. But I'll lay money that you'll probably prefer the Brut.

A good vintage in Bordeaux is also good in Burgundy
These two regions are separated the mountain range, the Massif Central, and enjoy completely different climates. In 1982, Bordeaux had a historic vintage for its red wines; Burgundy's reds were pleasant but far from great. Beware too of assuming that vintages are of consistent quality for all the styles produced in a single region. Burgundy's white wines were far better in 1992 than its reds; 1967 Sauternes were wonderful; the red Bordeaux of that year were often little short of appalling.

A hot summer means a good vintage
A cold, rainy summer and autumn will usually make for a bad year, but a hot month of August will not necessarily indicate a good one. Vintages depend on the weather being "right" at various phases of a grape's development, from the spring to the autumn. A late storm at the end of September can spoil what, at the beginning of that month, seemed set to be a great vintage.

Qualitätswein, Appellation Contrôlée, DO, DOC or DOCG on a label are a guarantee of quality
They should be; unfortunately all these expressions legally indicate only that the producer has ensured his wine conforms to a set of controls governing grape varieties, their origin and methods of production – not that he has to be a good wine-maker. Hence they can only really serve as a guide to what the wine is going to be like.

FRANCE

RY LISTING THE WORLD'S 10 best-known wine regions – without including Champagne, Bordeaux, Burgundy, Châteauneuf-du-Pape, Muscadet, Beaujolais, Sancerre, Sauternes, Chablis and Côtes du Rhône.

Yes, I know that Rioja, Chianti and the Mosel would be fighting pretty hard to get on that list too, along with Barolo, California's Napa Valley, Australia's Coonawarra and Portugal's Douro – but so would Pouilly-Fumé, Hermitage and Alsace. In other words, France is rather like one of the Hollywood studios of the 1940s that somehow managed to sign up Garbo, Gable and Grable, cornering the market in the stars most people wanted to see.

Despite the explosion of exciting wines from the New World, the renaissance of run-down wine regions of Europe and an unprecedented international readiness to question France's pre-eminence in the wine world, this is still the one country that no-one interested in wine can possibly ignore.

And, as if France's innately chauvinist wine-makers needed it, their confidence has also been increasingly boosted by the sincerest of all forms of flattery. What kinds of grapes do the wine-makers in California, Australia and Chile – and even such long-established wine-making countries as Spain, Italy and Greece – want to plant? The Chardonnay and Cabernet Sauvignon, the Pinot Noir, the Syrah and the Merlot: varieties historically most closely associated with France. And what styles of wine do they want to make? Those of Champagne, Bordeaux and Burgundy, the Loire and the Rhône.

But what today separates French wine-makers from many of the producers in the countries that have adopted their grapes is the way in which they have tended to plant them. In California and Australia, the Cabernet Sauvignon, Riesling and Chardonnay are often grown almost cheek-by-jowl in the same vineyards. In France, there have been centuries of natural selection to sort out what grows best where – and, for the last 50 years or so, strict legislation to ensure that no-one tries to experiment with Bordeaux grape varieties in Burgundy or vice versa.

Until the 1980s, when a few pioneers began to try their luck in what was once the wine morass of southern France, the Pinot Noir was only cultivated in a handful of regions, all of them in the northern, cooler half of the country; the Merlot was more or less restricted to Bordeaux; the Sauvignon Blanc rarely strayed beyond the Loire and Bordeaux and the Viognier was exclusively at home in a tiny region in the northern Rhône. Even now, the Riesling and the Gewürztraminer are grown almost nowhere outside Alsace.

And that has been one of France's great advantages – having all those different areas. It is the only country that successfully makes wine in both northern and southern Europe. The vineyards of Champagne, the Loire, Burgundy and Alsace are more or less as close to the North Pole as you can be and still make quality wine; those on the southern coast are a short drive from some of the sunniest beaches on the Continent.

La vie française: Inseparable from the grape

CLIMATE, SOILS AND TRADITIONS

The variation in climate between France's wine regions is enormous. The climates of regions such as Muscadet and Bordeaux, for example, benefit from the moderating effect of the Atlantic Ocean; those further east, such as Burgundy, Alsace and the northern Rhône, are subject to the more continental heat-chill conditions associated with areas surrounded by a mass of land.

Soil types vary, too, from the sands of the Mediterranean in which the *vin de sable* vines are grown, to the "pudding stone" pebbles of Châteauneuf-du-Pape, the gravel of the Graves in Bordeaux and the chalk of Champagne. The vineyards in some regions – the Médoc, for example – appear at first glance to be boringly flat while those of Alsace and the northern Rhône are perched on improbably steep slopes.

Finally, there are the diverse styles of wine-making that have evolved region by region, over the centuries. Some areas make white wines with varying shades of sweetness; others restrict themselves to dry wine. Some produce little but sparkling or rosé; others concentrate exclusively on red. Some use new oak barrels; others would never dream of doing so.

HISTORY

If the French cannot claim to have invented wine, they can, through a combination of luck and judgement, boast of having been, with a little help from the Romans and subsequent settlers, the first to isolate some of the best sites and grape varieties. All over the country, vineyard names reveal their ancient history: Corton Charlemagne, for example, one of Burgundy's finest white wine vineyards, is supposed to have been planted with white grapes by the emperor Charlemagne, who had an eye for a good vineyard site.

It was the Dutch who helped to provide the Médoc with the drainage ditches that converted what was often a bog into land fit for vines; it was a German who first experimented with making Sauternes in the style we know today, and it was Scots, English and Irish merchants and estate-owners who, with châteaux like Lynch-Bages, Smith Haut-Lafitte and Cantenac-Brown, were instrumental in creating the prestige of Bordeaux.

The success of particular regions, however, often had as much to do with ease of access as the quality of their wines. Regions like Cahors saw their wines sold as Bordeaux – because that was the port from

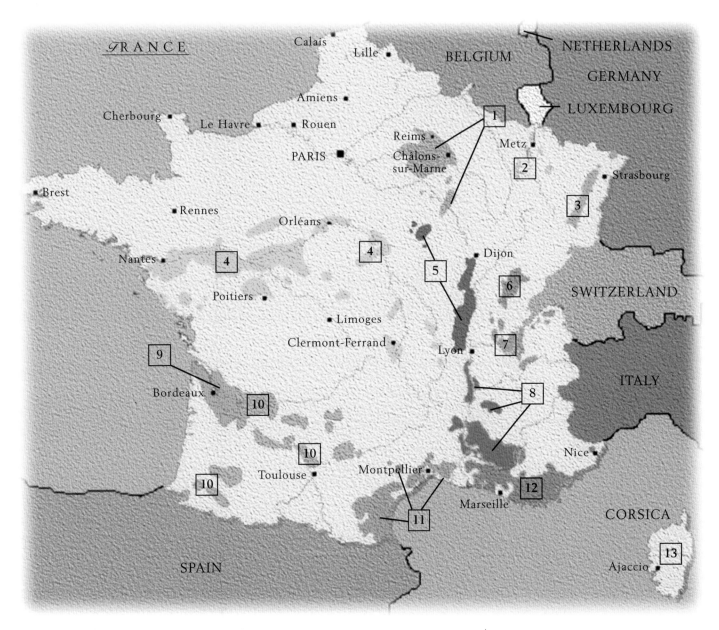

FRANCE

which they were shipped overseas. Likewise, wine made in Pommard bought at the market in Beaune might well have been sold as "Vin de Beaune". Areas close to Paris such as Chablis and Sancerre were far more heavily cultivated than they are today and, until a canal was opened linking Burgundy to the capital, there were sizeable areas of well-regarded vines in and around the city itself.

The first major change in the development of the French industry came with the French Revolution which redistributed large tracts of land which were previously in the hands of the church, and introduced inheritance laws which divided property equally among a deceased owner's heirs. While well-established domaines in Bordeaux survived these changes, there and

elsewhere, estates were split into tiny entities, most of which would rely on bigger merchants or, ultimately, co-operatives to handle their grapes or wine. Today, while California has a few hundred wineries, Bordeaux can boast some 20,000 individual producers, of whom just 4,000 ever get to see the name of their estate on the labels.

The second dramatic change came at the end of the nineteenth century with the arrival of the *phylloxera* louse which chomped its way through the roots of vineyards throughout Europe. After strenuous and fruitless efforts to combat the pest, the French finally acknowledged that the only solution was to graft traditional vines – or some of them at least – onto *phylloxera*-resistant rootstock imported from North America.

1	Champagne
2	Lorraine
3	Alsace
4	Loire
5	Burgundy
6	Jura
7	Savoie
8	Rhône Valley
9	Bordeaux
10	South-West France
11	Languedoc-Roussillon
12	Provence
13	Corsica

The *phylloxera* crisis provided France with the opportunity to tidy up its wine industry, reducing the size of Chablis' vineyards, for example, from 40,000 acres to 2,000, and the number of grape varieties grown in Bordeaux from 60 to fewer than a dozen.

TAKING CONTROLEE

Life for the newly replanted vineyards was not easy, however. In the financially strapped years between the two World Wars, wine was often hard to sell, and quality-conscious producers with vines in regions like Châteauneuf-du-Pape and Nuits-St-Georges increasingly found themselves competing against counterfeit versions of their wines.

The defence mechanism those disgruntled producers helped to invent was a quality hierarchy – the *Appellation Contrôlée* system – that has become the envy of wine-makers in other countries and, increasingly, the subject of heated debate. Almost from the outset, the system – usually referred to as AC or AOC – was based on the early discovery that certain pieces of land always seem to produce better wine, that particular climates and types of soil suit some grapes better than others and – this is the contentious part – that, given half a chance, wine-makers will cut corners and cheat.

There have been laws covering what could be planted and where for well over a millennium. The Emperor Charlemagne issued precise edicts in the ninth century; the English king Edward I defined the boundaries of St Emilion in 1289; and 100 years later, Philip the Bold, Duke of Burgundy, issued an ordinance banning the planting, in the region we now know as the Côte d'Or, of the heavy-cropping, easy-to-grow Gamay. This last variety may perform well in the granite soil of Beaujolais but produces dull fare in Beaune and Nuits-St-Georges where fourteenth-century growers were eagerly using it to supplant the more suitable traditional Pinot Noir.

In the 1930s, a Gamay-packed Beaune or Nuits-St-Georges might have been distinctly preferable to some of the wines masquerading under the names of these and other classic regions. As one visitor to Sète in southern France noted at the time, unscrupulous companies shamelessly filled smartly labelled bottles with blends of all manner of liquids and solids, many of them wholly unrelated to grapes, and some most likely poisonous.

This was the background against which France's *Appellation* system was born. To understand how it evolved, and the role it now holds today, however, you have to know something about the Gallic character. The French may have a healthy Latin disrespect for law, but there is an ingrained reverence for qualifications and official rank. I recall once buying bread in the general store of a tiny country village in southern France about eight kilometres from nowhere. In the window, there was a card advertising for a sales assistant – and

Light and shade: *Wheat and vines sharing the open hills of Champagne*

indicating the precise sales assistant's qualification required of anyone applying for the job.

Remember this when you are confronted by the confusing mass of qualifications to be found on French labels – *Appellation Contrôlée*, *VDQS*, *Vin de Pays*, *Grand* and *Premier Cru*, *Premier Grand Cru* and so on... To the French, these are all a cross between battle-medals, aristocratic pedigrees and professional qualifications. As such, they are not to be taken lightly.

At the foot of the quality pyramid, without even the faintest trace of blue blood, there are the *vins de table* – basic red and white wine made any old where from any old kinds of grapes and, usually, any old how. Traditionally, this was the stuff you got if you ordered "*un coup de rouge*" in a bar, the sinew-stiffener old drunks would buy in supermarkets by the alcoholic degree, and the major part of the nearly two-thirds of a bottle of wine consumed daily by the average Frenchman during the years following the Second World War.

Today, *vins de table* represent a steadily shrinking part of France's wine industry – even the internationally popular Piat d'Or has climbed out of this category – and regulations which bar producers from printing a vintage or a grape variety on the label of a *vin de table* hardly encourage producers to choose it.

These legislative handicaps, however, prevent French producers from competing on level terms against New-World companies such as Penfold's in Australia and Fetzer in California who unashamedly – and tastily – use blends of grapes grown in different regions to make highly successful wines whose labels include both vintage and grape. In France, when the Bordeaux firm of Dulong produced just such an innovative red blend called "Rebelle", its *vin de table* status ensured that no Gallic critic was even prepared to taste it.

Next come the 139 *vins de pays*, the country yeomanry which are supposedly representative of the region in which they are made and the varieties of grapes grown there. For the decade or so after the designation was created at the end of the 1960s, these wines were often produced by the same co-operatives as the *vins de table* and to the same low standards. Under the leadership of a few go-ahead co-ops, companies and estates, however, they underwent a quality revolution which leapfrogged a growing number into the international marketplace. These (to French traditionalists) non-aristocratic, under-qualified wines are still little appreciated in France itself. Thanks, however, to the relatively relaxed rules covering the grape varieties which may be used for them, *vins de pays* have proved particularly popular with innovative producers seeking to compete on level terms with "varietal" wines from the New World. Ironically, in countries like the US and Britain, *vin de pays* Chardonnay and Cabernet Sauvignon is often easier to sell, and at a higher price, than white Burgundy and red Bordeaux made from the same grapes.

Above the *vins de pays*, like the ornament nobody can quite find a way to get rid of, there are the VDQSs – *Vins Délimités de Qualité Supérieure*. Originally intended as a waiting-room between *vin de pays* and the heady peaks of *Appellation Contrôlée*, this has become a tiny anachronism, a limbo-land representing just 1.5 per cent of France's wines. No new VDQS has been created for a while. Some are indeed occasionally promoted, though others are more frequently bypassed by *vins de pays* like Limoux, which skip the waiting-room entirely to become instant *Appellations Contrôlées*.

This of course is the promotion to which the *vins de pays* and VDQS are supposed to aspire. *Appellation Contrôlée* wines, like those in both "inferior" categories, come from tightly specified regions, some as small as a single vineyard, others as big as Bordeaux, of which, in a single vintage, nearly one thousand million bottles may be produced.

AC wines also have to comply with strict rules covering the grapes from which they can be made, yields per acre and methods of wine-making. They are also, theoretically, subject to tasting and analysis. All of which, when taken with the promotional campaigns for AC regions and wines, could reasonably lead one to suppose that the words "*Appellation Contrôlée*" might provide some guarantee of quality.

Sadly, as even the more honest apologists for the system would concede, the only thing an *Appellation* is likely to guarantee – at best – is typicality. The supposedly rigorous tasting is frequently performed by friends and neighbours of the producer and takes place while the wine is still in barrel or tank. Perhaps unsurprisingly, only 2 per cent or so of the wines are rejected. Experienced wine enthusiasts know that anyone who orders a bottle of wine from even such well-known *Appellations* as Nuits-St-Georges, St Emilion, Sancerre or

A taste of France: The AC system is based on preserving the typicity of each wine

Champagne, without knowing the name of the producer, is flying as blind as if he asked for "Californian Chardonnay" or "Australian Cabernet". And with AC wines, maybe the risk of disappointment is even higher, because there are all too many people ready to make, sell and buy duff bottles of well-known French wines.

Added to which, the authorities in France subject French producers to handicaps rarely suffered by their competitors. New-World wine-makers may blend in limited quantities of grapes from other regions; neighbouring countries such as Spain and Italy allow the addition of small amounts of wine from other harvests. In France these procedures – potentially invaluable in tricky vintages – are outlawed. As is irrigation, even when vines are dying of thirst.

FIRST AMONG EQUALS

If France's *Appellations* form the tip of the quality pyramid, they are themselves often stratified with further sets of arcane mini-hierarchies. Within the regional *Appellation* of Burgundy – Bourgogne – for example, you should get better wine within the village *Appellation* of Gevrey-Chambertin, within whose boundaries you will find even finer stuff in one of the *Premier Cru* vineyards such as "les Cazetiers". "Premier" does not, however, as one might expect mean "first". For that, one has to look to a *Grand Cru* vineyard such as "le Chambertin" itself, whose wine really should be sublime. Well, that's the theory, and in many Burgundian cellars you can find examples of all four levels which really do illustrate the relative differences in quality and complexity.

But wander into the cellar of a less careful producer or of a less scrupulous merchant, and you could well taste a *Grand Cru* that's a lot less impressive than a good example of plain Bourgogne Rouge. The fault does not lie in the *Appellation* – time has proved that the *Grand Cru* vineyard is capable of yielding top class – but in the way its grapes have been handled.

Once you have learned about those Burgundian *Premiers* and *Grands Crus* – and taken on board the fact that villages as well known as Meursault and Beaune don't actually have any *Grands Crus* – you can then turn to the even more confusing world of Bordeaux, most of whose regions have hierarchies of their own. So, St Emilion has its regularly revised *Premier Grand Cru Classé* and *Grand Cru Classé* wines; the Médoc its 140-year-old table of *Premier*, *Deuxième*, *Troisième*, *Quatrième* and *Cinquième Crus* and Sauternes its *Grand Premier*, *Premier* and *Deuxième Crus*, while Pomerol, home of Château Pétrus, priciest Bordeaux of them all, exists quite nicely without any classification at all.

Then there are the anomalies dotted around France's wine regions. Don't go looking for Montagny's *Premier Cru* vineyards – there aren't any. But that's not to say that a wine-maker in that Burgundian village can't call his wine a *Premier Cru*; all he has to do is make sure that it is made from slightly riper grapes. Similarly, the words "*Grand Cru*" on a bottle of Banyuls simply refer to the grape variety and wine-making method.

After such a brutal exposé of its failings, it may come as a surprise to learn that I firmly believe in the principles of

Appellation Contrôlée. *Appellation* of some kind makes sense – the same kind of sense as the preservation orders even some of the youngest countries in the world slap on to their more interesting buildings. Without rules to prevent developers from bulldozing anything which stands in their way, San Francisco, Sydney and indeed Paris could all look as hateful as Singapore, a place where an "old" building is one that went up in the 1980s.

Unrestrained market forces would have the same effect on wines as on nineteenth- and early twentieth-century buildings. Little-known, uncommercial *Appellations* like Jurançon would, most probably disappear, along with Pacherenc de Vic Bilh and Crépy, as the marketeers replaced the quirky grapes from which they are made with easier-to-sell Chardonnay, Cabernet and Merlot.

But stopping people from pulling down buildings and killing off traditional wine styles is the easy part. The real challenge lies in overseeing the way those bits of heritage

Flower of Bordeaux: *Château Lafite is at the top of the Médoc hierarchy*

are maintained. Allow them to fall into disrepair and disrepute and you simply make life easier for the developer and the marketeer. Every bottle of sub-standard Bordeaux Rouge is an own-goal – and a point scored by a New-World Cabernet Sauvignon or a Vin de Pays Merlot.

In general, when considering *Appellations* in France or elsewhere, there are two essential rules. First, that *Appellations* are not all equal. Smaller ones like Meursault, Bergerac and Carneros in California generally make much more sense than larger, more diverse, ones such as Mâcon, Bordeaux and Napa. Second, that any *Appellation* refers to the potential quality of the piece of land, and not necessarily to the actual quality of the bottle in your hand. Remember these, and an *Appellation* system can serve as a useful guide from one style and quality level to another.

The Language of France

Appellation d'Origine Contrôlée (AOC/AC) Designation governing such factors as area of production, grape varieties, levels of alcohol, maximum yield etc. Supposedly the key French "quality" label.

Assemblage A blending of base wines that creates the desired *cuvée* – particularly in Champagne and Bordeaux.

Ban de vendange Officially declared regional date for the permitted start of grape-picking.

Barrique Wooden barrel holding 225 litres.

Baumé Measuring scale for the amount of sugar in grape must.

Blanc de Blancs White wine made from white grapes. Usually applied to sparkling wine.

Blanc de Noirs Relatively rare designation for white (usually sparkling) wine made from black grapes.

Brut Dry.

Cave Cellar.

Cepage Grape variety.

Chai Cellar/winery.

Chaptalization Addition of sugar to grape must to increase level of alcohol.

Clairet A pale red wine.

Climat Burgundian term for vineyard.

Clos A plot of land that is, or once was, enclosed by a wall.

Collage The fining of a wine.

Commune An administrative district within a *département*.

Confrérie A "brotherhood" or association.

Côte/Coteaux Hillside(s).

Courtier A broker who liaises between wine-makers and merchants.

Crémant Sparkling wine – in Champagne, traditionally indicated a less fizzy, more "frothy" style, but this usage has now been phased out following the granting of *Appellations* to the fully sparkling Crémant d'Alsace, de Loire and de Bourgogne.

Cru Literally a growth; refers to a particular wine.

Cru Classé An officially classified growth, or vineyard, in Bordeaux. Also an anachronistic designation in Provence.

Cuvaison/macération Period of time a red wine spends in contact with its skins.

Cuve (de fermentation) Vat.

Cuve close Bulk production method for sparkling wine also called after its inventor, Charmat, whereby second fermentation takes place in a tank.

Cuvée A special batch of wine or the contents of a vat.

Débourbage The period during which the solids are allowed to settle from the must *(moût)* during fermentation.

Dégorgement Stage in sparkling wine production when sediment is removed.

Demi-sec Half dry/half sweet.

Département Administrative region, similar to British county or US state.

Doux Sweet.

Elevage Maturation, rearing of a wine, often including racking and blending, before bottling – the job of the *négociant*.

Egrappoir A machine which removes stalks from grapes before they are pressed.

Encépagement Varietal blend.

En primeur Description of wines (particularly clarets) for sale before they have been finally bottled.

Foudre A large wooden cask.

Fouloir A long, revolving tube used to remove the juice in grapes.

Fût Barrel.

Goût de terroir Literally "taste of earth" but meaning that a wine has flavours reflecting a combination of soil, slope and climate.

Grand Cru A top-quality vineyard site: literally "great growth". The meaning has been debased due to lack of legislative control. It has specific status in Burgundy, Bordeaux, Champagne and Alsace.

INAO The *Institut National des Appellations d'Origine*, the body governing the *Appellation Contrôlée* system.

Jeunes vignes Young vines.

Lies Lees, or dead yeasts, left over from fermentation. Wine may be bottled "*sur lie'*.

Liquoreux Rich and sweet.

Macération carbonique Carbonic maceration – see *How Wine is Made* (pp 20–29).

Marc The detritus left after pressing grape skins – or the brandy distilled from it.

Méthode champenoise/traditionnelle/classique See *How Wine is Made* (pp 20–29).

Méthode rurale/gaillaçoise/dioise Variations on the *méthode champenoise*.

Mistelle Fresh grape juice which has had alcohol added prior to fermentation. Not technically a wine as it never ferments.

Millésime Vintage.

Mis en bouteilles (*au château*, or *domaine*) Bottled at the estate.

Moëlleux Semi-sweet.

Mousseux Sparkling, but not a *méthode champenoise* wine.

Moût Must.

Mutage The addition of alcohol to must to stop it from fermenting.

Négociant Trader or merchant.

Négociant-éleveur Merchant who buys wine post-fermentation and blends and bottles it for sale under his own label.

Nouveau Wine intended to be consumed in the months following harvest.

Passerillage The process of allowing grapes to overripen and shrivel.

Pelure d'oignon "Onion skin" – used to describe the colour of some rosés.

Perlant Very slightly sparkling.

Pétillant Slightly sparkling.

Pièce Cask.

Pourriture noble "Noble rot" – *botrytis cinerea*.

Premier Cru The highest level of the 1855 Bordeaux classification; the second level in Burgundy.

Primeur New wine.

Pressoir Grape press.

Pupitre Rack used for tilting sparkling wine bottles so that sediment falls on to the cork ready for *dégorgement*.

Rancio A taste created by controlled oxidation by heat of a wine in cask.

Ratafia Liqueur made from *marc* and grape juice in Champagne.

Récolte Harvest.

Remontage The pumping of the must over its skins to extract colour and flavour.

Remuage The manipulation of sparkling wine bottles by turning so as to deposit the sediment in the neck of the bottle.

Rendement The allowed yield of wine from a given area.

Rosé d'une nuit A rose created by macerating red grape juice briefly – overnight – with the skins.

Saignée Literally, "bleeding" – creating a rosé by drawing off lightly tinted surplus juice from a fermenting vat of red wine.

Sous-marque Secondary brand-name often used for wine not good enough for the producer's main label.

Sec Dry, or low in sugar.

Sélection de Grains Nobles See *Alsace*.

Soutirage Racking.

Sur lie Aged on its lees.

Supérieur/e A term which indicates a higher degree of alcohol.

Surmaturité Over-ripeness.

Tastevin A shallow, dimpled metal cup used primarily in Burgundy for tasting.

Terroir "Earth", but meaning the factors that affect a vine, e.g. soil, slope, climate.

Tête de cuvée The first and the finest flow of juice from the newly crushed grapes.

VDN See *vin doux naturel*.

VDQS *Vin Délimité de Qualité Supérieure*, quality level below AOC but above *vin de pays*.

Vendange Harvest.

Vendange tardive Late harvest.

Vieilles vignes The oldest and best vines.

Vigne Vine.

Vigneron Vineyard worker.

Vignoble Vineyard.

Vin de garde Classic wine capable of improvement if allowed to age.

Vin de pays "Country wine" with some regional character. Quality level above the basic *vin de table* and below VDQS.

Vin de presse Press wine.

Vin doux naturel A wine which has been fortified before all the sugar has been fermented out.

Vin gris A very pale rosé.

Vin de table/vin ordinaire Basic, everyday wine, from no particular area.

BORDEAUX

57 VARIETIES

TWO GLASSES. The one on the left contains a paleish red liquid that tastes of unripe berries, green pepper – and water. The wine on the right is quite different: dark, almost black, with a rich, deep smell of plum, mulberry, pencil shavings and spice. The flavour goes even further, creamily blending all of these flavours with ripe blackcurrant and maybe a touch of violet. There's power here, but there's subtlety too, in a combination never quite attained in even the best efforts of the New World.

Two clarets: a pair of examples from some 750,000,000 bottles of wine produced per year from the nearly 250,000 acres (100,000 ha) of vineyards which comprise the 57 different *Appellations* of Bordeaux. The one on the right is a St Emilion from Château Pavie, packed with the ripeness of the 1985 vintage; as for the watery stuff, that was a basic Bordeaux Rouge from the rainy harvest of 1993. Unfortunately, there's a lot more of the latter than the former; bobbing along in the wake of the 100 or so big-name flagship châteaux, whose wines regularly feature in restaurant wine lists and auctioneers' catalogues, there are 4,000 or so lesser-known estates, not to mention the

reds and whites made every year by some 15,000 producers whose names are never even seen on a label.

In warm vintages, most of these little wines are generally more or less acceptable, if often not as well made as they might be. In cooler wetter years, however, their failings – and the fundamental differences in quality between the soil and climate in which they are made, and that of the better-sited châteaux – become all too apparent. So, if there is one fundamental lesson to learn about Bordeaux it is: don't treat it as one region, but as several thousand variations on 57 themes.

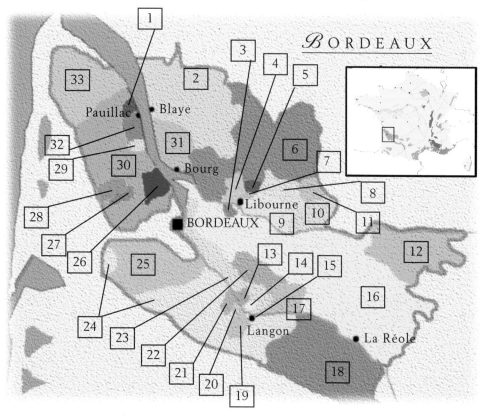

11 Bordeaux-Côtes de Francs
12 Ste-Foy-Bordeaux
13 Cadillac
14 Loupiac
15 Ste-Croix-Du-Mont
16 Entre-Deux-Mers
17 Côtes de Bordeaux-St-Macaire
18 Bordeaux/Bordeaux Supérieur/ Bordeaux Clairet
19 Sauternes
20 Barsac
21 Cérons
22 Bordeaux et Entre-Deux-Mers-Haut-Benauge
23 Premières Côtes de Bordeaux
24 Graves
25 Pessac-Léognan
26 Margaux
27 Moulis
28 Listrac
29 St-Julien
30 Haut-Médoc
31 Côtes de Bourg
32 Pauillac
33 (Bas) Médoc

1 St-Estèphe
2 Côtes et Premières Côtes de Blaye
3 Graves de Vayres
4 Fronsac/Canon Fronsac
5 Lalande de Pomerol
6 Bordeaux/Bordeaux Supérieur/ Bordeaux Clairet

7 Pomerol
8 Puisseguin-St-Emilion/ St-Georges-St-Emilion/ Montagne-St-Emilion/ Lussac-St-Emilion
9 St-Emilion
10 Côtes de Castillon

Bordeaux: Centuries of wine-based wealth have made it beautiful

THE HISTORY

Serious wine-making began in Bordeaux with the Romans, whose contribution can be seen in archeological remains – and on the labels of wines such as Château Ausone, named after the poet Ausonius who was born in St Emilion. Precisely what happened to the wines made in Bordeaux during the period between the days of the Roman occupation and the early twelfth century is unclear, but there are stories of eighth- and ninth-century exports to Ireland and the west of England.

Everything changed, however, when Henry II of England married Eleanor of Aquitaine, and Bordeaux became for 300 years what it sometimes still seems to be – a part of the British Isles. Richard *Coeur de Lion* regularly drank wine from Bordeaux and, under King John, the region's merchants were encouraged to send their barrels to England by an exemption from export tax. During the thirteenth and fourteenth centuries, thousands of casks of "Gascon wine" regularly crossed the Channel – six bottles per year for every English man, woman and child.

Most of the wine those early English Bordeaux drinkers would have enjoyed drinking at court, in inns and in their homes was of the style the French called *clairet*, a pale red made by leaving the skins in contact with the fermenting juice for only a day or so. It was from this name that the English took the term they still use for all red Bordeaux – "Claret".

In fact, though, much of that "Bordeaux" was actually produced nowhere near the city whose name it bore. At that time, Bordeaux was an internationally famous sea-port; its name was far more saleable than, say, that of a wine such as Cahors which was produced a long cart-ride inland. Ironically, while Bordeaux seems itself to have been predestined to produce a number of great wines, the region owes much to the seventeenth-century Dutch engineers who laid down a system of invaluable drainage ditches in the Médoc without which much of the land would still regularly become a bog. If the Bordelais often ungratefully overlook the part played by the Dutch, they rarely make much of the contribution of the English and Irish château-owners and merchants who helped to bring Bordeaux its international renown. Today, the names of such Bordeaux châteaux as Cantenac-Brown, Smith Haut-Lafitte, Léoville-Barton and Lynch-Bages give them the lie.

Surprisingly, for those who liken the French Revolution to its Russian counterpart, the grand estates of Bordeaux survived the removal of the monarchy surprisingly well: the Gallic revolutionaries harboured a far greater dislike of the church than of the similarly anti-clerical aristocracy. So, while the vineyards of Burgundy were redistributed among thousands of peasant-farmers, the great châteaux of Bordeaux continued to build their international reputation. During the nineteenth century, the market for their wines was sufficiently well established for the brokers and merchants of the city of Bordeaux periodically to draw up league tables to mark which regularly fetched the highest prices. For some reason, one such league table, drawn up for the Grand Exhibition of 1855, like that other supposedly temporary structure the Eiffel Tower, unexpectedly survived to become something of a national monument.

The arrival of *phylloxera* decimated the vineyards here, as elsewhere, but it also gave

WHAT IS A CHATEAU?

One of Bordeaux's more incidental gifts to the world has been the notion of the château. Visitors to Burgundy and the Rhône expect all the wine-makers in those and every other wine region of France to be based in châteaux. In fact, while there are wine-producing châteaux in other regions, the concept is still very Bordelais – and surprisingly recent. When the brokers were drawing up classifications of the best wines of the region in the nineteenth century, around half the estates they listed had no mention of "château" before their name. Gradually, however, the success of such grand properties as Château Margaux drove almost everyone to rename their estates. Today, although there is no rule that a Bordeaux estate has to call itself Château anything, wines like Domaine de Chevalier are the rare exceptions to the château-dominated rule.

Some "châteaux" look like palaces and castles; others are no more impressive than any of the cottages by which they are surrounded, while a number do not materially exist at all. According to the rules, the only necessary condition is that the name proposed for use is "linked to a specific vineyard that has been known for a very long time by the name in question".

Château Margaux: a very grand Médoc property

Where sheep may safely graze: *Next to valuable vineyard land in Pomerol*

the owners the opportunity to plan which of the 60 or so uprooted red and white grape varieties were worth replanting. Henceforth, red Bordeaux would have the now recognizable flavours of Cabernet and Merlot, and the white would be made principally from Sémillon and Sauvignon.

Wine-making was, however, still quite unsophisticated. As recently as the 1960s, for example, there were many producers who completely misunderstood the natural process of malolactic fermentation; they would talk straightfacedly of the wine in the barrel reacting in sympathy with the sap rising in the vines. The man who helped to drag the region into the twentieth century was Professor Emile Peynaud of Bordeaux University.

In the late 1970s and early 1980s, money was invested in cleaning up the *cuveries* which, even in some of the more famous châteaux, often looked as though they had last been modernized at some time during the nineteenth century. Cooling equipment was brought in for the fermentation vats in order to avoid the problems of overheating in hot years and, where relevant, to allow the production of crisp, dry white wines. Throughout the region, dirty old casks were replaced, either by cleanable tanks or, in the best properties, by a greater number of 225-litre barrels, a proportion of which would be replaced every year, giving the wine a touch of the spicy vanilla which had helped to win friends for those New-World reds.

Despite the influence of Peynaud and his successors at the University of Bordeaux, and the more recent introduction of such high-tech devices as must-concentrators which freeze and remove the watery component of wines produced in rainy years – the methods used to make the more basic wines have often remained ... well, fairly basic.

Responsibility for the lack of progress can be blamed largely on the *négociants* – the merchants, who have been happy to buy in ready-made wines from producers and co-operatives – and on their customers, especially in France, who have been remarkably tolerant of the frequent shortcomings of Bordeaux. It is revealing that the producers of Mouton Cadet continued to buy in the white wine sold under their label until the early 1990s – which helps to explain the traditionally uninspiring quality of that commercially successful brand.

BORDEAUX TODAY

There have been three recent key vintages in Bordeaux. The great 1945 – coming directly after the end of the war and 11 years after the last fine pre-hostility harvest – marked a triumphant return to normality. The 1961 vintage, for its part, changed the way top-class Bordeaux was bought. Traditionally the merchants of the region had routinely fixed a price per barrel "*sur souche*" – while the grapes were still on the vine. The method worked well enough until the agreements reached before the great, but woefully short crop of 1961 obliged them to sell the small quantities they had made at far less than their value. Thereafter, they began instead to offer their wine "*en primeur*", in the spring following the vintage, by which time it was possible to assess its quality and quantity.

Despite a boom in the early 1970s – and a scandal involving fraudulent labelling by one of the region's most respected merchants – the next most significant moment came in 1982, which brought a happy coincidence of fine weather, the fruits of all that modernization in the wineries, and the arrival on the scene of a new generation of well-off wine-drinkers.

Looking back at what is now acknowledged to be one of Bordeaux's great years, it is chastening to recall that when the 1982s were first tasted, traditionalists often found them too ripe, too approachable, too "New-World" in style. One man, however, disagreed. Robert Parker, a young American lawyer, waxed – highly – lyrical about their voluptuous flavour in his *Wine Advocate* newsletter. Parker's timing was impeccable. His recommendations were devoured by Americans with dollars to spend and a (readily admitted) lack of vinous experience.

Unlike their European counterparts, who still tended to rely for bespoke guidance on wine merchants and auctioneers, these novices wanted to be told precisely what they should and should not buy. This need was filled by Parker and subsequently by a glossy New York-based magazine called the *Wine Spectator*. Both employed a curious marking system adapted by the former lawyer from one used by US law schools. Erroneously known as the 100-point scale, it actually begins at 50 – the mark which would be given to a blend of pond water and sulphuric acid. Suddenly, a desirable new phenomenon was born, the "90+ point" wine.

The interest of the new wave of collectors and investors, not to mention the readiness of France's supermarket chains to sell off surplus stocks of even the grandest châteaux wines in their annual "*Foires aux Vins*", and a punitive system of death duties, were all instrumental in laying the ground for a change in the ownership of Bordeaux. To the horror of traditionalists, cash-strapped families sold out to insurance companies and industrial giants with a taste for diversification, including, *mon Dieu!*, Japanese whisky distillers.

Local traditionalists understandably and predictably bemoaned the disappearance of the families – conveniently forgetting that many of these had had little physically to do with their châteaux. When a subsidiary of the giant AXA insurance company took over Château Pichon-Longueville in the late 1980s, parts of the building were in the state in which they'd been abandoned by the German soldiers billeted there during a war which had ended nearly half a century earlier. More importantly for anyone interested in the flavour and quality of the stuff in the bottle, the newcomers were under no illusion that a wine estate had to be run in as businesslike a way as any of their other investments. Almost without exception their wines tasted better than the ones made during the previous few vintages by their predecessors. And they were certainly to the taste of the increasingly influential US gurus.

But were these, and other "modern" Bordeaux, as fine as the historic clarets of 1961 and 1945? Wasn't their immediate appeal achieved at the cost of the longevity found in those earlier vintages? And weren't all these new techniques leading to wines that all tasted more and more similar? The jury is still out on these questions, but those who argue that post-1982 red Bordeaux are all too soft and approachable have a tough time explaining the decidedly tougher, more "old-fashioned", style of years like 1983, 1986 and 1988.

Bordeaux is unquestionably making more fine red and white wine than ever before; despite a series of difficult harvests in the early 1990s, the top wines have reasserted their position securely atop the wine world. The lesser wines have improved too; unfortunately for their producers and fortunately for wine-drinkers, so – often far more dramatically – have their competitors and imitators from other regions.

WHAT GIVES BORDEAUX ITS FLAVOUR?

Most New-World wine-makers would give the greatest credit to the grape varieties that are grown here. For the red wines, these consist of the blackcurranty, sun-loving Cabernet Sauvignon; its easier-to-please, lighter-bodied "kid brother" the Cabernet Franc; the plummier Merlot, which ripens a little earlier and is an invaluable softening ingredient in any Bordeaux blend; and the Petit Verdot, which only ripens in the best vintages but imparts a wonderfully spicy

note, even when it makes up only 2 or 3 per cent of the wine. Also allowed are the now-unfashionable Malbec and the almost-impossible-to-find Carmenère

For the whites, the two key grapes are the rich, honeyed Sémillon, which can make great dry and sweet wines; and the tangier, more gooseberryish Sauvignon Blanc – better known as the variety used to make Sancerre in the Loire. The white counterpart to the Petit Verdot is the similarly spicy Muscadelle which, like that variety, is only ever used as a small component of a blend. The two also-rans here are the Colombard and, for some reason, the dull Ugni Blanc.

It is blending which sets Bordeaux apart from purely "varietal" wines produced elsewhere. There is, very rarely, no such thing as a 100 per cent Bordeaux Cabernet Sauvignon or 100 per cent Bordeaux Merlot; every top-quality claret you are ever likely to drink will be a blend of at least a couple of grape varieties. This tradition may have developed to enable the Bordelais to back two horses at once, so that in years when the Merlot fails to ripen (like 1986, say) or when rain hits the later-harvested Cabernet (as in 1994), they could still make good wine.

Whatever the reason, these marriages of complementary characteristics – unions ideally strengthened by careful maturation in barrel – contribute to the complexity (the wonderful mixture of flavours and smells that can be found in a single glass) that sets Bordeaux's best wines apart.

The Bordelais, however, would stress that it is not so much the grapes *per se* as the soil in which they grow – the well-drained gravel which covers clay or sand in the Médoc and Graves; the limestone and chalk of Sauternes and Barsac; and the clay and limestone in St Emilion and Pomerol – plus the way in which it nurtures the grape varieties that makes Bordeaux special. In fact, while the different soils clearly dictate the choice of which kind of grape to plant where, strenuous efforts to link quality to specific soil types have yet to bear fruit.

THE VINTAGE

Even within these regional *Appellations*, wine-making styles – and skills – vary. When buying Bordeaux, you need to look for the commune – or region, in the case, for instance, of the Médoc, Haut-Médoc and Graves – and the château (and possibly château-owner – the owner of one good estate may also have others). And, of course, the vintage.

Because of the size of the region and the range of soils and grapes, some vintages are more successful for some *Appellations* than they are for others. In 1964, for example, the pickers of St Emilion and Pomerol had already harvested their grapes when many of their neighbours in the Médoc (where the Cabernet Sauvignon ripens rather later) saw their crop washed out by torrential storms. Some vintages, like 1985, are acknowledged to be "Merlot years", while in others, like 1986 when that grape failed to flower consistently, the flavour of the Cabernet was often predominant. Similarly, vintages that are good for red wines are often disappointing for sweet whites – and vice versa.

The reputation of Bordeaux vintages is often greatly affected by their investment – in other words, long-term – potential. Wines made by the best estates in years such as 1987, 1992 and 1993, which were generally light-bodied and for early drinking, are often underestimated by the experts. When fairly priced, these can be well worth buying, particularly by those waiting for wines from "better" vintages to reach their peak – or by those who would like a taste of great Bordeaux style at a more affordable price.

THE MEDOC

"THAT MAN," my friend whispered conspiratorially across the restaurant table, "is worth over a billion dollars". Looking across at this colossus among millionaires, I felt strangely let down; he looked resolutely unexceptional – just like the newsagent from whom I bought my paper every day. The only evidence of tycoonal prestige lay in the evident quality of the briefcase propped against his chair-leg and a discreet but decidedly stylish watch.

My first visit to the Médoc left me with pretty much the same feeling of disappointment – and for pretty much the same reasons. The flat featureless landscape – the variation in altitude is no more than about 80 ft/25 metres – was like the unmemorable profile of the millionaire. And like the watch and briefcase, the occasional château did not somehow seem enough.

But there's no questioning the wealth and the potential of this region which easily outranks its neighbours, the Graves, St Emilion and Pomerol. This is the area that can boast Châteaux Lafite, Latour, Mouton Rothschild and Margaux, and in their wake a small fleet of other illustrious estates. When people think of Bordeaux this is the part most of them, consciously or unconsciously, have in mind.

So how do all those great wines come to be produced in a place that looks like a billiard table? Why don't they need the slopes of Burgundy and the Rhône? For the answer you have to look not at the lie of the land but at the land itself. As any Bordelais will tell you, the secret of the Médoc's success – and the particular level of success enjoyed by any specific château – has always come from the character of the soil in which its grapes are grown. While the Californian is often striving to express the flavour of the grape, the Bordeaux grower's aim is to convey the character of the *terroir* – the vineyard.

For around 1,300 years, while the Burgundians were busily cultivating vines and making wine in the Côte d'Or, most of the Médoc was no more than wild and lonely marshland. Even such now-illustrious estates as Margaux and Lafite were largely devoted to growing wheat. There wasn't even very much in the way of roads between the villages, and landowners travelled to their châteaux from Bordeaux by boat along the Garonne.

But, at the end of the sixteenth century, the wine-growing potential of the Médoc was finally realized by the ingenuity of a team of Dutchmen, who drained the marshes and then introduced the novel idea of planting vines in rows instead of in the higgledy-piggledy way the Bordelais had been doing.

The following two centuries were Bordeaux's – and the Médoc's – heyday as virtually the world's only source of great wine, and much of this success was directly attributable to the Irish, English and Scots families – the Johnstons, Lynches, Bartons, Smiths and the rest – who settled here and produced and sold wine to the rest of Europe.

The key date for the Médoc, however, was 1855, the year of the Great Exhibition in Paris, and the year which saw the publication of an official classification which divided the red wines of the Médoc into first, second, third, fourth and fifth growths – the *Crus Classés*. The red and white wines of the Graves and the white wines of Sauternes and Barsac also received their own classifications with just two levels – *Premier* and *Deuxième Cru*.

It is often supposed that these league tables were specially produced for the exhibition; in fact, they were merely official versions of lists the brokers of Bordeaux had

Château Latour: *This slope is what passes for a hill in the Médoc*

Château Lafite: These barriques contain some of the world's most valuable wines

long been using among themselves to establish the prices for which wine might be sold to local customers and to such distinguished foreigners as Thomas Jefferson.

Even in the previous century Médoc first-growths such as Latour and Lafite had been worth twice as much as second-growths, three times as much as the thirds and so on. Over the years, various wine writers have acknowledged the fact that the 1855 classification was merely the last and most widely publicized in a series of such lists, by drawing up hierarchies of their own. In France, where restaurants which omit the producers' names from their list of Burgundies rarely fail to suffix a Bordeaux château with its 1855 classification, this lack of reverence is considered distinctly *infra dig.*. Indeed when an American oil millionaire decided to hold a blind tasting in 1995 to reassess the *Crus Classés*, French commentators reacted as though he had pointed a howitzer at the palace of Versailles.

I suspect the people who would have the longest laugh at all this would be those 1855 brokers. After all, if they'd known their efforts were going to be taken quite this seriously close on a century and a half later, they might have laid down some rather tighter ground-rules. Back then, for instance, they took no account of the specific size and location of each château's vineyards. In other words, Château Margaux could sell off almost all of its best land and replace it with less good vineyards in the same commune, and still sell its wine with its First-Growth label. Château Margaux might not do that, but a former owner of Château Lascombes, for example, added substantial acreage of less-than-top-quality land without anyone suggesting that he might be jeopardizing the estate's second-growth status. (Revealingly, the current wine-maker, René Vanatelle, tastes all of the vats blind every year to decide which will go into the "*grand,*" and which into the "*second*" *vin* – and almost invariably finds that the rejects contain the fruit of those additional vineyards).

The Essentials
THE MEDOC

What to look for Complex, rich, yet subtle wines with flavours of blackcurrant and cedar. The iron fist in the velvet glove.

Official quality AOCs are Bordeaux, Bordeaux Supérieur, Haut-Médoc, Médoc, Moulis, Listrac, St-Estèphe, Pauillac, St-Julien and Margaux. Superimposed on these are the *Cru Bourgeois* and *Cru Classé* hierarchies, the latter in a strictly ranked league. No VDQS or *vins de pays* wines are produced, though there is talk of creating a Vin de Pays d'Aquitaine.

Style All *Appellations*, bar the first, are for red wine – the tiny amount of white made qualifies only as Bordeaux Blanc. Reds are blackcurranty/cedary and more or less tannic depending on the region and in proportion to the amount of Cabernet Sauvignon used. Styles are very site-specific, varying with each communal *Appellation* and with the care given to wine-making.

Climate Basically maritime, though the position, between two masses of water (the Atlantic and the estuary of the Gironde), moderates extremes of temperatures, creating a unique micro-climate. The Gulf Stream gives mild winters, warm summers and long autumns. The area is also fortunate in being shielded from westerly winds by the pine forest seaboard strip that runs parallel to the Gironde.

Cultivation Vineyards are planted on flattish land with occasional low, rolling hills. Soils are variable but principally composed of gravel over limestone and clay.

Grape varieties *Reds*: Cabernet Sauvignon, Cabernet Franc, Merlot, Malbec, Petit Verdot. *Whites*: (rare) Sauvignon, Sémillon.

Production/maturation Style of wine-making is very influential, the best wines being the most complex and concentrated, and those which have received the most new oak ageing – though use of new oak is dependent on the wine having sufficient concentration to handle it. Old oak is being gradually replaced, and stainless steel is now commonly used for fermentation.

Longevity Bordeaux Supérieur, Médoc and Haut-Médoc: 1–6 years; *Crus Bourgeois*, Moulis and Listrac 4–10 years (though good wines in good years can last longer); *Crus Classés* anything up to 25 years and sometimes more.

Vintage guide 78, 79, 82, 83, 85, 86, 88, 89, 90, 95.

My Top 19 For lots of different reasons, and in no particular order: Châteaux Margaux, Cos d'Estournel, Léoville-Lascases, Palmer, Léoville-Barton, Pichon-Longueville-Lalande, Pichon-Longueville, Angludet, Haut-Marbuzet, Labégorce-Zédé, Latour, Monbrison, Lynch-Bages, la Lagune, Mouton Rothschild, Chasse-Spleen, Grand-Puy-Lacoste, Pontet-Canet, Sociando-Mallet.

THE COMMUNES OF THE MEDOC

Driving north from Bordeaux, you have barely left the outskirts of the city before you find yourself in the gravelly soil of the Haut-Médoc. This *Appellation* – literally "High Médoc" – confusingly comprises the lower part of the overall region and includes the six higher-quality communal *Appellations* of Margaux, St-Julien, Pauillac, St-Estèphe, Moulis and Listrac, while the Médoc *Appellation* itself includes the lesser-quality area mostly further north.

Haut-Médoc wines from land that falls outside those six communes can offer some of the best value in Bordeaux. Only five are classed – the delicious La Lagune and Cantemerle, de Camensac, La Tour-Carnet and Belgrave – but several unclassed châteaux, like Caronne-Ste-Gemme, Beaumont and Lanessan, are easily better than some fifth- and even fourth-growth wines. ·

Château Cissac: To be called a château, it doesn't have to resemble a palace

The key words to look for on Haut-Médoc labels are, in descending order of quality, *Cru Grand Bourgeois Exceptionnel*, *Cru Grand Bourgeois* or *Cru Bourgeois*, all of which ought to indicate that the wine is a cut above the average. But a word of warning: there are two lists of *Crus Bourgeois* – one a 1932 classification, and the other a 1978 membership list of the *Syndicat des Crus Bourgeois*. According to the Syndicat, there are just 127 wines that can describe themselves as any kind of *Cru Bourgeois*; a significant number of the better wines from the 1932 list, such as Labégorce-Zédé and Siran in Margaux were excluded.

In addition, some châteaux which could call themselves *Cru Bourgeois* prefer not to be included among the "middle class", perhaps fearing that to do so might jeopardize their chances of ever being considered for inclusion in a revised classification of the classed growths.

As for basic Médoc, my advice is to beware – especially of anything but a really ripe vintage. Wines carrying this *Appellation* are rarely better than basic Bordeaux Supérieur and may even be worse. At least a producer of the latter could blend together wine from throughout the region.

A Pinch of Salt with Your Margaux

Margaux provides two perfect examples of why no one should place too much reliance on the 1855 classification. In 1811, an English Major General called Charles Palmer bought Château de Gasq from an attractive young widow he met on a train. Palmer renamed the château and, following the Prince Regent's misplaced advice, changed the vines and the wine-making style – and went bankrupt.

Today, Château Palmer is a third-growth next-door-neighbour of Château Margaux that makes wines of first-growth quality. I wonder how it would have been classed if the widow's companion had been a French Major General?

Château Margaux itself similarly demonstrates the dangers of treating the classification as gospel. Until the mid-1960s this first-growth estate, which had so impressed Thomas Jefferson, consistently produced one of the very best wines in Bordeaux; its 1953 was – and is – one of the finest wines ever made anywhere. However, in the 1960s and 1970s, things started to go wrong; neither the vineyards nor the winery were getting the care, attention and money they needed, and it showed in the wine. It was like a great restaurant with a tired chef and a broken-down range. Then, in 1978, the château was bought for a small fortune by the Mentzelopoulos family which then went on to spend another small fortune on putting everything to rights, employing the Bordeaux guru Professor Emile Peynaud as a consultant and, a few years later, the brilliant young Paul Pontallier as wine-maker. The medicine worked almost overnight. Critics who had been calling for Margaux's demotion were, and still are, rightly declaring it second to none. But it's a happy ending that won't improve the flavour of overpriced pre-Mentzelopoulos 1975 or 1976.

Château Cantenac Brown: *Outside Margaux village, but inside the "Appellation"*

MARGAUX

The first "classy" *Appellation* you reach after leaving Bordeaux is Margaux. The only one that shares its name with its best château, this, as countless hopelessly lost visitors have discovered to their exasperation, is actually more of a collection of villages than a single commune; wines from Arsac, Cantenac, Labarde, Soussans and Margaux itself can all call themselves Margaux. This occasionally raises a wry smile in the cafés of Labarde, Arsac and Cantenac – these quiet villages to the south of Margaux boast some of the juicier wines of the *Appellation*. Châteaux here such as Giscours, Siran, d'Angludet, du Tertre, d'Issan, Prieuré-Lichine, Kirwan and Brane-Cantenac can, and do, legitimately describe themselves as Margaux.

But it would be dangerous to overstate that juiciness; Margaux has a reputation for making the most delicate and perfumed wines of the Médoc, with a scent of violets and flavour of blackberries, rather than the more usual Bordeaux blackcurrant. The vines have to work hard for their nourishment, fighting their way through the gravelly soil, but, as the locals say, the plants never get their feet as wet here as they do in the clay soil of more northerly St-Estèphe.

Margaux is (relatively) big – the largest communal *Appellation* in the Médoc, and the most blessed with classed growths and top-quality *Crus Bourgeois*. Sadly, though, as some of its more forthright producers would admit, the quality of Margaux's land is often let down by some pretty poor wine-making, Apart from the glorious Château Margaux itself, and Château Palmer, its closest rival, the best classed wines are d'Issan, Lascombes, Rauzan-Segla, Malescot-St-Exupéry (the last two most particularly in recent vintages) and du Tertre. Prieuré-Lichine, which belonged to the great Russian-American wine-writer Alexis Lichine, is fairly priced, and good value can also be found in Château Notton and Pavillon Rouge du Château Margaux (the second wines respectively of Châteaux Brane-Cantenac and Margaux).

Among non-classed wines, seek out Château d'Angludet (made by Peter Sichel, who is also responsible for Château Palmer), La Gurgue, Labégorce-Zédé, Monbrison and Siran, all of which make wine of at least fourth-growth quality at far lower prices.

Before leaving Margaux, I have to mention the exception that proves the rule. The Médoc is emphatically not white-wine territory – but then there's Pavillon Blanc du Château Margaux, an extraordinary oaky, honeyed, tangy Sauvignon Blanc which has to be the ultimate "basic" Bordeaux Blanc (there is no *Appellation* for white Margaux or Médoc).

MOULIS AND LISTRAC

From Margaux the obvious next stop, quite a drive north, is St-Julien. Worth a diversion on the way, though, by turning off to the west into the forest, are two communes rarely mentioned in the old wine books – for the simple reason that neither includes any classed growths. But the villages of Moulis and Listrac-Médoc well repay a visit, because they both, in their different ways, can produce some very worthwhile wines.

Moulis and the village with which it shares its small *Appellation*, Grand Poujeaux, lie on gravelly soil, are bang next door to Margaux and have everything it takes to make wine of classed quality. Château Chasse-Spleen and, to a slightly lesser extent, Château Maucaillou prove what can be done here every year and Poujeaux and Gressier-Grand-Poujeaux are both good too. All these wines "come round" rather more quickly than Margaux, but good examples can last at least 15 years.

If Moulis wines can be enjoyed young, Listracs demand greater patience; they're much tougher, and much more closely related to those of St-Estèphe, a little further to the north. The Merlot grows well in the heavy soil here, but isn't used as much as it ought to be. Despite heavy investment at Château Clarke, these and wines like those of Châteaux Fonréaud, Fourcas-Hosten and Fourcas-Dupré remain daunting in all but the ripest vintages.

ST-JULIEN

You know that you've got to St-Julien when you round the bend in the road and see the smart gates, statuary and gardens of Château Beychevelle. Before continuing north, turn right just beyond the château and drive down to enjoy the peaceful view from the river bank. This is where it is said that passing boats obeyed the command to lower their sails ("Basse-les-Voiles") issued by the then owner of the château, the Duc d'Epéron, one of France's best-known admirals. Sadly, neither the story that this command gave the château its name, nor the one that the sailors occasionally dropped their trousers instead of the sails, is actually true.

Château Beychevelle is as good an introduction to the commune as you are likely to need. This is a place for grand, big châteaux though, surprisingly, no first-growth wines. But, if there are no firsts, there are certainly two famous "super-seconds" – second growths that make wine as good as the firsts – in the shape of Léoville-Lascases and Ducru-Beaucaillou; Léoville-Barton, a château I'd now place alongside that pair; the almost as impressive Gruaud-Larose; and a clutch of other richly wonderful wines in recent vintages, particularly Beychevelle, Léoville-Poyferré, Branaire-Ducru, Talbot and Lagrange.

This is Bordeaux the way the British have always liked it: blackcurrant, but cedary too, with the unmistakable sweet scent traditionally described as "cigar-box". Despite its smaller size, St-Julien is a more reliable source of good, fairly priced wine than Margaux – such as Langoa-Barton, Léoville-Barton's slightly lighter-weight stable-mate, Lalande-Borie, Terrey-Gros-Caillou, St-Pierre and Clos du Marquis, the second wine of Château Léoville-Lascases.

PAUILLAC

The town of Pauillac is disconcertingly like a sleepy seaside resort, with café terraces and fish merchants lining the bank of the Gironde. This looks far more like the kind of place that couples run away to for illicit weekends in French films than the town whose name appears on some of the world's greatest red wine.

It's not easy to know that you've arrived in Pauillac's vineyards; they run into those of St-Julien almost seamlessly, with only one of those Dutch drainage ditches to mark the join. Léoville-Lascases is right next door to Latour; indeed, according to some old maps, the latter estate really ought to be situated in St-Julien, but it was Pauillac that drew the better hand.

It is easy to understand why these wines have made so many friends for themselves; they are magnificent in the way that they manage to combine the intense flavour of blackcurrant with those of cedar and honey. Taste these against the best Cabernet Sauvignon from California and you will understand just how brilliantly this variety shines here – and how far the complex flavours of Pauillac can go beyond the simple Cabernet flavour of most of those New-World wonders.

Apart from Latour, Lafite and Mouton Rothschild, there is a second row of wines chasing hard on their heels: Pichon-

Château Pichon-Longeville: All French châteaux should look like this

Gigot d'Agneau Persillé

Leg of lamb baked in a parsley and herb crust

Thanks to its great wines, the fish and shellfish of the nearby Atlantic, its land rich in game, truffles, goose, duck and wild mushrooms (cèpes) and, especially, the young lamb fattened on the grass of the salt meadows, the Médoc provides some of the best eating to be enjoyed in the whole of France.

SERVES 6

3–4 lb/1.5–2 kg leg of lamb, trimmed of excess fat (which in France is cut into leaf shapes to decorate the joint)
salt and freshly ground black pepper
juice of 1 lemon
1 oz/25 g softened butter
2 tbsp plain flour
4 tbsp dried breadcrumbs
3 tbsp minced fresh parsley with sprigs to garnish, or 1½ tbsp dried parsley
1 tbsp minced fresh rosemary or 1 tsp dried rosemary

Dry the lamb with kitchen paper and squeeze the juice of the lemon all over the joint. Season with salt and pepper. In a bowl mix together the butter, flour, breadcrumbs, parsley and rosemary and spread it evenly over the lamb. Bake in an oven, preheated to 375°F/190°C/Gas mark 5, for 40 minutes. Remove from the oven and let it rest for 10 minutes before carving. Serve with boiled new potatoes, steamed courgettes and grilled tomatoes.

Longueville-Lalande is Pauillac's best-established "super-second", now rivalled by its neighbour Pichon-Longueville, which has recently been restored to its former prestige by Jean-Michel Cazes. Cazes' own Château Lynch-Bages, though on paper only a fourth growth, can also perform as well as many a second (and turn out an impressive white),

Château Cos d'Estournel: A souvenir of Zanzibar in the Médoc

while fine wines can be found at Clerc-Milon, Grand-Puy-Ducasse, Grand-Puy-Lacoste, Haut-Bages-Libéral, Haut-Batailley, d'Armailhac (the former Mouton Baron-Philippe) and Pontet-Canet. For a relatively affordable taste of Pauillac, try Reserve de la Comtesse, Haut-Bages-Averous and Les Forts de Latour, the second wines respectively of Châteaux Pichon-Longueville-Lalande, Lynch-Bages and Latour.

ST-ESTEPHE

St-Estèphe is the most attractive town in the Médoc, but it feels like a distant outpost. And the wine is like that too – distant and forbidding stuff that tempts me to use expressions like "austere" and "masculine" that I would normally avoid like the plague. It is distinctly cooler here and this, coupled with the generally less gravelly, more clayey, soil, makes for wines that can take forever to soften and become more friendly. I tend to think of these as "old-fashioned" wines, but many of them evidently failed to dazzle the drinkers of 1855 and their forebears; there are only five *Crus Classés*, a quarter of the number in Margaux which covers a similar amount of land.

The stars of the *Appellation* are Châteaux Calon-Ségur, Montrose and Cos d'Estournel. Of these, Calon-Ségur is the least immediately impressive, but in their different styles, Montrose and Cos d'Estournel are two of the finest wines in the Médoc. Montrose can be majestic stuff, more approachable in its youth than it used to be, but still packed with cedary, blackcurranty flavour.

It's a shame that so many Bordeaux lovers know what Cos (as it is known by aficionados, who pronounce it like the name of the lettuce) looks like – it is too easy to imagine that their descriptions of the wine as "spicy" are influenced by thoughts of the mock-oriental folly with its carved front door imported by its owner from Zanzibar.

In fact Cos benefits from its gravelly soil to make wines that are rather closer to Pauillac in style than they are to those of most of its neighbours. But their wonderful, spicy flavour is all their own.

Of St-Estèphe's unclassed wines, the best are Marbuzet, Haut-Marbuzet, Andron-Blanquet, Beau-Site, Le Boscq, Meyney, Les Ormes-de-Pez, de Pez and Lafon-Rochet.

Beyond St-Estèphe, where the gravel

A Touch of Class?

THE 1855 classification has remained largely unchanged since its inception; the most important modification being the elevation, in 1973, of Mouton Rothschild, to *Premier Cru* status. Some names have changed slightly, largely due to changes of ownership – for example, what was then Château d'Armailhac for a while became Mouton-Baronne-Philippe – or to distinguish them from other properties. Some of the original estates have been divided, through either sales or inheritance; the present Châteaux Boyd-Cantenac and Cantenac-Brown, for example, once made up the original Château Cantenac. In these cases, the two or more "new" châteaux have retained the original's ranking.

The following list includes the names of each château and its commune – and those of their "second label" wine(s) which, in many cases, can offer a more affordable, earlier-drinking taste, both of the château's *Grand Vin* and of the commune in which it is made.

First Growths (Premiers/1ers Crus)
Lafite-Rothschild, *Pauillac* (Carruades de Lafite); Latour, *Pauillac* (Les Forts de Latour); Margaux, *Margaux* (Pavillon Rouge de Château Margaux); Mouton Rothschild, *Pauillac*; (le Second de Mouton); Haut-Brion, *Pessac-Léognan* (Bahans-Haut-Brion).

Second Growths (Deuxièmes/2èmes Crus)
Rauzan-Ségla, *Margaux*; Rauzan-Gassies, *Margaux*; Léoville-Lascases, *St-Julien* (Clos du Marquis); Léoville-Poyferré, *St-Julien* (Moulin-Riche); Léoville-Barton, *St-Julien*; Durfort-Vivens, *Margaux* (Domaine de Curebourse); Lascombes, *Margaux* (La Gombaude); Gruaud-Larose, *St-Julien* (Sarget de Gruaud-Larose); Brane-Cantenac, *Margaux* (Domaine de Fontarney and Notton); Pichon-Longueville (Les Tourelles de Longueville), *Pauillac*; Pichon-Longueville-Lalande, *Pauillac* (Reserve de la Comtesse); Ducru-Beaucaillou, *St-Julien* (La Croix); Cos d'Estournel, *St-Estèphe*; Montrose, *St-Estèphe* (La Dame de Montrose).

Third Growths (Troisièmes/3èmes Crus)
Giscours, *Margaux*; Kirwan, *Margaux*; d'Issan, *Margaux*; Lagrange, *St-Julien* (Les Fiefs-de-Lagrange); Langoa-Barton, *St-Julien*; Malescot-St-Exupéry, *Margaux*; Cantenac-Brown, *Margaux*; Palmer, *Margaux*; La Lagune, *Haut-Médoc*; Desmirail, *Margaux* (Baudry); Calon-Ségur, *St-Estèphe*; Ferrière, *Margaux*; Marquis d'Alesme-Becker, *Margaux*; Boyd-Cantenac, *Margaux*.

Fourth Growths (Quatrièmes/4èmes Crus)
St-Pierre, *St-Julien*; Branaire-Ducru, *St-Julien*; Talbot, *St-Julien* (Connétable Talbot); Duhart-Milon-Rothschild, *Pauillac* (Moulin de Duhart); Pouget, *Margaux*; La Tour-Carnet, *Haut-Médoc* (Sire de Camin); Lafon Rochet, *St-Estèphe*; Beychevelle, *St-Julien*; Prieuré-Lichine, *Margaux* (de Clairfont and Haut Prieuré); Marquis-de-Terme, *Margaux*.

Fifth Growths (Cinquièmes/5èmes Crus)
Pontet-Canet, *Pauillac* (Les Hauts de Pontet); Batailley, *Pauillac*; Grand-Puy-Lacoste, *Pauillac* (Lacoste-Borie); Grand-Puy-Ducasse, *Pauillac* (Artigues-Arnaud); Haut-Batailley, *Pauillac* (La Tour d'Aspic); Lynch-Bages, *Pauillac* (Haut-Bages-Averous); Lynch-Moussas, *Pauillac*; Dauzac, *Margaux*; Mouton-Baronne-Philippe, *Pauillac*; du Tertre, *Margaux*; Haut-Bages-Libéral, *Pauillac*; Pédésclaux, *Pauillac* (Grand-Duroc-Milon and Bellerose); Belgrave, *Haut-Médoc*; de Camensac, *Haut-Médoc*; Cos-Labory, *St-Estèphe*; Clerc-Milon-Rothschild, *Pauillac*; Croizet-Bages, *Pauillac*; Cantemerle, *Haut-Médoc*.

The following unclassed Médoc châteaux are well worth seeking out; their wines can be very good value for money:
d'Angludet, Beaumont, Caronne-Ste-Gemme, Chasse-Spleen, Clarke, de Cordeillan, La Fleur-Milon, Fonbadet, Fonréaud, Gloria, La Gurgue, Hantaillan, Haut-Bages-Averous, Haut-Marbuzet, Labégorce-Zédé, Lalande-Borie, Lamarque, Lanessan, Maucaillou, Monbrison, Les-Ormes-de-Pez, de Pez, Les Ormes-Sorbet, Patache d'Aux, Potensac, Poujeaux, St-Bonnet, Siran, Sociando-Mallet, Terrey-Gros-Caillou, La Tour-de-By, La Tour de Haut Moulin, Châteaux Reysson, St Bonnet, Siran, Sociando-Mallet, Potensac, d'Angludet, Chasse-Spleen, Caronne Ste-Gemme, Beaumont, Labégorce-Zédé, Maucaillou, de Pez, La Tour-de-Mons, La Tour-St-Bonnet, La Tour du Haut Moulin, La Tour-de-By, Belgrave, Citran, Le Crock, Dutruch Grand Poujeaux, Fonbadet, Fonréaud, Gloria, Haut Marbuzet, Clos du Marquis, La Gurgue, Monbrison, Poujeaux.

---

gives way to clay and the Cabernet is supplanted by the Merlot, the wines can only be sold as Médoc; in theory, this northern counterpart to the Haut-Médoc really ought to be called the Bas (low) Médoc; it is where much of the wine that is sold as "Médoc" and "House Claret" is made.

There is very little of real class here, though there are occasional flashes of brilliance such as Château Potensac (made by the owner of Château Léoville-Lascases), La Tour Haut Caussin, La Tour-de-By, Castéra, Patache d'Aux, La Tour-St-Bonnet and Les Ormes-Sorbet. Most can be drunk young (thanks to their high Merlot content) but when well made they can be kept for a decade or longer. One that seems built to last is the St-Estèphe-like Château Cissac, but it has only seduced me in the ripest vintages. The pin-striped devotees of London's El Vino bars, however, relish even Cissac's toughest efforts; perhaps I went to the wrong school to appreciate its disciplinarian style.

THE EXTRAORDINARY BARON PHILIPPE

UNTIL 1973, Pauillac had only two first growths: Châteaux Lafite and Latour. Mouton Rothschild, though almost unanimously ranked alongside the firsts, was only a second growth. In that year, however, Baron Philippe de Rothschild achieved what had been thought to be impossible – he persuaded the powers-that-be and his Rothschild cousins at Lafite to right the injustice of 1855. The elevation of Mouton Rothschild is the only change to the 1855 classification since it was first drawn up. While the argument still rages over which (if any) of the other second growths deserve a similar dispensation, no one who has tasted Mouton's wines in recent years has ever denied that it is as great a first growth as its neighbours.

But Philippe de Rothschild was a pioneer in all kinds of ways. So many of the things everyone else has done since – both here in Bordeaux and throughout the wine-making world – he did first. He was the first to make a point of bottling all his estate's wines at the château rather than sell in barrel for other people to bottle – and possibly mistreat or adulterate – themselves. He was the first to create a wholly new kind of wine label, inviting well known and frequently unconventional artists such as Salvador Dali, Pablo Picasso and Andy Warhol, each to illustrate the label of a single vintage of Mouton Rothschild – a tradition which hit the headlines in 1996 when the 1993 illustration of a young female nude by Balthus fell foul of the authorities in the US who banned the importation of the wine.

He was the first (and still the only truly successful) person to create a branded Bordeaux. Mouton Cadet was born in 1934 when Rothschild blended the previous three (poor) vintages together to make a single, non-vintage wine. Today, Mouton Cadet is still the biggest-selling branded red Bordeaux. But don't expect it to taste anything like Mouton Rothschild – there isn't enough of that flavour to go round.

ST EMILION AND POMEROL

THE ATMOSPHERE of anti-cipation must have been extraordinary as the inhabitants of the little town of Libourne gathered on the platform of their newly built railway station in 1853 and listened for the whistle of the first train ever to stop there. For some of the crowd, the excitement must have been caused by the possibility for the first time of travelling directly to Paris along the new iron path – the *chemin de fer*. Most, though, were most likely relishing the idea of using the new mode of transport to carry them across the two rivers that separated them from the city of Bordeaux just 20 miles (30 km) away.

It was not only human passengers who were going to benefit from the train; the wine made in the nearby vineyards of St Emilion and Pomerol could make the journey too and finally take its place alongside the already well known clarets of the Médoc and Graves in the Gironde.

But not, it transpired, among the estates featured in the classification drawn up two years later by Bordeaux merchants, who were far more used to selling wines from their back yard and allowing the produce of these more easterly regions to make its own way north to Brussels and Amsterdam, where it was highly appreciated.

So, when the Great Exhibition opened in 1855, the best-known St Emilion châteaux such as Cheval Blanc, Ausone and Figeac, and Château Petrus in Pomerol, were never directly ranked alongside Latour, Lafite, Margaux and Haut-Brion.

To a historian this might seem rather unfair; after all, good wine-making has been going on here for rather longer than it has in the Médoc. One of the best châteaux, Ausone, owes its name to the Roman poet Ausonius, who was born near St Emilion, and ownership of the vineyards of another top château, Figeac, can be traced back to the same era. The wines of the region were already known abroad as early as the twelfth century and it was Edward I of England who, 700 years ago, as Duke of Gascony drew up the boundaries of St Emilion.

Apart from the problems of trans-portation – until the early 1900s the only way across the two rivers was by ferry – there are two other possible explanations

for the surprising second-class status the region as a whole retained until as recently as the years following the Second World War. Firstly, there was the small size of the estates; the average St Emilion château produces less far less wine than its Médoc equivalent and those in Pomerol are often positively tiny: the annual harvest at Château Pétrus yields just 25,000 bottles, a tenth of the quantity Château Margaux might make. With this limited a scale of production, it was rarely easy for an estate

St Emilion: Far more historical than the upstart Médoc

to make an international reputation for itself. Secondly and more importantly, there was the style of the wines.

The clay soil that covers most of the region does not suit the Cabernet Sauvignon; it simply doesn't ripen properly. Despite this, it was this variety and the uninspiring Malbec that were traditionally included in much of the wine. The St Emilions and Pomerols of the last century, and even of the first half of this, were often lean, unripe, rangy beasts.

The fortunes of the producers changed dramatically and unexpectedly in 1956, when vicious frosts wiped out large sections of the vineyards and obliged the growers to replant. When they did so, it was largely with the clay-loving Merlot along with some Cabernet Franc for the areas with limestone. As for the Cabernet Sauvignon, that was restricted to the few patches of gravel on which it would thrive. The new improved blend in the vineyards brought what was for many an equally new style of wine: one that was not only softer and more approachable than it had been, but riper and easier than the wines of the Médoc.

There was another incidental effect which is often insufficiently appreciated by people with credit-card sized vintage charts offering a single mark out of 10 for a Bordeaux of any given year. The Merlot naturally flowers before the Cabernets. On the one hand this can make for years like 1986 when it fails to develop properly – and the risk of increased damage from late frosts. On the other hand, early flowering leads to earlier ripening and picking – and the chance as in 1964 of getting the grapes safely into the winery long before the onset of rainstorms that can spoil the harvest in the Médoc.

CHACUN A SON GOUT

Today, with the further refinement of modern wine-making, the made-in-heaven marriage of soil and grape has created what can be some of the world's most immediately appealing serious wines. It is no accident that British claret-drinkers, for whom drinking anything before its sixteenth birthday is only just this side of illegal, still cleave to their favourite Médocs while, on the other side of the Atlantic, American drinkers who prefer more instant gratification opt for St Emilion and Pomerol.

The best way to appreciate the difference wrought by the change in grape varieties is to undertake what is in any case one of the most instructive tasting exercises of all: to compare a set of Bordeaux "blind" and to guess which side of the Gironde they come from. If the stuff in your glass is tannic and tastes of blackcurrant and cedar it's probably a Médoc; if its complex array of flavours make you think of ripe plums, honey and toffee, my money would be on it

coming from St Emilion or maybe Pomerol.

Having determined, as a Bordeaux buff would say, that the wine is from the right rather than the left bank of the Dordogne, your next task is to decide in which of the two communes it was made. This is a great deal trickier – indeed, it can flummox many experienced tasters. But, with practice, this too is an art you could master.

ST EMILION

This is one of the few parts of Bordeaux that looks like a proper wine region. The land has some contours to it and the vines run up and down slopes; the cosy old town is set right amongst the vineyards.

The vine-covered hillsides form one long south-facing slope, the Côtes, that contributes toward the quality of some of St Emilion's best, most long-lived wines: Ausone, Belair, Canon, Pavie, Pavie-Decesse and Magdelaine all include grapes grown on the Côtes. L'Arrosée is one of the very few châteaux to make good wine exclusively from the hillside.

Much of the rest of St Emilion's vineyard area is planted in sandy soil – the *sables* – that results in lighter, young-drinking wine. In theory, young-drinking Merlot should be delicious – provided yields are kept low. When – all too often – they aren't, the Merlot's toffee can take over from the plum and make for wine that's downright dull.

But there are two top-class St Emilion châteaux that are on neither the Côtes nor the *sables*. Cheval Blanc and Figeac both sit on the same long outcrop of gravel, and compete with Ausone for the commune's crown. It's an unfair fight, really, because Cheval Blanc always wins; its big, sumptuous flavours simply eclipse the other wines. But give Figeac time, taste it beyond Cheval Blanc's shadow, and its gentler, more perfumed character could well seduce one into calling the whole thing a draw.

However, both these wines are atypical St Emilions; neither is predominantly Merlot-based, and Cheval Blanc is a true rarity in being largely made from the Cabernet Franc. Other good St Emilions grown on gravelly soil include La Tour Figeac, Dominique, Soutard and de Grand Corbin, all of which can be rather less costly than Figeac or Cheval Blanc.

Finally, a word of warning. If St Emilion's best châteaux produce some of the finest wines in the world, bottles from lesser estates – even ones with a *Grand Cru* to

their name – are often woefully dull and horribly overpriced. Their only defence is that they may be a bit better than stuff that's simply labelled as St Emilion which is among the worst-value wine in France.

THE ST EMILION SATELLITES

Your money would be far better spent on a wine from Lussac, Montagne, Puisseguin or St Georges, a set of "satellite" villages which, until 1936, could sell their wine as St Emilion but now have to prefix it with their own names. The best of these more affordable *Appellations* is St Georges-St Emilion, where Château St Georges makes wine of soft, classed St Emilion quality. Montagne-St Emilion partly overlaps this *Appellation* and some châteaux have the choice of which label they prefer to use. Of the wines labelled as Montagne-St Emilion, I'd go for Vieux-Château-St-André, made by the oenologist at Château Pétrus. Lussac-St Emilion can produce attractively plummy wine too (try Château Cap de Merle). Puisseguin has traditionally been the weakest of the quartet but Château des Laurets is helping to lead a drive toward quality.

POMEROL

If the Médoc has a small fleet of flagships, Pomerol – a fraction of its size at just 2,000 acres – has just one: Château Pétrus, the world's most expensive red wine. But even as recently as 50 years ago, mentioning Pétrus would have aroused very little response among even some of the keenest British wine-drinkers; as a Pomerol, it was firmly stuck in the shadow of its more famous neighbours in St Emilion. Uniquely in Bordeaux, there is no quality classification here and no separate *Grand Cru Appellation*, though any open-minded comparison between a set of Pomerols and

---

The St Emilion Rules– Not so Grand?

*W*hat is the difference between a *St Emilion Grand Cru* and a *St Emilion Grand Cru Classé*? Give up? Well, the latter is situated in better-than-average soil and belongs to the official St Emilion classification which – unlike those of other parts of Bordeaux – is revised every decade or so. As for the former, it is a term that can be used by *any* château whose wine has passed a – possibly pretty lenient – annual tasting. Some *Grands Crus* may be almost indistinguishable from a basic St Emilion, others are better than wines that appear within the official classification. Confused? Don't blame me; I didn't make the rules.

---

supposed *Grands Crus* from St Emilion provides a perfect justification for sticking all such questionable tags straight in the bin.

It was America that discovered Pétrus – and wine buffs there fell head-over-heels for its extraordinary spicy-fruity-gamey intensity. Of course, they couldn't all actually drink it – the château makes only 20 or 30,000 bottles in a good year – but they fell in love with the idea of it, and with the rich, plummy, chocolatey, berryish Merlot flavour of the other Pomerols they proceeded to seek out.

Heretical though it may sound, blind tastings of Pétrus have always left me feeling a touch disappointed, given its astronomical price. Often I've felt as though I was looking for a little extra acceleration in a Ferrari. Even so, this is remarkable stuff, partly because of the careful way in which it is made, but more essentially because of the magic piece of clay soil in which its vines are planted. To look at, there doesn't appear to

---

be anything special about Pétrus's soil – nor about the château itself, which could easily be a modestly successful Bordeaux merchant's weekend retreat. But that's Pomerol's style. The land here is flatter and less picturesque than St Emilion, but its very flatness helpfully allows you to see just how small the estates are – you could pack at least half a dozen into the vineyards of the average Médoc château.

The soil is far less variable here than it is in St Emilion, but there are parts of the commune where the clay does contain all kinds of minerals that help to give the best Pomerols an extra dimension, a minerally edge which balances what could all too easily be jammy sweet fruit.

As there is no Pomerol classification, the commune's estates can all compete for the role of prince to Pétrus's king. Among a strong field, I favour Vieux-Château-Certan, Certan-de-May, La Conseillante, La Fleur Pétrus, L'Evangile, Le Pin, Trotanoy, Bon-Pasteur, Petit-Village, Clos-René, Lafleur, Feytit-Clinet, Clos du Clocher, Franc-Maillet, l'Eglise-Clinet and Clinet, Latour-à-Pomerol and La Grave Trigant de Boisset.

LALANDE-DE-POMEROL

What's in a name? Well, in this case, there's the recognizable name of Pomerol which, particularly in the USA, has helped to boost prices of this once-inexpensive *Appellation*. Even so, the wines of Lalande-de-Pomerol can still be delicious, plummily ripe buys for drinking earlier. There are lots of good examples, but I'd particularly recommend Châteaux Annereaux, Tournefeuille, Bel-Air and Siaurac.

FRONSAC

In the eighteenth century Fronsac was one of the classiest wines of Bordeaux and sold for a higher price than Pomerol. All that changed with the Revolution. From being scarce and good, Fronsac suddenly became plentiful and mediocre.

Today, though, with the support of Christian Moueix who's best known for Château Pétrus, Fronsac is making a gradual comeback with wines that often outclass all but the best of St Emilion. Try a bottle from Château la Rivière; better still, go and taste the wine at the château – it's straight out of

---

THE 1986 CLASSIFICATION OF ST EMILION

Premiers Grands Crus Classés (Class A)
Ausone; Cheval Blanc.
Premiers Grands Crus Classés (Class B)
Beauséjour (Duffau-Lagarrosse); Canon; Belair; Clos Fourtet; Figeac; la Gaffelière; Magdelaine; Pavie; Trottevieille.
Grands Crus Classés
L'Angélus; l'Arrosée; Balestard la Tonnelle; Beau-Séjour-Bécot; Bellevue; Bergat; Berliquet; Cadet-Piola; Canon-la-Gaffelière; Cap de Mourlin; le Châtelet; Chauvin; Clos des Jacobins; Clos la Madeleine; Clos de l'Oratoire; Clos Saint Martin; la Clotte; la Clusière; Corbin; Corbin-Michotte; Couvent des Jacobins; Croque-Michotte; Curé-Bon la

Madeleine; Dassault; la Dominique; Faurie de Souchard; Fonplégade; Fonroque; Franc-Mayne; Grand-Barrail-Lamarzelle-Figeac; Grand-Corbin-Despagne; Grand-Corbin; Grand-Mayne; Grand-Pontet; Guadet-St-Julien; Haut Corbin; Haut Sarpe; Laniote; Larcis-Ducasse; Lamarzelle; Laroze; Matras; Mauvezin; Moulin-du-Cadet; l'Oratoire; Pavie-Décesse; Pavie-Macquin; Pavillon-Cadet; Petit-Faurie de Soutard; le Prieuré; Ripeau; Sansonnet; St-Georges-Côte-Pavie; la Serre; Soutard; Tertre-Daugay; la Tour-du-Pin-Figeac (Giraud-Belivier); la Tour-du-Pin-Figeac (Moueix); Trimoulet; Troplong-Mondot; Villemaurine; Yon-Figeac.

Château Cheval Blanc: Leading St-Emilion (above)
Fronsac: Leading the also-ran regions (left)

one of Polanski's more Gothic films. Other Fronsacs to look out for include Villars, Mayne-Vieil and La Valade.

CANON-FRONSAC

This is a patch of hillside country within Fronsac itself. The style of the wines is somewhat similar to that of Pomerol, but rather more rustic, particularly when the wines are young. Give them time, though; they can be worth it. The best wine here is made by Christian Moueix at one of Bordeaux's several estates called Château Canon.

BORDEAUX-COTES-DE-CASTILLON

Castillon, almost hidden between St Emilion and the Dordogne river at Bergerac, seems such a sleepy little place that it is hard to imagine that, in 1453, this was the site of one of the most important battles in which English soldiers were ever involved; it was here that Aquitaine and the vineyards of Bordeaux were snatched back by the French after 300 years of English ownership. Today the town, or rather its hills, are known for Merlot-based, good-value reds from such châteaux as Robin, Belcier and Pitray.

BORDEAUX-COTES-DES-FRANCS

A name that even the best-informed Bordelais would rarely have known – until recently. Today, as vineyard and wine prices in the rest of Bordeaux climb steadily higher, this warm, dry farmland area that was once part of St Emilion has suddenly attracted new interest – from some very keen and skilful young wine-makers who come with a fine pedigree. Château de Francs was bought by the owners of the top St Emilion property Château Cheval Blanc, while Châteaux Puygueraud and La Claverie belong to the Thienpont family, whose Château Vieux-Château-Certan is one of the finest estates in Pomerol. The Merlot-packed wines are already impressive and surprisingly inexpensive.

GRAVES

THE FRENCH have an expression I've referred to elsewhere: *le goût de terroir*, "the flavour of the soil". For those of us who, unlike His Holiness the Pope, have never even kissed the dirt, let alone chewed a mouthful of it, this kind of language seems either fanciful or downright unhelpful. Until, that is, you get to this area to the south of the city of Bordeaux – and discover that the free-draining qualities of the gravel here are important enough for them to have named the region after it.

Time and a regard for accuracy have, however, slightly rearranged matters. The metropolis – in the shape of an airport, industrial parks, housing and shopping centres – has eaten into some of the best, gravelliest land and displaced over 150 châteaux. In 1988, the owners of the surviving properties in the north of the region acknowledged that the southern part of the Graves has more sand and clay than gravel – and created a new *Appellation* for themselves, frankly naming it after two of Bordeaux's duller (but authentically gravelly) suburbs: Pessac and Léognan. So, paradoxically, if you want to find the best wines of the gravel – the *crus classés* – the Graves is no longer the place to look.

The Graves is the oldest of the regions around Bordeaux, the one that, in the thirteenth century, produced all the best wine. Today it is still recognized as being the only bit of Bordeaux to make quality red *and* white. At least, that's the theory. In fact, until quite recently, close to half of what the Graves produced was, with a very few glorious exceptions, awful white that either smelled and possibly even tasted of damp, dirty dishcloths, or was simply an unripe travesty of Sauvignon Blanc.

Then, in the early 1980s, there was a revolution. Faced with the prospect of a major revision of the Classification of the Graves (still eagerly awaited in 1996), and influenced by three men – Peter Vinding-Diers, a Dane who'd worked in Australia; Pierre Coste, a wine merchant; and Denis Dubordieu, an oenologist at Bordeaux University – a small but growing band of producers introduced a number of changes to the way in which they made their wine.

First, they gave up the practice of picking too early – and instantly did away with those raw flavours. Second, they cooled down their fermentation tanks – and increased the flavour of their wine. Third, in some cases, they left the juice in contact with its skins (following Dubordieu's advice), fermented it with specially cultured yeasts (that was Vinding-Diers' idea) and even in oak barrels (in the same way as the Burgundians). And fourth, they cut down on the amount of sulphur dioxide they used, simultaneously casting out all those dirty dishrags.

The results were startling. Suddenly the Graves began to make wines that tasted ripe, buttery and peachy, with all the fascinating flavours of ripe Sémillon that had already dazzled visitors to Australia in the examples made there.

Today, as an increasing number of châteaux follow the revolutionaries' example, the only real debate concerns the choice of white grape. For some people, the Sémillon should be king; for others, including André Lurton, who makes great wine at several châteaux, including La Louvière and Couhins-Lurton (which, like Malartic-Lagravière and the fast-improving Smith-Haut-Lafite, is 100 per cent Sauvignon), the Sauvignon Blanc is essential. The authorities seem to have agreed with him, insisting that Pessac-Léognan whites contain at least 25 per cent Sauvignon Blanc.

But if the whites have been undergoing a revolution, the traditional focus of attention has remained on the reds. And the best place to discover how they should taste is more or less in the middle of a housing estate at Pessac, not far from Bordeaux's Mérignac airport.

On April 10, 1663, Samuel Pepys tasted "A sort of French wine, called Ho Bryan" and

A subtle red: The vineyards of Domaine de Chevalier, in Pessac-Léognan (opposite, top)

Pickers not pickets: Starting the harvest at Château Haut-Brion (left)

thought its flavour "good and most particular". Two centuries later, in 1855, Château Haut-Brion was the only Graves château to be ranked alongside Lafite, Latour and Margaux. Today, it is still quintessential Graves, combining the blackcurranty Cabernet fruit of the Médoc with the richer, softer approachability of Pomerol.

Haut-Brion is an easy wine to underestimate because, though dangerously easy to drink in its youth, it takes time to develop its host of complex flavours. Its next-door neighbour, La Mission-Haut-Brion, is tougher, as is Pape-Clément. All three can resemble top-class wines from Margaux, but with a honeyed, slightly minerally flavour of their own.

Down the road, in the commune of Léognan, there lies one of my favourite Bordeaux estates, Domaine de Chevalier, a small property that produces wonderfully subtle, raspberryish red and rich, peachy white wine almost every year. Domaine de Chevalier's neighbour, Châteaux Fieuzal, though classified for its red, was never recognized for its whites. Today they are among the region's oaky superstars. Château Haut-Bailly, another underrated favourite, makes a deliciously soft, approachable red wine, but no white.

Further south, you move into the Graves, and into affordability, early-drinking reds and innovative whites. It was in this area that Peter Vinding-Diers, with a little help from such now-famous Australians as Brian Croser and Len Evans, first showed the region how good well made, carefully oaked Sémillon could be at the unclassified Château Rahoul. Vinding-Diers has moved on to make impressive wine at Domaine La Grave and Château de Landiras.

Other wines from the south that are certainly worth looking out for include the reds from Châteaux Ferrande and Cardaillan; both reds and whites from Pierre Coste's châteaux, Montalivet and l'Etoile; Domaine de Gaillat; and Châteaux Chicane and Chantegrive. Some of these estates may

benefit as and when the authorities get around to reclassifying the region.

CERONS

Tucked away in the Graves, on the border with Barsac, Cérons is a sweet white *Appellation* that has largely switched its attention to making dry wine. It's a pity, really, because Cérons' sweet whites, which have to be made in the same way as Sauternes, can be a good cheap alternative to that wine; on the other hand, it's quite understandable because, unlike the Sauternais who can only call their dry white Bordeaux Blanc, the Cérons producers can call theirs Graves – and charge a higher price.

As for Graves Supérieur, this is a white wine *Appellation* that most wine-drinkers overlook – despite the fact that it applies to one in every five bottles of wine produced in this region. There are some reasonable dry examples made, but the best ones are sweet. Occasionally, examples like Clos St Georges can compete with Barsac – but not top-class Barsac.

THE CRUS CLASSÉS OF THE GRAVES

The Graves is the only Bordeaux region to award the *cru classé* distinction to both red and white wines; thus, certain châteaux appear in both lists. Haut-Brion is the most notable, though its fame has largely been achieved through its annexation, in 1855, into the *Premiers Crus Classés* of the Médoc. Most authorities agree that the long-awaited revision of the league table is well overdue – especially following the recent improvements in white wine-making. The name of each château is followed by that of its commune.

Red Wines
Bouscaut, *Cadaujac*; Carbonnieux, *Léognan*; Domaine de Chevalier, *Léognan*; de Fieuzal, *Léognan*; Haut-Bailly, *Léognan*; Haut-Brion, *Pessac*; La Mission-Haut-Brion, *Pessac*; La Tour-Haut-Brion, *Talence*; La Tour-Martillac, *Martillac*; Malartic-Lagravière, *Léognan*; Olivier, *Léognan*; Pape-Clément, *Pessac*; Smith-Haut-Lafitte, *Martillac*.

White Wines
Bouscaut, *Cadaujac*; Carbonnieux, *Léognan*; Domaine de Chevalier, *Léognan*; Couhins-Lurton, *Villenave d'Ornan*; Haut-Brion, *Pessac*; La Tour-Martillac, *Martillac*; Laville-Haut-Brion, *Talence*; Malartic-Lagravière, *Léognan*; Olivier, *Léognan*.

SAUTERNES AND BARSAC

A LIQUID CALLING ITSELF Sauternes almost put me off the whole idea of wine-drinking. On my eighth birthday, I was thought old enough to be treated to a glass of "Spanish Sauternes"; the mixture of sugary sweetness, sulphur and decaying meat was as effective a form of aversion therapy as even the most fiendish psychologist could have devised.

My dislike of what I thought of as Sauternes was only vanquished years later when I was introduced to "real" quality Sauternes – in the form of 1967 Château d'Yquem. Suddenly I realized what great sweet wine was all about – and, far more crucially, what it was not about. The differences lie in naturally ripe grapes, cleanness of flavour (no nastily obvious, meaty sulphur dioxide), balance (the harmony between refreshing acidity and honeyed sweetness) and complexity (the combination of several different flavours and smells).

Praying for humidity: Château d'Yquem

The people who make real Sauternes, the stuff that only comes from a hilly corner of Bordeaux, have long been a dedicated and masochistic bunch. If their main aim in life had been to make wine for profit, they'd have switched their attention to red or dry white ages ago, either of which would have enabled them to produce at least a bottle of wine per vine instead of just a glass or two of Sauternes. Until recently, with the exception of a few big-name châteaux, they

received little financial reward for their effort; in the 1980s, good Sauternes was famously undervalued. Today, happily for the producers and unhappily for the rest of us, this is a pleasure that has to be paid for. But it's worth it.

THE HISTORY

The gently hilly region of Sauternes has been making wine since the Roman occupation – but the wine we know today is a recent innovation. The wine-makers of 400 years ago had to add alcohol to their light, dryish white wine to stabilize it for the journey to the Netherlands, where much of it was drunk. With or without the alcohol,

---

NOBLE OR IGNOBLE

I t is, of course, quite possible to make Sauternes from grapes with very little, or even no, noble rot, and this is precisely the way in which cheaper commercial Sauternes is made in even the best vintages. Though it can never compare with the nobly-rotten stuff, well-made, rot-free Sauternes can be delicious. But beware of cheap basic Sauternes – and indeed of producers with unfamiliar names. These wines can be disappointing, sugary and over-sulphured. Only consider buying from shops that choose their wine very carefully.

But do treat yourself – even just once – to a finer example, that's redolent of honey and peaches, the hallmarks of the Sémillon, the deep, dried-apricot taste of the noble rot, the balancing, tangy gooseberryish fruit of the Sauvignon Blanc and the spiciness of the Muscadelle. Taste these in a young wine – or, if you're lucky, one that's 20, 30 or 40 years old – and you will enjoy a sweet wine that is much more complex than those produced anywhere else on earth. And, if ever you get the chance, look out for a bottle from Château Gilette, the extraordinary property whose wines are left to age for decades in large concrete tanks. Old bottles (and that is all anybody ever sees) taste extraordinarily fresh. They are fascinating to compare with other Sauternes of a similar age.

The Essentials
SAUTERNES AND BARSAC

Official quality AOC Sauternes and Barsac, which also share their own *cru* classification, drawn up in 1855 at the same time as that for the Médoc.
Style Very sweet, luscious whites, with tropical or marmalade aromas. The lusciousness and complexity depend upon the degree to which *botrytis cinerea* has affected the vintage and the care taken to restrict picking to nobly-rotten grapes. Barsac is perhaps lighter but can be of as high a quality as Sauternes. Barsac may be sold as Sauternes, but not vice versa. The little dry white produced may be sold only as Bordeaux Blanc, though it can be of high quality in its distinctive, nutty way.
Climate A warmer micro-climate within Bordeaux; the region is also peculiarly susceptible to morning mists rising from the Ciron river which, combined with warm afternoons, provide ideal conditions for the development and proliferation of *botrytis*.
Grape varieties Sémillon, plus Sauvignon Blanc and Muscadelle.

Cultivation Soil is of clay limestone to sandy gravel. The most experienced pickers are needed for the vintage here as, to make fine Sauternes, only the overripe and, when appropriate, botrytized grapes must be plucked from each bunch. Several sorties into the vineyard are made – at the best châteaux, as many as 10 – until all the grapes are harvested; these successive selective pickings are known as *tries*. In some years, though, noble rot never appears; when this happens, Château d'Yquem makes no vintage wine.
Production/maturation Grapes are whole-pressed and wood fermented and matured. New oak is increasingly being used.
Longevity Anything between 5 and 40 years.
Vintage guide 70, 75, 76, 78, 80, 81, 83, 85, 86, 88, 89, 90.
My Top 20 Château d'Yquem, Rieussec, Lafaurie-Peyraguey, Suduiraut, Coutet, Climens, Guiraud, Doisy-Daëne, Doisy-Védrines, D'Arche, de Malle, Nairac, Brousset, Raymond-Lafon, Gilette, Bastor-Lamontagne, Rabaud-Promis, Sigalas-Rabaud, Filhot, Rayne-Vigneau.

As in the Médoc, the original classification of 1855 has been modified to accommodate changes of name and divisions of estates. Thus the original Château Doisy is now three châteaux, Doisy-Daëne, Doisy-Dubroca and Doisy-Védrines. The name of each château is followed by its commune.

Grand Premier Cru Classé
D'Yquem, *Sauternes*.

Premiers Crus Classés
Climens, *Barsac*; Coutet, *Barsac*; Clos Haut-Peyraguey, Guiraud, *Sauternes*; Haut-Peyraguey, *Bommes*; Lafaurie-Peyraguey, *Bommes*; Rabaud-Promis, *Bommes*; Rayne-Vigneau, *Bommes*; Rieussec, *Fargues*; Sigalas-Rabaud, *Bommes*; Suduiraut, *Preignac*; La Tour Blanche, *Bommes*.

Deuxièmes Crus Classés
D'Arche, *Sauternes*; Broustet, *Barsac*; Caillou, *Barsac*; Doisy-Daëne, *Barsac*; Doisy-Dubroca, *Barsac*; Doisy-Védrines, *Barsac*; Filhot, *Sauternes*; Lamothe, *Sauternes*; Lamothe-Guignard, *Sauternes*; Nairac, *Barsac*; de Malle, *Preignac*; de Myrat, *Barsac*; Romer, *Fargues*; Romer du Hayot, *Fargues*; Suau, *Barsac*.

Dry Wines for a Rainy Day

Under *Appellation* law, dry wine made in Sauternes can only be sold as Bordeaux Blanc. It is, however, almost always identifiable by its smell and flavour, which combine – sometimes disconcertingly – the honey of the sweet wine with a dry nuttiness. The first and most famous of these dry wines was Yquem's "Y" (ask for it as "Ygrec"); Château Rieussec now has its "R", Guiraud "G" and so on. Other châteaux often simply label their dry wine with *"Le Vin Sec de"* tacked on to their names.

the stuff they were making must have tasted pretty good because, in 1787, Thomas Jefferson described Sauternes as one of the three best white wines in France – along with Hermitage and Champagne – and bought some for his cellar.

The switch from the style Jefferson enjoyed to the Yquem that converted me came some time in the 1800s, though no-one is quite certain of precisely how or when. According to one story, it was a German called Focke who, in 1836, recognizing noble rot in the vineyards, tried to recreate a German-style botrytized wine in France. The Sauternais don't like giving credit to a foreigner; they prefer to fix the date of the first "modern" Sauternes vintage to 1847, when a delay in the harvest at Château d'Yquem allowed the rot to develop in the vineyards. It was the combination of that rot and the skill they developed at handling sulphur dioxide, an essential protection against bacteria, that allowed the Sauternais to establish their tradition of sweet, unfortified wine.

Unfortunately, that skill with the sulphur dioxide has still not been mastered as widely and consistently as most modern wine-drinkers might wish. In the past, when wines were left to age for decades in their owners' cellars, the sulphur overdose from which even some of the biggest names suffered would have been less apparent; today, with younger bottles being opened, it can remove a large amount of the pleasure from the wine, quite obscuring the fascinating, spicy flavour of grapes that have been subject to noble rot.

But the capricious *botrytis cinerea* will not appear to order. Everything depends on the weather – and on the wine-maker's preparedness to wait for the warm, humid fog from the River Ciron that encourages *pourriture noble* to grow on the grapes.

In some years – 1985 is a good example – when the weather has been perfect for red wines, the crucial blanket of mist does not appear. In vintages like these, all but the best producers will simply make wine with little or no *botrytis* character, while the harvesters working with their more painstaking neighbours will wait patiently, making as many as six, eight or even more trips into the vineyards to pick only the *botrytis*-affected bunches.

If you are going to wait, though, Sauternes is a very pleasant place in which to do so. This is a far easier region to fall in love with than the flatlands of the Médoc or Pomerol. Even today, Sauternes itself is still

Foie de Volailles avec Raisins

Chicken livers with grapes

Sauternes goes particularly well with rich liver paté. The famous version from this area – *pâté de foie gras* – is usually made from goose or duck livers, but chicken livers can also be made into a good accompaniment for wines with a sweeter accent. This recipe makes a tasty starter.

Small knob of butter
4 chicken livers
1 triangle of bread, without crusts
and lightly toasted
8 white grapes, peeled and seeded if necessary
1 tsp brandy
Salt and freshly ground black pepper

Heat the butter in a frying pan without letting it brown. Fry the chicken livers until they are browned on the outside but still pink inside. Put the livers on the toast and keep warm. Add the grapes to the pan and heat them gently. When they are hot, place them on top of the livers. Add the brandy to the frying-pan juices, bring to the boil and scrape the pan with a wooden spoon or spatula. After one minute, reduce the heat to a gentle simmer and add salt and pepper to taste. Pour the sauce over the livers and grapes.

small and makes no great effort to flaunt its fame: there are just 600 inhabitants, the odd church and a town hall – and the *Maison du Sauternes*, which looks as though it only opens once a year. The meandering tourist might well pass it by in favour of the comparatively bustling village of Barsac down the road.

BARSAC

Barsac can produce wine under its own name which, when of the likes of Châteaux Coutet and Climens, can compete with the finest Sauternes, though with a slightly drier, less unctuous style. Other Barsac properties, however, often prefer to take advantage of the permission given to them and their wine-making neighbours, Fargues, Preignac and Bommes, to give their wines the better-known label. Which is perhaps a pity; Barsac certainly shouldn't be thought of as second-class Sauternes.

The elegance of Barsac: *Château Coutet*

THE OTHER WINES OF BORDEAUX

IN GOOD VINTAGES, vineyards throughout Bordeaux can make decent wine; the trick is to find the best value. In trickier years, however, the region can be a minefield in which value for money sometimes seems no longer to exist. In both cases, it is worth looking to regions like Blaye, Bourg and the Premières Côtes – but don't forget to carry our list of recommendations (or a reliable mine detector).

PREMIERES COTES DE BLAYE

A brief ferry ride from the Médoc, the lovely, old, walled citadel of Blaye ought to be on every wine-tourist's list of places to visit. On paper, as a wine region, Blaye has a great deal to offer too: a handy set of no fewer than four red and white *Appellations*, clay soil for the Merlot and limestone for the Sauvignon (with a bit of the Colombard which grows well here). Unfortunately, this is an area that has suffered from neglect. In the last century its vineyards were used to produce acidic white wine for distillation into brandy. Replanting was often haphazard and, all too often, other forms of agriculture – this is great asparagus country – were allowed to take over.

But take another look at that limestone, at the clay, at the slopes and at the red and white wines Château Haut Bertinerie is making. What Blaye needs is love and investment; given both, it can give several better-known Bordeaux regions a serious run for their money.

BOURG

The wine-makers of Bourg are an enterprising lot; they did what many other regions ought to consider doing and employed a team of market researchers to find out what people thought of their wine, The answer came back that Bourg, which has been making wine since Roman times, was thought now to be producing "rustic",

"country" wine that lacked the finesse most people look for in red Bordeaux. The solution, it seemed, was to learn a few lessons from their neighbours in Margaux, on the other side of the Gironde.

Today, the wines are decidedly classier in style than they used to be – and rather more so than those of the Blayais, which are produced all around them. Both the Cabernet and Merlot grow well here and styles vary depending on which of the two is used. The Tauriac co-operative is spearheading the move toward quality, and Château de Barbe is a model for the region as a whole. Most of the wine is red and sold as Côtes de Bourg, but the Bourg and Bourgeais *Appellations* also exist and there is a tiny amount of white Bourg made.

PREMIERES COTES DE BORDEAUX

Like the Graves, this is a region where land tends to be valued in two ways – as vineyards and, for rather higher sums, as building plots. As the city of Bordeaux expands, there seems little hope for the vines – particularly because this 30-mile-long strip of riverside land has no great reputation for its wines. However, the Premières Côtes have tremendous potential; not for the sort of wines it has traditionally made – sweet and semi-sweet whites – but for its blackcurranty reds and clairet rosés. Among the best châteaux at present are Lamothe, Barreyres, Grand-Mouëys, Tanesse, Fayau and de Bouteilley.

Blaye: More work needed

CADILLAC

Within the region of the Premières Côtes, Cadillac sits on the Garonne facing Sauternes. All the wine made here is sweet and semi-sweet white, and most is dull stuff – sales are difficult and there is little incentive for quality wine-making. One estate that is trying hard, though, is Château Fayau, which backs up its Yquem-style label with some pretty luscious wine – despite the evident absence of the *botrytis* that makes Sauternes special.

LOUPIAC

Making sweet white wine often referred to as "poor man's Sauternes", this island in the Premières Côtes perseveres, despite public indifference and the unwillingness of *botrytis* to visit its vineyards as often as it does Sauternes and Barsac. As those more famous sweet wines return to favour, hopefully the overall quality of Loupiac will rise too. Wines worth looking for now are the ones made by Château Loupiac-Gaudiet and de Ricaud.

STE-CROIX-DU-MONT

The third and best of the Premières Côtes *Appellations*, producing sweet and very sweet white wines. There is a little more *botrytis* here, and even when the rot doesn't appear, the wines can be well made and well balanced. The top château is Loubens; la Rame and des Tastes are good too.

ENTRE-DEUX-MERS

The name is misleading; there are no seas, only the rivers Garonne and Dordogne. In fact, it would make rather more sense to call this large region "Entre-Deux-Vins" in recognition of the way in which it separates

Ste-Croix-du-Mont: Beautiful scenery, but stick to the top producers

The Essentials
THE OTHER WINES OF BORDEAUX

What to look for Inexpensive fresh whites and improving reds to compete with Médoc, Haut Médoc and basic St Emilion.

Official quality AOCs are: Bourg; Côtes de Bourg; Blaye; Premières Côtes de Blaye; Côtes de Blaye; Blayais; Entre-Deux-Mers; Loupiac; Ste-Croix-du-Mont; Cadillac. Reds from Entre-Deux-Mers are sold as Bordeaux Rouge. Premières Côtes de Bordeaux can be red, pink or white.

Style Bourg and Blaye produce less refined versions of the Médoc style, rarely as supple, and lacking in complexity; Premières Côtes de Bordeaux are better than basic Bordeaux. Whites are principally from Entre-Deux-Mers, predominantly dry and light-bodied, and though rarely exciting can, when well made, be fresh and lively. Loupiac and Ste-Croix-du-Mont produce Sauternes-style wines, though rarely botrytized. Cadillac can produce unusually successful honeyed *demi-sec* wines, but these are rarely seen.

Climate Bourg and Blaye have a similar climate to the northern Médoc, while Entre-Deux-Mers is quite cool. Loupiac, Ste-Croix-du-Mont and Premières Côtes de Bordeaux enjoy a mild, dry climate.

Cultivation Rolling to steep hills with rich fertile soils.

Grape varieties *Red*: Cabernet Sauvignon, Cabernet Franc, Merlot, Malbec and Petit Verdot. *White*: Sémillon, Sauvignon Blanc, Muscadelle, Colombard and Merlot Blanc.

Production/maturation Stainless steel is increasingly used for fermentation: cool fermentation temperatures and early bottling are helping to improve the freshness of the whites. For reds, old oak for maturation; very little new wood is seen as yet.

Longevity Dry whites: between 1 and 3 years. Sweet whites and reds: generally 5–6 years depending on the producer. Wines from a good château may keep for 10 years.

Vintage guide *Red*: 82, 83, 85, 86, 87, 88, 89, 90, 95; *White*: 90, 94, 95.

My Top 31 *Bourg and Blaye*: Châteaux de Barbe, de Haut Sociando, Haut Guiraud, Tayac, Haut Bertinerie, Segonzac, Rousset and le Chay, Tauriac co-operative; *Entre-Deux-Mers*: Château du Barrail, Bonnet, La Tour Martines, de Sours, Tour de Mirambeau, Thieuley, Rose du Pin, les Gauthiers; *Loupiac and Ste-Croix-du-Mont*: Châteaux Ricaud, Rondillon, Lousteau Vieil, Mazarin, Clos Jean; *Cadillac*: Château Fayau, du Juge; *Premières Côtes de Bordeaux*: Châteaux Fayau, Grand-Mouëys, Birot, Reynon, du Juge, la Mothe, du Peyrat and Barreyres.

the Graves from St Emilion and Pomerol. Once a name that was synonymous with the most awful cheap, sweet white wines, Entre-Deux-Mers has recently gone through a between-two-seas-change to become a region that can produce perfectly decent dry white and a red and pink Bordeaux – but only when there is enough sun to ripen the grapes and low enough yields to provide concentrated flavours.

This is attractively varied country, where farmland competes with woods and vineyards and a growing number of small estates have to combat not only the frequent unwillingness of the grapes to ripen properly but also the readiness of some big customers to buy on price rather than quality. But quality is possible, as the Lurton family have proved at Château Bonnet, a property whose oaked white puts some famous Graves wines to shame.

Although it has been the whites that have put Entre-Deux-Mers back on the map, my own suspicion is that the future stars of this region will be red. Just taste the wines of Châteaux La Tour Martines, Thieuley and Toutigeac, and you'll see what I mean. Unfortunately for the area, these, like all of the other reds made here, can only be sold as Bordeaux Rouge and Bordeaux Supérieur, names that can be used for red wine made anywhere in Bordeaux. Perhaps one day soon, the authorities will allow them to call themselves Entre-Deux-Mers Rouge.

BURGUNDY

YOU CAN ALWAYS spot the true Burgundy lover in a wine shop. The claret fan relaxedly strolls across to pick up a bottle of Château This or That, pausing only to check the vintage. Back among the Burgundies, the enthusiast has pulled out his magnifying glass and his pocket guide, reading the small print on every label like a nervous householder examining an insurance certificate.

Every now and then, he probably glances across at the Bordeaux buyer, envying him the simplicity of his choice – but, until he's got to the last bottle on the shelf, he'll go on searching. He knows that, if he can find precisely the bottle he's looking for, it will give him far more

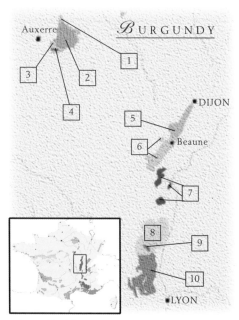

1   Chablis
2   Petit Chablis
3   Bourgogne-Irancy
4   Sauvignon de St. Bris
5   Côte de Nuits
6   Côte de Beaune
7   Côte Chalonnaise
8   Mâconnais
9   Pouilly
10   Beaujolais

pleasure and excitement than even the greatest Bordeaux. But if he gets it wrong, he'll end up with a few glasses of very expensive disappointment.

And that's it in a nutshell, really. Buying Bordeaux is a pretty simple process; all you have to do is remember the names of a few châteaux that make wine you enjoy and

Blue-blooded vine: Château de Pommard in Burgundy, most hierarchical of wine regions

follow them faithfully from year to year. Château Lynch-Bages, Château La Louvière, Château Rieussec ... apart from vintage variations (and they're traditionally less severe in temperate Bordeaux than in inland

Burgundy), the wines from any of these or a few hundred other estates should always taste recognizably the same.

At first glance, Burgundy ought to be just as simple; except that instead of the names of châteaux, it's villages you're looking for; villages like Nuits-St-Georges, Meursault and Gevrey-Chambertin. Unfortunately, it doesn't work like that. Every bottle of Château Lynch-Bages will taste the same for the simple reason that it was all made and bottled at the same place by the same person; a bottle labelled Gevrey-Chambertin could have been produced by any one of several hundred individual wine-growers, all of whom own their own little slices of land here.

Sometimes those growers bottle their own wine; sometimes they sell it to one of the region's *négociants*, or merchants, who will most likely blend it with other growers' wines from the same village in order to have enough wine to sell around the world.

Burgundy is a small-scale place. If you include Beaujolais, it produces around half as much wine as Bordeaux; if you exclude that sea of fruity young red, the figure drops to 25 per cent. And if you focus in on the tiny strip of the Côte d'Or, two dozen villages together produce less wine than only four – Margaux, Pauillac, St-Julien and St-Estèphe – do in the Médoc.

Visiting Burgundy cellars is very different to visiting ones in Bordeaux. And it takes longer. Even the tiniest estate probably makes at least five wines every year; some will produce a dozen – but in tiny quantities. In an average vintage, a Médoc château could easily produce 25,000 12-bottle cases of the same wine; an estate in Meursault might make just 250 cases each of 10 different ones.

The difference is all to do with eighteenth-century politics. Most Bordeaux estates escaped the wrath of the revolutionaries because they often belonged to anti-papist merchants with whom the new order had no quarrel. Burgundy, on the other hand, was church territory through and through.

The small plots into which the vineyards were divided among the gleeful villagers were made smaller still in subsequent generations, thanks to the new inheritance laws that guaranteed equal shares to all of a landowner's sons and daughters. The death of a man with 10 acres and 10 children could have resulted in 10 wine-makers, each with just an acre.

Clos de Lambrays, in Morey-St-Denis:
Châteaux are a rarity in Burgundy

The only reason, apart from the ability of heirs to come to common-sense agreements among themselves, that estates did not shrink to the size of postage stamps was the propensity for sons of wine-growers to marry wine-growers' daughters from the next village, combining names and vineyards to create new estates with new ranges of wines. This process (which continues to this day) not only explains the diverse range of wines, but also the confusing plethora of neighbouring domaines with similar double-barrelled names, such as Coche-Debord and Coche-Dury.

The diversity of wines would be rather less broad if the Burgundians had not discovered over the centuries that the differences in quality and character between vineyards could be so significant that each of the best plots, or *climats* (micro-climates), deserved to be known by its own *lieu-dit* – place-name. By the 1330s, when the Cistercians were building the stone walls to enclose their Clos de Vougeot vineyard, they had already identified most of the *climats* that are best known today, including Clos de Tart, Clos de Bèze, the Chambertin (Bertin's field) and Montrachet. When these vineyards were taken back from the church and split up and distributed among the villagers, the new owners were often more than happy to perpetuate their fame.

Indeed, the vineyards were often so much more famous than the villages in which they were sited that the villagers eventually decided to reflect a little glory on to their other wines by adopting the best plots' names; the little-known village of Gevrey became the well-known village of Gevrey-Chambertin, Nuits became Nuits-

Burgundy's Humbler Wines

Bourgogne Passetoutgrains and Bourgogne Aligoté are respectively the region's daily red and white. The former wine is a blend of two-thirds Gamay and one-third Pinot Noir (though the proportions do vary) that, when well made, can taste not surprisingly like a cross between a classy Beaujolais and a Bourgogne Rouge; the latter is made from the Aligoté grape. Good Aligoté can be like lemony-limey white Burgundy; some can be aggressively acidic and only really useful when blended with *cassis* – blackcurrant liqueur – in the region's *Kir* cocktail.

Crémant de Bourgogne is Burgundy's answer to Champagne; often rich, appley-creamy *méthode champenoise* Chardonnay and Pinot Noir.

St-Georges, and both Chassagne and Puligny added the name of the Montrachet to their own.

After the Revolution, marriages and inheritances, a grower might have ended up with small patches in three different *climats* of Gevrey, two in Morey-St-Denis, four in Vosne-Romanée and one in land that could only be called Bourgogne.

The problem with only making 10 barrels (3,000 bottles) each of 10 different wines is that it is hard not to frustrate one's customers – so the brighter growers began to buy in wine from the same village and to blend it with their own to produce a larger, more saleable amount. The *négociant-éleveur*, the merchant who literally "*élève*" or "brings up" the wine, was born.

For the following 200 years, the *négociants* more or less ran things, buying in barrel, blending and bottling. Some did the job shoddily, some did it well and honestly and some, caught between the frequent unwillingness of the Pinot Noir and Gamay to ripen and customers' demands for rich, alcoholic red, "helped" pallid wines along with judicious additions of beefier wine from further south.

Then, in the 1970s, a new generation of wine-drinkers decided that it was more *sympathique* to buy wine made by an individual in a little cellar rather than by a big company in a factory – only to discover that some of those little cellars were full of filthy barrels and filthier wine, and that some of the "factories" were producing the best wine in the region.

Today, it is a rare wine-lover who would want categorically to declare himself for or against either growers, *négociants* or co-operatives; most would acknowledge the need to seek out the best in each category.

THE QUALITY

So what makes one producer and his or her Burgundy better than the next one on the shelf? If there were no vines planted in France, and if a team of Californian experts were to visit on a mission to decide where to plant them, one thing is pretty certain; they wouldn't linger for long in Burgundy. Almost the entire region would be dismissed as being too cold, too damp, too frost-prone, too hail-prone, too variable... You can't grow the Cabernet Sauvignon here and even the Pinot Noir and Chardonnay rarely ripen sufficiently, so wine-growers have to unload sacks of sugar into their vats to boost the alcohol to an adequate level. The Californians would be just as dismissive of Burgundy, as many of them have been of the similarly cool, damp north-western state of Oregon where (just by coincidence?) the Pinot Noir is beginning to achieve a little of the success it has in Burgundy.

The climatic conditions shared by Burgundy and Oregon are officially described as "marginal"; in other words, both regions are right on the northernmost boundary that defines where great red wine can be made. This closeness to the edge coupled, in the case of Burgundy, with the character of the Pinot Noir and Chardonnay and the region's extraordinary range of soil types, can make for sharply defined fruit flavours and complexity rarely achieved in

Château Rocheport: Patterned roofs are typical of Burgundy's historic buildings

warmer, easier climates where the Pinot Noir, at least, tends to produce duller, jammier wine.

But a marginal climate is no place for a lazy, greedy or even unlucky wine-grower. Even when the vines escape the attentions of frost, rot and hail, they have to be pruned tightly. If they are allowed to overproduce, the red wine in particular will be thin, flavourless and low in natural sugar. To rectify this, the producers who are now (in theory at least) denied the possibility of adding stronger wine from the Rhône or North Africa, resort to the sugar bag. They are allowed to use cane sugar to raise the strength of a wine – to *chaptalize* it – by 2 per cent – for example, from a natural 10.5 per cent to 12.5 per cent. What they are not allowed to do is jack up a 9 per cent wine to 13 per cent.

A lot of nonsense is talked about chaptalization, particularly by Californians who pat themselves on the back for not having to add sugar to their ripe grapes, while conveniently overlooking the doses of tartaric acid with which they routinely have to balance their wines. The only sensible thing to be said on the subject is that, while with rare exceptions most good and even great Burgundy is chaptalized to a certain extent, there are still too many thin wines whose mouth-burning alcohol reveals a very heavy hand with the sugar bag.

Then there is the question of new barrels – to oak or not to oak. The flavour of new oak, like that of alcohol, can be overdone. On the other hand, top class red and white Burgundy can, like top class Bordeaux, broaden its range of flavours extraordinarily if enough of the wine spends just enough time in new enough wood.

THE REGIONS

Burgundy is a very disparate region, strung out like a series of lakes, beginning in Chablis, around 100 miles (160 km) south of Paris, and stretching down through the Côte d'Or (the heart and the greatest part of the region), the under-appreciated Côte Chalonnaise, the Mâconnais and Beaujolais, almost at the outskirts of Lyon and well within the southern half of France.

Today, it can be hard to imagine what Chablis has in common with Beaujolais. The answer in part is historical politics; both fell within the boundaries of what was once one of the most powerful states in the then-developed world. At its heyday in the fourteenth and fifteenth centuries, the Duchy of Burgundy extended all the way up to the coast of Flanders and the Duke of Burgundy was a major political player, who negotiated with the king of England and delivered him Joan of Arc.

But the style, the diminutive size of the estates and the varieties of grapes grown are common themes that run through all of Burgundy's regions. This is essentially a land of just four grape varieties; two greats – the Pinot Noir and Chardonnay – which are shared with Champagne and a growing number of wine regions throughout the world, and two – the red Gamay and the white Aligoté – which are allocated very specific roles. The former is used to make Beaujolais, a lot of red Mâcon and, in a two-thirds/one-third blend with the Pinot Noir, Bourgogne Passetoutgrains, traditionally most Burgundians' daily red in the days when they could afford to drink their own wines.

In the right hands, the Aligoté produces good, basic white that, at its rare ripest and best, can have a creaminess not unlike that of Chardonnay; more usually, its wines are light and acidic, and best drunk mixed with locally made *cassis* – blackcurrant – liqueur in a cocktail known as Kir. Apart from these four, there are a few Pinot Blanc and Pinot Gris vines around, as well as a few oddities such as the César and Tressot, grown in northern Burgundy, but wines made from these are very rare.

THE STYLES

Avoid anything labelled Bourgogne Grand Ordinaire; the odds are 250-to-one against it being any good and the only relevant part of its name is the "Ordinaire". Thankfully this catch-all, Gamay-dominated *Appellation* is rarely seen nowadays.

Bourgogne Rouge and Bourgogne Blanc, on the other hand, can range from basic to brilliant, depending on where they were made, how and by whom. Wine produced anywhere from the chilly hills of Chablis to the warm Mâconnais can bear these labels, provided that, in the case of the white, it has been made from the Chardonnay (or, in very rare instances, the Pinot Blanc or Pinot Gris, here called the Pinot Beurot), and in the case of the red that it has been produced from the Pinot Noir (or in the even rarer instances in the Chablis region, from the Tressot or César). There is one other peculiar exception; wines made in the Beaujolais *cru* villages, where only the Gamay is grown, may be declassified to Bourgogne Rouge.

The vineyards in which this basic red and white Burgundy are produced range from the flat land of the Côte d'Or to the hills of the Côte Chalonnaise. And then there are the "almost" wines made by top-class producers in the top-class villages of the Côte d'Or from grapes grown on vines that are just outside the legal limits of those villages. Occasionally, these producers may also decide to declassify some of their potentially higher-class wine that doesn't quite come up to scratch.

More tightly defined than Bourgogne are the *villages Appellations* for areas within the overall region. These include Beaujolais-Villages as well as smaller *Appellations* such as the Côte de Beaune-Villages and Côte de Nuits-Villages in the Côte d'Or.

Next come the *Appellations* centred around villages and towns, such as Chablis, Fleurie, Beaune and Pouilly-Fuissé, and, in some cases, the best vineyards within those *Appellations*. Some villages – like Pouilly-Fuissé, St-Romain and Fleurie – have no official recognition for their best *climats*, but may include a vineyard name – such as Morgon "Le Py" – on their labels.

Other, more fortunate communes – including Beaune, Meursault and Nuits-St-Georges – have sets of *Premier Cru* vineyards, whose names also feature on labels, usually, but not always, with the additional words "*Premier Cru*" – such as Beaune Grèves *Premier Cru* or Meursault Charmes. Some producers whose *Premiers Crus* have little-known names, or who blend wine from two or more *Premiers Crus* vineyards together, may simply choose to label a wine Beaune *Premier Cru*.

A very few communes – Aloxe-Corton, Gevrey-Chambertin and Chassagne-Montrachet for example – have *Premiers Crus* and *Grands Crus*. *Grands Crus* are considered to be so important that their labels don't need to mention the name of the village in which the wine was made. So Le Corton labels say nothing about Aloxe-Corton, and Richebourg labels don't say that the wine is made in Vosne-Romanée.

These *Grands Crus* are all situated in the grand vineyards of the Côte d'Or. Chablis has *Premier* and *Grand Cru* plots of its own – but helpfully tacks them on to the region's name – "Chablis *Grand Cru* Grenouilles", for example. In theory, if they were all lined up in the same cellar, the *Grand Cru* would have more complex flavours and greater potential longevity than the *Premier Cru* from the next-door vineyard; the *Premier Cru* would be a notch above the wine made from a humbler piece of land in the same village, and the village wine would have a more characterful flavour than one simply labelled Bourgogne.

Life gets trickier when you compare wines made by different producers; one man's carefully made Bourgogne Rouge is most likely better than his careless cousin's Vosne-Romanée – and even his Richebourg.

Winter côte: Each strip of vines belongs to a different producer

CHABLIS

YOU'LL RECOGNIZE the town of Chablis, because you've already been there – every time you've watched one of those old French films; black and white even when they're in colour; brightly lit cafés in empty, rainswept streets; and quiet country folk of the kind who have affairs with and murder each other.

But raise your eyes, and you'll see the reason for Chablis' fame – in the shape of the vineyard-covered hillside that overlooks the town, home to the *Grand Cru* vineyards with their mysterious and evocative names: Vaudésir, Valmur, Grenouilles, Blanchot, Les Clos, Bougros and Les Preuses. These are the epitome of what Chablis can be, the "big wines", the ones most worth keeping. Beneath them on the scale of excellence, there are the *Premiers Crus;* beneath these, plain Chablis and, most humble of all, Petit Chablis. And all must be made from Chardonnay grapes grown in this 4,000-acre Burgundian oasis, almost precisely mid-way between Paris and Beaune.

During the summer months, the owner of the town's best café gets rather bored by the stream of tourists – even French tourists – who ask for "a glass of red Chablis". American visitors are more likely to order "blush Chablis". Neither exists. Chablis comes in one style: dry and white.

Until a quarter of a century or so ago, Chablis was often little more than a convenient, easy-to-pronounce (and remember) name for almost any old white wine. The lazy attitude of pre-EC Britain still prevails in the US, where producers on either coast cynically make "Chablis" out of any old grapes, any old where, any old how. These forgers (for that is what they are) defend themselves by saying that what they are selling is a style of wine – and then shamelessly continue to sell sweet white and pink wine under the name of one of the driest white wines in the world.

Ironically, the more this abuse is practised, the more famous Chablis becomes, and the more the price of the real thing rockets, leaving its aficionados to bemoan the fact that their favourite tipple does not hail from a Burgundian village with a less approachable name – like Auxey-Duresses.

No backwater: The name of Chablis has been used world-wide

The unique quality of good, typical, authentic Chablis isn't easy to describe. It is absolutely dry, but with a suppleness and a fatty fullness that you seldom find in the dry wines of Sancerre and Pouilly-Fumé, both of which are little further away than Beaune or Nuits-St-Georges. But there's also a flinty flavour to Chablis, particularly when it is young, and the wine still has its characteristic green-tinged colour.

The flavour of Chablis has changed in recent years. The steely style has gradually given way to a softer, less demanding one, thanks to over-production, to a succession of ripe vintages, and to the decision of some wine-makers to allow their wine to undergo malolactic fermentation and, in a few cases, to ferment and age it in new oak barrels. To Chablisien purists, both techniques ought to be outlawed; in their view, producers who use them are merely trying to make Meursault-style wines 150 kilometres north of Meursault.

Also contributing to the change in style is the controversial authorization that

---

The Essentials
CHABLIS

What to look for Bone dry white – usually unoaked – wine which develops richness with age.
Location Centred on the town of Chablis, half-way between Paris and Beaune.
Official quality AOC Chablis, with a further hierarchy of *Grands* and *Premiers Crus (see below)*. Also AOC Petit Chablis, Irancy, Epineuil, Crémant de Bourgogne, and VDQS Sauvignon de St Bris.
Style Flavours range from steely and austere to pineappley and rounded, usually with either no or little clearly detectable oak (although new oak is finding favour with modernists). *Premier Cru* wines should have a minerally acidity and the capacity to develop with age. *Grands Crus* are the biggest. richest, most complex wines, yet are lean and restrained compared with white Burgundy from farther south. Sauvignon de St Bris is gooseberryish and Sancerre-like; Irancy and Epineuil are light reds though the latter can be white.
Climate Continental.
Cultivation Soils are of calcareous clay. Rivalry

exists over the benefits of the classic Kimmeridgian versus the more recently allowed Portlandian limestone. All the *Grands Crus* are on one south-west-facing slope.
Grape varieties Chardonnay for Chablis; Sauvignon Blanc in St Bris, Pinot Noir, Tressot and César for reds; Sacy for Crémant de Bourgogne.
Production/maturation Stainless steel has largely replaced oak for both, but new oak still has some fervent and successful supporters, notably William Fèvre.
Longevity Petit Chablis, Sauvignon de St Bris and red wines are intended to be drunk young. Chablis drinks from 1 to 8 years; *Premiers Crus* for up to 15; *Grands Crus* should be kept for 5 years, and can be drunk for a further 15.
Vintage guide 85, 86, 88, 89, 90, 92, 93, 95.
My Top 15 *Chablis*: Vincent and René Raveneau, William Fèvre, René Dauvissat, Domaine Laroche, Louis Pinson, Vocoret, Daniel Defaix, Joseph Drouhin, Louis Michel, Tremblay, Jean-Paul Droin, la Chablisienne Co-operative, Jean-Marc Brocard; *Sauvignon de St Bris*: Domaine Sorin, Jean-Marc Brocard.

The Grands Crus of Chablis

Bougros; Blanchot; Les Clos; Grenouilles; Les Preuses; Valmur and Vaudésir. One vineyard within the *Grands Crus*, La Moutonne, is not classified as such but, because of its status and position, is tacitly allowed to describe itself as "*Grand Cru* La Moutonne". (Spellings vary)

The Premiers Crus of Chablis

Beauroy; Côte de Léchet; *Fourchaume*; Les Fourneaux; Melinots; *Montée de Tonnerre*; *Montmains*; *Mont de Milieu*; Vaillons; Vaucoupin; Vaudevey and Vosgros. (Italics indicate the most reliable *Premiers Crus*. Spellings vary)

transformed what was previously Petit Chablis land into Chablis and Chablis *Premier Cru* vineyards. The crucial difference between the "new" land and the area from which the original, most typical, Chablis comes lies in the soil. Or, more precisely, beneath it.

The limestone bedrock on which Chablis rests has been the subject of a violent squabble between two groups of Chablisien wine-growers. The traditionalists claim, with the vehemence of real-ale campaigners, that "real" Chablis can only be grown on the small area of Kimmeridgian limestone which takes its name from the village in Dorset where it is also found. The modernists, like keen urban planners, argue that the Portland limestone that sits beneath the rest of the region can produce wine that

is just as good. Tasting the wines side by side, I tend to agree with the traditional line – but then again, the Portland faction are making wines that are certainly of good, if not great, quality. And, given the way that demand for this, the most famous white wine in the world, has forced its price through the roof, it's very tempting to allow the Chablisiens to expand their vineyards as much as they'd like.

Besides, a little over a century ago, the Chablis vineyard was perhaps 10 times its current size. The ravages of the *phylloxera* louse in the 1880s, then the depredations of two World Wars, took a heavy toll on the region's vines and vinegrowers. By the early 1960s, when thirsty Americans were already gulping back their version by the gallon, the area of Chablis vines had shrunk to less than 1,500 acres – less than the size of a modest Texan farm.

In those days, few men could rely on making a living simply from their vines. One of their biggest problems was frost, which could – and can – destroy a whole year's crop in a single night. The reason why Chablis is so subject to frost – as late as May in some years – is because of the way that the sheltered valley of the Serein traps and holds cold air.

At the end of rows of vines one can still see the archaic oil burners which are lit as soon as the temperature falls below zero. Now, however, many growers prefer to rely on sprinklers that protect the vines from frost by, paradoxically, allowing a thin layer of ice to form on them.

Wide blue Yonne: *Vineyards of the Yonne, near Chablis*

Saumon aux Herbes

Raw salmon marinated in herbs, olive oil and lemon juice

The flinty crispness of the wines of Chablis makes them very good with this marinated salmon dish which, although traditional in this region, has an almost Scandinavian character.

SERVES 6 AS A STARTER

*1 lb/500 g salmon fillet, skinned and boned
5 tbsp olive oil
2 tsp tinned green peppercorns, drained and crushed
2 tsp whole black peppercorns, coarsely crushed
juice of 1 lemon
3 tbsp fennel leaves, finely chopped, or 1 tbsp dried fennel seeds*

Dry the salmon with kitchen paper and coat it with olive oil. Rub in the green and black pepper, the lemon juice and fennel. Put the salmon in a glass or ceramic dish, covered, and refrigerate for at least four hours, turning occasionally. Serve thinly sliced as a starter with brown bread and butter or toast triangles.

THE OTHER WINES OF CHABLIS

Though none is allowed to be called Chablis, there are red and rosé wines made in this region. The best-known red is Bourgogne Irancy, a fruity and, in warm years, raspberryish wine that is usually made from the Pinot Noir, though it may include a generous dose of the duller local varieties Tressot and César. The village of Coulanges-La-Vineuse produces a similar red, while Epineuil makes red, white and *gris* (dustily pale pink) wines, all AOCs, though the leanness of their style in cool years could leave you wondering why. Especially when the dry white produced in the village of St Bris, which really deserves an AOC, has been denied one and remains a VDQS. Given the eccentricity of the AOC system, this is probably because it is made from the "wrong" grape. The Sauvignon, prized and pricy, though not always so carefully treated in nearby Sancerre, is underrated here.

THE COTE D'OR

SET OUT from Dijon on the *route nationale* heading south, with the east-facing vine-covered hills on your right and the humbler, flatter land on your left, and read the village signs as you pass: you're driving down a restaurant wine list. Even if you stick rigorously to the speed limit, there they are: one every two or three minutes – Gevrey-Chambertin, Morey-St-Denis, Chambolle-Musigny, Clos de Vougeot, Vosne-Romanée and Nuits-St-Georges...

But for more than signposts, take one of the narrow tracks to your right and follow the *Route des Vins* – past the weather-worn archways that punctuate the rough stone walls and indicate the name of the vineyard or of the proprietor of that particular segment. If it's autumn, bask in the colours, from green to bronze via the gold after which these hills were named. At dusk, stroll slowly between the vineyards and you may even sense the fractional but influential variations in temperature which led the Burgundians to refer to each piece of land as a *"climat"* – a climate. Pick up a handful of soil from each of a couple of neighbouring vineyards and see how the way the earth was folded here aeons ago has packed one with fossils which are almost completely absent in the other.

The Côte d'Or is divided into two parts: the 3,500 acres (1,400 ha) of the more northerly Côte de Nuits, in which most of Burgundy's greatest reds are made and where there is scarcely a drop of white, and the 7,500 acres (3,000 ha) of the Côte de Beaune, where the Pinot Noir still covers 75 per cent of the land, but a handful of villages produce the white wine that turns owners of Chardonnay vineyards in other countries green with envy.

Both Côtes produce simpler wine labelled as Bourgogne Rouge, Bourgogne Blanc, Bourgogne Passetoutgrains and Aligoté, from land that cannot legally produce wine of a grander *Appellation*; some of these can be delicious, especially when made by a grower who also makes loftier wines.

THE COTE DE NUITS

Apart from the wines produced in the "big-name" villages and those more basic reds and whites, the Côte de Nuits has two other *Appellations*.

Côte de Nuits-Villages can come from the villages of Marsannay, Fixin and Brochon just north of Gevrey-Chambertin, and from the marble-quarrying country around Comblanchien, Corgoloin and Prissy, immediately to the south of Nuits-St-Georges. Little of the wine does actually come from Fixin, which has an *Appellation* of its own, but Brochon and the more southerly communes can produce good-quality, blackcurrant, plummy wine with a recognizable family resemblance to the wines of the better-known villages along the Côte. These are the country cousins, dressed up for a day in the town.

Rather more rustic wines are also produced high in the hills behind the Côte in the Hautes Côtes de Nuits. These definitely have wisps of straw poking out of their hats sometimes, but they can also be the closest thing to a bargain Burgundy has

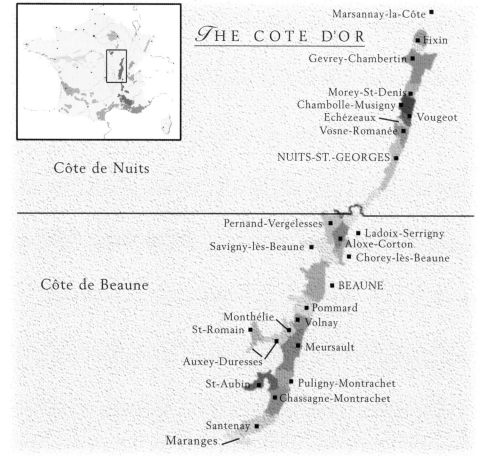

THE COTE D'OR

Marsannay-la-Côte ■
■ Fixin
Gevrey-Chambertin ■
Morey-St-Denis ■
Chambolle-Musigny ■
Echézeaux — ■ Vougeot
Vosne-Romanée ■
NUITS-ST.-GEORGES ■

Côte de Nuits

Pernand-Vergelesses ■
■ Ladoix-Serrigny
Savigny-lès-Beaune ■ Aloxe-Corton
■ Chorey-lès-Beaune

Côte de Beaune

■ BEAUNE
■ Pommard
Monthélie ■ ■ Volnay
St-Romain ■
■ Meursault
Auxey-Duresses
St-Aubin ■ ■ Puligny-Montrachet
■ Chassagne-Montrachet
Santenay ■
Maranges —

Burning the prunings: *The warmest part of a chilly task*

to offer. Stick to warm years; it can get quite chilly up here and lesser vintages tend to produce unripe-tasting wine. Almost all of the wine made here is red. The occasional white can make you wonder why they don't make more. Intriguingly, some of these whites don't taste quite like Burgundy, inspiring vinous know-it-alls to claim that they are made from Aligoté rather than Chardonnay. But the know-it-alls are wrong. If they used their tastebuds instead of regurgitating bits of half-digested information, they might just notice a resemblance between the stuff in their glass and white wine from Alsace – which is hardly surprising because dotted around there are still plantings of Pinot Blanc and Pinot Gris.

What was once called the Côte Dijonnaise is now largely full of the tyre-fitting operations, discount warehouses and *hypermarchés* that make Dijon's southern suburbs look like those of any medium-sized American town. Nowadays, the Côte d'Or officially begins with Marsannay, a village which is still celebrating its recent elevation to join its *Appellation Contrôlée* neighbours.

Marsannay's traditional reputation was for rosé, and that's arguably the one style it can claim as its own (pink Pinot Noir is a rarity). Its reds are still rather closer in quality to decent Bourgogne Rouge (the label they used to bear) than to the kind of stuff one might expect to find down the road in Fixin or Gevrey-Chambertin. One label to look out for (you're sure to notice it) is that from the "Montre Cul" vineyard, whose name – literally "show-arse" – refers to the steepness of the slope and the view male pickers got of their female companions' bloomers. Perversely, the authorities who oversee alcohol, firearms and tobacco in the US forbade the importation of this wine because the vaguely bawdy cartoon on the label apparently created too strong a connection between sex and alcohol. It's a ruling I remember sometimes when I read of the innocent victims of legally imported firearms.

Back to the wine. As one might gather, Marsannay's a fairly jolly place and so is its wine. Fixin, the next-door neighbour, comes as a bit of a shock. Wine merchants have a description for the wines of this village: "Hard to say (it's pronounced *Fissan*), harder to drink and almost impossible to sell". This is a good a place as any to learn about the effects of Burgundian micro-climates. When Gevrey-Chambertin starts to pick its grapes, those in Fixin across the track still need another week on the vine to ripen. Even when the grapes are ripe, they

Walled in: Chambertin's Clos de Bèze. A clos is a walled vineyard.

produce tough, uncompromising wine that seems to taste the way it must have done when the Cistercian monks first made it in the early twelfth century. Give it a decade or so and it can soften – a bit – but it's still Burgundy's answer to old-fashioned St-Estèphe.

Gevrey-Chambertin's much more fun. Or it ought to be. Sadly this, like Nuits-St-Georges, Beaujolais and Châteauneuf-du-Pape, has suffered from the fame syndrome. There are brilliant vineyards here – the *Grands Crus*, including the Chambertin itself, the more immediately appealing Charmes-Chambertin, the Chambertin-Clos de Bèze, Mazis-Chambertin and the Griotte-Chambertin (possibly named after, and certainly tasting of, bitter cherries), and the slightly lighter-weight but sometimes equally impressive *Premiers Crus* such as the Clos St Jacques and Cazetiers. But this is

one of the region's biggest villages and its *Appellation* includes a huge tract of flat land, including some which is on the other side of the *route nationale*, the side that usually only makes Bourgogne Rouge. Dull wine-making and over-production don't help either; Gevrey-Chambertin *should* be a rich cocktail of dark cherries and really ripe plums. Treat cheap examples with the respect you'd pay to the gold watches on offer from market stalls.

Morey-St-Denis is not a name that rings many bells with Burgundy fans, and nor is Clos-St-Denis, the *Grand Cru* that gave it its name, but here lovely village wines are vying for attention with often poorly made *Grands* and *Premiers Crus*. The best stuff from the Clos de la Roche *Grand Cru* can be majestic, deep wine – better than most Clos-St-Denis. The Clos Sorbès and Clos des Ormes are the best *Premiers Crus*.

Chambolle-Musigny provides your first chance to taste classy white Burgundy – of which a very few bottles are made in the

The Essentials
THE COTE D'OR

What to look for Fine examples of the Pinot Noir and rich, buttery Chardonnay.

Location In Burgundy, a narrow strip of land from Dijon in the north to Cheilly-les-Maranges 30 km south of Beaune.

Official quality Overall Côte d'Or AOCs: Bourgogne; Bourgogne Aligoté; Crémant de Bourgogne; Bourgogne Passetoutgrains. Principal Côte de Nuits AOCs: Chambertin*; Chambertin Clos de Bèze*; Charmes Chambertin*; Chambolle-Musigny; Clos de la Roche*; Clos de Vougeot*; Côte de Nuits-Villages; Echézeaux*; Fixin; Gevrey-Chambertin; Grands-Echézeaux*; Hautes-Côtes de Nuits; Marsannay; Morey St Denis; Nuits-St-Georges; Richebourg*; Romanée*; Vosne-Romanée. Principal Côte de Beaune AOCs: Ladoix; Aloxe-Corton; Auxey-Duresses; Bâtard Montrachet*; Beaune; Blagny; Chassagne-Montrachet; Chorey-lès-Beaune; Corton*; Corton-Charlemagne*; Côte de Beaune; Côte de Beaune-Villages; Hautes-Côtes de Beaune; Maranges; Meursault; Monthélie; Montrachet*; Pernand-Vergelesses; Pommard; Puligny-Montrachet; St Aubin, St Romain; Santenay; Savigny-lès-Beaune; Volnay. Superimposed on most of the *Appellations* is a complex structure of named vineyards: the *Grands* and *Premiers Crus*. The AOCs marked (*) are in themselves *Grands Crus*.

Style Whites, at their best, have a dazzling array of enticing flavours, with rich, buttery fruit, a creamy/nutty texture and splendid overtones of honey, vanilla and toasty oak. The reds are more varied in quality but should have delicate strawberry/raspberry fruit in the Côte de Beaune and a finer character, with greater depth and a sumptuous silky texture, in the Côte de Nuits. With bottle age, the reds develop a gamey flavour. Because of the myriad of small-plot owners, the producer's name is all-important and the best guide to quality. A general rule is that the wines are reasonably straightforward at village level, with greater complexity and depth of flavour to be expected from *Premier* and *Grand Cru* wines. Tiny

quantities of dry rosé, packed with soft currant and berry fruit flavours, are also made.

Climate Temperate continental climate with hot, sunny summers and long, cold winters. Hail and heavy rain can cause rot and dilute wines.

Cultivation Subtly varying marl, clay and calcareous soils overlay a limestone subsoil which underpins the east-facing slopes of the region. Vines generally grow at 200–400 m above sea level and vineyards generally face north-east or south-east. Vines are trained low to maximize heat reflected from the soil during the day.

Grape varieties The dominant red is the Pinot Noir, though the Gamay is also grown. Principal white is the Chardonnay; secondary white the Aligoté.

Production/maturation Traditional methods are used. For red wines the grapes are at least partially de-stemmed and the juice receives 8–14 days' skin contact. Some producers leave the black grapes for a period of a few hours to a few days at low temperature or beneath SO_2 before fermentation begins. Top whites are cask-fermented although stainless steel is used for lesser wines. Both reds and whites are matured in oak.

Longevity *Reds*: Village wines and basic Bourgogne: 4–17 years; *Premiers Crus*: 8–25 years; *Grands Crus*: 10–30+ years. *Whites*: Village wines: 3–11 years; *Premiers Crus*: 6–15 years; *Grands Crus*: 10–30+ years. *Rosés*: Up to 4 years.

Vintage guide *Reds*: 71, 76, 78, 79, 83, 85, 88, 89, 90, 92; *Whites*: 78, 79, 81, 82, 85, 86, 88, 89, 90, 92, 93.

My Top 32 *Côte de Nuits*: Jayer, Jayer-Gilles, Ponsot, Dujac, Patrice Rion, Méo-Camuset, Gros Frères, Mongeard-Mugneret, Domaine de la Romanée-Conti, Domaine Leroy, Jean Grivot, Alain Michelot, Henri Gouges, Joseph Drouhin, Jaffelin, Faiveley; *Côte de Beaune*: Bonneau du Martray, Lafarge, Mussy, Château de Chorey, Leflaive, Sauzet, Pothier Rieusset, Domaine de la Pousse d'Or, Domaine Bachelet, Ramonet, Comtes Lafon, Joseph Drouhin, Leroy, Chartron & Trébuchet, Michelot-Buisson, Louis Jadot.

Outliving the paper they're written on: *Old wines in storage*

ought to be soft and velvety with the flavours of ripe raspberries and plum. The château itself, which looks just like a ship sinking in a sea of vines, is worth visiting too, either by day to see its old presses, or by night when the local order of wine enthusiasts, the Chevaliers de Tastevin, dress up in mock medieval costumes for one of their banquets.

There isn't a lot of village at Flagey-Echézeaux – a few houses, a great café/restaurant and a church – and it's in the wrong place, down on the flat land, a fair distance from its *Grand Cru* Echézeaux and Grands Echézeaux vineyards up on the slopes. Both produce tiny amounts of gloriously rich, raspberryish, plum-flavoured wine with more than a hint of spice. They can be among the more affordable *Premiers Crus*, except when they are made by the Domaine de la Romanée-Conti, Burgundy's equivalent of Château Pétrus. Hidden away in a modest building in the heart of Vosne-Romanée, this is the shrine to which well-heeled Burgundy lovers flock to worship – and buy. Less-well-heeled enthusiasts merely stand and stare at the domaine's minuscule *Grand Cru* Romanée-Conti vineyard. If you want to taste that wine, you have to buy it from the domaine, where a bottle would cost you at least a week's wages. You can, however, discover the juicy, blackberryish flavour of Vosne-Romanée's wines a little more cheaply by going for a village wine, or one of the *Premier Crus*. My favourites are Beaux Monts, Suchots and Chaumes.

If you find yourself enjoying a glass of young Nuits-St-Georges, beware – it is unlikely to be a really good one. This is like

primarily red *Grand Cru* Musigny vineyard – and a red from one of the most romantically named *Premiers Crus*, Les Amoureuses. Chambolle-Musigny's wines should taste more like Côte de Beaune than Côte de Nuits, with that area's more delicate style. Bonnes Mares is the other top *Grand Cru*.

Clos de Vougeot is Burgundy's nearest to a Bordeaux-style château – or that's what it used to be in the days when the Cistercian monks owned this 125-acre (50-ha) walled vineyard and made wine here, carefully

separating the inferior grapes grown on the flatland from the best ones grown on the slopes. The French Revolution and inheritance laws changed all that; today there are seven dozen individual owners and seven dozen different wines, ranging from the poor (badly made and/or from the flattest parts) to the sublime (well made, generally from the slopes). But every drop is *Grand Cru*. Confusingly, there is also an *Appellation* for Vougeot wine made outside the walls, 90 per cent of which is classified as *Premier Cru*. Good Clos de Vougeot

Fixin with class; tough, broody wine that usually needs at least five years to soften. But when they do, the mulberry-and-plum wines of Nuits itself, or the ones made at Prémeaux just down the Côte – also sold as Nuits-St-Georges – are among the best buys in Burgundy. Nuits has no *Grands Crus*. This is an injustice; examples of Les St Georges, Les Vaucrains and Les Pruliers all regularly outclass plenty of *Grand Cru* Corton – about which I shall have a little more to say.

As you leave Prémeaux, past the marble quarries which reveal the limestone lying beneath the soil, you leave the big-name villages of the Côte de Nuits and pass through a tract of Côte de Nuits-Villages before imperceptibly crossing the border into the Côte de Beaune, just south of the village of Corgoloin.

THE COTE DE BEAUNE

Like its Côte de Nuits counterpart, Côte de Beaune-Villages is a rag-bag *Appellation* for wine produced almost throughout this half of the Côte d'Or. Unlike the Côte de Nuits, however, it only covers red wines, despite the fact that this bit of Burgundy is where all of the best whites are made; white wines that ought to be sold as Côte de Beaune-Villages are stuck with plain Bourgogne Blanc. The hillside *Appellation*, Hautes-Côtes de Beaune, does include wines of both colours – or rather all three, because a little light, raspberryish clairet and rosé is made here. All are pleasant in warm years, and lean in cool ones.

The first Côte de Beaune village is Ladoix-Serrigny, whose unfamiliar wines are usually sold as Ladoix. They actually *taste* as though they are made on the border; they combine some of the gentle, raspberryish flavours of Beaune with the toughness of Nuits-St-Georges, but in rather a rustic way. With time they can, however, sometimes outclass some of the less impressive wines from its neighbour Aloxe-Corton.

A village that is quite literally in the shadow of its *Grands Crus*, grown in vineyards which extend rather too far around the hill of the Corton itself, Aloxe (pronounced Aloss)-Corton makes red wines that, like those of Nuits-St-Georges, can take forever to come round. The better examples of the *Grands Crus* Corton, Corton-Vergennes, Corton Bressandes *et al* (there are 21 different bits of the Corton vineyard) do eventually develop glorious richness of flavour; others remain perpetually comatose. The more reliably exciting wine is the white Corton-Charlemagne – made in, it is implausibly said, vineyards that belonged to the emperor and were named after him, following his conversion from red to white wine by his wife who complained at the undignified red stains on his snowy imperial beard.

If Aloxe-Corton makes tough wine, the little-known *Appellation* of Chorey-lès-Beaune, (*lès*, by the way, is old Burgundian for "near") produced from grapes grown on the flat land on the east of the *nationale*, is a place to look for lovely, soft, raspberryish Pinot Noir which, drunk young, is one of the region's classiest bargains.

Back in the hills, Pernand-Vergelesses also produces soft, approachable reds, some of which can be so soft that they taste a bit too much like damson jam and make you wonder if their makers are not over-compensating for the tough Cortons most of them produce from the part of that *Grand Cru* vineyard that strays into their village. The best wine here is the white, which can be very distinguished – hazelnutty and buttery, sometimes with a hint of the quality of the Corton-Charlemagne many of its producers make too. Les Vergelesses and Ile

Seeking the spotlight: *Lesser-known villages like Monthélie are coming into their own*

𝒜 Burgundy Buyer's Guide

*T*he process of choosing Burgundy can be frustrating and, often, very disappointing. If you follow the advice below, I cannot guarantee that you will always end up with a good and, more importantly, a good-value bottle of Burgundy (I've wasted my money on far too many bad ones ever to imagine there to be any foolproof route through the maze), but it should improve the odds in your favour.

Good and Bad Value Villages
Some villages do offer better value than others; seek out reds and whites from St Aubin, Savigny-lès-Beaune, Monthélie, Auxey-Duresses, Mercurey, Rully, Givry, Ladoix; reds from Fixin, Chorey-lès-Beaune and Meursault; whites from St Aubin, Rully, Pernand-Vergelesses and Montagny. Beware of Puligny and Chassagne-Montrachet, Meursault, Pommard and Gevrey-Chambertin.

Vignerons Versus Négociants
Once upon a time, almost all of Burgundy's wines were sold by the region's merchants – the *négociants*. More recently, the trend has been toward buying from individual growers – the *vignerons*. Neither group has a monopoly over good Burgundy; each has its superstars – and its knaves, fools and people who simply don't care very much about the quality of what they are selling.

Who's Who? or, Just Say No to Dregs
If the price is high, you've never heard of the grower or merchant and you have no reason to trust the buying skills of the restaurant or shop, just say no thank you. The chances of a random bottle of Gevrey-Chambertin being worth its money are very slim. Unfamiliar *négociants* should be treated with suspicion; most Burgundy merchants have sets of fictitious names they can legally stick on labels for their customers.

Beware, too, of apparently familiar labels. Most growers use the same few printers and many are happy to use the same basic label (complete with heraldry, grapes, parchment or whatever) as their neighbours.

Château Corton-André: In Alox-Corton

des Vergelesses are the best *Premiers Crus*.

The village of Savigny-lès-Beaune is just beneath Pernand-Vergelesses and has a good *Premier Cru*, Les Basses Vergelesses. Red Savigny can be – and often is – like a classier version of Chorey-lès-Beaune (several estates make both), with lovely, ripe, blackberryish, mulberryish sweetness, but some examples are rather too jammy for their price. There is very little white wine

made here, but it's worth looking out for – and unusual in being made from the Pinot Blanc, a variety usually associated with Alsace.

From just above Savigny-lès-Beaune, you can see the old walled town of Beaune, its church and its most famous building, the Hospice at which, every November, wines of the most recent vintage from various Côte de Beaune vineyards (and one Côte de Nuits plot) are auctioned in aid of the town's hospital.

Like Nuits-St-Georges, Beaune has no *Grands Crus*; also like that *Appellation*, it has at least three contenders in Theurons, Grèves and Bressandes. None really fits the mould of *Grand Cru* Côte de Nuits wines, however, because these are far less "big" wines; they whisper rather than roar. My classic tasting note for a mature Beaune is of the smell of faded roses and the flavour of wild raspberries and honey.

Perhaps because most of Burgundy's best-known merchants have their cellars in a rabbit warren beneath the town, and more crucially because they almost all have large vineyard holdings here and so are often making wine from their own grapes, Beaune remains one of the most reliable labels in Burgundy. A tiny amount of white Beaune is

made too; it tastes a little like a leaner version of Meursault.

Apart from the *Appellation* of Beaune itself, there is the tiny anomaly called simply Côte de Beaune that includes a small set of vineyards in the hills overlooking the town. Often quite understandably confused with Côte de Beaune-Villages, Côte de Beaune can be good value.

Pommard is a little like Gevrey-Chambertin, a well-known village too much of whose wine comes from the wrong side of the *nationale*, except that here any grapes that cross the road do so illegally. Good Pommard, like Aloxe-Corton, is sturdy stuff. Like Aloxe-Corton, these wines need time and sensitive wine-making to bring out the plummy fruit that's hiding behind all that muscle. The best *Premiers Crus* are Les Epenots, Les Rugiens and Les Arvelets.

Many of Pommard's growers produce prettier wine a few yards further south in Volnay, a village that can make some of the greatest red Burgundy of all. The *Premier Cru* Les Santenots – which, confusingly, is actually in Meursault – should be a *Grand Cru*, but it too rarely dazzles as most Côte de Nuits *Grands Crus* are expected to, because of a lightness of touch, attributable to its very, very shallow topsoil and deep limestone. The best Volnay combines ripe plums and violets; the Côte de Beaune's counterpart to Vosne-Romanée, with which it is often confused.

On the same hillside, you next arrive in the village of Monthélie, which makes little-known wines that used to be sold as Volnay. Tasting them you can see why it was subsequently decided to sell these more rustic wines under their own name, but they still often offer good value. The rare whites can be tasty too.

Auxey-Duresses is a victim of its hard-to-pronounce name (as elsewhere round here the "x" sounds like "ss"). Prices are often lower for well-made whites than they are for fairly basic Meursault, but the quality is more variable, as much because of a lack of care by the wine-growers, as because of the poor siting of some of the vineyards. The reds, which make up a quarter of the wine, can be good and juicy, but rarely delicate.

Further up in the hills, among the Hautes-Côtes de Beaune, St Romain is a glorious place to picnic and watch hungry birds circling over the vines. The reds can be fruitily appealing, but only in warm years; in cool ones, the grapes don't ripen well. The whites are better, in their lean way – provided they aren't over-exposed to the new oak barrels made by the village success-story, Jean François, most of whose toasty casks end up being used for the Californian and Australian Chardonnays that are big enough to handle them.

The wine many of those New-World wine-makers really want to make is Meursault. They just love the fat, buttery, hazelnutty style of this wine, but sometimes miss the point that Meursault shouldn't just be buttered toast and oak; it should also be

No entry: Latricières-Chambertin, a grand cru vineyard

about subtlety and complexity. For these qualities, sidestep the obvious appeal of most village Meursault and the immediately seductive Charmes (these names do mean something) and try the *Premiers Crus* Genevrières, Goutte d'Or and Perrières, all of which could be *Grands Crus* if Meursault had any. Incidentally, if Meursault's *Premiers Crus* are undervalued, so are some of its village wines, many of which proudly print their non-*Premier Cru* names on their labels. Red Meursault is a rare oddity, but try some if you get the chance – it can be like drinking liquidized wild raspberries; pure Pinot Noir.

Puligny-Montrachet and Chassagne-Montrachet *do* have *Grands Crus* of their own – but they have to share the small plot of land that gave them their name. The 18.5-acre (7.5-ha) Le Montrachet vineyard, and its oddly named neighbours – Bâtard (bastard) Montrachet; Bienvenue Bâtard (welcome bastard) Montrachet; Criots Bâtard (cries of the bastard) Montrachet and Chevalier (Knight) Montrachet – can produce the greatest dry white wine in the world. The flavour is almost impossible to describe, an explosive marriage of ripe, peachy, appley, peary fruit, butter, roasted nuts, digestive biscuits and honey. Drink it when it's at least 10 years old.

Tasting village or *Premier Cru* wine from Puligny- or Chassagne-Montrachet alongside one of the *Grands Crus* is a little like looking at a black-and-white photograph next to a colour one, especially since worldwide popularity has allowed greedy *vignerons* to overproduce. Even given good examples, telling a Puligny-Montrachet from a Chassagne-Montrachet can be tricky; as a rule, the latter is toastier in style and the former is slightly more floral. Both tend to be ferociously priced.

Red Chassagne-Montrachet (around half the production) can be good, if rarely delicate, but beware disappointing examples forced on to merchants by producers who refuse to offer their white to anyone who won't take the red too.

Slightly off the beaten track, close to the village of Gamay – said to be the birthplace of the Beaujolais grape – St Aubin is one white-wine-producing village I wasn't going to mention. Because I'm not certain if I want the secret of this commune's nutty, buttery wines to spread too far. When well made, they can show up a Meursault, Chassagne or Puligny – for a far lower price. The reds (of which there are far more) are a little less impressive, but can still be good value.

Santenay is the last important commune on the Côte. The reds here from the

Ragôut de Canard aux Navets

Duck and turnip stew

Some have called this region of Burgundy the heart of French gastronomy, so rich is the tradition of great wines matched with sumptuous food. The richness of this duck recipe will do justice to the deep wines of the Côte de Nuits.

SERVES 4

*8 oz/225 g unsmoked bacon, diced
1 medium onion, peeled and sliced
3 garlic cloves, peeled and minced
1 tbsp olive oil
1 oz/25 g butter
2 lb/1 kg duck, cut into pieces
4 tbsp plain flour
4 tbsp fresh parsley, chopped
1 bay leaf
2 juniper berries, crushed
Salt and freshly ground black pepper
3 wine glasses of dry white wine
1½ lb/750 g small whole turnips, peeled, or larger turnips peeled and cut into quarters*

In a large pan, sauté the bacon, onion and garlic in the olive oil until the onion is lightly browned. Remove from the pan with a slotted slice or spoon. Dredge the duck pieces in flour and brown in the pan. Pour off excess fat if necessary. Return the bacon, onion and garlic to the pan and add the parsley, bay leaf, juniper berries, salt and pepper and wine and cook, uncovered, for about 45 minutes. Add the turnips, cover the pan and cook at a bare simmer for about an hour.

Premiers Crus Clos Tavannes, Gravières and Commes can be good, straight-down-the-line wines, but too many Santenays are a bit dull and earthy. The whites are, if anything, less impressive, but Santenay is worth a visit – by anyone who fancies a flutter at the casino or a dip in the spa.

Beyond Santenay, Dézize-les-Maranges, Sampigny-les-Maranges and Cheilly-les-Maranges unaccountably share their own Maranges *Appellation* and even some *Premiers Crus*. Sensible producers, however, sell their often rather basic wine as Côte de Beaune-Villages.

SOUTHERN BURGUNDY

AS YOU DRIVE away from the Côte d'Or and into the Côte Chalonnaise just outside the small town of Chagny, past the three-star Lameloise restaurant, you cross the invisible border that separates "smart" Burgundy from the rest.

But 'twas not ever thus. This is a region of might-have-been places. Tourists flock to the magnificent medieval abbey of Cluny – but it's a ruin; the town of Autun was intended, Brasilia-like, by the Romans to be a "Rome of the West"; today, all that remains is the Forum and bits of an amphitheatre. As for Chalon-sur-Saône itself, its industrial heyday is long past.

To an eighteenth-century Frenchman, though, names like Mercurey, Rully and Givry would have rung louder bells than some of today's superstar villages of the Côte d'Or. Henri IV, the French king who made the name of Sancerre's wines, was a particular fan of Givry; his mistress lived there. The *négociants* of Beaune, Nuits-St-Georges and Mâcon have always treated the Côte Chalonnaise rather as though it were their mistress: a region to be taken advantage of and not referred to in public. And their attitude was understandable. This area has always been a good minor source (20 per cent of the crop) of Chardonnay and Aligoté and more plentiful

Picking the white stuff: *The harvest in Montagny*

red Burgundy, almost all of which (even the humblest Bourgogne Rouge) is grown on hillsides.

In the mid-1980s, as prices rose for the wines of the Côte d'Or, bargain-hunters inevitably began to head south. Today, a decent bottle from the Côte Chalonnaise costs as much as many a bottle from smarter villages up north.

There is, however, one style of Côte Chalonnaise wine with which the Côte d'Or cannot easily compete. The Aligoté, Burgundy's secondary white grape, has, since 1979, had its very own *Appellation* in the shape of Bourgogne Aligoté de Bouzeron. The village of Bouzeron, northernmost commune of the region, is a perfect place to discover how good this light, lemony variety can be.

Rully is not so much little-known as almost unknown outside the region. Which is a pity, because this village – whose vines were planted by the Romans – makes Chablis-like Chardonnay, pleasantly plummy and rather "pretty" Pinot Noir, and a large quantity of good Crémant de Bourgogne fizz.

Rully's wines used to be sold under the name of the far larger, more southerly commune of Mercurey, a quiet town whose historic credentials are confirmed by the presence of a Roman temple dedicated to the messenger of the gods from whom it took its name.

It was traditionally said that there were three types of Mercurey: for masters, for servants and for washing horses' hooves – and, until quite recently, the masters took little interest in it. Today, however, it is increasingly acknowledged that the tiny quantity of this buttery white can compete with Meursault, while the beefier red can put some Pommard to shame.

Givry used to be thought the equal of wines from the Côte d'Or. Well, perhaps... Its jammy, easy-drinking reds can match some of the less exciting stuff from Pernand-Vergelesses, but it's a far cry from Beaune or Volnay – but then again, so is the price. There is a tiny amount of white wine made; for the most part, nutty, up-market Bourgogne Blanc.

The Essentials
SOUTHERN BURGUNDY

What to look for From the Côte Chalonnaise, better than average "basic" Bourgogne Rouge and Blanc, and good if rarely complex village wines. From the Mâconnais: mostly run-of-the-mill whites and rustic reds, though the best village wines can be as good as some Côte de Beaune examples.

Official quality AOCs: Crémant de Bourgogne; Bourgogne Passetoutgrains; Bourgogne Aligoté de Bouzeron; Givry; Mercurey; Montagny; Mâcon; Mâcon-Villages; Mâcon + village name (may be used by 42 specified villages, e.g. Mâcon-Viré, Mâcon-Lugny, Mâcon-Clessé); Pouilly-Fuissé; Pouilly-Loché; Pouilly-Vinzelles; St-Véran; Rully.

Style Dry whites are soft, but with good acidity, and can achieve a fair degree of richness in good years and in the hands of the right producer. For example, the intense, richly flavoured Château Fuissé Vieilles Vignes, with its delicious creamy-vanilla and honey aromas, can match many whites from the Côte d'Or. Virtually no sweet white is produced, though Jean Thevenet has made small quantities of a botrytized white at Mâcon in hot years. Reds are – at best – generally light-bodied with soft raspberry fruit; white Mâcons from named villages have greater depth and complexity and should, but often do not, offer excellent value.

Climate Drier than the Côte d'Or, these more southerly regions enjoy some Mediterranean influences.

Cultivation Gentle rolling hills with clay, alluvial and iron deposits covering a limestone subsoil. All the red vines of the Côte Chalonnaise are planted on hillsides.

Grape varieties Pinot Noir, Gamay, Aligoté and Chardonnay.

Production/maturation Similar to the Côte de Beaune in that the very top whites are barrel-fermented. Most, though, are fermented in stainless steel and bottled early to retain acidity and freshness. Reds are vinified using the *macération carbonique* technique.

Longevity *Whites*: Mâcon-Villages and lesser wines: up to 4 years. Montagny, Mercurey, Rully, Pouilly-Fuissé: 4–12 years; *Reds*: Mâcon-Villages and lesser wines: up to 6 years. Mercurey, Rully, Mercurey *Premiers Crus*: 5–15 years.

Vintage guide *Reds*: 83, 85, 88, 89, 90, 92, 93. *Whites*: 85, 88, 89, 90, 91, 92, 93.

My Top 29 *Aligoté de Bouzeron*: A & P Villaine, Chanzy; *Mercurey*: Faiveley, Antonin Rodet, Juillot, de Suremain; *Rully*: Jadot, Antonin Rodet, Chanzy, Cogny, Domaine de la Folie; *Givry*: Joblot, Thénard; *Montagny*: Louis Latour, Michel, Vachet; *Mâconnais*: Jean Thevenet, Georges Duboeuf, Louis Latour, André Bonhomme, Henri Goyard, Château de Viré; *Pouilly-Fuissé*: Château Fuissé/Marcel Vincent, Domaine Ferret, Luquet, Noblet, Guffens-Heynen, Léger-Plumet; *St Véran*: Corsin, Lycée Viticole.

For good white, travel a little further to the hillside village of Montagny where they make nothing else. Of at least basic Chablis quality, though with a slightly nuttier, more buttery richness, this is another good buy. But don't get taken in by the words "*Premier Cru*" on the label; they only indicate a higher natural alcohol level.

Montagny is the southernmost *Appellation* of the Côte Chalonnaise, but in the unrecognized village of Buxy, the go-ahead co-operative produces large quantities of good Bourgogne Rouge, including some that has been matured in new oak.

THE MACONNAIS

The region of Mâcon has one of the longest-established wine traditions in Burgundy – Ausonius, the Roman poet who was born in Bordeaux, wrote about it in the fourth century and, in 1660, a grower called Claude Brosse travelled to Versailles and introduced it to the court. Brosse, it is said, was a giant who was noticed in church by the king when, because of his height, he appeared not to be kneeling.

In Brosse's day – and even in the last century – the region was thrice as big as it is today. Now, it's very varied in its agriculture; the fields surrounding the savage hill of Solutré, over which primitive man chased hundreds of horses in religious ritual, are now inhabited by goats and creamy-white

Charolais cattle. The main style here used to be dull red, made from the Gamay, but without using the *macération carbonique* technique. Today, however, two-thirds of the vineyards have been given over to Chardonnay. Mâcon Blanc and the rather better Mâcon-Villages are many people's idea of affordable white Burgundy. Both these wines can be perfectly pleasant but, made in large quantities by 15 co-operatives, they are rarely exciting – and they still cost Burgundian prices.

Ignore the suffix "*Supérieur*" which merely refers to the wine's strength. Look instead for Mâcons from communes such as Lugny, Prissé and Viré and Chardonnay (the last thought to be the grape's birthplace), which can tack their names onto the Mâcon *Appellation*, and particularly Clessé, where the Domaine de la Bongran produces extraordinary Sauternes-style, late-harvest Chardonnay.

The wines of St-Véran should be a cut above these Mâcon villages, but they're not. A relatively recent *Appellation*, created as an alternative for wines which might otherwise call themselves Beaujolais Blanc, this is often seen as a cheaper alternative to Pouilly-Fuissé. It can indeed outclass poor Pouilly-Fuissé, but can't compete with one that's half-way good.

Pouilly-Fuissé's problem (the inhabitants wouldn't call it a problem) is its inexplicable ease of pronunciation by Anglo-Saxons. At its best, made and oak-aged at the Château Fuissé or Domaine

Suprèmes de Volaille à l'Epinard et au Fromage

Chicken breasts stuffed with spinach and cheese

*T*he lighter meats that go so well with Beaujolais are also suitable for the wines of the Mâconnais. Ham, veal and chicken are equally good with either the whites or the reds.

SERVES 4

8 oz/225g fresh spinach, washed and stemmed, or an equal weight of frozen leaf spinach
2 tbsp double cream
Salt and freshly ground black pepper
4 chicken breasts, beaten flat to an even thickness of about 5 mm
4 slices of Gruyère or Emmenthal cheese, cut to the size of the flattened chicken breasts
1 oz/25g butter

In a large saucepan, steam the fresh spinach with only the water remaining on its leaves from washing until it is just wilted (if using frozen, heat thoroughly until most of the moisture is evaporated). Squeeze it as dry as possible and chop. Combine it with the cream and season with salt and pepper. Divide the spinach mixture equally between the chicken breasts and spread in an even layer. Place a slice of cheese on top and roll up the breasts, securing each one with a wooden toothpick. In a frying pan, heat the butter until the foam subsides and cook the breasts, turning occasionally, for about 12 minutes or until they are browned and cooked through. Serve with whole baked tomatoes, first coated with olive oil and rolled in dried thyme.

Ferret, its wines do deserve their international fame and Meursault-level prices; they can be wonderfully ripe, at once peachy and nuttily spicy – and quite "serious". Far too much, however, is made in bulk to be sold to people who don't notice that they are paying through the nose for stuff that tastes no better than Mâcon-Villages.

Bargain hunters are often pointed toward the wines of Pouilly-Vinzelles and Pouilly-Loché, but the harvest of both *Appellations* is unambitiously vinified by the Loché co-operative and sold as Pouilly-Vinzelles whichever commune the grapes come from. The style and quality is like that of St-Véran.

Pouilly-Fuissé: *Too often over-produced, over-hyped and over-priced*

BEAUJOLAIS

I HAVE A SURE-FIRE way of spotting a wine snob – just ask him what he thinks of Beaujolais. If his nose turns up by as much as a millimetre, you know that you're talking to a label-lover, to someone who cares more about what the wine is called than about the way it tastes. Because that's what Beaujolais – and most especially Beaujolais Nouveau, the target of some of the sniffiest disdain – ought to be all about: taste. It should quite simply be the tastiest, fruitiest red wine of them all, stuff for gulping back by the chilled glassful and enjoying without snobbery or inhibitions.

But Beaujolais has been misunderstood for a long time. For over 200 years, from the time vines were first planted on the gentle hills of this region in the seventeenth century, this was a wine that rarely saw a bottle; it was driven up to Lyon in a cart and shipped up to Paris by river and canal, to be drawn directly from the barrel and served from jugs over the zinc-topped bars of cafés in both cities.

It was when it reached other countries that Beaujolais was found wanting; this purple-red cherry juice was nothing like what British, Belgian and Dutch wine-drinkers thought of as "real" wine. It wasn't alcoholic enough, it was too vibrantly fruity, and its colour was wrong.

So, they – or the merchants from whom they were buying the Beaujolais – turned it into "real" wine, quite simply by dosing it up with a good dollop of red from North Africa or the Rhône. Served at room temperature, from a bottle with a label, Beaujolais became just another soft, anonymous red.

Its proud producers quite naturally took exception to this "everyday" image. In the 1960s, the drum-beats of revolution were heard when the wine-makers, co-operatives and merchants of the region, led by pioneers like Georges Duboeuf, began to take control of their wine – and their destiny.

For many people, it took some time to get used to the new style, and to the idea that it was, and still is, best drunk young and chilled. It is quite possible that the flavour would never have really caught on, but for the invention of a marvellous marketing gimmick: Beaujolais Nouveau.

For around 20 years, this instant release of wine made from grapes picked a few weeks earlier has focused international attention on the region's wine and enabled producers to raise prices to levels way above those asked for basic Bordeaux. Today, thanks in part to those prices, the novelty of Nouveau has worn thin: at one time half the region's wine was sold in this form, now it's a still impressive one bottle in three.

THE STYLES

Beaujolais is the basic stuff, well over half of which is sold within weeks of the harvest as Beaujolais Nouveau or Primeur, which is exactly the same as any other kind of Beaujolais but made to be ready to drink early. After New Year's Eve, wine merchants and producers can legally relabel any unsold Nouveau or Primeur as plain Beaujolais.

Wines labelled Beaujolais-Villages come from vineyards surrounding a select group of better-sited communes; they are usually worth their slightly higher price. Some Beaujolais-Villages Nouveau is also made and this, too, is usually a cut above plain Nouveau.

Beaujolais Blanc is very rare – for the simple reason that most is quite legally sold as St-Véran. Whatever the label, this is pleasant Chardonnay; a tad better than most Mâcon-Villages.

THE CRU VILLAGES

These 10 communes make better wine than the Beaujolais villages further north. There are no *Premiers Crus* within these communes, but there are quite certainly vineyards with their own characteristics;

The Essentials
BEAUJOLAIS

What to look for Fresh, fruity reds with vibrant cherry fruit.
Official quality AOCs: Beaujolais; Beaujolais Supérieur; Beaujolais-Villages; Coteaux du Lyonnais. There are 10 named *cru* villages – Brouilly; Chénas; Chiroubles; Côte de Brouilly; Fleurie; Juliénas; Morgon; Moulin-à-Vent; Regnié; St Amour.
Style Reds are soft, full of attractive, juicy raspberry fruit with smooth, supple character and fresh acidity. Generic Beaujolais, made by the *macération carbonique* method, has a characteristic "pear-drop" aroma. *Cru* wines are firmer, more complex and compact. White Beaujolais is rare; the best – often sold as St-Véran – is dry and peachy.
Climate A temperate continental climate with temperatures and rainfall that are ideal for wine-growing, although the influence of the Mediterranean leads to the occasional storm and problematic hail.
Cultivation Traditional, on rolling hills of granite-based soils. Vines are "spur-trained" following a single main branch for plain Beaujolais; *villages* and *cru* vines follow the "gobelet" bush pattern and the fruit is generally hand-harvested.

Grape varieties The dominant red grape is the Gamay; Pinot Noir may be used in *cru* wines, though it never does as well here as it does further north. Whites are from the Chardonnay.
Production/maturation The *macération carbonique* method is widely used although *cru* Beaujolais producers frequently employ traditional vinification methods. Experiments are now being carried out with new oak for the *crus* by go-ahead producers like Duboeuf.
Longevity Generic Beaujolais – including Nouveau – is intended for early consumption (within two years). *Crus* are capable of ageing for up to 10 years – up to 15 in great vintages like 1983 and 1985. With age, these wines become more Burgundian in style – but seldom, it must be said, like terribly good Burgundy.
Vintage guide 85, 88, 89, 90, 94, 95.
My Top 22 Georges Duboeuf, Château de la Plume, Domaine Jambon, Domaine Labruyère, Louis Tête, Château des Jacques, Jacques Depagneux, Chanut, Sylvain Fessy, Eventail, André Large, Jean Garlon, Champagnon, Janodet, Foillard, Château du Moulin à Vent, La Tour du Bief, Trichard, Chauvet, Charvet, Hospices de Beaujeu, Château des Tours.

Simple cru: Chiroubles is best drunk young and fresh

just compare a Fleurie La Madone with one from the Pointe du Jour.

Similarly, wine-making styles vary, from wines that are light, fruity and made for immediate consumption to fuller-bodied, longer-vatted, traditionally fermented wines which seem to want to be taken as seriously as Burgundy.

Chiroubles is classically the lightest Beaujolais *cru* and the one to offer at any blind tasting as the best example of what young Beaujolais is supposed to be. But drink it young. Wonderfully named, Fleurie really can smell and taste the way you'd imagine a wine made from a bowlful of flowers immersed in plenty of cherry juice.

Another glorious name – taken from that of a Roman centurion – is St Amour, as romantic as it sounds, though it's a surprisingly little-known *cru*.

Brouilly is less exciting – up-market Beaujolais-Villages sold at Beaujolais *cru* prices. The vineyards are too big, too flat and too far south to compete with the best. Better to spend just a little more on Côte de Brouilly, produced on the volcanic hillside in the middle of the Brouilly vines; it's just as fruity, but richer and longer-lasting.

Regnié is controversial because it was only recently promoted to *cru* status. Some examples do support its case for promotion, but more taste like good Beaujolais-Villages, the label under which it was previously sold. Chénas has never been an easy sale – indeed much of the small amount of wine made here has, in the past, legally been sold by Beaune merchants as Bourgogne Rouge. Its style is – for a Beaujolais – rather tough, particularly when young.

Juliénas isn't immediately seductive but, like Chénas, can be an ugly duckling that needs three years or so to develop into a splendid swan.

There isn't a village of Moulin à Vent, but there is still a windmill. The vineyards make some of the richest, most "serious" wines in the region. Drink a bottle at two or three years old and you'll enjoy its cherryish, chocolatey flavour.

Another "big" Beaujolais, Morgon, has even given its name to a verb – *morgonner* – which describes the way the wine develops a cherryish flavour that, with time, really does vaguely resemble wine from the Côte de Nuits.

Just to the south of the Beaujolais, there are the Coteaux du Lyonnais, which produce lightweight versions of that region's wines and some pleasant, fruity rosé.

The way the wind blows: *The windmill at Moulin-à-Vent*

Jambon à la Crème de Bourgogne

Ham in a cream and mushroom sauce

The fruity tang of a chilled glass of young Beaujolais goes particularly well with the ham and cream combination of this simple and absolutely delicious Burgundian dish.

SERVES 4

4 good thick slices of cooked ham
Sauce
1 medium onion, minced
2 juniper berries, crushed
6 tbsp white wine vinegar
2 tbsp butter
2 tbsp plain flour
10 fl oz/275 ml chicken stock, heated
8 tbsp dry white wine
2 oz/50 g mushrooms, thinly sliced
Salt and freshly ground black pepper
10 fl oz/275 ml double cream
2 tbsp dried breadcrumbs
Knob of butter

Put the ham slices into a shallow ovenproof dish. In a saucepan, simmer the onions and juniper berries in the wine vinegar until the liquid has evaporated. Remove from the heat. In another pan, melt the butter and stir in the flour, cooking gently and stirring until the mixture just begins to brown. Gradually pour in the stock, little by little, stirring constantly. Add the wine, the onion and juniper berries and the mushrooms and cook over a low heat, stirring occasionally, for 30 minutes. In a small saucepan, bring the cream to the boil and remove from heat. Add the knob of butter and stir. Add the cream to the sauce, stir and pour over the ham. Sprinkle with breadcrumbs and grill until golden brown. Serve with boiled new potatoes and young peas.

𝒯HE LOIRE

𝓘F SOMEONE were handing out prizes for Most Half-Understood Region in France, the Loire would get my nomination. How many diners in smart restaurants, ordering an obligatory Sancerre to go with their monkfish, know that they could have had the pigeon instead – and washed it down with a red Sancerre, made from the same grape as Nuits-St-Georges? How many Nouveau fans realize that there are wine-makers in the Loire using the Gamay to make red wines that could make some Beaujolais blush? How many restaurateurs offer sweet white Loires as alternatives to their Sauternes?

The best way to explore the Loire is to get in a car at Nantes in Muscadet country, and to head along the river toward Sancerre. At the end of a long and somewhat tortuous journey, you'd have tasted wines made from the Chardonnay, the improbably named Melon de Bourgogne, the Chenin Blanc, the Sauvignon Blanc, the Pinot Noir, the Gamay, the Cabernet Franc and the Malbec. In other words, you'd have discovered wines that are directly related to Champagne, to red and white Burgundy, to Bordeaux and Cahors, but all with their own distinctive styles. Some, like most of the Muscadet pro-duced nowadays, are wines to be taken more or less for granted; others, like Savennières and dry Vouvray can be among the most exciting – and demanding – in the world.

MUSCADET

If Muscadet has a red cousin, it has to be Beaujolais. Both are light, easy-going and perfect to drink within a few months of the harvest, and they've both come a long way from where they started out. A hundred years ago neither wine would have found its way into a bottle; Muscadet's the stuff Brittany fishermen and poor Montmartre artists would have been given by the jugful as basic "house white".

Since then, like Beaujolais, Muscadet has become an international star. Sometimes it's difficult to understand why. New Beaujolais tastes of a bowlful of fresh fruit, while Muscadet tastes of … well, it's rather difficult to define precisely what it does taste of. Eventually, it is all too easy to fall back on

Any colour as long as it's white: *Wine for sale in Muscadet*

the description of it as prototypical "dry white wine".

But Muscadet matured in a certain way can have its own, distinctive character. Most newly fermented white wine is removed from its lees – solid yeasts – as quickly as possible; good, typical Muscadet is left to sit for several months on this yeast, picking up a nutty, biscuity flavour and a slight fizz in the process. Unfortunately, until the rules were tightened up in the early 1990s, there

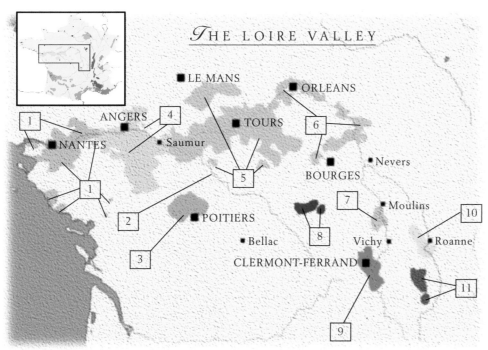

1	Pays Nantais
2	River Loire
3	Haut-Poitou
4	Anjou-Saumur
5	Touraine
6	Central Vineyards
7	St Pourçain
8	Châteaumeillant
9	Côtes d'Auvergne
10	Côtes Roannaises
11	Côtes du Forez

The Essentials
MUSCADET

What to look for Fresh, young, zingy white alternative to modern, "fruit-driven" Chardonnay and Sauvignon.
Location The Pays Nantais; a 40km sweep around Nantes encompassing the Loire estuary.
Official quality AOCs are: Muscadet; Muscadet Côtes de Grand Lieu; Muscadet de Sèvre et Maine (which, though officially the best part of the region, actually covers 85 per cent of its overall area); Muscadet des Coteaux de la Loire. All may be bottled, and bear the designation, *sur lie*. VDQSs are: Gros Plant du Pays Nantais; Coteaux d'Ancenis and Fiefs Vendéens.
Style Whites are crisp and dry, light-bodied and modestly fruity, occasionally slightly *pétillant*. The best are bone-dry (but not tart), lemony and fresh. *Sur lie* wines should have a yeasty, more complex character; Muscadet de Sèvre et Maine should be better than straight Muscadet. Coteaux d'Ancenis and Fiefs Vendéens reds and rosés are dry, light-to-medium-bodied, lively and often grassy.
Climate Maritime.
Cultivation On the flat land around Nantes mechanical harvesting has been introduced with ease. The vineyard area stretches away to the gentle Sèvre et Maine hills; soils are mainly sandy overlying schist and volcanic subsoils.
Grape varieties Primarily the white Muscadet (Melon de Bourgogne) and Folle Blanche (Gros Plant). Coteaux d'Ancenis and the Fiefs Vendéens use a mix of Loire and classic Bordeaux and Burgundian varieties for reds, rosés and whites.
Production/maturation Stainless steel is increasingly used for fermentation. *Sur lie* wines are aged on their lees – yeasts – until, traditionally, the February 15 following the harvest; the process by which the yeasts affect the wine's character is known as autolysis. Bottling is direct from the tank; new oak is very occasionally found.
Longevity Most of these wines are best young or in their first 2 years.
Vintage guide 94, 95.
My Top 10 Bossard, Sauvion et Fils, Donatien Bahuaud, Luneau, Chéreau-Carré, Louis Métaireau, Marquis de Goulaine, Domaines de la Dimerie, Chasseloir, des Dorices.

were far more bottles of Muscadet which claimed to have been "*mis en bouteilles sur lie*" – bottled on their lees – than had the biscuity flavour those words theoretically ought to promise.

Like Beaujolais, there are a few key villages that make better, more characterful wine than the surrounding area. Unlike Beaujolais, they don't feature helpfully on the labels as *crus*. So, as elsewhere in France, it is essential to look for the name of the producer. But if you've got a plate of fresh Atlantic oysters in prospect, it's worth taking the trouble; good, fresh, young Muscadet will do them far more justice than many a smarter Chardonnay or Sauvignon.

Oaked and Aged Muscadet

At the Château de Chasseloir, the Domaine Chéreau-Carré, one of the best in the region, has proved that good Muscadet can taste even better with a little ageing in oak. Other producers complain that Muscadet and oak don't mix. The debate between the two camps is fierce; I tend to agree, though, that the innate neutrality of the Melon de Bourgogne grape makes it all too easy for the flavour of the wood to dominate the wine.

Another argument in the region is over the ageability of Muscadet. Many of the best estates proudly like to uncork 10-year-old bottles in precisely the same way – and to much the same effect – as Beaujolais producers opening venerable examples of Beaujolais-Villages. There are exceptions to the rule, of course, but generally, all these bottles prove is that good Muscadet doesn't die after five years in the cellar; most taste convincingly like old white Burgundy, but not like particularly *good* old white Burgundy.

River of wine: *Barrels at Château de Chenonceau in Touraine*

Mussels a l'Armoricaine

Mussels in an onion and tomato sauce

The wine grown here, around the estuary of the Loire as it enters the Atlantic, was made for shellfish, especially oysters. But if you cannot get oysters, this recipe for mussels complements these crisp white wines beautifully.

SERVES 4 AS A MAIN COURSE

6½ lb/3 kg mussels
2 oz/50 g butter
1 medium onion, coarsely chopped
3 large tomatoes, seeded, peeled and chopped
or a 16 oz/500 g tin of tomatoes,
drained and chopped
Freshly ground black pepper

Scrub the mussels and remove the small blackish tassle (the "beard"). Soak in frequent changes of clean cold water for several hours, discarding any which have opened or are cracked or broken. Melt the butter in a large heavy-bottomed pan. Sauté the onion until it is transparent. Add the tomatoes and the mussels. Cook covered, shaking the pan occasionally, until the mussels have opened (discard any that do not open). Season with pepper and serve, perhaps with crusty French bread and a green salad.

And if you're in France and you want something even simpler with which to wash down your seafood, you could always save a few francs by buying the Nantes region's lesser white, Gros Plant. This bone-dry VDQS, made from the Folle Blanche, is generally even less fruity than the Muscadet. When well made *sur lie*, however, it can give some stale Muscadets a run for their money.

Other regional VDQS wines include the light red, rosé and white Coteaux d'Ancenis, often made from the Gamay, the Pinot Gris (here called the Malvoisie) and the Chenin Blanc (or Pineau de la Loire), and the Fiefs Vendéens, with its attractive dry rosé, Cabernet-influenced red and less dazzling dry white.

THE MIDDLE LOIRE

ANJOU

FOLLOWING THE river Loire eastwards through a vinous no-man's-land surrounding the village of Ancenis, within a few miles you will be deep in the heart of one of the most abused wine *Appellations* in France – Anjou, the area that helped to give the colour pink such a bad name that the Californians had to rename their rosé as "white" or "blush".

In fact, Anjou Rosé is also a relatively modern invention, created earlier this century by wine-makers who found they were unable to sell their dry red wines.

In the Loire, though, the change of style must have come as a shock to those used to the red and white wines Anjou had been producing for nearly 2,000 years. In the sixteenth and seventeenth centuries the Dutch had developed a taste for the region's sweet whites. As buyers, they were evidently more quality-conscious than some of today's customers for Anjou Rosé; in those days, the region's wines were divided into *vins pour la mer* (the stuff that was considered good enough for foreigners) and *vins pour Paris* (the dregs, kept back for the easy-going domestic market).

The innovative Bordeaux-born wine-maker Jacques Lurton proved that it is possible to make interesting dry Anjou Rosé but even that effort displayed the hard-edged shortcomings of the Groslot grape. Pay a little more for the potentially far better Cabernet d'Anjou (one of the few rosés which genuinely does age), or the slightly lighter Cabernet de Saumur from just along the river. At their best, these pink wines are crunchily blackcurranty, as is Anjou Rouge when it is made from the Cabernet varieties. When Anjou Rouge is made from the Gamay, however, and by the same method as Beaujolais, the effort to match that more southerly wine rarely quite works – because neither climate nor soil suit the grape so well here. Look instead for Anjou-Villages, which can only be made from the Cabernets and can taste like good summer-picnic claret.

FROM PINK TO WHITE

Anjou Blanc provides a good introduction to the often difficult character of the Chenin Blanc. Throughout the region, modern wine-makers are learning to work with the Chenin, allowing the skins to remain in contact with the juice before fermentation or, in Anjou, adding a proportion of Chardonnay or Sauvignon Blanc to the blend. These wines range from bone-dry to intensely sweet and from dire

Safely gathered in: Harvest time at Roche aux Moines in Anjou

Flowing sweetly: Conditions at Rochefort-sur-Loire allow sweet wines to be made almost every year

to delicious; they can be inexpensive, fresh and clean tasting and a good showcase for the Chenin hallmarks of apple and honey. Pure Chenin Blancs of slightly higher quality are labelled Anjou Coteaux de la Loire; these can be good, cheaper alternatives to Vouvray.

For top-class sweet wines, though, turn your back on the Loire and visit a set of villages that face each other across the River Layon, surrounded by vineyards that produce rich, honeyed, semi-sweet-to-luscious Chenin appropriately called Coteaux du Layon. The best of these villages, Rochefort-sur-Loire, has a micro-climate that allows the grapes to ripen almost every year, and sometimes to develop noble rot, thus producing a pair of more intense wines: Coteaux du Layon Chaume and Quarts de Chaume, which owes its name to the local lord who used to extort a quarter of the tiny harvests.

At their best, these wines are at once apricotty, rich and floral, with a surprisingly attractive hint of zesty bitterness; they can keep for at least 10 – more like 20 – years. Bonnezeaux (disconcertingly pronounced "Bonzo"), though often as well thought of, is rarely quite as good. The few great examples, however, are extraordinary honey-and-spice cocktails that last for decades.

For a lower price than any of these, and built on a lighter scale, Coteaux de l'Aubance provides good, cellarable, *demi-sec* Chenin Blanc – but in small and diminishing quantities.

The sweet style of these wines was once shared by Savennières which is now made dry or *demi-sec*. It's "difficult" wine that can often taste bitterly like unripe limes until it

has been given a decade or so to soften; of 15 producers, only five survive by making and selling wine alone. One of these, Nicolas Joly, proves what can be done here using biodynamic methods with his fruit-and-flower, dry Sauternes-like *Grand Cru* Coulée de Serrant, which slightly outclasses Savennières' other larger *Grand Cru*, La Roche aux Moines.

SAUMUR

Saumur once enjoyed the same prestige as Vouvray, but today neither the white nor the red produced under this *Appellation* is inspiring, and sparkling wine has become the focus of attention. Links with Champagne go back to 1811, when a wine-maker called Jean Ackerman, who had worked there, decided to use its techniques on grapes grown in the similarly chalky soil of his native Saumur. His wine was sold as Champagne; today the rules are stricter, yet Champagne houses like Bollinger and Taittinger own sparkling Saumur houses here, making fizz labelled until very recently with the now-banned words "méthode champenoise".

Even at its best, sparkling Saumur never really matches even the most modestly successful of Champagnes, largely because the Chenin Blanc and the red Cabernet grapes simply aren't as good at the job as the Chardonnay and Pinots. On the other hand, the quality is rarely less than adequate, thanks to the combination of the Chenin, the chalky soil and the cool(ish) climate. Coteaux de Saumur, Saumur's *Appellation*

Rillettes

Potted pork pâté

This land of châteaux and tranquil rivers has often been called the garden of France. Pike, bream, salmon and carp abound in the Loire River and its tributaries. *Andouillette* (a tripe sausage), *boudin de volaille* (a sausage made of chicken breast, truffles and mushrooms) and *rillettes* (a delicious and easily made country pâté) are just some typical dishes of this beautiful region.

SERVES 8–10 AS A STARTER

2 lb/1 kg belly pork, cut into thick strips
2 juniper berries, crushed
2 garlic cloves, peeled and halved
Bouquet garni sachet, or a bundle made of 1 sprig of rosemary,
2 sprigs parsley and 1 bay leaf tied together with cotton
Salt and freshly ground black pepper

Put at least 5 mm of water into a heavy-bottomed casserole dish. Add the pork, juniper berries, garlic and bouquet garni. Cook, covered, in an oven at 300°F/150°C/Gas mark 2 for 4–5 hours until the meat is very soft. Allow to cool slightly and pour the contents into a sieve over a large bowl. When drained, shred the lean meat off with two forks. Season the meat well with salt and pepper and put into small bowls (individual ramekins are useful). Pour over the reserved juices until the meat is completely covered. Cover each bowl with foil and refrigerate when cool enough. Serve with crusty French bread and gherkins, or as a more substantial lunch dish with crisp green salad and new potatoes.

for its sweet wines, was once the priciest in the Loire, partly thanks to the enthusiasm of Edward VII, a loyal customer, and partly to the reputation of the curious Clos des Murs, a set of 11 100-metre-long walls along which vines were trained to obtain as much sheltered sunshine as possible. Today, sadly, examples are very, very rare, but the vineyard is still worth a visit.

Apart from its sparkling and still whites and pinks, Saumur also produces two reds, Saumur Rouge and Saumur Champigny. The former is rarely impressive Cabernet Franc-dominated stuff. Champigny, however, is much classier – either young, or after five years or so (though not between the two), this can be gorgeously crunchy, black-currant wine. To taste Saumur Champigny at its best, look out for Filliatreau's Vieilles Vignes, made from old vines.

South of Saumur, in stark contrast to the

Summer wine: The River Loire flowing through the centre of Anjou

small scale of some of the region's estates, there stands the Loire's biggest modern co-operative, the Cave du Haut Poitou. The success here has been the Sauvignon Blanc, a wine that has on occasion shown the potential to fight its corner against pricier examples from Sancerre but it still never rises above workaday levels. The Chardonnay is less impressive, but there is a reliable *méthode champenoise* sparkling wine.

The modest and little-known VDQS, Vin du Thouarsais, similar in style to basic Anjou, but slightly cheaper, certainly deserves a backward glance as one crosses the frontier into the next of the Loire's major regions.

TOURAINE

If Touraine had no other claim to vinous fame, it would have been sure of a place in the history books because it was here that, according to local legend, St Martin invented vine-pruning, after discovering that he made better wine from vines that had been partially nibbled away by his donkey.

Today, the region owes much of the success of its blanket *Appellation* to the Oisly et Thesée co-operative whose *directeur*, Jacques Choquet, took the rare and brave step of enforcing a quality test for

his member-growers' grapes. His audacity was all the more impressive given the ever-present financial temptations to the producers to uproot their vines and replace them with other crops. Oisly et Thesée Sauvignon and Chenin (here called Pineau de la Loire) are among the most reliably affordable whites in the region, and the blended reds are also worthwhile, thanks to the way in which the Cabernet is allowed to make up for the failings of the Malbec (here known as the Cot) and the Gamay. Experiments with Pinot Noir and sparkling wine are interesting too.

The Touraine vineyards cover around a tenth of the land they would have occupied a century or so ago. It is a striking polyculture, with easy-to-grow, easy-to-sell strawberries, sun-flowers, asparagus and wheat all competing for space on level terms with vines. From a distance, the layers of gold, yellow and green crops make the countryside here look like nothing so much as a slice of vegetable terrine. The Touraine *Appellation* – and its three village *Appellations*, Azay-Le-Rideau, Amboise and Mesland – can produce fair to excellent dry and *demi-sec* Chenin Blanc and, in the case of Amboise, good, fruity Cabernet Franc.

Non-wine-buff visitors to the region are often unknowingly led by their guide books to the source of the Loire's best reds, Chinon whose castle some readers may remember from the play or film of *The Lion in Winter*. Almost all of Chinon's wines are red, combining – in ripe years – rich flavours of mulberry, blackberry and blackcurrant,

with just a hint of earthiness. There is a little rosé and white, the latter made in a floral-spicy style said to have been popular with Rabelais.

Like Chinon, red Bourgueil is built to last and can take as long as a decade to soften. But in good vintages it's worth waiting for, delivering a real mouthful of wonderfully jammy damson and black-currant fruit. St-Nicolas-de-Bourgueil is usually less impressive, less intense and less long-lived but can be more approachable than Bourgueil when young.

VOUVRAY

Before my first visit to Vouvray, I had never quite believed in the tales I had heard of the town's community of cave dwellers. But there they were – modern Frenchmen and women who not only make and store wine, but also live in homes burrowed deep into the sides of cliffs. Of course, these are twentieth-century troglodytes, with video recorders, shiny new Citroëns and central heating flues channelled up through the chalk, but there is still something deeply traditional about their wines.

Vouvray comes in just about every white style you could want – and several you wouldn't. But whatever they are like – dry

HONEY, NUTS AND APPLE

*I*f the Chenin Blanc were only used to make dry wine, it would probably have been relegated to the ranks of "potentially good but difficult" varieties, along with such other non-household names as the Marsanne and Arneis. It certainly wouldn't feature among the world's greats. There are two problems associated with the Chenin. First, there's the Chenin's tendency to produce an unpalatable gluey smell and taste when, as often, it is subjected to an over-generous dose of sulphur dioxide by heavy-handed wine-makers. And second, there's the reluctance of this variety to ripen in any but the best sites and warmest years. Even given those ideal conditions, it can still produce wines with tooth-scaling, appley acidity or a dull nuttiness which is the opposite of refreshing.

In good examples, however, the acidity can be balanced by a unique honeyed character to produce some of the most extraordinary white wines in the world. Everything depends on the ripeness of the vintage and the skill of the wine-maker.

Stone age: *The same limestone rock gives character and longevity to many Loire wines*

(*sec*), semi-sweet (*demi-sec*), sweet (*moëlleux*) or sparkling (*crémant*) – they provide an invaluable insight into what the Chenin Blanc is really like. And how difficult it is to get right. The dry style can have all the mean, cooking-apple character of the grape, while the *demi-sec* and *moëlleux* can be respectively honeyed and dull, and sweetly honeyed and dull. At its least successful, semi-sweet Vouvray can make you long for a glass of fairly basic Liebfraumilch.

Then, just as you decide to drive further west to Sancerre, you stop and have lunch at a little roadside restaurant, order a last bottle – and discover what the estate made famous by the mayor of the village, Gaston Huët (pronounced "wet"), or the Domaine des Aubuisiers can do with the Chenin Blanc. Suddenly both wine and grape make sense. These Vouvray *secs* have the rich, creamy texture of Chardonnay and the appley bite of the Chenin. The *demi-secs* are beautifully well balanced – sweet but not cloyingly so – and the *moëlleux* have the luscious intensity of noble rot. All of these, but particularly the *moëlleux*, are made to last – "for 50 years or so" as they say in Vouvray.

Huët also makes great sparkling wine. Bubbles are very saleable around here – as the producers of nearby Montlouis have

discovered to their delight. Turning their back on the still wines they used to make lighter, less acidic, less long-lived versions of Vouvray, they have switched to sparkling wine, so successfully that of the 4.2 million bottles of Montlouis made every year, only 700,000 come without bubbles.

Having come to terms with dry Chenin Blanc in Vouvray, you could put yourself to a further test with Jasnières, a wine that can be so bitingly acidic in cool years that only a masochist or a drinker with a palate lined with elephant hide could enjoy it. But, in

warmer vintages, and – this is essential – given a decade or so in the bottle, Jasnières can be one of the most exciting, dry yet honeyed, wines of all.

Of the region's other wines, VDQS Chéverny can be good, lightly floral, still and sparkling white, despite the presence in the blend of the "characterful" Romarantin, which seems to work against the fresh appeal of the Sauvignon, Chenin and Chardonnay with which it shares the vat. Sales are growing fast, though this owes much to buyers confusing it with Chardonnay.

The Essentials
THE MIDDLE LOIRE

What to look for Honeyed late-harvest and dry Chenin Blanc whites; crunchy young Cabernet-based reds, some of which age surprisingly well; sparkling wines.

Location Surrounding the Loire River and its tributaries, particularly the Cher, largely between Angers and Tours.

Official quality AOCs: Anjou; Anjou Coteaux de la Loire; Anjou Gamay; Anjou Mousseux; Cabernet d'Anjou and Cabernet d'Anjou-Val-de-Loire; Rosé d'Anjou and Rosé d'Anjou Pétillant; Bonnezeaux; Bourgueil; Chinon; Coteaux de l'Aubance, Coteaux du Loire; Coteaux du Layon and Coteaux du Layon-Chaume; Crémant de Loire; Jasnières; Montlouis; sparkling Montlouis; Quarts de Chaume; Rosé de Loire; Saumur, Saumur Champigny, sparkling Saumur; Cabernet de Saumur, Coteaux de Saumur; Savennières; Savennières-Coulée-de-Serrant and Savennières-Roche-aux-Moines; St-Nicolas-de-Bourgueil; Touraine; Touraine-Amboise; Touraine-Azay-le-Rideau; Touraine-Mesland; sparkling Touraine; Vouvray; sparkling Vouvray. VDQSs and *vins de pays*: Cheverny; Coteaux du Vendômois; Valençay; Vin du Haut Poitou; Vin du Thouarsais. *Vin de pays* du Jardin de la France.

Style The Cabernet Franc produces cool reds which have clean, blackcurrant fruit and an appealing herbaceous freshness. The best are undoubtedly Chinon, Bourgueil and Saumur-Champigny. Though pleasant when young, these tend to need ageing to lose their early earthiness. The dry and medium white wines are generally light, fresh and for early consumption. Savennières and Jasnières have a stark acidity in youth but open out with age into rich and honeyed, yet still dry wines; Vouvray, Quarts de Chaume and Bonnezeaux are the best sweet styles, and again need ageing, often lasting for decades. Rosés, both dry and medium, can be appealing and very fruity, though many are over-sweetened and dull. The best sparkling wines – Saumur, Vouvray and Crémant de Loire – are soft and approachable but with good acidity.

Climate Influenced by the Atlantic, though less maritime than Muscadet. Warm summers and autumns and little rain.

Cultivation Crammed between fields full of other crops in this agricultural region, the best sites are south-facing on gentle slopes or terraced on steeper slopes, as in the schist soils of the Layon valley. Elsewhere, soils vary from chalk to clay overlying sand and gravel.

Grape varieties Arbois, Aligoté, Cabernet Franc, Cabernet Sauvignon, Chambourcin, Chenin Blanc (Pineau de la Loire), Chardonnay, Gamay, Grolleau/Groslot, Gros Plant, Malbec, Meslier, Pineau d'Aunis, Pinot Blanc, Pinot Gris, Pinot Meunier, Pinot Noir, Plantet, Romorantin, Sauvignon Blanc.

Production/maturation Though old wood is still used for fermentation and maturation, stainless steel and new oak are becoming more common. To make Bonnezeaux and Quarts de Chaume, Chenin grapes are left on the vines until late October to await noble rot. Fermentation takes at least 3 months and the wines are bottled the following October.

Longevity Lesser reds, dry and medium whites and rosé should be drunk within 3 years. Chinon, Bourgueil and St-Nicolas-de-Bourgueil will last at least 5 years. Sweet Bonnezeaux, Chaume and Layon and the dry Savennières and Jasnières will develop over a decade and beyond.

Vintage guide *White*: 76, 78, 82, 83, 85, 88, 89, 90, 93, 94, 95; *Red*: 78, 82, 83, 85, 88, 89, 90, 95.

My Top 25 *Anjou*: Richou, Cailleau, Daviau, Ackerman-Laurance; *Savennières*: Clos de la Coulée-de-Serrant, Roche aux Moines, Domaine Bizolière, Château Chamboureau; *Vouvray*: Huët, Domaines des Aubuisières, Champalou, Foreau, Mabille; *Chinon*: Olga and Jean-Maurice Raffault, Couly-Dutheil, Joguet; *Bonnezeaux*: Renou, Château de Fesles; *Quarts de Chaume*: Domaine Echarderie; *Coteaux de Layon*: Vincent Ogereau, Domaine Jolivet; *Saumur*: Bouvet-Ladubay, Gratin-Meyer, Langlois-Château, Filliatreau.

THE UPPER LOIRE

WINE CAN BE as much of a victim of fashion as any reader of Vogue or Vanity Fair. It just takes a little longer. For most wine buffs, Sancerre and Pouilly are almost synonymous with the extraordinarily gooseberryish, blackcurranty, asparagussy Sauvignon Blanc. Wine-makers from around the world regularly make pilgrimages to this easternmost part of the Loire to marvel at the perfect marriage of grape, chalky soils and climate. A century or so ago, though, what they'd have found was a bulging ragbag of red-wine grapes including lots of Pinot Noir – and a few acres of featureless Chasselas.

Today, Sancerre and Pouilly-Fumé have become world-famous, easy-option whites. But this newly acquired fashionability is already proving fragile. Over the last few years both wines have lost fans to the New World. In the US, people who find the Sauvignon's innate zinginess too "herbaceous" have opted for local efforts which often taste like understudy Chardonnays.

Elsewhere, it has been the New Zealanders, South Africans, and cool-climate Australians that have become flavours of the month.

It's a pity because the best Loire Sauvignons ought to be packed with the same kind of zappy gooseberry fruit as the Sauvignons from New Zealand – but in a far less obvious way. Their steely backbone and complexity should make them more interesting to drink, long after the palate has tired of the simplicity of some of those New-World flavours.

The Loire classics have been handicapped by the readiness of the region's less commendable producers to produce dilute, over-sulphured, over-priced, soft, fat, dull versions of their wine – and by the authorities' preparedness to allow these travesties onto the market. The same authorities, mark you, who chose to obstruct one of Pouilly-Fumé's best producers, Didier Dagueneau, when he experimented with late-harvest versions of his organically produced wine. Perhaps they might have

done well to read up a little of their local history and discover how well the Upper Loire has done out of the fashion pioneers of the past.

SANCERRE

Sancerre is not so much a single *Appellation* as a collection of 14 villages with slightly differing versions of the same chalky soil, on varying slopes that surround the hill-top town itself. If this were Beaujolais, and if the inhabitants of these villages had their way, at least a few of them would be promoted to *cru* status. The strongest contenders for any such promotion are the village of Bué and a cluster of houses called Chavignol, locally famous for its little round goat's cheeses, Crottins de Chavignol, and for wines which would, it was said by the wine-loving French King Henri IV, if drunk by the entire populace, put an instant stop to religious wars. Chavignol's best wines come from its Les Monts Damnés, Clos Beaujeu and Clos du Paradis vineyards; Bué's finest vineyards are the Clos du Chêne Marchand and Le Grand Chemarin. Other villages worth looking out for include Champtin, Sury-en-Vaux, Reigny, Ménétréol and Verdigny.

Sancerre also makes small quantities of pink and red wines from its old mainstay, the Pinot Noir. The former are pleasant, raspberryish versions of the grape, but woefully overpriced, thanks – *again!* – to their fashionability in Paris restaurants; the latter have much of the style of good, basic Bourgogne Rouge, but with less stuffing.

Down on the Loire itself, the featureless town of Pouilly-sur-Loire still confuses even those wine-drinkers who know the difference between Pouilly-Fumé and Pouilly-Fuissé by using Chasselas grapes to produce an unmemorable wine called Pouilly-sur-Loire.

The "Fumé" in Pouilly-Fumé is said to come from the smoky dust from the grapes that hangs over the vineyards during the harvest or, more popularly, from the smoky flavour of the wine. I prefer the latter explanation; these wines really can taste as though they have spent a while in a salmon smokery. Some descriptions also refer to

---

The Essentials
THE UPPER LOIRE

What to look for Crisp, dry Sauvignons with the occasional light Pinot Noir red or rosé.
Location At the eastern end of the Loire Valley toward Burgundy: Sancerre and Pouilly-Fumé face each other across the river.
Official quality AOCs: Ménétou Salon; Pouilly-Fumé; Pouilly-sur-Loire; Quincy; Reuilly and Sancerre. VDQSs are: Châteaumeillant; Coteaux du Giennois; Côte Roannaise; Côtes d'Auvergne; Côtes du Forez; St-Pourçain-sur-Sioule; Vins d'Orléanais. *Vins de pays*: Coteaux du Cher et l'Arnon; Coteaux Charitois.
Style Classic Sancerre and Pouilly-Fumé rank among the most exciting Sauvignons in the world, with a smoky aroma and full of gooseberry and asparagus flavours. Bué, Chavignol, Les Loges, Tracy and Les Berthiers are noted for quality. Lesser whites may capture a little of this style and are generally crisp, herbaceous and appealing. Do not confuse Pouilly-sur-Loire. a rather ordinary Chasselas, with Pouilly-Fumé. Red and rosé wines, from Sancerre, are quite Burgundian.
Climate Continental, with short, hot summers.

Cultivation Soils are mainly chalk and clay with a lot of limestone. The vineyards are on mainly south-facing, often steep, slopes, with other crops being grown on the opposite side of the valley. Picking is usually done by hand.
Grape varieties Aligoté, Cabernet Franc, Chardonnay, Chasselas, Chenin Blanc, Gamay Noir à Jus Blanc, Gamay, Pinot Gris, Pinot Meunier, Pinot Noir, Sauvignon Blanc, Tresallier.
Production/maturation Stainless steel is widely used, although some of the red wines spend up to 18 months in oak and Didier Dagueneau is experimenting with new oak for his whites.
Longevity Most wines are at their best within 3 years. Although the top wines will continue to develop. they may lose their initial freshness.
Vintage guide 95.
My Top 22 *Sancerre:* Vacheron, Alain and Pierre Dézat, Laporte, Jean Thomas, Bourgeois, Crochet, Gitton, Jean-Max Roger, Pinard, Jean Vatan, Henri Natter; *Pouilly-Fumé:* Didier Dagueneau, Château de Nozet (Ladoucette), Pabiot, Château de Tracy; *Menetou-Salon:* Domaine H Pellé, Teiller, de Chatenoy; *Reuilly:* Lafond, Beurdin; *Quincy:* Pichard, Rouzé.

Rooms with a view: *The town of Sancerre, and its vineyards*

gun-flint and, even without having tasted any, I know what they mean; this character is reckoned to come from the flintier, lighter clay content of some of Pouilly's best slopes. To taste the mixture of smoke and flint at its best, look for wines whose labels mention *silex*, the term for this kind of soil.

Pouilly-Fumé is said to be the Loire Sauvignon with the best potential for ageing – which really means that the wines here develop their flavours of asparagus rather more slowly. With rare exceptions, though, I prefer to drink this wine, like Sancerre, within three years of the harvest.

The best of Pouilly's communes, and the ones you are most likely to see mentioned on labels, are Les Berthiers and Les Loges. For the quintessence of Pouilly-Fumé, splash out on a bottle of Didier Dagueneau's "Silex" or "Baron de L" from the Baron de Ladoucette's Château de Nozet. And remember their flavours the next time you taste a "Blanc-Fumé" from California or Australia; warm-climate Sauvignon Blanc plus new oak does not equal the sheer complexity of this variety grown in the cooler conditions and the best soil of the Loire.

Reuilly needs your support: its growers have to be encouraged to stop growing vegetables and to turn their attention back to the vines that used to cover this commune. Reuilly's soil is very similar to that of Sancerre or Pouilly-Fumé, and most of the vines are the same variety – the Sauvignon Blanc – so there seems little reason why its wines shouldn't be every bit as fine.

In fact, the slightly greater limestone content here makes for lighter, leaner wines that rarely have the richness of its more famous neighbours. What Reuilly can make, however, is that most unfashionable style, rosé, produced not (as in Sancerre) exclusively from the Pinot Noir, but with a generous dose of the pink-skinned grape known here as the Pinot Beurot and more

readily found in Alsace, where it's called the Tokay-Pinot Gris.

The small (250-acre/l00-ha) *Appellation* of Menetou-Salon has the same *terre blanche* soil as Reuilly, and an even longer history; its growers proudly yet wrily point out that Menetou-Salon had its *Appellation* before any of its neighbours. Often, the wines taste rather rustic, but at their best they can be cheaper alternatives to good – but not great – Sancerre; the Pinot Noir reds are disappointing.

Quincy should be inexpensive, ultra-gooseberryish Sauvignon Blanc, grown on the gravelly soil of vineyards overlooking the river Cher. Unfortunately, too few examples are well-enough made; too many taste raw and green, or earthy and dull.

Leaving Pouilly and heading up the river toward Odans, you pass through the VDQS vineyards of Coteaux du Giennois and Côtes de Gien on either side of the Loire. The pink produced from these grapes can be light and pleasant; the white usually tastes raw and uninteresting. Châteaumeillant's red and pink Gamay is better and the *vin gris* rosé is worth looking out for.

The wines of Orleans itself – the *vins de l'Orléanais* – were once thought equal to those of Beaune. Today they are less exalted, but the pale pink Pinot Meunier is a rare treat; the white Auvernat Blanc, however, is unimpressive. This is the local alias for the Chardonnay, though from tasting the wine you'd never guess.

Among the other lesser-known wines in this part of the Loire, the Côtes Roannaises and Côtes du Forez both make easy-going wines from the Gamay. St Pourcain Blanc is a weird blend of Chardonnay, Sauvignon and the oddly smoky Tressalier. It's very dry, and very much an acquired taste. Minuscule

quantities of Gamay-Pinot Noir rosé are made too.

Even more obscure, high among the ski slopes of the Massif Central in the Côtes d'Auvergne, the villages of Châteaugay, Chanturgues, Mandargues and Corent – make fresh white wine from the Chardonnay and light raspberryish rosé from the Gamay. There are two *vins de pays* made nearby: the Coteaux du Cher et l'Arnon, producing Sauvignon Blanc whites and red and pink wines from the Gamay; further east is the exclusively white wine region of the Coteaux Charitois. Quality is rising steadily, but there are no superstars.

THE RHONE

IT'S SOMETIMES said that the French are a Latin people but, talking to some of the starchily mannered gentlemen of Bordeaux and Champagne, it's an idea I find very difficult to accept. And then I arrive back in the Rhône, the land of terracotta roof tiles, of fresh herbs growing at the roadside, of olive oil and garlic and ripe, tasty tomatoes, and I know I'm in the land of the sun – savage country that must look just as it did when the Romans arrived.

The vineyards of the Rhône valley begin just beyond the southern suburbs of Lyon and follow the river south almost as far as the Mediterranean. But to talk of the Rhône as though it were a single region is misleading. Like the Loire, the river is more of a link between very different wine-making areas: in this instance, the northern and southern Rhône.

The essential differences between the two regions lie in the grape varieties, and the land in which they are planted. The north, like Burgundy, is a region in which wine-growers use just one kind of black grape – in this case, the smoky, brooding Syrah. With it they produce long-lived red wines such as Côte-Rôtie, Hermitage and Cornas, and their more approachable but still muscular neighbours, Crozes-Hermitage and St-Joseph.

If the wines are tough, so is making them; the vineyards are some of the most spectacular in the world, rivalling those of the Rhine and Douro in the way they cling to the perilously steep slopes that overlook the river as it snakes its way southward.

Down south, in the Côtes du Rhône-Villages (the more select area within the

Roasted artichokes: The hill of Côte-Rôtie, and a crop of artichokes in the foreground

broad Côtes du Rhône *Appellation*), Gigondas and Châteauneuf-du-Pape, it is another grape, the peppery, berryish Grenache, that holds sway, but as the captain of a team that also includes the Mourvèdre, the Cinsault and, of course, the Syrah.

Here, as in Bordeaux, wine-makers have to be as skilled at the art of blending as they are at growing grapes. In some cases, for example in many Côtes du Rhônes, the Grenache is allowed to trumpet its presence in juicy-fruity reds that are almost indecently easy to drink. In Châteauneuf-du-Pape, on the other hand, the blender's art can be taken to absurd lengths, with a total of 13 permitted grapes to choose from. Very few producers use even half this number – one, Château Rayas, focuses almost exclusively on the Grenache – but, even with three or four to play with, they can make wonderful wine that takes you straight to the spice bazaar.

The flat vineyards of the south are different too, and they're a revelation. Until you see them, you would never believe that vines – or any plants for that matter – could grow in what looks just like the uncom-fortable pebbles that cover some of Europe's least hospitable beaches.

But if the Rhône is best known for characterful reds (and for its readiness, in times gone by, to supply them to wine-growers in Burgundy and Bordeaux whose own wines needed a little body-building and "beefing-up"), it's also the place to find an extraordinary range of other styles. Muscat de Beaumes de Venise, now a favourite inexpensive alternative to Sauternes, comes from a village that makes good red Côtes du Rhône-Villages; Clairette de Die, a less pungently perfumed counterpart to Asti Spumante, comes from here too. So do the strange and wonderful creamy-spicy dry whites of Condrieu and the dry, peppery rosés of Lirac.

But ultimately the reds have always been the Rhône's strong suit. Unfortunately, in the past, too much of the wine was dull and disappointing; Châteauneuf-du-Pape, for example, once rivalled Beaujolais for the prize for best-known, worst-made red. The problem was that no one paid these wines much respect. Old-timers recalled the days when Hermitage sold for a higher price than

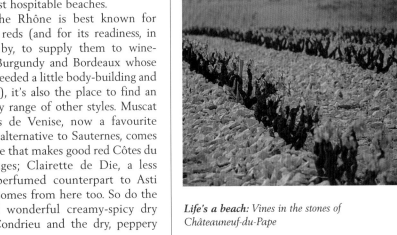

Life's a beach: *Vines in the stones of* *Châteauneuf-du-Pape*

the best Bordeaux, and when a dollop of their wine could raise the value of a barrel of Lafite – and shrugged their shoulders.

Today, though, the Rhône is back in fashion. The region's growers, merchants and co-operatives are tidying themselves up and, despite the size of the area – it's nearly 150 miles (240 km) long – and the amount it makes (over 200 million bottles of Côtes du Rhône each year), this has become one of the world's most reliable, good-value wine regions. And people have begun to notice.

America's wine guru, Robert Parker, is the author of what has been described as the "definitive" guide to Bordeaux. What would you find if you looked in his cellars – nothing but claret? No, they're packed wall-to-wall with Rhônes, red and white. And what kind of grape varieties are California's most pioneering wineries all falling over each other to plant? Yes, you guessed – Syrah, Viognier, Mourvèdre and Cinsault.

The prices of the best wines of the northern Rhône already reflect this growing success and popularity, but they're still rising fast. Buy now before everyone gets the taste for them. And stock up on a few dozen cheap bottles of Côtes du Rhône to enjoy while you wait for your brooding monsters to soften.

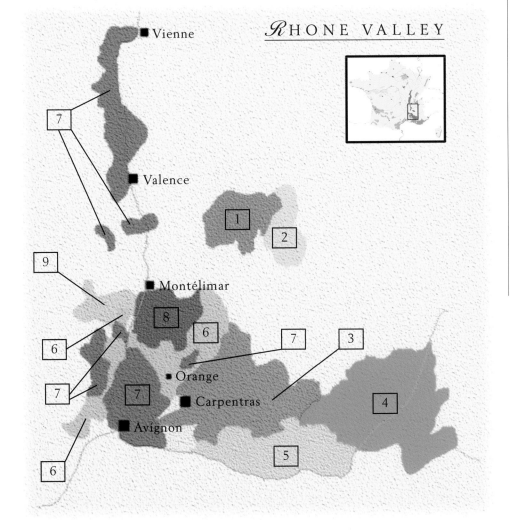

RHONE VALLEY

1   Clairette de Die

2   Châtillon-en-Diois

3   Côtes du Ventoux

4   Coteaux de Pierrevert

5   Côtes du Lubéron

6   Côtes du Rhône-Villages

7   Côtes du Rhône

8   Coteaux du Tricastin

9   Côtes du Vivarais

THE NORTHERN RHONE

IT TAKES a couple of days to drive south from the quiet, riverside town of Vienne to the Mediterranean coast. At least that's how long it always seems to take me, though I guess if you put your foot down on the *autoroute* you could probably do it in four or five hours. But if there's any romance in your soul, you won't be on the *autoroute*; like me, you'll be following the broad Rhône on the old *route nationale* and you won't even be on that for long. No, you'll be forever heading off and up into the vineyards at almost every bend in the river.

The first temptation will strike on the west bank, on the sheer "roasted hillside" of Côte Rôtie. Only a masochist would ever have wanted to plant vines up here – but what else could anyone have done with this land? The men and women who prune the Syrah vines and harvest their grapes deserve every penny they can get for their wine, and not just for their talents as mountaineers. The 250 acres (100 ha) of vineyards here are very, very exposed. In the summer, as the sun blazes down, you soon learn how the Côte got its name – and then there's the 90 mph mistral wind and the winter frosts. But the efforts pay off. The flavour of the Syrah, tempered slightly by the addition of up to 20 per cent of the perfumed white Viognier grapes, is a cocktail of ripe, dark berries and wild flowers, with just a hint of woodsmoke.

The Viognier's role in red Côte Rôtie is generally unrecognized, but this curious

Château-Grillet: A very small vineyard, but not the best

variety gets the credit for the two white wines that are made, on similarly steep slopes, a little further down the river at Condrieu and Château-Grillet. The former *Appellation* is small at just 25 acres (10 ha), but the latter is tiny, with just six and a half acres (2.5 ha) of terraced vineyards. This diminutive size only partly explains Château-Grillet's astronomical price; the fact that there is only one producer (Château-Grillet) has some bearing too.

My advice would be to save some money and go for a Condrieu (particularly from Georges Vernay) which, judging by recent unimpressive vintages of Château-Grillet, will give you a better taste of the Viognier's weird aromatic perfume and peach, apple and cream cheese flavours. Try it, and you'll see just why all those Chardonnay-sated Californians are turning to it in their droves.

The *Appellation* of St-Joseph overlaps that of Condrieu or, to be more precise, runs along beneath it on the flat land by the river. Elsewhere, close to Tournon and Mauves, between Hermitage and Valence, it runs up into the hills on its way to Valence. It is in these hills that the best wines are made: spicy, peachy whites from Marsanne and Roussanne, and intensely blackcurrant,

The Essentials
NORTHERN RHONE

What to look for Big, rich, spicy, smoky Syrah reds and rich, perfumed whites.
What to buy Go for the big reds; they'll cost you but they're worth it. There are some good-value St-Josephs and Crozes-Hermitages too.
Location From Vienne, just below Lyons, to Valence in the south.
Official quality AOCs: Chatillon-en-Diois; Château Grillet; Clairette de Die; Condrieu; Cornas; Côtes du Rhône; Côtes du Rhône-Villages; Coteaux du Tricastin; Crozes-Hermitage; Hermitage; St-Joseph; St-Péray and St-Péray Mousseux.
Style Reds vary from the cheap and cheerful to the mighty – Hermitage and Côte Rôtie are two of France's greatest wines. Immensely tannic in youth, Hermitage matures into an approachable but serious wine, with a cocktail of rich fruit flavours and characteristic smokiness. Côte Rôtie is slightly softer but even smokier. (Look for wines from the best slopes, the Côtes Brune et Blonde.) More affordable, but still showing good Syrah character, are St-Joseph and Crozes-Hermitage. The white wines are dry and quite full in style. Condrieu, in particular, produces rich yet dry wines with an inviting tropical fruit aroma. Sweet, grapey sparkling Clairette de Die is infinitely superior to plain Crémant de Die.
Climate Continental, with hot summers and cold winters.
Cultivation Varied soil, but mainly granite. The vineyards are set into the steep slopes of the

rocky hillsides, though some extend beyond.
Grape varieties Aligoté, Bourboulenc, Calitor, Camarèse, Carignan, Chardonnay, Cinsault, Clairette, Counoise, Gamay, Grenache, Marsanne, Mauzac, Mourvèdre, Muscardin, Muscat Blanc à Petits Grains, Pascal Blanc, Picardan, Picpoul, Pinot Blanc, Pinot Noir, Roussanne, Syrah, Terret Noir, Ugni Blanc, Vacarèse, Viognier.
Production/maturation Traditional methods prevail, with less emphasis on new oak than elsewhere.
Longevity Lesser whites should be drunk as young as possible and even the better white wines tend to peak before 5 years. Côtes du Rhône, Crozes-Hermitage and St-Joseph will be drinkable at 3 years but, as the quality of the wine increases, so does its ageing potential.
Vintage guide *Reds*: 78, 80, 82, 85, 88, 89, 90, 91; *Whites*: 78, 82, 83, 87, 88, 89, 90, 91.
My Top 30 *Hermitage*: Jaboulet Aîné, Chapoutier, Guigal, Chave, Grippat, Delas, Sorrel, Desmeure, Gray; *Côte Rôtie*: Jasmin, Jamet & Barge, Vidal-Fleury, Jaboulet Aîné, Guigal, Delas, Rostaing, Dervieux-Thaize, Georges Vernay, Burgaud, Champet; *Condrieu*: de Rozay, Dumazet, Georges Vernay, Guigal; *St-Joseph*: Chave, Coursodin, Grippat, Jaboulet Aîné, Co-op St-Désirat-Champagne; *Crozes-Hermitage*: Guigal, Desmeure, Graillot, Tardy & Ange, Delas, Fayolle, Jaboulet Aîné; *Cornas*: Clape, Juge, Guy de Barjac, Alain Voge, Colombo.

spicy ("spicy" can't help being an overworked word round here) reds from the Syrah. Most examples of St-Joseph are good; some are much more chunky and long-lived than others.

HERMITAGE

The next site of pilgrimage is Hermitage. Stand beside the huge statue of the Madonna in the hills here and you can see steep terraces dotted with long signs proclaiming the names of the region's biggest merchants: Jaboulet-Aîné, Chapoutier, Guigal... The tiny chapel high on the hill stands in the middle of Hermitage's most famous plot. Jaboulet-Aîné's "La Chapelle" vineyard produces one of the very best Hermitages. And the view from here at dusk is one of the most unforgettable sights in the vinous world.

Red Hermitage is usually made exclusively from the Syrah, though growers are allowed to add a little Marsanne and Roussanne, the grapes from which the *Appellation*'s white is made. Good red Hermitage is astonishing – classy, but raunchy too, combining just about every berry and spice you can imagine. There's tannin, but also a sweet ripeness; in all but the lightest years, you should allow these wines 10 or 15 years for flavours to develop.

White Hermitage is rarely as exciting an experience but, like the red, it too can need time. When young, it can taste dull and earthy but, given 10 years or so, the earthiness can miraculously turn into all kinds of floral, herby, peachy smells and flavours.

The easiest way to describe Crozes-Hermitage is that it is – usually – scaled-down Hermitage. The wine-making rules are the same, and so is the region, more or less, except that the Crozes *Appellation* extends eastward behind Hermitage and away from the river. The wine still has those flavours of berries and spice, but you can get at them earlier, and they don't usually last as long. For a taste of wines that give the lie to those "usuallys", try ones made by Alain Graillot. White Crozes-Hermitage is for early drinking.

CORNAS

As outsiders have discovered Hermitage and Côte Rôtie, the last remaining semi-secret red of the northern Rhône is the tiny (165-acre/67-ha) region of Cornas. Critics complain that the wines here are more "rustic" than their northern neighbours, and that they take even longer to come round. Those critics obviously haven't tasted the smoky, blackberryish wines made by Auguste Clape, Guy de Barjac and Alain Voge.

South of Cornas, the interesting reds dry up and it's time to move on to fizz. St-Péray, whose vineyards rub shoulders with the suburbs of Valence, makes full-flavoured still wine and fizz from the Marsanne and Roussanne that sell well enough in local restaurants but are decidedly unfashionable elsewhere, so it's hard to blame the growers for selling out to house-builders.

More commercial stuff is produced down to the south-west, along the Drôme river, in Clairette de Die and Chatillon-en-Diois,

Steak Diane

Steak in a brandy sauce

*T*he dark, robust wines of the region need to be accompanied by a dish with a character rich enough to do them justice.

SERVES 4

5fl oz/150 ml beef stock
4 tsp Worcestershire sauce
2 tsp lemon juice
2 tsp Dijon mustard
3 tsp brandy
3 tsp sherry (preferably amontillado)
1 tsp cornflour
1 oz/25 g butter
1 tbsp olive oil
Four 6 oz/175 g sirloin or entrecôte steaks,
flattened to about 5 mm thick
1 medium onion, peeled and finely sliced
1 tbsp fresh parsley, minced

In a bowl, mix the stock, Worcestershire sauce, lemon juice, mustard, brandy, sherry and cornflour. In a large frying pan heat the butter until the foam subsides and sauté the steaks for about 25 seconds on each side (for medium-rare) and transfer them to a heated serving dish or individual plates. In the pan juices, cook the onion over moderate heat until it is softened and add to it the mixture from the bowl. Bring to the boil, stirring, until it thickens and then pour it over the steaks. Garnish with the parsley and serve with sautéed potatoes and a purée of fennel or celery.

close to the village of Bourdeaux. Avoid straight Crémant de Die itself; made from at least 75 per cent of the neutral Clairette, it's lighter than St-Péray, but with less fruit. The stuff to buy is Clairette de Die. Made primarily from Muscat grapes, this can be first-class, emphatically grapey wine, produced by the traditional *méthode dioise*, in which the wine is bottled before its first fermentation is complete.

Getting away from it all: *The hermitage at Hermitage, overlooking the river*

THE SOUTHERN RHONE

ACCORDING TO the *Appellation Contrôlée* maps, the area directly to the south of the northern Rhône is a grapeless no-vine's-land. In fact, although there is no AOC wine made here, there are two *vins de pays*: the Collines Rhodaniennes (easy red from the Gamay and Syrah) and the Coteaux de l'Ardèche which, apart from the reds it makes from the Gamay and from Rhône and Bordeaux varieties can, thanks to Louis Latour and his fellow Burgundians, now boast Chardonnay vines galore and, thanks to Georges Duboeuf, the world's biggest planting of Viognier. A little further south, there is the up-and-coming new *Appellation Contrôlée* of the Coteaux du Tricastin, source of some first-class, pure, smoky Syrah.

Wines labelled Côtes du Rhône can

Nearly new: The castle at Châteauneuf, now a crumbling ruin

legally be made in a number of areas along the Rhône valley; in practice most come from the flat land on either side of the river south of Montélimar. This is a huge area, and quality and styles can vary enormously. The same *Appellation* can be used to label a Syrah that tastes just like Hermitage's kid brother and a blend of the Grenache, Cinsault and Carignan that's first cousin to Beaujolais Nouveau.

The key to knowing what you are going to find in the bottle is to look for wines from good individual estates, or to pay a little extra for a Côtes du Rhône-Villages, which legally has to come from one of 17 named villages, be made from grapes that come from lower-yielding vines and be a blend that includes at least 25 per cent of Syrah, Mourvèdre and Cinsault.

The wine-makers of the 17 villages are nothing if not individualists, and are active promoters of the wines of their communes, driven on by the example of Gigondas and Vacqueyras which have both been promoted from Côtes du Rhône-Villages to have their own *Appellation*. It is easy to understand why Gigondas was the first of the pair to get its *Appellation*; its red wines do taste a bit more "serious", and its (rare) rosés are first-class. Good examples are a much better buy than many a wine sold under the label of Châteauneuf-du-Pape.

Several villages, most notably Visan, Cairanne, Valréas and Seguret, take advantage of the rules that let them print their commune's name on the labels of their wines; each could make a case for the quality of its reds. Chusclan deserves an *Appellation* for the rosé made by its co-operative (better than a great deal of Tavel), and Laudun merits one for its white. Ironically, Beaumes de Venise and Rasteau, which make decent reds, have had *Appellations* of their own for nearly 50 years, but not for their unfortified wines; both make *vins doux naturels*, fortified wines made by adding pure grape spirit to partly fermented juice. Muscat de Beaumes de Venise is a world-famous success story; Rasteau's fortified Grenache is less immediately appealing but has a plummy, port-like charm.

The Essentials
SOUTHERN RHONE

What to look for Spicy reds, New Wave *vins de pays* de l'Ardèche.

Location South-eastern France, north of Avignon.

Official quality AOCs: Châteauneuf-du-Pape; Côtes du Rhône; Côtes du Rhône-Villages (named villages include Cairanne, Vacqueyras, Séguret, Visan, Valréas, Chusclan and Laudun); Côtes du Lubéron; Côtes du Ventoux; Gigondas; Lirac; Tavel. Côtes du Vivarais is the VDQS, while *vins de pays* include Coteaux de l'Ardèche, Vaucluse, Collines Rhodaniennes and Bouches-du-Rhône.

Style Ripe, full-bodied red wines are produced, warmer and softer than their northern Rhône neighbours, simple in style though with more depth and complexity in Gigondas, Châteauneuf-du-Pape and some of the better Côtes du Rhône-Villages, such as Cairanne and Séguret. There are also some soft, fresh and fragrant whites, most notably in Châteauneuf-du-Pape and Lirac. The most famous rosé is Tavel, though neighbouring Lirac can be better. The now-famous sweet white Muscat de Beaumes de Venise is arguably the best and classiest of France's *vins doux naturels*, luscious yet elegant, while the area's other *vdn*, Rasteau, can be almost port-like.

Climate Mediterranean with very long, hot summers.

Cultivation Arid chalk and clay soils covered with large, round "pudding-stone" pebbles which reflect and intensify the heat. As the river widens the vineyard slopes become less steep.

Grape varieties As for northern Rhône; 13 varieties are designated for use in Châteauneuf-du-Pape, chiefly Carignan, Cinsault, Grenache, Mourvèdre and Syrah. Whites are principally from Muscat, Clairette, Picpoul and Bourboulenc.

Production/maturation Increasing use of stainless steel with old wood being used for maturation.

Longevity Reds, apart from the best village *Appellations* and Châteauneuf-du-Pape, peak after about 3 years. Good village wines will last beyond 5 years, and the best Châteauneuf-du-Pape beyond a decade. White and rosé wines are for early consumption.

Vintage guide 81, 83, 85, 86, 88, 89, 90.

My Top 30 *Châteauneuf-du-Pape*: Rayas, Beaucastel, Font de Michelle, Fortia, Clos des Papes, Clos du Mont Olivet, Guigal, Vieux Télégraphe, Chante-Cigale, Bosquet des Papes, Sabon, Delas, Guigal, Jaboulet Aîné; *Gigondas*: Gouberts, St Gayan, de Montmirail, Faraud, de Piaugier, Guigal; *Beaumes de Venise*: Vidal-Fleury, Co-operative; *Côtes du Rhône*: Jaboulet Aîné, Ste-Anne, Rabasse-Charavin, Ameillaud, Cru de Coudoulet, Grand Moulas, Guigal; *Ardèche*: Georges Duboeuf, Louis Latour; *Lirac*: Maby, Méjan.

CHATEAUNEUF-DU-PAPE

Châteauneuf-du-Pape is one of the world's famous wine names – but, until quite recently, despite their embossed keys and their price, the wines here were often a little like the Pope's castle itself; impressive from a distance and a hollow ruin when viewed at close range.

Châteauneuf should be brilliant stuff. The "pudding stones" covering the vineyards, which release heat during the night, help to ensure perfectly ripe grapes – and wines of up to 14.5 per cent alcohol. The local *Appellation* laws, the first to be drawn up in France, further guarantee the quality of the fruit (in a way unique to Châteauneuf) by obliging producers to use the least-ripe 5 to 20 per cent of the crop to make *vin de table*. The rules also strictly control yields and restrict the use of grape varieties to eight reds and five whites.

The fact that these rules had to be drawn up as early as 1923 illustrates the well-established tradition of abusing the reputation of what has long been a house-hold name. Today, fortunately, the merchants who were largely guilty of that abuse are prevented from doing so by the keenness of the individual estates to make and bottle their own wine. This has made for a huge improvement in quality, but today's Châteauneuf is still rather two-faced; some are big, packed with pizza herbs, bitter chocolate and oriental spice; others, made by the *macération carbonique* method, taste rather like peppered Beaujolais. There's nothing wrong with these lighter versions, but they don't really do justice to Châteauneuf. The biggest examples from the best estates are worth keeping for a decade or so but, unlike their counterparts from the northern Rhône, they can all be broached by the time they are 5 years old.

White Châteauneuf-du-Pape is very rare – maybe two or three bottles in a hundred – but good modern examples can be worth looking for; their mixture of spice, flowers and lemon is delicious for the first few years after the harvest.

TAVEL

The traditional claims for Tavel are first that it is one of the world's only rosés that can age, and second that it is a cut above its neighbour Lirac. As far as I'm concerned, both claims fail the taste test. Old Tavel tastes duller than young Tavel, and young Tavel often tastes duller than young Lirac. The trouble is that the producers at Tavel now try too hard to make "serious" pink wine. Sadly, the wine-makers at Lirac, who do produce good rosé, are increasingly turning their attention to red instead.

Not quite alone: *Domaine de la Solitude in Châteauneuf-du-Pape, plus neighbours*

Crème aux Fruits

A light cream with summer fruits and brandy

One of the great stars among the wines of the southern Rhône – in fact, one of the greatest dessert wines – is Muscat de Beaumes de Venise. To say it is merely sweet is like saying Champagne is merely sparkling. This dessert has a lightness which complements the wine deliciously.

SERVES 4

12 oz/350 g raspberries or strawberries; fresh or thawed from frozen, mashed and sieved
10 fl oz/275 ml double cream
1 egg white
2 oz caster sugar
1 tsp orange liqueur (e.g. Cointreau or Triple Sec)
12 sponge fingers

Whisk cream until it thickens. Fold in the egg white, sieved fruit pulp, caster sugar and liqueur. Arrange sponge fingers in a serving dish or on individual plates and pile mixture on top.

OTHER WINES

There are several "lesser" *Appellations* and VDQSs in the region for which bargain-hunters ought to keep their eyes open. The Côtes du Ventoux benefit from limestone soil to make light, but still quite spicy, red which can outclass many a basic Côtes du Rhône. The Côtes du Lubéron, between Avignon and Aix-en-Provence, got their brand new AOC largely through the efforts of vegetable-oil millionaire Jean-Louis Chancel of Château Val Joanis, where he makes pleasant, if unexceptional, early-drinking red, white and rosé. Still VDQS, the Côtes du Vivarais behave as if they were AOC by having a set of *crus* – Orgnac, St Montant and St Remèze – which produce attractive lightweight reds and rosés. Finally, up in the mountains, the VDQS of the Coteaux de Pierrevert could serve you a jugful of refreshing rosé.

ALSACE

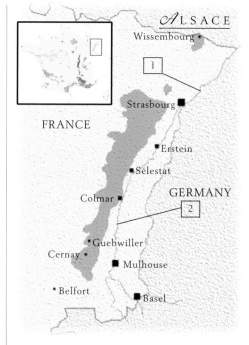

1 River Rhine **2** River Ill

S WINE-MAKERS everywhere else have seemingly given up naming their wines after places and begun to call them after the grape varieties from which they are made, the Alsatians smile knowingly to themselves. They invented "varietal" labels long before the Californians and Australians; indeed, in Alsace more or less the only way wine is sold is by its grape variety, be it the Riesling, the Pinot Gris, Blanc and Noir, the Muscat, the Gewürztraminer or, to a decreasing extent, the Sylvaner.

Talk to the Alsatians about their German neighbours' recent conversion to dry wines and again they will smile; round here, dry Riesling is no novelty and, as they will point out, in Alsace's warm climate the grapes actually ripen much more easily than they do on the other side of the Rhine.

THE HISTORY

The Alsatians have a way with knowing, if wry, smiles, and when you consider their history, it's hard to blame them. Over the years their region has been a territorial ping-pong ball; they've seen it all. As early as the fourteenth and fifteenth centuries, Strasbourg was at the heart of a thriving wine-producing area that included vineyards on both sides of the Rhine, exporting 100 million litres a year from its river docks.

But this early prosperity did not last. When the French took control in 1648 at the end of the Thirty Years' War, Alsace was no prize acquisition. The war had so devastated the region that immigrants from neighbouring lands were offered free land to encourage them to cultivate it once more.

Fortified Alsace: The church at Hunawihr speaks volumes about Alsace's history

However hard these times were, they did not deter some from starting wine businesses; among the family firms that are still in operation today, Hugel, Dopff, Trimbach, Zind-Humbrecht and Kuen had all opened their doors by 1700. Over the following century, they learned to work with another immigrant – the Riesling grape, from the Rheingau on the other side of the river. The end of the Franco-Prussian war in 1871 brought a return to German rule. Less than 50 years later, at the end of the First World War, Alsace became French again – only to fall back into German hands in 1940. The Second World War brought some of the worst times Alsace has ever known; villages were fought for house by house. In Bennwihr, precious wine literally boiled in the cellars as the buildings were burned to the ground.

Today, some of the people speak French; others retain a Germanic dialect – but, whatever the language, they are all quick to stress that they are, above all, Alsatian. And perhaps that's the best image for Alsace wines, too: German spoken with a French accent. Or vice versa.

THE BEST OF BOTH WORLDS

This dual nationality is just as apparent in the villages; both in their names and their appearance. This is one of the few parts of the world in which holiday brochure expressions like "fairy tale" and "picturesque" actually do ring true; the narrow streets, the crooked, half-timbered houses, often painted pink, yellow or blue, with their gilded signs are straight out of an illustrated volume of stories by the Brothers Grimm. And overlooking all of the villages, there are vineyards, basking in the sun that, thanks to the shelter of the Vosges mountains, gives the vines one of the driest, warmest environments they could want.

In the autumn, these vineyards are packed with families sharing the task of picking. The slopes are too steep for mechanical harvesters; besides, most of the plots are too small for their owners to afford a machine. Although the soils of particular villages can suit particular varieties (for example, the Muscat does particularly well in both Mittelwihr and Gueberschwihr), most growers produce wines from several different grapes.

But here, there is another contrast with Germany. Whereas the liberal German wine laws have allowed wine-growers in even the best parts of the Rhine and Mosel to replace their Riesling with a range of new, easy-to-grow varieties, in Alsace, the trend has been toward the Pinot Blanc and the region's four traditionally best white grapes, the Riesling, Pinot Gris, Muscat and Gewürztraminer.

There are no new varieties here, and indeed even traditional ones such as the dull Sylvaner and Chasselas are now treated as second-class citizens; neither can be used to make Alsace's recently established *Grands Crus*.

With these *Grand Cru* vineyards, first introduced in 1983 and fast growing in number, the Alsatians have characteristically put together an *Appellation* system that's half-French, half-German too. Although it is often imagined that each of the region's grape varieties has an *Appellation* of its own, in fact it is the region of Alsace as a whole to which the *Appellation* applies. The names of individual villages, thus, have no legal significance, but those of the 50 *Grand Cru* vineyards (see box) around those villages do – provided that the wines made there are produced from one of the four permitted varieties.

So much for the French-style part of the rules; the Germanic part is all to do with the

Grimm reality: Eguisheim is a typically fairy-tale Alsace village

The Essentials
ALSACE

What to look for Rich, spicy, dry whites and sweet late-harvest wines, plus occasional good fizz and even more occasional light Pinot Noir reds.

Location North-eastern France, on the border with Germany, along lower slopes of the Vosges mountains.

Official quality AOC Alsace, usually followed by the name of the wine's grape variety. Crémant d'Alsace is the region's sparkling AOC. Around 50 vineyard sites are currently entitled to use an additional *Grand Cru Appellation*, adding their name to that of the grape variety. Although the growers of Alsace would like this designation extended to cover yet more sites, outside observers feel that even the current figure is too high, thus devaluing the *Appellation*. There is nothing to prevent wine-makers printing their vineyard name on a wine's label, be it *Grand Cru* or not, and, in view of the fact that *cru* status has in some cases been granted somewhat arbitrarily, this seems excusable. However, it does confuse matters for the average wine-drinker, who might in turn be forgiven for not committing to memory all 50 (and rising) *Grand Cru* names. In similar vein, *Réserve or Cuvée Personelle/Spéciale/Particulière* are commonly seen, indicating the producer's favourite wines but having no official significance. Ironically, while these anomalies would be cause for concern almost anywhere else, Alsace as a region has one of the best reputations for honest and reliable wine-making in France, although yields from one vineyard can be on the high side.

Style Rich, spicy, dry still whites, usually from a single grape variety (Edelzwicker, a blend, is losing favour); usually sweet Vendange Tardive; always sweet Sélection de Grains Nobles. Light-bodied Pinot Noir reds. Crémant d'Alsace is a *méthode champenoise* sparkling wine, dry and often quite full-bodied. Though little seen, it can be good value.

Climate Continental: sheltered by the Vosges mountains, this area is warmer and drier than the surrounding countryside.

Cultivation Middle and lower hillside vineyards, usually south or south-easterly in aspect. Soils are diverse and complex.

Grape varieties *Predominantly white*: Riesling, Gewürztraminer, Muscat, Pinot Blanc, Tokay-Pinot Gris (Tokay d'Alsace), Auxerrois, Knipperlé, Sylvaner, Chasselas and a little Chardonnay; *Red*: Pinot Noir.

Production/maturation Traditionalists prefer old oak for fermentation and maturation while modernists use stainless steel. The jury is still out over which is better. Crémant d'Alsace fizz can be good. Some new oak is being used for Pinot Noir.

Longevity Riesling: 5–20 years; Gewürztraminer: 3–5; Pinot Gris: 5–10. Most Muscat, Sylvaner and Pinot Blanc are best drunk young, though the last can keep for up to 4 or 5 years, as can the reds.

Vintage guide 79, 81, 83, 85, 88, 89, 90, 92, 94.

My Top 23 Adam, Deiss, Albrecht, Blanck, Cattin, Zind-Humbrecht, Ostertag, Josmeyer, Hugel, Trimbach, Faller, Muré, Rolly Gassmann, Kreidenweiss, Schaller, Schlumberger, Dopff & Irion, Weinbach, Sick-Dreyer, Kientzler. The co-operatives at Turckheim, Eguisheim and Pfaffenheim produce reliable, sometimes excellent, wine.

Soaking up the sun: Alsace grows some of the richest, ripest dry wines in France

reverse is true. Whichever is correct (and it is grown in Hungary – where it is called the "Greyfriar"), this pale-pink-skinned grape produces some of the spiciest, smokiest wine in Alsace. Like the Riesling, it's worth waiting for, but far easier to drink when young. Ostertag, Kreydenweiss, Schlumberger and Muré make good examples.

Gewürztraminer

I remember tasting Gewürztraminer with a Burgundian who had never encountered it before. "Bizarre!" he said. "Is this wine or is it perfume?" I know what he meant, and I know why a fair number of people are put off by the sweet-yet-dry, pungent smell and taste of wines made from this dark-pink-skinned grape. It is over-the-top, but unashamedly so. The words that often appear on tasters' notes are "grapey", "lychees", "Parma violets", "rose water" and, above all, "spice". And that's how it's supposed to taste; the word "Gewürz" in German means "spice", and thus one can deduce that this is the spicy version of the Traminer grape. If it didn't taste this way, it simply wouldn't be living up to its name. For a taste of Gewürztraminer at its best, try

ripeness of the grapes – in other words, their natural sweetness. Although Alsace is almost exclusively a dry wine region, the Alsatians love to prove that they can make sweet wine that's every bit as luscious as the stuff produced across the Rhine.

SWEET ALSACE

These sweet Alsace wines have two designations, Vendange Tardive – literally "late-harvest", the equivalent of Germany's Spätlese; and Sélection de Grains Nobles – "selection of nobly rotten grapes", similar in style to a German Beerenauslese or Trockenbeerenauslese. Beyond just two more terms – the increasingly rare Edelzwicker (used for a basic blend of various varieties) and Crémant d'Alsace (the region's often excellent *méthode champenoise* sparkling wine) – there is almost nothing else to learn. Expressions such as the commonly seen Réserve Personelle and Cuvée Speciale have no legal significance, but they should indicate that the producer believes the wine to be a cut above the rest of his production.

Comparing Alsace's dry and sweet white wines with their German counterparts is a fascinating experience, and one that sends writers scurrying in search of similes. One somewhat pretentious analogy that nevertheless makes sense to me likens the wines of the Mosel and Rhine to Mozart quartets, and those of Alsace to Beethoven symphonies.

The difference is all to do with volume and richness. The peculiar warm, dry micro-

climate created by the Vosges mountains allows the grapes to develop those few extra grammes of sugar almost every year and that, in turn, makes for a higher level of alcohol and a richness rarely attained in northern Germany; if a wine seems Germanic, yet exotically spicy and tangibly oily in texture, there's a strong chance that it comes from Alsace. And if you are looking for a wine to go with food, you've come to the right place.

THE GRAPES

Riesling

Is this the greatest of Alsace's varieties – or should that honour go to the Pinot Gris? I'm not certain, but I've a pretty clear idea what the Riesling would say. Tasted young, Alsace Rieslings can be forbidding, hiding their richness behind their acidity. Leave them to sulk for a few years and you'll be rewarded with an extraordinary appley, spicy glassful that can smell – not unpleasantly – just like petrol. Weinbach, Blanck, Sick-Dreyer, Trimbach and Kientzler make good examples.

Tokay-Pinot Gris/Tokay d'Alsace

Until recently confusingly known as the Tokay, this is no relation of the Hungarian wine of that name (which is made from the Furmint, another variety altogether). Some stories say that the Pinot Gris was imported from Hungary to Alsace; others that the

THE GRANDS CRUS OF ALSACE

The names of any of the following 50 *Grand Cru* vineyards could appear on a label and, if linked to that of a good producer, should indicate a better wine. Some owners of *Grand Cru* land, however, prefer to put the emphasis on their own names and on terms such as "Reserve Personelle" and "Vendange Tardive".

Altenberg de Bergbieten; Altenberg de Bergheim; Altenberg de Wolxheim; Brand; Bruderthal; Eichberg; Engelberg; Florimont; Frankstein; Froehn; Furstentum; Geisberg; Gloeckelberg; Goldert; Hatschbourg; Hengst; Kanzlerberg; Kastelberg; Kessler; Kirchberg de Barr; Kirchberg de Ribeauvillé; Kitterlé; Mambourg; Mandelberg; Markrain; Moenchberg; Muenchberg; Ollwiller; Osterberg; Pfersigberg; Pfingstberg; Praeletenberg; Rangen; Rosacker; Saering; Schlossberg; Schoenenbourg; Sommerberg; Sonnenglanz; Spiegel; Sporen; Steinert; Steingrubler; Steinklotz; Vorbourg; Wiebelsberg; Wineck-Schlossberg; Winzerberg; Zinnkoepflé; Zotzenberg.

Riquewihr: The vineyards run straight up to the edges of the forest

it made by Schlumberger, Zind-Humbrecht, Schleret, Trimbach or Faller.

Muscat

The Muscat has all the Gewürztraminer's grapiness – and then some – but far, far less of its spice. Tasting Alsatian Muscat alongside a Muscat de Beaumes de Venise is like seeing a great actor in two very different roles. Here, unless it is late-picked, the style will be dry and wonderfully refreshing. But there is not a lot made, so you may have to search a little to find a bottle. Names to look for include Kuentz-Bas, Dopff & Irion and Zind-Humbrecht.

Pinot Blanc

The least characterful, and thus the most immediately approachable of Alsace grapes, this cousin of the Pinot Noir is the same variety that the Italians often misleadingly label as Chardonnay (here, confusingly, producers can legally do the reverse). Alsace Pinot Blanc always reminds me of the fatty, hard-to-define flavour of Brazil nuts and offers an affordable introduction to Alsace for people who are deterred by the spice and perfume of some of the region's more characterful varieties. Among my favourites are examples from the Cave de Turckheim, Hugel and Kreydenweiss.

Sylvaner

This rather earthy-flavoured grape used to be one of the most widely grown here, but is rapidly going out of favour. Good examples can have a rich style of their own but they are rarely exciting. Rolly Gassmann makes a good one.

Chasselas

Another, and rather duller, traditional resident that has been chased out by more attractive newcomers.

Pinot Noir

The one style that seems to unite Germany and France in Alsace is red wine; on both sides of the Rhine, the Pinot Noir produces wines that, in warm years and when yields are kept low, can be very raspberryish and attractive like a light-to-middleweight Burgundy. Good examples benefit from being matured in new oak too – provided that they have enough guts to carry the woody flavour. Look out for examples from Hugel, Rolly Gassmann and the Turckheim co-operative.

OTHER WINES OF THE REGION

Crémant d'Alsace sparkling wine is often underrated. There are two VDQS regions close to Alsace. Côtes de Toul, in what was once the huge wine-growing region of Lorraine, can produce pleasant light red and rosé (*vin gris*). And in Lorraine the Mosel crosses the border into France to become the Moselle – but the wine of this name, made on the banks of the river, is very dull.

Beckenhoff

Pork, lamb and potato casserole in wine sauce

*I*n a region so close to Germany (and at times in its history actually part of it), it is not surprising to see a Germanic influence in the food here: *choucroute* (sauerkraut), saddle of hare in cream sauce, sausages, noodles, pastries and, above all, pork.

SERVES 6–8

2½ lb/1.25 kg potatoes (King Edwards or similar)
3 medium onions, peeled and sliced
Bouquet garni sachet, or a bundle made of 1 sprig of rosemary, 2 sprigs of parsley and 1 bay leaf tied together with cotton
1½ lb/750 g pork fillet or tenderloin
1½ lb/750 g boned shoulder of lamb
2 wineglasses of dry white wine
Salt and freshly ground black pepper
1 oz/25 g butter

Peel and slice the potatoes (not too thinly) and put half of them in a layer in an ovenproof dish. Put half of the onion on top followed by the bouquet garni. Now put in all the meat in an even layer, followed by the rest of the onion, and then the remaining potato. Pour in the wine, and add salt and pepper. Dot the potato with the butter. Cover with tinfoil and a lid. Cook in a pre-heated oven at 350°F/180°C/Gas mark 4 for about 4 hours or until the meat is very tender. Serve with steamed broccoli.

CHAMPAGNE

EVERYBODY HAS their own image of Champagne. The word itself, with its connotations of luxury, the sound of the cork popping out of the bottle, the stream of foam fired at the crowds by victorious racing drivers, the glass raised to toast a bride and groom… All of these take Champagne out of the wine rack and turn it into something that really is rather magical.

What's more, however hard they have tried, however often they have turned out wine that outclasses poor-quality Champagne, none of the world's would-be sparkling wine-makers – including overseas subsidiaries of the Champenois themselves – has yet produced anything that quite compares with Champagne at its best.

So what is it that gives Champagne its edge? Well, the one thing it is most emphatically not is the way in which the wine is made. The Champagne method – what used to be called the *méthode champenoise* and is now more often known as *méthode classique* or *traditionnelle* – is used all over the place, often by those subsidiaries. No, the answer lies in a peculiar combination of climate, soil and grape varieties which are particular to the region of Champagne itself.

The climate in this northern part of France is ideal for making fizz, simply

Champagne: Exposed, chalky and chilly

because it's not much good for any other kind of wine; it's just too cold and damp for the grapes to ripen properly. But acidic grapes that have partially ripened in a cool climate are just what you want for sparkling wine – far better than the juicier sweet ones grown in warmer climes.

Then there is the soil – the deep chalk that gives the wines their lightness and delicacy – and lastly, there are the grape varieties: Burgundy's Pinot Noir and Chardonnay, and the Pinot Noir's paler-skinned cousin, the Pinot Meunier.

Put all, or even some, of these elements together somewhere else and you might begin to make a wine that is a little like Champagne. But you'd still have to learn one of the Champenois' other tricks: the art of blending that they call *assemblage*. The closest parallel to this is to be found in Bordeaux, where wine-makers marry together varying proportions of Cabernet Sauvignon, Cabernet

---

The Essentials
CHAMPAGNE

What to look for Creamy, ideally biscuity, fizz which is at once rich and fresh.
Location Centred on Epernay and Reims, 90 miles north-east of Paris.
Quality Within the Champagne AOC, villages may be further classified as *Grands* or *Premiers Crus*. Practically, this is less important than elsewhere because of the blending of wines from different areas. AOCs for still wines are Coteaux Champenois, Bouzy Rouge and Rosé de Riceys.
Style Champagne varies from the very dry Brut Zéro, which has no *dosage*, through Brut – the most common – to the dessert styles Demi-Sec and Doux. It varies greatly in quality but, from the better non-vintage Champagnes upward, should be biscuity with soft, ripe fruit (particularly if from the Chardonnay grape) and clean, balancing acidity. Coteaux Champenois is white, bone-dry and fiercely acidic; Rosé de Riceys and Bouzy Rouge can be fair to good examples of Pinot Noir, but are usually wildly overpriced.
Climate Similar to that of southern England with long, often cool summers and cold, wet winters. Frost may be a problem at times.
Cultivation Because of the inhospitable climate, vines need careful placing and vineyards are normally on south- or south-east-facing slopes. Soil is mainly of chalk with occasionally sandy topsoil. To combat the effects of frost, growers now employ sprinklers. AOC Champagne regulations forbid mechanical harvesting.
Grape varieties Chardonnay, Pinot Noir and Pinot Meunier.
Production/maturation Champagne production is an exact science. The grapes are quickly and carefully pressed. Fermentation is mainly in stainless steel and lasts approximately 10 days. The still wines are then blended to make a particular style of *cuvée*. A sugar, yeast and wine solution, the *liqueur de tirage*, is then added to make the bottled wine undergo a second fermentation. The bottles are stacked on special racks in the cellars during which time *remuage* takes place. This involves turning and tapping each bottle of wine, while gradually inverting it so the sludge containing the dead yeast cells from the second fermentation falls on to the cap. Traditionally this was done by hand; now machines called *giropalettes* are more common. Then the bottle neck is placed in freezing brine to freeze the sludge; the bottle is turned upright and the cap, and with it the sludge plug, is removed. This is called *dégorgement*. Finally, the *dosage* is added to the wine.
Longevity In basic terms, the better the base wine, the longer the finished Champagne will last. Most Champagne, including non-vintage, will benefit from up to 3 years' ageing before drinking.
Vintage guide 75, 76, 79, 81, 82, 83, 85, 88, 89, 90.
My Top 22 Krug, Bollinger, Henriot, Louis Roederer, Gosset, Jacquesson, Pol Roger, Ayala, Laurent Perrier, Alfred Gratien, Boizel, Deutz, Billecart-Salmon, Jacquesson, Jacques Selosses, Ruinart, Salon, Moët & Chandon, Taittinger, Comtes de Champagne, Veuve Clicquot-Ponsardin, Charles Heidsieck, Pommery & Greno.

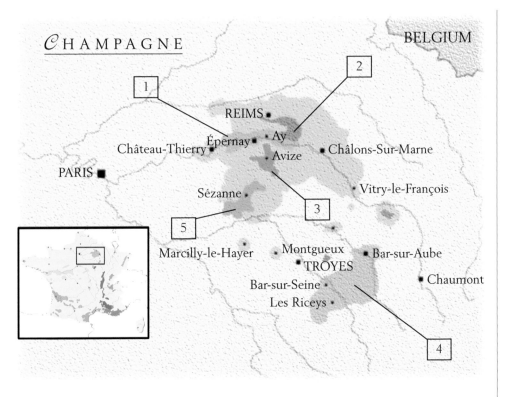

CHAMPAGNE

BELGIUM

REIMS
Château-Thierry • Épernay • Ay
PARIS ■
Avize • Châlons-Sur-Marne
Sézanne • Vitry-le-François
Marcilly-le-Hayer • Montgueux • Bar-sur-Aube
TROYES
Bar-sur-Seine • Chaumont
Les Riceys

1   Vallée de la Marne
2   Montagne de Reims
3   Côte des Blancs
4   Aube Vineyards
5   Côte de Sézanne

Franc, Merlot and Petit Verdot from a number of vineyards within the same commune. The difference in Champagne is that here, the blend is often of wines from villages scores of miles apart and, in the case of non-vintage Champagne (the vast majority of the region's production), from different years. The winemakers of Champagne share with the port producers of the Douro a peculiar habit of not making vintage wine every year, but of only "declaring" a vintage when they think its wine is good enough.

Of course, every Champagne producer is delighted to be able to declare a vintage and to bottle a batch of wine from a single harvest, but the greatest compliment you can pay him is to say that the most recent glass of his non-vintage wine tastes exactly the same as the one you had a year ago.

What every Champagne house is selling is a combination of a recognizable style and consistency. (The Krug brothers, who run one of the greatest Champagne houses of all, believe this so strongly that they price their non-vintage wine nearly as highly – and it *is* highly – as their vintage.) Most producers believe that the best way to achieve that consistency is to blend wines made from two or three of the region's grape varieties, produced in several vintages, and in vineyards throughout the region.

The Language of Champagne

Assemblage Mixing of base wines to create the desired blend, or *cuvée*.
Atmosphere 1 atmosphere = 15 pounds per square inch. The average Champagne is under 6 atmospheres of pressure – more than you'd find in the tyre of a fully laden London bus.
Autolysis The flavour-imparting process of ageing wines on their lees.
Bead The size of the bubbles.
Blanc de blancs Champagne made purely from the Chardonnay grape.
Blanc de noirs Champagne made purely from the black grapes Pinot Meunier and/or Pinot Noir. The wine itself is white.
Brut Very common sparkling wine term – literally "dry" but in practice not bone-dry.
B.O.B. "Buyer's own brand" wine.
Cuvée The assembled or blended wine.
Cuvée de prestige/deluxe The flagships of the Champagne houses. Supposed to be the finest *cuvées*. Sometimes very great (Roederer Cristal and Dom Pérignon) and always very expensive.
Dégorgement Removal of the yeast lees created during the second fermentation.
Dosage Wine added to top up Champagne after disgorging, setting sweetness level.
Giropalette Remuage machine.

Grande marque Literally "great brand", a grouping of recognized producers whose names should be a guarantee of quality. Usually the name of the house or grower but it may be a brand name.
Liqueur de tirage Mixture of sugar, yeast and wine added to still Champagne to create the sparkle.
Matriculation number This number, mandatory on all Champagne labels, reveals, by the two letters preceding it, the origins of the contents of a bottle of Champagne. NM = *négociant-manipulant*; wine from all over the region was bought and blended by a commercial house. CM = *co-opérative-manipulant*; a group of growers "pool" their grapes/wine to produce a blend. RM = *récoltant-manipulant*; a grower/producer who grows, vinifies and sells his own wine. MA = *marque auxiliaire*; a brand name owned by the producer or purchaser.
Microbilles See pille.
Mousse The effervescence of Champagne.
Non-dosage A term for wines without sugar added at dosage – also called Brut Zéro or Brut Sauvage.
Non-vintage The objective of these blends is to keep to a uniform "house" style. A blend will be

based on one vintage, normally the last, plus wine from older vintage(s). "NV" accounts for over 80 per cent of the region's production.
Pille A membrane-coated yeast capsule under experimentation in Champagne.
Pupitre The racks which hold Champagne bottles on end while *remuage* takes place.
Ratafia Liqueur made in Champagne by blending grape must and *marc*.
Récemment dégorgé Recently disgorged. Bollinger has registered the abbreviation "RD" as a trademark.
Remuage The "riddling" – twiddling – of bottles of Champagne undergoing the secondary fermentation to move the yeast deposit on to the corks. A laborious task by hand, it is today increasingly done by *giropalettes*.
Rosé Pink champagne. Uniquely in EC wine law, may be made in this region by blending white and red wines. To some, however, the best method is to use only black grapes, as with Blanc de Noirs, but allowing minimal maceration.
Vintage Wine from a single "declared" vintage. Must have more bottle-age than non-vintage, with strict quality control of the *cuvée*. No more than 80 per cent of the harvest can be sold as vintage.

The Monk and the Widow

*D*ESPITE what wine writers tend to say, Dom Pierre Pérignon did not invent fizz; more or less sparkling wine of one kind or another was already being made in various parts of France and Spain before he arrived to take up responsibility as treasurer at the Abbey of Hautvilliers in 1668. On the other hand, Dom Pérignon did accidentally invent a wine that was very similar to the Champagne we know today.

Ironically, the last thing the monk was aiming to make was fizzy wine; what he wanted to do was produce a white wine that was as good as the best red Burgundy. Discovering that white grapes made stuff that turned yellow, he restricted himself to the black-skinned Pinot Noir grapes, devising grape presses that crushed them gently enough for the skins not to tint the wine. Tasting the grapes that were picked, he discovered that the best wine could be produced from a blend of wines from different parts of the region. And lastly, most crucially, he bottled the wine as quickly as possible, knowing that the old barrels in which it was stored had a tiring effect on its flavour.

This early bottling, soon after the harvest, usually meant that the wine still contained a little yeast and had not quite finished fermenting; this was not apparent in the autumn and winter but was very much so in the warmer weather of the spring when the stuff in the bottle began to fizz.

Despite Dom Pérignon's initial dismay, his wine proved popular and fetched a higher price than any other in the region. However, in these early days its fizziness would have been far less vigorous than that of today's Champagne – largely because the French bottles of the time weren't tough enough to withstand much pressure. In England, however, thanks to the development of a new glass-making process, bottles were far stronger and heavier – and far better suited to withstand the carbon dioxide in the "Champaign" that was shipped to England in barrels. Thus it was in London that modern Champagne was first tasted and appreciated.

During the eighteenth century producers, including such now-familiar names as Ruinart, Roederer, Heidsieck and Moët, had begun to include white grapes in their blends because they made fizzier wine (which was one of the reasons why Dom Pérignon had excluded them), and to age the wine in bottle-shaped quarries left beneath Reims by the Romans.

The only drawback to the Champagne of this time was its variability of style and the residue of dead yeast whose presence required the wine to be decanted, thus losing some of its precious bubbles. However popular the wine had become, its production was still very much a cottage industry. Then, in 1805, a little-known producer called Ponsardin died, leaving his 27-year-old wife in charge of the firm.

Veuve-Clicquot: *The process of remuage was developed here*

Nicole-Barbe Clicquot-Ponsardin, soon to become internationally renowned as "the widow", devoted herself to her firm and its wines for over 60 years, during which time, with the help of her wine-maker, Antoine de Müller, she created the first efficient Champagne production line and certainly the first that guaranteed clean wine.

De Müller discovered that standing the bottles on their corks – *cul en air*; literally "bottoms up" – allowed the yeast to settle in the neck. Even so, some stuck stubbornly to the sides of the bottles, so he experimented with standing the bottles neck-downward in holes drilled in the top of a kitchen table. Lifting them out daily for a few weeks, shaking them and letting them drop heavily back into the holes shifted the dead yeasts down to the cork, whence they could easily be *degorgé* – "disgorged" – from the bottles.

The kitchen table was replaced by more sophisticated A-shaped wooden racks called *pupitres* in which the bottles could be rurned as well as shaken in a process known as *remuage*. Pupitres are still used in Champagne today, but in recent years they have more often that not been replaced by machines called *giropalettes*.

But, whether the task is done manually or mechanically, the principle of shaking the yeast out of the wine remains unchanged. And unless and until new experimental techniques using yeast capsules called *microbilles* are put into practice, Champagne and *méthode champenoise* bottles will go on being shaken for the foreseeable future.

Despite this innovation – a Clicquot trade-secret until 1821 – Champagne-making remained a hit-or-miss affair because there was no way of being certain of the strength of the bottle and the pressure in the wine; in 1828, 80 per cent of the bottles exploded in the cellars. Forty years later, the failure rate had dropped to 15 or 20 per cent but sensible visitors to Champagne cellars in the spring still wore protective face masks.

During the nineteenth century, however, the Champagne producers gradually sophisticated their art. A method was devised – by one Armand Walfart – of freezing the liquid and yeast in the necks of the bottles, thus simplifying *dégorgement*. Wine-makers learned how to start with dry wine to which was added a precisely blended mixture of Champagne, sugar and yeast called the *liqueur de tirage*. And they perfected the essential trick of *dosage*, of topping up the bottles after *dégorgement* with a *liqueur d'expédition*, made from older wine, cane sugar and (then but seldom nowadays) brandy, thus sweetening and softening what can be aggressively dry wine.

In the early 1800s, most Champagne would have seemed astonishingly sweet to modern tastes; indeed, served almost frozen, it would have tasted like a cross between a sorbet and Asti Spumante. It was the Russians who were responsible for encouraging the production of sweet fizz – and the British who popularized their own taste for dry Champagne, though even today most examples contain at least a little sugar.

THE REGIONS

If you were to ask the Champenois pro-ducers where they go for the wines to blend, for white grapes, they might well look to the Côte des Blancs, the Chardonnay-covered slopes south of Epernay where, in villages like Cramant and Le Mesnil-sur-Oger, the best *blanc de blancs* – white wine made from white grapes – is made.

For the Pinot Noir, they'd probably head north to the Montagne de Reims where, in villages like Bouzy, Verzenay and Mailly, this hard-to-ripen grape can surprisingly – though only occasionally – produce red wines with almost as much depth as some Burgundy. Most of the Pinot Noir goes into blends, but occasionally you can find a *blanc de noirs* or a rosé that will give you a taste of what the grape can do here.

West of Epernay, following the Marne river toward Château-Thierry, there is the essential, but unsung, region of the Valle de la Marne, where huge quantities of Pinot Meunier are grown. The Champenois rarely say much about the Pinot Meunier, a grape grown in England as the "Dusty Miller" because of the fine white powder that covers its skin (*meunier* means "miller" too), and they certainly don't mention the fact that it is the most widely planted grape in Champagne.

Vision of prosperity: Avise, Côtes des Blancs

The advantage of the Pinot Meunier is that it ripens well in clayey soil that the Chardonnay and Pinot Noir disdain. It can give a soft fullness to any blend; its disadvantage is that, in itself, it doesn't have much to offer in the way of fruity flavour. Most cheap Champagnes contain a fair whack of Pinot Meunier; but only Rémy Krug acknowledges the essential role it plays in his wine.

If most of Rémy Krug's fellow producers refrain from mentioning the Pinot Meunier, they are just as reticent about the Aube region, way to the south of Epernay. If pressed, they might mumble something about the vineyards there being quite good for the Pinot Noir (because they are a little warmer) but imply in the same breath that Aube wines lack delicacy. A glance at some of their annual shopping lists will reveal, however, that most of them are very happy to put Aube Pinot Noir in their blend. The proportion may vary from year to year, but few Champagne houses own enough land to supply the grapes for more than a fraction of their production; most like to buy the same varieties from the same regions every year.

The quality of each vineyard and the price of its grapes is officially designated on a percentage scale, known as the *échelle*. Those

BREAKING THE CHAMPAGNE CODE

At the bottom of every Champagne label there is a line of small print that reveals the identity of the person or firm that made the wine; unfortunately it does so in a code that seems impenetrable. Here's how to break it.

"NM" stands for *négociant-manipulant*, in other words, a company that has bought grapes or freshly-crushed juice, fermented and blended it and turned it into Champagne. All of the big-name or *grande marque* Champagne houses, such as Moët & Chandon, Krug and Bollinger, are NMs.

On both "own-label" bottles and some convincingly individual-looking labels, the letters MA – *marque auxiliaire* – reveal that the company whose name appears does not exist in its own right as a Champagne producer, and that the name on the label is merely a "brand".

"CM" indicates a *co-operative-manipulant*. This features on a wide range of labels; it tells you that the wine has been made by one of Champagne's big co-operatives, some of which make wine that is every bit as good as that produced by prestigious Champagne houses.

Finally, there is the "RM" – *récoltant-manipulant* – an individual domaine that has made its own Champagne exclusively from grapes grown in its own vineyards.

All that bubbles...
Sadly, the custodians of a region whose wine is synonymous with "the best", the Champenois themselves, have been less than assiduous when it comes to ensuring that Champagne is as good as it ought to be. Makers of quality sparkling wine in the New World, for example, take care to allow their fizz plenty of time in contact with its lees before dégorgement. In Champagne, even the members of the supposedly quality-conscious Syndicat des Grandes Marques, however, accept the regional minimum of 12 months which will give the wine little if any of the biscuity yeast-autolysis which is – or should be – the hallmark of fine Champagne.

of Champagne's 18,500 growers lucky enough to own a vineyard in one of the 17 villages, including Bouzy, Cramant, Le Mesnil-sur-Oger and Ay, that are rated as *Grands Crus* receive 100 per cent of the annually agreed price per kilo of grapes. Their neighbours in the 140 *Premier Cru* villages, whose land is rated at 90–99 per cent, get proportionately less money per kilo while those unfortunates in the rest of Champagne's vineyards, including most in the Aube, are rated at 80–89 per cent.

THE STYLES

Brut

This is the most common dry Champagne style but, however dry they may taste to some people (and there are examples that can scrape your teeth cleaner than any dentist), all Brut Champagnes are slightly sweetened.

Extra Dry, Brut Zéro, Brut Sauvage

They sound similar, but for a taste of bone-dry Champagne, don't try Extra Dry – which is, in fact, slightly sweeter than Brut. Look for Brut Zéro or Brut Sauvage. These wines are sugar-free and are thus sometimes recommended to diabetics; for most people, however, they are too dry to be enjoyable.

Demi-Sec, Doux, Rich

For the sweeter-toothed, Demi-Sec is, as its name suggests, semi-sweet while the rarer Doux and Rich are really very sweet indeed. Good examples of these styles are rare.

Blanc de Blancs and Blanc de Noirs

The words *blanc de blancs* feature on so many white wines nowadays that it is worth remembering that the expression is only relevant to sparkling white wines – for the simple reason that these are almost the only ones that can ever be made from anything other than white grapes.

A *blanc de blancs* Champagne will be made exclusively from the Chardonnay, while the rarer *blanc de noirs* can be made from a blend of Pinot Noir and Pinot Meunier.

Prestige Cuvée

The first "Prestige Cuvée", or super-Champagne, was Dom Pérignon, the 1921 vintage of which was launched, after much hesitation, by Moët & Chandon in 1937. After the Second World War, Roederer entered the competition with its Cristal, a wine originally created for the Tsar of Russia and, over the last 50 years, almost every Champagne house has felt constrained to have a vintage or non-vintage prestige cuvée.

Some of these wines can be sublime: Dom Pérignon, despite its image of being every newly famous pop star's first choice, *is* a great Champagne, as are Taittinger's Comtes de Champagne, Roederer's Cristal and Bollinger's Grande Année Rare.

Rosé

While other pink wines – or at least the ones that haven't renamed themselves "blush" – have gone out of style, rosé Champagne has caught the public fancy in a way that has surprised even the Champenois, who don't really approve of the style, possibly because of the effort they take to keep the pink colour out of their wine. Rosé Champagne can be made in two ways. You either crush the grapes as if you were going to make white Champagne, but leave the skins in the

SPARKLING SERVICES

Cool but not too cool is the rule, particularly for vintage Champagne; an hour or so in the fridge or 10 minutes in a bucket full of ice and water should do the trick. A half-hour in the freezer may be similarly effective, but potentially very dangerous; if you allow it to freeze, it could explode.

When opening Champagne bottles, treat them with as much care as you would a firework. From the moment you remove the wire capsule, the cork could fly out at any moment. So don't leave it unattended. Point the bottle away from people and valuables and, holding it at an angle of 45 degrees, gently turn it while keeping a firm grip on the cork (there are special plier-like grips to help this part of the operation).

Unless you are a racing driver, avoid spraying anyone with wine. Let the cork out gently; keeping the bottle at that 45-degree angle should reduce its keenness to froth over.

All Champagne, vintage and non-vintage, is sold ready to drink. Most will benefit from a further year or so in your rack at home – provided (and this is crucial) that you buy it from a supplier who has a swift turnover.

juice for just long enough to tint the wine, thus producing what the Champenois call Rosé de Noir; or you simply blend a little of the region's red wine into the white fizz. Purists prefer the first of these methods; unfortunately, their preference is not supported by blind tastings in which skilled judges are often unable to differentiate between the best wines of both styles.

Vintage

Vintage Champagne can be made by any producer in any year reckoned to be up to the mark. Small domaines tend to produce a vintage fizz every year simply because they lack the old stock with which to blend a good non-vintage. Thus there is no guarantee that a vintage Champagne will be better than a good non-vintage, but it should have been made from the best available grapes harvested in a ripe year. Just as crucially, it must have been aged on its lees – or yeasts – for at least 36 months, which should give it a richer, yeastier, nuttier flavour than non-vintage, which enjoys a legal minimum of just 12 months'

Sunset strip: *The valley of the Marne, near Bouzy (left)*
Not RIP: *A vineyard marker, showing ownership of vines (right)*

yeast contact (though good Champagne houses will aim to give their non-vintage fizz three years or so too).

The non-sparkling wines of Champagne

Coteaux Champenois Blanc
At its best, Coteaux Champenois Blanc can be a little like Chablis, but rarely like top-class Chablis. In cooler vintages, a glass could save you from having to visit the dentist; do-it-yourself teeth-scaler. Laurent Perrier's version comes in a pretty bottle; Saran and Ruinart are usually better.

Coteaux Champenois Rouge
If the white grapes find it hard to ripen, the Pinot Noir and Pinot Meunier have very little chance of doing so. In some ripe years, however, Coteaux Champenois Rouge can be made, which has some of the character of basic red Burgundy – but at a much higher price. Bouzy Rouge is the one to look for, if only because of its delicious name, but several other villages – for example, Ay and Ambonnay – proudly put their name to their own reds.

Rosé de Riceys
Rosé de Riceys is a more interesting wine, if only because Pinot Noir rosé is quite rare. It is produced in the Aube, a region which is not generally thought to make the best Champagne. Like its still red and white neighbours, it can be lean stuff – and expensive – but good examples are juicily raspberryish.

Filets de Sole Champagne

Sole fillets in a Champagne, cream and mushroom sauce

Although its wine is distinctive, the Champagne region does not have a cuisine that is quite as individual. This is not to say that the countryside is not well endowed. Pork dishes are prominent, as is game, such as wild boar and venison, and there is plenty of fish – pike and trout in particular – from its rivers. The following recipe need not be made with Champagne, but is certainly delicious if it is accompanied by a glass or two.

SERVES 6
*12 unskinned sole fillets
salt and freshly ground black pepper
8 oz/225 g mushrooms, sliced
(include the left-over stems)
18 button mushroom caps
2 small onions finely diced
2 oz/50 g butter
juice of half a lemon
3 wine-glasses of dry Champagne or
a good dry white wine
10 fl oz/275 ml double cream
2 tbsp brandy
2 egg yolks
chopped fresh parsley to garnish*

Season the fillets with salt and pepper. Mix the chopped mushrooms with the onion in a bowl. Melt half the butter in a small frying pan. Add the mushroom caps and sauté gently. Remove the pan from the heat after about 4 minutes and keep warm. With the remaining butter, grease a shallow flameproof dish and spread the onion and mushroom mixture in it evenly. Sprinkle with lemon juice and arrange the fillets on top. Pour in the wine and bring to the boil, then immediately reduce to a simmer. Cook gently for about 4 minutes or until the fish is just cooked through. Remove the fillets with a slotted slice and place on a warmed serving dish. In a small saucepan mix the cream, brandy and egg yolks and, while cooking gently, stirring all the time, gradually add the juices from the pan in which the fish was cooked. Simmer and stir until the sauce thickens. Pour over the fillets, add the mushrooms and garnish with the parsley. Serve with boiled potatoes and a carrot purée.

EASTERN FRANCE

*T*HE JURA is caught in a time warp, making eccentric, old-fashioned wine in precisely the same way it has done for centuries. But the Jura has a place in wine history because it was in this region of vineyards and dairy cattle that Louis Pasteur was born, and it was here that he carried out his first experiments on ways to prevent milk from going bad, and wine from oxidizing.

The wines that fascinated Pasteur were the dry, but curranty-raisiny *vins de paille* still produced (though rarely nowadays), like some of Italy's most traditional wines, from grapes laid out to dry on straw mats beneath the autumn sun and, more particularly, *vin jaune* which, like *fino* sherry, is allowed to oxidize in its barrels beneath a film of scum-like yeasts that the Spanish call *flor*.

Vin jaune is an exception that proves a pretty reliable rule. Leave almost any other red or white wine in a cask that hasn't been topped up properly and you will end up with vinegar; *vin jaune* is protected from harmful bacteria by its blanket of yeast during the 18 months it can take to ferment and the six years that it has to be matured. The flavour of *vin jaune* is inevitably more like that of sherry than any other white wine, but it's lighter in alcohol (not having been fortified) and packed with more of a punch of flavour because, unlike the neutral Palomino used for *fino* sherry, the French wine is made from the assertive Savagnin grape. Some people hate it; others revel in its extraordinary nutty, salty, woody, flower-and-leaf flavours.

The best *vin jaune* is made (in tiny quantities) at Château-Chalon and l'Etoile, but examples from the small market town of Arbois and the regional Côtes du Jura are slightly less rare. Despite efforts at standardization by the authorities in Brussels, all *vin jaune* comes in the eccentric 62 cl clavelin bottle, because, the Juraçiens claim, six years' evaporation from the barrels "costs" them 13 cl a time.

Of the Jura's other wines, the whites, even when they are made from the Chardonnay, seem to have unwanted *vin jaune* character – and get sent back in restaurants for being oxidized. L'Etoile is,

again, the one *Appellation* that gets it richly right, often by blending the Savagnin with Chardonnay and even a little of the red-wine Poulsard grape.

There is no red l'Etoile, but Arbois makes red and rosé wines from the Pinot Noir, sometimes blended with the Pinot Gris, both of which taste a little like middle-weight Pinot Noir from Alsace and rarely repay ageing. Arbois reds made from the Trousseau and Poulsard vary in style, depending on the blend; the former makes heavy, tannic wines with little discernible flavour, while the latter can be delicate and floral, but with a hint of woodsmoke; a marriage of the two is decidedly characterful. The Pupillin Co-operative makes a good example.

SAVOIE

Far less bizarre, but even less well known beyond this region, are the wines of Savoie. Of course, every year, there are a whole lot of people who discover these wines for the first time – because this is winter sports

Arbois: A market town in the mountains, making yellow wine

country, and if you ask for a bottle of something white as an *après-ski* refresher in Val d'Isère, this tangy, floral and often slightly sparkling wine is what you'll probably be given. But, as the skiers pack up their goggles, their boots and their recipe for Glühwein, they tend to forget the wines they drank on holiday. Even in Paris, bottles labelled Crépy and Chignin-Bergeron are rare.

It would be easier for the Savoyards if those vineyards were all in a single area, but instead they're scattered around the valleys and on the slopes like patches of melting snow left over from what was once a far larger area; in the eighteenth century, there were around 22,500 acres (9,000 ha) of vines; today the figure is just over 2,500 acres (1,000 ha).

The local grapes are a curious bunch too: the Jacquère, Roussanne, Roussette, Cacabboué, Gringet, Mondeuse and Persan and the Petite-Sainte-Marie. This last may sound like the most obscure of them all, but actually the Little-Saint-Mary is one of the

The Essentials

EASTERN FRANCE

What to look for Fresh, light, if overpriced, young Savoie white and reds, and pleasant Pinot Noir, rich fizz and nutty, sherry-like whites from Arbois.

Location To the east of, and running parallel to, Burgundy: Savoie comprises a series of small wine-producing areas from Lac Léman (Lake Geneva) south to Grenoble; Arbois lies within the Côtes du Jura to the north of Savoie, on the slopes of the Jura mountain range.

Official quality AOCs: Arbois and Arbois Mousseux; Arbois Pupillin; Côtes du Jura and Côtes du Jura Mousseux; L'Etoile; Château-Chalon (*vin jaune*); Crépy; Roussette de Savoie (and *cru*); Seyssel; Seyssel Mousseux; Vin de Savoie (of which the most widely seen *cru* is Apremont) and Vin de Savoie Mousseux. The best-known VDQS is Bugey (and *cru*); Bugey Mousseux is also made.

Style Still and sparkling white wines are very fresh, floral and light, reminiscent of the wines of nearby Switzerland; more traditional wood-aged Jura whites are slightly fuller. Jura reds and rosés are light and vaguely Burgundian, while Savoie reds can sometimes be quite robust. *Vin jaune* and *vin de paille* are the Jura's speciality styles; the former, though unfortified, has been called France's answer to *fino* sherry, while the latter is extremely sweet with an appealing nuttiness. Arbois Pupillin reds can be characterful, if rustic.

Climate The area is affected by the proximity of the Alps and, while the summers are warm, it can be very damp, cold and frosty during the winter and spring.

Cultivation The vineyards are found on gentle lower slopes. The soil is predominantly clay, with some limestone and marl.

Grape varieties Cacabboué, Chardonnay, Chasselas, Gringet, Jacquère, Molette, Mondeuse, Mondeuse Blanche, Pinot Blanc, Pinot Noir, Poulsard, Roussanne, Roussette (Altesse), Savagnin, Tressot, Trousseau.

Production/maturation Stainless steel and, in the Jura, large wood is used for fermentation. Sparkling wines are made by the *méthode champenoise*. Côtes du Jura Mousseux is the best sparkling wine *Appellation* here. *Vin jaune* must be matured for at least six years in oak with no topping up, and a yeast *flor* develops, as in *fino* sherry; *vin de paille* is made from bunches of grapes that have been laid out to dry for up to six months while the sugar concentration intensifies. *Vin jaune* is made entirely from the Savagnin grape, while *vin de paille* is generally made from a blend of grapes, but always including the Savagnin. Labour-intensive to produce, these are fairly rare, expensive wines.

Longevity All Savoie whites should be drunk as young as possible, as should rosés. Red wines will last for between 3 and 6 years, while *vin jaune* and *vin de paille* appear to last almost indefinitely.

Vintage guide 95.

My Top 10 *Arbois*: Château d'Arlay, Jean Bourdy, Château de l'Etoile, Henri Maire, Aubin Co-operative, Pupillin Co-operative, Domaine de Montbourgeau; *Savoie*: Pierre Boniface, Goy, Mercier.

Gratin aux Cèpes

Baked sliced potatoes in a mushroom and cream sauce

The crisp, white wines of the region go splendidly with trout, crayfish and char from the lakes and mountain streams. They also complement the region's dairy produce, which is often teamed up with the area's particularly good potatoes.

SERVES 6

2 lb/1 kg peeled and thinly sliced potatoes
1½ lb/750 g mushrooms, sliced
(cultivated will do if cèpes are unobtainable)
4 tbsp finely chopped onion
6 tbsp grated Gruyère or Emmenthal cheese
1 garlic clove, peeled and minced
Salt and freshly ground black pepper
1 pt/575 ml double cream
2 tbsp milk
½ tsp grated nutmeg
1 oz/25 g butter
4 tbsp chopped parsley

Butter a shallow ovenproof dish. Layer potatoes with mushroom sprinkled with onion, cheese, garlic, salt and pepper. Mix the cream and milk in a saucepan and bring almost to the boil. Pour over the dish. Sprinkle on the nutmeg. Dot with butter and bake in a preheated oven at 350°F/180°C/Gas mark 4 for about 1¼ hours. Remove from oven and sprinkle with parsley. Serve either as a lunch dish with salad or as an accompaniment to roast lamb or beef.

only two that are grown anywhere else; it's the local name for the Chardonnay. And the other one? The usually dull Chasselas.

There's something about the cool climate of Savoie, as in nearby Switzerland, that lets this variety shine. Here, it's used as an ingredient in a wide range of tangily floral whites; but it's not the one that gives them their distinctive spicy character; that comes from the obscure Roussette (also known as the Altesse) and Jacquère, and in some cases, the Pinot Gris. The blanket regional *Appellation* of Vin de Savoie includes some good, lightweight but emphatically refreshing *méthode champenoise pétillant* and *mousseux* whites made from blends of local grapes; and reds and rosés that combine the Gamay and Pinot Noir with local red and even (up to 20 per cent) white varieties. There are a number of individual villages whose names can appear on labels. Of these, the best are Ayze (which makes good sparkling wine) Apremont, Abymes and Chignin-Bergeron (whose

Putting on the ritz: *Abymes, one of the best crus of Savoie*

white offers a rare chance to experience pure Roussanne).

Best-known of Savoie's other *Appellations* is Crépy, which, like Muscadet, is bottled *sur lie* and is thus very slightly sparkling. But it's got bags more flowery freshness than most Muscadet. For the flavour of pure Roussette, try the dry, flowery Seyssel; the *mousseux* made here can be good but slightly less distinctive, probably because of its high Chasselas content. Roussette de Savoie and Roussette de Bugey can both (with the exception of a few specified villages) include Chardonnay, which tends to make for a creamier, less tangy flavour. The Vins du Bugey are often single-varietals, including some first-class pure Chardonnay, but the label also appears on some refreshingly fruity Gamay/Pinot Noir/Poulsard/Mondeuse blends.

Heading south, there are also the *vins de pays* de la Haute-Sâone, du Franche-Comté, du Jura, de l'Ain, de la Haute Savoie, de Savoie, de l'Allobrogie, des Balmes Dauphinoises, and des Coteaux du Grésivadan. The majority of these wines (red, pink and white) are fairly lightweight, the whites being made from the same local grapes as the region's *Appellations*, and the reds and rosés being mostly Pinot Noir and Gamay.

PROVENCE AND CORSICA

PROVENCE

SOMEWHERE, close to the village of Cassis, so the locals say, there's a staircase to Heaven built by God to facilitate deliveries of His favourite wine. Sitting at a café on the seafront here, watching the fishing boats bobbing away, with a plateful of olives on the table and a glass of chilled, fresh peppery Côtes de Provence pink in your hand, it's extremely easy to imagine that they are right.

For most people, thoughts of Provence's wines are all too often wrapped up in memories or conjured-up images of sun-baked holidays. When they actually taste the same wines on a chilly day in London, New York or Paris, doubts begin to creep in. Is it the wine that's changed, or is it me? It's probably a bit of both – but no matter which, the wines never taste as good without the accompaniment of olives and sunshine.

This is far too easy a region in which to be lazy. And then, there are all the traditional ways that no one wants to cast

Gold in them thar hills: Or at least bauxite. Vines at Les Baux

---

The Essentials
PROVENCE AND CORSICA

What to look for Fresh Provence rosés, traditional Rhône-style reds and modern blends. New-wave efforts at traditional Corsican grape varieties.

Location The south-east corner of France, bounded by the Rhône and the Italian border. The Mediterranean island of Corsica lies 110 km off the coast, south-east of Provence.

Official quality *Provence* AOCs: Bandol; Bellet; Cassis; Côtes de Provence, Coteaux d'Aix-en-Provence; Les Baux de Provence; Palette. The best-known VDQSs are Coteaux de Pierrevert and Coteaux Varois. *Vins de pays* include: Bouches-du-Rhône, Mont Caume, Oc, Var and Maures. *Corsica* AOCs: Vin de Corse (with a number of suffixes) – Aiaccio and Patrimonio are the best-known; the *vins de pays* de l'Ile de Beauté and of Pieves, however, include some of Corsica's more interesting wines, from Cabernet Sauvignon, Syrah, Chardonnay and Sauvignon Blanc. *Vins doux naturels* are from Patrimonio and Cap Corse.

Style The red wines of Corsica and Provence are generally deep, dense and ripe, varying in style from Bandol, which must contain at least 50 per cent Mourvèdre, to the excellent Château Vignelaure, made from Cabernet Sauvignon. Provence rosés tend to be dry, often with an evocative herby character, while the white wines, although rarely exciting, are pleasantly aromatic.

Climate The Mediterranean influence ensures mild winters and springs and long, hot summers and autumns. The vines are planted on both hillside and plain sites. The soil is mainly composed of sand and granite, plus some limestone.

Grape varieties Aramon, Aramon Gris, Barbarossa, Barbaroux, Barbaroux Rosa, Bourboulenc, Braquet, Brun-Fourcat, Cabernet Sauvignon, Calitor, Carignan, Chardonnay, Cinsault, Clairette, Clairette à Gros Grains, Clairette à Petits Grains, Clairette de Trans, Colombard, Counoise, Doucillon, Durif, Folle Noir, Fuella, Grenache, Grenache Blanc, Marsanne, Mayorquin, Mourvèdre, Muscat d'Aubagne, Muscat Blanc à Petits Grains, Muscat de Frontignan, Muscat de Die, Muscat de Hamburg, Muscat de Marseille, Muscat Noir de Provence, Muscat Rosé à Petits Grains, Nielluccio, Panse Muscado, Pascal Blanc, Petit Brun, Picardan, Picpoul, Pignol, Rolle (Vermentino), Roussanne, Sauvignon Blanc, Sémillon, Sciacarello, Syrah, Teoulier, Terret Blanc, Terret Gris, Terret Noir, Tener Ramenée, Tibouren, Ugni Blanc, Ugni Rosé.

Production/maturation New-tech applied to traditional grapes and styles is producing some exciting reds. Provence rosés are benefiting from the introduction of cool-vinification methods, although large old wood is still widely used for fermentation and maturation of other wines. Red Bandol must be matured in cask for a minimum of 18 months.

Longevity White and rosé wines should be drunk within 3 years; red wines generally within 5, although Bandol and the wines of the producers starred (*) below will last a decade.

Vintage guide 92, 94, 95.

My Top 14 *Provence:* Domaine Ott*, Château Simone, Domaine de Trévallon*, Château Vignelaure*, Domaine Tempier*, Terres Blanches, Mas de Gourgonnier, Mas de la Dame, de Beapré, Fonscolombe, du Seuil. *Corsica:* Domaine Comte Peraldi, Skalli-Fortant de France, UVAL.

off – such as allowing dull, local, white grapes to ferment at high temperatures, of leaving the reds for too long in old casks and allowing the rosés to become bronze-coloured and stale.

The Provençaux are at last beginning to get their act together, making consistently better, fruitier wines from fruitier grapes. Côtes de Provence is not all rosé; a fifth of the wine made here is red and a tenth, white. Too much of the red and pink is still made from the Carignan, but growers are busily planting Cabernet Sauvignon, Syrah and Mourvèdre, and taking more care of their Grenache. Cool fermentation and a little Sémillon and Sauvignon have arrived for the whites too, to help the workhorses, Ugni Blanc and Clairette.

Much the same could be said for two recent AOC promotions, Coteaux d'Aix-en-Provence and its enclave, Les Baux de Provence. Both already made adequate-to-good whites and rosés, but the focus now is on fruity, spicy, modern reds, made from blends of Grenache, Syrah, Mourvèdre, Cinsault and lots – up to 60 per cent in Coteaux d'Aix-en-Provence – of Cabernet Sauvignon. The flagship estate here, Château Vignelaure, is back on form after a dull patch and other investment is moving in fast.

The marriage of Syrah and Cabernet, once acceptable for Bordeaux such as Château Cos d'Estournel and now familiar in Australia, is given its most dramatic French showcase in Les Baux de Provence at the Domaine de Trévallon, a wine which can fetch a higher price than many a claret.

Palette is curious stuff, and very characterful. Its best wine is the rosé which, like the white, is exclusively made and aged in oak by Château Simone. Both these wines are very herby in flavour, but pleasantly so; the red is simply herby and dry.

Bandol proudly claims the best climate of the Côte d'Azur. Californian wine-makers hasten from one cellar to another. What brings them here is the chance to sample a grape that they've heard a lot about in the Rhône. Red Bandol has to include at least 50 per cent Mourvèdre (the rest is made up by Grenache, Cinsault and Syrah) and should reveal that variety's spicy, herby flavour and, in good examples, its ability to age. The rosé, made from the same grapes, is similarly good (but expensive).

On the maps of wine regions, Bellet looks huge, covering 17,500 acres (700 ha) of steep slopes around Nice. And there's the rub; the land here is worth too much as gardens for millionaires' villas. A mere two dozen producers farm just 125 acres (50 ha)

to make these crisp whites and rosés, using the local Rolle, Roussanne, Pignerol and Mayorquin for the former, and Braquet and Folle Noire for the latter. Prices, like those for almost everything else in Nice, are very high.

Lastly, there are the country wines here at the mouth of the Rhône and heading eastwards and westwards along the coast: the variable *vins de pays* des Bouches du Rhône, excellent de Mont Caume and *vins de pays* des Sables du Golfe du Lion, in which is situated the large Listel winery, near the tourist-trap walled town of Aigues Mortes.

CORSICA

Corsica is part of Italy. I know that's not what they believe in Paris, and I know the Corsicans would probably (just) prefer to be French than Italian, but the wine-makers of this glorious island have far more in common with their neighbours in Campania than their counterparts on the French mainland.

The names of the producers, Torraccia, Peraldi, Gentile – and of the grape varieties, Nielluccio, Sciacarello, Vermentino – and the styles of most of the traditional wines – dull, oxidized whites and rosés and big, alcoholic reds – all support Corsica's case as a long-lost cousin of Sardinia and Sicily.

And so does the extraordinary generosity with which the *Appellation Contrôlée* authorities have dished out no less than eight inadequate *Appellations*, deftly avoiding giving one to the only style that actually deserves it, the raisiny Muscat produced in various parts of the island.

What Corsica has needed is modernization. Unfortunately, until quite recently, neither Corsicans nor the North African immigrant wine-makers have been keen on ideas like that.

The wines are improving fast, though. For the best examples, and the best value, apart from the Muscat, go for the offerings of Skalli-Fortant de France, the wonderfully

Rouget à la Niçoise

Sautéed red mullet in a tomato and herb sauce

The heat of the south of France gives the region's classic ingredients – garlic, tomatoes, olives and herbs – such an intensity of taste that Provençale dishes seem to be soaked in the sun.

SERVES 6

12 small whole red mullet or 12 fillets, scaled and cleaned
Salt and freshly ground black pepper
Plain flour
Olive oil, enough to cover a frying pan to a depth of ½ in/1 cm
2 lb/1 kg tomatoes, peeled, seeded and chopped, or tinned tomatoes, drained and chopped
Dried thyme
12 anchovy fillets
6 black olives, pitted
6 tsp capers
Juice of 1 lemon
Chopped fresh parsley to garnish

Season fish with salt and pepper and then dust lightly with flour. In a frying pan heat the oil until it is almost smoking. Put in a batch of fish, turning until they are browned on both sides. Remove with a slotted slice and drain on kitchen paper. Repeat until all the fish are cooked. Put them in a shallow ovenproof dish. Pour over the tomato and sprinkle a pinch of thyme on each piece of fish, then place on each an anchovy fillet, 3 olives and ½ tsp capers. Sprinkle with the lemon juice. Bake, uncovered, in a pre-heated oven at 325°F/170°C/Gas mark 3 for about 20 minutes, until the flesh of the fish parts easily from the bone or, if filleted, is just flaking. Serve with boiled rice.

named *vins de pays* de l'Ile de Beauté, made by the UVAL co-operatives, and now featuring Chardonnay, Syrah and Cabernet alongside the local varieties. And if you're there and want a Corsican classic with your dinner, try the good but overpriced, very old-fashioned reds and even a carefully oaked white from the Domaine Comte Peraldi.

Corsica: If only the wines would inspire like the scenery

SOUTHERN FRANCE

ONE OF the sadder figures in the wine world is the Burgundy or Bordeaux producer with an obsession about the competition his region is now facing from New-World countries such as the Americas, the Antipodes and South Africa. It is a little like a jealous husband who's worried about being cuckolded by a rival from another country when the true challenge lives in the house next door.

It is easy to sympathize with the Burgundians and Bordelais for underestimating Languedoc-Roussillon: a few years ago, it may have been the world's biggest single vineyard region, but it was also a major tributary of the wine lake. Every year wine-makers, whose French accent was almost as impenetrable to a Parisian as it would be to any foreigner, got on with the business of producing huge quantities of wine, most of which might just as well have been turned directly into industrial alcohol.

The plug began to be removed from the lake in the 1980s, as an increasing number of farmers switched their attention from growing unwanted wine-grapes to planting orchards. And, while the bulk-wine producers reduced their production, their younger, keener neighbours began, with a bit of help from a growing number of newcomers, to think quality, They studied modern wine-making at the nearby University of Montpellier, tasted wines grown in other warm parts of the world like California and Australia, compared their region to the Barossa and Napa Valleys and thought "Why not us?"

HIDDEN STRENGTHS

But before considering the new wines the new-wave producers are now making, let's look at the wines which were never at risk of ending up in any lake. First of these were the *vins doux naturels*. Ironically, while the sweet, fortified Muscat for which France is best known comes from Beaumes de Venise in the Rhône, the far wider range of sometimes richer Muscats here goes almost unnoticed.

The Muscat de Frontignan was once well enough known to have given its name to the finer kind of Muscat, the Muscat à Petits Grains. As in Beaumes de Venise, the co-operative makes almost all of the wine, but an independent jury tastes each year's production to ensure regularity of quality which is generally good, but not quite as zingy as the wine from the Rhône. The rather bigger, richer, Muscat de Mireval owes its style to the way in which it is matured at often very warm outdoor temperatures for two years before bottling. Like the far more delicate Muscat de St Jean de Minervois, however, it is produced in very small quantities.

There are two other Muscats, both of which claim to be the best in France: the light Muscat de Lunel and the beefier Muscat de Rivesaltes. They come in white and pink styles and are usually of at least good quality – and often rather better than wine that is just labelled Rivesaltes which is made in red, white, pink and tawny styles from a rag-bag of local varieties, and accounts for half of France's *vins doux naturels*. The mixture of Grenache and

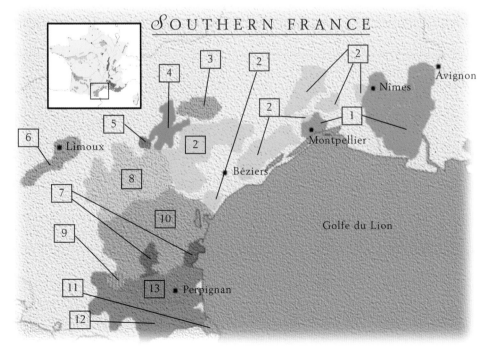

1 Costières de Nîmes
2 Coteaux du Languedoc
3 Faugères
4 St-Chinian
5 Muscat de St-Jean de Minervois
6 Blanquette de Limoux
7 Fitou
8 Minervois
9 Maury (including Rivesaltes)
10 Corbières
11 Collioure and Banyuls
12 Côtes du Roussillon (including Rivesaltes)
13 Côtes du Roussillon-Villages (including Rivesaltes)

Muscat used for the red and pink tends to make for emphatically old-fashioned flavours that seem reminiscent of stewed fruits, though the Maccabeo white can taste fascinatingly like currants and spice. Rivesaltes is also a good place to discover the style the French call "rancio", produced by ageing *vin doux naturel* in barrel and intentionally allowing it to oxidize. This sweet sherry-like stuff is an acquired taste, but good examples can have lots of spicy, plummy flavour.

Banyuls, the *Appellation* that's usually described as France's answer to port, also comes in a *rancio* style. The interesting wine here, though, is the red which, made primarily from the Grenache, tastes the way cheap ruby port would if that wine were better made. Sadly, really good examples are rare, but look for the words "*Grand Cru*" on the label; they indicate that there's at least 75 per cent Grenache and 30 months' ageing in wood. The Grenache is used to make the fortified red and rosé at Maury too – and some *rancio*. All three are curiously spicy – but they have their fans.

FROM DULL TO DIVINE

Grapes for Banyuls are picked late; earlier-harvested fruit from the same vineyards can be sold as Collioure, taking its name from the tiniest and least-spoiled fishing village of this region. There's very little made, but what is produced is wonderfully intense red wine. Clairette du Languedoc is made from the Clairette grape in three styles: dull table wine, dull fortified and dull *rancio*. All are, however, more impressive than the even duller unfortified wine made from the same grape at Clairette de Bellegarde.

The Clairette was once used in the sparkling wines of Blanquette de Limoux which are now made mostly from the local Mauzac. The banning of the Clairette in 1978 led to an instant improvement in what claims to be the oldest sparkling wine of all, though styles and quality vary depending on how much Chenin Blanc or (increasingly) Chardonnay feature in the blend. The efforts made to improve quality, and the modernization of the highly impressive Limoux co-operative, have been rewarded by the award of a separate *Appellation* to the Chardonnay which previously was merely a *vin de pays*. The coolish climate and the limestone both suit the variety well and make for wines that often have little

The Essentials
SOUTHERN FRANCE

What to look for Traditional reds, fresh modern styles, especially varietals, rich fortified Muscats and fast-improving fizz.
Official quality AOCs: Banyuls (VDN – *vin doux naturel*); Blanquette de Limoux; Clairette de Bellegarde; Clairette du Languedoc; Collioure; Corbières; Costières de Nîmes; Coteaux du Languedoc; Côtes du Roussillon; Côtes du Roussillon-Villages; Faugères; Fitou; Limoux; Maury (VDN); Minervois; Muscat de Frontignan (VDN); Muscat de Lunel (VDN); Muscat de Mireval (VDN); Muscat de St-Jean-de-Minervois (VDN); Muscat de Rivesaltes (VDN); St Chinian; Vin Noble du Minervois. VDQSs include: Costières du Gard; Côtes de la Malepère; Cabardès. *Vins de pays* include: Gard; Coteaux Flaviens; Hérault; Coteaux de Murviel; Côtes de Thongue; Aude; Vallée de Paradis; Oc; Pyrénées Orientales; des Sables du Golfe de Lion.
Style The majority of wines produced are red. At their best, Corbières or Côtes du Roussillon-Villages for example, they are firm, rounded, deeply coloured and packed full of spicy, peppery fruit. White and rosé wines may be dry or medium-dry and are improving fast. Sparkling Blanquette de Limoux is produced using a local (and ancient) variation on the *méthode champenoise*; appley-lemony, sometimes quite full and earthy, it can more resemble Spanish Cava than more northerly French sparkling wines. Some of the region's most interesting wines are its *vins doux naturels* from Banyuls, Maury and Rivesaltes; deep, dark and raisiny-sweet. Muscat de Frontignan is lighter but just as intensely sweet. Bordeaux grapes – especially Merlot – are increasingly being planted in the Midi and more modern vinification techniques are being incorporated into the wineries. The resulting wines are cleaner, fresher and decidedly fruitier. These southern French wines are some of the best value-for-money wines to be found anywhere.
Climate Influenced by the Mediterranean and also the savage marine and mistral winds.
Cultivation Vineyards are found on the alluvial soils of the plains and on slopes above valleys such as the Aude.
Grape varieties Alicante-Bouschet, Aspiran Gris, Aspiran Noir, Auban, Bourboulenc, Cabernet Franc, Cabernet Sauvignon, Carignan, Carignan Blanc, Cinsault, Clairette, Couderc, Grenache Blanc, Grenache Rosé, Fer, Lladoner Pelut, Malbec, Malvoisie, Maccabeo, Marsanne, Mauzac Blanc, Merlot, Mourvèdre, Muscat d'Alexandre, Muscat Blanc à Petits Grains, Muscat de Frontignan, Muscat Rosé à Petits Grains, Négrette, Oeillade, Palomino, Picpoul, Picpoul Noir, Roussanne, Syrah, Terret, Terret Noir, Tourbat, Ugni Blanc, Villard Blanc.
Production/maturation While (old) wooden vats are still sometimes used for fermentation, stainless steel and new oak are now common. *Vins doux naturels* (VDN) are half-fermented, then a very strong spirit is added to stun the yeasts and raise the alcohol level.
Longevity Most wines are made to drink within 3 years, although some of the better reds may last beyond 5. If a VDN is non-vintage it should be ready to drink, but vintage VDNs can continue to develop in bottle for decades.
Vintage guide 94, 95.
My Top 12 *Languedoc*: Pech-Redon, Abbaye de Valmagne; *Roussillon:* Cazes Frères, Château de Jau, Corneilla, Dom Gauby; *Vin de Pays de l'Hérault:* Mas de Daumas Gassac; *Minervois:* Château de Gourgazaud; *Corbières:* Château de Lastours; *Vin de Pays d'Oc:* Skalli-Fortant de France, Domaine de la Baume, Domaine Virginie.

Corbières: The ruins of Nôtre Dame des Ouilles

difficulty in outclassing basic Chablis.

Back toward the coast, in the mountainous region around Perpignan, you know you're close to the Spanish border. Some of the villagers speak Catalan, some speak heavily accented French, but it makes little difference – both are almost equally unintelligible even to a Frenchman from a few hundred miles away. The Côtes du

Roussillon is the place to find some fast-improving, good-value, juicy-fruity reds and rosés – and some aniseedy whites that need drinking straight from the co-operative vat before they lose their freshness. The Côtes du Roussillon Villages, especially from the communes of Caramany and Latour de France, produce the *Appellation*'s best wines but these too need drinking young.

Fitou has a reputation for flavour and value, too, which seems slightly surprising, given the fact that this *Appellation*'s reds have to be made from 70 per cent of the usually derided Carignan and aged for 18 months in (usually old) wood. Fitou isn't specifically fruity, but it is big-bodied and rich, and everyone's holiday-driven idea of how good, southern red should taste.

Climbing up: *The Coteaux de Languedoc has a way to go but is improving*

Corbières got its *Appellation* after Fitou, but the wines made in this savage region are also Carignan-dominated and have a similar style, except that here, lighter, fruitier wines are being made. For real class, though, go to the Château de Lastours, a home for the mentally handicapped whose residents helped to produce a red wine good enough to beat the world at the 1989 *Wine Magazine* International Challenge.

Minervois is improving, too, thanks to a number of innovative producers, including the Châteaux de Gourgazaud, de Blomac and Ste Eulalie, which are producing reds with all kinds of rich flavours. For far finer fare, though, head for the hills, to Faugères and St Chinian, two villages that compete in making fruity, plum-'n'-cherry reds, using traditional blends of Carignan and Rhône varieties. Faugères, in particular, is a beautiful, made-for-vines region, where I'd certainly spend a windfall on buying an estate. The berryish wines produced so far are only scraping the surface of what could be achieved. Watch this space.

On the coast, the Coteaux de Languedoc is a region – and a collection of villages including the commune of La Clape – which, in the Middle Ages, was actually an island, connected to the mainland by a bridge. Malvasia and Terret Blanc are used to make distinctively grapey whites that can last. The reds and rosés lean heavily on the Carignan but include Cinsault and Grenache. La Clape is the region's only

white wine; of the other villages, the best are St Saturnin which makes a good, light *vin d'une nuit* rosé by leaving the juice with the skins overnight, St Drézéry, with a 24-hour rosé, St-Christol (a favourite, for what it's worth, of Tsar Nicholas II of Russia) Quatourze, Coteaux de Verargues and Cabrières, famous in the fourteenth century for its "bronze" rosé, and still the place to sample the local Oeillade grape.

Of the region's VDQSs, the best are the Costières du Gard which can be perfectly pleasant, if sometimes dull, reds, whites and pinks from mixed assortments of local grapes. The wines of the Côtes de la Malepère can be more impressive – and in the case of the red, a bit more Bordeaux-like – as can the Rhône-like Cabardès.

BRAVE NEW WORLD

So much for the improved and improving classics of the regions. Now let's get back to those revolutionaries. Professor Emile Peynaud, the genius behind the modernization of Bordeaux, once elegantly defined tradition as "an experiment that has worked". Mahler had an alternative view: for him, tradition was laziness. Until the 1960s, the vineyards of southern France proved both men right. An experiment in making wine lazily had succeeded quite well. For as long as people were prepared to buy flavourless, often quite vinegary, stuff, the men and women of Languedoc-

Roussillon could provide it without too much difficulty. Things became trickier when customers at home and abroad began to demand flavour and freshness – qualities their particular tradition of shoddy wine-making simply could not provide.

Fortunately, examples of those traditional wines are becoming rarer with every year, but I'd like to collect up a set of them and force a glass past the lips of every critic I hear complain about modernists who are making everything taste the same. I suppose there are people who feel nostalgic for the sort of cars Skoda made in the good old days of Communism when taking a bend at over 40 mph often involved defying death. Personally, I prefer the way they are made today.

Several people deserve credit for introducing southern France to the modern world of wine. Aimé Guibert, the foxy creator of Mas de Daumas Gassac, the self-termed *"Grand Cru"* Vin de Pays de l'Hérault, which sells for the price you might expect to pay for a classy Bordeaux or Burgundy, proved that one did not have to go to the classic wine regions to find "special" soil – and that you didn't have to follow the classic recipes of which grapes could go into which blends. If his red tastes better because he's included Pinot Noir and Cabernet, well, why not do it?

Guibert's influence has been enormous, and helped to inspire the giant Australian

The heart of Minervois: *The town of Minerve itself, bathed in sunlight*

firm Penfold's when it came to make its own, large-production versions of Guibert's blends in partnership with Val d'Orbieu, one of the biggest, most dynamic firms in the south.

The collection of co-operatives brought together by Val d'Orbieu is today highly successful, using New-World techniques to make modern varietals and more traditional local styles. What it has so far failed to do is create an international brand for its wines – unlike Skalli-Fortant de France which, under the leadership of Robert Skalli, a canny, Corsican, marketing genius, has introduced wine-drinkers in Europe, the Far East, the US and, most significantly, France, to the idea of buying a reliable, smartly packaged, fairly priced bottle of Vin de Pays d'Oc Chardonnay, Merlot or Viognier rather than a potentially unreliable *Appellation* wine from a supposedly "better" region.

Finally, but just as crucially, there have been the foreigners, mostly Australians, who have brought their money, skills and enthusiasm to the region. If James Herrick had not planted one of the world's biggest Chardonnay vineyards, if BRL Hardy had not bought its Domaine de la Baume, if Antipodean wine-making had not been introduced at Domaines Virginie, and if countless Flying Wine-makers had never been deployed throughout the region on behalf of British and Dutch buyers, by men like Hugh Ryman, Kym Milne and Jacques Lurton, I doubt we'd be seeing half the exciting wines that are now emerging from Languedoc-Roussillon, nor the creation of a wholly new set of traditions and exciting experiments.

UP FROM THE COUNTRY

The one thing the revolutionaries all have in common is that they have been working outside the straitlaced *Appellation Contrôlée* system which has, until now, been the sole focus of attention for France's wine experts and critics. The new wines are, among some 125 *vins de pays*, the "country wines" of France.

Some of these regions encompass huge swathes of land that seem to stretch from one end of France to the other, while others are tucked away in small, obscure corners you only ever find your way to by accident. Whatever the relative sizes of the *vin de pays* areas, however, their rules all allow far greater experimentation with grape types than those governing *Appellation Contrôlée* wines – and,

unlike *Appellation* wines, they permit reference to two grape varieties on the label.

The larger regions, such as the prettily named Vin du Pays du Jardin de la France in the Loire, tend to offer something of a lucky dip: some of their Sauvignon Blancs and Chardonnays can be good examples of these varieties, while others – most of the Chenin Blanc, for example – can be either dull or downright poor.

The most interesting *vin de pays* regions, however, are down here in Languedoc-Roussillon in the warmer, southern part of France where the grapes ripen far more reliably than the ones in most of the more marginal *Appellations* further north. The quality of these wines depends less on vintages than on the attitude of the producers.

Ironically, while the motor that is supposed to drive the *vins de pays* to improve the standard of their wines is the knowledge that they might one day, like Limoux, climb the ladder to become a fully-fledged *Appellation Contrôlée*, many now relish the New-World freedom allowed to the humbler designation.

Although there are *vins de pays* throughout France, the ones I find most reliable are the ones from Catalan, Coteaux du Quercy (in its tough, "old-fashioned" way), Côtes de Gascogne (from Yves Grassa's various domaines, and from the Plaimont co-operative), Côtes de Thongue, Drôme, Gard, Hérault, Ile de Beauté, Principauté d'Orange, Vaucluse, Collines Rhodaniennes, Mont Caume (especially the Cabernet Sauvignon from the Bunan estate), Sables du Golfe du Lion, Uzège, Mont Bouquet, Coteaux de Peyriac, and Vallée du Paradis. The common Vin de Pays d'Oc covers far too large a region to offer much in the way of reliability; best buys here are to be found by looking for the names of reliable producers like Skalli-Fortant de France, Val d'Orbieu, Dom de la Baume and Dom Virginie.

To the east and north-east, there are some first-class, spicy, Rhône-like wines from the Coteaux de l'Ardêche and Bouches du Rhône that easily compete with good Côtes du Rhône, but neither region could be described as reliable. Further north, the whites of the Loire-Atlantique, Charentais, Loire-et-Cher and Maine-et-Loire can be good – if acidic – alternatives to Muscadet. Finally, I've never had a memorable bottle of wine from the Côtes du Brian, but I love its name so much that I'm still looking for one. Sadly, importers shy away from importing it into English-speaking countries, so it has to be sold under its alternative name of Coteaux de Peyriac.

Cassoulet

Hearty bean and meat casserole

Like its wines, the cooking of Languedoc is robust and no-nonsense. Cassoulet, a rich bean and meat stew, traditionally contains preserved duck; this is a simpler version and a tasty complement to the red wines that come from this region.

SERVES 8–10

1½ lb/750 g dried white haricot beans
1 tbsp olive oil
1 lb/500 g unsmoked bacon, cut into pieces
10 chicken pieces
1¾ pt/1 l chicken stock
1 large onion, peeled and pierced with 3 cloves
1 carrot, peeled and cut into chunks
4 garlic cloves, peeled and coarsely chopped
1 lb/500 g pork spare ribs, cut into bite-sized pieces
1 lb/500 g breast of lamb, cut into bite-sized pieces
1 lb/500 g garlic sausage (Spanish chorizo is good), cut into chunks
1½ lb/750 g tomatoes, skinned, seeded and chopped, or drained and chopped tinned tomatoes
Salt and freshly ground black pepper
Fresh breadcrumbs
Butter

Wash the beans under cold running water. In a frying pan brown the chicken pieces and bacon in the olive oil. Put the beans, onion, carrot and garlic in a large casserole and pour in the stock, topping up with water if necessary until the contents are covered. Add the lamb and spare ribs and cook gently on top of the stove for about an hour, adding water if it seems to be drying out. Turn off the heat and add the chicken, bacon and sausage, tomato, salt and pepper. Sprinkle enough breadcrumbs over the surface to give a ½ in/1 cm crust. Dot with butter and cook, uncovered, in a pre-heated oven at 350°F/180°C/Gas mark 4 for about 1½ hours. The crust should be golden. Serve with crusty French bread and a watercress salad.

THE SOUTH-WEST

THE SOUTH-WEST of France is rather like one of those disaster movies in which as disparate a group of people as might ever be found in the same ship, airplane or skyscraper are all gathered together in order to add interest to the plot.

Apart from finding themselves within this area of France, wines like Cahors, Vin de Pays des Côtes de Gascogne and Monbazillac have almost nothing in common except that, like the people in the movie, they all have readily defined characters of their own. Until now, few of the wines have been known outside their own patch but, as the prices of good Bordeaux have continued to rise and the quality of wine-making in the South-West has improved, this has quietly become one of France's most interesting up-and-coming regions – and one that will certainly repay a little study.

Perhaps the easiest way of dealing with the South-West is to separate its wines into two groups: ancient and modern. Among the "ancient", I would include the *Appellations* with names like Pacherenc du Vic-Bilh, made from local grapes such as the Gros Manseng and the Petit Manseng. The "modern" group principally includes wines

Facing the sun: The South-West boasts some of France's most original wines

SOUTH-WEST FRANCE

BORDEAUX

Mont-de-Marsan

Bayonne

Pau

TOULOUSE

SPAIN

1 Pécharmant
2 Bergerac
3 Cahors
4 Gaillac
5 Côtes de Duras
6 Monbazillac
7 Côtes du Marmandais
8 Côtes de Buzet
9 Béarn
10 Côtes du Frontonnais
11 Côtes de St-Mont
12 Madiran
13 Jurançon
14 Irouleguy

made from Bordeaux-style varieties and/or by up-to-date methods.

Cahors was until recently one of the most ancient styles of all. The "great black" wine, drunk by the Romans, was once either sold as Bordeaux or used to beef up Bordeaux. Made from the Tannat and the Malbec (Bordeaux's unwanted red variety), Cahors has always had the reputation of being extremely old-fashioned: tannic, tough, and sweetly tobacco-spicy – more Italian in style than French. In fact, however, this old-timer has had a partial face-lift; some of its wines taste the way they used to and some taste light, fruity and very agreeable. They're more approachable – and less interesting.

For light, fruity reds, I'd rather go to Gaillac, another ancient *Appellation* whose name means "fertile place" in Gallic. All sorts of odd grapes are used, from the wonderfully named, tangy L'En de l'Elh ("far from the eye"), to the rather dull Mauzac. Of white Gaillacs, the best are probably the slightly sparkling Perlé, the semi-sweet *méthode rurale* fizz (made by allowing the wine to finish fermenting in the bottle), and some good attempts at wines with low alcohol. The sweeter versions are rarely exciting. Of the reds, the

best are the Beaujolais-style *macération carbonique* wines, made from the local Duras, the Gamay, Syrah and Cabernets.

Sweet Pacherenc du Vic-Bilh sounds more like Normandy cider than wine. Its name refers to the fact that this was one of the first places to plant vines in rows ("piquets en rangs") and is rather more memorable than "Madiran Blanc" which is what it really is. It is made from the Gros and Petit Manseng and the local Arrufiat, often "*sur lie*" and, when young, has attractive soft, peachy, peary flavours.

Côtes de St Mont is mostly (and well) made by the large Plaimont co-operative, according to the same rules as Pacherenc, but makes more use of less outlandish grape varieties such as the Sémillon and Sauvignon. The red, which can be similarly good, is made from a blend of the local Tannat and Fer grapes softened considerably by the Bordeaux varieties.

Madiran is now making a comeback after almost disappearing in the late 1940s. Today, it's still resolutely tough stuff, thanks to the presence of the Tannat and Fer grapes, but the Cabernet Franc is making inroads, rounding off the style and adding a touch of blackcurrant fruit. The star turn here is unquestionably Alain Brumont

whose Château Montus has the sophisticated country appeal of Gérard Depardieu in a well-cut suit. Mind you, the Plaimont co-operative doesn't do a bad job. As for Béarn reds, they contain more Tannat, are lighter in weight, but even tougher. The rosés are pleasant though, as are the Gros and Petit Manseng whites. Tursan is similar.

Finally, like the unexpected hero in the disaster movie, there has been the unpredictable commercial success story of Vin de Pays des Côtes de Gascogne, which was probably the first significant example in France of New-World wine-making techniques being applied to pretty basic grapes. Until the Plaimont co-operative and Yves Grassa separately began to exercise their skills on them, the Ugni Blanc grapes were thought best suited for distillation into Armagnac – or for sale at rock-bottom prices as an ingredient of very basic sparkling wine.

For several years in the 1980s, these clean, fruity, slightly off-dry white wines made instant friends for themselves, especially in countries like Britain where wine-drinkers were often graduating from far sweeter German efforts. Today, their future is slightly less certain, now that they have to compete with a new wave of similarly priced Chardonnays from the warmer regions of Languedoc-Roussillon. All of which is not to say that this hero is likely to expire before the final reel, but it'll take a lot more heroics for it to survive.

JURANCON

Jurançon is Manseng country too, and an *Appellation* that has survived by swapping the emphasis from sweet to dry. Good examples of both can be oddly spicy with flavours of tropical fruits and a refreshing whack of acidity that allows the sweet versions to last for aeons. But beware; it is easy to buy sweet Jurançon when you want the (less interesting) dry. Unless the label says "sec", the wine isn't. Up in the Pyrenées, Irouléguy makes interesting, earthy-but-spicy reds and rosés and dull whites. Côtes du Frontonnais reds are much more fun; lovely juicy, rich wine, made from the unusual Négrette.

There are four VDQSs here, the basic Vin d'Entraygues et du Fel, Vin d'Estaing, and Vin de Marcillac, and the rather better Négrette-dominated Vin de Lavilledieu.

The softening of Cahors: The black wines have become civilized and approachable

THE SHADOW OF BORDEAUX

The town of Bergerac has, like Cyrano himself, always been kept out of the limelight in which Bordeaux, made on the other side of the Dordogne from the same grape varieties, has so happily basked. Edward III, an English king who ruled this part of France during the Middle Ages, banned the passage of wine, fruit, men, women and children across the river. In the seventeenth century, in a similar mood, the local authorities sneakily obliged Bergerac's wine-makers to use smaller casks than the Bordelais; at the time, tax was levied per barrel, irrespective of size.

Despite these handicaps, Bergerac, which now grows one in six of France's strawberries and a fair amount of tobacco (it even has a tobacco museum!), made a

market for its wines in the Netherlands, where the sweet wines we now know as Monbazillac first became popular. In post-war years it fell out of favour and its unimpressive dry successor made little impact and few new friends.

Ironically, Bergerac owes its current renaissance to the enthusiasm of an Englishman, Nick Ryman, his son Hugh, and a visiting young wine-maker from Australia who, between them, proved that Ryman's Château de la Jaubertie Bergerac Blanc could compete with all but the best Graves, and that his juicy, blackcurranty red – though less impressive – could beat many a bottle labelled Haut Médoc. Others are following Ryman's lead with Bergerac Sec, which explains why the local, slightly sweeter alternative *Appellation* of Saussignac is fast disappearing. Still surviving near here though, is Pécharmant, which really can be of Médoc *petit château* standard.

Thanks to the growing popularity – and sadly the rising price – of Sauternes, the wine-makers of Monbazillac have finally found the patience necessary to wait for *botrytis* to develop and the skills required to make better, cleaner wines. Good examples easily outclass many shamelessly poor efforts in that illustrious Bordeaux *Appellation*. Nearby Rosette makes tiny (and shrinking) quantities of pleasant, delicate, Cadillac-like *demi-sec* rather more successfully than the various sweet and dry wines made at Montravel which, when compared to most modern white Bordeaux, taste quaintly old-fashioned. And generally dull.

Côtes de Duras can be good basic red and white Bordeaux-by-any-other-name, produced from the same kinds of grapes grown in the same kind of soil; only the fact that it's just over the border in the next *département* denies it the *Appellation*. Buy some and try to tell the difference between

Château de Monbazillac: *The example of Sauternes is raising standards and expectations*

a red made here and a cheap basic claret. If you can't, do me a favour and let the Bordeaux *Appellation Contrôlée* authorities know; I'm sure they'd love to hear from you. The same applies to the generally excellent Côtes du Marmandais, and the Côtes de Buzet, produced within the region of Armagnac (but only for the Buzet reds and rosés; the whites are dull). The Côtes du Brulhois makes no white, but its rosé is pleasantly light and Cabernet-ish and rather better than the rustic red made here from the same varieties.

Of the South-West *vins de pays*, there are the region-wide Vin de Pays du Comte Tolosan and the Vin de Pays des Côtes de Gascogne which, as I mentioned above, have revolutionized their region. Vin de Pays d'Agenais can be either Bordeaux-style or old-fashioned, depending on the grapes that are used. Vin de Pays de Dordogne is similar in style to Bergerac; Coteaux de Quercy and tiny Coteaux de Glanes are

Cahors with pigeon: *Pigeon loft at Château Lagrezette*

The Essentials
SOUTH-WEST FRANCE

What to look for Distinctive, if sometimes rustic, reds and whites made from indigenous grape varieties, plus alternatives to Bordeaux.
Official quality AOCs: Béarn; Bergerac; Cahors; Côtes de Bergerac; Côtes de Saussignac; Côtes de Buzet; Côtes de Duras; Montravel; Côtes du Frontonnais; Gaillac; Irouléguy; Jurançon; Madiran; Monbazillac; Pacherenc du Vic-Bilh; Pécharmant; Rosette. VDQSs: Côtes du Brulhois; Côtes de St Mont; Côtes du Marmandais; Tursan; Vin d'Entraygues et du Fel; Vin d'Estaing; Vin de Lavilledieu; Marcillac. The best-known *vins de pays* are Côtes de Gascogne, Charentais and Tarn.
Style Dry white wines are generally fresh, crisp and Bordeaux-like, the exception being dry Jurançon which has a spicy, honeyed quality. Sweet Jurançon is rich and raisiny while the best examples of Monbazillac resemble Sauternes. Red wines vary from the rustic to Bordeaux-style; from good producers, these can be good-value alternatives to Bordeaux *petit château* or *cru bourgeois* wines. The wines of Cahors, made primarily from the Malbec grape, tend now to be lighter in style. In Irouléguy, it is again the reds to look out for; rather earthy, spicy wines made from the Tannat grape. Gaillac can produce good Gamay.
Climate Atlantic-influenced, with warm and long summers but wet winters and springs.
Cultivation Soils are varied. Vineyard sites facing east or south-east offer protection from the Atlantic.
Grape varieties Abouriou, Arrufiac, Baroque, Cabernet Franc, Cabernet Sauvignon, Camaralet, Chardonnay, Chenin Blanc, Cinsault, Clairette, Caret des Gens, Claverie, Colombard, Courbu Blanc, Courbu Noir, Crachiner, Duras, Fer, Folle Blanche, Fuella, Gamay, Grapput, Gros Manseng, Jurançon Noir, Lauzet, L'En de l'Elh, Malbec, Manseng Noir, Mauzac, Mauzac Rosé, Merille, Merlot, Milgranet, Mouyssaguès, Muscadelle, Négrette, Ondenc, Petit Manseng, Picpoul, Pinot Noir, Raffiat, Roussellou, Sauvignon Blanc, Sémillon, Syrah, Tannat, Ugni Blanc, Valdiguié, Villard Noir.
Production/maturation White wines and some red wines are produced by modern methods as in Bordeaux. Sparkling wines are made by the *méthode champenoise*.
Longevity Most red wines are at their best between 3 and 5 years, although some of the heavier wines, notably Cahors and Madiran, can last beyond 10. The dry white wines should be drunk within 3 years. Good Monbazillac and sweet Jurançon will last for at least a decade.
Vintage guide 83, 85, 86, 88, 89, 90, 92.
My Top 29 *Cahors*: Triguedina, Haute-Serre, Cayrou; *Bergerac*: Château la Jaubertie, Court les Mûts, Panisseau, Gouyat, Priorat; *Jurançon*: Domaine Cauhapé, Cru Lamouroux, Jolys; *Madiran*: Montus/Bouscassé, Plaimont; *Pacherenc du Vic-Bilh*: Crampilh; *Gaillac*: Domaine Jean Cros, Labastide de Lévis, Plageoloes; *Monbazillac*: Château de Monbazillac, Château la Jaubertie, Château Hébras, Haut Roaly; *Vin de Pays des Côtes de Gascogne*: Grassa, Plaimont; *Côtes du Frontannais* Château Montauriol, Bellevue la Forêt; *Irouléguy*: Iturrite, Brana, Mignaberry; *Buzet*: Co-operative de Buzet; *Montravel*: Gouyat.

Poule au Pot
Le Roi Henri IV

King Henry's chicken casserole

*I*t was Henri IV, king of France in the sixteenth century, who vowed to his subjects that he would put "a chicken in every pot". The king came from Béarn in the South-West, and this dish will go very well with the good robust reds of the region.

SERVES 6

1 large chicken, 4–5 lb/2–2.5 kg
Salt and freshly ground black pepper
6 pt/3.5 l chicken stock

Stuffing
4 slices ham (Bayonne is traditional but not essential), chopped
8 oz/225 g veal, minced
8 oz/225 g pork, minced
2 chicken livers, chopped
1 oz/25 g butter
2 medium onions, chopped
2 garlic cloves, crushed
4 oz/100 g dried breadcrumbs
1 tsp dried tarragon
1 tsp crumbled dried sage
1 tbsp single cream
2 tbsp brandy (Armagnac is traditional but not essential)
½ tsp grated nutmeg
2 egg yolks
Salt and freshly ground black pepper

Season the bird inside and out with salt and pepper. In a large bowl combine all the ingredients for the stuffing. Mix well and leave to stand, covered, for at least 30 minutes. Stuff the bird and put it in a large flameproof casserole. Close the opening through which the bird was stuffed by pulling the flap of skin across the opening and tucking it under the bird. Pour over the stock. Bring to a boil and then reduce to a moderate simmer and cook, covered, for 2–2½ hours. Remove the chicken to a serving plate (keep the stock for soup) and serve with creamed potatoes and steamed cabbage.

---

good Gamay- and Merlot-influenced reds; Bigorre is like mini-Madiran; Côtes Condomois are old-fashioned Tannat reds and dull Ugni Blanc whites, and Côtes de Montestruc include unusual, beefy reds made partly from the dark-fleshed Alicanté Bouschet. Close to Toulouse, the Côtes du Tarn combines local and Bordeaux varieties with, for some reason, the Portugais Bleu, and Saint-Sardos produces traditional reds, whites and rosés from local varieties.

ITALY

Italy is the most gloriously confusing country on earth – except that, like Germany, as would-be national leaders have increasingly discovered in recent years, it is not so much a country as a collection of disparate regions, seemingly stuck together with experimental glue. What realistic link could there be between the German-speaking, *lederhosen*-clad producers of Lagrein Dunkel in the mountains of the South Tyrol on the Austrian border, the Franco-Italian wine-makers of Valle d'Aosta who give their wines French names like Enfer d'Arvier, the Sardinians who use the Spanish Garnacha grape for their Cannonau, and the peasants of Sicily, who farm grape varieties such as the Frappato and Perricone, that have never been seen on the mainland of Italy?

It would be tempting to file Italy in the "too hard" basket and switch to the easier subject of California or Australia, if it weren't for all those fascinating flavours and styles which, like Italy's myriad dishes, are found nowhere else.

LATIN LABYRINTH

The more closely you look at Italy's wines and wine regions, the more confusing it all becomes. You could, of course, start as you would in other countries, by learning the names of the regions – but, unlike France, for example, the ones listed in the atlases rarely feature on labels. Bordeaux comes from Bordeaux, Champagne from Champagne and Rioja from Rioja; Barolo, on the other hand, comes from Piedmont and Chianti from Tuscany.

Of course, you could bone up on Italy's 1,000 or so different grapes, but you'd still end up banging your head against the wall in frustration. The Montepulciano grape is used to make Montepulciano d'Abruzzo, but not for Vino Nobile di Montepulciano which is made from another variety altogether. The same grape can be called the Nebbiolo in one Piedmont vineyard and Spanna in the one next door.

HOLES IN THE DOC NET

In 1415, long before Christopher Columbus sailed for America, Chianti became the first wine region in the world whose boundaries and production were controlled by law. Five centuries later, in 1924, Italy began to lay the ground rules for regional designations

Under the DOC umbrella: *Italy is at last tackling the problems created by her wine laws*

that finally led to the allocation in 1966 of the first DOC – *Denominazione di Origine Controllata* – to the Tuscan white wine of Vernaccia di San Gimignano.

If the DOC had achieved its objective of fulfilling the same role as France's *Appellation Contrôlée*, it would today provide at least some kind of indication of where one ought to look to find Italy's

better wines. The list of DOCs, however, included so many wines – good, bad and indifferent – that a "super-DOC" called DOCG (*Denominazione di Origine Controllata e Garantita*) had to be created. This, too, was soon allocated over-generously, for political reasons, to entire regions and to generally dull wines like Albana di Romagna.

Worse still, even when the DOCs and DOCGs made geographical sense – as in the case of Chianti and Bardolino, for example – they included all sorts of rules and regulations requiring producers to make their wines in ways that had everything to do with politics – again! – and the worst aspects of tradition. So, to earn the term "*superiore*", Bardolino has to spend at least a year in barrel, despite the fact that, ideally, this fruit-packed wine's true role in life is to compete with Beaujolais; like that wine, most of it should be in the bottle and on the streets as young as possible. With few exceptions, for "*superiore*" read "*inferiore*". The same idiocy has been apparent in the requirement for Chianti producers to include flavourless white grapes in the recipe for their red wine.

Perhaps unsurprisingly, given the Italian attitude to authority, the meaninglessness of the legal designations and frequently the downright silliness of the wine-making rules associated with them, the makers of many of Italy's best, most innovative and often priciest wines have preferred to sidestep the system completely by labelling their bottles as *vino da tavola* –"table wine" – ludicrously setting them alongside the cheapest plonk on the market.

What these pioneers are fighting against is the steady trend away from wine quality of the last 50 years. For them, as recently as the early 1980s, their country's wines were still suffering from the mistakes made during the years after the Second World War when, almost throughout the land, the call was for productivity; for vines and vine varieties that would yield plenty of bottles.

In some regions – Soave, for example – wine-growers took over areas previously used to grow maize; in others, such as Chianti, anaemic red wines were beefed up with heady stuff from the southern parts of the country. The more wine people made, the more problems they had; space was short, and so was the money to pay for the bottles, so a single vintage would often be bottled in several sessions spread over two, three and even four years – during which time the quality of the wine in the barrels could and would change and deteriorate. So, three bottles of identically labelled Chianti, of the same vintage and producer, could taste completely different.

THE RENAISSANCE

The renaissance of Italian wine brought cooling equipment which helped to make fresh, clean white wines rather than fat, flabby ones. It brought a new understanding of the texture of red wines – and the knowledge that tough-and-tannic is not a description that has to apply to high-quality, young, red wine. Highly skilled oenologists were employed to advise on every stage of production: today a winery owner sometimes seems to be prouder of his consultant than of his house, his vineyard or even his wife. Under the watchful eyes of these experts, old barrels were thrown out and replaced by clean new ones. Throughout Italy, wine-makers planted Chardonnay and Cabernet Sauvignon and started to make wines that competed with white Burgundy, red Bordeaux and the best varietals of California.

Traditionalists began to complain that this sudden rush to make "international"-style wine was undermining Italy's own vinous heritage. Almost as if anticipating this, pioneers like Paolo di Marchi in Tuscany fixed their attention on the indigenous grapes that had for so long been under-exploited – and revealed some extraordinary unsuspected potential. The uninspiring flavour of most pre-1980 Chianti could, it was discovered, be attributed to the fact that a large proportion of the wine was not made from the flavoursome clones of the Sangiovese today's wine-makers' grandparents would have grown, but from more productive, lower-quality efforts created by clever nurserymen.

New-wave Chiantis and "Super-Tuscan" reds – *vino da tavola* wines made from the old clones of Sangiovese and nothing else (and consequently barred by the silly DOC laws from carrying an official designation) –

did not just impress open-minded Italians; they dazzled critics overseas. Suddenly, Californians who had been obsessively planting Merlot and Cabernet Sauvignon in their attempts to mimic Bordeaux cleared space in their Napa Valley vineyards for Sangiovese.

Elsewhere, almost throughout the country, individualists experimented with the potential of Italy's indigenous grapes. In Piedmont, for example, Angelo Gaja startled his neighbours by producing a range of stunning single-vineyard wines which sold internationally at prices higher than those paid for top-flight claret. Packed with glorious berry fruit and sweet new oak, these had nothing whatsoever to do with the tough, dried-out husks traditionally

associated with the region. If Gaja had achieved this feat in Barolo, traditional emperor of the region's red wines, it would have been impressive but unsurprising; in fact, though, he had made these world-beaters in Barbaresco, traditionally Barolo's humbler neighbour.

Gaja's influence on the entire region – and on Italy as a whole – cannot be under-estimated. With Antinori, the leading mould-breaker of Tuscany, he proved that Italy's wines could break free of the bargain shelf and local pizzeria and stake a claim on the most serious wine lists and dining tables in the world. This self-confidence was soon exhibited in other ways by countless Italian producers who discovered that a smart new label and bottle could do as much for their

1	Valle D'Aosta	2	Lombardy	3	Trentino-Alto Adige
4	Friuli-Venezia Giulia	5	Veneto	6	Piedmont
7	Emilia-Romagna	8	Liguria	9	Tuscany
10	Marches	11	Umbria	12	Latium
13	Abruzzo	14	Molise	15	Sardinia
16	Campania	17	Apulia	18	Basilicata
19	Calabria	20	Sicily		

House red: *The simplest Italian wine, in wicker-covered demijohns*

*A*nother debate that has surrounded Italian wines over the last decade or so has been their potential for ageing. Until recently, with the exception of a few regions such as Barolo and Brunello di Montalcino, and *vini da tavola* Super-Tuscans such as Sassicaia, most Italian wines were thought of as stuff to drink within a few years of the harvest.

Attempts to age Chianti Classico, for example, were generally repaid in the form of bronze-hued, dried-out, flavourless stuff which couldn't have frightened a comatose goose, let alone stood up to a herb-redolent pizza. Even when wines were supposedly built to last, their producers often seemed unwilling to demonstrate the fact. On one famous occasion, for example, a group of British Masters of Wine, used to being offered illustrative tastings by wine-makers from Sauternes to Sonoma, were surprised to be denied the possibility of sampling old examples of wine at the Biondi-Santi estate in Montacino.

Fortunately, the makers of the Super-Tuscans took a less arrogant stance; unless you count as arrogance their ambition to make wines of the quality and longevity of top-class Bordeaux. It did not take long, however, for the skills they applied to their innovative, generally Cabernet-influenced wines, to be used on wines like Chianti and Barbaresco. Today, as many American wine enthusiasts know, Italian wines can repay cellaring, financially as well as in the glass.

wines as a new wardrobe from Armani could do for them. Visitors to the annual Vinitaly fair in Verona return with their heads reeling

Spurred on – or should I say shamed? – by the success of these wines, in the mid-1990s, the authorities took another look at the system, proposing to reallocate DOCG far more precisely and to bring in another new designation – IGT or *Indicazione Geografica Tipica* – to cover those "super *vino da tavola*" wines.

On paper, the new proposals had much to be said for them and might indeed be worth considering by would-be reformers in France and Germany. However, one must never forget that this is Italy where any new measures will have to be introduced region by region by more or (frequently) less willing and efficient local organizations who are hardly likely to run them with any great rigour.

THE BURDEN OF TRADITION

Over the last few years, Italy has seen the most extraordinary three-way battle between a new wave of wine-makers whose obsession has been the flavour of their regions' indigenous grape varieties, neighbours who have been seduced by the Californian notion of recreating Burgundy and Bordeaux, and the old guard who'd like wine to taste the way it did in the old days when you could taste the (old) wood of the barrel rather than the fruit of the grape – whatever its variety.

Unlike those of Germany and France, Italy's wine laws have not officially acknowledged the identity of specific vineyard sites. The closest they have come to recognizing that some parts of a DOC make better wines than others is the set of Classico sub-regions – such as Chianti Classico, Soave Classico and Valpolicella Classico – whose French equivalent is the

"Villages" (Beaujolais Villages, Côtes du Rhône Villages) *Appellation*.

What there is not, however, is the system of prestigious *Grand Cru* and *Premier Cru* vineyards on which the French have built their vinous reputation. Burgundy's vineyards are divided into good, better and best; those of Barolo have – so far – all been considered equal. By everyone, that is, except the wine-makers who, as elsewhere, have just gone right ahead and printed the names of their particular bits of land on their labels. Unfortunately, and inevitably, this has allowed all sorts of fudging to go on, and all sorts of meaningless and misleading references to non-existent or no-better-than-ordinary pieces of land. So while one Barolo Cannubi, from a good part of the Cannubi hill, could be the equivalent of a *Grand Cru* Burgundy, another, from a less well-exposed section of the same hill, might be no better than an ordinary Barolo.

As it happens, the wine-growers of Barolo and nearby Barbaresco have tidied

Barolo and Barbaresco: Altare, Clerico, Aldo Conterno, Conterno Fantino, Aldo and Giuseppe Mascarello, Gaja, Giacosa, Moccagatta; *Chianti and Brunello:* Castello di Ama, Fontodi, Fonterutoli, Felsina Berardenga, Frescobaldi, Isole e Olena, Altesino, Caparzo, Banfi, Ciacci Piccolomini, Villa di Capezzana, Selvapiana; *Vino da tavola*: Cepparello, Cabreo il Borgo, Coltassala, Vigna l'Apparita, Camartina, Flaccianello, Ornellaia, Sammarco, Sangioveto, Solaia, Sassicaia, Tignanello, La Poja, Maurizio Zanella, Bricco dell'Uccellone; *Amarone*: Quintarelli, Masi, Allegrini, Bertani, Dal Forno.

this up by establishing their own list of top-class vineyards – but that's not to say that there aren't going to be heated battles between producers on the right and wrong side of the newly laid tracks. So, there's every reason to welcome the creation of the new DOCGs which are intended to give recognition to particularly good vineyards.

THE UNOFFICIAL ELITE

In response to the often lax regulations, growers in some regions have formed *consorzii* – associations – that are supposedly devoted both to improving quality and to promoting their local wines. The best-known of these is the Chianti Classico Gallo Nero Consorzio, membership of which is proclaimed by the presence of a collar depicting a black cockerel around the neck of the bottle. Unfortunately, even the best *consorzii* rarely include all the producers of their region (Antinori, probably the biggest name in Chianti Classico, is not a member) and some seem to be all promotion and little quality.

One much more reliable national alternative to the *consorzii* is the VIDE association, the wines of whose 30 members have to be tasted and analyzed before they are allowed to carry the VIDE symbol on their labels.

Hung up to dry: *These grapes, when shrivelled, will be made into Vin Santo*

The Language of Italy

Abboccato Semi-sweet.
Amabile Semi-sweet, but usually sweeter than *abboccato*.
Amarone Bitter.
Annato Year.
Asciutto Bone-dry.
Azienda/Azienda Agricola Estate/winery.
Azienda Vitivinicola Specialist wine estate.
Barrique Denotes ageing in new oak.
Bianco White.
Bric Piedmont term for hill.
Cantina Cellar, winery.
Cantina Sociale Co-operative winery.
Cascina Farm or estate (northern Italy).
Cérasuolo Cherry-red.
Chiaretto Somewhere between rosé and very light red.
Classico Wine from a restricted area within a DOC. Usually the central area and often the source of the best wines.
Colli Hilly area.
Consorzio Group of producers who control and promote the wines in their particular region.
Cru Vineyard.
Denominazione di Origine Controllata (DOC) Controlled wine region. The DOC system has been recognized as having many faults, notably that it patently fails to acknowledge some of the best wines in Italy and that it has been granted to some areas more for their wine tradition than for their present quality. The best guarantee of quality is the name of the producer.
Denominazione di Origine Controllata e Garantita (DOCG) Theoretically a superior classification to DOC but this was cast into doubt when the first white DOCG was granted to the undistinguished Albana di Romagna. Nevertheless, it does recognize some of the best Italian reds, for example Barolo, Barbaresco and Brunello di Montalcino. In future it should apply to specific, higher-quality sub-regions.
Dolce Very sweet.
Enoteca Literally a "wine library" – most commonly a wine shop but sometimes a local wine "institute" or regulatory body.
Fattoria Farm.
Fermentazione Naturale Natural fermentation, but can be in bottle or tank.
Flore Literally "flower", refers to the first pressing of grapes.
Frizzante Semi-sparkling.
Frizzantino Very lightly sparkling.
Gradi Percentage of alcohol by volume.
Imbottigliato Bottled.
Indicazione Geografica Tipica (IGT) New quality designation below DOC but above vino da tavola
Liquoroso Sweet and fortified, or a dry white wine high in alcohol.
Località (also **Ronco** and **Vigneto**) Single vineyard.
Metodo Classico The *méthode champenoise*.
Passito Strong, sweet wine made from semi-dried (*passito*) grapes.
Pastoso Medium-sweet.
Podere Small farm or estate.
Ramato Copper-coloured wines made from Pinot Grigio grapes briefly macerated on their skins.
Recioto (della Valpolicella, di Soave) Speciality styles of the Veneto made from semi-dried grapes. Can be dry and bitter (*amarone*), sweet (*amabile*) or an intermediate style (*amandorlato*). All are characterized by strong, concentrated flavours and high alcohol levels.
Ripasso Wine fermented on the lees of a *recioto*.
Riserva/Riserva Speciale DOC wine matured for a statutory number of years in a barrel.
Rosato Rosé.
Rosso Red.
Secco Dry.
Semi-secco Medium-dry.
Sori Piedmont term for hillside.
Spumante Fully sparkling wine.
Stravecchio Very old.
Superiore DOC wines meeting certain additional conditions, such as higher alcohol content.
Uvaggio Wine blended from a number of grape varieties.
Uvas Grapes.
Vecchio Old.
Vendemmia Vintage.
Vigna Vineyard.
Vin Santo/Vino Santo Traditionally sweet – although can be dry – white from *passito* grapes stored in sealed casks that have not been topped up for several years. Literally means "holy wine", as it was traditionally racked during Holy Week before Easter.
Vini tipici Equivalent of French *vins de pays* – "country wines" with some regional character. A new designation which may or may not catch on.
Vino novello New, "*nouveau-style*" wine.
Vino da arrosto A robust red that is a "wine for roast meat".
Vino da pasta Ordinary "meal-time" wine.
Vino da tavola Literally means "table wine" but includes some of Italy's finest wines since the DOC laws place onerous restrictions on the use of non-traditional grape varieties and innovative methods.

THE NORTH-EAST

*T*HE NORTH-EASTERN corner of Italy is a crazy, mixed-up part of the world, full of people who refuse to speak Italian, call their wines by all sorts of confusing names and, in the Veneto at least, have for a long time seemed actively to have sought to ensure that the wines anyone is likely to have heard of, such as Valpolicella and Soave, are often the ones that taste worst.

To complicate matters further, this is also a region of false starts where sparks of promise often seem to go unfulfilled. And yet this is a great region for vinous explorers – for people who are ready to brave the labyrinth of language for the sake of excitingly different flavours.

ALTO ADIGE

In deference to the official maps, I shall call this former Austrian region the Alto Adige, but the majority of its inhabitants prefer it to be known as the Sud Tirol, and many of the wines they make bear such un-Italian

Red and white: *The Veneto produces all styles*

names as Vernatsch, Müller-Thurgau and Lagrein Dunkel. Thankfully, those labelled Pinot Grigio, Chardonnay, Cabernet Sauvignon and Franc, Traminer and Sauvignon are reason-ably straightforward.

But then there is the oddly and deliciously smoke-and-cherry-flavoured Schiava, or Vernatsch, grape which makes wine most outsiders would describe as deep rosé but the locals insist is red. Some of the best examples come from St Magdalener (or Santa Maddalena), and from the region around the Kalterersee (Lago di Caldaro).

The wild-berry-flavoured Lagrein makes light, raspberryish rosé (Kretzer or Rosato) and beefy reds (Dunkel or Scuro) and can do wonders for Schiava. It might also be beneficial blended with some of the region's Cabernet Sauvignons and Cabernet Francs, some of which can taste a little raw. A few of these can be impressive though – as, in their light, raspberryish way, can the Pinot Noirs.

Betwixt red and white there is an extraordinary wine that is made almost nowhere else. Rosenmuskateller is the nearest I have ever found to a liquid rose garden. My favourites are the dry example made by Tiefenbrunner and Graf Kuenberg's sweeter versions, which can last for a decade or more developing all kinds of fascinating rose-petal flavours (yes, flavours) and smells.

Of Alto Adige whites, the ones that have received the greatest media attention have been the oaked and unoaked Chardonnays. I am less convinced than some of the enthu-siasts; the unwooded versions taste light and pineappley, and are hard to distinguish from the Pinot Biancos made by the same produ-cers in the same region. A few of the better examples, such as those from Tiefenbrunner and Lageder, can handle ageing in oak, but most seem to be overpowered by the experience. The wines that excite me more are those made from more aromatic vari-eties such as the Muscat, the Pinot Gris, the Gewürztraminer (the grape that is supposed to have its origins here in the town of Tramin), the Riesling and, believe it or not, the Müller-Thurgau. Anyone who doubts that this variety can make special wine should try the one made by Herbert Tiefenbrunner from grapes grown in his mountain-top Feldmarshall vineyard.

Unfortunately, despite the excitement the region created in the early 1980s, fine, concentrated wines such as this are not as common in the Alto Adige as the region's

NORTH-EAST ITALY

SWITZERLAND

Bolzano

Trento

Udine

Trieste

Vicenza

Verona

Padova

VENICE

1 Trentino-Alto Adige   2 Friuli-Venezia Giulia   3 Veneto

apologists like to claim; far too many show the signs of vines that have been allowed to produce far too much juice. There are signs of improvement, however, particularly among the co-operatives. Maybe, one day soon, we'll see a lot more characterful examples of the varied wines that can be made in this region of hills and valleys.

TRENTINO

South of the Alto Adige, Trentino is a warm, productive area where huge amounts of anonymous fizz are made, usually from a blend of Chardonnay, Pinot Bianco and Pinot Grigio. The climate and the terrain make Trentino an easy place to grow grapes; unfortunately, most of the farmers here prefer to grow as many as they can per hectare and leave the wine-making to co-operatives such as Càvit which processes over half the region's crop. There is very little wrong with any of the wines Càvit makes, but most have the typical over-cropped Trentino characteristic of tasting pleasantly bland. The Lavis co-operative, by contrast, is trying to raise quality by limiting yields. So far, the growers' reaction has been to take their flavourless grapes elsewhere, but, in a wine-glutted world, I suspect that the young team at Lavis will have the last laugh.

Trentino's reds have more to offer, provided that you generally sidestep such "French" varieties as the Cabernets, Merlot and Pinot Noir and turn to the characterful local grapes. The Teroldego, used to make Teroldego Rotaliano, and grown almost nowhere else, is one of Italy's underrated varieties. Its wines are rich and fairly spicy, as are those from the almost mentholly Marzemino.

THE WINE OF MEDITATION

The term *recioto* is used to describe the strong and naturally sweet wines produced from grapes taken from the ears ("*recie*" comes from "*orecchie*") of the bunches. These upper parts of the bunch receive the most sun, and have much higher sugar levels than the others. When picked, the grapes are hung indoors in lofts or barns to allow them to dry partially and to concentrate the sugars. The semi-dried grapes – the *passito* – are then pressed and fermented very slowly to produce the strongest natural wine

Aiming high: Valpolicella can be outstanding

possible (up to 17 per cent alcohol).

Recioto is a speciality of the Veneto region and can be made from either red or white grapes. Classic, creamy, honeyed, Recioto de Soave dei Capitelli is made by Anselmi, while Maculan produces the rather finer Torcolato. The red Recioto della Valpolicella from producers such as Quintarelli, Masi and Tedeschi ranks among the greatest and most unusual wines of Italy. If all the sugar is fermented out of the wine,

it is known as *amarone* and combines the fascinating smells and flavours of bitter chocolate, plums, raisins, cherries and smoky charcoal. Wines that do not undergo a second fermentation remain sweet and are termed *amabile*. An intermediate bitter-sweet, sweet and sour version is *amandorlato*. Neither style is an ideal accompaniment to food, but both are ideal *vini da meditazione* for sipping at by the fireside.

Valpolicella *ripasso* is produced by pumping young Valpolicella over the lees of a *recioto* to precipitate a second fermentation. Such wines have a higher alcohol content and take on some *recioto* character but can only be sold as *vino da tavola*.

VENETO

The greatest red wine of the Veneto has one of the most abused wine names in Italy. If your only experience of Valpolicella is of dull, flavourless stuff from a two-litre bottle, you'd be forgiven for finding it hard to believe that this wine is capable of any kind of real drinkability, let alone greatness.

Back in the 1960s, the authorities generously extended the name Valpolicella to a huge area of undistinguished land, effectively undermining the reputation of the good producers with individual vine-yards within the original Valpolicella Classico zone. Today, those producers, such as Masi, Allegrini and Boscaini, are still making serious Valpolicella with lots of plummy, cherryish flavour and a fascinating bitter, almondy twist, but they sensibly focus wine-drinkers' attention on the names of their vineyards rather than that of the region; some labels barely seem to mention Valpolicella at all.

For really great Valpolicella, seek out the rather rarer Recioto della Valpolicella, made from grapes dried in barns and slowly fermented. Wines bearing this label are sweet and raisiny; those also labelled *amarone* are dry. Both can be as alcoholic and intense as some fortified wines, amply deserving their local name of *vini da meditazione*; wines to sip at thoughtfully.

Bardolino – and pink *Chiaretto* – is a lighter-weight red cousin of Valpolicella, made from the same grape varieties a few miles to the west of that region. Good examples can be packed with cherry fruit and compete easily with Beaujolais, though without ever quite losing the characteristic

bitter twist of the region. Buy young vintages labelled *Classico*, but avoid *Superiore* wines, which legally have had to spend a year in barrel losing their flavour. The only exceptions are the single-vineyard wines from a few quality-conscious producers, such as Masi, Boscaini, Portalupi and Guerrieri-Rizzardi. Even these need drinking long before their fifth birthday.

If Valpolicella is a debased name, Soave has been dragged through the dirt. Sadly, until recently, almost no one except Leonaldo Pieropan was making anything other than the poorest, dullest wine the Garganega and Trebbiano di Soave grapes can produce. Today a few other producers have come to Soave's rescue, producing rich-yet-fresh wines with lovely lemony flavours. Look for young examples of Soave Classico from individual vineyards made by producers such as Anselmi, Allegrini, Masi and Boscaini. And look too for the rare, honeyed, curranty Recioto di Soave, the white version of Recioto della Valpolicella. If you are looking for better alternatives to basic Soave, try the Garganega-based Gambellara and Bianco di Custoza.

One producer – Maculan – has almost single-handedly put the region of Breganze on the map. My own favourite of the range of wines made here is the gorgeous, raisiny-honeyed Torcolato, made from a blend of this region's native Vespaiola and Tocai grapes that have been left to dry before fermentation and maturation in new oak. But the Maculan Cabernet reds are just as impressive, and the oak-aged white Prato di Canzio shows what the Tocai can do in a blend if it is given the chance.

Piave's interesting grape is the Raboso, which can pack a real punch of rustic fruity flavour. The white Verduzzo is locally just as well thought of, but its naturally low acidity tends to make for soft, dull wine; if you want a white from Piave, stick to the Pinot Bianco or Grigio, or the Tocai.

Lison-Pramaggiore is in the Veneto, but only just. The attitudes here – and the styles of wine – are far more akin to those of Friuli; varietals are the order of the day, with a firm emphasis being placed on Cabernet, Merlot and Tocai.

FRIULI-VENEZIA GIULIA

If the Alto Adige is overtly Austrian in style, parts of this easterly region – usually referred to simply as Friuli – are Slovenian in all but name. But who cares about nationalities when there's a glassful of flavour to be drunk? And Friuli is all about flavour and tip-top wine-making. While wine-writers have taken a growing interest in this region's wines, its unwieldy name has yet to make its mark with most wine-drinkers. The reason for this is that Friuli has no identifiable regional style; all you really have to remember is the name of the grape variety you enjoy drinking, and take your pick. No one quite knows precisely how large a number you can choose from, but it's certainly over 70. Unlike the Alto Adige, though, Friuli doesn't complicate matters by swapping around the names of its grapes, but it does confuse newcomers with its major white variety, the Tocai, which isn't the Tokay of Hungary, the Tokay-Pinot Gris of Alsace, or the Liqueur Tokay-Muscadelle of Australia. No, this is another variety altogether. Grown here and in the Veneto, it can make dull wine, but it can also produce unusual, rich, figgy, pear-flavoured stuff.

Of Friuli's seven regional zones, the one to start with is the large, flattish area of

Head for the hills: High quality in Friuli

Grave del Friuli, where the red varieties of Bordeaux produce refreshing, unpretentious wines with plenty of crunchy berry fruit; there's some pleasant, similarly undemanding Chardonnay here, too, that can be every bit as good as, and rather cheaper than, examples from the Alto Adige.

The black grape the locals would prefer you to concentrate on, though, is the tough, spicy Refosco dal Peduncolo Rosso (its friends just call it Refosco) which is indigenous to the region. There are some good examples of this variety produced in Grave de Friuli, but, like all of the region's best wines, the ones to write home about are the intensely fruity examples made up in the hills of Collio and the Colli Orientali (the eastern hills) on the Slovenian border.

There are all sorts of familiar flavours to be found here, ranging from crunchy blackcurranty Cabernets and plummy Merlots to creamy Pinot Bianco and spicy Pinot Grigio. But the unfamiliar ones are worth looking at too. Try the Refosco, the tangy white Ribolla, the spicy-berryish Schioppettino and the limey-lemony sweet or dry Verduzzo di Ramandolo. If you aren't paying, take a sip or two of Picolit and try to imagine why this grape's wine has been compared not just to any old Sauternes, but to Château d'Yquem. It can be lovely honeyed, perfumed stuff – but you'll still need a really vivid imagination.

Finally, a word or two about Silvio

Fegato alla Veneziana

Sautéed liver and onion, Venetian style

*I*n this classic dish of the Veneto, use the very best calves' liver available. The thinner it is sliced, the quicker it cooks and the sweeter it tastes. It is a simple dish, the success of which depends on the quality of its ingredients.

SERVES 4

5 tbsp olive oil
2 lb/1 kg medium onions, peeled, and thinly sliced
1½ lb/750 g calves' liver, thinly sliced
4 portions of risotto rice

In a shallow flameproof pan (large enough to take the liver slices in one layer) heat 3 tbsp of olive oil and sauté the onions over a low heat until they are soft (about 3 minutes). Remove them with a slotted slice or spoon and keep warm. Add the remaining oil to the pan and turn up the heat until the oil is very hot. Add the liver slices in one layer. As soon as the bottom of the liver turns grey, turn it over. The total cooking time will be about 1 minute if the slices are less than 5 mm thick. Serve immediately with the onions and risotto rice.

Jermann and Francesco Gravner, two of Italy's best, and least-vaunted, producers, who have arguably made their greatest wines by blending various grapes together. Jermann's unoaked Vintage Tunina and Gravner's Vino Gradberg are among the most deliciously intriguing white wines in the world.

Borgo Conventi: High quality in Friuli

The Essentials
FRIULI–VENEZIA GIULIA

What to look for Exciting, tangy and richer, fuller-bodied whites, good reds from "French" varieties and and spicy reds from indigenous grapes.
Location North-east Italy, on the Slovenian border.
Quality One-third of production is from seven DOC areas – Grave del Friuli, Carso, Collio, Colli Orientali, Latisana, Isonzo and Aquilea.
Style Whites are crisp and dry at best, with tangy lemon fruit. There is also a fine pair of new-wave *vino da tavola* whites: Ronco delle Acacie, which combines this appealing fresh fruit with understated new oak, and Vintage Tunina, which has the added weight and richness of Chardonnay. Some dessert wines, notably the very pricy Picolit and Verduzzo di Ramandolo, are also produced. Reds are generally light, refreshing and slightly grassy, but the local Schioppettino produces a big, spicy wine with rich fruit flavours which can mature extremely well. Friuli produces some of Italy's best varietal Cabernets and Merlots.
Climate Cool European climate with warm summers and cold winters. Extremes are moderated by the Adriatic. Lack of sun may be a problem for reds in some years.
Cultivation Flat, alluvial plains with the better vineyards in the hills.
Grape varieties *Red*: Merlot, Cabernet Franc, Cabernet Sauvignon, Pinot Noir, Refosco, Schioppettino; *White*: Chardonnay, Sauvignon, Tocai, Pinot Grigio, Malvasia, Pinot Bianco, Picolit, Ribolla, Traminer, Müller-Thurgau, Verduzzo.
Production/maturation Stainless steel and cold-fermentation have been widely adopted to the detriment, in some cases, of the personalities of the grape varieties. More recently there has been some experimentation with oak in order to add complexity to the fruit flavours.
Longevity Reds may last for 8 years – Schioppettino can be kept for 5–15 years – although most are best drunk within 3–5 years. Whites are at their best within 1–3 years of the vintage. The "super-deluxe" *vino da tavola* whites can benefit from up to 8 years' ageing.
Vintage guide *Reds*: 85, 86, 88, 90, 91, 93, 94, 95.
My Top 7 Jermann, Schioppetto, Marco Felluga, Collavini, Gravner, Dri, Puiatti.

THE NORTH-WEST

I HAVE FALLEN in love with far too many places, but none has slid beneath my skin quite like Piemonte in November. The *nebbia*, the fog after which the Nebbiolo grape is named, was skulking between the hills inspiring operatic melancholy, but it wasn't the view that seduced me. No, it was the flavours I encountered – of red peppers, tomatoes, truffles, sardines, artichoke and garlic *bagna cauda*, fresh young olive oil, and just as fascinatingly varied a set of wines.

To my mind, the North-West is by far the most exciting part of Italy. I suppose, though, that I ought to come clean and admit to the enthusiasm of a convert. For too long, my prejudices had me believing that Piemonte had little to offer apart from Asti – a sweet and grapey unde-manding fizz I could never persuade my more sophisticated friends to drink – and the tough, tannic, flavourless Barolo with which I washed down my *osso bucco* in the local Italian restaurant.

Then a kind Italophile friend introduced me to a range of "modern" wines from different producers and communes sur-rounding the village of Barolo. And I discovered the Nebbiolo grape, one of the most exciting and most frustrating varieties of them all.

Suddenly I was back in Burgundy, where the similarly pernickety Pinot Noir is just as difficult to grow, just as easy to get wrong, just as influenced by the precise character of the piece of soil in which it is planted and, when everything goes right, just as fascinating in the variety of its flavours.

Despite the differences in flavour, the links between Barolo and red Burgundy are actually remarkably close. Both are wines made from a single grape and both have long suffered by being adulterated with beefier wines from further south. Like Burgundy, Barolo used to be a far lighter wine – indeed until the early twentieth century the wines bearing this name would have been sweet and slightly fizzy. Then in the 1930s Barolo slid into the phase of trying to be too big for its boots. The grapes were over-pressed to extract every possible ounce of tannin and the wines were left to age for far too long in barrel. That was the way people liked them – until Professor

---

The Best Vineyards of Barolo and Barbaresco

The following are the pieces of land which deserve to be recognized as *Premiers* or *Grands Crus*.

Barolo: Bricco Fiasco, Bricco Rocche, Brunate, Bussia Soprana, Cannubi, Cascia-Francia, Ginestra, Marcenasco, Marenca-Rivette, Monfalletto, Monprivato, Rocche, La Serra, Sperss, Vigna Rionda, Villero.

Barbaresco: Asili, Basarin, Bricco di Neve, Costa Russi, Marcarino, Martinenga, Moccagatta, Rabaja, Rio Sordo, Roncagliette, Santo Stefano, Secondine, Serraboella, Sori San Lorenzo, Sori Tildin.

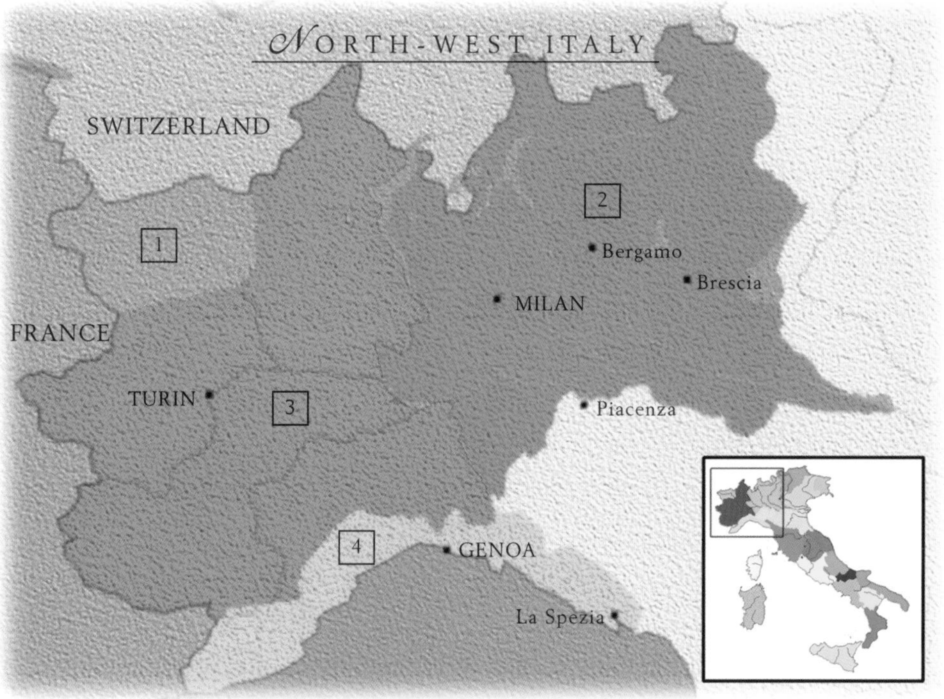

Emile Peynaud arrived from Bordeaux and shocked his hosts by declaring some of the most illustrious wines to be oxidized.

Since the French guru's visit there have been all manner of discussions about the way Barolo ought to be made. Should it be fermented for a long time with the grape skins to extract as much tannin as possible, and aged for several years in large *botti* casks to be softened by oxidation? Or should it be handled in much the same way as Bordeaux, and matured less lengthily in small (new) oak barrels? The local jury is still out on all these questions, but outsiders are rapidly coming to their verdict; what they like is wines with personality and fruit that age well, but can be enjoyed in their youth. In practice many of these are usually from single vineyards, and made by producers like Mascarello, Clerico, Roberto Voerzio, Aldo Conterno and Elio Altare who fight to prevent their wine from oxidizing as it matures, bending the rules if necessary by allowing it to spend less than the regulation two years in cask.

Under present law all Barolos are equal. Until, that is, you begin to read the labels and find yourself immersed in such names as Cannubi and La Morra. But hold on, say some of the traditionalists, "real" Barolo shouldn't come from a single vineyard; it ought, like Champagne, to be a blend of

---

NORTH-WEST ITALY

SWITZERLAND

FRANCE

[1]

[2]

[3]

[4]

• Bergamo

• MILAN

• Brescia

TURIN •

• Piacenza

• GENOA

La Spezia •

1 Valle D'Aosta **2** Trentino-Alto Adige **3** Piemonte **4** Liguria

wines grown in various plots. That argument is still raging; as always, both sides can make a convincing case for themselves, the blenders claiming that some of the vineyard names appearing on labels are far from special, while the plotters talk keenly about the way the new DOCG rules will finally help ennoble the best pieces of land.

THE KID BROTHER

The traditional view of Barbaresco is that it is a more approachable, lighter-weight version of Barolo. But if good examples of Barolo have been hard to come by, good Barbaresco has been rarer still. One man who has done more than any to stake a claim for Barbaresco is Angelo Gaja, who makes a range of extraordinarily pricy single-vineyard wines here. At their best, these are excitingly spicy, intense wines that benefit from legislation allowing them to go into bottle after one year rather than Barolo's two.

Those who question Barbaresco's potential for greatness cheekily point out that Gaja has committed the sacrilege of planting Chardonnay here, and that he has "disloyally" begun to make Barolo. Gaja's supporters fairly reply that it is traditional for producers in Piedmont to make several styles of wine and that his Chardonnay is one of Italy's most successful whites.

If Barolo and Barbaresco are the potentially daunting Everest and K2 of wine here, there are some wonderfully individual, far less demanding, smaller peaks among the region's reds that are just as worth exploring. You can find various versions of less-matured wines sold with a DOC as Nebbiolo d'Alba, or as *vino da tavola* as Nebbiolo delle Langhe.

Up in the north of the region, Carema, Gattinara, Ghemme, Bramaterra and Fara all make floral, delicate wines based on the Nebbiolo, but that also include Bonarda and, in a few instances, Vespolina. *Vino da tavola* wines made here from this kind of blend (with a fair dollop of the Aglianico) tend to be sold as Spanna and can be of very variable quality.

Even the lightest Nebbiolo can be a bit of a mouthful, though, which makes the Barbera such a very welcome alternative. But Barberas vary too, depending on where and how they are made. Some versions are best classified as basic table wine to be drunk by the jugful; some are really quite serious. Look out for Barbera d'Asti, Barbera d'Alba and Barbera del Monferrato from producers such as Bava.

The icing on the cake: The Alps form a backdrop to the town of Alba

Five other varieties make wine for easy drinking. The Dolcetto sounds as though its wines ought to be sweet. They're not, but when well made, they are so perfumed and so packed with plummy, chocolatey, raspberryish flavours that they taste as though they can't be 100 per cent dry. Look for Dolcetto d'Alba, Dolcetto di Dogliani and Dolcetto delle Langhe Monregalesi.

The Freisa, for its part, sounds as though it ought to taste of strawberries; actually, I reckon raspberries or mulberries are closer to the mark – but, whichever fruit it is, Freisa wines are more tightly packed with it than many a pot of jam. Like many of the wines in this region, Freisa used to be be sweet and fizzy; sadly, few producers make it that way now but, whatever the style, good Freisa should have a lovely, refreshing acid bite of not-quite-ripe fruit. Try examples from Bava, Voerzio and Vajra.

Ruche is a variety that very few of the books ever bothered to mention, for the simple reason that it was so rarely grown. According to some local producers, it was brought to the region from Burgundy, and I believe them; Bava's example tastes like one of the best, most creamy and floral Beaujolais.

Grignolino has always been a name that

The Essentials
PIEMONTE

What to look for Rich, tannic reds; lighter, juicy reds from Dolcetto; crisp, dry whites; aromatic, grapey fizz.

Location North-west Italy, in the foothills of the Alps around Turin.

Official quality Barolo and Barbaresco are two of only five Italian reds with the top level DOCG designation. Around 25 per cent of production is DOC, notably Asti Spumante, Barbera, Gavi, Gattinara, Ghemme, Moscato d'Asti, Dolcetto, Arneis and Freisa.

Style Some dry, lemony whites are produced at Gavi, while a rich and full-flavoured wine is made from the Arneis, an ancient grape variety grown in the foothills of the Alps, north of Alba. The region around Asti is renowned for its light, refreshing, grapey *spumante* wines. Equally famous are the massive, chewy reds of Barolo and Barbaresco, wines that can take many years to reveal all of their complexities. Rich in tannins and high in acidity, both have a variety of fruit flavours – raisins, plums, prunes, blackberries – together with liquorice, chocolate and a whiff of smoke. Also from the Nebbiolo grape, but more readily approachable, are Gattinara, Ghemme, Nebbiolo d'Alba and Spanna, the local name for Nebbiolo. Barbera from Alba, Asti and Monferrato can produce a rich, raisiny wine with good underlying acidity. The Dolcetto makes soft, juicy wines which at their best combine succulent cherry fruit with bitter chocolate.

Climate Severe winters with plenty of fog – the *"nebbia"* of Nebbiolo – relatively hot summers and long autumns, although lack of sunshine can cause problems.

Cultivation The best vineyards, in Barolo, are situated on free-draining, south-facing hillsides. Around Asti the hills are much gentler. Soils are varied, but calcareous marl mixed with sand and clay predominates.

Grape varieties *Red*: Nebbiolo, Barbera, Dolcetto, Bonarda, Vespolina. *White*: Moscato, Arneis, Cortese, Chardonnay, Pinot Bianco.

Production/maturation Traditionally, Barolo spent a long ageing period in wooden vats; today, ordinary Barolo is released at 3 years old, *riserva* at 4 years old and *riserva speciale* at 5 years old, and there has been a move away from oak to bottle age. Barbaresco must be aged for a minimum of 2 years, one of which must be in oak. Asti is made by the *cuve close* method.

Longevity *Reds*: drink Dolcetto within 3 years, but most other reds (Barbera, Ghemme, Gattinara, good Spanna) require 4–12 years. Barbaresco can be kept 5–20 years while Barolos are capable of ageing for between 8 and 25 years. *Whites*: Asti and Moscato d'Asti should be drunk within a year. Gavi requires 2–3 years.

Vintage guide *Reds*: 78, 82, 83, 85, 86, 88, 89, 90. *Whites*: 94, 95.

My Top 36 *Barolo*: Giacosa, Ceretto, Ratti, Fontanafredda, Pio Cesare, Pira, Roberto Voerzio, Borgogno, Altare, Clerico, Scavino, Poggio, G Mascarello, B Mascarello, Vajra, Vietti, Aldo Conterno, G Conterno, Conterno Fantino, Sandrone, Prunotto, Gaja, Elio Grasso; *Barbaresco*: Gaja, Moccagatta, di Gresy, Ceretto, Giacosa, Castello di Neive, Pio Cesare; *Other reds*: Vallana, Brugo, Dessilani, Bava, Bricco dell'Uccellone, Vigna Arborina, Darmagi; *Dry whites*: Gaja, Bava; *Asti/Moscato*: Fontanafredda, Duca d'Asti, Cantina Sociale Canelli, Bava.

seemed to promise juicy-fruity flavours, but most of the ones I have tasted have seemed disappointingly unripe. Try one from Vietti, though, with a plate of antipasto prepared

with good olive oil, and you might just develop a taste for it. I prefer Brachetto, both in its dry and wonderfully grapey-floral sweet styles. Blended with the black Muscat, this is one of the best arguments for sweet red wine. Low-alcohol (5.5 per cent) versions compete on level terms with Moscato d'Asti and Asti.

Both these wines provide one of my favourite means of testing for wine snobbery; the moment you see the nose begin to lift at the mention of sweet fizz, you know that you are in the presence of a label drinker. Great Asti is quite simply one of the most unpretentious, fun drinks I know; served chilled on a warm summer's afternoon it's the nearest thing to drinking ripe grapes. And that's hardly surprising because the Muscat grape from which both wines are made is quite simply the grapiest grape of them all.

Apart from Asti and Moscato d'Asti, Piemonte is not usually thought of as white-wine country. There are, however, two characterful whites that are worth looking out for. Gavi's gain – and most wine-drinkers' loss – was to be likened to white Burgundy. This meant that this perfectly pleasant, dry, creamy, appley wine made from the local Cortese grape rapidly became a "smart", over-priced, pleasant, dry, creamy, appley wine. Some bottles are labelled Gavi, some as Gavi di Gavi, which is a sort of Chianti Classico-style desig-nation for wines from the village itself. The latter are rarely worth their extra price.

I'd rather opt for the far more distinctive Arneis di Roero made in small quantities from the Arneis grape, whose name in local

dialect actually means "little difficult one". It may be difficult to grow, but I've always found it remarkably easy to drink – and one of the freshest, most spicy mouthfuls in the world. Try the ones from Gianni Voerzio or Deltetto.

LOMBARDY

Lombardy is to Milan what Chianti is to Florence and Barolo is to Turin: the city's vinous backyard. Surprisingly, given the thirst of the Milanese, their historic mercantile fortune, and the tourist attrac-tion of the lakes, none of the region's wines have achieved as much fame as their counterparts in other parts of the country. The problem is perhaps one of definition; too many of the wines of Lombardy are often too like – if frequently better than – more famous stuff produced elsewhere.

So Lugana, in the east, is fairly described as up-market Soave (good Trebbiano in other words); in the Oltrepò Pavese hills there is a mass of varietals – Riesling, Pinot Grigio, Moscato *et al.* – producing pleasant wines that could be made almost anywhere in Italy. In Valtellina, up in the mountains, close to Switzerland, a quartet of villages called Grumello, Inferno, Sassella and Valgella produce wine that is at once delicate, floral and fruity – like a water-colour version of Barolo. Bottles labelled Valtellina Sfursat can command a higher price because of their beefier flavour and alcohol,

Dolcetto: The wine has a bitter-cherry twist

Cinqueterra in Liguria: Few wines escape from the region

characteristics that, to my mind, rather diminish the appeal.

Lombardy does have some very characterful wines of its own, though even here they often owe their individuality to the fact that they are blends of grapes that elsewhere rarely share a blending vat. The reds made in Oltrepò Pavese, for example, are produced from blends of the Barbera and the Bonarda, a variety normally only found in the Veneto. And then there is the fact that many of these wines are slightly sparkling. Judged on their own terms, like real Lambrusco, they can be refreshingly fruity wines with just enough of an acid bite to balance their juicy, plummy fruit. The whites often fizz here too; indeed Franciacorta is one of Italy's best-known sparklers. For a good example, try Maurizio Zanella's Ca' del Bosco, then take a deep breath, forget your bank manager and buy one of his brilliant Pinot Noir, Chardonnay or Cabernet table wines.

LIGURIA

The crescent-shaped region of the coast around Genoa is arguably the least well-known of all the wine-making areas of northern Italy. The most characterful wines here are the fragrant, floral red Rossese (reputedly the wine Napoleon drank when he wasn't sipping at his watered-down Chambertin) and two whites: the light,

lemony Vermentino (no relation of the Sardinian grape of the same name) and the rather heavier Pigato. All three need to be drunk with rich Genovese cooking and are, in any case, rarely seen outside the region.

VALLE D'AOSTA

This is such a tiny region, with less than 2,500 acres (1,000 hectares) of steeply sloping vineyards, that it is hardly surprising that a single DOC bearing its name is used for all of the various wines produced here. Unfortunately, the range is so wide that the DOC is really rather meaningless. Linguistically this is tricky country too; Valle d'Aosta is as French as it's Italian.

Unfortunately, too, this is another of those regions where vine-growing is an endangered occupation. Tucked away among the eminently skiable mountains, Valle d'Aosta is a far from easy place in which to grow grapes. Trained monkeys might be happy working these terraces and slopes that overlook the Dora Baltea river, and they might even enjoy leaping between the pergolas on which the vines are trained; the young men of the 1990s tend to prefer a monthly pay-packet from Fiat.

There is, as I say, no such thing as a

typical Valle d'Aosta wine, but you could start your exploration of the region by trying the Donnaz or an Arnad-Montjovet, both of which give a different accent to the Nebbiolo, allowing it to display a pungently distinctive, violetty perfume. From those semi-familiar flavours you could progress to Chambave Rosso, Torrette and Enfer d'Arvier (all of which are made from the local Petit Rouge), the Nus Rosso (made from the Vien de Nus) and thence to such obscure whites as Blanc de Morgex (from the grape of the same name) and Nus, which will bring you back to the familiar territory of the Pinot Grigio. (See what I mean about it being varied?) And then, of course, there's the Pinot Nero (used to make red, pink and white – yes, white), the Gamay and even the Müller-Thurgau.

Carbonata di Manzo

Hearty beef casserole with wine and vegetables

*W*hite truffles, gnocchi (tiny potato dumplings), risotto and polenta (a savoury cornmeal cake), as well as beef, venison and poultry, are characteristic of an area renowned for its hearty, no-nonsense eating, with wines to match.

SERVES 4–6

6 tbsp olive oil
2 lb/1 kg stewing beef, cut into chunks
10 fl oz/275 ml red wine (Barbera is traditional though not essential, but use a wine with body)
1 lb/500 g pickling or other small onions, peeled and whole
2 oz/50 g butter
4 medium carrots, scraped and cut into thick rings
4 celery stalks, cut in chunks (remove strings if necessary)
1 lb/500 g fresh or frozen peas
Salt and freshly ground black pepper

Put 4 tbsp of olive oil into a frying pan and heat until hot but not smoking. Brown the meat in batches and transfer it to a plate. Pour off the fat and add half the wine to the pan. Bring it to the boil and scrape up any solids. Turn off the heat. In a large flameproof casserole, mix the remaining olive oil, the browned meat, the juices from the frying pan, onions, butter, carrots and the remaining wine. Cover and cook over a low heat for 20 minutes. Add the celery and cook, covered, for 45 minutes. When the meat is tender, add the peas and cook for 5 minutes. Season to taste with salt and pepper. Serve with rice or noodles.

CENTRAL ITALY

SHUT YOUR EYES and imagine Italy; then think of this part of the country – the part that includes the regions of Emilia-Romagna, Latium and Tuscany – and I'll bet the two visions overlap almost perfectly. There are Roman-tiled villas, dramatic landscapes and that extraordinary Italian co-existence of style and scruffiness to be found in every town. And such traditionally famous (and in some cases infamous) wines as Chianti, Frascati and Lambrusco, plus some of Italy's most exciting new wines, the "Super-Tuscans".

TUSCANY

Tuscany is Renaissance country – in every way. The towns, the villages, the terracotta-roofed houses and the absurdly hummocky hills have changed little since the days when Leonardo da Vinci painted them, but this is also the heart of the renaissance of Italian wine. During the years when Italy seemed to be sliding down the same slope of mediocrity as Germany, fans of the classics

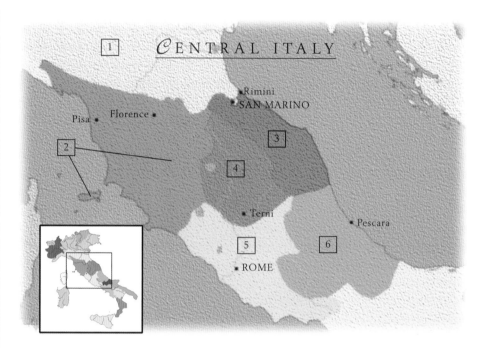

CENTRAL ITALY

| 1 | Emilia-Romagna | 3 | Marches | 5 | Latium |
| 2 | Tuscany | 4 | Umbria | 6 | Abruzzi |

of France lamented the paucity of Italian wines that could be realistically compared to the best of Bordeaux and Burgundy. And the region that attracted most of the flak was Tuscany.

Chianti's shortcomings had been less evident in the old days when most of the wine was sold cheaply in straw-covered *fiasco* bottles. But when the region's producers became pretentious enough to introduce Bordeaux-style bottles and to spend money promoting the black cockerel emblem of the supposedly quality-oriented Chianti Classico consortium, the general reaction among outsiders was that they were simply dressing their mutton as lamb.

The late 1970s saw a reassessment of what Chianti could and should be. The definition of where Chianti might legally be produced had been more or less established for nearly 700 years; the region had, however, grown in that time and split into

Pale and interesting: San Gimignano's Vernaccia is best drunk young

segments including the central Chianti Classico and the Chianti Rufina zones. What remained questionable was the grape varieties from which this region's wines ought to be made. The principal and traditional variety, the Sangiovese, seemed unwilling to provide much in the way of flavour, which explains why some of the producers began to think about adding Cabernet Sauvignon to their vats. The only problem was that to do so in any bottle labelled as Chianti would have involved breaking the law.

But the Cabernet campaigners, maintained that, even if their wines could only be sold as *vini da tavola*, they could still gain a reputation of their own and sell for a higher price than most Chianti. Thus were born the Super-Tuscans, that have catapulted Italy's wines back onto the world stage and are still giving the law-makers headaches.

During the 1970s, among the long list of wine-makers who turned to making Bordeaux-style *vini da tavola*, the most

The Essentials
TUSCANY

What to look for Good traditional and excitingly made modern reds. Pleasant, whites.
Official quality Possesses 3 of the 6 DOCGs in Brunello di Montalcino, Chianti Classico and Vino Nobile di Montepulciano. Notable DOCs are Carmignano, Pomino and Vernaccia di San Gimignano. There are also some red *vini da tavola* ("Super-Tuscans") such as Solaia and Tignanello which, like Sassicaia should soon get their own DOCs.
Style Vernaccia di San Gimignano is the most famous local white. Smooth and nutty, with lots of fresh fruit and a hint of honey, it should be drunk within 2 to 3 years. Galestro and Pomino, a blend of Trebbiano, Pinot Bianco and Chardonnay, are both good. Chianti is by far the most important Italian red but, as a consequence of its large production, quality varies considerably. However, single-estate and *riserva* wines show good depth of raspberry and cherry fruit, gentle oak and a whiff of tobacco. Produced nearby, Carmignano gains chocolatey richness from around 10 per cent Cabernet Sauvignon, while Vino Nobile di Montepulciano has a richer, generous fruit character in its finest wines. Mature Brunello di Montalcino, at its best, is rich, heady and complex, full of concentrated dried fruit, plum and tobacco flavours. Some of the best wines of Tuscany, though, are the new-wave, barrique-aged wines from a handful of producers using Sangiovese, Cabernet Sauvignon or a blend of the two. The sherry-like Vin Santo, a red or white *passito* wine, can be dry, semi-sweet or

sweet and, at its best, has a fine concentrated richness.
Climate Summers are long and fairly dry. Winters are cold.
Cultivation The best vineyards are on free-draining exposed hillsides where altitude moderates the long, hot growing season. Soils are complex; galestro, a crystalline rocky soil, dominates the best vineyards.
Grape varieties *Red*: Sangiovese, Cabernet Sauvignon, Brunello, Canaiolo Nero, Colorino, Mammolo; *White*: Trebbiano, Malvasia, Vernaccia, Grechetto, Chardonnay, Pinot Grigio, Pinot Bianco, Sauvignon Blanc.
Production/maturation Barrique-ageing has become much more common. Vin Santo is still very traditional, with grapes being dried indoors and the wine being aged for up to 6 years in sealed casks.
Longevity *Reds*: Chianti: 3–6 years for ordinary Chianti, but up to 20 for the best; Brunello di Montalcino: 10–25 years; Vino Nobile 6–25 years; barrique-aged reds: 5–25 years; other reds: 3–10 years; *Whites*: up to 5 years, although Vin Santo can last far longer.
Vintage guide 85, 87, 88, 90, 91, 94, 95.
My Top 23 Antinori, Avignonesi, Castello di Volpaia, Marchese Incisa della Rochetta, Isole e Olena, Villa di Capezzana, Il Poggio, Vinattieri, Altesino, Badia a Coltibuono, Ruffino, Fontodi, Castelli di Ama, Castell'in Villa, Castellare, Felsina Berardenga, Monte Vertine, Argiano, Fattoria dei Barbi, Val di Suga, Talenti.

famous was Piero Antinori, whose ancestor had used Cabernet in his Chianti at the beginning of the century. Antinori's Sangiovese-Cabernet Sauvignon blend, Tignanello, was instantly acknowledged to be one of Italy's finest reds – and proof that you could sell a *vino da tavola* at a higher price than a DOC. The authorities belatedly read the writing on the wall, granting a DOC to the Chianti Montabano region of Carmignano for wines made from a blend of Sangiovese and Cabernet.

Just as it began to seem as though

Worth the money? *Biondi-Santi, producers of Brunello di Montalcino*

Chianti would become Cabernet country, in which all the best wines would owe at least some of their flavour to the Bordeaux variety, Antinori and a number of his fellow producers began to experiment with different clones, including old Sangioveto (Sangiovese Toscano) vines, and to make pure Sangioveto wines, which they aged in small, new oak barrels. These managed to blend regional typicity with the ultra-fashionable flavour of new oak.

Tuscany is now an anarchic mess. Chianti Classico has been promoted to a DOCG, producers are now allowed to add 10 per cent of Cabernet to their vats, and a blind eye is turned to those who neglect to put in the obligatory white grapes. These developments have finally encouraged a move toward higher-quality Chianti – both in the Chianti Classico region and in other parts of the area – but they haven't deterred anyone from making at least one *vino da*

Petti di Pollo alla Fiorentina

Chicken breasts sautéed with spinach

*O*live oil, beef from the Val di Chiana, chicken, herbs and game from the wooded hills are the hallmarks of Tuscan food. This recipe comes from the capital of the region – Florence – where the use of spinach, a local speciality, is often signalled by the phrase "alla Fiorentina".

SERVES 4

2 lb/1 kg fresh spinach, washed and destalked, or equal weight of frozen leaf spinach
4 tbsp olive oil
1 clove garlic, peeled and minced
3 tbsp single cream
Salt and freshly ground black pepper
1 oz/25 g butter
4 skinless chicken breasts, slightly flattened

If fresh spinach is used, cook it in a covered saucepan over a low heat with only the water left on the leaves from washing. Toss to prevent scorching and cook until wilted and most of the moisture has evaporated. If frozen spinach is used, heat until most of the water has evaporated. In a frying pan, heat 2 tbsp of olive oil until it is hot but not smoking. Sauté the garlic for 2–3 minutes (without burning) and reduce the heat. Add the spinach and cook for 3–4 minutes. Stir in the cream, seasoning with salt and pepper to taste. Cook for 2–3 minutes. Remove contents with a slotted spoon or slice to a bowl and keep warm. Add the remaining oil and butter to the pan and heat. When the butter foam has subsided add the chicken and cook over a high heat for about 3–4 minutes on each side or until browned. Cover the pan, reduce the heat to moderate and cook for a further 10 minutes or until the chicken is cooked through. Remove to a serving dish and dress with the spinach. Serve with sautéed potatoes.

tavola that, until new rules are sorted out to allow it a *denominazione* of its own, stands outside the DOC system. In fact, today Tuscan wineries have Bordeaux-style or pure Sangioveto wines like newly fledged republics have airlines. At their best, these wines are some of the tastiest reds in the world with a distinctly "Italian" flavour of blackcurrants, and fresh herbs. At their worst, they are impeccably packaged, shamelessly overpriced imposters.

Ask most well-read wine-drinkers to name Italy's greatest wine and some, at least, are sure to come up with the estate of Biondi-Santi in Brunello di Montalcino. Then ask them when they last tasted a bottle of its wine. Biondi-Santi and Brunello (as the DOCG is known) have lived on their reputations for a very long time, relying on the sheer muscle of their wines and the requirement that they be aged for four years in wood to convince people that they were the best in the region. What used to make Brunello special was the fine character of the grape, the brown-skinned clone of the Sangiovese.

Today, as other Tuscans pay greater heed to their clones, Brunello's producers have had to work hard to compete. Some of the old-fashioned, long-aged wines can shed their tannic husks to develop glorious herby, spicy, dried-fruit flavours; some never make it. If you are impatient, or not much of a gambler, try more modern examples from producers like Altesino or Tenuta Caparzo – or the less woody, more immediately approachable Rosso di Montalcino. Old Biondi-Santi wines are worth tasting if you are offered the chance, if only because they provide an insight into the way wines used to taste here.

Until quite recently, the least noble thing about the wonderful hilltop town of Montepulciano was its Vino Nobile di Montepulciano. In blind tastings, few people

Fifty years on: Wines ageing at Montalcino, where wine has been made for generations

Top of the hill: Early spring in the vineyards of Montalcino

could tell the difference between Vino Nobile and fairly basic Chianti; both were dull, over-aged and often oxidized. Becoming a DOCG (the first in Italy) has changed things here, too, just as it did in Chianti. Spurred on by the quality of Avignonesi's wines, Montepulciano's producers have begun to make finer, spicier, more intense wines. Some are still left for too long in barrel, but a new DOC – Rosso di Montepulciano – now gives an incentive for all but the very best wine to be bottled earlier.

There is no longer any such wine as white Chianti, but that's what Galestro is in all but name. Light, slightly Muscadet-like (though with even less character than the best examples of that wine), Galestro is the commercial brainchild of a group of Chianti producers who sought a way to dispose of a surplus of white grapes.

For the moment it has no DOC, but is controlled by an association of its makers. Its quality rarely rises above, nor descends below, a basic level of adequacy. Vernaccia di San

Gimignano (from the extraordinary town of that name whose medieval towers dominate the landscape like so many ancient skyscrapers), on the other hand, is a white wine that has both a DOC and the delicious, tangy flavour of the Vernaccia grape.

Before leaving Tuscany, don't miss the chance to taste the local examples of the sweet or (less impressive) dry Vin Santo. These wines' sherry-like flavour comes partly from intentional slight oxidation, and partly from the fact that good producers use a type of *solera* system, adding a little "*madre*" (mother) of the previous year's wine to the new cask. Dunk a *cantuccini* almond biscuit in a top-quality Vin Santo (Avignonesi makes an especially good one) and you will wonder why this wine is so little known. Taste the cheap, syrupy versions served in most restaurants and you'll wonder why anyone drinks it at all.

UMBRIA

Umbria has never quite had the magic of Tuscany; Perugia has yet to gain the cachet of Siena and Florence. But, as the more northerly region increasingly deserves John Mortimer's witty description of it as "Chiantishire", the focus of attention is bound to shift downward. And when it does, hopefully Orvieto, one of Italy's most ancient wines, will be taken more seriously. Sadly, most modern Orvieto lacks the honeyed, nutty character that earned this town's wines their reputation. The occasional sweet, nobly rotten examples can be good, but the more usual medium-dry *abboccato* or dry examples are unmemorable. Antinori's is pleasant, but uninspiring; for a more special experience, try the Terre Vinati from Palazone.

But it isn't Orvieto that is attracting the attention these days, it is Torgiano, a region that owes its reputation almost exclusively to the efforts of Dr Giorgio Lungarotti, whose extraordinarily successful wines – notably the Rubesco reds – have become so established that he has single-handedly won Torgiano its own DOCG.

LATIUM

Rome's backyard is a surprisingly barren source of good wine. The one DOC almost everyone has heard of, Frascati, has, like Soave, sadly become "just one of those cheap Italian whites", produced and drunk in bulk by people who care little about quality. Actually, Frascati is, if anything, often an even worse buy than Soave, because, while the latter wine is rarely worse than dull, the former can be just the other side of likeable because of its odd sour-cream character. And don't imagine that paying a little extra for Frascati Superiore will buy you anything better; it won't – just a wine that's a little more alcoholic.

The problem, as so often in Italy, is silly local laws; if you make wine in this region exclusively from the local Malvasia del Lazio, it can be terrific – but it's illegal as Frascati, because the rules limit its proportion to 30 per cent. To produce a wine that can call itself Frascati, you have to use the lesser quality Malvasia di Candia or, worse still, the Trebbiano. In other words, the less palatable it tastes, the more likely it is to be genuine.

Fortunately, there are Frascati-makers who get their Malvasias mixed up and sidestep the law by using the good Malvasia

---

The Essentials
UMBRIA/LATIUM

What to look for Characterful whites and – from Lungarotti – tasty modern reds.
Official quality Approximately 10 per cent of production is DOC, the best-known of which are Orvieto, Torgiano, Est!Est!!Est!!! and Frascati.
Style Frascati is the most significant white of Latium. Often very dull, it can have soft, refreshing citrus fruit. Est! Est!! Est!!! is the most memorable name – but the same cannot be said of this often disappointing dry or semi-sweet wine itself. Orvieto, sadly, is rarely seen at its best, when it has a lovely fat richness to it, combining honey and peaches with nutty overtones. It can be dry or semi-sweet (*abboccato/amabile*), the latter style often including botrytized grapes. Two good oaked Chardonnays are produced by Antinori and Lungarotti. Torgiano, the Umbrian DOC created and virtually wholly owned by Dr Lungarotti, produces well-structured reds that are packed with soft, plummy fruit coupled with a good portion of oak. Lungarotti also makes a fine Cabernet Sauvignon, rich, perfumed and well-balanced. Torre Ercolana and Fiorano are good Cabernet-Merlot blends produced in Latium. Falerno, by contrast, is rich and rustic.
Climate Hot, dry summers and warm autumns. Winters are fairly mild.
Cultivation Soils vary greatly but outcrops of limestone, clay and gravel are frequent. Most vineyards are located on hillsides for drainage and exposure to the sun while altitude is used to moderate the heat.
Grape varieties *Red*: Sangiovese, Canaiolo, Cabernet Sauvignon, Merlot, Cesanese, Montepulciano, Barbera, Aglianico, Aliegiolo; *White*: Trebbiano, Malvasia, Grechetto, Chardonnay, Pinot Bianco.
Production/maturation Modern vinification techniques are resulting in a general improvement in the quality of wines. Experimental blending of foreign grapes with indigenous varieties has shown what potential can be realized by wine-makers in Italy and has given added impetus to similar experimentation elsewhere.
Longevity Most whites should be drunk young, within 1 to 3 years. Some Orvieto *abboccato* can be aged for up to 10 years while the few examples of oak-aged Chardonnay can be matured for 3 to 8 years. The majority of basic reds can be drunk within 5 years though Torgiano can be kept for 3 to 8 years, the *riserva* for 5 to 12 and Torre Ercolana and Fiorano require some 5 years to show their class and can last for 12 to 15 years.
Vintage guide *Reds*: 90, 91, 93, 94, 95.
My Top 8 Colli di Catone (Colle Gaio), Fontana Candida (Santa Teresa), Lungarotti, Antinori, Bigi, Decugnano del Barbi, Cantina Colacicchi, Boncompagni Ludovisi.

---

del Lazio instead of the di Candia. And, as in Soave, there is a move toward wines from individual vineyards, such as Fontana Candida's Santa Teresa. Even so, it does not bode well for Frascati's image that Colle Gaio, the best wine to come out of the region recently, makes almost no mention of Frascati on its label.

Marino and Montecompatri can both be better buys – provided that they are caught young. Traditional writers like to pretend that Est! Est!! Est!!! di Montefiascone is one of the region's finest wines, recounting the old story that it owes its name to the enthusiasm of a visitor who shouted, with growing enthusiasm, "It is! It is!! It is!!!". For most of the examples on offer today, the words "Boring! Boring!! Boring!!!" would be rather more appropriate.

There is so little Aleatico di Gradoli produced that it is hardly worth mentioning, but for the fact that this is one of Italy's more unusual grapes, and the fortified and unfortified sweet whites it produces close to Rome boast a perfumey, grapey character.

Up in the Castelli Romani hills, Velletri's is a name that deserves to be better-known. The Wine Research Institute of Latium has experimental vineyards here and makes tasty reds from a blend of Cesanese, Sangiovese and Montepulciano, and a rich white from the Malvasia and Trebbiano that is immeasurably better than all but the very best Frascati. The Cesanese is also used to make a number of other reds, such as Cesanese di Olevano Romano, Cesanese di Affile, Cesanese del Piglio and, with a little help from the Montepulciano and the Nero Buono di Cori, Cori Rosso.

Noble cellar: Barrels at Montepulciano

EMILIA-ROMAGNA

Think of Parma ham, of Parmesan, of Spaghetti Bolognese... Emilia-Romagna is the home of all of these, and of the barrel-aged, intense balsamic vinegar of Modena, and of one of the world's most commercially successful wines: Lambrusco, the sweet, frothy red, white or pink stuff drunk directly from its screwtop bottle by countless thirsty drunks in Britain and the USA. But the stuff those drunks enjoy would be unrecognizable to an Italian; his version of Lambrusco has a DOC, comes in a bottle with a cork and is bone-dry, with an unripe-plum acidity that takes a lot of getting used to. The best comes from Cavicchioli.

Beyond Lambrusco, Emilia-Romagna – a hot, flat swathe of land – has some worthwhile wines to offer. The place not to look for good wine is, paradoxically, Italy's first white DOCG, Albana di Romagna, which is rarely other than pleasantly boring. Much the same (though without the "pleasantly") could be said for Trebbiano di Romagna. The red Sangiovese di Romagna is better, but don't go expecting it to taste like Chianti; the clone is different and the style lighter. Fattoria Paradiso makes one of the few decent ones.

Down in the south-west of the region, Bianco di Scandiano proves that the Sauvignon can make good wine in the warmer parts of Italy, but it is up in the Colli (the hills) that most of the region's tastiest wines are to be found. Close to Umbria, Colli Piacenti produces dry and *amabile*, slighty fizzy whites, in which the aromatic qualities of grapes such as the Malvasia and Moscato are sometimes smothered by the ubiquitous Trebbiano. The reds – particularly

Gutturnio, a tobaccoey-fruity blend of the Bonarda and local varieties – are more interesting.

There is some first-class red, too, made by Terre Rosse and Tenuta Bissera from the Cabernet Sauvignon in Bologna's hills – the Colli Bolognesi, a DOC that confusingly encompasses the DOCs of Monte San Pietro and Castelli Medioevali. Other varieties, including the Malvasia and (unofficially, because it is not allowed by the

DOC) Chardonnay, are similarly well handled, but it is the Sauvignon that is the real star, both here and in nearby Colli di Parma, provided you aren't looking for wines with the bite of good Sancerre.

The Essentials
EMILIA-ROMAGNA

What to look for Light, tangy reds (including "real" Lambrusco) and tasty Sauvignon whites.
Location The region surrounding Bologna in central-east Italy.
Official quality Contains the first white DOCG, Albana di Romagna, and a number of DOCs but the bulk of the production is *vino da tavola*. DOCs you may come across are Colli Bolognesi and Sangiovese di Romagna.
Style Straightforward commercial wines of all types, including sparkling and semi-sparkling. The generally dull Albana di Romagna typifies much of the white-wine production. It comes in either a dry or semi-sweet version that may be *spumante*. Fortunately there are a few outstanding wines, such as the buttery Terre Rosse Chardonnay or Baldi's rich, balanced Sangiovese reds. Lambrusco is by far the most well-known wine produced in the region and may be dry, semi-sweet or sweet, red, white or rosato, barely *frizzantino* or virtually sparkling. Traditional red Lambrusco is low in alcohol, off-dry and full of ripe, cherry-flavoured fruit. "Commercial" Lambrusco, recognizable by its screwcap, is more like fizzy pop.
Climate Hot, dry Mediterranean summers, the effects of which are alleviated by altitude and aspect. Winters are cool.
Cultivation Flat plains of rich alluvial soil, notably in the valley of the river Po, result in abundant yields. The best vineyards are, however, located in the well-drained foothills of the Appennines.
Grape varieties *Red*: Sangiovese, Barbera, Bonarda, Cabernet Sauvignon, Pinot Nero, Cabernet Franc; *White*: Trebbiano, Lambrusco, Albana, Malvasia, Chardonnay, Sauvignon, Pinot Bianco, Pinot Grigio, Müller-Thurgau.
Production/maturation Viticultural practices and vinification techniques are as varied as the quality of the reds. Bulk-blending is used for the commercial wines but elsewhere traditional practices are maintained with the adoption of modern methods where necessary.
Longevity Most wines – red, white or rosato – are best drunk young, although the quality reds of producers like Baldi, Vallania and Vallunga may need up to 15 years to be at their best. Terre Rosse Chardonnay requires 2–5 years.
Vintage guide Vintages have little effect on the majority of commercial or blended wines from this fertile area.
My Top 6 Fattoria Paradiso, Baldi, Vallania, Vallunga, Il Moro, Cavicchioli.

MARCHE

For some reason Verdicchio has achieved greater fame and popularity in the USA than it has in Britain or even in Italy itself. Outsiders imagine that the shape of the recognizable bottle is traditional, and based on that of ancient *amphorae*. Older Italians wink knowingly; they refer to it as the "Gina Lollobrigida", after the spectacularly proportioned Italian actress, and recall its introduction back in the 1950s.

There are actually several kinds of Verdicchio, all made in this hilly region from the Verdicchio grape, a high-acid variety that needs careful handling. Used carelessly, its wines taste the way they sound – green, or "verde". The fact that a wine comes from the castles of Jesus – Castelli di Jesi – or from the lesser-known DOC of Verdicchio di Matelica means little too. Everything

Mostly Sangiovese: *Harvesting in Montepulciano*

The Essentials
MARCHE/ABRUZZI-MOLISE

What to look for Rich, traditional reds to drink with game and light appley whites.
Location Central-east Italy.
Official quality The majority of wines are *vini da tavola* but around 12 per cent are DOC, notably Montepulciano d'Abruzzo, Rosso Conero, Rosso Piceno, Verdicchio dei Castelli di Jesi and Biferno.
Style Verdicchio del Castelli di Jesi is the most famous wine of Marche which, at its best, has a full appley flavour with hints of honey and nut. Rosso Piceno produces firm, fruity, some-times herby reds with good acidity. Those from Rosso Conero are richer, more complex, com-bining under-ripe plums, dried fruit and herbs with a pinch of spice. Montepulciano d'Abruzzo ought to be the only wine of real quality from the Abruzzi region; at its best it can be full of ripe, plummy fruit with a velvety texture and fine balancing acidity. The rosato is called Cerasuolo. Molise produces tannic reds and dry rosatos that as yet have proved unexciting.
Climate Typical Mediterranean climate with dry, hot summers and cool winters. Cooler micro-climates occur at higher altitudes.

Cultivation Limestone and granite outcrops occur often in these hilly regions, although alluvial soils dominate in the coastal plains.
Grape varieties *Red*: Montepulciano, Sangiovese, Ciliegiolo, Merlot; *White*: Trebbiano, Malvasia, Verdicchio, Pinot Grigio, Riesling Italico.
Production/maturation Still a traditional area, although modern methods are beginning to creep in. Barrique-ageing is employed for Rosso Conero, Rosso Piceno and for some whites. Molise in particular requires considerable investment to improve its poorly equipped wine industry.
Longevity *Reds*: Rosso Conero and Rosso Piceno: 5–15 years; Montepulciano d'Abruzzo: 4–20 years, depending on the style and the producer; other reds: up to 8 years; *Whites*: Verdicchio: 2–3 years; other whites: within 4 years of the vintage, though most are best drunk young.
Vintage guide *Reds*: 90, 91, 93, 94, 95.
My Top 11 Mecvini, Umani Ronchi, Marchetti, Tatta, Tenuta S. Agnese, Valentini, Pepe, Illuminati, Masseria di Majo Norante, Barone Cornacchia, Villa Pigna.

depends on the producer; Umani Ronchi has proved that Verdicchio from a good single vineyard, such as his Casal di Serra, can handle new oak and can even age quite well; others are taking advantage of the variety's acidity to use it for sparkling wine. Another local grape, the Bianchello, also produces pleasant, if unexciting, light white wines that are labelled as Bianchello del Metauro.

Marche reds are blends of the Montepulciano and the Sangiovese, and vary depending on which of the two grape varieties has been allowed to take charge. Rosso Conero has bags of rich depth, thanks to the 85 per cent of Montepulciano that it has to contain; Rosso Piceno is more common, lighter and less emphatically fruity because of its higher Sangiovese content.

It is also worth looking out for Cumaro, Umani Ronchi's answer to the Super-Tuscans, and the pure Montepulciano Vellutato from Villa Pigna. This last winery is also breaking new ground in a very Tuscan style with a Cabernet/Sangiovese/Montepulciano blend called Tenuta di Pongelli. Watch these two wineries; I've a hunch that they may be the forerunners of a wave of interesting Marche wines.

ABRUZZI

One day soon – when it catches up with the last decade of wine-making progress in Tuscany and Piemonte – this empty, mountainous region on the Adriatic coast is going to be worth knowing about. There are two main grape varieties grown here, the red Montepulciano, used for Montepulciano d'Abruzzo, and the local clone of the Trebbiano, from which the white Trebbiano d'Abruzzo is made. The former wine can be rich, peppery and chocolatey (from producers such as Valentini and Barone Cornacchia), but the latter is rarely better than dull.

MOLISE

This tiny region is better known for its pasta and honey than for the two DOCs – Pentro and Biferno – that it received years after every other part of Italy had been allotted its quota. Pentro certainly deserved to remain unknown, but Biferno is of greater interest, partly because of the proximity of its vines to the sea and partly because one estate, Masseria di Majo Norante, is using

Ragú Bolognese

A classic pasta sauce from Bologna

*B*ologna – the centre of Emilia-Romagna – is considered by many to offer the finest cooking in all Italy. This traditional recipe for pasta sauce has many variations, all of which go equally well with a glass of robust red wine.

SERVES 4

2 tbsp olive oil
1 oz/25 g butter
3 bacon rashers, rind removed, diced
1 medium onion, peeled and chopped
1 celery stalk, thinly sliced (remove strings if necessary)
1 carrot, scraped and diced
8 oz/225 g minced beef
4 oz/100 g chicken livers, thawed if frozen, chopped
2 oz/50 g mushrooms, sliced
1 tbsp tomato purée
1 tsp dried oregano
5 fl oz/150 ml chicken stock
1 wine glass of dry white wine
Salt and freshly ground black pepper
Grated nutmeg

In a large flameproof casserole or pan, heat the oil and melt the butter. Add the bacon and cook until the fat is transparent. Add the onion, celery and carrot and cook over a moderate heat for about 5 minutes. Add the beef and chicken livers and sauté until browned. Stir in the mushrooms, tomato purée, oregano, stock and wine. Cover and cook at a simmer for about 45 minutes, stirring occasionally. Season with salt and pepper and a pinch or two of grated nutmeg. Cook, stirring, for another minute or two. Serve with spaghetti, fettucine or tagliatelle and a good grating of sharp Parmesan or pecorino cheese.

Montepulciano and Sangiovese to make a first-class red called Ramitello. The spicy white made here from Trebbiano, Malvasia and Falanghina, is good too, but has no DOC because of the presence of the Falanghina. Such are the rules.

THE SOUTH

THE PROBABLE birthplace of California's Zinfandel, this poor, sun-baked region was, until recently, handicapped by a lack of equipment and modern wine-making know-how and, most crucially, an absence of the will to produce better wine. And why should the wine-growers here bother? For far too long, they had a ready market for the thick, alcoholic soup with which the northerners repaired the defects in their own cooler-climate reds. Fortunately, however, as some more enterprising producers have recently rediscovered, they also had characterful grape varieties grown nowhere else.

CAMPANIA

The region overlooked by Mount Vesuvius is one of the cradles of Italian wine-making and the home of the ancient Falerno del Massico, whose three styles provide the opportunity to taste the local grape varieties. The old-fashioned, woody reds and rosés are made from the Aglianico, the Piedirosso and the Primitivo; the dull white is 100 per cent Falanghina. Far more interesting than these, though, is the pure Aglianico Taurasi, which can display all sorts of plummy, spicy flavours. Mastroberardino, who makes most of the Taurasi, also produces the white Fiano di Avellino and the spicily attractive Greco di Tufo.

CALABRIA

This poor, windy and mountainous region deserves to be better known for its success with one grape, the Greco. With the help of equipment to cool the fermentation tanks, producers are now using this variety to make creamy-peachy dry wines in the shape of Melissa and the rather more intense Ciro Bianco, and gloriously sweet and fairly alcoholic bianco in Greco di Bianco (look for examples from Umberto Ceratti).

Calabria's reds are mostly made from the local Gaglioppo grape. Best of these potentially chocolatey wines are Ciro Rosso and Savuto.

BASILICATA

If Calabria appears poor, this scrubby region seems positively poverty-stricken. It's not a good place to farm anything really; some areas are parched by the sun and drought; others, on the hills, are astonishingly cool. But it is on the extinct volcano of Mount Vulture here that the Aglianico can make its most impressive wine. Donato d'Angelo makes long-lived, deep spicy, chocolatey Aglianico del Vulture here and a *vino da tavola* called Cannetto, which is one of the south's most exciting "modern" wines.

PUGLIA

The heel of the Italian boot has long been considered the source of blending wine for the north, but modern wine-making techniques are beginning to pay off. Castel del Monte is a good DOC for red (mostly Montepulciano), rosé (made from the Uva di Troia) and, to a lesser extent, white. Look for the Il Falcone made by Rivera, this region's best producer. Brindisi is very characterful stuff, largely made from the Negroamaro. The best example is probably Taurino's Patriglione in which the bitterness is toned down with a little Malvasia Nera. The Gravina co-operative is proving that a little disrespect for the official rules – they leave out a couple of dull grape varieties – makes for characterful white, aromatic yet dry Greco di Tufo. Look out too for the fresh inexpensive wines, including a delicious rosé made here by Australian-born Flying Wine-maker Kym Milne.

SICILY

Sicily is trying to improve its image by funding one of Italy's most go-ahead wine-research stations, with a brief to find the most modern methods to bring out the best

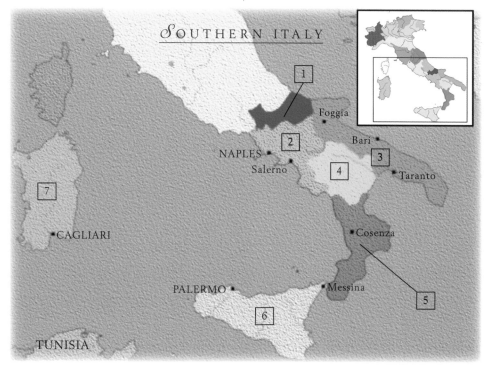

SOUTHERN ITALY

Foggia

NAPLES

Salerno

Bari

Taranto

CAGLIARI

Cosenza

PALERMO

Messina

TUNISIA

1	Molise	3	Apulia	5	Calabria	7	Sardinia
2	Campania	4	Basilicata	6	Sicily		

in indigenous grapes such as the Nero Mascalese, the Frappato and the Perricone.

These are all varieties you'll have encountered in wines from Corvo – as the Casa Vinicola Duca di Salaparuta prefers to be known. This range of *vini da tavola* wines has been so well marketed internationally that the company name is widely thought to be a DOC. None of the wines is bad – but they're pricy. The red and white *vini da tavola* of Regaleali are cheaper and worth trying, as are the more modern Terre de Ginestra and the increasingly attractive offerings of the Settesoli co-operative.

The best-known Sicilian wine, though, is of course, Marsala. A potentially great fortified wine, Marsala's name has been debased by the limited aspirations of its producers and consumers and by wrapping itself up in silly and lax laws (you can use almost any grape variety, make almost any style and bottle it at almost any age). For a taste of the real stuff, look out for Marco de Bartoli's great fortified Moscato Passito called Bukkuram.

For similarly fine sweet wines go to the volcanic Lipari islands where Carlo Hauner's Malvasia delle Lipari is one of the prettiest raisiny wines I've tasted. Florio's Erba di Luce runs it a close race, though.

SARDINIA

Until recently this was a better place for a holiday than for wine. Today thankfully, as

---

The Essentials
SOUTHERN ITALY

What to look for Hefty reds, a few traditional, characterful Greco whites, sweet and fortified wines and, most excitingly, the impact of modern wine-making on unusual indigenous grape varieties.
Official quality The vast majority is *vino da tavola* with small quantities of DOC wine. DOCs include: Castel del Monte, Primitivo di Manduria, Salice Salentino, and Squinzano in Apulia; Aglianico del Vulture, Cirò and Greco di Bianco in Basilicata; Greco di Tufo, Taurasi and Vesuvio in Campania; Marsala, Malvasia di Lipori and Etna in Sicily; and Cannonau di Sardegna in Sardinia.
Style Most whites are dull and flabby while the reds are rich, heady concoctions. Nevertheless, there are a growing number of crisper, more characterful wines. Apulia produces a great deal of ordinary wine but Il Falcone, Castel del Monte Riserva and Favorio are good, fruity exceptions. Full-bodied, robust reds of good quality can also be found from Squinzano, Salice Salentino and Manduria. A light, well-balanced and fragrantly fruity rosato is produced by Calo as Rosa del Golfo. Famous for Lacrima Christi del Vesuvio, which is produced in all styles, Campania's best wines are the robust and rustic Falerno and the vigorous Taurasi with its rich chocolate, liquorice and herby flavours. Greco di Tufo and Fiano di Avellano are good, dry, fruity whites. The rich, bitter-sweet, chocolate-cherry Aglianico del Vulture from d'Angelo is Basilicata's only wine of real quality while the same can be said of Calabria's luscious and vibrantly sweet Greco di Bianco. Sicily is famous for its fortified Marsalas but produces full, smooth and fruity reds – Corvo and Regaleali – and the nearby island of Lipari makes some great, grapey Malvasia and some well-made crisp, dry whites. Sardinia produces a full range of styles: best are the improving, Beaujolais-style Cannonau, the aromatic Moscato, the dry, slightly bitter Vernaccia, and Sella e Mosca's port-like Anghelu Ruju.
Climate The hottest and driest part of Italy, though altitude and sea-breezes have some moderating effect.
Cultivation Apulia has fertile plains and gentle slopes but much of the rest of this area is composed of volcanic hills and outcrops of granite. The best vineyard sites are located on the cooler, higher north-facing slopes. New grape varieties and earlier harvesting, which preserves what acidity the grapes can muster in this hot climate, have been employed to good effect.
Grape varieties *Red*: Aglianico, Barbera, Negroamaro, Primitivo, Malvasia Nera, Cannonau, Cabernet Franc, Malbec, Pinot Nero, Carignan, Montepulciano, Monica; *White:* Pinot Bianco, Chardonnay Trebbiano, Greco, Vernaccia, Vermentino, Torbato, Sauvignon, Moscato, Malvasia, Fiano, Inzolia, Grillo, Catarratto.
Production/maturation Poverty, together with unrelenting heat, results in a large amount of ordinary wine. But considerable modernization of equipment has been undertaken in some areas, notably in Sicily and Sardinia, with evident improvements in quality. Temperature-controlled fermentation and early bottling are beginning to show improved results.
Longevity *Reds*: Most should be drunk within 5 years. The following are exceptions – Il Falcone, Aglianico del Vulture, Taurasi: 8 to 20 years; Favorito: 3 to 10 years. *Whites*: Most are for drinking within 1 to 3 years, though Greco di Bianco requires 3–5 years.
Vintage guide 81, 82, 83, 85, 86, 88, 90, 92, 94.
My Top 12 *Sicily*: Terre di Ginestra, Regaleali, de Bartoli, Hauner, Florio; *Sardinia*: Sella e Mosca; *Taurasi*: Mastroberardino; *Aglianico del Vulture*: Fratelli d'Angelo; *Greco di Bianco*: Ceratti; *Puglia*: Rivera, Taurino, the Gravina co-operative.

Pasta Siciliana

Anchovy, garlic, hot pepper, tomato and olive sauce

This dish combines ingredients which are particularly characteristic of Sicily – anchovies, tomatoes, garlic, olives and capers. They combine to make a tasty pasta sauce which does justice to the robust red wines of the region.

SERVES 4–6

16 tinned anchovy fillets, chopped, with their oil
½ tbsp olive oil
2 cloves garlic, peeled and minced
1 tbsp capers, chopped
1 lb/500 g tomatoes, skinned, seeded and chopped, or drained and chopped tinned tomatoes
12 black olives, stoned and chopped
1 fresh chilli pepper, seeded and chopped, or ¼ tsp dried red pepper flakes
2 tbsp parsley, minced
1 wine glass of dry white wine

Drain the oil from the anchovies into a flameproof pan. Add the olive oil and heat. Add the anchovies and garlic. Cook and stir for 2–3 minutes. Add the capers, tomatoes, olives, chilli pepper (or pepper flakes), parsley and white wine. Cook uncovered until the mixture is quite thick. Serve over spaghetti or pasta shells.

in Sicily, there's a busy wine-research station helping a growing number of producers to discover new ways of using the island's grapes. Arguably the best wines being made in Sardinia today are from Sella e Mosca, whose Anghelu Ruju, an extraordinary port-like wine made from the Cannonau (the Spanish Garnacha and the French Grenache), has now been joined by a dry red called Marchese di Villamagna, good enough to beat many a Super-Tuscan. Nuragus di Cagliari, the best-known of Sardinia's whites, is cleaner and fresher than in the past, but is still pretty anonymous; Vermentino can be better. For something a little different, try the sherry-like Vernaccia di Oristano and the Malvasia and Moscati.

GERMANY

"MADE IN GERMANY". Three words which, when applied to a car, a washing machine or a piece of hi-fi equipment, are synonymous with the highest quality – albeit at some of the highest prices. But high quality and high prices are hardly the words which spring to mind when most non-Germans think of the wines of the Rhine and Mosel.

Sadly, over the last 50 years, the vast mass of Germany's wine sold outside its borders has increasingly and shamefully lived down to a basic image of cheap, sugary plonk which has helped to edge finer examples off the pages of smart wine lists.

Ironically, the style of wine for which Germany has become best-known is not the stuff the Germans like to drink themselves, nor the style their northern European vineyards are best suited to produce. It's as though Robert de Niro had developed a reputation as a performer in tacky musicals.

THE QUALITY COMPROMISE

Some years, trying to ripen grapes in Germany can be a little like trying to grill a steak over a candle. Which might seem to be a pretty good reason for not making wine here at all – except that, like the Loire and Burgundy, Germany enjoys the benefits of a "marginal" climate. Like a racing driver whose skills come to the fore when his car is closest to its top speed, grapes tend to produce their most impressive feats of flavour in the testing conditions provided by regions where they cannot ripen too easily.

Before the Second World War, Germany used to produce two kinds of wine: dry and often rather raw-tasting stuff in the frequent cool years, and sweeter, sometimes gloriously sweet, wines in the rare years when the sun shone sufficiently to ripen the grapes and, more especially, when noble rot (here called *Edelfäule*) appeared in the autumn to give the wines their characteristic, rich intensity of flavour.

Unfortunately, those rare years came far too rarely to guarantee grape-growers a decent livelihood and, after the war, the rest of the world was not overly eager to buy German wines of any description. It was hardly surprising, therefore, that the growers embraced any new idea that promised to make their lives easier. First came the simple but radical decision to begin replacing the Riesling, which had made Germany's reputation, with a range of easier-to-grow, easier-to-ripen varieties such as the Müller-Thurgau, Optima and Reichensteiner, all of which were especially developed to be reliable producers of large quantities of fruit even in the least hospitable climates. None of these new grapes were used to make wine that was remotely as good as Riesling – even when they were capable of doing so.

Then, the wine-makers developed ways of countering the quality problem. Following Mary Poppins' advice, they added a spoonful of sugar – or, to be more precise, two spoonfuls. The first was of granulated sugar, to raise the alcohol level (the same legitimate process of chaptalization that has long been used in such northern French regions as Burgundy), while the second was in the form of sweet grape juice, or *süssreserve* which, "backblended" with the wine, gave it an appealing grapiness that would either make a good but not-quite-ripe wine taste better, or turn a dull, unripe dry wine into an equally dull sweet one. It was this combination of the new grape varieties with the widespread adoption of backblending, and thus sweeter flavours, that revolutionized the style of German wine.

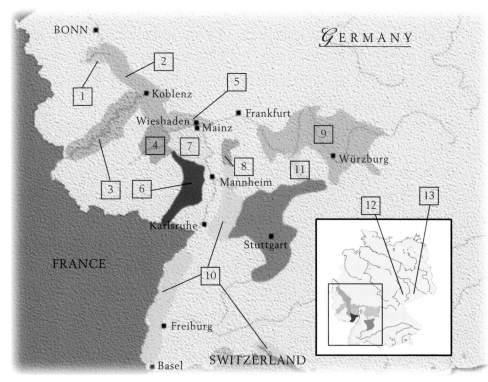

1	Ahr	7	Rheinhessen	12	Saale-Unstrut
2	Mittelrhein	8	Hessische Bergstrasse		(Formerly East
3	Mosel-Saar-Ruwer	9	Franken		Germany)
4	Nahe	10	Baden	13	Sachsen
5	Rheingau	11	Württemberg		(Formerly East
6	Pfalz				Germany)

Don't look down: Mosel slopes are so steep that every vine needs its own stake

A LACK OF DEFINITION

"Quality wine from a given area"? Isn't that the equivalent of France's AOC? No – for the simple reason that the "given area" in question encompasses all of Germany's recognized vine-growing land. It is the "quality" (ripeness) factor that earns the wine its designation. In all but the very best or very worst vintages, around 80 per cent of Germany's wine – including every drop of Liebfraumilch – is legally sold as QbA, with the finer QmP wines and the two most basic, least ripe categories, *Landwein* and *Tafelwein*, making up the remaining 20 per cent. In a great, warm year like 1990 or 1993, for instance, around half of Germany's production could be sold as QmP and nary a drop had to languish as *Landwein* or *Tafelwein*. In France, by comparison, much less than a third of the national annual harvest can ever be sold as *Appellation Contrôlée*, and there is in France no national "super-AOC" equivalent of QmP.

Supporters of the way the German laws have been drawn up claim, quite reasonably, that the ripeness rules themselves help to sort out the good, well-sited, hillside vineyards (which get a lot of sun) from those on poor, flat land (which don't). This may well be true for the Riesling, but it conveniently ignores the readiness of those newer varieties to ripen in cooler places.

For the egalitarianism of German wine law also extends to the kinds of grapes that are grown. In the regions of France, there exists what could be called viticultural

THE GERMAN WINE LAWS

None of this would, however, have been possible without the rather eccentric set of wine laws drawn up in 1971 and vainly amended as recently as 1989. The best way to understand these laws is to compare them with those of Germany's neighbour on the other side of the Rhine. France's vinous legislation is unashamedly class-conscious; if you are Château Latour, or a slice of a Burgundy *Grand Cru* vineyard such as Le Corton or Le Montrachet, your wine will be classed among the French wine nobility because, for hundreds of years, these particular vineyards have consistently made the best wine. But if you are a parcel of land on the other, the middle-class, side of the tracks, then, however well your vines are tended and your wine is made, it will never earn you the respect paid to a true aristocrat.

In Germany, almost all vineyards are created equal. Although, as in France, there are inevitably slopes and parts of slopes that have a centuries-old reputation for making the best wines in their regions, German

legislation, unlike French law, recognizes no such inherent superiority. In other words, a piece of poorly situated, flat land could theoretically produce a wine of the same legally designated "quality" as one on the finest hillside in the country.

RIPENESS IS ALL

Why? Because the only criterion is ripeness. The more natural sugar the grapes contain, the higher the quality designation the wine can claim. So, a wine labelled as *Auslese*, for example, will have been made from riper, sweeter grapes than one labelled as *Spätlese*, which would, in turn, have been produced from riper ones than a *Kabinett*.

All three of these designations, along with the still riper *Beerenauslese*, *Trockenbeerenauslese* and *Eiswein*, fall into Germany's top category of QmP – *Qualitätswein mit Prädikat* (literally, "quality wine with distinction") – and are subject to (somewhat) stricter regulation than wines that are simply labelled QbA – *Qualitätswein bestimmter Anbaugebiete* ("quality wine from a given area").

THE AP NUMBER

*A*mong all the confusing verbiage that you may encounter on a German wine label, there is a set of numbers that can be genuinely helpful. Every wine that is bottled in Germany has to have an *Amtliche Prüfungsnummer* – AP – number which, for anyone who has the code books to decipher it, reveals the identity of the producers, as well as the date and place it was bottled.

In order to receive its AP number, every wine has to undergo what is officially described as a "strict" blind tasting, though quite how strict outsiders would consider the required pass mark of 1.5 out of five to be is another question.

apartheid. If you want to make Gevrey-Chambertin, you have to use the Pinot Noir; if your label says Sauternes, there are only four grape varieties you can legally grow. In Germany it's almost a free-for-all. All of which makes buying German wine pretty complicated, as anyone who has wondered what on earth all those words on the label mean will testify.

GOTHIC HORROR

Apart from the vintage and producer, there is the region (one of a possible 13), the district and/or village and/or vineyard (of which there are over 2,500, most of which have dauntingly long and complicated names by themselves, let alone in combination), the grape variety, the quality level (in other words, the ripeness) and, quite possibly, an indication of the wine's sweetness or dryness in the form of such terms as *Kabinett*, *Spätlese* and *Auslese*, *Trocken* and *Halbtrocken*.

And this is where it all gets more complicated still. Most wine books equate the ripeness "quality ladder" with an ascending order of sweetness – hence an *Auslese* will be sweeter than a *Spätlese*, which will, in turn, be sweeter than a *Kabinett*. Except that the amount of natural sugar in the grape may not have any bearing on the sweetness of the finished wine; the super-ripe grapes of the sunny Rhône, after all, make wines that are more alcoholic – not "sweeter" – than those of cooler Burgundy. And, in recent years, the Germans have increasingly turned to making "*Trocken*" (dry) and "*Halbtrocken*" (off-dry) wines to compete with white Burgundy and Sancerre. So an *Auslese Trocken* will be a bone-dry wine made from (much) riper grapes than a decidedly sweet traditional *Kabinett*.

Is it any wonder that the average wine-drinker just feels too confused to dare to buy a bottle of finer German wine? (If it's to accompany a meal, knowing how sweet a wine is in advance can be crucial.) The German authorities have handicapped their producers still further by interpreting EC wine laws so literally that they forbid a German wine-maker (or his British or other European importer) to describe his wines in the same way as, say, the Australians or Californians do.

So a producer in the Mosel cannot even print a back-label telling potential customers that his wine is "dry and appley" – because, the authorities claim, he might possibly mislead consumers into thinking that it was

---

The Language of Germany

Amtliche Prufungsnummer Literally means "official proof number" – and refers to the unique code given to batches of wine that have passed statutory tests for the area of origin. Usually referred to as the AP number.

Anbaugebiet Wine region, e.g. the Rheingau or Baden.

Auslese Third step on the QmP quality ladder: wine made from grapes with a high natural sugar content. The wines are usually rich and concentrated.

Beerenauslese Fourth step on the QmP quality ladder: wine made from individually selected overripe grapes with up to 16 per cent potential alcohol. Such wines are rich and very sweet.

Bereich Grouping of villages or a district within an Anbaugebiet, e.g. Bernkastel.

Bundesweinprämierung German state wine award.

Charta Organization of Rheingau estates whose members make drier (*Halbtrocken*) styles, observing higher standards than the legal minimum.

Deutscher Sekt Sparkling wine made from 100 per cent German grapes.

Deutscher Tafelwein Lowest grade of German wine.

Deutsches Weinsiegel Quality seal around the neck of a bottle for wines that have passed certain tasting tests.

Domäne Domaine or estate.

Edelfäule Noble rot – *botrytis cinerea*.

Einzellage "Single site" or individual vineyard, usually following name of a specific town or village: e.g. Graacher *Himmelreich*.

Eiswein Literally, "ice wine", made from grapes of at least *Beerenauslese* ripeness, picked while the water content is frozen thus leaving the concentrated sugar, acids and flavour. Eiswein is rare and expensive.

Erzeugerabfüllung Estate-bottled.

Flurbereinigung Government-assisted replanting of slopes to up-and-down rows instead of terracing.

Gemeinde Commune or parish.

Grosslage A group of neighbouring *Einzellagen* producing wines of similar style and character – a group site, e.g. Piesporter *Michelsberg*.

Halbtrocken Half-dry.

Herb German equivalent of Brut.

Hock English term for a wine from the Rhine, derived from Hochheim.

Kabinett First step on the QmP quality ladder. The equivalent of reserve wines, *Kabinetts* are the lightest and driest of the naturally unsugared QmP wines.

Kellerei Winery.

Landwein German equivalent of French *vin de pays*: *Trocken* or *Halbtrocken* wines of a higher quality than *Tafelwein* and produced in a specific region.

Lieblich Wine of medium sweetness, equivalent to the French *moëlleux*.

Oechsle German measure of the ripeness of grapes used as the basis for determining the quality level of individual wines.

Perlwein Semi-sparkling wine.

Qualitätswein bestimmter Anbaugebiete (QbA) Quality level below QmP for wines that satisfy certain controls, such as area of origin, but which have had sugar added for extra alcohol.

Qualitätswein mit Prädikat (QmP) Wines made from grapes that are ripe enough not to require any additional sugar. Meaning "a quality wine predicated by ripeness", these top wines are further classified into the categories *Kabinett* to *Trockenbeerenauslese*.

Rotling Rosé.

Rotwein Red wine.

Schaumwein Sparkling wine.

Sekt Sparkling wine, usually made by the *cuve close* method, which, if not prefixed by "*Deutscher*", can be produced from grapes grown outside Germany. Little of it is any good.

Spätlese The second step on the QmP ladder; literally means "late-picked". Sweet or dry and full-flavoured, these wines are balanced with fine acidity.

Spritz/Spritzig Light sparkle.

Süss Sweet.

Süssreserve Pure, unfermented grape juice used to sweeten basic German wines. Also used by English wine-makers.

Tafelwein Table wine that, even if bottled in Germany, may be a blend of wines from different EC countries. *Deutscher Tafelwein* must be 100 per cent German.

Trocken Dry.

Trockenbeerenauslese Fifth and highest step on the QmP quality ladder. Made from "shrivelled single overripe berries" affected by *botrytis*, these intense, complex wines are extremely rare and expensive, with a potential alcohol of at least 21.5 per cent, although only 5.5 per cent need be actual alcohol. The high level of residual sugar produces rich wine with wonderfully intense honey, raisin and caramel flavours.

Weingut Wine estate. Can only be used on labels where all the grapes are grown on that estate.

Weinkellerei Wine cellar or winery.

Weissherbst Rosé of QbA standard or above produced from a single variety of black grape.

Weisswein White wine.

Winzergenossenschaft Wine-growers' co-operative.

made from apples rather than grapes.

In this bedlam, it sometimes seemed as though the only people who were doing well out of the German wine industry were the companies who specialized in holding tastings in the homes of unsuspecting people, who were persuaded to pay way over the odds for wines often made from decidedly ordinary grapes in decidedly ordinary vineyards. Meanwhile, some of Germany's finest estates, by contrast, annually fought off financial disaster.

PRODUCERS TAKE THE LEAD

Rescue for these estates came, in at least one case, in the form of investment from Japan. Meanwhile a growing number of producers have begun to take matters into their own hands to dissociate themselves from the Liebfraumilch lobby, to create new styles and revive traditional ones, to devise clearer labels and, above all, to rehabilitate Germany's reputation as a producer of some of the most uniquely exciting wines in the world.

Thanks to demand for new styles from German wine-drinkers themselves, to the enthusiasm of importers in other countries – particularly Britain – and to a series of good and very good vintages, the range and quality of German wines is improving by the year. Today, wine-drinkers can find dry German whites that compete for quality and price with Muscadet, Chardonnays and, more particularly, Pinot Noirs, to worry quite a few producers in Burgundy; juicy reds made from such varieties as the Dornfelder and Lemberger; and versions of the Pinot Gris and Gewürztraminer that are excitingly different from the Alsatian examples most people have encountered.

THE NEW WINES

And then, of course, there are the Rieslings, the wines that still set Germany apart and that now come in almost any style you could desire: dry (*Trocken*), off-dry (*Halbtrocken*), with or without the vanilla of new oak barrels... You name it, somebody is probably trying to make it from the Riesling somewhere in Germany, extracting all the nuances of flavour they can find in what, in the right hands, can be the most aristocratic white grape of them all.

The good guys who are making these

wines get precious little help from their government – which is anxious to keep the votes of the rather more numerous and vociferous bulk-wine brigade – so they have set up their own self-help, self-regulating associations.

One of these, the Charta association of the Rheingau, is responsible for what could be a most constructive initiative: an attempt to introduce a French-style system of vineyard classification – probably limited initially at least to *Grands Crus* – which

Look, no vines: Not all the Mosel is planted with grapes. This is Cochem.

would recognize the best sites, the kinds of grapes grown in them, and the quan-tity of wine they can produce every year.

The day on which these efforts are granted official recognition will be a red-letter one for those people dismayed at the prospect of a world in which there are only two kinds of white wine – Liebfraumilch and Chardonnay.

THE MOSEL

F THE RHINE is the most famous wine river in Germany, it is the Mosel that is the most exciting, and the most dramatic. Rivers all over the world are so often said to curve like snakes that the description has become a cliché, which is a pity, because the Mosel genuinely is just about the nearest thing to a liquid boa constrictor you would ever want to see. From Perl, the meeting point of Luxembourg, France and Germany, it carves its way sinuously for 145 miles (233 km) north-eastwards to meet the Rhine at Koblenz. On its way it passes forests, castles, tiny precariously perched villages, and sheer slopes covered with vineyards facing in every direction.

These slopes, and the Riesling grape grown on them, are the Mosel's greatest gifts and its greatest curse. Even when it is planted on flattish, easy land, the Riesling is not the easiest of grapes to grow, and far from the most productive; when it is grown on slopes that rise almost vertically from the river, the challenge is well-nigh impossible.

At its very best, Mosel is precisely what the Riesling is all about: a glorious mixture of crisp apples, of flowers and honey,

coupled with the "slatey" character derived from the soil. And it is here that many of Germany's most impressive wines are now being made.

Green carpet: Intensive planting at Piesport, in the Mosel Valley

The essence of these wines is their acidity; the Mosel is not the region to go looking for rich, fleshily ripe wines, or for Germany's best dry or red wines; most of these come from the warmer vineyards further south. No, the words most applicable to the Mosel's wines are "racy", "elegant" and "finesse" – terms that I normally struggle to avoid. Another word that springs to mind is "perfume", because of their floral style. Interestingly, when perfumiers talk about the precious liquids in their bottles, they traditionally divide them between daytime perfumes, such as Nina Ricci's *l'Air du Temps*, most of which they call "green", and evening scents, such as *Chanel No. 5* or *Poison*, which they generally term "brown". If you apply the perfumiers' rules to wine, it seems highly appropriate that the riper, more spicy wines of the Rhine are bottled in brown glass and those of the Mosel always come in green bottles. These are the "daytime" wines – the ones I most crave on warm summer afternoons.

All of these descriptive terms are worth remembering when you are tasting Mosel wines, because all too often they won't apply, for the simple reason that far too many wines from the Mosel are pale shadows of what they ought to be. In many cases they are handicapped by being made from the Müller-Thurgau rather than the Riesling; all too often the vines will have been so overburdened with flavourless fruit that they taste like dilute apple juice.

The slopes of the Mosel should be covered with Riesling vines that are physically incapable of this kind of over-production, but in the "good old days", when the growers here did tend Riesling vines on their hillsides, they got precious few thanks for doing so. Most years the wretched grapes never ripened sufficiently

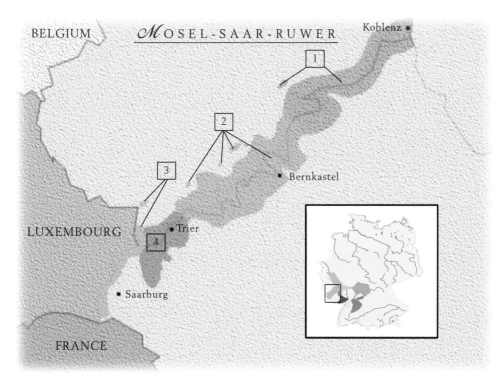

1   Zell

2   Bernkastel

3   Obermosel/Moseltor

4   Saar-Ruwer

to make wine of even *Kabinett* level and, even when the climate did allow good, naturally sweet wines to be produced, no one was rushing to pay a price for them that repaid the work, struggle and risk their production had entailed. So when it was suggested (by Professor Helmut Becker at the Geisenheim Wine School) that the growers replace their old Riesling with some new Müller-Thurgau, who could blame them for saying yes?

The change in the make-up of the region was dramatic. The Riesling used to cover so much of the Mosel that producers didn't even bother to mention its presence on their labels, any more than a grower in Burgundy might tell people that his Nuits-St-Georges is made from the Pinot Noir. Today less than half of the Mosel's vineyards, and far less than half of its wines, are Riesling. Any label that doesn't name a grape variety today is almost certainly hiding the fact that the wine is at least partly made from the Müller-Thurgau.

So the first lesson when buying Mosel is "look for the Riesling". This is not to say that good wines are not being made from other varieties – some Müller-Thurgau can be refreshingly drinkable if it has been treated with care – but they won't give you the peculiar Mosel cocktail of apple, flowers, honey and slate.

Fortunately, the chances of your finding it are slightly brighter than they appeared a few years ago, when the onward march of the Müller-Thurgau seemed almost unstoppable. Today, the advent of *Trocken* and *Halbtrocken* wines has made producers stop and think; these dry styles suit the Riesling far better than the newcomer. The decision to replant with Riesling has been made easier, too, by the development of new, easier-to-work and more productive vineyards that run vertically rather than horizontally – and by generous local government grants toward the costs of replanting.

Bleak midwinter: The cold Saar Valley near Wiltingen

Well over three-quarters of the region's vineyards have been transformed in this way, and the success of the scheme has been great enough to ensure that terraced vineyards will disappear from all but the very steepest slopes. This modernization of the way vines are grown was the first dramatic change in the vineyards since wine-growing was introduced to the Mosel by the Romans 2,000 years ago. It was the Romans who invented the system of using individual stakes to support the vines that is still used here – and almost nowhere else in the world.

Among the other aspects of life in the Mosel that have barely changed over the centuries has been the ownership of the vineyards. There are co-operatives here, but they are less powerful than they are elsewhere and account for just one bottle in every five that are produced. Wine-making here remains in the hands of the church, the state, old families (some of which can prove ownership over 12 generations) and mer-chants, including, most notably, the innovative and quality-conscious Wegeler-Deinhard in Koblenz. Between them, this disparate band produce one of the most diverse collections of wines of any of Europe's wine regions.

THE REGIONS

Moseltor and Obermosel

These two *Bereiche* in the southernmost part of the Mosel both produce basic, light, acidic wine, most of which, thankfully, ends up having bubbles put into it by the producers of Sekt. The only interest here lies in the continued presence in the Obermosel of the Elbling, the grape variety the Romans grew here; if you ever wonder what Roman wine may have tasted like, try a modern example from this region – it'll make you believe in progress.

The Essentials
MOSEL-SAAR-RUWER

What to look for Delicate, floral, off-dry and lusciously sweet Riesling.
Location Western Germany, from Koblenz south to the French border.
Quality Mostly QbA, although there are some exceptional QmP wines in the best years.
Style White wine only: Rieslings from the northerly vineyards of the Mosel-Saar-Ruwer are pale and light-bodied, with racy acidity and surprisingly intense flavours of crisp apples, steel and slate with a hint of honey. In hotter years some superb wines of *Auslese* quality or above are produced which retain vitality and freshness amidst the luscious, honeyed flavour of the overripe grapes. Mosel-Saar-Ruwer wines, never fat and overblown, age extremely well and can be superb. The Doctor vineyard in Bernkastel produces Germany's most famous and most expensive wine. Müller-Thurgau, only introduced in the nineteenth century, is now almost as widespread as the Riesling, but its rather angular mixture of thick grapiness, flowery overtones and an unnerving sharpness does not produce very exciting wines.
Climate Temperate, with modest rainfall. The steep valley sides provide protection for the vines and also allow rapid warming during the day.
Cultivation Soils are varied, with sandstone, limestone and marl in the upper Mosel giving way to slate and clay soils in the lower reaches. There are, in addition, alluvial and gravel soils. The best sites for Riesling are the slatey slopes of the Saar-Ruwer and Bernkastel *Bereiche*. The valley has very steep sides (at Bernkastel rising 700 ft above the river as a virtually sheer face), giving altitudes of 100–350 m (330–1,150 ft) and making cultivation laborious; in some places, tractors have to be winched up the vineyards.
Grape varieties Riesling, Müller-Thurgau, Bacchus, Kerner, Optima, Elbling, Auxerrois, Ortega.
Production/maturation Cool fermentation results naturally from the early onset of winter. Individual growers – most with long family traditions of wine-making – predominate, although co-operatives flourish and play an important role. There are some important merchants with the best, like Deinhard, amongst the leading producers.
Longevity Mosel-Saar-Ruwer wines generally age better than their counterparts in the Rhine because of their higher acidity. *Deutscher Tafelwein* and *Landwein* should be drunk immediately; QbA wines: within 1–3 years; *Kabinetts*: 2–10 years; *Spätlesen*: 3–15 years; *Auslesen*: 5–20 years; *Beerenauslesen*: 10–35 years; *Trockenbeerenauslesen, Eiswein*: 10–50 years.
Vintage guide 71, 76, 79, 83, 85, 86, 88, 89, 90, 93, 94.
My Top 22 Wegeler-Deinhard, Pauly-Bergweiler, Dr H Thanisch, J J Prum, S A Prum, Friedrich-Wilhelm Gymnasium, Von Schubert/Maximin Grünhaus, Dr Loosen, Bischöfliches Priesterseminar, Lauerburg, Max Ferd Richter, Bert Simon, Selbach-Oster, Schloss Saarstein, Von Kesselstatt, Peter Nicolay, Grans-Fassian, Egon Müller-Scharzhof, J Lauerberg, Mönchhof, Bischöfliches Konvikt Trier, Eitelsbacher Karthauserhof.

Saar-Ruwer

This *Bereich* is the one part of the region that involves rivers other than the Mosel. Both the Saar and the Ruwer deserve to stand alongside the Mosel as part of a great region because they produce some of the best, least-well-known wines here.

The Ruwer would be worth visiting, if only to spend an hour or so in the Roman town of Trier. There are vines around the town itself, but these produce fairly run-of-the-mill wine; for the good stuff you have to head down to the water. The Ruwer has one *Grosslage* – Romerlay – within which are situated the Maximin Grünhaus, Karthaushofberg (notable for its bottles that wear nothing but a neck label) and Marienholtz vineyards, all of which can, in the right hands, make sublime, steely wines. The "right hands" here, as elsewhere in Germany, are generally the state domaines, the old family estates and the church. Names to look out for include Von Schubert, Bert Simon, Bischöfliches Konvikt Trier and Eitelsbacher Karthauserhof.

Very few producers market their wine under the *Grosslage* name – as they do in Bernkastel for example – because they make so little; by the same token, they have no need to sell much to merchants, and the co-operatives have little role to play here. For all these reasons, the odds on getting a good wine from the Ruwer are among the best in Germany.

The same cannot quite be said of the Saar, partly because producers do off-load fair quantities of unimpressive wine under the *Grosslage* name of Wiltingen Scharzberg, and partly because the climate tends to be cooler, so, in all but the ripest years, the wines can taste a bit raw. But when the sun hangs around for long enough at the end of the year, the Saar can produce some of Germany's most intense, longest-lived wines.

As elsewhere, the best vines are grown on the slopes, a fact that is emphasized by the vineyards that are named Kupp after the round-topped hillsides. Among these, the best are Ayler Kupp, Wiltingen Scharzhofberger, Wiltingen Braune Kupp, Filzener Herrenberg, Serriger Herrenberg and Schloss Saarfelser, Saarburger Rausch and Ockfener Bockstein. Look for wines made by Egon Müller, Hohe Domkirche-Trier, Reichsgraf von Kesselstatt and Staatl. Weinbaudomäne.

Bernkastel

This name, which must be the most famous *Bereich* in the Mosel, covers the whole region of the Mittelmosel, the central stretch of the river's course from the frontier to Koblenz. In the confusing jungle of German wine, few words are more misunderstood than the name of this small town. On the one hand there is the great Bernkasteler Doctor vineyard that overlooks the town and river and makes one of Germany's finest wines, and on the other, there are the oceans of dull wine legally labelled as Bereich Bernkastel produced in vineyards nowhere near the town of Bernkastel at all – which ought to bear the regional name of Mittelmosel they were allowed in the 1960s.

There are two *Grosslagen* here: Kurfürstlay and Badstube. The former contains the least interesting of Bernkasteler's vineyards and the best of those of Brauneberg; the great Doctor vineyard and Bernkasteler Lay are both in the *Grosslage* Badstube. Named after the supposedly healing qualities of its wine, this sheer, slate-soiled, 3.5-acre (1.4-ha) vineyard is the German equivalent of Burgundy's Romanée-Conti. In ripe years its wines are everything that the Mosel should be: rich, honeyed and as "slatey" as the roofs the vines overlook, but with a balancing acidity that makes this a wine to keep for decades. The Bernkasteler Doctor should long ago, like the Romanée-Conti, have been recognized as some kind of

Between the woods and the water: Saarburg, on the River Saar

Grand Cru or First Growth to distinguish it from its neighbours. Instead, it found itself at the centre of a ludicrous court case begun because the German authorities decreed in 1971 that no vineyard could be smaller than 12.5 acres (5 ha).

Instead of changing the rules to fit the tiny size of this particular plot, the authorities then sought to justify expanding it. Hardly surprisingly, they were supported in this by the

Bernkastel: Superb at its best

13 owners of the neighbouring vines, who were keen to sell their wine as Bernkasteler Doctor. Ultimately – it took 13 years and considerable effort on the part of the three original owners of the Doctor vineyard – a compromise was agreed, whereby the size of the plot was increased to 8 acres (3.24 ha). The story says a great deal about everything that has been wrong with the German wine industry since the war. The official prestige of a piece of vine-growing soil should be judged by the quality of the wine it produces, not by its ability to fit legal criteria drawn up by those for whom numbers and neatness are all-important.

There is a very similar problem at Piesport, another wine-producing village within the *Bereich* of Bernkastel. Look at the bottles on the shelf: on the left, there's Piesporter Michelsberg, on the right there's Piesporter Goldtropfchen. Both seem to come from Piesport, so which should you buy? The answer is that the Goldtropfchen ("golden droplets") is a single, hillside vineyard that produces wine that should taste distinctive and wonderful, while the Michelsberg is a huge, flat *Grosslage*, most of whose wines are produced in enormous quantities and rarely have much more flavour than tap water. Unfortunately the international fame of Piesporter Michelsberg has not only debased the wine of that name; bottles of Piesporter Goldtropfchen don't always come up to scratch either.

Brauneberg is less well known than either Bernkastel or Piesport and consequently often a better buy. The best vineyard here is the Juffer, which overlooks the village of Brauneberg itself from the other side of the river and produces delicate wines that once sold for higher prices than those of the Bernkasteler Doctor. It still competes at the equivalent of First Growth level with that vineyard, but at a (relatively) lower price.

The *Grosslage* of Munzlay boasts some of the region's best estates and three riverside villages – Graach, Wehlen and Zeltingen – all of which can produce some of the finest, ripest, wines in the Mosel. Graach's best vineyards are the Domprobst, the Josephshofer and the Himmelreich. Zeltinger Himmelreich is worth looking out for too, as is Wehlener Sonnenuhr, named after the vineyard clock that ensures the pickers are never late for lunch. Best producers include Max Ferd Richter and Dr Loosen.

Collectors of bizarre wine labels will appreciate the *Grosslage* Nacktarsch, which, literally translated, means "naked arse" and whose label depicts a small boy having that particular part of his anatomy spanked. Unfortunately, the wine made here is far less exceptional than either the name or the label.

Zell

The village of Zell used to be better known outside Germany than it is today, thanks to the success of one of its wines, the Zeller Schwarze Katz. Recognizable by the black cat on its label, this wine is supposed to owe its name to an occasion when three merchants could not make up their minds over which of three barrels to buy. As they asked for another sample from one of the casks, the grower's cat sprang onto it, hissed, arched its back and generally treated the merchants as though they were Dobermanns intent on stealing a kitten. This, the men decided, must be the best wine in the cellar.

Until quite recently, the producers of Zell adopted a slightly more scientific method of selecting the wine that could call itself Schwarze Katz – by holding a blind tasting. The region of Zell has now been expanded by the addition of the villages of Merl and Kaimt and, sadly, the tasting is no longer held. The cat can now grace the labels of any wine from this *Grosslage* and today you would be far better advised to opt for a bottle of Zeller Domherrenberg. Elsewhere within the *Bereich* of Zell, the best wine probably comes from the village of Neef, whose Neefer Frauenberg can be great Riesling.

Salm in Saurer Sahne

Salmon in a sour cream sauce

*T*he valley of the Mosel is close to the French regions of Alsace and Lorraine, and the cooking of this part of Germany has a lightness perfectly in tune with the wines that are produced here.

SERVES 6

6 salmon steaks
Salt and freshly ground black pepper
Juice of 1 lemon
1 oz/25 g solid butter
2 tbsp mixed grated Parmesan and Gruyère cheese
2 tbsp dried breadcrumbs
3 oz/75 g melted butter
5fl oz/150 ml sour cream
1 tbsp plain flour
5fl oz/150 ml dry white wine
Chopped parsley to garnish

Season the steaks on both sides with salt and pepper, and sprinkle them with lemon juice. With the solid butter, grease a shallow ovenproof dish, into which you place the fish. Sprinkle with the grated cheese and breadcrumbs. Dribble the melted butter over and pour the sour cream between the steaks. Bake uncovered in an oven preheated to 350°F/180°C/Gas mark 4 for about 25 minutes, until the fish just begins to flake but is still firm. Remove the steaks with a slotted slice to a warm serving dish. In a saucepan mix the wine and flour to a smooth sauce and add what remains in the baking dish. Bring to the boil and immediately reduce to a simmer, stirring, until the sauce begins to thicken. Remove from the heat and stir in the parsley. Pour over the fish. Serve with new potatoes and steamed courgettes.

A Liebfraumilch-equivalent called Moselblumchen can be found throughout the Mosel. It should be treated with the same suspicion as Liebfraumilch. However, bottles bearing this label will probably be no worse, and cheaper, than many that abuse the name of Bereich Bernkastel and Piesporter Michelsberg.

THE RHINE

FORGET Liebfraumilch and basic bottles of hock. OK, so they're all made here, but to associate the wines for which the vineyards of the Rhine are best known outside Germany with the kind of glorious, unique wines produced by the regions of the Rheingau, Rheinpfalz and Rheinhessen is like imagining there to be some kind of link between a bottle of "French dry red" and top-class Bordeaux or Burgundy. There is nothing actually wrong with the better-made examples of these cheap wines provided that you treat them as what they are: white plonk developed almost exclusively for foreigners.

In a sense, though, the success of these wines has probably done less damage to the image of the rest of the Rhine's wines than the generally mediocre quality of the contents of bottles bearing such apparently "classier" names as Niersteiner Gütes Domtal and Bereich Johannisberg, and the less than entirely successful attempt by some of the most quality-conscious producers during the 1980s and early 1990s to compete with the rest of the world by switching from their

Haardt work: *The Haardt mountains in the Pfalz*

characteristic sweet and off-sweet wines to ones that were bone-dry – often teeth-scouringly so.

Let's set the plonk-purveyors and the dry-brigade largely to one side, however, and focus our attention on the main regions of the Rhine, each of which should produce identifiably different styles of wine of a quality and flavour found nowhere else in the world.

THE REGIONS

The Rheingau

This ought to be the "best bit" of the Rhine – if not of the whole of Germany. In the eighth century the Emperor Charlemagne recognized the potential of the slopes and decreed that they should be planted with the vines that have been there ever since. The emperor was quite a visionary; how did he come to appreciate the way in which the mountains shielded the vineyards from the wind and the river reflected the sunlight? How could he have known that the rocky – often slatey – subsoil was so perfect for the Riesling? Or that the tricky set of fragmented hillsides might include vineyards with unique qualities of their own – some of which might be helped by the mist to attract noble rot? Maybe he just struck lucky – like he did in that other area to which he took a liking, the Côte d'Or in Burgundy.

The link with Burgundy is worth pursuing. The Cistercians who founded Clos de Vougeot and helped to develop the best vineyards of the Côte de Nuits were just as instrumental here, choosing the ideal spots in which to plant vines close to their monastery at Kloster Eberbach. Those spots, and others along the banks of the river, have always been the places to look for the best wines.

The Rheingau distinguishes itself from other parts of the Rhine in several ways. It is far smaller than its neighbours, with only a little over 10 per cent of the vineyard area of either the Rheinhessen or Rheinpfalz; and the Riesling is still the major grape variety, producing yields of around 350

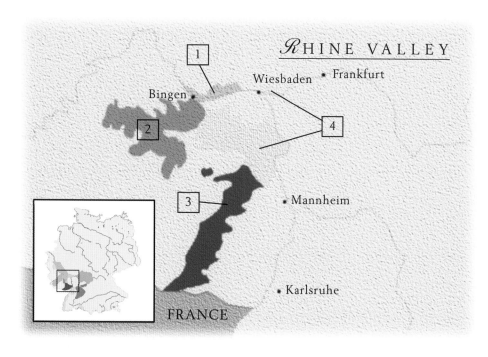

RHINE VALLEY

Wiesbaden • Frankfurt

Bingen

Mannheim

Karlsruhe

FRANCE

| 1 | Rheingau | 2 | Nahe | 3 | Pfalz | 4 | Rheinhessen |

Castle on a hill: Schloss Johannisberg in the Rheingau

cases per acre (140 per hectare), compared to around 430 and 500 (174 and 200) respectively for the other Rhine regions. Thanks to these factors, and to the individualism of the Rheingau's 500 estates and 2,500 growers, the co-operatives have not achieved the stranglehold on production and marketing here that they have elsewhere, so quality has every reason to be higher than almost anywhere else in Germany. And so, occasionally, it is. The mark of a typical Rheingau will be the same appley-grapey flavour that the Riesling produces in the Mosel, but with more honeyed richness, and less of that region's acid bite. At their best, particularly at *Spätlese* and *Auslese* levels of sweetness, these can be the most exquisitely well-balanced and refreshing wines – but not cheap.

Unfortunately, sales of such wines are less than brisk – which helps to explain why a group of Rheingau producers decided to switch their emphasis from sweet to dry, announcing their decision to the world with the establishment in 1983 of the Association of Charta Estates, whose recognizable seal appears on members' *Trocken* and *Halbtrocken* wines.

The first thing to be said about Charta wines is that, apart from being dry, they will always be produced from the Riesling (this is obligatory), and are likely to be more carefully made than many of the Rhine's other wines. The second thing to be said about them, though, is that their dryness has all too often made them far less enjoyable to drink when they are young than slightly sweeter wines made from similar grapes – or than dry French wines that achieve a higher natural level of ripeness.

Dry wines of equal or greater than *Spätlese* ripeness can compete with their counterparts from Alsace, and genuinely do achieve their object of being a good accompaniment to food. As QbAs, too, they can be softened up sufficiently to make them drinkable.

Even so, to most non-Germans, these

The Essentials
THE RHINE

What to look for Rieslings with a wonderfully taut balance between fruit and acidity. They are richer in the Pfalz, softer in the Rheinhessen and majestic in the Rheingau.
Location Western Germany, bordering Switzerland.
Official quality Plenty of *Deutscher Tafelwein* and QbA but also the full range of QmP styles.
Style As elsewhere in Germany, apart from the Ahr which produces pale, light, cherryish reds, almost all wine produced is white. The Mittelrhein and Nahe make good, slatey, refreshing Riesling. The Pfalz and Rheinhessen produce virtually all of Germany's Liebfraumilch, whose dull sweetness or, if they are more fortunate, mild, flowery grapiness is the first introduction to wine-drinking for many people. From the Rheinhessen, too, comes Niersteiner Gütes Domtal, produced in dull and dubiously large quantities, a wine that has debased the good name of the Nierstein vineyards as bulk Liebfraumilch has the original Liebfrauenstift wines. Further up the quality scale, around 16 per cent of production is Riesling of *Kabinett* and *Spätlese* standard, full of soft, honeyed, floral fruit in Rheinhessen, riper and spicier in the Pfalz, more delicate in the Rheingau, with underlying acidity and steeliness to balance the richness of the fruit. Intensely rich, honeyed and unctuous wines of *Auslese* quality and above are produced in small quantities (around 5 per cent of total production and only in the very best years) in the Rhine from famous vineyards such as Schloss Vollrads and Schloss Johannisberg in the Rheingau, and Forster Jesuitengarten in the Pfalz. A tiny quantity of light red wine is produced, and an increasing amount of *Trocken* and *Halbtrocken* (dry and semi-dry) white is made, with a steelier, mineral character to it.

Climate Temperate, due to the moderating effects of the river, the protection of the Taunus mountains to the north and local forests.
Cultivation Soils are varied, with quartzite and slate at higher levels and loams, clay bess and sandy gravel below. Vineyards are located on the flat hinterlands and gentle slopes of the Rhine, the best sites being the south-facing river banks. New crosses of grapes such as Kerner and Scheurebe have been introduced since the 1960s.
Grape varieties *White*: Riesling, Müller-Thurgau, Silvaner, Kerner, Bacchus, Huxelrebe, Morio-Muskat, Scheurebe, Muskateller, Gewürztraminer; *Reds* are from the Spätburgunder and Portugieser; *Ahr*: Riesling, Müller-Thurgau, Kerner, Silvaner, Scheurebe, Rulander, Blauer Portugieser, Spätburgunder, Ahr Domina, Dornfelder.
Production/maturation The finest-quality wines are produced in minute quantities, allowing for great attention to detail. Many of the independent producers market their own wines as well. At the other extreme, a great deal of bulk-blended generic wine, such as Liebfraumilch and Niersteiner, is produced.
Longevity *Deutscher Tafelwein* and *Landwein*: drink immediately; QbA: 1–3 years; *Kabinetts*: 2–8 years; *Spätlesen*: 3–12 years; *Auslesen*: 5–18 years; *Beerenauslesen*: 10–30 years; *Trockenbeerenauslesen, Eiswein*: 10–50 years.
Vintage guide 85, 86, 88, 89, 90, 92, 93, 94, 95.
My Top 17 *Ahr*: Winzergenossenschaft Heimersheim; *Mittelrhein*: Heinrich Weiler, Toni Jost; *Nahe*: Staatliche Weinbaudomäne/Graf Von Plettenberg, Diel, Kruger-Rumpf; *Rheingau*: von Bretano, Künstler, Deinhard, von Simmern; *Rheinhessen*: Carl Sittman, Bruder Dr Becker; *Pfalz*: Lingenfelder, Kurt Darting, Müller-Catoir, Neckerauer, Bürklin-Wolf.

---

still tend to be rather like Japanese films – to be admired and talked about rather than enjoyed. If you have ever thought a Chablis or a Sancerre dry and acidic, you would find it hard to imagine the meanness of some of these wines.

Charta members counter any such comments from visitors with the argument that these wines need time to soften and that, in any case, they are being ordered by the cellarful by German restaurants, whose customers seem ready to pay high prices, patriotically drinking them instead of a French import. Today the dry Rheingaus are indeed selling so well that most of the people making them have cut their production of sweeter wine to just 30 or 40 per cent of the total. The Rheingau is now, quite literally, going dry; tragically, its producers

seem resolute in their desire to rewrite history by claiming that their region's wines were traditionally made without any remaining sweetness. Maybe in cool, unripe, years this was the case; in warmer ones, however, as anyone who has been lucky enough to pull the cork on a glorious, petrolly, 30- or 40-year-old *Auslese* or *Spätlese* knows, they were still producing the kind of sweet, part-fermented wines that had so enchanted the Romans 2,000 years earlier.

When buying Rheingau wines, beware of wines labelled as Bereich Johannisberg; although some are good, they could come from literally anywhere in the region – this is the Rheingau's only *Bereich*. Look out instead for wines from individual villages – but not necessarily villages such as Lorch and Lorchhausen, both of which are close to the border with the Mittelrhein and produce good, but unexceptional, Riesling.

Assmannshausen has a local reputation for the quality of its Pinot Noir reds, few of which stand comparison with good examples from the Rheinpfalz, let alone those from across the French border. As you round the elbow of the river, however, you come to the tourist town of Rüdesheim, with its street of wine bars and its steep Berg vineyard, source of some of the biggest-tasting wines of the region.

Next stop on the river is Geisenheim, site of Germany's top wine school and research institute, and the place where vine experts labour to create new kinds of easy-to-grow grapes that are ideally adapted to these northerly conditions. The best vineyard here is probably the Mauerchen.

Beyond Geisenheim, you arrive at Winkel and its Hasensprung vineyard, and two German oddities: Schloss Johannisberg and Schloss Vollrads, old-established estates that are allowed to print their own names rather than that of an individual vineyard on their labels. Both are in the forefront of the dry-wine movement. Today the Steinberg vineyard planted by the monks houses the German Wine School and a wine museum, but it still produces full-flavoured, honeyed wine with a dash of slate and flowery acidity that is sold as Steinberger.

The nearby riverside villages of Oestrich and Hattenheim make similar, if less intense, wines. Hattenheim is also the place to come in June for its annual Erdbeerfest – strawberry and wine fair. The Nussbrunnen and Wisselbrunnen are the top vineyards here. The little hillside villages of Hallgarten and Kiedrich make great, if slightly more spicy and floral, less honeyed Riesling, especially good examples of which come from the Sandgrub and Grafenberg vineyards, while Erbach has the Rheingau's greatest plot of vines, the Marcobrunn, as well as Schloss Rheinhausen, one of its oldest (eighth-century) and best estates. The Rieslings and dry Chardonnays here are impressive.

Eltville's claims to fame include the fact that it was the home of Johannes Gutenberg; it is also the place to find one of Germany's best state-owned estates, the Staatsweinguter, which makes a wide range of top-class wines – including, when possible, extra-ordinary Eiswein.

Back in the hills, Rauenthal makes small quantities of intensely flavoured wines that need longer to soften than those made closer to the river – but they're worth the wait. Nearby, Walluf boasts two of the oldest vineyards in the region, while Martinsthal has the impressive Wildsau vineyard.

Finally, on the River Main close to Wiesbaden, is Hochheim, the town that gave the English "hock" – their easy-to-remember term for the wines of the Rhine. Like all the vineyards on the Main, Hochheim makes "earthier" wine than the rest of the Rheingau, but the flavours can be rich and tangily refreshing.

Rheinhessen

The biggest wine region in Germany – with some 165 vine-growing villages, 11,000 growers and around a quarter of the annual production – this is also one of the oldest. Historically, at least, the Rheinhessen could be called the heartland of the Rhine. Fifty per cent of all Liebfraumilch is made here, and millions more bottles of undistinguished wine are labelled Bereich Nierstein or Niersteiner Gütes Domtal.

The weather here is comparatively mild, with neither the frosts suffered in the Mosel, nor the greater warmth enjoyed by the Pfalz. The Riesling can fare well; unfortunately, this is lazy wine-making country in which bulk-oriented merchants and co-operatives hold sway and the Müller-Thurgau and its recently developed fellow varieties have taken over in the largely flat, featureless vineyards. Just one vine in 20 is now a Riesling and most of these are grouped around a set of nine riverside towns and villages called the Rhein Terrasse. These include Auflangen Bodenheim, Nackenheim, Oppenheim and Nierstein, the lovely old town whose 150 growers more or less lost their birthright when their neighbours stole the name of Nierstein and that of one of its least distinguished vineyards, the Gütes Domtal, and applied them indiscriminately to an enormous amount of mediocre Müller-Thurgau produced throughout a large chunk of the Rheinhessen. Nierstein's real wines are worth seeking out, as are those of Oppenheim and nearby Ingleheim, where the speciality is Spätburgunder.

Pfalz

The most exciting region in Germany today, the Pfalz, is benefiting both from its climate, and from the presence of some of Germany's most go-ahead wine-makers. Just across the southern border from Alsace, and in the same rain shadow provided by the range the French call the Vosges and the Germans know as the Haardt mountains, the Pfalz is warmer country. Grapes ripen better here, taking on the richer, spicier character often found in Alsace. Picking out a wine from the Pfalz "blind" can be one of the easiest of tasting party-tricks; if there seems to be more body to the wine and more spice, the odds of it being from the Pfalz are pretty good. And the more spice and perfume you find, the greater the likelihood that it was made by a maverick like Müller-Catoir, Kimich, Koehler-Ruprecht or Kurt Darting, quite possibly from some new-fangled grape variety like the Rieslaner or Scheurebe, both of which can make exceptional wines here.

Beyond those rising superstars, though, you have to pick and choose. That ripeness can mean a lack of fresh acidity; much of the wine here is soft, dull Müller-Thurgau – basic Liebfraumilch in name or nature. This is not only Germany's second largest wine region, but also, on occasion, its most productive, thanks to the combination of the sun and those generous Müller-Thurgau vines. It is also co-operative country – as you

Mild weather, mild landscape: The Rheinhessen

Middle of the road: The Burg Guttenfels and a midstream toll post, Mittelrhein

might expect from any region whose 25,000 wine-growers have less than two and a half acres (one hectare) of vines each, where the wine-makers know that their grapes are likely to ripen most years, in a climatically privileged part of Germany, and whose pre-eminence, they would argue, was recognized 2,000 years ago by the Romans and, more recently, by Napoleon.

Just as the Mosel has its best part in the Mittelmosel, the Pfalz's finest vineyards are to be found around a set of half a dozen villages in the *Bereich* Mittelhaardt-Deutsche Weinstrasse to the north of Neustadt. Inevitably, however, the allocation of *Bereichen* was as mishandled here as it was elsewhere, and this one takes in the whole of the northern half of the Pfalz, leaving the south to the *Bereich* Südliche Weinstrasse. The most northerly vineyards of the *Bereich* Mittelhaardt-Deutsche Weinstrasse are an undistinguished bunch, and the first village of any interest is Kallstadt, whose Annaberg vineyard produces great Riesling. Unusually, the labels of the wines made in the Annaberg, like those of a Burgundian *Grand Cru* such as the Corton, do not need to include the name of a village. Which is just as well because, while most of the rest of Kallstadt's vineyards are in the *Grosslage* Kobnert, the Annaberg confusingly falls into the *Grosslage* Freurberg, along with Bad Durckheim, another source of potentially great wine.

It is in the next most southern *Grosslage*, the Mariengarten (Forst an der Weinstrasse), and in Wachenheim, Forst and Deidesheim, most specifically, that the wine-making fireworks really begin. Other wines produced in the Rheinpfalz may

equal the best made here; none beats them. The secret of these vineyards lies in their exposure to the sun, to the black basalt of Forst's vineyards – especially in the Forster Jesuitengarten – that helps to give the grapes a little extra ripeness, and to the quality of the producers. The names of the estates with vines here – Basserman-Jordan, Reichsrat von Buhl, Bürklin-Wolf – read like a roll-call of Germany's vinous aristocracy, though not necessarily of Germany's present-day best.

Nahe

The wines of the Nahe don't really have a style of their own, despite the characteristically unhelpful creation of a single *Bereich* Nahetal designation covering all of its wines. In fact, the region is a meeting point of the Mosel and the Rhine; some wines taste like basic Rheinhessen, while others combine the depth of fruit of the Rheingau with the acid bite of the Mosel. The Riesling is a newcomer here, but at its best – in villages such as Bad Münster and Münster Sarmsheim – it can be richly intense. Another speciality of the region is its grapefruity Scheurebe.

Good wine is, however, the exception to the Nahe rule. A lot of what is made here is fairly basic – particularly when it bears such convincing-sounding labels as Rüdesheimer Rosengarten (which is sold on the reputation of the great Rüdesheim of the Rheingau) and Schlossböckelheim. Look for Rieslings from the cellars of Hans Crusius (especially from the Traiser Rotenfels and Traiser Bastei vineyards) and von Plettenberg (from Schlossböckelheimer Kupfergrube and Bad Kreuznacher Narrenkappe).

MITTELRHEIN

From its name, one might expect this region to be as important a part of the Rhine as the Mittelmosel is of the Mosel. But in fact, the Mittelrhein is best described as tourist country, the Germany on which Hollywood based its version of Grimms' fairy tales. Its riverside villages are almost too well kept, but so, thankfully, are the sheer, sloping vineyards in which the Riesling still holds sway. Unfortunately, the wines produced here are rather less spectacular. The best – from villages such as Braubach, Bacharach, Boppard and Oberwesel – can be quite intensely, if often rather acidically, reminiscent of the Mosel, but very little is made, and very few bottles escape the grasp of the region's landlords,

Gebäckenes Schweinsfilet im Broselteig

Tenderloin of roast pork baked in a herb crust

The sandy soils of some parts of the Rhine valley are perfect not only for vines but also for that other great Rhineland delicacy – asparagus – which accompanies this dish to perfection.

SERVES 4–6

3 lb/1.5 kg pork tenderloin or fillet
Olive oil
Salt and freshly ground black pepper
1 onion, peeled and halved
1 bay leaf
2 egg yolks
½ tsp dried sage
½ tsp dried marjoram
2 oz/50 g dried breadcrumbs
1 glass dry white wine

Rub the meat all over with olive oil and season with salt and pepper. Place in a roasting tin with the onion and bay leaf and put into an oven pre-heated to 425°F/210°C/Gas mark 7 for about 1½ hours. Remove and allow to cool a little. In a large bowl mix all the other ingredients except the wine until it forms a spreadable paste (if too wet, add more breadcrumbs; if too dry, a little water). Season this mixture with salt and pepper and spread over the meat. Return the joint to an oven pre-heated to 450°F/230°C/Gas mark 5 for 15 minutes, basting regularly. Remove the meat to a heated dish. Add the wine to the roasting tin, bring to the boil and scrape up any solids. Strain the juices over the meat and serve with steamed young asparagus and noodles.

who have no difficulty in selling them. For the moment, the region's one international star remains Toni Jost.

Ahr

The wines from this area rarely leave German soil either, partly because Ahr is so tiny – under 1,000 acres (400 ha) of vines are divided among nearly 1,000 growers – and partly because over two-thirds of its wine is red (pink) Weissherbst, made either from the Portugieser or Spätburgunder (Pinot Noir).

Making red wines this far north, even in the favourable micro-climate provided by the valley slopes of the river after which the region is named, is impracticable. The producers might do better to concentrate a little more on their pleasant Riesling and Müller-Thurgau whites.

THE OTHER WINES OF GERMANY

*I*F THE wine-makers of the Rhine and Mosel went on strike, would-be German wine-drinkers would still have a surprisingly wide range of bottles from which to choose – a far wider range, in fact, than either of those regions could ever begin to offer.

FRANKEN

Poor old Franken. Very, very few people know its wines and at least some of those who do imagine that this region stole its Bocksbeutel bottle design from Mateus Rosé rather than vice versa. The earthy Silvaner grape still occupies much of the land, producing often similarly earthy wine; but, like the Chasselas in Switzerland, the Silvaner does its very best here, producing dry wines that go well with the region's heavy Bavarian dishes.

WURTTEMBERG

When German wine-drinkers want a red wine produced by their countrymen, this is the region to which they look. The only problem, to an outside observer, is that, while the locals accept the stuff they are given as red, most non-Germans would call it sweet and pink. The handicaps here are the heavy-handed influence of the co-operatives (half the growers have vineyards of less than half an acre) and the range of grapes that is used. The main varieties are the Trollinger, the Pinot Meunier (here known as the Schwarzriesling) and the Lemberger, all of which make better rosé than red. Some decent Pinot Noir is made, and some better Riesling – particularly in the *Grosslage* of Heuchelberg and in the Stuttgart suburb *Einzellagen* of Berg, Goldberg, Hinterer Berg, Steinhalde, Wetzstein and Zuckerle – but these wines are rarely seen outside the region.

HESSISCHE BERGSTRASSE

"The spring garden of Germany", this is orchard country where the 1,000 acres (400 ha) of grapes have to compete with a wide range of fruits and vegetables. The Riesling can ripen well enough, but its wines (most of which are made by two co-operatives) are rarely better than middle-of-the-road Rhines.

BADEN

For decades now, under the guidance of its huge Badische Winzerkeller co-operative, Baden has gone its own way. While other regions were busily planting Müller-Thurgau with which to make semi-sweet plonk, Baden has been increasing its acreage of Riesling, and concentrating its attention on making dry and off-dry wines, including some increas-ingly impressive Pinot Noir. Today, of course, growers throughout the rest of Germany have followed Baden's example; unfortu-nately for them, few enjoy the warm climate of this region.

Few, too, enjoy seeing their countrymen sending their wine overseas in Burgundy-shaped bottles whose labels seem to go out of their way to hide their Germanic origins. To a Rhine or Mosel traditionalist, these Baden bottles are turncoats; to many a casual overseas wine-drinker, they are a far more attractive prospect than the more classic German bottle whose value has been undermined by too many unhappy experiences with cheap-and-nasty Liebfraumilch.

It would be wrong to paint too rosy a picture of Baden's wines, however – many of the co-operatives' 500 different wines are neutral, dry, Müller-Thurgau, Gutedel, or unexciting red or pink Weissherbst – but both the Riesling and Rülander can make really tasty wine here. Look out for slightly sparkling *spritzig* examples.

SACHSEN

If the name is unfamiliar, don't worry; it wouldn't ring loud bells with most German wine-drinkers either – certainly not the ones living in what used to be known as West Germany, on the other side of the old Iron Curtain. Once upon a time, this was one of the more significant wine regions, with vineyards covering some four times as much land as Sancerre does today. Sachsen had

The Kaiserstuhl: *This extinct volcano provides some of Baden's best vineyards*

The Essentials
OTHER GERMAN REGIONS

What to look for Richer than usual (for Germany) whites from Baden and earthy, spicy distinctive wines from Franken.
Official quality Overwhelmingly QbA, although *Kabinett* wines are made in reasonable quantities in hot years. Very little *Auslese* or above.
Style Württemberg produces a light, grapey red from the Trollinger grape and a characterful, soft summer fruit Schillerwein. These regions also produce classic racy Riesling, aromatic with piercing green apple fruit, in contrast to the richer Riesling made in Hessische Bergstrasse, which is full of soft, almost tropical fruit flavours. Baden's wide range is rarely seen outside the region. Franken produces full, earthy, dry wines. Riesling from warm years can be excellent.
Climate These regions are characterized by sheltered, temperate climates although the climate of Franken, Sachsen and Saale-Unstrut is more continental.
Cultivation Most vineyards are located on gentle slopes or south-facing hillsides of river valleys.
Grape varieties *Hessische Bergstrasse:* Ehrenfelser, Gewürztraminer; *Franken:* Bacchus, Silvaner, Ortega, Perle, Riesling, Rieslaner;

Württemberg: Trollinger, Müllerrebe, Lemberger, Pinot Meunier; *Baden:* Gutedel, Silvaner, Riesling, Nobling; *Sachsen:* Riesling, Gutedel, Portugieser, Müller-Thurgau, Traminer; *Saale-Unstrut:* Riesling, Müller-Thurgau, Weissburgunder, Silvaner, Portugieser, Gutedel, Traminer.
Production/maturation Much of the wine in these regions is produced by technically proficient co-operatives from grapes grown by small growers who use labour-intensive methods. In Sachsen and Saale-Unstrut, however, efficiency in both vineyard and winery is still a novelty.
Longevity Varies enormously, depending on the style of the wine. Most reds and whites made from "new" varieties should be drunk young.
Vintage guide 71, 76, 83, 85, 88, 89, 90, 92, 93, 94.
My Top 13: *Franken:* Ernst Popp, Hans Wirsching, Juliusspital, Bürgerspital, Castell; *Württemberg:* Dautz-Able, Staatliche Weinbau Lehrund Versuchsanstadt Weinsberg, Adelmann; *Baden:* Bezirkskellerei Markgräflerland, Johner, Dörflinger, Heger, Durbach.

---

already shrunk before Communism did its inefficient worst, but today, there are just 300 acres, a 20th of what it had in its prime. There's Riesling here along with Gutedel and Traminer but, despite low yields, wines are unexciting and unmemorable. Still, the tourists following the new Wine Route will probably lap them up.

SAALE-UNSTRUT

Another wine region that came from the cold of East Germany, Saale-Unstrut is slightly larger, but suffers from the effects of the same 50 years of neglect. Apart from the Riesling and Müller-Thurgau, there's also a bit of Silvaner which might prove to be the region's strongest suit.

SEKT

This is not a region, but a peculiarly ignoble style of wine which confirms everything the most cynical critic has ever said about the German wine industry. Before going any further, I'd like to point out that the banning of the harmless words *méthode champenoise* from the labels of classically made fizz was originally instigated, not by the Champenois

Facing forward: Baden wines are riper and drier

as one might have expected, but by German fizz-makers who were desperate to protect their (non-Champagne-method) wines

---

Königsberger Klopse

Meatballs in a creamy caper sauce

*B*erlin, cosmopolitan crossroads of East and West, first adopted this dish (originally brought in by East Prussian immigrants) as its own, but today variants on this tasty recipe with its piquant sauce are served throughout Germany.

SERVES 6

8 oz/225 g minced beef
8 oz/225 g minced pork
8 oz/225 g minced veal
2 slices stale white bread, crust removed, soaked in water and squeezed dry
4 tbsp dried breadcrumbs
2 medium onions, finely minced
2 eggs
3 anchovy fillets, finely chopped
2 tbsp melted butter
Salt and freshly ground black pepper
25 fl oz/700 ml beef stock
2 egg yolks
2 tbsp capers
Lemon juice

In a large bowl, mix the meats, the bread, 1 tbsp breadcrumbs, onion, eggs, anchovy and melted butter. Season with salt and pepper and shape into balls. In a large saucepan bring the stock to the boil and lower in the meatballs with a spoon or ladle. Cook for about 20 minutes and then lift them out with a slotted spoon and keep warm. Stir the remaining breadcrumbs into the stock and simmer and stir until the sauce begins to thicken. Remove from the heat. Beat the egg yolks well and add a spoonful of the stock and mix well. Add this mixture to the stock and simmer gently, stirring constantly, until it just begins to thicken. Do not let it boil. Add the capers and a few drops of lemon juice, then add the meatballs to the sauce. Serve with noodles and broccoli.

---

from competition (Champagne-method) wines such as Cava from Spain.

What those Sekt producers hated to admit was that the very worst Cava is a million times more drinkable than most German sparkling wine. At its finest, *flaschengarung* – champagne-method – Riesling can be both delicious and refreshingly different but, unfortunately, such examples are very, very rare; most Sekt is made by the *cuve close* method from dull, unripe Müller-Thurgau or Elbling. And, unless the label says *Deutscher Sekt*, the mass of the wine in the bottle won't even be German. Try the ones made by Deinhard and Schloss Rheinhartshausen or stick to Cava.

SPAIN

SOMETHING STRANGE and wonderful is happening to Spain. If you watched the flamboyant finale of the 1992 Olympics, in Barcelona, or have relished the culinary wit of the cooking at restaurants like the Michelin-bestarred El Bulli, not far from that city, or wandered through the new architecture of Seville, you'd have to be blind to have missed sensing a new mood. As you would if you'd spent any time talking to the sophisticated young Spaniards who throng the colourfully tiled bars in the heart of Madrid. It seems fanciful, I know, but it is almost as though an entire country is slowly shrugging off its heavy shroud of melancholy and somehow swapping the heavy dark oils of El Greco for the gaiety of Joan Miró.

Now taste a glass of the Marques de Riscal's white wine from Rueda; of Berberana's various fruitily young unoaked Tempranillos; of Martinez Bujanda's unofficial Cabernet Sauvignon Rioja; of Chivite's new wave Chardonnay from Navarra or Lagar de Cervera's Albariño from Galicia. These are all fresh, fruit-packed wines that have nothing to do with the dull, woody efforts of which Spain's wine-makers were often so proud. And just the stuff to take over from some of the increasingly tired players who were slowing down the Spanish team and preventing it from being fully competitive with both the Old and New World.

The new wines arrived in the nick of time – at the moment when the European authorities were demanding the uprooting of large sections of the vineyards of La Mancha, and when increasing numbers of wine-drinkers were switching allegiance to

The new Spain: French-style barriques at Torres, Penedés

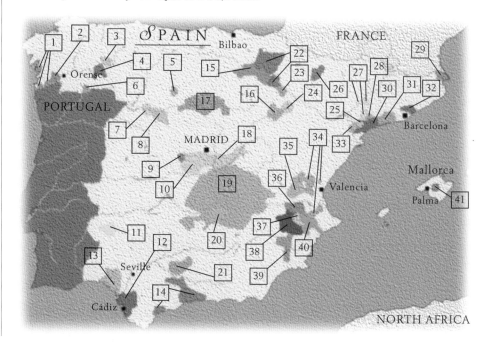

1 Rias Baixas	10 Mentrida	19 La Mancha
2 Ribeiro	11 Tierra de Barros	20 Valdepeñas
3 Bierzo	12 Jerez y Manzanilla	21 Montilla-Moriles
4 Valdeorras	13 Condado de Huelva	22 Navarra
5 Cigales	14 Málaga	23 Campo de Borja
6 Valle de Monterrey	15 Rioja	24 Cariñena
7 Toro	16 Calatayud	25 Priorato
8 Rueda	17 Ribera del Duero	26 Somontano
9 Cebreros	18 Vinos de Madrid	27 Costers del Segre

28 Conca de Barberá	36 Almansa
29 Ampurdán-Costa Brava	37 Yecla
30 Tarragona	38 Jumilla
31 Penedés	39 Bullas
32 Alella	40 Alicante
33 Terra Alta	41 Binissalem
34 Valencia	
35 Utiel Requena	

Australia, California and Southern France. Mind you, Spain's more old-fashioned wines had performed well enough for a very long time. The reds were for decades the easy-going seducers of the wine world, the wines that gently led countless white-wine-drinkers down the path toward more "sophisticated" claret and Chianti. The point was that while, to many novice drinkers, those French and Italian wines were dauntingly tannic, Spain's reds were soft and, to use a term cherished by the hacks who write the descriptive labels on the backs of bottles, "mellow". They were, above all, very, very approachable. The trouble was that once those novice drinkers (of whom I was one) had been introduced to red wine, where did they go next? Straight to claret.

So what was wrong? Well, if an independent analyst had been called in to define the problem, he or she would undoubtedly have initially focused on the raw materials – Spain's indigenous grape varieties, of which there are over 600. This may sound like a wealth of choice, until you go on to discover that just 20 of these cover 80 per cent of the vineyards. And these 20 produce wine as monotonous and undemanding as the contents of an average Top Twenty pop chart. The Airén, for example, the most widely planted grape in the world, covers nearly a third of the country's vineyards – and makes dreadfully dull white wine.

The second most widespread variety, the Garnacha – the grape the growers of the Rhône know as the Grenache – covers around 10 per cent of the vineyards and is rarely encouraged to make wine of any great distinction. And none, apart from Priorato, built to last. The only red grape of note, the Tempranillo, accounts for around a fifth as much land as the Garnacha, and only achieves real recognition for its essential contribution to the flavour of Rioja and Ribera del Duero, despite the fact that, under one alias or another, it is grown almost throughout Spain's vineyards. Italy and Portugal's widely planted grape varieties are a far more interesting lot. Spain does have top-class grapes, to be sure – varieties like the Graciano, Loureira, Verdejo and Albariño – but it has done far too little to exploit them.

So, while the rest of the world lapped up Cabernets, Merlots, Chardonnays and Sauvignons made almost anywhere, and highly priced designer Italian reds in designer bottles, Spain's wines remained, if not in the bargain basement, at least among the cheaper wines on the shelf, vulnerable to competition from more flavoursome, fashionable fare. Cava, Spain's sparkling wine made by the Champagne method but from dull indigenous grapes, did sell well internationally, but usually at lower prices than many New-World offerings which were made in the same way, but from Champagne grape varieties.

There were, thankfully, a few pioneering wine-makers who took a broader view. Miguel Torres, for example, proved what could be done with Gewürztraminer, Riesling, Cabernet Sauvignon, Sauvignon, Pinot Noir and Chardonnay, and his lead was followed by Jean León, by Carlos Falco at his Marques de Griñon estate and by Raimat, a sizeable subsidiary of the huge sparkling wine producer Codorníu, which broke ranks by introducing a pure Chardonnay fizz. Despite a strong reactionary backlash – in 1996 there was a major public

Old Spain: Theme-park-style harvest festivities in Jerez

row between Codorníu and its main rival Freixenet over the legitimacy of using Chardonnay in Cava – the international success of these wines encouraged experimentation.

The region in which this bore the most impressive fruit was Navarra, whose high-tech Evena research station helped growers to convert the DO from one that was associated with cheap rosé to one in which firms like Chivite made world-class Cabernet Sauvignon and Chardonnay. Across the regional boundary in Rioja, there was a grudging acknowledgement that the Cabernet Sauvignon that had been a major component of the prize-winning Riojas of the nineteenth century might just possibly be legally used to make their twentieth-century counterparts.

Encouragingly, though, the "international" varieties were not the only beneficiaries of this wind of change. In the best parts of Rioja, the easy-to-grow Garnacha, which had largely supplanted the finer Graciano and Mazuela, was pushed back to allow those varieties to return – and to give more

emphasis to the Tempranillo. Elsewhere, there were successful efforts to exploit the often underrated potential of the Verdejo and Viura grapes.

If the grape varieties were a handicap, so too were the ways in which the wine was produced and matured. To most older Spaniards, an old wine is, by definition, better than a young wine. And a wine that has been matured for a long time in oak barrels is best of all. Spain's recently updated *Denominación de Origen* system – its equivalent of France's *Appellation Contrôlée* – has traditionally had age as one of its central tenets, officially designating wines that have undergone the required period of maturation with the words *Con Crianza*, *Reserva* or *Gran Reserva*.

All three terms may indicate higher-than-usual quality – based on the assumption that the *bodegas* only produce *Reservas* and *Gran Reservas* in the best vintages. All too often, however, the same terms and rules are applied to wines made from grapes that have no natural propensity for ageing. Visitors from other countries often left the

tasting rooms of *bodegas* – wineries – shaking their heads in dismay that the wine-makers insisted on keeping ready-to-drink young wine to flatten out and lose its fruit in cask. But it's hard to blame the wine-makers; the oak-aged wine not only sold for a higher price, but did so very easily on the local market.

In the past, this Hispanic keenness on ageing was catered for by displaying on the labels of wine bottles not a vintage, but that the wine was a "2nd", "3rd" or "4th" *Año*, or "year", meaning that it had been matured for two, three or four years. When vintages did appear, they were often used in what one might call a rather "relaxed" fashion, with a single batch of labels being used on wines from a succession of harvests. But what did it matter? After all, the wines were almost always ready to drink when they were sold and all but the best producers liked to promote the erroneous idea that there was little variation in wines of different vintages. Indeed, one quite go-ahead wine-maker freely admitted having blended together wines of two or three years so as to maintain a commercially successful flavour. As he said, people liked the 1982, so he made the 1983 taste as similar to it as he could.

There was work to be done too in the *bodegas*. Some lacked the equipment needed to make good wine; others lacked the know-how or will. In 1995 I watched a modern conveyor-belt system, of which any Californian winery would be proud, carry to the press a mixture of rotten and healthy grapes no Californian would countenance for an instant. Elsewhere, trucks full of grapes stood cooking in the sun while the wine-makers enjoyed a long, leisurely lunch. Pipes that should have been washed through thoroughly every day were cleaned only at the beginning and end of the harvest.

A PRIDE OF WINE-MAKERS

This easy-going attitude began to change, however, when overseas customers unintentionally bruised the most sensitive part of any male Spaniard – his pride. Foreigners openly suggested that Spanish wine-makers did not know how to do their job properly. In one famous joint venture, a French co-operative so distrusted its partners across the border that, having supervised the crushing of the grapes and the fermentation in Spain, it shipped the

The Language of Spain

Abocado Medium-sweet.
Añejado por Aged by.
Año Year.
Blanco White.
Bodega Wine shop, firm or cellar.
Cepa Vine.
Clarete Very light red.
Consejo Regulador Official organization controlling each region's system of *Denominación de Origen*.
Cosecha Harvest, vintage.
Criada por Matured by.
Crianza A red wine with a minimum of 2 years in the barrel (6 months for whites).
Denominación de Origen (DO) Controlled quality wine region, equivalent to France's AOC. Every such region possesses its own quality stamp.
Denominación de Origen Calificada (DOC) A superior quality level, created in 1988, and confusingly similar to Italy's DOCG. So far Rioja is the only region.
Doble Pasta A wine macerated with twice the normal proportion of grape skins to juice during fermentation.
Dulce Sweet.
Embotellado Bottled.
Espumoso Sparkling.
Elaborado por Made by.
Flor Wine yeast peculiar to sherry that is vital to the development of the *fino* style.
Garantia de Origen Simple wines that have received little or no oak ageing.

Generoso Fortified.
Gran Reserva The top quality level for wines. Reds must have spent 2 years in oak and 3 years in bottle, or vice versa. Whites must have been aged for 4 years with at least 6 months in cask.
Granvas Sparkling wine made by the *cuve close* method.
Joven Young wine – unwooded, fresh, fruity and modern.
Nuevo "Nouveau-style" red.
Reserva Reds matured for a minimum of 3 years, of which at least 1 is spent in cask. Whites and rosados receive 2 years' ageing with at least 6 months in cask.
Rosado Rosé.
Seco Dry.
Semi-seco Medium-dry.
Sin Crianza Without wood ageing.
Solera Traditional system of producing consistent style of sherry or Málaga whereby increasingly mature barrels are topped up – refreshed – with slightly younger wine.
Tintillo Light red (like *clarete).*
Tinto Red.
Vendimia Harvest, vintage.
Viejo Old.
Viña/Viñedo Vineyard.
Vino de aguja Wine with a slight sparkle.
Vino de mesa Table wine.
Vino de pasta Ordinary, inexpensive wine, usually light in style.
Vino de la Tierra Equivalent of France's *vin de pays;* "country wine" with some regional character.

wine back home to take care of it until bottling. Elsewhere, wines intended for sale in Britain and the Netherlands were fully produced and bottled on Spanish soil – but under the supervision of young Australian and French "Flying Wine-makers". In Australia, wineries do not shut for an instant during the vintage; in Spain, they traditionally close at lunch, for the weekend and for saint's day fiestas, whatever is going on in the vats. When one young Antipodean was denied access to his fermenting wine on a Sunday, he simply smashed a window, climbed inside – and telephoned the boss of the *bodega* to warn him to hand over a key, or expect a lot more break-ins.

In Eastern Europe when visiting foreigners made such efforts beyond the call of local wine-making duty, the response was usually an apathetic shrug. In Spain, they had a more direct impact. As did the international success of wines like the Rueda whites made by Jacques Lurton and by Hugh Ryman for the Marques de Riscal. The huge Bodegas y Bebidas group, for example, swiftly decided that anything the foreigners could do, they could do just as well – if not better – and proved it with a fresh new-wave Rioja called Albor and a set of pure varietals made from local grapes which would have been inconceivable a few years earlier.

Taking a more traditional route, Telmo Rodriguez of the great family-owned Remelluri estate undertook research into the tannins in the Tempranillo grape and the effect various systems of fermentation had on a wine's ultimate toughness or softness. Where his neighbours were throwing out old wooden vats to install stainless steel, Rodriguez was doing the opposite – except that his vats were clean, well-kept and their contents overseen as though they were a new-born baby in an incubator.

TINY PRODUCTION

Quality-conscious Spanish wine-makers following in Rodriguez's footsteps faced two other barriers, however: one connived at, and one wholly created by the DO system. The authorities not only favour large *bodegas*, but make life very difficult for small ones. Ageing *bodegas* in Rioja, for example, are legally obliged to stock a minimum of 2,250 hectolitres – or around 1,000 225-litre barrels. Even spread over several vintages, 1,000 barrels could hold the production of four or five estates in Burgundy or St Emilion. And without a legally recognized ageing *bodega*, you can't

Clearer future: Rioja quality is at last improving

use those magic *Con Crianza*, *Reserva* and *Gran Reserva* labels that guarantee a valuable extra few pesetas per bottle. The inevitable consequence of this is that Spain still has had far too few maverick wineries to pioneer new developments; compared with Italy, for example, it has a pitifully small band – less than a dozen strong – of internationally recognized superstars.

Then there are the vineyards. Yields in Spain are very low – on average only 25 hl/ha or half those of Burgundy, for example. It is these low yields that explain why, although Spain has more vineyards than any other country in Europe and nearly half as many again as France, its annual production is far smaller than it ought to be. This limited production is directly attributable to the lack of rain. But even when it is available, irrigation has, until 1996, been against the law in the denominated regions. This might seem reasonable enough, were it not for the international success of wines made at Raimat whose huge swathes of vineyards would have a hard time supporting cactus if it weren't for the "experimental" irrigation system. In other words, some vine-growers could water their vines while others could not.

In the early 1990s, however, as I say, the bubble burst. Wine-makers in Rioja and elsewhere introduced their own equally "experimental" irrigation schemes so successfully that the authorities conceded that the ban on adding water might have to be reconsidered. Newly planted Cabernet

Sauvignon vines made their contribution to new-wave Riojas (even if their presence too was deemed "experimental"); smaller estates like José Puig's Augustus in the Penedés joined Torres's Milmanda in producing world-class Chardonnays; and, in Rueda, a whole new white-wine region was born.

It will take time for these revolutionary tendencies to make an impact throughout Spain, and courage for more *bodegas* to flout custom by offering better wines with less oak-ageing. The first regions to escape from the shadow of Rioja have been Ribera del Duero and Navarra, but Rueda is on track with its whites and could soon prove to be just as good a place to make reds. Galicia will gain an international reputation for its white wines, as will previously unknown areas like Conca de Barberá (where Torres makes his Milmanda Chardonnay) and Somontano. Who knows? Valencia's sweet Muscats may finally get the recognition they deserve as lighter alternatives to France's Beaumes de Venise.

Spain has recently followed Italy's (questionable) lead by upgrading Rioja from plain DO – *Denominación de Origen* – to the first DOC – *Denominación de Origen Calificada* – and tightened the controls on the way it is made. All that's needed now is a version of the newer Italian rules that shift the emphasis toward the intrinsic quality of particular pieces of land and away from the way a wine has been made and matured.

RIOJA AND NAVARRA

AFTER A CERTAIN POINT, good old wines all begin to look alike. Judging by its appearance, I'd have guessed the stuff in my glass to have been made in the 1960s or the 1940s. But it wasn't; it was an 1871. At 125 years of age that bottle of Marques de Riscal Rioja and the 1924 that I tasted alongside it were two of the most impressive old wines I have ever tasted.

The difference in quality and character of the wines had little to do with *when* or indeed where they were made, but everything to do with the grape varieties from which they had been produced. Under modern law, both those wines would have been illegal – at least, they would if anyone were to reveal the amount of Cabernet Sauvignon the Tempranillo-dominant wines contained because, despite the part played by the French grape in the award-winning Riojas of the nineteenth century, today it may not be used other than on an "experimental" basis.

Rioja's history could be separated into four phases. There was the period during the last century when the region produced simple wine, most of which was for early drinking by the jugful. Then, in the 1860s, expertise – and grape varieties – were imported from Bordeaux, just across the Pyrénées. The newcomers, many of whom came to Spain when their own vineyards first fell prey to the *phylloxera* louse, introduced novel ideas such as the prolonged ageing of the wine in small (50-gallon/225-litre) casks and the practice of crushing the grapes rather than the Beaujolais-style method of fermenting them whole. Rioja became a wine worth keeping.

The third phase – from the early part of this century until quite recently – was often one of chauvinism and laziness: it saw the expulsion of the Cabernet Sauvignon, the relegation of the (characterful) Graciano to the sidelines, and the promotion of the easy-to-grow, but often featureless, Garnacha. By the early 1970s, Rioja was an internationally acknowledged, softly attractive wine with a sweet oaky flavour – but little justifiable claim to stand among the great wines of the world.

Today, faced with competition from regions elsewhere in Spain, and from overseas, the Riojanos have finally begun to

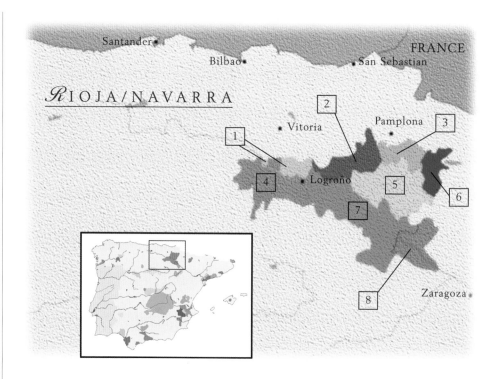

1	Rioja Alavesa	5	Navarra/Ribera Alta
2	Navarra/Tierra Estella	6	Navarra/Baja Montana
3	Navarra/Valdizarbe	7	Rioja Baja
4	Rioja Alta	8	Navarra/Ribera Baja

raise their game. Despite the big-is-beautiful rule which obliges any *bodega* that is going to mature wine that will sell as *Crianza*, *Reserva* or *Gran Reserva* to hold at least 1,000 barrels of wine in stock at any given time, smaller individual estates have been established (generally by the big companies which used to run the region). The Garnacha's horns have been trimmed, the Graciano encouraged and there has even – though this is rarely acknowledged openly – been a return of the Cabernet Sauvignon. Just as important has been the acknowledgement that, alongside its traditional oak-aged *Crianza*, *Reserva* or *Gran Reserva* wines, the region should exploit the lovely strawberry flavour of young, unoaked – "*sin crianza*" – Tempranillo.

There are now four Riojas: the autonomous region which does not precisely match the DOC, the overall wine area of the same name which in parts stretches beyond it – and elsewhere stops short; and the three component parts, the Rioja Alta, the lower Rioja Baja and the Rioja Alavesa. Most Riojanos traditionally used to maintain that the best Rioja is a blend of wines from two or three of the regions. The Rioja Alta's calcium-rich soil is well suited to the Tempranillo and produces fine, long-lived red wines, while the Alavesa, shaded by mountains, has fewer extremes of temperature and makes the plummiest, best early-drinking wines. That leaves the Baja, which some unfairly say lives down to its "low" name by making the region's most basic wine.

The oaky flavour associated with red Rioja was once also the mark of the region's whites. For these, the ageing requirements are slightly less stringent; sadly only a handful of *bodegas* now make good oaky,

RIOJA AND NAVARRA

What to look for Rich, soft, oaky, and juicy *"joven"* unoaked Riojas, and increasingly impressive "new-wave" Navarra reds and whites.

Official quality Navarra is classified as *Denominación de Origen* (DO) while Rioja is now a *Denominacion de Origen Califica* (DOC). Rioja is divided into 3 sub-regions.,the Rioja Baja, Alavesa and Alta, in ascending order of quality.

Style Red Rioja should have soft strawberry and raspberry fruit with rich vanilla overtones from ageing in American oak barriques. There are two very different styles of white Rioja. One is the very clean, cool-fermented, anonymous new-wave style exemplified by Marqués de Cacerés. The other is the traditional *reserva* style with a very deep golden colour and intense vanilla flavour imparted by oak. Some wines, such as CVNE'S Monopole, successfully combine the two styles, producing fruity wines that have an attractive creamy vanilla character. The wines of Navarra tend to be more overtly modern, reflecting the flavours of the (diverse set of) grape varieties grown here.

Climate The Pyrenées and the Cantabrian mountains moderate the climate, offering protection from the Atlantic winds and the excessive heat of the Mediterranean. The climate becomes hotter and drier as one moves toward the coast.

Cultivation Topography in the region ranges widely, from the foothills of the Pyrenées to the flatter, hotter Rioja Baja. The best vineyards are in the central hill country of Rioja Alta and Alavesa. Limestone is the dominant component of the soils with additional sand and clays in Alta and Alavesa and silty alluvium deposits in Baja and Navarra.

Grape varieties *Red:* Tempranillo, Garnacha Tinta, Graciano, Mazuelo, Cabernet Sauvignon; *White:* Viura, Malvasia, Garnacha Blanca, Muscat Blanc à Petits Grains.

Production/maturation Ageing in Bordeaux-style barriques imparts the characteristic vanilla flavour to the wines of Rioja, where the new-style whites are cold-fermented. A lowering of minimum ageing periods in cask and bottle has, some say, resulted in a lessening of quality and character in red Riojas, many of which are now sold much younger than previously.

Longevity *Red Rioja Crianza*: 3–8 years; *Reserva*: 5–30 years; *Gran Reserva*: 8–30 years. New-wave white Rioja is for drinking young (within 3 years); the traditional white can be kept for 15 years but good examples are rare; *Navarra reds*: 3–10 years; whites: 1–3 years.

Vintage guide 82, 83, 85, 86, 87, 89, 90, 91, 94.

My Top 22 *Rioja:* Lopez de Heredia, La Rioja Alta, CVNE, Remelluri, Contino, Campillo, Marqués de Cacerés, Marqués de Riscal, Riojanas, Martinez Bujanda, Marqués de Villamagna, Amézola de la Mora, Campillo, Navajas, Baron de Ley; *Navarra:* Chivite, Senorio de Sarria, Ochoa, Guelbenzu, Palacio de la Vega, Agramont.

---

traditional wine that conforms to these rules, but firms like Berberana are spearheading a renaissance of white Rioja.

NAVARRA

Every now and then, when I hear right-wing politicians ranting about the evils of "intervention", I'd love to lead them to the old kingdom of Navarra, birthplace of Spanish wine-making, next-door neighbour to Rioja and, until the 1980s, one of the most run-down wine regions in the country. Left to the devices of the free market, this varied region devoted itself to the production of dull rosés and duller reds.

Then the local government became involved and sank substantial sums into a world-class research station called EVENA where men and women in white coats were employed to discover why Navarra's wines always tasted so recognizably different to – and less impressive than – the wines of

Navarra: Incentives are paying off

Rioja. It didn't take long to discover the answer; 80 per cent of the region's growers farmed less than one hectare (2.5 acres) and delivered mostly Garnacha grapes. Then, 90 per cent of its wine was made by ill-equipped and old-fashioned co-operatives. Having defined the problem, EVENA had a solution: further planting of the Garnacha was to be banned and growers were to be given financial incentives to plant better varieties, principally the Tempranillo, but also newcomers such as the Cabernet Sauvignon and Chardonnay and undervalued local varieties like the Graciano.

Lomo de Cerdo con Pimentos

Pork chops with a tomato, olive and red pepper sauce

*T*he Rioja region of Spain is blessed with not only luscious, oaky wines but also fruit and vegetables, particularly peppers, which add a subtle sweetness to this traditional recipe.

SERVES 6

6 pork loin chops
Salt and freshly ground black pepper
2 oz/50 g plain flour
3 tbsp olive oil
2 medium onions, minced
2 cloves garlic, peeled and minced
2 tomatoes, peeled, seeded and chopped or
2 tinned tomatoes, drained and chopped
1½ lb/750 g red peppers,
seeded and chopped
6 tbsp dry white wine
10fl oz/275 ml water
1 bay leaf
1 hard-boiled egg, finely chopped
2 tbsp parsley, chopped
12 black olives, pitted and halved

Season the chops with salt and pepper. Dredge them in the flour and shake to remove any excess. In a flameproof casserole, heat the oil until it is hot but not smoking. Brown the chops, turning regularly. Transfer the chops to a plate. To the casserole dish, add the onions and garlic and cook until the onions are soft but not brown. Add the tomatoes and peppers and cook over a moderate heat for about 5 minutes. Stir in the wine, water, bay leaf, egg, parsley and olives and bring to the boil. Immediately reduce to a simmer and add the chops (ensuring they are well-basted with the sauce). Cook gently for 30–40 minutes or until the chops are tender. Serve with rice and steamed courgettes.

EVENA would advise on what would grow best, and where and how the wine should be made, and – *pour encourager les autres* – the government would invest its own money in Cenalsa, a new showcase blending and bottling *bodega* that sells 20 per cent of all the Navarra wine sold in Spain.

And what did all this intervention achieve? Well, just taste some of Navarra's fruity and emphatically "modern" whites and rosés which have often leapfrogged over their more famous counterparts from Rioja. Try the young, unoaked reds that are among the most plummily refreshing in Spain. Some of the big *bodegas* of Rioja should look to their laurels. Navarra is quietly regaining Spain's vinous crown.

CATALONIA

$\mathcal{F}$IRST THINGS first. According to the Madrid govern-ment, Catalonia may appear to be part of Spain – but that's not the way the Catalans see it. They have their own capital in Barcelona, their own language and, from the way it looked to many observers, they had their own Olympic games.

A decade or so ago, though, before autonomy was on the menu, wine pundits were predicting that the Penedés, Catalonia's most famous wine area, would soon become one of the world's most exciting wine regions. In fact, after a promising start, the Penedés has had to watch some of its neighbours catch up and even overtake it, almost from a standing start.

THE REGIONS

There are nine Catalonian DOs, ranging from the huge Penedés to tiny Costers del Segre and Conca de Barberá, both of which owed their DO to the presence of a single large producer. Only one bottle in 10 leaves

Cava: Gaining sparkle at last

the winery without a regional *denominación* to its name. but ask most Spaniards to name as many as three of these regions and you'll be lucky to get much of a reply.

Penedés

This is the most successful part of Catalonia, thanks almost exclusively to the efforts of its Cava – sparkling wine – producers and to the dynamic Miguel Torres, the man who persuaded his neighbours of the benefits of clean, temperature-controlled fermentation; who proved, by winning international

tastings against the best of Bordeaux with his Gran Coronas Black Label (now called Mas La Plana), that the Cabernet Sauvignon could make top-class wine in the Penedés; and who, following a spell in France, took a fresh look at the local varieties.

A few small estates, such as Puig i Roca, have followed in Torres' footsteps toward the Cabernet Sauvignon and Chardonnay, but none of the big *bodegas* – with the exception of Codorníu's Raimat winery – has even begun to compete on any kind of major scale. And yet there are few regions in the Old World in which an adventurous wine-maker would have greater scope to experiment; between them, the Upper, Middle and Lower Penedés really do offer an extraordinarily broad range of climates. Down near the coast in the Lower Penedés, it's hot, ripe country – ideal for Muscat, but less suited to even medium-bodied reds and whites. For better examples of either of these styles, you have to cross the hills to the white-wine country where the grapes for Cava are grown, and where Torres has produced his prize-winning Cabernet Sauvignon. Even here the temperature is still a bit high for really fine whites; these are to be found in the Upper Penedés at 2,000–2,600 ft (600–800 m).

Surprisingly, the one style Torres has never marketed has been Cava, the Penedés *méthode champenoise* sparkling wine. Cava's early success merely served to confirm to a few cynical critics, who maintained that these wines tasted earthy, dull and unrefreshing, how easy it is to sell bubbles. Old-fashioned wineries (including co-operatives) do little to maintain the wine's freshness and flavour and the climate where the grapes are grown is also less than ideal, but the main problem is the grape varieties – the Parellada, the Macabeo and the dull, alcoholic Xarel-lo.

When the Raimat winery introduced its Chardonnay Brut Nature, few who tasted it blind recognized it as a Cava and non-Spaniards, used to Champagne, declared it a winner. Today, despite howls of anguish from conservatives like Freixenet, Chardonnay is rapidly appearing in all sorts of Cavas, and efforts are being made by newcomers like Moët & Chandon to improve the quality of wine made from the traditional varieties. Even so, too many producers are still

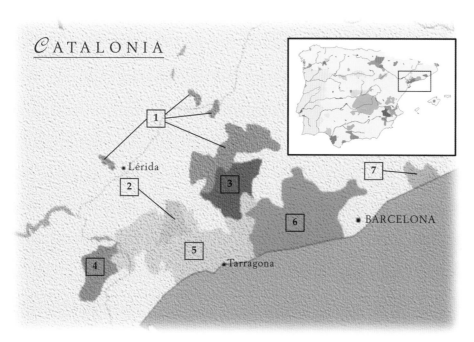

1	Costers del Segre	3	Conca de Barberá	5	Tarragona	7	Ampurdán-Costa
2	Priorato	4	Terra Alta	6	Penedés		Brava

The Essentials
CATALONIA

What to look for Varied and possibly quite innovative red and white wines whose character and quality can depend on altitude as much as grape variety and wine-making.

Official quality Penedés, Alella, Terra Alta and Priorato are notable areas with DO status.

Style Both red and white wines are varied, ranging from light and fruity to full, oak-matured to oak-free, dry to juicy-sweet. Although Catalonia is renowned as being Spain's most go-ahead wine-making region, most wines tend to be little more than sound and commercial. A significant difference can be seen in those wines from producers such as Torres and Jean León who use foreign grape varieties, oak-ageing and the latest techniques. Cava is the largest source of sparkling wine outside Champagne. Most are dry although there are sweet and rosado versions. Once recognizable by a characteristic earthy flavour, Cava has improved remarkably in recent years. The area around Tarragona is the source for much of the world's sacramental wine. Similarly rich and dark reds are produced at Terra Alta and Priorato.

Climate A relatively mild Mediterranean climate on the coast, becoming more continental further inland, with frost an increasing hazard. High-altitude vineyards are cool enough for Riesling.

Cultivation A wide variety of soils ranging from the granite of Alella to the limestone chalk and clay of Penedés and Tarragona, where there are, in addition, alluvial deposits. There is a similar variety of relief, ranging from the highest vineyards of Alto Penedés, which benefit from cooler temperatures, to the flat plains of Campo de Tarragona.

Grape varieties *Red*: Cabernet Sauvignon, Merlot, Tempranillo, Garnacha, Monastrell, Pinot Noir, Cabernet Franc; *White*: the Parellada predominates, with some Chardonnay, Sauvignon, Gewürztraminer, Muscat, Riesling, Garnacha Blanca, Macabeo, Malvasia and Xarel-lo.

Production/maturation With the exception of the very traditional Priorato, techniques are modern. Torres introduced cool-fermentation to Spain while the Cava companies have invented their own apparatus and methods besides adopting some – for example, the *méthode champenoise* – from outside. The Raimat estate at Lerida exemplifies the good use of ultra-modern vinification techniques.

Longevity *Reds*: up to 5 years for most, but top-class Penedés wines can last for 15; *Whites*: best drunk early, but between 3 and 8 years for fine whites such as Jean León's Chardonnay; *Cava*: within 1 to 3 years for non-vintage. Old vintage Cava is generally earthy and dull and unrecommendable to anyone who enjoys fizz with freshness and fruit or the kind of rich biscuitiness to be found in mature Champagne.

Vintage guide *Penedés: Reds* 82, 85, 87, 91, 94, 95; *Whites*: 91, 94, 95.

Top producers *Penedés:* Torres, Jean León, Marqués de Monistrol, Puig Roca; *Alella*: Raimat; *Cava*: Torre de Gall (a.k.a. Cava Chandon), Masia Bach, Codorníu, Freixenet, Castellblanch, Juve i Camps, Rovellats.

---

promoting old-fashioned vintage *cavas* and "special reserves". Save money and stick to young non-vintage examples from Raimat, Codorníu, Freixenet and Segura Viudas.

Conca de Barberá

Some day, the name of this almond-growing region ought to be as well known as that of the Penedés. This is the cool area from which Torres gets the grapes to make Milmanda, its top-of-the-range Chardonnay, and in which Flying Wine-maker Hugh Ryman has made some successful commercial whites.

Costers del Segre

This one-estate *denominación* to the west of the Penedés owes its reputation to the success of the wines made at Raimat. The Raventos family of Codorníu, who own this ultra-modern *bodega*, today have over 5,000 acres (2,000 ha) of vineyards, where they make good reds (from Cabernet Sauvignon and Tempranillo), pure still and sparkling Chardonnay. Interestingly, it would be quite impossible to grow anything very much here without the benefit of – theoretically illegal – irrigation. Raimat was highly fortunate in being allowed the "experimental" status which permitted it to install its sophisticated irrigation system.

Tarragona and Terra Alta

Despite their dusty, hot summers, two of Tarragona's three regions specialize in white wine. Little of it is worth going out of your way to find, however, and much the same can be said for the Cariñena- and Garnacha-based reds. Look for the dry, grapey Moscatel Seco from De Muller and Viña Montalt Blanco Seco from Pedro Rovira.

Though technically within Tarragona, the hot dry region of Terra Alta has its own DO for the fairly hefty whites and dullish reds it produces. The *denominación* is more deserved by its organically produced, sweet, lightly fortified altar wines.

Priorato

Primitive wine from a primitive region, in which olive trees, men and vines struggle to survive on steep, rocky slopes. Lack of rainfall, an intensely hot climate and slatey soil mean tiny yields, mostly of Garnacha and Cariñena, which are used to make wines that are highly alcoholic – often up to 18 per cent.

Alella and Ampurdán-Costa Brava

Alella has become a doomed wine region; over the last 25 years over half of its vineyards have been stolen to extend Barcelona. True, the world can live without the sort of dull, wood-aged, semi-sweet wine made by the Alella co-operative, but the Marqués de Alella makes a range of dry whites, including promising Chardonnay, and good Cava from its sister company Parxet.

Ampurdán-Costa Brava is a parched inland region whose co-operatives make big, alcoholic rosé, big, dull whites and big, unsubtle, fortified wine.

Alta wine: Terra Alta makes dry reds and whites

THE OTHER WINES OF SPAIN

TRAVELLING through the rest of Spain's wine regions can be as frustrating as it is fascinating. Every region seems to have its own official denomination, irrespective of the quality of wines being produced – and despite the fact that a *vino de tierra* might well be a better buy. But the trip is worthwhile, if only to watch how the wine revolution is gradually taking hold of the country as a whole.

THE NORTH-WEST

Rias Baixas

Up in Galicia far too many of this cool, damp region's wines have traditionally been made from European hybrid grapes left over from the days following the ravages of the *phylloxera*. For a taste of what Galicia can produce, seek out the spicy Albariño made by Bodegas Cardallal and the "Martin Codax" from Bodegas de Vilariño-Cambados.

Dry wine country: Parched Mentrida vineyards

Ribeiro

This warm, dry region has high aspirations. The reds – made from the Brencellão, Caino and Souson – can be light and herby, but the trend is toward white wines. Those made from the Albariño, Godello, Treixadura and Torrentés are promising, but the Palominos are as dull as almost every other non-fortified example of this variety.

Valdeorras

The Palomino is just as prevalent in the mountainous vineyards here, along with the dark-fleshed Garnacha Tintorera. Sadly, while the growers of Ribeiro are experimenting with new varieties and more modern wine-making techniques, the producers up here are handicapped by low yields, low prices and land that's almost too difficult to tend.

El Bierzo

The Bodegas Palacio de Arganza, the best *bodega* here, is most widely respected for its skills at blending, ageing and bottling wines from various other regions. The red wines produced from the local Mencia grapes are pleasantly light and grassy but hardly distinguished enough to justify El Bierzo's promotion from *vino de tierra* to *Denominación de Origen*.

Toro

This is another "new" region (it received its DO in 1987) that hopes to benefit from the success of its eastern neighbour Ribera del Duero. The grape here, known as the Tinto de Toro, is that region's Tinto Fino – and indeed the Tempranillo of just about everywhere else. The lower altitude and rainfall, and the use of up to 25 per cent Garnacha, tend to give Toro's wines a softer, more beefily alcoholic style. Wines made by Bodegas Fariña, including the oaky Gran Colegiata, show this is a region to watch.

León

The unhappy acronym VILE – for Vinos de León – appears on every bottle from this region's modern co-operative. The reds, mostly made from the Prieto Picudo, are soft, woody and comparable to some mid-range Rioja.

Rueda

Once exclusively the source for unimpressive sherry-like fortified wine, Rueda has, partly thanks to the encouragement of the Bordeaux guru Emile Peynaud, pinned its colours to the mast of modern white wine-making. In this, the region's producers have a great advantage over their neighbours in the Penedés; their Verdejo grape (not to be confused with Portugal's Verdelho) has far more character than the latter region's Parellada and Xarel-lo. Even so, many producers still choose to add tangy Sauvignon Blanc to the blend. Marqués de Griñon is one of the best examples of young, pure Verdejo, while Marqués de Riscal has proved that this aromatic grape can take ageing in new oak.

Cigales

Like Toro, this name ought to be one to remember; a recent DO, it's close to Ribera del Duero, grows the same grape varieties (reds have to contain at least 75 per cent Tempranillo), and can produce high-quality pink rosados – which, for the moment at least, are still its strongest suit. Progress is being made, on reds and whites.

Ribera del Duero

Historically almost unknown to many Rioja drinkers, Ribera del Duero has long been famous among Spanish wine buffs as the region that produces Spain's most historically illustrious and expensive wine, Vega Sicilia The success of that *bodega* has somewhat confused outsiders because its wine is actually rather atypical of its region, due to the fact that 40 per cent of its blend is made up from such Bordeaux interlopers as the Cabernet Sauvignon, Merlot and Malbec.

The traditional grape variety here is the Tempranillo (locally known as the Tinto Fino) and that's what's used, for example, in Protos, the over-praised wine made by the Bodega Ribera Duero. Vega Sicilia's position as the region's top *bodega* has been challenged by the sudden stardom of Pesquera, a wine made by another *bodega* from local varieties, but with much less ageing in oak. The description of Pesquera by American wine guru Robert Parker as "the Château Pétrus of Spain" ensured that bottles of this wine would be grabbed from the shelves despite a sudden hike in price. Today, led by these two and a growing number of other increasingly impressive wines, the region is rapidly developing a reputation for its red wines that ought to worry the Riojanos.

THE NORTH-EAST

Campo de Borja

Alcohol levels of the dull Garnacha-based red and pink wines here have traditionally been too high. There are hopes that good wine-making – especially Beaujolais-style fermentation – will make for lighter, fresher styles. Whites show promise too.

Cariñena

This hot, dry region was where the Carignan grape apparently got its name. The red wine varieties used here are – inevitably – the Cariñena, the Tempranillo and, more particularly, the Garnacha, though the Cabernet is making (welcome) inroads. Few wines are better than basic hefty, table fare, though the softly fruity Don Mendo red and pink from Bodegas San Valero show what can be done. Nearby, the recent DO of Calatayud has no such flagships, but it makes plain, acceptable wines.

Somontano

Cool, green Somontano is Aragón's most exciting region, though its potential is only beginning to become apparent. Wine-making techniques are still pretty old-fashioned, and too much of the production remains in the hands of the co-operative. Even so, the local co-operative is producing decent reds from Tempranillo, Moristel and Macabeo while the go-ahead COVISA is proving what can be done with foreign grapes such as the Chenin Blanc, Gewürztraminer and Chardonnay. Look for the Viñas del Vero label.

THE CENTRE

Madrid

Despite their DO status, the wines produced to the south and east of the capital have more in common with the most backward village in the country than with the restless modernity of Madrid, but there are a few improving exceptions to a dull, rustic rule. Look out for Ricardo Benito's light young reds. Nearby Cebreros is primitive country that makes primitive wines.

Mentrida

I can't imagine many people getting too ecstatic about pink wine that, at a strength of 18–24 per cent, packs more of a punch

---

---

than some vermouth, but the wine-drinkers here seem keen enough on the style, which they enjoy with medieval-style dishes such as stuffed partridge and game stew. The region also makes a similarly strong red, often adding tannic bite to the alcohol by drawing off half the juice at the beginning of fermentation and thus doubling the proportion of skins to juice.

La Mancha

La Mancha's indigenous Airén grape is, incredibly, the world's most widely planted variety and the region itself is the largest appellation in Europe. But it's far from the most productive; the lack of water, the high summer and low winter temperatures make for tiny yields. In addition, the authorities

Far horizons: The huge La Mancha plateau can, with proper investment, make decent wine

have until recently decided that – even when available – irrigation is forbidden.

The area as a whole is woefully underexploited. Only one in 10 of the bottles made in La Mancha can carry the distinctive Don Quixote logo of the *Consejo Regulador de la Denominación de Origen*, for the simple reason that most of the wine is still made in apparently medieval *bodegas*, where the juice of over-ripe, intrinsically flavourless Airén grapes is fermented in *tinajas* (*amphorae*), with only the most rudimentary attempts at cooling.

These methods of wine-making can, when carefully employed, produce creditable reds, but are less well suited to the production of dry white wine. If you like young wine with the colour of ochre, the flavour of nuts that have been left to mature for a few years in a dusty loft and the alcoholic kick of a lethargic mule, traditional La Mancha whites are for you. But not for long.

Today, a fight is on between the region's wine-producers and the European bureaucrats who want to see a large proportion of the vines uprooted. While sympathizing with the growers who'll have a hard time finding a replacement crop, it has to be said that they've stubbornly gone on making bad white wine, much of which has been taken straight to the distillery, while they could have turned their attention to the red wine varieties for which the region is better suited – and for which there is more demand.

Valdepeñas

The "Valley of Stones" is white, Airén, country too, but its reputation was won by the red and pink wines made from the Cencibel grape. The Bodegas Félix Solís and

Los Llanos provide the best chance to try this variety's red wines in their *Reserva* and *Gran Reserva* form, but most Valdepeñas reds should be caught as young as possible, and bought with care, too, because the use of Airén white grapes in their production makes many of them taste flat and earthy.

It's a good idea to avoid the *clarete* pink wine too; it's often only Airén dyed with a little Cencibel.

THE SOUTH-WEST

Condado de Huelva

Interesting sherry-like versions of *fino* and *oloroso* are produced here, as well as some promising whites that display a triumph of modern wine-making over dull local grapes and hot summers. Ignore the Extramedura, close to the Portuguese border; its wines are boring bruisers.

THE SOUTH-EAST

Valencia

This is the region into which Swiss investors have pumped enormous amounts of money, and the one in which the Swiss and Spanish exporters have combined forces to discover the kinds of wine they should be selling to the USA. The Valencians are – unusually for Spain – more interested in producing wines

---

The Essentials
OTHER SPANISH DOs

Official quality Ribera del Duero, Toro, Rueda, Ribeiro and Rias Baixas are the notable DO areas.
Style Some of these areas are producing good-quality, even exciting, wines. Good Ribera del Duero reds are packed with rich plummy fruit and have a velvety texture which, when combined with generous oaking, has resulted in a wine – Pesquera – which has been compared to Pétrus by Robert Parker. Toro is capable of producing similarly generous wines, which are often oak-aged, while neighbouring Rueda makes good-quality whites from classic and local grape varieties. Ribeiro and Valdeorras are both located in Galicia, producing fresh, aromatic and slightly sparkling whites, resembling the *vinhos verdes* of Portugal, and attractively fresh and fruity reds. Few of these wines are exported but as boredom and dissatisfaction grow with Rioja, hopefully, they will attract greater attention.
Climate Ribera del Duero, Toro and Rueda have typical continental climates – hot summers and cold winters. Ribeiro and Rias Baixas in the far north-western tip of Spain, influenced by the Atlantic, have a warm wet climate.
Cultivation Ribera del Duero and Rueda

compare favourably to Penedés in terms of innovative use of foreign grape varieties.
Grape varieties *Ribera del Duero*: Albillo, Cabernet Sauvignon, Garnacha, Malbec, Merlot, Tinto del Pais; *Toro*: Albillo, Garnacha, Malvasia, Palomino, Tinto de Toro (Tempranillo), Verdejo; *Rueda*: Cabernet Sauvignon, Chardonnay, Palomino, Sauvignon, Verdejo, Viura; *Galicia*: Albariño, Albilla, Caiño, Garnacha, Godello, Mencia, Merenzão, Palomino, Sousão, Tempranillo, Treixadura, Valenciano.
Production/maturation These areas show what can be achieved in Spain by the adoption of modern vinification methods and the use of the latest knowledge, combined, in some cases, with the best of local wine-making tradition. The wines of Bodegas Alejandro Fernandez, sold as Tinto Pesquera, are the result of both old and new techniques; Vega Sicilia Unico is produced combining an age-old formula requiring 10 years' oak-ageing with the local Tinto Fino and French grape varieties.
Longevity *Reds*: Ribera del Duero: 3–25 years; Toro: 3–8 years; *Whites*: Rueda: 1–3 years; Galicia: within 2 years.
Vintage guide *Reds*: Ribera del Duero 85, 87, 90, 91, 94.

that sell than in making styles with a specifically identifiable regional character. Unfortunately, with the exception of the Moscatel which can be every wine-drinker's ideal Sunday afternoon drink, Valencia is handicapped by a surplus of dull local grapes. A little Navarra-style diversification in the vineyards would not go amiss.

Utiel-Requena

The wines of this neighbouring region have often been sold under the better-known name of Valencia, despite its right to bear its own DO. But a combination of a high altitude that is ideal for crisp wine-making, the Bobal, one of Spain's few underrated grapes, and reasonably plentiful Tempranillo are helping Utiel-Requena to develop a growing reputation for its reds and rosados. The whites are – so far – less worthwhile.

Signs of improvement: *Valencia will never make great wine, but it's getting better*

Almansa

This is the place to go for a real taste of the Garnacha Tintorera; this variety is widely planted here and used, along with the Monastrell and Cencibel, to make beefy, unsubtle red wines. Bodegas Piqueras proves itself to be the exception to the local rule by making lighter-bodied, oak-aged reds.

Jumilla

It says much about Jumilla's isolation from the rest of wine-making Europe that it was by-passed by the *phylloxera* louse when it munched its way through the rest of the continent. But now it's arrived at this dry, old-fashioned region, whole vineyards have been wiped out. New vines are being grafted onto the same kinds of resistant

rootstock that are used elsewhere, and the opportunity has been taken to introduce experimental plantings of foreign grape varieties to supplement the traditional Monastrell which has conspired with "traditional" wine-making methods to make tough, often unlovable, stuff.

Yecla

Another recent DO, Yecla is, nevertheless, still at risk of extinction. The altitude is high (at 2,000 ft/650 m above sea level) and the soil stony, so yields are uneconomical. The hope for the area lies in the modern Bodegas Ochoa, which makes and exports large quantities of soft reds, and the huge Co-operative La Purisima, which, despite a tendency to over-age its wines, can produce fairly rich red wine.

Alicante

This is not only the name of a region, but also that of a grape that was traditionally prized by wine-makers in Burgundy and Bordeaux. The variety, which is also known as the Garnacha Tintorera, is still grown here, though it is the Monastrell that is more frequently used to make the region's big, dark, alcoholic reds. The most interesting drink made from grapes in Alicante, though, is Fundillon, a cask-aged liqueur.

THE ISLANDS

Majorca

What most tourists miss is a range of ripe reds and fresh, young *vino joven* wines, produced in the hot, windmill-bestrewn land around Binissalem on a plateau nearly 500 ft (150 m) above sea level. Most are made from the good-quality, local Manto Negro and Callet grapes and the dull Fogoneu, though both the Jaume Mesquida and José Ferrer wineries have been quite successful with Cabernet Sauvignon, while the Swedish-owned Santa Catalina winery has made some reasonable Chardonnay. Other wine grapes are Moll, Xarel-lo and Parellada.

Canary Isles

Some of the most interesting-looking vineyards are to be found here – because of the black volcanic soil in which Lanzarote's vines are planted – but they produce some of the least interesting-tasting wines. The

Tortilla con Chorizo

Potato "omelette" with spicy sausage

This wonderfully versatile dish is found all over Spain. It can have innumerable additions, such as shrimp or ham (here we have used the traditional spicy sausage of Spain – chorizo). It can be eaten cold as a starter or hot as a main course and it has the advantage of going well with lighter reds, whites or rosados.

SERVES 4–6

8 tbsp olive oil
1 medium onion, peeled and finely chopped
2 garlic cloves, peeled and minced
3 oz/75 g spicy sausage (Spanish chorizo is traditional but not essential)
2 lb/1 kg large potatoes, peeled, thinly sliced, washed and dried on kitchen paper
5 eggs
Salt and freshly ground black pepper

In a frying pan, heat 5 tbsp of olive oil and sauté the garlic, onion and sausage for 5 minutes. Add the potato and cook until browned. Remove the contents of the pan to a colander and drain off excess oil. In a large bowl, beat the eggs well and add the potato mixture. Stir well and season with salt and pepper. Heat the remaining oil in the frying pan until it is very hot (but not smoking). Pour in the mixture, shaking the pan to prevent sticking, and cook until the bottom is browned. Slide the tortilla on to a large plate, invert another plate on top of the tortilla and turn them over. The uncooked side is now on the bottom and the tortilla can be slid back into the pan and cooked until the bottom browns. Serve with a large green salad.

problem in the Tacoronte-Acentejo region to the north-east of Tenerife is partly the grapes – Listan Blanco and Negro and Negramoll – and partly the way they are vinified. This is holiday wine, to be drunk very cold – if at all. Lanzarote's Malvasias can be appealingly nutty, dry and rich.

SHERRY

$\mathcal{L}$ET'S PLAY a word-association game. I'll say "sherry", and you reply with the first word that comes into your head. If you're British, it's almost even odds that you would say "vicar", "maiden aunt", "Bristol Cream" or "trifle". If, on the other hand, you were brought up on the other side of the Atlantic, I'll bet that your mind shoots straight to Bowery bums drinking locally produced headache-juice hidden in a brown paper bag. And if you were French, you'd more than likely be thinking of an ingredient to use in the kitchen.

The word that probably wouldn't have occurred to you, unless you happen to be Spanish, is "wine". It's precisely the one most Spaniards – but no-one else – would come up with; they not only think of sherry as wine, they drink it that way – bone-dry, with food, and out of glasses that hold a proper mouthful of liquid.

So put all those Anglo-American pre-judices out of your mind and try to look at sherry through Spanish eyes. Which means accepting right away that, just as one small corner of north-eastern France is the only place in the world that makes genuine Champagne, the only source of real sherry is a similarly small area around Cadiz, near the southernmost point of Spain. And, like Champagne, the best sherries (particularly *fino*, the region's main style) have traditionally been dry.

Nor does either region make table wine of any great quality; while Champagne's grape varieties produce thin, acidic stuff in their cold-climate region, sherry's dull Palomino makes even duller wine in the near-drought conditions of vineyards where there are only 10 weeks of the year when the sun doesn't shine. Both wines owe their natural lightness of touch to the fact that they are made from grapes that have been grown on some of the chalkiest soils in the world – in sherry's case, on the brilliantly white *albariza* that covers much of the vineyards. Both are made in a peculiar way that depends on prolonged contact with yeast, and both are essentially non-vintage wines that call for great expertise in blending different vintages – usually by merchants with huge stocks of wine. And if you agree that not only is Champagne a

wine, but a great and historic one, then you're half-way to being convinced that so, too, is sherry.

THE HISTORY

Sherry is one of the oldest wines of all. The town of Cadiz had been founded by the Phoenicians before 1200 BC, and a thousand years later a wine called Ceretanum which almost certainly came from Ceret – Jerez – was being exported to Rome to be praised by the Roman poet Martial.

In the fourteenth century, the naturally high alcohol levels of wine from this hot region made it travel well, and sherry had become a firm favourite in Britain. Chaucer wrote of the wine of Lepe (a village near

Seeking the shade: *Part of the Gonzalez Byass bodega in hot Jerez*

Jerez) *"of which there riseth such fumositee"* that three draughts were enough to confuse a drinker as to whether he was in La Rochelle, Bordeaux or home in bed.

In 1587, a short-term supply was assured when Sir Francis Drake took Cadiz and captured 2,900 butts of what was by then known as "sherris" or "sack" after the Spanish word for export, "*saca*". Ten years later, it was given its first testimonial under its new name when Shakespeare's Sir John Falstaff declared, in *Henry IV, Part 2*: *"If I had a thousand sons, the first humane principle I would teach them would be to foreswear thin potations and addict themselves to sack."* In Shakespeare's day, this naturally dry wine was already being sweetened for the English palate; at the Boar's Head Tavern in Eastcheap, where Falstaff supposedly lived, sugar was sometimes added, as were pieces of toast and even egg (vividly described by Sir John as "*pullet-sperm*").

During the eighteenth century, the English and Irish moved into Jerez in much the same way as they moved into Bordeaux; soon, the *bodegas* of Thomas Osborne, William Garvey, Sir James Duff and James Gordon were shipping wine to England where, in the port of Bristol, firms like Harvey's and Avery's had established their own blending and ageing cellars.

STYLES

It was in these cellars in both countries that the styles of sherry we know today gradually evolved. Some barrels developed an unpleasant-looking white scum on their surface – it was later discovered to be a kind of yeast which, unlike the other kinds of bacteria that attack wine, actually kept it fresh and fragrant.

In honour of this quality, the Jerezanos dubbed the scum *flor*, or "flower". The wine it made was thought the finest in the cellars, and so, quite naturally, was called *fino*, though the slightly lighter version made and aged a little further up the coast, at Sanlúcar, became known for some reason as "the little apple", *manzanilla*, a word still used elsewhere in Spain for camomile tea. These wines were said to be saltier because of the sea air; this character and the lightness may, however, be attributable to the

fact that the yeast grows more thickly here.

Usually, the inhabitants of Jerez drank the wine soon after it was made; when they left it in its barrel for a few years, the wine darkened and took on a nutty flavour. By topping up last year's *fino* barrels with this year's *flor*-affected wine, however, they found that the freshness could be maintained. Soon, they developed the *solera* system, keeping back a number of casks every year from which to refresh the wine of the preceding vintage, and from there to the vintage before that, and so on.

Today, the oldest barrels are never emptied – indeed, no more than a third is ever removed from them – and the transfer is always made from one year's casks to that of the year before. Somehow – and no one is quite certain precisely why – provided the quality of the initial wines is carefully chosen and the chain of ever-older barrels – the *solera* – is well maintained, this relay-race gives the oldest casks the vinous equivalent of immortality, allowing *bodegas* to sell a consistent style every year.

The blending of *flor*-affected wines of different ages remains the basis of *fino* sherry production today, but a great many of the barrels did – and do – not develop *flor*; these are fortified by the addition of brandy. These stronger, darker, wines were called *oloroso*, or "fragrant", but they were never as well-considered by the Jerezanos as their *fino* and *manzanilla*. A third style, a cross between *fino* and *oloroso*, was invented too. *Amontillado*, literally "in the fashion of Montilla"*(see below)*, was made by leaving *fino* unrefreshed by younger wine to develop a deeper colour and a rich, nutty flavour.

Neither *fino* nor *manzanilla*, with a natural strength of around 15 per cent alcohol, were sturdy enough to ship overseas; without the protection of their *flor*, they oxidized very quickly. So, the Jerezanos developed a tradition of fortifying them and of sweetening them up with cooked grape juice. This not only created a number of new styles, but had the useful side-effect of masking any defects in taste or style.

Today, too many non-Spaniards still expect sherry to be sweet, and many firms in Jerez and England still obligingly sweeten all of their styles for the British palate. It can be infuriating, when one expects the bone-dry, nutty tang of a good *fino*, to find a sweetened or an over-alcoholic version. Thankfully, today, while sweet and over-fortified dry sherry can still be found, real,

Montilla: Wines that are similar to sherry, but with less pungency

(see below)

Tapas

The term "*tapa*" originally referred to the piece of bread placed over a glass of wine in order to keep flies out, but *tapas* are now the appetizers of Spain – little mouthfuls of delightful tastes.

They are designed to be eaten with a glass of chilled *manzanilla* or *fino* sherry or a glass of wine (they make the perfect cocktail party snacks). These are some of the classics.

CHAMPINONES RELLENOS
Mushroom caps filled with slices of spicy chorizo sausage, which are then grilled.

ALBONDIGAS
Garlicky little balls of minced beef, fried and served with a home-made tomato sauce.

POLLO AL AJILLO
Small chunks of chicken sautéed in olive oil and garlic and coated in chopped parsley.

JAMON SERRANO
Cured raw ham, grilled in pieces and served with a garlic mayonnaise.

BOQUERONES
Fresh anchovies (or whitebait) dipped in batter and deep-fried.

CHORIZO
Spicy Spanish pork sausage cut into slices and grilled.

GAMBAS AL AJILLO
Unshelled prawns sautéed in olive oil and garlic.

lower-strength examples are increasingly available throughout the world.

But don't dismiss all sweet sherries out of hand. Gonzalez Byass's Matusalem and Noë and Osborne's Pedro Ximénez, for example, are packed to the brim with the sweetness of the best fruit cake and molasses; these are among the world's most delicious, indulgent yet demanding drinks. Or, to be more accurate, "wines".

The grape and the olive: *A typical landscape in southern Spain. This is Montilla.*

The Essentials
SOUTHERN SPAIN

What to look for Fresh zingy pale *fino* and *manzanilla*; rich, nutty, raisiny *oloroso* and *amontillado* and Christmas puddingy Pedro Ximénez.

Location Spain's south-west corner, from Condado de Huelva near the Portuguese border south-west to Málaga and inland to Montilla-Moriles.

Official quality DOs are Jerez, Manzanilla, Condado de Huelva, Málaga, Montilla-Moriles.

Style Sherry is one of the world's greatest and, in England at least, most misunderstood fortified wines. Its style varies enormously (*see box*); in general, dry *manzanilla* sherries are thought to be lighter and more delicate than their Jerezano counterparts. Montilla-Moriles, to the north-east of Jerez, produces a similar range of wines, but they are generally softer and lower in alcohol – they may or may not be fortified. Málaga makes wonderful sweet wines with a strong raisiny flavour which are still underrated.

Climate The Mediterranean climate makes southern Spain the hottest wine region in the country, although the climate is moderated by the Atlantic toward Portugal. The Atlantic *poñete* wind is wet and encourages the *flor* yeast that produces *fino* sherry to grow on the surface of the wines. The easterly *levante* wind is hotter and drier and partially dries the grapes on the vines while they ripen, concentrating their sugars.

Cultivation The land of southern Spain is generally flat, but ranges in altitude from the low-lying coastal plains near Sanlúcar de Barrameda to the plateau of Málaga at some 1,650 feet. The unique *albariza* soil of Andalusia is a lime-rich marl that is able to soak up and retain moisture, while its brilliant white colour reflects the sun on to the lower parts of the vines, helping the grapes to ripen.

Grape varieties Principally the white Palomino (Listan), plus Moscatel Fino, Pedro Ximénez, Baladi, Garrido Fino, Lairén, Mantuo, Torrontés, Zalerna.

Production/maturation Sherry-making involves the art of mastering wine and naturally occurring yeast. The *solera* system, coupled with skilful blending, ensures that a consistent style of sherry is produced over a number of years, though *Almacenista* wines, from a single, unblended *solera*, are worth seeking out for their characterful individuality, particularly if shipped by Lustau. Sweetening and colouring agents – usually thick, concentrated wines from grapes such as Pedro Ximénez or Moscatel – may also be added.

Longevity *Fino* sherries should ideally be drunk soon after they are bottled. An opened bottle should be consumed within a very few days. Sweeter, more alcoholic, traditionally made styles can be kept indefinitely but will not normally improve in the bottle.

My Top 13 *Sherry:* Lustau, Diez-Merito, Osborne, Harvey's, Hidalgo, Garvey, Gonzalez Byass, Valdespino, Diez Merito, Domecq, Caballero, Barbadillo; *Montilla-Moriles*: Gracia Hermanos.

THE BUSINESS OF SHERRY

Most sherry is produced by big sherry houses, some of which have *soleras* that were begun in the last century. The size of the companies is partly dictated by rules that require any *bodega* to store a minimum of 100,000 litres of wine. There are, however, around 50 smaller *Almacenistas*, small maturers that buy wine from co-operatives or small producers and age it, selling most for blending by the bigger *bodegas*, but bottling a little themselves. These *Almacenista* wines, because of their small-scale production, can be some of the most exciting sherries on the market.

Montilla-Moriles

Montilla-Moriles – or plain Montilla, as it is more generally known – is the region and the style that gave its name to *amontillado*. The wines produced here are often quite reasonably considered to be "poor man's sherry", because they tend to be low-priced and of fairly basic quality. They can be not only good, but indeed better and more delicate than poorly made sherry. Montilla's producers use grapes grown in chalky soil to make a range of styles that are just like those of Jerez – from *flor*-affected *fino* to rich dry *oloroso*.

There are, though, two differences. First, the Pedro Ximénez grape, used almost exclusively here, ripens so well that

Montilla can often achieve the same strengths as sherry without fortification. And second, there's the continuing tradition of fermenting Montilla in large terracotta *tinajas*, which are nothing more nor less than the same kind of *amphorae* the Greeks and Romans would have used to ferment their wine, over 2,000 years ago. But despite this evidence of tradition, the Jerezanos until quite recently managed to prevent the Montilla producers from using the term "*amontillado*", which was a little like the *parfumiers* of France barring their counterparts in Cologne from selling eau de Cologne.

What Montilla needs most urgently is to be taken seriously. Sales of the most illustrious wines of Jerez and Sanlúcar are far from brisk, and the need for cheap alternatives reduces every year. Watch out for wines labelled Moriles. Produced in the village of that name and rarely seen elsewhere, they can be more delicate than those from the town of Montilla – and lighter and more evidently wine-like than many sherries.

Málaga

Málaga was being shipped from the port of the same name as early as 1500 and was first sold in Britain as "sack", then as "Mountain". In the eighteenth century, when sherry fell out of favour and the British turned to port, the harbour town of Málaga lowered its export duties and effectively stole the London "sack" market from Jerez. But everything went wrong late in the following century, when the *phylloxera* louse made Málaga its first Spanish port of call. The vineyards were never properly replanted; today, they cover just 3,000 hectares, compared with 112,000 before the arrival of the louse.

The wine has gone out of fashion too, and standards of wine-making have often dropped to accommodate a small, undemanding market. Unlike their counterparts in Jerez, the Málaga *bodegas* have mostly turned their backs on tradition, and make little effort to attract the attention of

tourists. But when Málaga is good – as it was from the now sadly defunct Scholtz Hermanos – it can be wonderful, molasses-rich wine. The *solera* system is used here, on wine that is often a mixture of dry wine and grape juice, part of which has been boiled until it has turned into sweet treacle (*arrope*), and part (the *vino maestro*) fortified in a very similar way to sherry.

Málaga can vary enormously both in colour, which ranges from white (*blanco*) to black (*negro*), rough golden (*dorado*), tawny (*rojo-dorado*) and dark (*oscuro*), and sweetness (from *seco* to *dulce*). Bottles labelled *dulce color* are pretty simple in their syrupy style; ones that describe themselves as *lágrima* ought to be of far higher quality, and are made without recourse to a press, from free-run juice. The difference in flavour between a good example of *lágrima* and a basic Málaga is as great as that between a top-class Bordeaux and a house claret. The finest Málagas have an intensity of flavour and a balancing acidity which combine to prevent the sweetness being in any way cloying.

"Solera" wines are common too; examples like the excellent Scholtz Hermanos Solera 1855 proudly proclaimed the year in which their particular *solera* was founded. Unfortunately, none of the other Solera Málagas are of anything like as high a quality as the Scholtz Hermanos.

Pedro Ximénez grapes: Leaving them out in the sun shrivels them and concentrates their sweetness

---

SHERRY STYLES

Fino
A *fino* should be light, dry and delicate. It develops beneath the light-coloured film of the *flor* which gives the *fino* its yeast character and absorbs any residual sugar. *Fino* is generally made from 100 per cent Palomino grapes and ranges in alcoholic strength from 15.5 per cent to 18 per cent. It is at its fragrant best when first bottled. *Fino* does not keep.

Manzanilla
The two main styles of wines from the port of Sanlúcar de Barrameda are *fino* and *pasada* (*fino-amontillado*), although there are intermediate styles.

The *fino* is pale and light in body with a bitter, salty flavour. These wines tend to be between 15.5 per cent and 17 per cent in alcohol, depending on the level of fortification. *Manzanilla fino* is also distinguished from traditional Jerez *fino* by the more vigorous nature of the *flor* and the greater amount used per cask.

Manzanilla sherries are said to have a salty tang, purportedly from the sea air of the town.

Amontillado
An *amontillado* is a *fino* which, as a result of ageing for over 8 years "without refreshment" (the *flor* having died after 2 to 3 years, and fallen to the bottom of the cask), has developed an amber colour and a dry, nutty flavour. *Amontillado* is fuller-bodied at a strength of 16 to 18 per cent. There is an intermediate *fino-amontillado* stage characterized by amber colour but not the nutty character or body.

Oloroso
Oloroso is the darkest, richest and most full-bodied of the natural sherry styles. Literally meaning "fragrant", it is completely dry but with an appealing soft richness from the higher fortification and glycerine content. These are wines that grow very little or no *flor* and, as a result, are fortified with a higher spirit strength

(up to 18 per cent). The wines are allowed to oxidize and to take on the characteristic nutty, raisin and caramel flavours.

Cream sherries
Originally developed for the UK market but now popular elsewhere, cream sherries are made in two ways. Pale cream is poor-quality *fino* sweetened artificially. Dark cream is a far superior sherry made from *oloroso* sweetened with Pedro Ximénez.

Pedro Ximénez
Pedro Ximénez is the traditional sweetening agent for sherry, but occasionally a pure Pedro Ximénez is released with delicious flavours of dried fruit and Muscovado brown sugar.

Palo Cortado
This is a naturally occurring rare, nutty, dry sherry; only one butt in a thousand is said to turn into a true *palo cortado*.

PORTUGAL

"*YOU SEE*, Señor, we are a calm, conservative people. Even when we have a revolution we avoid making too much fuss and noise." The Portuguese wine-maker raised the subject of the almost violence-free political upheaval of 1974 to illustrate the fundamental quality of his countrymen's character: they are people who aren't terribly fond of change. Wine-makers in other countries may have been importing tons of cooling equipment and thousands of new oak barrels for decades; the Portuguese have, until recently, preferred to go on drinking the kind of wine they've always drunk. And doing so in some quantity; this is the seventh largest wine-producing country in the world and its small population has always done a pretty good job of making sure that none of its produce goes to waste.

The Portuguese divide their wine into two very different styles: the stuff they sell to foreigners, and the stuff they drink themselves. The off-dry, slightly sparkling

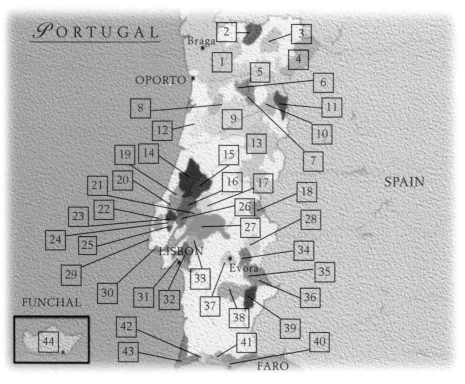

P O R T U G A L

Braga
OPORTO
LISBON
Evora
FUNCHAL
FARO
SPAIN

1 Vinhos Verdes	10 Pinhel	22 Torres	34 Redondo
2 Chaves	11 Castelo Rodrigo	23 Alenquer	35 Reguengos
3 Valpaços	12 Bairrada	24 Arruda	36 Granja-
4 Planalto-	13 Cova da Beira	25 Bucelas	Amareleja
Mirandes	14 Encostas d'Aire	26 Cartaxo	37 Evora
5 Port and the	15 Tomar	27 Coruche	38 Vidigueira
Douro	16 Santarém	28 Borba	39 Moura
6 Varosa	17 Chamusca	29 Colares	40 Tavira
7 Encostas da	18 Portalegre	30 Carcavelos	41 Lagoa
Nave	19 Alcobaça	31 Arrabida	42 Portimão
8 Lafoes	20 Obidos	32 Setúbal	43 Lagos
9 Dão	21 Almeirim	33 Palmela	44 Madeira

rosé and white wines that most people associate with Portugal are treated very sniffily by the Portuguese themselves. The wine they enjoy most is still either the mouth-scouringly dry, red Vinho Verde (traditionally made in far greater quantities than the white, but unsaleable anywhere outside Portugal and its former colonies), or tough, inky dark, venerable reds from Dão, Bairrada or the Douro.

To understand the Portuguese taste for these wines you have to have experienced Portuguese cooking. Until you have ploughed your way through a deep bowl or three of *caldo verde* vegetable soup, a platter piled high with *bacalhão* (the national dish of salt-cod), half a suckling pig and a pudding that can best be described as half-cooked cream caramel, you can never imagine the essential role those tannic, high-acid reds manfully perform.

Of course, few people outside Portugal live on a diet of salt-cod and suckling pig, which explains why, in the middle of this century, a few Portuguese producers cleverly created the export styles of light, sweetish pink and white wine with which most foreigners have become familiar..

Today, as wine-drinkers around the world increasingly turn away from off-dry pink and white wine, and as the increasingly health-conscious Portuguese themselves cut back on the suckling pig, Portugal's wine-makers are beginning to take a fresh look at the kind of stuff they are making. They know that they have one tremendous advantage over their Spanish neighbours; theirs is a far more interesting arsenal of grape varieties.

To exploit these varieties, however, the Portuguese have had to launch another "calm revolution" – in the vineyards and wineries. First, they have had to sort out the system of regional appellations, the *regiãos demarcadas*. Portugal more or less invented the idea of *Appellation Contrôlée* years before the French got around to it. Until the beginning of the 1990s, however, the whole country had just 11 such regions, of which four – Bucelas, Carcavelos, Colares and Moscatel de Setúbal – produced tiny amounts of wine, while another – the Algarve – made appalling wine and owed its legal recognition solely to its importance as a tourist region. Not surprisingly, many of Portugal's best wines have carried no regional denomination at all, and the label of Barca Velha, Portugal's top red, doesn't trouble to mention that it comes from the demarcated region of the Douro. For most Portuguese, the word "*garrafeira*", indicating a mature, special-reserve wine, curried more favour than any mention of a particular area.

The Language of Portugal

Adamado Sweet.
Adega Cellar, winery.
Branco White.
Carvalho Oak.
Clarete Light red wine.
Colheita Vintage.
DOC (Denominação de Origem Controlada) Portugal's new appellation system which replaced the old RD.
Dolce Sweet.
Engarrafado na Origem Estate-bottled.
Espumante Sparkling.
Garrafeira A wine made from one or more areas and matured for 3 years including one in bottle if red, and for one year including 6 months in bottle if white. Wines must bear a vintage date and have 0.5 per cent alcohol above the minimum. Often, the *garrafeira* is the "private reserve" of the merchant.
IPR (Indicação de Proviência Regulamentada) The second layer of Portugal's new DOC appellation system.
Licoroso Sweet fortified wine.
Maduro Matured (in vat).
Quinta Farm.
RD (Região Demarcada) Now-defunct appellation system, replaced by DOC (qv).
Reserva A wine from one or several areas from an outstanding vintage. It must contain 0.5 per cent alcohol above the minimum.
Rosado Rosé.
Seco Dry.
Tinto Red.
Velho Old. Reds must be over 3 years old, whites over 2 years old before they may use the term on the label.
Verde Young, "green" (as in Vinho Verde).
Vinho consumo Ordinary wine.
Vinho generoso Fortified aperitif or dessert wine.
Vinho de mesa Table wine.
Vinhos Regionãos Roughly equivalent to the French *vins de pays*.

The second problem is the way in which the industry has been held in a virtual stranglehold by a small number of giant co-operatives that bought in most of the grapes and made most of the wine, selling it to an even smaller number of merchants, whose creative input has often been restricted to the way in which they have aged and

Piled high: *Cork bark stacked to dry*

bottled it. Inevitably, this has encouraged the Iberian tradition of keeping wine for a long time before bottling. Quite often this is far more appropriate here than in Spain, because a lengthy period in tank will generally allow a tough red to shed some of its impenetrable tannic husk. In some cases the final result is a wine with fascinating, mature, tobaccoey flavours. Far too often, though, it makes for dull wines that lose their fruit along with the tannin. Portugal is a great place to buy inexpensive old wine; some of it tastes attractively old, but some tastes of almost nothing at all.

In recent years a growing number of small producers and innovative merchants have begun to wrest back control from the co-operatives and to take a more careful look at their grapes and the best ways to extract as much fruit as possible from them, however long the wine is going to be aged.

For the first time, too, the Portuguese are looking overseas for inspiration. For the moment at least, they are not falling into the trap of copying everybody else with lookalike Chardonnays and Cabernets, but they *are* discovering the methods of modern wine-making from people such as Peter Bright and David Baverstock, who learned to make wine in their native Australia and are now independently producing some of the most exciting wines in Portugal.

The tough, old-fashioned reds and the semi-sweet pinks and whites are finally making way for fruity young wines that can compete with Beaujolais, for clean, dry whites that have nothing to do with Vinho Verde, and for deep, richly flavoured red wines that stand comparison with the best from Italy. Of course, as you'd expect in a "calm, conservative" country, the wine revolution is a leisurely, undramatic affair. Given time and encouragement, though, Portugal is steadily becoming one of the most exciting wine countries of all, with one of the broadest ranges of different flavours. Companies such as Sogrape, JM da Fonseca, JP Vinhos (the winery at which Peter Bright makes his wines) and the huge Herdade do Esperão estate (where David Baverstock produces some of his) are already proving what can be done – and at prices that are low enough to encourage even the most timid wine-drinker to risk buying a bottle.

THE NORTH

VINHO VERDE

AMONG the first of Portugal's less commercial wines to be shipped overseas in any quantity was the "real" Vinho Verde on which Guedes had based Mateus. Surprisingly to foreigners, who rarely encounter it, most Vinho Verde is red (the "verde" part of its name refers to "green" youth, not colour), though the proportion of white has increased dramatically in recent years. Made in the (relatively) cool Minho region in the north of the country, from grapes grown on high trellises and among the trees so as to allow the farmers to plant cabbages and other vegetables at

High wire act: *Picking red grapes for Vinho Verde, made in the "cool" Minho region*

ground level, these wines give an insight into the way wine might have tasted a thousand or so years ago.

All sorts of local grapes were – and still are – used and, if asked, few of the growers (most of whom farm garden-sized plots) could name any of them. The traditional wine-making techniques were pretty basic too, but their peculiarity was the fact that the wine was bottled during, rather than after, the malolactic fermentation, which transforms the natural appley malic into creamier lactic acid.

The flavour, the fizz and the unpredictability from one bottle to the next were often as reminiscent of home-made cider as of wine. Unfortunately, the flavour of unripe apples and plum skins (of the red) and of unripe apple and lime (of the white) took more getting used to than most non-Portuguese drinkers were prepared to allow. Hence the switch to more modern wine-making techniques, the use of CO_2 canisters to provide the bubbles, and the generous dollops of sugar that go into the whites that are to be sent overseas (little of the red is exported).

Vinho Verde seemed destined to become another commercial drink. Fortunately, under the leadership of estates such as the Palacio da Brejoeira and the Solar das Bouças, and of Peter Bright, the Australian wine-maker at JP Vinhos, a small band of producers have begun to take Vinho Verde seriously, growing the vines more conventionally and concentrating on the best varieties – the Alvarinho and Loureiro.

Whichever colour you buy, though, try to ensure that it is of the most recent harvest, which is not always an easy task, given the producers' tendency to print the vintage in tiny figures on the back label or, more frequently, nowhere at all.

DOURO

Portugal's top red wine is made here, but you'd never know it from the bottle. The only hint that Barca Velha comes from the same part of Portugal as Taylor's and Dow's port lies in the presence on the label of the producer's name Ferreira and its address in the port-shipping centre of Vila Nova da Gaia; otherwise it might come from anywhere in Portugal. The precedent of a port producer making a first-class red has, however, been followed by a number of other companies, all of whom have, to one extent or another, produced wines that are packed with berry flavours and, when young, taste like a cross between ruby port without the sweetness, and freshly made Bordeaux. First off the stocks was the Quinta da Cotto whose table wine is rather better than its somewhat rustic port. Next, and with far more balanced quality, was the Quinta de la Rosa which, like the even more successful Quinta do Crasto, is made by David Baverstock, one of those two Australians. These are wines to watch: Europe's answer to some of Australia's bigger reds.

TRAS OS MONTES

Baking summers and freezing winters in this, one of Portugal's northernmost regions, situated just "behind the mountains" and the Spanish frontier, make for impoverished agriculture. Vines survive here and their fruit is used to produce Valpaços, Planalto-Mirandês and Chaves, none of which are much seen outside the region. Neither the wines nor the region are worth a hedonistic detour.

BAIRRADA

When Bairrada finally joins the ranks of the world's internationally recognized wine regions, three producers will share the credit for dragging the region into the late twentieth century. The wine-makers at Caves Alianca and Caves São João have been unusually quality-conscious and Luis Pato has seen the wines made at his estate thrown out of local tastings – because the overly conservative judges, many of whose own Bairradas tasted of nothing at all, could not come to terms with the blend of new oak and plummy-herby fruit they found in them. Hopefully, Bairrada's characterful

How green was my valley: The Douro Valley produces both port and table wines

Baga grape will soon be given rather more opportunities to show off these flavours. In the meantime, stick to the reds from these three producers, and explore their lemony whites and often impressive *méthode champenoise* fizz.

DAO

Until Portugal joined the EC, local protectionist rules more or less restricted the production of Dão to the region's co-operatives. Almost incredibly, given Dão's reputation as one of Portugal's best appellations, there was only one individual estate, the Conde de Santar; its wines rarely did the region much credit. The rest of the wine was made by the co-operatives who then sold it to the merchants; they, in their turn, matured, bottled and sold it. Blind tastings of Dão were so monotonous.

Sogrape, the company behind Mateus, tried to improve the quality of the wine it was buying by supervising the wine-making at the Tazem co-operative, where its Grão Vasco is made, and managed to transform

the region's flabby nutty whites into fresher, more lemony versions. Finally, in the late 1980s, Portugal's entry into the Common Market, and the banning of that restrictive monopoly, has allowed Sogrape and others to concentrate on buying the best grape varieties – including two that are used to make port, the Touriga Nacional and the Tinta Roriz which is thought to be Spain's Tempranillo – and to make their own wine. At last, Dão has the chance to show what it can do.

THE CENTRE AND SOUTH

RIBATEJO

THE TEMPERATE climate region of the banks of the Tagus – the Ribatejo – is gradually earning the recognition it deserves for making fruity, easier-going wines than most other parts of the country. For the moment, there are just three names to look out for: the huge co-operative at Almeirim, Caves Velhas (producers of the reliable Romeira red and some good *garrafeiras*) and the Heredeiros de Dom Luis de Margaride estate, where the local João de Santarem and Fernão Pires grapes

Beach babies: Vines at Colares, growing in desert sand

are successfully used alongside such imports as the Cabernet Franc and Merlot.

Arruda and Torres, which like so many other Portuguese regions were given their original demarcation because the largest co-operative asked for it, both make pleasant, light, "modern" wines of a style that goes down better abroad than locally.

COLARES

Colares's immunity to the *phylloxera* is explained by the desert sand in which the vines are grown, but these conditions can make it pretty difficult for people too; the sand is up to 16 ft (5 m) deep and every time an old vine has to be replaced a hole has to be dug down to the clay beneath. The reds they make are tough and tannic and need at least a decade to soften enough for their intense, plummy fruit to become (vaguely) apparent.

BUCELAS

Twenty miles (32 km) from Lisbon, this tiny region produces just half a million bottles of exclusively white wine, from around 420 acres (170 ha) of vines. Confusingly, the young wine made here by Caves Velhas, the

region's biggest producer, is labelled as Bucellas Velho, combining an archaic spelling of the region's name with a misleading implication that the wine is old. At its best, Bucelas can marry a fatty, almost Chardonnay-like, texture to some fairly biting, lemony acidity. Even so, it takes some imagination to understand how, a century ago, British gentlemen drank it as an alternative to hock. Neighbouring Carcavelos is of only passing interest – as the source of generally unimpressive fortified wine which may soon cease to exist if eager local urban developers get their way.

SETUBAL/TERRAS DO SADO

Made from vines grown almost in Lisbon's backyard, the Moscatel here is one of Portugal's – and the world's – most famous fortified wines, competing directly against Muscat de Beaumes de Venise, but with far greater age on its side. Almost all of the production is in the hands of a single firm: José Maria da Fonseca, whose go-ahead winery also produces a range of table wines from this region, most notably the Periquita, and Camarate reds (and the TE and CO *garrafeira* reserve versions), as well as Pasmados and Quinta de Camarate, both of which are worth looking out for in red and white versions. Also nearby is JP Vinhos, the winery at which Peter Bright makes the excellent Bordeaux-like Quinta da Bacalhôa, the João Pires unfortified white Muscat, the good Ma Partilha Merlot and some impressive attempts at Chardonnay.

ALENTEJO

JM da Fonseca's ultra-traditional JS Rosado Fernandes estate is typical of the kind of *adega* with which this warm southern region is associated. The grapes are still trodden by foot and fermented in terracotta *amphorae* precisely like the ones the Romans would have used. The only concession to modernity is the careful way in which the *amphorae* are hosed down to cool the temperature of the fermentation, and a concentration on red rather than the white that was more usually produced here. When they are under the control of the

Californian-trained wine-maker at JM da Fonseca the old ways clearly work; the high-strength Tinto Velho is, given five years or so in the cellar, one of Portugal's more impressive reds. Elsewhere, however, wines made in these ways live down to the regional reputation of "country of bad bread and bad wine".

Fortunately, better wine is being made by more modern methods – such as Peter Bright's Tinto da Anfora and Santa Marta, and his countryman David Baverstock's efforts at the huge Esporão estate where he has some 40 varieties of grapes to play with. For lovers of wines with aristocratic connections, there's the Quinta do Carmo in which Château Lafite Rothschild is involved and, for democrats, there are the improving co-operatives of Borba, Reguengos and Redondo.

BUCACO

Lovers of grand hotels, over-the-top architecture and good wine can indulge themselves in all three at the extraordinary

Breaking up the cap: Alentejo wine gets better

Bolinos de Bacalhôa

Cod balls with parsley, coriander and mint

*W*ith one of its borders entirely taken up by the Atlantic, it is not surprising that cod – particularly salt cod – features prominently in Portuguese cooking.

SERVES 6

1 lb/500 g skinned and boned salt cod
2 oz/50 g dried breadcrumbs
3 tbsp fresh coriander leaves, minced, or
1 tsp crushed coriander seeds
2 tbsp parsley, chopped
2 tsp fresh mint, minced, or 1 tsp dried mint
2 cloves garlic, peeled and crushed
Salt and freshly ground black pepper
8 tbsp olive oil

The day before, immerse the salt cod in water for at least 12 hours in a glass, ceramic or stainless steel bowl or pan, changing the water three or four times. Drain and rinse the cod and place it in a saucepan with enough water to cover. Bring to the boil, then reduce to a simmer and cook for about 20 minutes or until the fish flakes. In a large bowl, mix 4 tbsps of the olive oil and breadcrumbs and leave until the breadcrumbs have absorbed the oil. Drain the cod and flake it into the breadcrumb mixture. Stir in the coriander, parsley, mint and garlic, adding salt and pepper to taste. Form the mixture into balls. In a frying pan, heat the remaining oil until it is hot but not smoking. Sauté the cod balls until they are browned all over. Serve with ratatouille.

Buçaco Palace Hotel, tucked away in the Buçaco forest. The rich red and white wines are made – very traditionally – by the hotel general manager, José Santos, and they last for ever, taking on an increasingly piney flavour from the mixture of beeswax and resin with which the bottles are sealed. But don't go looking for these wines in the shops; they are only available at this and three other Portuguese hotels.

ALGARVE

The kindest way to deal with the wines of the Algarve would be to say nothing about them at all. They owe their demarcation to local politics, are (poorly) made from the Tinta Negra Mole, and are among the least impressive of the entire country.

PORT

O UNDERSTAND PORT you have to take the slow train up alongside the Douro River to the farms or *quintas* where it is made. Before you do so, however, wangle your way into the Oporto Lawn Tennis and Cricket Club down on the coast. Previously known as the British Club, this is a good place to watch the Portuguese play the British at tennis, and to watch the British play each other at cricket. The nuance translates directly to port. The Portuguese drink copious amounts of wine; little of it is port and even less is remotely comparable to the kind of vintage port most British wine-drinkers would recognize and enjoy. Port is a drink invented by and for Anglo-Saxons.

THE HISTORY OF PORT

Although Portuguese wines from various regions had been shipped to Britain since the days of Chaucer, the first Anglo-Saxons to discover the wines of the Douro were sixteenth-century merchants – or "factors" – visiting the market town of Viana do Castelo in search of olive oil and fruit. By 1666 there were sufficient of these factors to start a club, called the Factory House, at which their successors still meet every week for lunch and a decanter or three of port.

When the first shipments of "pipes" – the region's rugby-ball-shaped, 115-gallon (522-litre) casks – arrived on British soil, the wine was called *Vinho do Porto*, after Porto, the harbour town from which it was shipped. It would have had some of the plummy, damsony flavour of the port we know today, but none of the sweetness or the strength it now gets from its fortification with brandy.

There are several stories to explain how brandy was first added to the Douro wine. According to one explanation, two British merchants chanced upon a monastery at Pinhão that was making particularly delectable wine. To satisfy the abbot's sweet tooth, some of the sugar and the grapes had been preserved during fermentation by

adding spirit before it had all been fermented out. Another more prosaic, but probably more credible, explanation was that the naturally sweet wine continued to ferment while being transported in barrels across the Atlantic to Newfoundland, where the ships used to stock up on cod, the fish that the Portuguese needed for their national dish of *bacalhão*. The addition of brandy before the wine left Portugal was intended to stop the fermentation and thus to prevent

Douro terraces: Dry stone walls curve round hills

the casks exploding in mid-ocean.

We know that the sweet strong wine had already begun to create a small market for itself in Britain by 1677, when French wines were banned in what could fairly be described as a seventeenth-century cold war between Britain and France. The 10 years of hostilities that followed meant a heyday for the Portuguese wine-makers, who, in 1683, despite the poor quality of most of their wine, apparently managed to sell the British some eleven and a half million bottles of the stuff.

The signing of the Methuen Treaty in 1686 more or less gave the Portuguese a monopoly of wine sales to Britain, in return for which the British received a similar concession for the export of woollen textiles to Portugal. (The tax on French wines was set at a hefty £55 per tun while importers of Portuguese wines had to pay only £7.) The British (and a few Dutch) merchants were not slow to take advantage of this privilege. During the early years of the eighteenth century, they established offices and warehouses – "lodges" (*loja* in Portuguese means storehouse) – for themselves in the village of Vila Nova de Gaia on the south bank of the Douro opposite the harbour town.

During the 1750s the market for port grew too quickly and, perhaps inevitably, the lack of scruples of the growers (who adulterated their wine with elderberries) and of the merchants (who paid little attention to the quality of what they bought) led to a slump. The growers blamed the merchants, the merchants blamed the growers, and the already questionable quality of the wine deteriorated still further. The man who rescued port was the Portuguese Chief Minister, the Marqués de Pombal. In 1756 he started the Douro Wine Company and effectively wrested back control of the region's wines from the foreigners, who were allowed to buy and ship port only once it had been tasted by officials of the company.

The late eighteenth century was a heyday for the port trade, with 50,000 pipes

---

The Essentials
THE DOURO

What to look for Rich, deep plummy vintage styles and nutty, tangy tawny.

Location The Douro valley traverses northern Portugal.

Quality *Região demarcado* (RD) for port, which is further classified, in descending order of quality, from A to F. Unfortified table wines are *vinhos de mesa* only, but can be good.

Style Red port comes in a variety of styles (*see page 201*). In most of its forms, it is classic after-dinner drinking, full of rich, spicy sweetness. The best old tawnies have faded in wood to a dry yet mellow smoothness. White port can be sweet or dry and is commonly drunk chilled as an aperitif, often mixed with tonic water. A few unfortified Douro reds are of very high quality and all are characterized by weighty berry fruit. The white wines are dry and again can have good fruit.

Climate High summer temperatures and rainfall. Winters can be surprisingly cold.

Cultivation The steeper and more inaccessible vineyards higher up the valley have better-quality schist soils which produce the finest ports. Thus production of Douro table wines is concentrated on the granite soil of the lower valley.

Grape varieties *Port*: of the over 40 permitted red port grapes the best are Tinta Amarela, Tinta Barroca, Tinto Cão, Tinta Roriz, Touriga Francesa, Touriga Nacional. *White port* is made from a ragbag of varieties. Little selection is practised. *Red table wines*: as for red port plus Tinta Francesa, Bastardo, Mourisco Tinto, Alvarelhão, Comifesto, Donzelinho, Donzelinho Tinto, Malvasia, Malvasia Preta, Mourisca de Semente, Periquita, Rufete, Sousão, Tinta Barca, Tinta Carvalha, Touriga Brasileira. *White table wines*: Arinto, Boal, Cercial, Codega, Donzelinho Branco, Esgana Cão, Folgosão, Fernão Pires, Malvasia Corada, Malvasia Fina, Malvasia Parda, Moscatel Galego, Rabigato, Rabo de Ovelha, Verdelho, Viosinho.

Production/maturation Port grapes are brought back to the central *quinta* where they are in many cases still trodden by foot in stone troughs, or *lagares*. Fermentation takes place at temperatures up to 32°C until the alcohol content reaches 6 per cent. It is at this stage that the wine is fortified with clear grape spirit (*aguardente*). The port is then matured and bottled at Vila Nova de Gaia, a suburb of Oporto.

Longevity The best vintage ports will last at least 20 years and often double that. White port should be drunk young; the unfortified white wines should be drunk within 3 years and the red wines between 2 and 10 years.

Vintage guide The best of recently declared port vintages are 63, 66, 77, 85, 91, 94. *Red table wine*: 80, 83, 84, 85, 91, 92, 94, 95.

My Top 14 *Port*: Taylor, Warre, Graham, Dow, Fonseca, Noval, Ramos Pinto, Fonseca-Guimaraens, Niepoort, Quinta do Crasto, Quinta do Vesuvio, Quinta do Bomfim, Quinta da Vargelas, Quinta de la Rosa; *Table wine*: Quinta do Crasto, Quinta de la Rosa.

(nearly 36 million bottles) being shipped to Britain each year – three times as much as is exported today. Port's popularity owed much to the development in 1775 of a new way of blowing bottles. Until then, bottles were squat containers that could only be stored standing up, and for a limited period of time. That year, the first port bottle – purpose-designed for laying down – was made and, with it, the first vintage port.

HOW PORT IS MADE

Every bottle of wine legally labelled as port comes from grapes grown in vineyards planted along a 45-mile (72 km) stretch of the River Douro as it ambles its way from Spain. On the western, Oporto, side of the town of Regua, the region is known as the Lower Douro; it is this part of the river that produces the more basic styles of ruby and tawny port. To the east of Regua is the Upper Douro, where grapes used for vintage, crusted and top-quality tawny port are grown.

The Upper Douro is extraordinary, savagely beautiful country, good for nothing

Port side: *All port used to be moved like this*

but grape-growing and goats. The steep banks that were once fought over by the armies of Napoleon and Wellington are now covered with terraces of vines, but the lot of the vineyard worker is scarcely more enviable than that of the eighteenth-century soldier. There could actually be 10 times as much vineyard land, but the dry-stone walls are crumbling, allowing the vertical steps to erode under the elements. The terraces cannot be worked by machines, and there are few Portuguese men who fancy the work.

The salvation of the region, as in the steeply sloping vineyards of the Rhine, has been the reorganization of the slopes to enable the vineyards to be planted the other way – up and down, rather than along the hills. All this work in the vineyards has inevitably redirected attention to the kinds of grapes that are planted.

No fewer than 88 different varieties are permitted for the production of port; in older vineyards perhaps a dozen or more different types will be planted side by side on the same hillside, and all will be vinified together. Top-class port, like most top-class claret, will never be made from a single variety. Now, though, the port shippers increasingly concentrate on isolating which – probably the Touriga Nacional, the Roriz, the Mourisco, and the Tinta Francesa, which is rather dubiously said to be related to the Pinot Noir – make the best wine.

The grapes are grown on quite small *quintas* or farms, which belong either to the port houses themselves or to the 28,000 peasant-farmers. Each shipper carefully oversees the yearly cycle and knows precisely when the harvest will begin (generally about September 20th) in each vineyard. Bands of pickers called *rogas*, headed by a *rogador*, bring the grapes into the farm for crushing.

Until 1960, all crushing took place by foot in low, open, concrete or wooden troughs called *lagares*. About 14 men per *lagare* would trample back and forth to the accompaniment of an accordion, four hours on, four hours off, until the grapes were crushed and the juice floated on top of the solids. When a sufficiently high alcohol level had been achieved, still leaving a good deal of sugar in the must, the wine would be run off into wooden vats and blended with neutral *aguardente* – grape brandy – at 77 per cent strength. The spirit stops the fermentation process, leaving the strong sweet liquid that is port.

Today, most of the annual harvest is crushed and fermented mechanically and the *lagares* are paradoxically only used by the most primitive farms and by the best port shippers for the grapes from their best vineyards.

Following the harvest, the port shippers travel around the *quintas* to gain an overall impression of the tannic new wines. In the spring following the harvest, most of the wine is shipped down the Douro to the lodges in Vila Nova de Gaia. Originally, the trip would have been made on *Barco Rabelo* sailboats, but since the building of roads and railway track these picturesque boats have been relegated to use as mobile advertising hoardings for the producers.

Once in the port lodge, the wine of each "pipe" is tasted again to decide on its future. Top-quality wines are separated from the others, blended only among themselves, held for 18 months, and re-tasted to establish whether they are potentially good enough to be sold as vintage port, late-

bottled vintage, or whether they will be kept in wood for long enough to become tawny.

TYPES OF PORT

In 1877 a visiting English writer called Henry Vizetelly complained that there were "almost as many styles of port as shades of ribbon in a haberdasher's shop". Today, thankfully, the range is narrower, but it still offers ample scope for confusion.

Theoretically, port can be divided into two fundamentally different styles: wood-aged – wine that has been matured in barrel – and bottle-aged – wine that has been bottled young, with a significant amount of the solid matter that will eventually drop out in the form of a deposit.

Unfortunately, nothing is that simple. There are several types of bottle-aged, and several types of wood-aged, wine and their producers have traditionally made little effort to make it clear to prospective customers which are which. Until recently, the producers used to defend their ways with the explanation that "most port drinkers know what they are buying". So saying, they shrugged off any criticism of their indiscriminate labelling as tawny of both old, wood-aged wine and young blends of white and ruby, and any complaint that terms such as "fine old" really ought to mean something. Today labelling is a little clearer, but it's still far from precise. So a bottle of

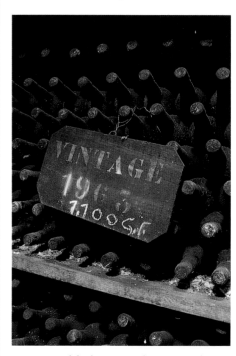

1963: One of the finest years this century. These are from Burmester

Taylor's (and just about everybody else's) Late-Bottled Port will have been filtered to ensure that it needs no decanting, while one bearing the same words from Warre's or Smith Woodhouse will have as much of a deposit as any vintage port – and taste twice as delicious as most other shipped LBVs.

Ruby port

Ruby is yesterday's basic port style – the stuff people used to drink in British pubs as half of that memorable cocktail, the "port 'n' lemon". The snootier members of the port trade would naturally never have dreamed of drinking their wine in this way – but it didn't stop them from making vast amounts of a raw, spirity drink that needed a good dose of lemon to help disguise what would otherwise be fairly awful.

White port

White port is supposed to be a "smart" drink, to be sipped at by elegant folk at the right kind of cocktail party. I only wish it were. Revealingly, its makers routinely serve it with a handful of ice cubes and a generous dollop of tonic or soda. In other words, white port is a very pricy alternative to vermouth – and one that has the added disadvantage of coming in unpredictable levels of sweetness and freshness.

Tawny port

Port labelled as "Tawny", "Fine Old Tawny", "Superior Old Tawny" and so on, is another of the port men's little jokes. Unlike real tawny, which owes its name, its colour and its tangy, nutty flavour to its prolonged sojourn in barrel, this stuff is simply a blend of young white and ruby ports, mixed to look and taste vaguely like the genuine article. A specific age of 10 or 20 years old will ensure that you are getting the real thing. Real tawny is a delicious alternative to vintage, but in the heat of the Douro the shippers often surprise visitors by serving it chilled.

There is another style of tawny less frequently encountered overseas: *Colheita* ports, or tawny port with a vintage date. To the traditionalists, the very idea makes no sense because, in theory at least, the best tawny is always a blend of ports of different ages (according to the rules, it only has to have the character of the age it claims) and, in fact, younger tawnies are often tastier than older ones. But that doesn't stop those same traditionalists from selling their own *Colheita* ports in countries such as France and Portugal.

Quinta de Bon Retiro: A "quinta" is simply a single estate

Vintage port

Even in a very good year, no shipper will declare a vintage as soon as the wine is made. Instead he wants to see how the juvenile protégé develops after 18 months, and then, if both he and the Instituto do Vinho do Porto agree that the wine of a given year is exceptional enough, a vintage is declared, and the wine of that single year is bottled during the following year. For some reason, although British port houses often disagree over which vintage to declare, none will ever declare in two consecutive years. Vintage ports take considerably longer to mature than wood-aged ports, though their longevity does vary from one vintage to another. All vintage ports throw a sediment in the bottle and need decanting anything up to a day before drinking.

Late-bottled vintage port

This is wine from a single vintage, matured in wood for between four and six years. The result is usually a wine that has been filtered and consequently has less character and weight than vintage port and lacks the fine nuttiness of good tawny. Look out, though, for traditional, earlier-bottled, unfiltered examples made by Warre's and Smith Woodhouse.

Crusted port

Crusted port is a blend of good wines from different vintages. Bottled young, it retains a lot of body and should be decanted. It offers

one of the best alternatives to real vintage port.

Single-quinta port

Vintage port produced at a single *quinta* or farm (as opposed to blends of wines from several different farms). Until quite recently, most single-quinta ports were produced and sold by well-known port houses in years when they had chosen not to declare a vintage, Now, however, these ports are facing strong competition from a growing number of privately owned, single-estate *quintas* whose wines are never sold off for blending. Among these, the best are Quinta de la Rosa, Quinta do Crasto and Quinta do Vesuvio (which belongs to the Symington family, owners of Dow's, Graham's and Warre's). Of the "off-year" single-*quintas*, Taylor's Vargellas, Warre's Cavadinha and Dow's Bomfim all offer real vintage style for a lower price.

MADEIRA

ONCE THE FAVOURITE tipple of American and English gentlemen, Madeira would have been the staple of every self-respecting dinner table of the late eighteenth and nineteenth centuries. George Washington, for example, a man described by his friend Samuel Stearns as "very regular, temperate and industrious", used to dine every day at three, drinking "half a pint to a pint of Madeira wine, this with a small glass of punch, a draught of beer, and two dishes of tea".

But what would Washington's "Madeira wine" have tasted like? According to one Edward Vernon Harcourt, whose A *Sketch of Madeira* was published in 1851, it would have been made from a mixture of three grapes: the Verdelho (for "body"), the Tinta, and the Bual (both for "flavour"). This use of several different grape varieties in a single blend may come as a surprise anyone who has learned that each of the four principal types of Madeira – Sercial, Verdelho, Bual and Malmsey – is named after, and made from, its own grape. But our ancestors would have known about wines with those names, *as well as* one known simply as "Madeira";

such names were fairly loosely applied.

In the late nineteenth century there was also a Madeira Burgundy, made from the Tinta Negra Mole, a grape supposedly grown originally in France as the Pinot Noir. Always less well thought of than the quartet of better-known "Castas Nobles", the Tinta wine was said by one contemporary author to have "the astringent property of port", losing some of its fine aroma and delicate flavour "after its first or second year". Even further down the quality scale were the colourfully named Bastardo and Moscatel. Wine simply called "Madeira" would have been made from a mixture of any or all of these. Casks that had had the benefit of the warm voyage through the tropics were sold as either "East" or "West India Madeira"; Madeira that had not taken either trip was simply styled "London Particular".

As the years passed, and as producers discovered that the wine could be "cooked", Madeira passed from being the preserve of the Anglo-Saxon gentleman to that of the Gallic or German cook. The quality of the

Famous name: The Madeira Wine Company

The Essentials
MADEIRA

What to look for Rich, concentrated wine with a marmaladey tang – whatever the level of sweetness.

Location This Atlantic island under Portuguese jurisdiction lies 370 miles off the coast of Morocco.

Quality Denominação de Origen Controlada (DOC).

Style Table wines rarely leave the island, which is chiefly famous for its classic fortified wines. These vary in style *(see box)* from dry Sercial and Verdelho, for drinking chilled as an aperitif, through to lusciously sweet, after-dinner Bual and Malmsey. All have extraordinary ageing potential and good balancing acidity.

Climate Hot summers and mild winters. High rainfall.

Cultivation Terraced vineyards hug the island's cliffs, the best sites being in the south of the island. The soil is fertile, due in part to its volcanic origins and the fire-raising of the island's first settlers. Vines are trained on trellises to allow other crops to be grown underneath.

Grape varieties The four quality grapes are Sercial, Bual, Verdelho and Malmsey. Should a bottle not specify any of these, it will probably be produced from the Tinta Negra Mole, either on its own or blended.

Production/maturation The grapes are fermented and then placed in a heated storeroom – an *estufa* – heated gradually to 45°C and then cooled. Fortification takes place before this *estufagem* "baking" for dry Madeira, and afterward for the sweeter styles. The wine enters a *solera* system, similar to that used in Jerez, 18 months after cooling.

Longevity Madeira, vintage or otherwise, is ready to drink when it is bottled. After this time it will keep almost indefinitely; it is also one of the rare wines that still taste good – sometimes better – even weeks after the bottle has been opened, since air contact is such a crucial and desirable factor in its style.

Vintage guide Most Madeiras are a product of the *solera* system, although there are still a few old single-vintage wines available.

Top Producers Henriques & Henriques, Rutherford & Miles, Cossart Gordon, Blandy, Artur Barros e Souza, d'Oliveira.

Madeira: Steep, rainy and sub-tropical

it, to the dynamic Symington family who own the Dow's, Graham's and Warre's port houses on the mainland.

Among Portuguese Madeira houses, the best – and best-known – is Henriques & Henriques where visitors can compare run-of-the-mill Madeira, sold on price, with 30- and 40-year-old examples of Bual and Malmsey that fill both mouth and memories with their richness and orangey tang. Some people on the island say that such *solera* wines are a thing of the past, that from here onward the best commercial wines will be like tawny port and fine whisky in declaring an age (10 years old for instance) rather than a specific *solera* year. It would be a great pity if they were to disappear because, like some of the real vintage wines, they offer delicious proof that, thanks to the way that it is made, Madeira can be the longest-lived drink of them all.

The taste of cheap, "cooking" Madeira hints at a wine that is capable of better things – but only hints. Tasting the real stuff is something else again, an experience like sampling the finest table wines in the world. Cooking wine will always have its place – in the saucepan rather than the glass – but fine Madeira has a far more important role to play. Try a bottle of the finest 10-year-old or older and you may be converted for life.

wine inevitably fell, and the four difficult-to-grow fine varieties – the "Castas Nobles" – were gradually replaced by the easier Tinta Negra Mole. After all, so the producers often thought, the wine it produces can be pretty similar and, once it's in the soup, who's going to notice?

For the true Madeira-lover, the more serious wine-lodges continued to produce Madeira of a remarkable quality, using the "noble" grapes and a *solera* system, and wines bearing specified vintages were made in good years. Even so, it was not until the late 1970s that the island's wine-makers finally decided to take a firm grip on the situation and concentrate on quality – or rather on reminding the rest of the world about the quality they had never really stopped producing. Suddenly, wines such as Blandy's 10-year-old Malmsey began to appear: beautifully packaged, fairly highly priced, but, most essentially of all, with the depth of flavour that Madeira shares with no other fortified wine. Where sherry has its own kind of identifiable savoury woodiness, and port its stemmy, tannic acidity, Madeira has a unique quality – a nutty, old-English marmaladey "tang" that can be quite addictive.

This concentration on reinstating Madeira in the public mind as a quality product stems partly from the fact that the costs of production of even the most mediocre wine on the island are so high that it can never be sold as cheaply as port or sherry, and partly from the accession of Portugal into the EEC. Among the more meddlesome of European laws, there is one that states that a product must conform to the description that appears on its label. So Sercial, for instance, has to be made 85 per cent from the Sercial grape. (Traditionally, the amount of pure Sercial in an average bottle bearing that name might well have been as low as 10 per cent or even less.) Equally, the Eurosnoops have not been as lenient as the Portuguese authorities toward some of the "vintaged" Madeira that used to fill the shops on the island. Rows of bottles, each proclaiming its vintage as 1884, inevitably inspired suspicion.

The island's future success or failure lies in well-tested hands. The Madeira Wine Company – which embraces no fewer than 26 brands, including such well-known names as Blandy, Cossart Gordon and Rutherford & Miles – was recently sold by Richard Blandy, a descendant of the subaltern who founded

---

MADEIRA STYLES

Sercial Made from a grape thought to be related to the Riesling, this is the driest, palest and most perfumed style of Madeira. Ideal as an alternative aperitif to *fino* sherry – or as an accompaniment to *consommé*.

Verdelho Also drinkable as an aperitif, this is slightly sweeter, with a hint of the lime flavour that is the mark of this variety.

Bual/Boal The second-sweetest type of Madeira, smoky and complex, with a typical marmaladey tang of acidity that sets it distinctly apart from sherries of similar levels of sweetness.

Malmsey The original and sweetest Madeira style, made from the Malvasia grape. Rich, dark and brown-sugary but, like the Bual, with a tangy vein of balancing acidity that makes it a far easier drink than vintage port.

Rainwater US name for a dryish blend of Sercial and Verdelho, so named because the casks were stood outside in the rain.

Reserve At least 5 years old.

Special Reserve At least 10 years old.

Exceptional Reserve At least 15 years old.

Vintage At least 20 years in cask and 2 in bottle.

THE UNITED KINGDOM

THE BRITISH are a strange race. Given a choice when buying anything – a car, a cheese, a beer, a computer – they all too frequently opt for an import; foreign is best. In no instance is this more marked than that of wine. A growing number of English and Welsh men and women have thrown themselves body, soul and savings account into wine-making over the last few years, only to be rewarded with the almost total indifference of their countrymen.

Of course, Britain's characteristically grey skies and chilly temperatures do little to dispel prejudice; surely the climate cannot be warm enough to ripen grapes? But the people who hold this view clearly have not spent much time in such classic cool wine regions as Champagne, Chablis and northern Germany, where producers regularly manage to use what seem to be inhospitable conditions to make fine wine.

No, the problem facing England's wine industry has been a deadly blend of the cottage-industry mentality of many of the growers themselves and the unwillingness of British governments to help them. Wine-makers in other parts of Europe are feather-bedded in all sorts of ways; in Britain, they are told to stand on their own two feet – and, just for good measure, given a few hefty blows to the ankles by the revenue-gathering arms of the state.

Supporters of English (which confusingly also means Welsh) wine never tire of proudly reminding those who scoff that the Roman and Norman invaders made wine here, that Henry VIII probably drank it – until he dissolved the monasteries and put a stop to its production – and that Vine Street, the City of London thoroughfare familiar to generations of English Monopoly players, was once a place in which were grown good, ripe grapes.

So what? The kind of wine medieval monks enjoyed would, I'm pretty certain, fare no better in most modern wine bars than the food they ate. No, the modern British wine industry dates firmly from the late 1960s and early 1970s – at around the time when wine suddenly began to interest a broader range of Britons who previously thought of it as something exotic and "foreign".

In those early days, farmers all too often simply expelled a pony from its paddock and planted a few vines without applying any real thought – let alone expertise – to the question of whether the grape variety and the plot of land were remotely suited to each other. Hardly auspicious beginnings. But luckily, more sensible would-be wine-growers did seek advice, perhaps inevitably looking to Germany, a country they rightly saw as having similar climatic conditions and whose viticultural tradition seemed entirely appropriate to English conditions.

It was immediately clear that Germany's greatest grape, the Riesling, would not ripen in England, but the experts at the Geisenheim Wine School on the Rhine saw no reason why newer varieties developed for Germany's cold climate should not succeed. In particular, they set great store by the Müller-Thurgau, the variety which was rapidly supplanting the Riesling almost throughout Germany.

The combination of Germanic grapes and advice meant, inevitably, that most of the early efforts were semi-sweet versions of wines that were already being imported from the Rhine and Mosel. Like the producers of many of those wines, the English could only make their wines sweet by "backblending", adding *süssreserve* – sweet grape juice – which they generally imported from Germany.

While the quality of these wines was often comparable to that of the German examples they were mimicking, the price was almost invariably higher than that, for example, of a mass-produced Piesporter. Why then, English wine-drinkers asked with a degree of logic, should we buy a local

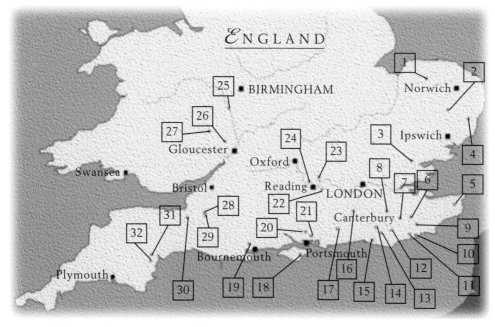

1	Elmham Park	9	Tenterden
2	Pulham	10	Carr Taylor
3	New Hall	11	Leeford
4	Bruisyard	12	Sedlescombe
5	Staple Vineyard	13	Barkham Manor
6	Biddenden	14	Rock Lodge
7	Lamberhurst	15	Breaky Bottom
8	Penshurst	16	Denbies

17	Nutbourne Manor	25	Astley
18	Adgestone	26	Three Choirs
19	Horton Estate	27	Bodenham
20	Meon Valley	28	Wootton
21	Hambledon Wines	29	Pilton Manor
22	Thames Valley	30	Moorlynch
23	Chiltern Valley	31	Sharpham
24	Cane End	32	Beenleigh Manor

product instead of the cheaper import?

During the second half of the 1980s, however, the business of making English wine became more businesslike. Hobbyists tired of what no longer seemed such a romantic occupation; the vines grew older and, like all mature vines, began to produce richer wine; and, most important of all, many of the English wine-growers, who were growing in confidence, decided to stop copying the Germans.

And when they did their own thing, hey presto! Their Germanic grapes began to produce dry and off-dry wines that seemed a whole lot closer in style to the Loire than to the Rhine. At their best – and that's an increasing proportion – these new styles are packed with the flavour of (ripe) grapefruit and gooseberries. The acidity – which was always their hallmark – is now balanced by a smokiness and a fatty richness that you'd never expect from cold-climate vineyards. Most growers still add *süssreserve*, but some most emphatically don't; both groups, thanks partly to (in German terms) tiny

Lamberhurst: A traditional Kent oasthouse, and very modern wines

yields, partly to increasingly skilful wine-making and partly, ironically, to the cool climate, seem consistently to produce intensely flavoured, good-quality wine with a capacity to age that surprises even their makers. Late-harvest wines are succeeding, as are – perhaps predictably, given the chalky soil southern England shares with Champagne – sparkling wines. The only cul-de-sac is presented by the eccentric reds, produced at high cost and effort from grapes grown, like tomatoes, in plastic tunnels.

Today there are 2,500 acres of British vines – well over 200 times as many as there were when a dozen pioneers gathered, in 1967, to launch the English Vineyards Association, the body that still oversees the quality of English, Welsh and Channel Island wines through the allocation of its gold seals of approval.

If the future for English wine looks bright, it is thanks to the growing professionalism of the wine-makers. John Worontschak, an ambitious young Australian, has proven both at Thames Valley Vineyards and with the dozen wineries which form the Harvest Wine Group that skilled wine-making can transform the quality of English wine. Elsewhere, after a bumpy start, the heavy investment began to pay off at the Denbies winery-cum-vinous-theme-park in Surrey and, for the first time, a number of the biggest producers actually agreed to co-operate in trying to market their wines to a surprisingly receptive market on the European mainland. All that's needed now is for the Britons themselves to take their country's wines as seriously as some of those Europeans do.

The Essentials
THE UNITED KINGDOM

What to look for Fresh, floral dry and off-dry wines possibly with a flavour of grapefruit and/or gooseberry.
Location The majority of English vineyards lie south of Birmingham, all the way down to the Isle of Wight. Many of the areas now cultivating vines are the same areas used for wine-making in the Middle Ages. Fertile Kent and Sussex are particularly well-populated with English wine-makers. The handful of Welsh vineyards, particularly those around the Monnow Valley – and usually lumped together with the English – should not be overlooked by any means.
Official quality A Quality Wine Scheme was introduced in 1992, the year England's production broke through the European Union's 25,000 hectolitre threshold. However, several producers have opted out of the Scheme and it remains largely irrelevant to English wine production as a whole. The English Vineyards Association awards seals of approval and various trophies to particularly good wines. Accept only "English" wine: "British wine" is made from foreign grape juice diluted with British water, and should be avoided.
Style Whites range from dry, even austere, through clean, fruity Loire-style to Germanic, medium-sweet wines. Many are made from a single grape, though blends can be very successful. *Süssreserve* is used by some producers to soften the high acidity, and chaptalization is essential to raise the alcohol level in grapes which can never produce enough sugar by themselves. There is proven potential for sparkling and, in warm years, dessert styles.

A little light red is made.
Climate Maritime, at – cynics say beyond – the northerly extreme of table-wine production. Even some warmer areas of south-west England can get l00 in/254 cm of rain a year.
Cultivation Wide range of soils, including chalk, limestone, gravel and granite. Slopes play an important role as suntraps and windbreaks.
Grape varieties Principally white and Germanic, though there is some experimentation with French varieties. Kerner, Müller-Thurgau, Scheurebe, Reichensteiner, Schönburger, Huxelrebe and Madeleine Angevine are most commonly seen. Despite the opposition of the EU to hybrids, the Seyval Blanc is still successfully grown. Reds including Pinot Noir, Gamay, Merlot and Cabernet Sauvignon are grown – mostly beneath plastic sheeting.
Production/maturation Stainless steel predominates. Occasional efforts with new oak are surprisingly promising.
Longevity Surprisingly high – 1 to 8 years, thanks to the wines' high acidity.
Vintage guide 88, 89, 90, 92, 93, 94.
My Top 29 Astley, Carr Taylor, Hambledon, Breaky Bottom, Lamberhurst, Three Choirs, Thames Valley, Ditchling, Pulham, Wootton, Penshurst, Adgestone, Bruisyard, Berwick Glebe, Pilton Manor, Staple, Nutbourne Manor, Chiltern Valley, Wickham, Bodenham, Biddenden, Headcorn, Shawsgate, Tenterden, Chilsdown, Wraxall, Elmham Park, Bruisyard St Peter, English Vineyard.

The Flavour of English Wines

Schönburger Peachy aromas with soft acidity.
Müller-Thurgau Flowery, light, grapefruit/gooseberry fruit.
Seyval Blanc Lighter than Müller-Thurgau, grapefruity acidity.
Reichensteiner Floral aromas and Müller-Thurgau-like flavour.
Huxelrebe Fat, gently Germanic.
Scheurebe Very grapefruity – good in the late-harvest style.

AUSTRIA, SWITZERLAND & LUXEMBOURG

AUSTRIA

"*I*T'S EITHER Burgundy or a really top-class Australian or North American Pinot Noir, but I'm damned if I can place it precisely." One of the most distinguished palates in Britain was clearly flummoxed by the stuff in his glass, but he and his fellow tasters were sufficiently impressed to make it share the Pinot Noir Trophy for the 1995 International Wine Challenge with a *Grand Cru* Burgundy. I shall never forget the look of consternation on his and his fellow tasters' faces when they learned that the wine that had beaten an impressive field of Old- and New-World Pinots was not even a Pinot Noir – it was made from the little-known St Laurent – and came from a winery called Umathum in Austria, of all places. A decade or so after the so-called anti-freeze scandal Austria, as Mr Schwarzenegger might put it, was decidedly back.

The exciting thing about the manner of its return, though, is the way Austria has cast off its old role as purveyor of cheap, sweetish, German taste-alikes and the illegal means to beef up inadequate offerings from

Bird scarer at work: *An evocative scene high in the Austrian hills*

the Rhine. Using grapes little-known in western Europe, like the St Laurent, and taking full advantage of the far easier climate enjoyed here than across the frontier in Germany, a new wave of producers is determinedly aiming high.

Visitors may still enjoy Austrian wine the way the Austrians do, as young and as cool and dry as possible and by the jugful in Heurigen ("*nouveau*") taverns, but for the really interesting stuff, the first place to go is to the wineries of the north-east – Niederösterreich – where they'll find all sorts of examples of the spicy, dry Grüner

Veltliner, Austria's true white wine speciality. Steiermark – Styria – is the place to look for good Sauvignon and a white called Morillon that tastes rather familiar – for the simple reason that it is a local alias for the Chardonnay. While there, they could try a glass (one will probably suffice) of bone-dry Schilcher rosé made from the local Blauer Wildbach grape.

Then there's the Wachau and Krems which offer dry Rieslings richer than most of those of Germany but less aromatic than versions from Alsace. There are reds made in the Weinviertel, but for Austria's best efforts at these, the key region is the warm southern area of Burgenland where the local berryish red Blaufränkisch is now competing with imports such as the Cabernet Sauvignon.

Finally, of course, there's the jewel in Austria's crown: the Neusiedler See, a lakeside area whose foggy conditions are made for producing late-harvest wines to match the best of France and Germany – but far more reliably. Some of the wines made here are simple and lusciously delectable; others, like those of Willi Opitz, Lang and Kracher, offer explosive taste experiences that do for the taste buds what pricier and less legal substances do for the brain.

SWITZERLAND

It is easy to see why the Swiss like holding referenda – and hard to imagine how they work. Theirs is, after all, a country that has three names for just about everything, depending on the region and its language. So, the German-speakers call the Pinot Noir the Klevner or the Blauburgunder and have Rauschling as an alternative name for the Elbling, while the widely grown Chasselas is known as the Fendant, the Gutedel (in Bern), the Perlan (in the regions of Geneva and Neuchâtel) and the Dorin (in the Vaud). Another popular Swiss style, the red blend of Pinot Noir and Gamay, is variously called Dôle, Goron and Savagnin (allowing further confusion with Sauvignon, which isn't grown here).

The wines produced from all these grapes are less confusing. In fact, they are

SWITZERLAND AND AUSTRIA

SWITZERLAND		AUSTRIA	
1 Geneva	9 Thurgau	1 Weststeiermark	8 Donauland
2 Fribourg	10 St Gallen	2 Neusiedlersee-	9 Weinviertel
3 Neuchâtel	11 Graubünden	Hügelland	10 Wien
4 Bern	(or Grisons)	3 Thermenregion	11 Neusiedler See
5 Jura	12 Zurich	4 Carnuntum	12 Mittelburgenland
6 Basel	13 Ticino	5 Wachau	13 Südburgenland
7 Aargau	14 Valais	6 Kremstal	14 Süd-
8 Schaffhausen	15 Vaud	7 Kamptal	Oststeiermark
			15 Südsteiermark

precisely what you'd expect them to be: impeccably made, meticulously clean – and expensive, given their lightness of body and lack of longevity, both of which have been exacerbated by a tendency to over-produce. Following a glut of such wines in the 1980s, however, (somewhat) tighter rules were introduced and the flavour (somewhat) intensified.

Although they find it hard to compete on pure price with wines made in neighbouring France, Germany and Austria, Switzerland's wines can at least offer a range of styles and flavours not often found in those countries.

The real success story has to be the Chasselas. French versions of the Chasselas are generally dull but, in the hands of the meticulous Swiss, this grape can sometimes produce surprisingly refreshing and long-lived wines. Look out for the slightly sparkling examples that have been bottled *sur lie* – on their yeast. Of Switzerland's other whites, try the Malvoisie (the local

name in the Valais for sweet wines made from the Pinot Gris), the (quite rare) Riesling and the Riesling-Sylvaner known elsewhere as Müller-Thurgau, produced around Thurgau, the home of Dr Müller, its inventor.

In Geneva and Neuchâtel the Chardonnay is also producing some tasty, pineappley wines not unlike the best examples from north-east Italy. If you like Beaujolais and don't mind paying classy Burgundy prices, you should enjoy some of the Dôle blends of Pinot Noir and Gamay.

LUXEMBOURG

Luxembourg is another of the world's more quietly efficient, wine-producing countries: nearly three-quarters of the annual production is drunk within the Duchy and most of the rest is exported to Belgium. The

Gruyère Cheese Puffs

In the country that gave us fondue cooking, cheese has always played an important part. This recipe is very easy and will do wonders for a wine and cheese party. It uses one of the great Swiss cheeses, Gruyère, but any hard cheese can be substituted.

MAKES 16

5fl oz/150 ml milk
5 tbsp water
4 oz/100 g butter
½ tsp salt
6 oz/175 g flour
4 eggs
8 oz/225 g Gruyère or other hard cheese, grated
7 tsp cayenne pepper (optional)

In a saucepan, combine the milk, water, butter and salt and bring to the boil. Reduce the heat to moderate and add the flour all at once. Mix vigorously with a wooden spoon until the mixture comes away from the side of the bowl and forms a ball. Put the mixture in a bowl and whisk in the eggs, one at a time. Mix the cheese and cayenne (if using) into the dough. Form 16 balls of dough (about 1 dessertspoon each ball), place them on a buttered baking sheet, and bake in an oven preheated to 400°F/200°C/Gas mark 6 for 30 minutes, or until the puffs are golden.

key grapes are the Elbling, the Riesling-Sylvaner (here often called the Rivaner), the Auxerrois, the Pinot Blanc and Pinot Gris (here, as in Germany, known as the Rülander), the Traminer and the Riesling. Of these, the most successful are probably the Riesling and the Pinot Gris, both of whose wines have more substance than the rather neutral ones made from the Elbling and Auxerrois. Even so, Luxembourg is not the place to come looking for full-flavoured wines; the key style, whatever the grape, is lightweight. Also beware of "Luxembourg" sparkling wines, which, like "British" wine, can be made from imported juices.

EASTERN EUROPE

$\mathcal{A}$T THE beginning of the 1990s, pundits throughout the wine world rushed to book flights to Budapest, Sofia, Sarajevo and Prague, following the return of capitalism to Eastern Europe, and eagerly began to predict the imminent arrival of a wave of wonderful new wines. All that was needed, they choroused, was a bit of free-market encouragement and the right kind of investment.

Heading for a decade later, the wave is still a long way offshore; indeed, while some areas have benefited enormously from an inflow of money and expertise, others seem, if anything, to be making worse wine than ever.

Among the first post-cold-war initiatives were the unashamedly opportunistic attempts by Western firms to buy up complete regions including – incredible as it may seem – such internationally celebrated ones as Tokaj in Hungary. (Just imagine every bottle from Sauternes being made by the same firm!) That deal foundered; others progressed somewhat further, including a short-lived agreement by a Dutchman with a minister in Moldova to take responsibility for all of that newly (semi-) independent country's wines.

In theory, little could be worse than the old collectivist system under which Soviet-Bloc states routinely swapped wine for petrol on a gallon-for-gallon basis. Vineyards were often appallingly managed and planted with varieties whose primary quality was their ease of farming.

Do not, however, imagine that no one cared about the quality of the wines they were making. Not a bit of it. Every year, wineries throughout the region submitted their best efforts to a so-called "international"

Built on rock: Vines on Brac Island, Croatia

wine competition in Ljubljana in former Yugoslavia where, if they were liquid and reasonably transparent, they stood a good chance of picking up at least some kind of award. Unfortunately, the certificates of which the wine-makers were so touchingly proud cut little ice with foreign buyers. Wines rarely had to compete seriously with overseas efforts on any basis apart from price.

Even when good wines were produced, one of the major problems – as in other Communist-run industries – was the relaxed attitude toward quality control. Wines were often as reliable as the dress shirt I once bought in Poland, three of whose buttons were carefully stitched to the wrong side of the fabric. Travellers who remember some of the stuff they bought in Eastern Europe in the 1980s may be interested to know about the birds which used to fly around the bottling hall of at least one winery, occasionally leaving their mark on – and in – the unprotected bottles on the conveyor belts below. Fortunately, few such establishments managed to sell their wines overseas. Today, the battle is to raise the standards overall, and few people have done more to achieve that than the teams of young Australians and New Zealanders who are annually sent in by – principally British – customers to supervise the wine-making in wineries throughout the region.

THE REGIONS

The Balkan states

Before Yugoslavia fell to pieces, it was collectively best-known to foreigners for white wines whose dubious role was to undercut the cheapest Liebfraumilch. Tiger Milk, Laski, Lutomer or Olascz Riesling as these wines were known before EC officials sensibly insisted on a change to "Rizling", not only helped to besmirch the reputation of wines made from the real Riesling (to which they are no more related than I am to Prince Charles), they also gave a totally false impression of the kind of wine the inhabitants of these states like to make and drink.

EASTERN EUROPE

GERMANY
POLAND
CZECH REPUBLIC
UKRAINE
RUSSIA
SLOVAK REPUBLIC
AUSTRIA HUNGARY
MOLDOVA
SLOVENIA
ITALY CROATIA
ROMANIA
BOSNIA - HERZEGOVINA
F.R. of YUGOSLAVIA
BLACK SEA
GEORGIA
BULGARIA
MACEDONIA
AZERBAIJAN
ALBANIA
GREECE
TURKEY
ARMENIA

Slovenia: The best wines of the former Yugoslavia come from here

This is not light, sugar-watery, white-wine country; it's a land of big, hefty reds that are about as approachable as some of the political leaders were under the old regime. Among the most typical of these heavyweights are the wines made from the local Plavac Mali in Dalmatia, from such regions as Pitovske Plaze, Bol, Vis, Brela, Postup, Dingac, Lastovo and Sveta. Another popular local variety is the Prokupac (once known as the "national vine of Serbia"), but this too is now rapidly giving way to the Cabernet Sauvignon, Merlot, Gamay and Pinot Noir.

In Croatia, apart from the Plavac Mali and a raft of apparently obscure local varieties, some of which might be related to ones we know elsewhere, the most familiar grapes are the Cabernet Sauvignon, Merlot and Pinot Noir. Success stories are rare – so far. In Serbia, the province of Kosmet on the Albanian border makes full-bodied Cabernet Sauvignons and Merlots, and Montenegro's Vranac is one of the region's best fuller-bodied reds.

CIS

Ironically, one of the regions whose wine industry suffered most in the first stages of the transition from hard-line Communism was the old Soviet Union. Under Mikhail Gorbachev, Moscow imposed a set of draconian measures to combat Russia's endemic alcoholism. Huge areas of vines were ripped up and wineries mothballed.

Despite the internationally acknowledged leniency of President Yeltsin's attitude toward alcohol, the industry has yet to recover. The stuff most visitors to the old Soviet Union remember – Krim "Champagnski" fizz, from Crimea – is as unpredictable and indeed "grim", as it was more familiarly known by foreign correspondents, as ever. Modern Crimean wine-makers have yet to recreate the great sweet and dry, fortified and unfortified wines of the past.

Georgia, the supposed birthplace of wine-making, is still proudly treating white grapes as though they were red, fermenting them with their skins to make strange, golden wine that, 12 months after the harvest, looks like century-old Château d'Yquem. And – to non-Georgians – is only just on the drinkable side of the line that separates interesting from disgusting. Reds are better but still far from suited to Western tastes for fresh fruit or subtle richness of flavour. Kazakhstan, Azerbaijan

The Essentials
EASTERN EUROPE/CIS

What to look for A bewildering array of indigenous grape varieties – and examples of familiar Western styles – all at affordable prices.
Official quality Under Communism, quality control tended to be non-existent in what were almost always directly or indirectly state-run industries. Capitalism has brought greater awareness of the importance of this aspect but it is taking time to change hardened attitudes – which is why so much of the best wine has thus far been produced by or under the supervision of foreigners. However, Bulgaria, in line with its success in Western markets, had already established a quality system under the old regime: "Country Wine" is table wine from a particular area; DGO or Declared Geographical Origin indicates a specified village appellation; and Controliran is wine from a designated grape from a specific DGO. A time-honoured hierarchy exists for Tokaji: the higher the *puttonyo* number on the bottle, the sweeter the wine.
Style White wines are generally "international" or Germanic in style, from off-dry and medium with basic fresh fruit through to lusciously sweet wines, such as the Romanian *edelbeerenauslese*. Bulgaria produces some passable but dull Chardonnay; Hungary's efforts with Sauvignon, Chardonnay and Riesling have been more successful. There are also several sparkling wines produced in these countries, particularly in the former Czechoslovakia and USSR, the latter producing sweet, red sparkling wine called "Champagnski" and "Krim". Hungarian Tokaji is made from *aszu* – semi-dried (somewhat) *botrytis*-affected grapes mixed, in varying quantities, with a dry base wine to make a number of styles. *Szamorodni* is made in the

Tokaj region from the same grapes but is rarely botrytized. Eastern European red wines are generally full-bodied and approachable with lots of ripe, rich fruit though they are traditionally spoiled by sweetness and oxidation. Bulgarian red wines owe not a little to Bordeaux, in terms of both style and grape varieties: putting up spirited competition to these is the local Mavrud grape. Modern examples of the famous Bull's Blood from Eger in Hungary are improving.
Climate The wine-growing areas of Romania, Hungary, Bulgaria, the Czech and Slovak republics, southern Yugoslavia and Russia have a warm continental climate. Hungary's climate is particularly affected by Lake Balaton, which is the largest in Europe.
Grape varieties Too many to list in full, but including: Aligoté, Cabernet Sauvignon, Chardonnay, Dingac, Furmint, Gamza, Gewürztraminer, Grüner Veltliner, Kratosija, Laski Rizling, Lenyka, Mavrud, Melnik, Merlot, Misket, Muskat Ottonel, Pinot Blanc, Pinot Gris, Pinot Noir, Plavac Mali, Plovdina, Prokupac, Riesling, Saperavi, Sauvignon Blanc, St Laurent, Ugni Blanc, Vranac, Zilavka.
Production/maturation Varies from mediaeval to ultra-modern.
Longevity Drink dry and medium whites within 3 years. Good-quality sweet wines and Tokaji will age for at least 5 years. Red wines are often non-vintage and are released when ready to drink. Most will keep at least 2 years in bottle.
My Top 9 *Tokaj*: Disznókó, Royal Tokaji Wine Co, Oremus; *Other Hungarian*: Gyöngyös Estate; *Bulgaria*: Russe, Suhindol, Svichtov; *Moldova*: Hincesti; *Slovakia*: Nitra.

and Uzbekistan are similarly caught in the time warp of trying to produce wines with as much modern appeal as some of the lard-and-gizzard offerings served up with pride by the cooks of earlier centuries.

Despite the efforts of the aforementioned Dutchman to control the market, an influx of Australian and German investment into Moldova has helped the Hincesti winery to modernize its equipment and to create a successful, if unambitious, brand of its own, while using an Anglo-Saxon name for the bottles it sends to the US where buyers of cheap Chardonnay rarely trouble to read the small print at the foot of the label. So far, no one has managed to produce current wines as impressive as some of the 30-year-old Moldovan reds that reappeared in the early 1990s, but conditions here are perfect and one day the vast areas of vine-covered hillside – over a tenth of the countryside – will once again produce world-class wine.

Hungary

The first Eastern European country to sell its wines successfully in the West was Hungary which, trading on the prestige achieved by what used to be known as Tokay – the "king of wines and wine of kings" in the days of the Austro-Hungarian empire – exported huge quantities of a red called Bull's Blood. This internationally familiar wine, from Transdanubia in the north of the country, is made from a blend of Kadarka, Kékfrankos, Cabernet Franc and Merlot (known here as "Médoc Noir") and owes its name to the strength it was supposed to have given the defenders of a besieged town to beat off their attackers.

Under Communism, Bull's Blood – or to give it its full name, "Egri Bikaver" or "Bull's Blood of Eger" – was anaemic stuff, but privatization is bringing progress here as it is with Hungary's other reds, particularly the Merlot and the local Kadarka and Kékfrankos from the pre-Roman vineyards of Villanyi-Siklos. Another grape grown here with some success is the Pinot Noir.

Small quantities of this variety have also been produced successfully with Antipodean help at the Gyöngyös winery by Hugh Ryman, the young Australian- and French-trained Englishman behind the rejuvenated Hincesti winery in Moldova. The most successful Gyöngyös wines so far, however, have been the Sauvignons and Chardonnays, both of which have been among the best, most consistent, dry whites to come out of Eastern Europe.

None of these wines are of top

international class, however. Tokay – or, as it is now more commonly known, Tokaji – should be, though this could rarely be said of examples made by the all-powerful co-operative under the old collective system. Quite unrelated to the Tokays produced in Alsace and Australia, Hungarian Tokaji is produced in the region of Tokaj close to the River Bodrog, from a blend of the local Furmint, Hárslevelú and Yellow Muscat, all of which are regularly attacked by noble rot, thanks to the mist that rolls off the water. Unlike Sauternes and other top-quality sweet wines, Tokaji is made by turning the nobly rotted grapes into a paste – aszu – which is then blended by the 35-litre hodful – puttonyo – in varying proportions into 140-litre containers of dry – szarnorodni – wine. The sweetness of the Tokaj is measured in puttonyos, the most intense being a "six puttonyo". Aszu Essencia is a kind of "super-Tokaji" made in the best years, while Tokaji Essencia is a

Door of opportunity: *Many are open for investors in Tokaj*

phenomenally pricy syrup made exclusively from nobly rotted grapes which is supposed to work wonders on the (presumably wealthy) male libido.

Everything changed for Tokaj with the arrival of an army of investors, principally from Britain, Spain and France where wine-makers were eager to lay their hands on the equivalent of *Grand Cru* vineyards. From the outset, the foreigners, including Jean-Michel Cazes of Château Lynch Bages,

raised fundamental stylistic questions. The old guard of the co-operative believed that Tokaji was supposed to taste oxidized – like sherry – and made their wine accordingly. The newcomers disagreed – and used old papers and old bottles to prove that, in its heyday, Tokaji would have been no more sherry-like than Sauternes.

The battle is far from over, but the first releases – Tokaj takes a long time to mature – certainly support the Western Europeans' views. More immediately, the introduction of modern methods has led to the renaissance of a forgotten style of light dry wine, made from the pleasantly aromatic Furmint.

Romania

At first sight, the slowcoach of Eastern Europe – watching peasants collecting water from roadside wells is very reminiscent of Bruegel – Romania has, despite the handicaps of outdated and inefficient equipment, quietly begun to show signs of becoming one of the most dynamic as well as the largest wine-producing countries of the region. Much of the progress here can be attributed to the state research centres of Murfatlar and Valea Calugareasca which have introduced Romania's wine-makers to such Western varietals as the Cabernet Sauvignon, Merlot and Pinot Noir. Previously, the vineyards, which were first planted even before the arrival of the Greeks in the seventh century BC, tended to be filled with local grape varieties like the Babeasca de Nicoresti, Negru Virtos, Frincusa, Tamiioaca Romaesca, Feteasca Negra and Kadarka.

The climate, though northerly, is well suited to the production of both red and white wines, but the best regions for reds are Murfatlar, close to the Black Sea where both Pinot Noir and Cabernet Sauvignon have been good; Banat, which makes Cabernet Sauvignon and the locally famous Kadarka de Banat; Vrancea where the Pinot Noir and Cabernet Sauvignon are grown as well as the Babeasca de Nicoresti and Feteasca Negra; and Dealut-Mare on the lower slopes of the Carpathians where the biggest, richest Cabernet Sauvignons and Pinot Noirs tend to be produced. Until recently, this last grape in particular was generally used to make sugary, jammy stuff which was popular among Germans and sweet-toothed Eastern Europeans. Today, more modern versions are dry and better than some less successful, but far pricier, New-World efforts.

What Romania needs now is some flagship wines. Maybe some of those French investors in Tokaj will direct their attention,

Tokaji grapes: Quality has been transformed

skills and cash to Cotnari whose now under-exploited sweet wines were once among the most famous in the world.

Bulgaria

Bulgaria, the success story of the Eastern Bloc, thanks to the provision (by Pepsi Cola of all people) of Californian wine-making know-how, had a surprisingly bumpy return to capitalism. At the root of the problem was land restitution – and the way in which the Communist monopoly over distribution somehow became a post-Communist duopoly.

Let's hope these are short-term problems, because the potential here is enormous. Conditions are fundamentally ideal for wine-making. The Black Sea is a crucial influencing factor on the land to the east of the Balkans, while the region to the west of the mountains is more affected by the Atlantic. Throughout the country, however, while conditions are typical of a continental climate, with warm summers and cool winters, local micro-climates are produced by hilly and mountainous regions.

The two most widely planted black grape varieties are the Gamza which is used to make daily-drinking, lightweight reds, and the more serious Mavrud which produces long-lasting, hefty wines. Further south, the Pamid and Saperavi are both good for simple fare, but the key red grapes for quality wines are now the Merlot and, more particularly, the Cabernet Sauvignon.

The best wines from these varieties can be rich and almost Bordeaux-like. And very good value. Whites – even when made from internationally vaunted varieties like Chardonnay and Sauvignon by visiting Australians – so far remain resolutely unrecommendable. Until smaller estates are recreated, the best way to find a worthwhile red is to look for the names of the best wineries: Russe, Suhindol and Svichtov would be my recommendations.

The Czech Republic and Slovakia

The two parts of what was once known as Czechoslovakia are regions to watch as their vineyards begin to develop their modern potential, and to exploit a micro-climate not unlike those of Austria and Alsace. At present, the greatest successes have been in Slovakia in the Nitra region where light, characterful Grüner Veltliner, Pinot Gris, Pinot Blanc and Pinot Noir are all grown, as well as good examples of the grapey Irsay Oliver. St Laurent is another berryish red to look out for.

Albania

Albania's isolation from the rest of the world has denied outsiders the opportunity to sample its wines, of which there were reportedly once quite large quantities. But

---

Csirke Paprikas

Paprika chicken

*T*his dish from Hungary combines two of the most popular ingredients used in Eastern Europe – paprika, made from dried sweet peppers, and the fresh sweet peppers themselves – in a typical goulash that goes equally well with the red and white wines of this and neighbouring countries.

SERVES 4

1 medium onion, peeled and chopped
2 tbsp olive or vegetable oil
2 tbsp paprika
10 fl oz/300 ml chicken stock
8 chicken pieces
2 green peppers, seeded and cut into thin strips
3 tomatoes, skinned, seeded and chopped, or 3 tinned tomatoes, drained and chopped
5 fl oz/150 ml sour cream
1 tbsp flour
Salt and freshly ground black pepper

In a flameproof pan, cook the onion in the oil until it is softened. Remove from the heat and stir in the paprika. Stir in the stock, return to the heat and cook, stirring occasionally, for 2 to 3 minutes. Add the chicken, peppers, tomatoes and salt to taste. Cook, covered, for about 30 minutes or until the chicken is cooked through. Reduce the heat and remove the chicken pieces with tongs or a slotted spoon to a warmed serving dish. In a bowl, whisk together the cream and flour, then stir the cream mixture into the vegetable mixture. Simmer and stir for 3 to 4 minutes. Add more salt and pepper to taste and spoon over the chicken. Serve with rice or noodles.

living and working under the longest-lasting, hardest-line Communist regime has not made for the most quality-conscious, co-operative of attitudes amongst wine-makers. An Australian wine-maker did produce one vintage there in the mid-1990s. The wine never left the country and the experiment was not, so far as I know, repeated.

THE EASTERN MEDITERRANEAN

THIS, OF COURSE, is where it all started – where man first got involved in the business of turning grapes into wine. The trouble is that, having begun there, wine-making never really developed beyond infancy. For hundreds of years, the general impoverishment of the region following the Mongol invasions of the thirteenth century and the lack of enthusiasm for wine of the Turkish Empire more or less put a stop to the development of wine-making. Visiting some wineries in this region and drinking their wines can be rather like wandering around a wine museum – fascinating, but tough on the taste-buds. Thankfully, things are changing...

GREECE

After centuries of arrested development, Greek wine-making finally encountered international modernity when John Carras converted some of the money he had made out of shipping into an ambitious vineyard planned by the great Professor Emile Peynaud and using the Bordeaux grapes with which the Frenchman was most familiar. A quarter of a century after the first vintage of the now famous Château Carras, it is interesting to see that a new wave of pioneering producers have – thank goodness – mostly preferred to concentrate on indigenous varieties, some of which are probably as old as any in the world. Throughout Greece and the islands, exciting wines are beginning to appear from bigger producers like Kourtakis (with its Kouros brand), Boutari, Tsantalis and Achaia Clauss, and more especially from smaller estates like Gentilini, Hatzimichali and Papaioannou, most of whom are exploring the benefits of higher altitude and wind-cooled vineyards.

Tasting these wines and those made from the Xynomavro grape by the Naoussa co-operative is like witnessing the restoration of a series of old masters, as fascinatingly unfamiliar flavours are revealed. But we ain't seen nothin' yet. Over the next few years, there will be a lot more where these came from. Who knows? We might even find some enthusiastic Californian marketeer declaring the Assyritiko or Tsaoussi

grape to be flavour of the month and planting it in the Napa Valley. In the meantime, seek out the recommendations in the *Essentials* box, and don't forget the great traditional Samos Muscats, the sweet dark Mavrodaphnes and, dare I say it, fresh examples of well-made Retsina.

CYPRUS

Forget the Cyprus "sherry" and "British" wines which have traditionally offered employment to a large proportion of the island's grapes. Forget, too, most of the table wines, many of which are handicapped by the grape varieties from which they are made. No, stride past all of these and head straight for the Commandaria, a potentially delicious fortified wine made from Xynistyeri and Mavron grapes that have been allowed to dry in the sun. It tastes the way you wish Bristol Cream did. For something lighter, look out for the youngest available bottles of table wines from Keo and Etko whose efforts at modernizing their styles are beginning to pay off.

MALTA

Maltese wines were once famous for the minimal use of grapes grown on the island. Today,

there are signs of local vinous pride – as shown by the efforts of the Delicata winery.

TURKEY

Tourism is guilty of all manner of cultural vandalism throughout the world, but if the recent rise in popularity of Turkey among young Northern Europeans has helped to encourage a few go-ahead producers there to make crisp, modern white wine, I'll raise a glass to Thomas Cook and American Express. None is memorable as yet, but all are preferable to the dull, yellow stuff they have begun to supplant. The mostly stewy, earthy reds need more work, but they do come with a built-in sobriety test: just try saying Oküzgözü – the name of one of the main grapes used in Buzbag, the best-known red – without having first swallowed a few glasses.

LEBANON

As Beirut tries to regain its role as the hedonistic capital of the Middle East, the world should see more of the wines of Lebanon's three best wineries, Château Musar, Kefraya and Ksara. Of these, it is Château Musar which has the strongest and longest claim to inter-national fame, thanks to Serge Hochar's bravery in making wine in the Bekaa Valley despite tanks and bullets – and his bravery in doing so in his own highly individual Bordeaux-meets-Rhône style. Lebanese whites still lag behind the reds, making it hard to judge the validity of local claims that the Obaideh is the ancestor of the Chardonnay.

ISRAEL

There is a lot to be said for playing to a captive audience – such as the international community of strictly orthodox Jews who cannot drink any wine that has not been produced by kosher methods and under the control of a rabbi. But for far too long, despite high-profile investment by the Rothschilds and characteristically ingenious irrigation schemes, Israel's (mostly) kosher wine producers got away with producing wine of dismal quality.

The change came in the mid-1980s when the Golan Heights winery showed what Californian know-how could achieve. Since then, the high-altitude vineyards have turned out a consistently respectable set of wines under the Yarden and Gamla labels including a Yarden Cabernet good enough to compete with the best of the New and Old Worlds. The huge Carmel winery, which is responsible for nearly three out of every four bottles of Israeli wines, has also learned to make wine of at least adequate quality, though Askalon and Baron Wine Cellars are both better bets.

SYRIA, JORDAN, EGYPT AND IRAN

There is some wine made in Syria – from Muscat grapes left over from this country's fairly sizeable table-grape industry – and in Jordan. But far less than in the past.

One day, some charitable soul will remind the present generation of Egyptian wine-makers of the care which their ancestors apparently devoted to wine-making. For the moment at least, modern

Kuzu Kapama

Leg of lamb baked with tomatoes, onions and coriander

This dish is traditional in Turkey, but its main ingredients – lamb, tomatoes, onion and olive oil – are used extensively throughout the Eastern Mediterranean, as is the practice of baking meat with vegetables.

SERVES 4–6

2–3 tbsp olive oil
12 spring onions, chopped
4 garlic cloves, peeled and minced
6 tomatoes, sliced
2 tbsp parsley, chopped fine
Salt and freshly ground black pepper
4 lb/2 kg leg of lamb
2 tsp coriander seeds, crushed
6 tbsp lamb or chicken stock

Coat a large roasting pan with the olive oil. Mix the spring onions with half the garlic and sprinkle the mixture over the bottom of the pan. Next, add the tomatoes in a layer. Top with the parsley and salt and pepper to taste. Rub the leg of lamb all over with the remaining garlic, the crushed coriander seeds and salt and pepper. Put the lamb on to the bed of vegetables and pour over the stock. Bake uncovered in an oven preheated to 350°F/180°C/Gas mark 4 for about 1 hour 20 minutes (20 minutes per pound if you prefer your lamb pink), basting occasionally with the juices. Serve with potatoes or bulgar (cracked wheat).

The Essentials
EASTERN MEDITERRANEAN AND THE LEVANT

What to look for Wines made using modern methods which bring out the flavour of indigenous grapes.
Official quality Greece alone has a broad Appellation of Origin system; the term Traditional Appellation is specific to Retsina.
Style Most Greek wines, whether white or red, are flabby, alcoholic and frequently oxidized, suiting local tastes. Greek Muscats can have an attractive raisiny character. Some full-bodied, richly flavoured reds, notably from Macedonia, are made, while Mavrodaphne can resemble Recioto della Valpolicella and Château Carras has made progress with Cabernet Sauvignon. Most traditional Turkish wines are flabby and alcoholic but Trakya, a dry white Sémillon, and the reds, Buzbag and Hozbag, are better, as is the Gamay from Villa Doluca. Cyprus is starting to produce clean, fruity whites and reds as well as the traditional strong wines, such as Commandaria, and Cyprus "sherry". Good-quality Israeli Sauvignons, Cabernets and Grenaches are now being made, while in Lebanon, though Domaine des Tourelles and Domaine de Kefraya reds are improving, quality wine-making is restricted to Château Musar.
Climate Very hot and dry, although moderated by the Mediterranean and by the mountain slopes of these countries.
Cultivation A variety of soils – volcanic, alluvial and gravelly – and vines grown at all altitudes, from flat coastal plains to mountain slopes. The more innovative wine-makers have grasped that sites enjoying cooler micro-climates produce better wine.
Grape varieties *Greece*: Xynomavro, Agiorgitiko, Mavrodaphne, Cabernet Franc, Cabernet Sauvignon, Cinsault, Grenache, Vertzami, Mandilaria, Savatiano, Rhoditis, Assyritiko, Moschophilero, Muscat, Robola; *Turkey*: Papazkarasi, Hasandede, Gamay, Sémillon, Karalhana, Altintas, Cinsault, Carignan, Cabernet Sauvignon; *Cyprus*: Mavron, Maratheftikon, Xynisteri, Cabernet Sauvignon, Cabernet Franc, Grenache, Muscat, Ugni Blanc, Palomino, Mataro; *Lebanon*: Cabernet Sauvignon, Carignan, Cinsault, Pinot Noir, Muscat, Chasselas, Chardonnay, Sauvignon, Ugni Blanc, Aramon; *Israel*: Cabernet Sauvignon, Sauvignon, Grenache, Clairette, Muscat.
Production/maturation Temperature-controlled fermentation and earlier bottling are being employed to produce lighter, fresher wines.
Longevity Most wines lack the acidity to be long-lasting although Musar and the best Greek reds can last for some 8 to 20 years.
Vintage guide Vintages have less effect than wine-making on quality.
My Top 24 *Greece*: Château Carras, the co-operatives of Samos, Naoussa and Zitsa, Korinthiaki, Kourtakis (Kouros), Boutari, Laziridis, Tsantalis, Achaia Clauss, Strofilia, Château Vatis, Gentilini, Hatzimichali and Papaioannou; *Turkey*: Kavaklidere, Diren, Villa Doluca; *Lebanon*: Château Musar, Kefraya; *Israel*: Yarden, Gamla, Baron; *Malta*: Delicata.

Egyptian wines are best avoided – especially when, as in the case of a Cabernet Sauvignon which killed a Briton in 1996, they turn out to be laced with poisonous methanol.

In 1948, the wine writer André Simon wrote of what was then known as Persia that "Once upon a time the country was famous for its wines; today the making and sale of wine is not allowed to Persians, but there are a few Armenians who make and Jews who sell wine". Fifty years later, the only wine being produced is made in secret, which is a pity because there are at least a few lovers of Australian wine who would like to visit the hillside town of Shiraz, purported birthplace of the grape of that name.

NORTH AMERICA

$\mathcal{O}$NCE UPON A TIME (in the late 1930s), two young brothers decided to start a winery. Their sense of time and place were impeccable; they were in California, the grape-growing heart of a nation that had just been freed from 14 years of Prohibition. If they could make the right kind of wine, there was a huge and very thirsty market, including plenty of immigrants, who were ready to buy it by the gallon.

Today one of those same brothers still owns and personally controls the world's largest winery. And the second largest. And the third. Every year his company makes more wine than the entire region of Champagne; the annual production of New Zealand would barely fill one of its larger vats.

A short drive from those giant wineries, there's a small estate whose owner lovingly produces just 1,500 bottles of wine per year – around half the annual output of Château Pétrus, the fabled Pomerol property whose scarcity value is beyond peer among the larger, Bordeaux estates.

The big wineries belong to E & J Gallo; the tiny one to the Lambourne family. And I'll bet that, until Ernest Gallo decided to start exporting overseas in the late 1980s,

Cactus hedge: North America boasts every sort of climate, from cool to sub-tropical

unless you lived or spent time in North America, you'd almost certainly have heard of neither their wines nor the Lambourne's.

That's the first crucial thing to remember about the wine industry of North America; it's huge, varied and as challenging to would-be explorers as the continent itself. And, as with so many other industries in that country, it is remarkably self-sufficient.

The second thing to bear in mind is that, while the Gallo and the Lambourne operations are as different as they could possibly be, they share, with every other US winery from the smallest to the most humungous, that peculiarly American spirit of pioneering possibility, the belief in the key words: "can-do".

In some states this kind of confidence is entirely justified; in California, where almost any kind of farmer can grow almost any kind of crop, there is little excuse for not making good wine. Elsewhere, however, the climatic handicaps are often so severe that "can-do" seems rather reminiscent of the sickly child who stubbornly believes that he is going to grow up to be a champion heavyweight boxer.

But climate has not been the only handicap would-be wine-makers have had to overcome. Throughout North America

UNITED STATES & CANADA

VANCOUVER

Portland

MONTREAL

OTTAWA

Minneapolis

DETROIT

BOSTON

CHICAGO

Salt Lake City

PHILADELPHIA

NEW YORK

Denver

Kansas City

WASHINGTON DC

St. Louis

SAN FRANCISCO

Richmond

Santa Fe

Little Rock

LOS ANGELES

Phoenix

DALLAS

Atlanta

Pacific
Ocean

Austin

Atlantic
Ocean

HOUSTON

MEXICO

Miami

there is a deeply puritanical resistance to alcohol that has, of course, led to its total ban in the past. In more recent years, though, this has been immeasurably strengthened by healthy-living and road-safety campaigners who, for the best of motives, have endeavoured to ensure that wine is never treated as casually as it is in the Old World.

North America is riddled with a confusing mass of restrictions that vary from state to state and even from county to county. Some counties have remained "dry" since Prohibition finally ended in 1933; elsewhere, wine sales are controlled by state monopolies; shops that sell wine are forbidden to sell peanuts or glasses (or vice versa); importers are barred from trading as wholesalers and retailers (and vice versa); and there is almost nowhere that a young man or woman can buy a bottle or glass of wine until they are 21 years old.

With hurdles like these to be cleared, most European producers and merchants might be forgiven for thanking their lucky stars that they are still allowed to ply their trade in the relative freedom of the Old World.

But the North Americans have their own advantages. Selling wine may some-times be less than straightforward, but there's very little to stop would-be producers from making the stuff in any way they choose. A Bordeaux château would encounter all kinds of problems if it wanted to plant a few acres of Chardonnay, and it certainly couldn't label the wine made from that grape as "Bordeaux". A wine-maker in North America can take his – or her – pick from all of the varieties on offer in the nursery, and (unless they're in the state of Oregon) call the wine more or less anything they like. So, if it's got bubbles, label it "Champagne", if it's sweet and pink, dub it "Blush Chablis".

And then there's the Madison Avenue factor. Wine-makers in the Old World are often still far more firmly rooted in the era of feudalism than that of twentieth-century marketing. If your father, grandfather and great-grandfather made Barolo in a partic-ular way from the Nebbiolo grape, and sold it to a local merchant for whatever he was prepared to pay, that's what you would most probably go on doing. And if one of those forebears had taken the brave step of deciding to bottle his wine himself, then you'd more than likely go on using the label he chose from the local printer. The words "promotional budget" almost certainly

wouldn't feature in your vocabulary; your entire marketing effort might well consist of a hand-painted roadside sign to tell passers-by that you have wine to sell, and a few printed cards bearing the name of your estate.

In North America, there is a far greater appreciation of the fact that while wine-making is part of an agricultural tradition, it also inhabits the same, hard-selling business world as the motor, computer or even enter-tainment industries. So the 1995 vintage Cabernet Sauvignon from the Mondavi winery will be described and marketed as that producer's latest "release" – just as though it were a pop record or a movie.

And if the success of a feature film can lie in the hands of the critics, so can that of a wine. If Robert Parker, author and publisher of an enormously influential newsletter called *The Wine Advocate*, and leading Internet pundit, or the contributors to the glossy *Wine Spectator* magazine give a new wine a top mark, it can sell out before the first case reaches the shops. And if they

decide that a wine isn't up to scratch, woe betide the unfortunate salesman who's trying to persuade a wine-retailer to stock it.

This critical spotlight, coupled with the US enthusiasm for all things fresh and new, has not only led to a wine industry in which scarcely a week goes by without another new winery opening its doors, but one in which wine-makers are constantly aware of the style of wine the public wants to buy at any given moment. While his Italian cousin in Barolo remains wedded to the Nebbiolo vines he inherited from his father, the US producer can decide, almost from one vintage to the next, to switch production from Zinfandel to Chardonnay, or from Chenin Blanc to Cabernet Sauvignon. In Europe, even if legal, such an upheaval would not only be unlikely; it would also be time-consuming, as the land is normally left to rest for three or four years between the pulling-up of the old vines and the planting of new ones which, in their turn, would take another three or four years to begin producing good wine.

Go north-west, young man: *Vineyards in Oregon*

Sonorra signage: You're never far from a winery

there are regions of north America where *vinifera* grapes simply will not grow. In parts of Canada and the northern states of the USA, the winters can be so cold that the plants freeze to death. Elsewhere, perversely, the weather can be too good for them. One of the main reasons why Florida has become such a popular holiday destination also explains why that state has never been able to attract top-quality wine-makers. The virtual absence of winter denies the vines the essential period of dormancy that protects them against disease. Only one type of vine can survive in this tender trap, and this, a native variety with the wonderful name of Scuppernong, produces less than wonderful wine.

Earlier this century, the USA was broadly divided between those regions that could produce good wine from *vinifera* grapes, and those that could make poor-to-

THE BEAST IS BACK

*I*f the US wine industry owes much of its success to the efforts of the Davis campus of the University of California, it could reasonably complain about the unreliability of some of that establishment's supposedly authoritative advice and about its emphasis on wine-making rather than vine-growing and quantity rather than quality. Oregon's wine-makers, for example, were advised to grow Chardonnay vines appropriate to the warm climate of the Napa Valley but wholly wrong for the cooler conditions of the more northerly region. Far more catastrophic, though, was the way the UC Davis experts recommended the planting of a productive "AXR" rootstock, despite warnings from their counterparts in France that it might prove vulnerable to *phylloxera*.

Time and the aphid have proved the French right. In the 1980s, vineyards throughout the Napa Valley of California began to fall prey to a new "biotype" prosaically called *phylloxera B* whose progress through the valley could lead to the replanting of 75 per cent of its vines. For some middle-aged wine-makers, the pest has removed any chance of making wine from truly mature vines; others more philosophically relish the chance to reconsider the way their vineyards were originally planted – and to introduce new varieties of grapes.

Ironically, though, there will be another incidental beneficiary in the shape of some of California's other regions such as Sonoma, Santa Barbara and Mendocino whose growers rarely used the AXR rootstock.

In California, particularly, where the vineyards are almost all much younger, the switch is sometimes made far more simply, by a process known as "T-budding" which involves grafting a new variety on to the old one, possibly even for one vintage, producing two kinds of grape on the same rootstock.

This expertise at grafting vines might seem shockingly new-fangled to a European traditionalist but, ironically, harks right back to a historical link between European and US vine-growing – a link which was perhaps the most significant development in vinous world history.

Vines were growing on North American soil before the earliest European settlers arrived. These were of the *vitis labrusca* species – producing table grapes, rather than the wine-making *vitis vinifera* traditionally grown in Europe – hardy plants that were tough enough to survive cold winters and sweltering summers. In particular, they were resistant to various kinds of disease and pest, most notably the locally prevalent and voracious *phylloxera vastatrix*, a louse that simply loves to kill vines by chomping away at their roots.

Until the late nineteenth century, thanks to the ocean separating the two continents, the vineyards of Europe were as untroubled by the *phylloxera* as British kennels are by rabies. Then disaster struck: the louse was

carried over the water and, in the space of a few decades, lived up to the *vastatrix* part of its name by devastating almost all of Europe's traditional vine-growing regions.

All kinds of remedies were tried; ultimately the only avenues left open to the Europeans led back to the source of the problem. If the louse didn't kill the vines in America, why not plant these American vines and use them to make wine in Europe?

The answer to this was simple. Although the American vines were easy to grow and their grapes pleasant to eat, the wine produced from their grapes tasted rather awful. But it wasn't the grapes the Europeans were interested in; what they wanted was the rootstock on to which – and this was the clever part – they grafted their good *vinifera* vines. This combination of resistant American rootstock and quality *vinifera* vine was soon adopted by wine-makers everywhere. Today, almost every top-quality vineyard in the world (with the exception of areas of South America and the Antipodes and tiny pockets of Europe that escaped the attentions of the louse) is planted in this way.

Initially, this was thought to be a two-way solution, engendering visions among US planters of an America gushing forth quality *vinifera* wine wherever the hardy *labrusca* flourished. Unfortunately, however,

mediocre stuff from *labrusca*. Expertise in the nursery improved matters considerably by creating hybrid vines with one *labrusca* and one *vinifera* parent whose wines tasted better than those made from the former, but less good than those of the latter.

Similarly, increased knowledge of vine-growing and of cloning, and improved pest-icides and fungicides, permitted producers to plant *vinifera* vines in some regions where it had previously been impossible.

Today, there are vineyards in no fewer than 43 US states and in three regions of Canada. Of these, though, California remains far and away the most important in terms of both quality and quantity. It not only produces around 95 per cent of all the wine made in North America, but it is also the area in which two of the world's best oenological colleges have been established and where the country's greatest wines have all been made.

The supremacy of California is easily explained. Quite apart from the quality (and the useful diversity) of its climate, wine-making here has benefited from what might be called the Hollywood effect. The fact that Hollywood has a thriving film industry has encouraged thousands of talented and ambitious actors and directors to flock there – which has, in turn, helped to ensure Hollywood's continued success.

The Napa and Sonoma Valleys are the Hollywood of California's wine world, the magnets that have not only attracted wine-makers from other parts of the USA, but also such illustrious overseas investors as Baron Philippe de Rothschild of Château Mouton-Rothschild and a clutch of some of the best-known producers in Champagne. And, with every new release from every new winery, the "can-do" confidence grows; it's a foolhardy man who'll tell a top Napa Valley wine-maker that he'll never make a wine to compete with Château Pétrus or Le Montrachet. Quite often he's half-convinced that he's already made it – and has a quote from a well-known wine critic to prove it.

Over the last few years, however, Californians have begun to find themselves facing increasingly stiff domestic compe-tition from other states. Further north, Véronique Drouhin, one of the biggest names in Burgundy, is helping to prove how well Oregon's cool climate and red soil suit the Pinot Noir. Also on the western coast, Washington state's wine-makers are taking advantage of a com-pletely different set of climatic conditions to make classy Chardonnays, Sauvignons, Rieslings, Cabernet Sauvignons and varieties (especially Merlots) that also seem to flourish on the eastern seaboard, in the micro-climate the Gulf Stream annually creates on Long Island.

Throughout North America, this growing understanding of the varying climatic requirements of different types of grapes and the readiness of producers to explore new regions has led to the creation of *Appellation Contrôlée*-style districts called AVAs – Approved Viticultural Areas – each of which is supposed to have its own identifiable characteristics.

In some cases, as in Long Island and Carneros in California, both of which genuinely do have micro-climates of their own, the existence of their AVA designation makes perfect sense. Elsewhere, there are all sorts of curious boundary definitions that seem horribly reminiscent of the political way in which DOCs and DOCGs have been doled out in Italy.

In general, though, the scheme has been well-received. All the same, the prosaic "Approved Viticultural Area" does not have the same ring to it as, say, "*Premier Grand Cru*". Just as democratic America is fascinated by the class divisions of Europe, so there are a few US wine-makers who are beginning to murmur about a hierarchy of estates with some of the social nuances of, say, French wine law.

Such a development seems distant at present, but one never knows... The only certainty about North America is that whatever you saw and learned today will have changed by tomorrow. If not before.

Where's the beef? Springtime mustard in flower in a vineyard in the Napa Valley

CALIFORNIA

ACCORDING to atlases of North America, California is neither more nor less than one of the 50 states of the union. In reality, as anyone who has come into even the slightest contact with this uniquely privileged part of North America will have discovered, California is far more like a nation within a nation. And a highly successful one at that.

Apart from movies, computers and oranges, its 250,000 square kilometres (160,000 square miles) produce sufficient grapes to keep hospital bedsides amply supplied in several countries, while still allowing California's wineries to make this the sixth-biggest wine-producing nation on earth, with an annual production approaching some three billion bottles of wine.

As any Californian will readily tell you, this state has all of the attributes a farmer could ask for: an ideal climate – or rather a

Moving to the hills: *Duckhorn at Howell Mountain has opted to grow vines up on the slopes*

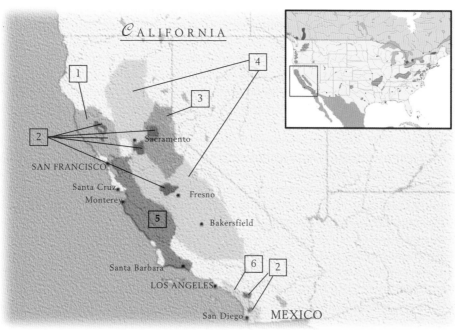

1	North Coast	4	Central Valley
2	Delimited AVA Wine Regions	5	Central Coast
3	Sierra Foothills	6	Southern California

range of different ideal climates – relatively inexpensive Mexican immigrant labour, two of the world's most advanced training colleges and plentiful local investment. Perhaps most valuably, though, California has the extraordinary self-confidence that comes from being the choicest segment of the chosen land that is the USA.

It was the brilliant Californian wines made by pioneering wineries like Mondavi, Stag's Leap, Heitz and Ridge in the 1970s that, more than anything else, helped to launch wine-making in the rest of the New World, and to revolutionize methods and attitudes in some of Europe's most traditional wineries and estates.

If California's wine industry is an undeniable success story, it unfortunately sometimes seems to have more in common with Hollywood than with Silicon Valley. Far too many wines have been made according to a formula that has worked elsewhere – like sequels to box-office hits or, very often, like the US remakes of French movies.

Ask almost any Californian wine-maker with aspirations to quality what styles he sells most easily and it's a dollar to a dime that top of his list will be Chardonnay and

Cabernet Sauvignon. Then wander out and look at what's being planted and grafted in the vineyards – that's right, more Cabernet and more Chardonnay.

Ask him about his ambitions and, all too often, you'll find that they are focused on making wines that will successfully compete with the best of Burgundy or Bordeaux – or more recently, the Rhône and Tuscany. Apart from the Zinfandel – California's "own" grape variety – there are far too few reds and whites that do not either closely conform to models already established in Europe – or represent "commercial" (for which, with white wines, you might often read "sweet") versions of those wines.

When the Australian wine-maker at Geyser Peak, reprising a formula that had worked at home in the Antipodes, introduced Semchard, a Bordeaux-meets-Burgundy blend of Sémillon and Chardonnay, the general reaction among his peers was that the public would never catch on to it; they'd be too busy wondering where to find Sémillon on the map. Even today, few competitors have so far had the courage to launch similarly offbeat blends.

If Chardonnay and Cabernet have been the object of too obsessive a focus, so has Napa, a politically defined county which is treated as though its every corner was somehow predestined to make better wine than that produced elsewhere in the state.

Fortunately for those of us who dread the idea of living in a world where wines all taste the same – even if that sole flavour were that of the finest Meursault or Pauillac – in the late 1980s and early 1990s, California in general and Napa in particular were given an unexpected opportunity to take a fresh look at the styles and wines they were making. The catastrophic reappearance of the *Phylloxera vastatrix* louse in vines which, according to the experts at the University of California, were supposed to resist it has led to the replanting of well over three-quarters of the Napa Valley.

It remains to be seen whether, when they come to choose what they are going to plant and where, the vine-growers and wine-makers find the courage required to explore new varieties, styles and blends, and to create wines that owe nothing to Bordeaux, Burgundy, or anywhere else.

THE HISTORY

Wine-making began in California in the late eighteenth century, following – or so it is generally believed – the arrival of Franciscan missionaries from Mexico. Initially, the grapes planted were the same, basic, Criolla variety that was grown in Mexico (though here it soon became known as the Mission) but, in the early 1800s, higher-quality French varieties were introduced from the east coast by an appropriately named Bordelais wine-maker called Jean-Louis Vignes, and an eccentric Hungarian who liked to be known as "Colonel" or "Count" Agoston Haraszthy and reputedly ended his days as a meal for alligators in Nicaragua.

However he died, Haraszthy's legacy to California's infant wine industry was a 250-hectare (400-acre) nursery, stocked with some 300 different types of grape brought back from a three-month expedition to Europe, and the still-functioning Buena

THROUGHOUT its early history, the Californian wine industry, like those of Australia and New Zealand, unashamedly labelled its wines as "Champagne", "Burgundy" and "Claret". Although this kind of labelling still goes on today – the giant Gallo winery has no compunction in selling "Hearty Red Burgundy" and the ludicrous "Blush Chablis" – the quality-conscious producers of the 1970s began to market their wines in a rather different way.

Faced with the choice of whether to use the names of European styles or of Californian towns and villages of which few people would ever have heard, they did neither. Instead they resorted to printing the names of the grape varieties from which the wines were made. Today, in a wine world awash with Cabernet Sauvignon and Chardonnay, it is worth recalling that Alsace is one of the few parts of Europe in which wine-makers have traditionally referred to grapes rather than places.

Labels on bottles of red Burgundy never referred to the Pinot Noir and few of the people who drank Château Latour had any reason or desire to know that it was principally made from grapes known as Cabernet Sauvignon and Merlot. What the Californians had done was to invent a new concept: "varietal labelling". Wines made from particularly popular grapes were dubbed the "fighting varietals".

Vista Winery in Sonoma County. Surprisingly, though, the one grape the Hungarian probably did not introduce to California was the Zinfandel, a variety which is thought to have originated in Italy as the Primitivo.

The mid-nineteenth century was the first heyday of Californian wine-making. Using Haraszthy's cuttings and the widely planted Mission grape, a large number of such familiar names as Paul Masson, Wente and Almaden dug the foundations of the industry we know today. In the 1870s, however, their progress was halted by the devastation of the vineyards by the *Phylloxera vastatrix* louse which had already begun to put a halt to wine-making in Europe. Half a century later, the louse's work was completed by the introduction of full-scale Prohibition in 1920.

The Prohibition years were a time of keen amateur wine-making, and of similarly keen overnight conversion to almost any religion that used sacramental wine. It was

Drive-in wine region: *This sign greets visitors to the Napa Valley*

Not just ornamental: *Newton Vineyards makes wines high above the Napa Valley*

wryly said that there was scarcely an apartment block in Manhattan that didn't have a resident rabbi or priest, and scarcely a household that wasn't experimenting with do-it-yourself kits that included a block of dried grapes and some powdered yeast, along with the strict injunction not to allow the two to come into contact with each other, lest they ferment.

After Repeal in 1933, although a few of the old-established wineries, such as Inglenook and Beaulieu, continued to produce wine from high-quality varieties, most preferred the more versatile table grapes that could be turned into poor-quality wine, juice or jelly depending on what the market demanded.

It was not until the 1960s and 1970s that a new generation of wine-makers began to explore the potential that Vignes and Haraszthy had revealed over a century earlier. The region that attracted most of their interest during those years was the Napa Valley, despite the fact that some of

the most successful pioneering producers, including Haraszthy, had made their wine in neighbouring Sonoma County.

Over the following couple of decades, the Napa Valley consolidated its reputation, attracting big-money investors whose architectural follies sometimes seemed to attract far more reverence than the wines produced in them deserved – and far too much public attention. By the mid-1990s, however, the return of the *phylloxera* louse to Napa's vineyards (other regions had planted more resistant rootstock) had helped to redress the balance. Today, sensible wine-buyers choose good wines produced throughout a wide variety of Californian regions.

The Regions

If far too many of California's wines taste alike, the regions where they are made could hardly be more varied. Visitors who drive up from San Francisco to the Napa Valley wander around the one or two well-known wineries – and imagine that they have "seen" vinous California. In fact, there

are vineyards and producers throughout the state, and even the big names in the Napa buy grapes from other regions to broaden their range.

The climate varies enormously, too. There are vineyards that are as cool as those of northern Germany, vineyards with growing periods similar to Bordeaux, and others which have everything in common with the oven-like conditions of north Africa. Elsewhere in the northern hemisphere, you might reasonably expect the temperature to rise as you head south. In California, latitude has far less of a role to play than the situation of the vineyard in relationship to the coast and to the range of mountains that runs parallel to it. Almost all of the best vineyards of the Napa Valley and Sonoma County benefit from the cooling effect of fogs. Without them, the viability of most of the state of California as a quality wine region would be very questionable.

Until recently, the majority of wine-makers tended to believe that the difference between any two wines lay in the grapes

One-Track Wines

California has a growing number of mavericks, thank goodness. Like the reactionaries who persist in using California's "own" variety to make big, dark, Zinfandel with spicy flavours encountered nowhere else, and the small group of individualists like Randy Grahm at Bonny Doone who are exploring such European varieties as the Syrah, the Viognier, the Nebbiolo and the Sangiovese. And, thankfully, there are people like Patrick Campbell at Laurel Glen and David Coleman at Adler Fels, who use the Chardonnay and Cabernet to make wines that do not fit the identikit picture dictated by the market.

Now that every winery has a Chardonnay or three, and grape prices regularly go through the roof (most producers buy their fruit from farmers), the variety's name stands in danger of losing its cachet. This became apparent in the late 1980s when the Sebastiani winery unblushingly launched a wine labelled "Domaine Chardonnay" that contained not a single drop of that variety; the effort was foiled by the authorities, but not without considerable discussion. Today, any wine labelled as Chardonnay, or as any other grape variety, has to contain at least 75 per cent of that grape. These rules have not prevented at least one successful winery from selling Chardonnay that tastes as though it is made from 100 per cent Muscat. Nor, for that matter, is there any legislation to deter producers from taking their own regions' names in vain. Ironically, a wine sold in the USA as Napa Ridge has to change its name to Coastal Ridge when it is exported to Europe, where the officials are rather fussy about the fact that, contrary to what one might suppose, it has little or nothing to do with the Napa Valley.

Fog alert: Pacific fogs cool the McDowell Valley

from which they were made, the style of wine-making and the climate. Today, acknowledging that maybe the Europeans who talked about such things had a point, they are giving greater recognition to the effect of the soil.

So, within each of California's wine-making regions, the authorities have allocated AVAs – "Approved Viticultural Areas" – in a manner that recalls a mediaeval monarch creating dukes and earls. The legitimacy of some AVAs, like Stags Leap in the Napa Valley, for example, is unquestionable; that of some others, like Lodi in the bulk-wine region of the Central Valley, smacks of local politics.

The Essentials
NAPA, SONOMA, LAKE & MENDOCINO COUNTIES

What to look for Top-class Cabernets, Chardonnays and Pinot Noirs.
Official quality Principal Napa AVAs and sub-AVAs are: Carneros (Napa and Sonoma); Rutherford; Oakville; Mount Veeder; Spring Mountain; Howell Mountain; Napa Valley; Stags Leap District; Atlas Peak; McDowell Valley; Potter Valley; Sonoma Alexander Valley; Chalk Hill; Dry Creek Valley; Knight's Valley; Los Carneros; Northern Sonoma; Russian River Valley; Sonoma Coast; Sonoma County Green Valley; Sonoma Mountain; Sonoma Valley; Mendocino and Lake; Cole Ranch; Clear Lake; Guenoc Valley; Anderson Valley.
Style Dry whites and reds, with small quantities of botrytized whites. Some sparkling blush rosé or white wines are also made. Wines tend to be rich and powerful with maximum varietal expression. Chardonnays have good fruit character and the best, particularly from the cool Carneros region, have good acidity and balance. At their best, the Sauvignons are fresh and grassy with an attractive softness. Some rich, intense, botrytized Johannisberg Rieslings can also be found. Napa County produces some of the finest North American reds, particularly good Cabernet Sauvignons. Good Pinots are made in the cool Carneros region which is shared by Sonoma. Wines from Sonoma are generally softer and more approachable than their Napa counterparts. Chardonnays are well structured with good fruit and acidity, and, at their best, are stunning. Quite good "Fumé-style" Sauvignons are also made. Cabernet Sauvignons tend to be soft and juicy, although denser and more austere styles are made. Excellent Zinfandels with rich, spicy varietal character, and seductively soft Merlots are produced by several wineries. Pinot Noirs can be spectacularly good, too.
Cultivation Vines tend to be grown at altitudes ranging from sea level near the bay to 125 m (409 ft) at Calistoga. Soils consist of gravel loams in the north and more fertile silt loams in the south. Most vines in Sonoma are grown on the floors or the gentle lower slopes of the Sonoma and Russian River Valleys. Soils vary considerably from loams to alluvial deposits; there are also local varieties such as Dry Creek Conglomerate.
Grape varieties *Red*: Cabernet Sauvignon, Merlot, Pinot Noir, Zinfandel, Syrah, Petite Sirah, Grenache, Barbera, Sangiovese, Alicante Bouschet, Cabernet Granc, Carignan, Gamay Beaujolais, Malbec; *White*: Chardonnay, Sauvignon Blanc, Chenin Blanc, Johannisberg Riesling, Gewürztraminer, Muscat, Sémillon, Pinot Blanc, French Colombard, Viognier.
Production/maturation Methods, like the size of wineries, vary widely, although small "boutique" wineries increasingly tend to employ "European" methods (including natural yeasts, barrel-fermentation etc.) where possible, while large firms use the latest, high-tech methods.
Longevity *Red*: many are approachable when young, but the best are capable of ageing for up to 20 years, though some tannic reds have proved to be surprisingly short-lived. *White*: At their best (Simi, Kistler, Sonoma Cutrer, Saintsbury, Mondavi, Beringer, Clos du Val Chardonnays, some Trefethens) they can last for 10 or more years. Others have died early.
Vintage guide *Red*: 74, 76, 84, 85, 87, 88, 89, 90, 93, 95; *White*: 89, 91, 92, 94, 95.
My Top 86 *Napa*: Caymus, Cuvaison, Beringer, Dominus (post-1990), Dunn, Flora Springs, Heitz, Long, Mayacamas, Mount Veeder, Château Potells, Robert Mondavi, Joseph Phelps, Silver Oak, Stag's Leap Wine Cellars, Sterling (Reserve wines), Newton, Saintsbury, Fetzer, Château Montelena, Crichton Hall, Niebaum Coppola, Peter Michael, Schramsberg, Grgich Hills, Hills, Forman, Cain 5, Franciscan, Beringer, Clos du Val, Shafer, La Jota, Acacia, Duckhorn (post-1990), Far Niente, Lamborne Family Vineyards, Frog's Leap, Opus One, Villa Mount Eden, Chappellet, Mumm Domaine Napa (good value), Domaine Chandon (recent wines), Atlas Peak, Spottswoode, Kent Rasmussen, Swanson; *Sonoma*: Alexander Valley Vineyards, Buena Vista (Chardonnay), de Loach, Chalk Hill, Gundlach Bundschu, Carmenet, Arrowood, Benziger, Voss, Château St Jean, Nalle, Clos du Bois, Dry Creek, Laurel Glen, Mark West, Matanzas Creek, Ravenswood, Sonoma Cutrer, Kistler, Preston, Iron Horse, Kenwood, Quivira, Simi, Rochioli, Joseph Swan, Seghesio (Zinfandel), Duxoup, Gallo Sonoma (single-vineyard wines), Jordan ("J" sparkling and Cabernet), Rafanelli (Zinfandel), Geyser Peak, Williams Selyem (Pinot Noir), Marimar Torres; *Other*: Monteviña, Madrona, Scharffenberger, Domaine Roederer, Calera, Jekel.

Napa Valley

Napa is about the same size as the Médoc, but that is only one of several parallels between the two regions: both are uninspiringly flat, though Napa has the advantage of being surrounded by picturesque hills; both have large numbers of impressive buildings associated with their wines; and both regularly produce a limited number of stunning red wines – and far larger amounts of frankly ordinary fare.

There are, however, some equally crucial differences. The climate in the Médoc is relatively constant from one end to the other, while Napa includes regions as warm as North Africa and as cool as Germany. In the Médoc, prices are based on a well-established hierarchy; in the Napa, they often have rather more to do with the skills of the winery's architect, label designer and marketing team.

So, my advice is to forget about Napa as

Gothic romance: Beringer has one of the oldest buildings in the Napa Valley

an appellation – or treat it with no more respect than you would the Médoc – and concentrate instead on the sub-regions and producers that have proved their worth over time. There are some really special vineyards here, both on the valley floor, such as those around Oakville, Rutherford and Yountville, and in Stags Leap, as well as the extraordinary Martha's Vineyard where Heitz produced a 1974 Cabernet Sauvignon which was one of the finest red wines I have ever tasted. Other wineries to follow include Caymus, Swanson and the Mondavi-Rothschild Opus One.

Elsewhere on the flatter land, however, the soil is often too productive and grapes often simply fail to mature properly, developing plenty of alcohol, while never losing the stringy character of unripe skins. Until quite recently, these unbalanced wines were treated over-charitably by local critics who believed that they would soften after a few years in the cellar. Unfortunately, time told a different story and, while California's great reds from producers like Mondavi and

Beaulieu's Georges de Latour Reserve wines stayed the course magnificently, the tough youngsters merely turned directly into embittered pensioners before their time.

Today, while acknowledging the potential of the best parts of the valley floor, producers here, as in other parts of the New World, have increasingly begun to head for the hills – to regions like Mount Veeder where Mayacamas, Mount Veeder, Château Potelle and the Hess Collection wines are made, and to Howell Mountain where La Jota is a name to watch. Given time, I am sure it will be from these hillsides that some of Napa's best and most sought-after wines will be made, long after the lustre has worn off some of today's less well-sited superstars.

For other top producers, see the Essentials box.

Carneros

White wines are made throughout Napa with widely varying success: Frog's Leap and Franciscan both, for example, show how

brilliantly Chardonnay can perform without the addition of cultured yeasts, and Swanson and Beringer have both hit the target impressively with this variety. Even so, for consistency, few would argue that the one part of the Napa Valley which bears comparison with the greatest white-wine regions on earth is Carneros. Here the mists that roll in reliably from the bay keep the temperatures low enough to suit both the Chardonnay and Pinot Noir – and, for most producers, to deter even the notion of growing Cabernet, though Cuvaison has made some fine Merlot to set alongside its Chardonnay.

To Carneros's credit, too, this is a region whose producers take a collective attitude towards quality, jointly producing, for example, a prototypical Pinot Noir to serve as a benchmark for any winery attempting to make wine from this trickiest of red varieties. For a taste of what Carneros can do, head straight for Saintsbury's matchless Pinots and Chardonnays, and for the wines of Acacia, Kent Rasmussen, Etude, Carneros Creek (Fleur de Carneros) and the excellent Domaine Carneros fizz.

Sonoma

If Napa has happily taken the credit for Carneros, few non-Californian wine-buffs are aware that this region actually – like the Montrachet vineyard in Burgundy – straddles two counties: Napa and the lesser-known Sonoma, where Agoston Haraszthy made wine at the Buena Vista winery.

True lovers of Californian wines have, however, long known about Sonoma. Their cellars probably included bottles of Chardonnay from wineries such as Simi, Clos du Bois, Kistler, Hanzell and Sonoma Cutrer, Sauvignon from Dry Creek and Adler Fels, Zinfandel from Ravenswood, Joseph Swan, Nalle, Quivira and Rafanelli, Merlot from Matanzas Creek, Cabernet from Simi and Kenwood, Bordeaux blends from Carmenet and Laurel Glen, Pinot Noir from wineries like Rochioli and Duxoup and sparkling wine from Iron Horse and Jordan.

If some or most of these names are unfamiliar to you, I'm not surprised; that's what Sonoma is all about. If Napa does its best to be, like the Médoc, a couple of parallel roads punctuated by big-name wineries, Sonoma is far more like St Emilion and Sauternes: a fragmented region that's full of often small-scale discoveries, some of which produce tiny quantities of top-class wine.

In the mid-1990s, however, Sonoma was yanked from Napa's shadow by the arrival of a giant, in the shape of a huge vineyard physically remodelled and planted by E & J Gallo who are now marketing the region's name for all it is worth. Gallo's first efforts in Sonoma are already impressive – light-years away from the dull fare from its base in Modesto.

Sub-regions to look out for are Russian River (a cool region for Chardonnay, Pinot Noir and fizz), Dry Creek (Sauvignon Blanc and Zinfandel), Alexander Valley (Chardonnay, Cabernet and Merlot – especially from Clos du Bois, Simi and Geyser Peak),

Running parallel: The Sonoma Valley and vines at Hacienda Winery

Sonoma Mountain (Cabernet from Laurel Glen), Sonoma Valley (Cabernet and Zinfandel from Kenwood) and Knight's Valley (Cabernet from Beringer).

Lake County

Taking its name – and a welcoming cooling effect – from the biggest lake in the state, this is one of the most quietly interesting regions of California. The actress Lillie Langtry started wine-making here around a century ago, and a label depicting her face still helps to sell bottles of Cabernet Sauvignon and Chardonnay made at the Guenoc Winery. The Kendall Jackson winery needs no such help to sell its wines; it relies instead on making "dry" white wines that strike Europeans as tasting positively sweet. Today, another up-and-coming winery to watch is Konocti, whose lesser-priced wines can be among the best value in the state.

Mendocino

One of the frequently quoted "facts" about this schizophrenic region which, through a fluke of geology, can produce rich reds and lean whites, is that marijuana actually features in official records as one of the county's most widely grown crops. Well, I'll believe it – given the laid-back, 1970s atmosphere that still prevails throughout

The Essentials

The Essentials
SOUTH CENTRAL, SOUTHERN &
OTHER PARTS OF CALIFORNIA

What to look for Rich Zinfandels, quirky wines from Rhône varieties, and everyday jug wines.
Official quality AVAs: Edna Valley; Paso Robles; Santa Maria Valley; Santa Ynez Valley; York Mountain; San Pasqual Valley; South Coast; Temecula; Arroyo Seco; Carmel Valley; Chalone; Cienega Valley; Lime Kiln Valley; Livermore Valley; Monterey; Paicines; San Benito; San Lucas; Santa Cruz Mountains; Sierra Foothills, El Dorado; Fiddletown; Shenandoah Valley; Merced; Clarksburg; Lodi; Madera; Merritt Island; Solano-Green Valley; Suisun Valley.
Style The warm South Central Coast region produces rich, ripe and powerful wines with plenty of varietal character. Chardonnays are rich and toasty while Johannisberg Rieslings can be either tangy and grapey, yet still dry, or luscious and rich when late-harvested. Reds are generally good but unexciting with warm and rounded fruit flavours. Exceptions are the Pinot Noirs and Zinfandels grown in the higher-altitude locations of San Luis Obispo, which have intense fruit flavours because of the longer growing season. Small amounts of fine dessert wine are also produced. Whites can show good varietal character with plenty of fruit extract and good acidity. The Chardonnays, in particular, are full of flavour and the complex examples from Chalone and Mount Eden rank amongst the best made anywhere in the States. Some juicy Cabernet Sauvignons are made, but the region is better-known for its Zinfandels and Pinot Noirs, the former rich in berry fruit and needing aging, and the latter packed with velvety fruit. The remarkable Bonny Doon vineyard produces some brilliant wines, notably a rich, perfumed "Vin de Glacière" sweet style and a large range of Rhône varietals including Syrah, Marsanne and Roussanne. The Central Valley produces commercial "jug" wine but could, particularly around Lodi, make better-quality fare if given the chance and effort.
Climate The coastal area is generally warm, though cooler at altitude or where fog encroaches inland.
Cultivation Soils are largely fertile, sandy or silty loams. Hillside locations, generally south-facing, are favoured in the South Central Coast area.
Grape varieties *Red*: Cabernet Sauvignon, Barbera, Pinot Noir, Syrah, Sangiovese, Carignan, Napa Gamay, Grenache, Zinfandel, Mourvèdre; *White*: Chardonnay, Chenin Blanc, French Colombard, Riesling, Sauvignon Blanc, Gewürztraminer, Sémillon, Silvaner, Pinot Blanc.
Production/maturation The coastal area uses oak for maturation and is a hotbed of experimentation with premium grape varieties, notably those from the Rhône. Bonny Doon is a fine example of this kind of innovative wine-making. The larger producers of the Central Valley tend to use high-volume equipment that is ill-suited to producing quality wine.
Longevity *Jug wines*: drink immediately; *Whites*: up to 10 years for the better-quality Chardonnays; *Reds*: up to 15 years for the top wines.
Vintage guide *Red*: 74, 76, 84, 85, 87, 88, 89, 90, 93, 95; *White*: 89, 91, 92, 94.
My Top 21 Edna Valley Vineyard, Firestone, Carey, Sanford, Foxen, Qupé, Zaca Mesa, Au Bon Climat, Meridian, Rancho Sisquoc, Byron, Ojai, Bonny Doon, Wild Horse, Chalone, Jekel, Mount Eden, Ridge, Maison Deutz, Martin Brothers, Central Valley Quady.

Some talk of Alexander: *La Colline Biaci, Alexander Valley*

the region. Just take a look at those *Easy Rider* chopper bikes parked outside the (excellent) micro-brewery in Hopland – and look at the Woodstock hairstyles sported by their owners. But the 1970s ethos runs deeper than that: this is where some of the early ecological ideals have survived – in the form of California's first major organic vineyard which was started here by the dynamic Fetzer family.

Fetzer hits the mark with Chardonnays and red blends, while Parducci produces a textbook, spicy Petite Sirah; for many, though, the region's most impressive wines come with bubbles. This is where the Champagne house of Roederer set up shop, and it is the place to find Scharffenberger, maker of another of California's best fizzes. The coastal range protects red-wine districts from the cooling fog, while a gap in the hills allows it to have its beneficial effect on the heat-sensitive white grapes in the Anderson Valley. So, when the obsession for Chardonnay eases up, this may be the place to look for Alsace-style Gewürztraminer (try the ones from Husch and Navarro), Riesling (Hidden Cellars) and Pinot Gris.

Sierra Foothills

A large region to the east of the Napa Valley, this is old gold-mining country where, if you hurry, in El Dorado, Fiddletown and the Shenandoah Valley of Amador County, you can still find thick, port-like Zinfandels made the way they liked them in the days when real men panned for gold and never did the washing-up. Sutter Home atones for the crime of inventing so-called "white Zinfandel" (most examples of which taste nothing like that grape) by using the variety to make top-class red. Monteviña and Madrona are other names to look for, as is Karly and, for Italian varieties, Noceto.

The Bay Area

Some of the roots of California's wine-making are to be found here, in Livermore, in wineries like Wente and Concannon, both of which were founded in the 1880s. Today, Concannon still produces some really fine, full-flavoured Cabernet and brilliant Petite Sirah. Wente preferred for a while to con-centrate its efforts on more commercial fare, though more recent efforts have included some classier reds.

For the jewel in the region's crown, though, get a good map or directions (I get lost every time), head for Santa Clara County, and drive up the mountain track to the Ridge winery. It's grown a bit grander in recent years, but visitors are still surprised to find the wooden shed that serves as headquarters for one of California's best-known wineries – and vineyards situated almost precisely on the San Andreas fault. Some spectacular Zinfandel, Cabernet and Merlot is made here and in vineyards elsewhere in the state. If I had to choose a wine from just one Californian producer, it would be a Ridge Zinfandel.

North Central Coast

Once written off as too cold and dry and the source of "vegetal" wines, the region of Monterey to the south of San Francisco actually has conditions that vary from those of Champagne to those of the Rhône; the trick has been to sort out precisely which grapes to grow where, and how to train the vines to grow best. Jekel was the pioneer here and, after a sticky period, it's a name to look for again for juicy Cabernets and clean, fruity Rieslings produced in Arroyo Seco. Another trailblazer close by was Chalone whose founders planted Pinot Noir and Chardonnay on one of California's rare bits of limestone and at a cool 600-m (2,000-ft) altitude.

For another version of limestone Pinot Noir, head for the AVA of San Benito County where Joseph Jensen of Calera makes individual-vineyard examples of Burgundy standard, as well as a fine Viognier. And don't miss out on Bonny Doon, in mountainous Santa Cruz County, where Randall Grahm is producing wittily labelled Rhône- and Italian-style reds that have helped to spawn a movement unofficially known as ABC – "Anything But Chardonnay".

SOUTH CENTRAL COAST

Santa Barbara

Santa Barbara is an old region that has recently come into its own. Once dismissed as being too cool for quality wine, it has two AVAs, Santa Maria and Santa Ynez, which have become a focus of attention for would-be Pinot Noir- and Chardonnay-makers, following the success of Au Bon Climat in Santa Maria and Sanford in Santa Ynez. In fact, while the Pinot can thrive in similar conditions in the two regions, they actually enjoy quite different climates. Where Santa Maria is generally mild, as Firestone has

proved, parts of Santa Ynez can be warm enough to make ripe, Bordeaux-style reds, too. Other names to watch out for include Carey, Qupé (source of pioneering Rhône-style reds), Meridian (Pinot Noir), Robert Mondavi's Byron winery and Kendall Jackson's Cambria, Foxen and Rancho Sisquoc.

Paso Robles, San Luis Obispo

Dick Graff, founder of Chalone and a Burgundiphile to his fingertips, found a bit more Burgundy-style limestone at Edna Valley and produced one of California's biggest, butteriest Chardonnays. Today, the butter is a little less rich, but this is still a terrific wine, as is the Maison Deutz fizz made in Arroyo Grande, directly to the south west, which takes advantage of chalky soil conditions far closer than most in California to those its parent company is familiar with in Champagne.

Parts of Arroyo Grande are warm enough to ripen Zinfandel but, for reds like this, Paso Robles is a far better choice, which helps to explain why the owners of Château de Beaucastel in Châteauneuf-du-Pape have picked this region to plant their Rhône varieties. Elsewhere the accent is on rich reds, especially Cabernets, Zinfandels, Syrahs (good value from Meridian), and Italian varieties such as Barbera, Nebbiolo and Sangiovese. Names to follow include Wild Horse, Eberle and Martin Brothers, who make good Sauvignon Blanc and Nebbiolo.

Central Valley and Southern California

The warm, fertile, "jug-wine" region of the Central Valley produces around two-thirds of California's wines, almost none of it worthy of note. It is hard to say quite why the Central Valley wines should be so much poorer than those produced in the apparently similar conditions of Australia's irrigated riverland regions, though I suspect that quality could be improved by a little more work in the vineyard, and by less heavy-handed, industrial wine-making by the major wineries. Unfortunately, tasting the wines, it is hard to believe that most of the producers are even trying to make anything of better than very basic quality. Robert Mondavi's white Woodbridge wines, for example, though pleasant, bear far less family resemblance to the Reserve wines produced in Napa than do the cheapest Penfold's or BRL Hardy reds to the top-of-the-range wines from those Australian firms.

It may teach some of these bigger

Ceviche

Marinated fish salad

*W*ith its abundant fish, shellfish, vegetables and fruit, California is the most innovative part of America as far as cookery is concerned. With its emphasis on lightness and freshness, it has pioneered a healthy style of eclectic cuisine that is now increasingly popular elsewhere.

SERVES 6–8 AS A STARTER

1 lb/ 500 g white fish fillets, skinned and boned (halibut, monkfish, hake or cod are good)
8 oz/225 g scallops
Juice of 4 limes
8 tbsp olive oil
1 garlic clove, peeled and crushed
1/2 tsp oregano
1/2 tsp dried thyme
1 tsp ground coriander seeds
1/2 green pepper, seeded and finely chopped
1/2 red pepper, seeded and finely chopped
4 spring onions
2 tomatoes, chopped
2 tbsp fresh parsley, finely chopped
Freshly ground black pepper to taste

Cut the fish and scallops into thin slices and place in a large glass or ceramic serving dish. Pour the lime juice over the fish, cover the dish with clingfilm and put in the refrigerator for 2 hours. Mix the remaining ingredients and stir into the marinated fish. Re-cover and refrigerate for at least an hour before serving.

companies a lesson to learn that when an Australian wine-maker was commissioned to make a set of wines at the Arciero winery, under the "King's Canyon" label, the resulting efforts were good enough to beat pricier wines from starrier regions to pick up medals at the 1996 International Wine Challenge in London.

The only other name worth remembering is that of Quady, the winery that makes spectacular, sweet Essensia Orange Muscat. Southern California is mostly hot and dry, too, but the Temecula Valley has a cooler micro-climate, allowing Callaway to make good, crisp wines.

PACIFIC NORTH-WEST

IF ANYONE ever tries to convince you that all Americans are the same, send him or her on a journey north from Los Angeles to Boise, Idaho – from the hub of the world's movie business to a place where the proud boast of every car registration plate is that its driver lives in a state that's good at growing potatoes. Along the way, your bigoted friend will have driven through the northern European climate of Oregon and western Washington State (Seattle's unofficial emblem is a slug) and across the mountains to what looks like desert land where the only successful agriculture happens beneath huge circular irrigators.

The people he'll have met will be quite unlike those southern Californians too. Oregon is the kind of country where the nearest you get to a fashion statement is the purchase of a pair of sandals and an annual trim for the beard. In Washington State there will have been successful wine-makers with a winery that's a converted garage and a home-made basket-press cobbled together from scrap bits of stainless steel. And then there are the empty spaces of Idaho, where Clint Eastwood runs to get away from Hollywood...

OREGON

Oregon is Pinot Noir country, and the red soil of the Dundee hills in this part of the Willamette Valley has produced Pinots that have held their own in tastings against top-class Burgundies. But as recently as the early 1960s, the only grape thought suited to the cold, damp conditions here was the Riesling, and the potential of even this relatively hardy variety was disputed by the experts at the University of California, who more or less discounted Oregon's chances to make it in the big time of quality wine-making.

In 1965, however, a Califomia-trained wine-maker called David Lett, recognizing similarities between the Oregon climate and that of Burgundy, resolved to prove those experts wrong by establishing the Willamette Valley's first vineyards – and planting them with Pinot Noir vines. Over the following two decades Lett was joined by a succession of fellow pioneers, almost all of whom shared his passion for the elusive wild raspberry flavour. Almost from the beginning, these producers proved successful in replicating Burgundy in a remarkable number of ways. Their estates were small, their vintages were varied (though astonishingly similar to those of Burgundy itself), their prices were high, and they often had little idea of why one wine had turned out to be so much better than the next.

Partly as an attempt to expand their knowledge, and partly as a piece of public relations, the Oregonians launched an annual Pinot Noir celebration in the small town of McMinville and invited wine-makers from around the world to participate in seminars covering every aspect of wine-making. It was a brilliant coup, which bought instant credibility for the region – and helped to encourage Robert Drouhin and his daughter to come and make what has become the state's top Pinot Noir in their own winery.

Despite the attention Oregon received from US pundits (Robert Parker has an interest in a winery here), and despite the competition success of a number of wines, for a long time the state promised far more than it could deliver. Its hand-crafted, high-price Pinots often tasted too similar to basic rather than top-class Burgundy; wine-lovers seeking value for money often found it more easily in the increasingly successful efforts from California.

But the Oregonians are nothing if not stubborn experimenters. Techniques were sharpened, new clones tried and, sure enough, a growing number of wineries began to prove that what frequent visitor James Halliday said of the Yarra Valley was just as true here: this is one of the rare places in which the Pinot Noir has found a natural home.

Other grapes are looking better too, especially now that the Chardonnay clone mistakenly proposed by the experts from UC Davis in California is being replaced by

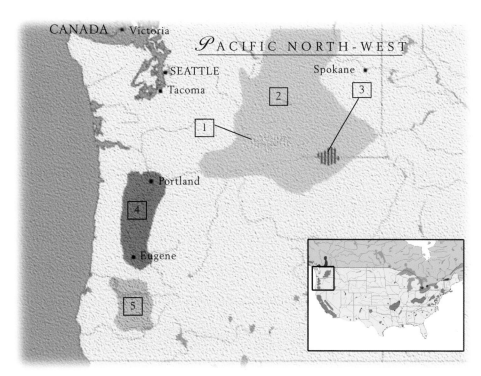

1   Yakima Valley

2   Columbia Valley

3   Walla Walla Valley

4   Willamette Valley

5   Umpqua Valley

one that ripens properly in Oregon (Shafer's and Bethel Heights make good ones). The Pinot Gris (especially from Adelsheim and Eyrie) is worth watching, as are fizzes from producers like Australia's Brian Croser at Argyll and Laurent Perrier. Oregon's wines will never be cheap – the cost of land and the often unfriendly climate both keep prices high – but nor are the wines they most closely resemble. The combination of keenness, soil and climate give them every reason to be world-class.

Oregon: *The aptly-named Red House Vineyard*

WASHINGTON

Washington State is the place to bring anyone who ever fell asleep during their geography classes. You remember the teacher saying something about rain forests? Well, Seattle's got one. And you recall a reference to "rain shadows"? Well, there's a king-sized one of those too – on the east side of the Cascade Mountains. In fact, when you consider the Scotland-meets-Algeria mixture of climates, you might fairly conclude that the person who snored most loudly during those lessons was the one who drew up the state boundaries.

The Cascade Mountains provide the key to Washington State. On the west, the condi-tions are cool, damp and attractive only to a small group of masochists led by Joan Wolverton of Salishan Vineyards, who, like her counterparts in Oregon, believes that this kind of "marginal" weather does wonders for grape varieties such as Pinot Noir and Chardonnay.

It is the area east of the Cascades, however, that produces most of the wines. At first glance this looks like land in which nothing thirstier than a cactus could ever be farmed. But there's sophisticated irrigation from the nearby river; half-mile long sprinklers pivot on the centre of the vineyards, feeding them a steady mist of life-preserving moisture. Little could be further from the European model of a vineyard, but the results speak for themselves.

Mind you, no good wine was made here until 1969 – partly because the farmers had not troubled to plant high-quality grape varieties, and partly because local laws effectively prevented producers from selling their wine anywhere other than in bars. These rules more or less obliged would-be wine-drinkers to make their own. So, Columbia, one of the state's biggest wineries, was started by a group of academics who formed themselves a company they named Associated Vintners.

From the beginning, one of Washington's greatest successes has been the Riesling, with some wonderful late-harvest versions being made by Kiona, for example. But Washington's wine-makers are having just as much success with buttery Chardonnay (try the one from Hogue Cellars), green, gooseberryish Sauvignon Blanc (from Columbia Crest) and, perhaps most par-ticularly, Merlot (from Gordon Brothers, Stewart, Quilceda Creek and Leonetti), Sémillon and Gewürztraminer. At their best these wines are packed with fruit, but with a bite of fresh acidity often lacking in California. And don't underestimate the seriousness of these producers: wines like those of Woodward Canyon and Leonetti achieve world-class complexity.

Land in Washington is cheap, the weather and irrigation are reliable and the wine-makers are – so far at least – unaffected by the hype that has pushed prices up elsewhere, so the future for tasty, affordable wine looks bright.

IDAHO

Idaho's wines come mostly from the savagely barren Snake Valley in the east of the state, from vineyards planted at an altitude of 2,300 ft (700 m). According to the Winkler scale of heat units, which acknowledges only the average amount of heat received by the grapes, this oughtn't to matter. In practice, however, this is T-shirt at noon, sweater-at-seven country; when the temperature is too hot or too cold the fruit simply fails to ripen. So despite the fact that the sun-tanned Idaho residents complain of the highest incidence of skin cancer in the USA, the grapes they grow produce wine that tastes as though it comes from somewhere far cooler.

One solution has been to ship in grapes from Washington and Oregon – which one producer famously forgot to mention on its label. Today Ste Chapelle – the winery responsible for that lapse of memory – uses local fruit to make good sparkling wine and Riesling, and "Washington Cabernet" now

---

openly and unashamedly graces the labels of its deep, rich reds. The Rose Creek winery has also been spectacularly successful with Cabernet, and Hell's Canyon is doing well with a light Chardonnay many a Californian would be proud to have made.

THE OTHER WINES OF NORTH AMERICA

COMPARED TO Australia where five out of seven states lay justifiable claim to making world-class wine, in the US the focus is pretty tightly on just three: California, which produces 95 per cent of the nation's wine, Washington State and Oregon. So it may come as a surprise to learn that there are wine-makers in some 43 other US states all doing their best to compete. Some are quietly outclassing the west-coast superstars; many simply serve the vinous needs of a loyally undemanding local populace, while others recall Dr Johnson's comment about a dog walking on its hind legs: "It is not done well; but you are surprised to find it done at all".

THE NORTH-EAST

There are two main wine-making regions of New York State: the Finger Lakes in the far north of the state and Long Island just over the bridge from Manhattan. The former area can be very chilly, but it produces good Germanic-style whites and, at the Wagner winery, some wonderfully fruit-salady Chardonnay. The Gulf Stream gives Long Island a Bordeaux-like micro-climate that allows wine-makers such as Alex Hargrave to make top-class Merlot and Chardonnay. This is curious country where land is traditionally used either to grow potatoes or for million-dollar holiday homes for week-ending New Yorkers. If wineries survive as the meat in this sandwich, this could be one of the most exciting small wine-making regions in the USA.

Elsewhere on the north-east coast, Connecticut has lots of hybrids and *labrusca* and the Crosswoods winery, which makes good Chardonnay, Pinot Noir and Gamay. Massachusetts is the region where, in 1602, Bartholomew found a vine-covered island he called Martha's Vineyard. Today various *vinifera* are grown and made into wine here by the Chicama winery; their Chardonnay is particularly good.

New Hampshire has little to offer the wine-lover, but several wineries in New Jersey are trying hard with *vinifera*. The best of these are probably Tewksbury, Renault

New York, New England: The Finger Lakes (above) and a Vermont winery (left)

and Alba. William Penn believed that the state to which he gave his name could make wine "as good as any European countries of the same latitude", but there appeared to be few grounds for that confidence until this century. Today good Pennsylvania Rieslings are made on Lake Erie, while less hardy varieties do better in the south-east of the state. Names to look out for here are Chadds Ford, Allegro, Naylor and Presque Isle.

THE SOUTH-EAST

Despite the curious allocation of the first AVA on the east coast to Mississippi, a state where all of the wine is made from the low-quality local Muscadine, there are few friendly places for quality grapes in the south-east. In Virginia, however, there is still a vineyard and winery at Monticello, the old home of the wine-loving President Jefferson. This state is gearing itself up to compete with Oregon and New York state as a good cool-climate region. Whites are generally better than reds, but wineries such as Meredyth have been successful with Cabernet Sauvignon. Elsewhere, Monthray Wine Cellars have made Riesling Ice Wine in Maryland, while in Arkansas, where the winters can be cold enough to kill fruit trees, there are warmer micro-climates that allow the Post Winery and Wiederkehr Wine Cellars to persevere with Cabernet Sauvignon.

THE MID-WEST

Few of the states here have proved successful with *vinifera*, but cool Michigan has wineries such as Boskydel, Fenn Valley and

Tabor Hill making good Riesling, while Ohio, once the biggest wine-making state of the Union, has Firelands, Grand River and Markko, all of which are making impressive Chardonnay and are progressing with other quality varieties.

THE SOUTH-WEST

The wines of Texas and Arizona stand as tributes to the self-belief of the residents of these states; it's a brave man who'll tell a Texan that he can't make anything bigger and better than a Californian. So, despite the hot climate of both states, cool, high-altitude sites have been found where decent, if not great, wines can be made. In Arizona, look for Cabernet Sauvignon made near Tucson by Sonoita Vineyard and Riesling produced in the Four Corners region by RW Webb. In Texas, a joint venture between the Bordeaux firm of Cordier and the State University has made successful Sauvignon Blanc, and Pheasant Ridge and Llano Estacado have produced good reds.

Hawaiian wine may sound like a joke, but the Tedeschi Vineyard makes sparkling wine using the Carnelian grape. It is not one of the world's greatest fizzes, but it's well enough made.

CANADA

The readiness of Canadians to drink "Canadian" wine made from imported grape concentrate for a long time offered little incentive to quality-oriented producers to test their skills against winter temperatures cold enough to kill vines. Fortunately, a few wineries in Ontario and British Columbia have persevered with vineyards situated in warmer micro-climates – and been rewarded with prize-winning sparkling wines, Rieslings and Chardonnays, and even some promising reds. The explanation lies, as in Long Island, in micro-climates where conditions can be surprisingly friendly to grapes. The best wines – so far – are white, late-harvested and – a speciality this – ice wine. And if you don't believe how good they can be, seek out a bottle of Summerhill's British Columbian fizz or of Reif Estate 1993 Ice Wine which, despite being made from the Vidal, a hybrid variety despised by Eurocrats, managed to beat a number of classic Europeans to take one of a small number of gold medals at the 1995 International Wine Challenge in London.

The Essentials
THE REST OF
THE UNITED STATES AND CANADA

Official quality North-east AVAs: Catoctin, Cayuga Lake, Central Delaware Valley, Cumberland Valley, Fennville, Finger Lakes, Grand River Valley, Hudson River Region, Isle St George, Kanawha River Valley, Lake Erie, Lake Michigan Shore, Lancaster Valley, Leelanau Peninsula, Linganore, Loramie Creek, Martha's Vineyard, Monticello, Northern Neck George Washington Birthplace, North Fork of Long Island, Ohio River Valley. Other AVAs: *Arizona:* Sonoita; *Arkansas:* Altus, Arkansas Mountain, Ozark Mountain; *Mississippi:* Mississippi Delta; *Missouri:* Augusta, Hermann, Old Mission Peninsula, Ozark Highlands; *New Mexico:* Middle Rio Grande Valley, Mimbres Valley; *Texas:* Bell Mountain, Fredericksburg, Mesilla Valley; *Canada,* despite a laudable voluntary Vintners' Quality Alliance created by the wineries, is hampered by having archaic liquor legislation instead of quality-control laws. The main wine-producing areas are: Niagara Peninsula, Ontario; Okanagan Valley, British Columbia; Alberta and Nova Scotia.
Style The white wines produced in the states of the Atlantic seaboard tend to be crisp and light, although the Hudson River area produces richer, toasty Chardonnays. Reds are similarly light and acidic. The best wines come from Long Island, notably some lovely grassy Sauvignons and crisp, intense and oaky Chardonnays. Cabernet Sauvignons and Pinot Noirs tend to be rather green. Sound sparkling wines are produced along with tiny quantities of sweet Riesling or Gewürztraminer. Elsewhere, most wines are made from classic grape varieties with some creamy Chardonnays coming from Texas and decent Cabernet Sauvignons from Arkansas and Texas. Both these states show good potential for the future. In Canada, plenty of *labrusca* wine is produced although some good dry whites and light fruity reds are made in the Niagara region. Canadian Chardonnays often show good fruit character with a restrained oaky richness. Rieslings can be made dry or rich and honeyed if harvested late as "ice wines". Some good-quality sparkling wines are produced from Chardonnay. Light, fruity reds are made from Pinot Noir, Gamay and Cabernet Sauvignon. Imported grape concentrate is also used. *Labrusca* varieties are used for sparkling and sweet wines.
Climate Obviously, varies considerably. In the north-east, it is continental, with severe winters moderated by the tempering effects of the Atlantic Ocean and the large areas of inland waters, such as the Finger Lakes and Lake Michigan, to produce suitable vine-growing micro-climates. Elsewhere, Texas and New Mexico are hot and fairly dry, the other states of the south-east being wetter. In Canada, near-European conditions may prevail: despite cold winters, parts of Ontario can enjoy a surprisingly temperate climate similar to that of Tuscany, with the Niagara Escarpment acting as a wind-break. Similarly, the Okanagan Valley of British Columbia has hot days and cold nights.
Cultivation In the north-east, vines are mainly grown on the flat shores of lakes or the lower slopes of mountain ranges. Soils vary considerably with limestone-based soils in Pennsylvania, Ohio and Virginia, glacial scree in Michigan and a mixture of shale, slate and limestone in New York. Silty loams and gravel are also found, mainly in Virginia. Elsewhere, vines are grown on a variety of soils. Canadian vines tend to grow on lakeside slopes, where the main soil types are sandy loams and gravel.
Grape varieties North-east, *vinifera:* Chardonnay, Cabernet Sauvignon, Gewürztraminer, Merlot, Pinot Noir, Riesling; *Labrusca:* Concord, Catawba, Delaware, Ives; *Hybrids:* Vidal Blanc, Aurore, Seyval Blanc, Baco Noir, Marechal Foch and Chelois. Elsewhere, *Red:* Cabernet Sauvignon, Carignan, Grenache, Merlot, Zinfandel; *White:* Chardonnay, Chenin Blanc, Gewürztraminer, Moscato, Riesling, Sauvignon Blanc. Canada also grows the *vinifera* Aligoté, Cabernet Franc, Chasselas, Gamay, Petite Sirah, Pinot Gris and Pinot Noir, as well as the *labrusca* Agawama, Alden, Buffalo, Catawba, Concord, Delaware, Elvira, Niagara, Patricia and President.
Production/maturation Most wineries have modern equipment with stainless steel fermentation and wood maturation in common use. In the cool, damp north-east the vines sometimes have to be buried under several feet of earth in order to survive the harsh winters.
Longevity Varied.
Vintage Guide This is a huge area and few wines are made to last long. Drink the youngest available.
Top producers *Maryland:* Catoctin, Elk Run, Boordy; *Michigan:* Lakeside Vineyard, Tabor Hill; *Hudson/New York Finger Lakes:* Rivandell, Millbrook, Gold Seal, Knapp, Treleaven, Wagner, Swedish Hill, and Hermann Wiemer; *New York Long Island:* Hargrave, Bridgehampton, Gristina, Palmer, Pindar, Lenz, Glenora, Bedell, Bidwell; *Arizona:* RW Webb; *Ohio:* Firelands, Debonné; *Pennsylvania:* Allegro, Chaddsford; *Arkansas:* Wiederkehr Wine Cellars; *Mississippi:* Almarla Vineyards, Clairbone; *Missouri:* Mt Pleasant Vineyards, Stone Hill, Hermannhof; *New Mexico:* Anderson Valley Vineyards, La Vina; *Texas:* Pheasant Ridge, Sanchez Creek, Llano Estacado, Fall Creek, Cordier Estates/Ste Genevieve.
Canada: *British Columbia:* Gray Monk, Gehringer Bros, Summerhill, Calona Wines, Mission Hill; *Ontario:* Brights Wines, Château des Charmes, Hillebrand, Inniskillin, Sumac Ridge, Cave Spring, Pillitteri, Vineland Estates, Konzelmann, Henry of Pelham, Reif Estate.

$\mathcal{S}$OUTH AND CENTRAL AMERICA

$\mathcal{O}$NE OF the things which most upsets some of the more precious wine-makers of California is to be included among the wine regions of the "New World"; they resent anything which sets them apart from their role models in Bordeaux and Burgundy. Tinkering with previously acceptable names is perhaps unsurprising at a time when short people are unsmilingly described as vertically challenged. Even so, until the Californians get round to dropping the more popular description of Dvorak's Ninth Symphony, I for one am going to continue to refer to the New World when talking about their state which is, after all, the most avowedly experimental and high-tech wine region on earth.

The wine-producing countries of South and Central America, on the other hand, have a far stronger case for inclusion in the Old World. After all, vines were being planted in Venezuela in 1523, long before most of the châteaux of Bordeaux were dreamed of.

Venezuelan wine has not, it has to be admitted, enjoyed quite as starry a reputation over the last four and a half centuries

New World wine: *Harvest at Viña Capena, Chile*

as Bordeaux or, in more recent times, California, but other countries in South and Central America are increasingly beginning to make wine that is worth taking seriously. Chile, in particular, is rapidly building a name as one of the world's most serious wine-making countries and has attracted the efforts and investment of an impressive array of big names from France and California. Argentina, historically – if surprisingly – one of the planet's five biggest wine-producers, is also, with outside help and investment, developing an internationally

competitive wine industry, while producers in both Uruguay and Brazil have now entered the international arena with wines that certainly bear comparison with some of the less lustrous efforts of supposedly "classic" regions of the Old World.

CHILE

Chile's reputation as anything more than a source of inexpensive, old-fashioned, Spanish-style reds and whites has, until recently, relied not so much on its wines as on its vineyards. A combination of mountain ranges and ocean provides a *cordon sanitaire* against the *phylloxera* beetle and other pests, making this a living horticultural museum. Visitors from France were sur-prised to see vines growing on their own roots as they were in Bordeaux a century ago, and internationally respected critics like Hugh Johnson declared Chile's vineyards to be a national treasure worthy of preser-vation. Conveniently, though, in their enthusiasm, Mr Johnson and others over-looked the fact that, *phylloxera* or no *phylloxera*, most of the wines which were being produced by the grapes grown in those vineyards were downright ordinary.

Part of the problem, ironically, lay in the fact that quite apart from the absent menace of *phylloxera* and a host of other pests, Chile is simply too easy a place to grow grapes. The clement climate of the best regions of the Central Valley might have been made to measure for the growing of Bordeaux and Burgundy-style wines. As Bruno Prats of Château Cos d'Estournel in St-Estèphe explains, the weather in an average Chilean vintage is like that of a top-class year in the Médoc. And those "average" Chilean vintages come along nine years in 10 – about thrice as often as good years in Bordeaux.

Throughout the Old World and even in New-World regions like Marlborough in New Zealand and the Hunter Valley in Australia, grape-growers are at the mercy of untimely rainstorms late in the growing season and during the harvest. In Chile there is almost no rainfall. Unlike other dry

VENEZUELA — GUYANA
— SURINAM
COLOMBIA — — FRENCH GUIANA

ECUADOR

PERU

BRAZIL

BOLIVIA

CHILE

$\mathcal{S}$OUTH
AMERICA

URUGUAY

ARGENTINA

regions, however, there is no risk of drought: as the snow melts on the Andes, it provides an unlimited source of the irrigation water which flows through the vineyards in an elaborate network of trenches.

So far, so good. Unfortunately, just as there might be a surfeit of milk and honey in Paradise, all this water has frequently proved to be too much of a good thing. Grape-growers with no interest in the quality of the wine produced from their fruit tend to pour water into the ground to increase yields.

To be fair to those grape-growers, until the outside world began to take a serious interest in buying Chilean wines in the mid-1980s, a major part of every year's harvest was sold in the same kind of cartons most of us associate with milk and orange juice. There was supposedly finer fare, but a lack of temperature control in the vats and cellars, and the European tradition of prolonged ageing in old casks made from the local raule wood, ensured that most of that more ambitious wine lost whatever fruit it may ever have had.

This Hispanic attitude – that an older wine is by definition a better wine – was coupled with another belief familiar in Spain and Portugal: that, when it came to wine-producers, big was decidedly beautiful.

BACK TO THE FUTURE

Chile's first internationally successful reds may have been made from the Cabernet Sauvignon, but my guess is that the starriest wines in future will probably be made from the Merlot – or from another Bordeaux variety unfamiliar to most Bordelais. One of the hidden treasures uncovered by producers like Alvaro Espinoza at Carmen and by Paul Pontallier and Bruno Prats are plantings of the Carmenaire, a grape which is still legally permitted in Bordeaux but which is no longer to be found almost anywhere in the region. Carmen's Grand Vidure provides a taste of the berryish, blackcurranty flavours the Carmenaire might have to offer; before long, there will be a great many more examples with which to compare it. And a wine style that will be as unique to Chile as the Zinfandel is to California.

Southern sun: Viña Undarraga, Chile

So, almost the entire industry remained in the hands of fewer than a dozen key producers who concentrated very nearly all their efforts on selling wine to their countrymen. As recently as 1982, less than 1.5 per cent of Chile's wines were drunk beyond its frontiers.

The French – and Spanish – connection

There is a dangerous – not to say condescending – tendency to attribute almost all of the credit for the modernization of the Chilean wine industry to the wealth of foreign expertise and investment the country has attracted in recent years; even so, there is little question that it was the arrival in 1978 of Miguel Torres from Spain that first helped to change local attitudes – and to stimulate a taste for exports.

Torres brought with him techniques learned in Montpellier in France, a genuinely international outlook, stainless steel tanks, cooling equipment and small oak barrels – all of which were then still novelties to the Chileans. Soon after the launch of Miguel Torres's South American winery, Agustin Huneeus, the similarly open-minded Chilean-born head of the Franciscan winery in California, became involved as a joint-venture partner with the local firm of Errazuriz in the Caliterra winery. Next, in 1988, in a highly publicized deal, Eric de Rothschild of Château Lafite bought 50 per cent, and took over the running, of Los Vascos, one of Chile's few smaller estates.

Mistakenly likened by observers to the Opus One collaboration between Eric's cousin Philippe and Robert Mondavi in California, this was in fact a very different operation from that quality-at-all-costs effort. Only a few insiders knew that the Franco-Chilean marriage was not entirely unconnected to a debt the owners of Los Vascos had to the Rothschild Bank – and to Eric de Rothschild's desire for a relatively low-price, high-volume, cash-cow wine brand he could sell internationally with a Lafite-style label.

Since Rothschild's arrival, and despite much scurrying around by wine-makers

from Bordeaux, Los Vascos has produced uninspiring reds, and whites of which even a less illustrious name ought to have been thoroughly ashamed.

While other Frenchmen and Californians began to take a serious look at Chile, a number of younger Chilean wine-makers were already showing that they

Andes view: Cousiño Macul, Chile

needed little help or instruction to make top-class wine. Most famous of these is the charismatic Ignacio Recabarren who, after a spell at Santa Rita, has gone on to make wines or advise on wine-making at a wide range of wineries, while taking full responsibility for the Casablanca operation.

It was Recabarren who first proved what Chile could achieve with its white wines. Cousiño Macul had long made fine traditional reds and Paul Draper of Ridge Vineyards in California recalls, as a young man, producing a top-class Cabernet while he was in Chile. International-quality whites, however, for a long time remained stubbornly beyond the Chileans' grasp. Part of the problem lay in the vineyard: the wrong grapes were often planted in the right places – as in the case of the Sauvignonasse, a lesser variety erroneously identified as Sauvignon Blanc – or vice versa. In the wineries, there was either a lack of cooling equipment or a tendency to over-filter and to remove flavour.

Recabarren and progressive vineyard managers, like Pablo Morande of Concha y Toro, addressed the first problem by seeking out – and planting – the right grapes in the right places (such as real Sauvignon in the cool Casablanca Valley) and, with equally progressive wine-makers like Alvaro Espinoza at Carmen, solved the second by using New Zealand and Australian techniques to preserve as much as possible of the wine's natural fruit. To understand the difference in philosophy this has required, all you have to do is taste a dull, traditional Chilean white alongside one of Recabarren's

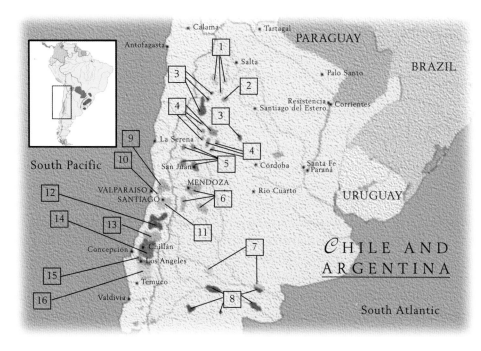

ARGENTINA

1 Salta
2 Tucumán
3 Catamarca
4 La Rioja
5 San Juan
6 Mendoza
7 La Pampa
8 Río Negro

CHILE

9 Aconcagua Valley
10 Casablanca Valley
11 Maipo Valley
12 Rapel Valley
13 Curicó Valley
14 Maule Valley
15 Itata Valley
16 Bio Bio Valley

perfumed new Casablanca Gewürztraminers.

While recognizing the skills of Chile's best wine-makers, it would be wrong to underestimate the part played by visitors like Hugh Ryman (who helped to add zing to Montes's Sauvignon); Kym Milne and Brian Bicknell who separately brought New Zealand techniques to Errazuriz; Gaetane Carron, the Frenchwoman who did much at Concha y Toro; Michel Rolland, the Bordeaux superstar consultant at Casa Lapostolle; Jacques Lurton, his neighbour, who has been sweeping a new broom through the once hide-bound San Pedro winery; and Paul Pontallier of Château Margaux and Bruno Prats of Château Cos d'Estournel whose Paul Bruno/Aquitania winery looks set to achieve everything one might have hoped for from Los Vascos.

No other wine-making country has attracted so much global expertise in such a short time – even without taking into account the investment of such high-profile Californians as Robert Mondavi, William Hill and Agustin Huneeus of Franciscan (now in his own right).

Unfortunately, so far at least, some of the efforts of these Chilean and non-Chilean wine-makers have been undermined by the demands of Chile's thirstiest customers. While Americans Paul Hobbs and Ed Flaherty were respectively helping to make and making high-quality wine at Valdivieso and Cono Sur, most of their compatriot wine-merchants were concentrating on obtaining the cheapest possible commercial reds and whites they could find. So vines which might have produced delicious, blackcurrenty wine were over-irrigated to increase production and the grapes were squeezed tightly to extract as much juice as possible. Whites sent north to the US were light, off-dry and simple.

By 1996, US critic Robert Parker was dismissing Chile almost out of hand. Revealingly, Parker's shortlist of recommended producers included the disappointing Los Vascos and excluded some of Chile's most exciting newer-wave wineries. His (mis)judgement, however, was based on what he tasted in the US. If he had travelled to Chile or sampled some of the wines on offer in London, his impressions might have been rather different.

In 1995, spurred on by the desire for international recognition and by the success enjoyed by recently created AVAs – appellations – in California, the Chilean authorities introduced a system of designated wine regions. In part, this move was a laudable step toward regularizing an industry which had historically often

The Essentials
SOUTH AND CENTRAL AMERICA

What to look for Improving reds and whites, especially from Chile and Argentina.
Official quality Only Chile has a form of quality control – and a recently launched programme of controlled appellations.
Style Chile is best known for its slightly earthy, soft, fruity reds made from Cabernet Sauvignon, Merlot and Malbec. Clean but dull Sauvignons and some Chardonnay and Gewürztraminer are also made. Argentina produces a large amount of inexpensive and generally well-made wine. The whites are soft and rounded and may lack acidity: the reds are better, medium-weight with good fruit. Mexico has a long history of wine-production but much of it is distilled into brandy or Tequila. Recent investment by European companies has produced red and white wines of decent quality. Brazil and Uruguay produce large amounts of wine; the whites tend to be rather dull but the reds show more promise.
Climate Widely varying in most countries with extreme fluctuations of temperature and either too much or too little rain causing great problems. Chile is particularly variable. The north is hot and arid while the south receives a great deal of rain. Around Santiago it is dry, frost-free and sunny. Argentina's Mendoza district has a semi-desert climate, with lower rain levels than Chile, although it is spread over the growing season.
Cultivation Vines are generally cultivated on flatter lands, notably coastal and valley plains, but some hillside sites are used in Chile. Soils vary considerably, although sand, clay and alluvial soils are common. Chile has good limestone-based soils.
Grape varieties *Red*: Barbera, Bonarda, Cabernet Franc, Cabernet Sauvignon, Carignan, Grenache, Malbec, Merlot, Nebbiolo, Pais, Petite Sirah, Pinot Gris, Pinot Noir, Syrah, Tempranillo, Zinfandel; *White*: Chardonnay, Chenin Blanc, Riesling, Lambrusco, Sauvignon Blanc, Pinot Blanc, Sémillon, Ugni Blanc, Palomino.
Production/maturation Recent interest in wine-production in these regions means that modern equipment and methods are fairly widespread, but Chile and Argentina still use traditional methods as well. Irrigation is widely used, as is cold fermentation, resulting in fresher, fruitier wines.
Longevity *Whites* are best drunk within 2 to 3 years and *reds* within 4 to 5 years, though some can develop for 10 years or more.
Top producers *Chile*: Casablanca, Caliterra, Cono Sur, Valdivieso, Concha y Toro, Cousiño Macul, Paul Bruno, Santa Rita, Miguel Torres, San Pedro, Errazuriz, Nogales/Montes, Santa Carolina, La Fortuna, Canepa, Carmen, Viña Porta; *Argentina*: Esmeralda/Catena, Navarro Correas, Finca Flichman, San Telmo, Norton, Chandon, Weinert, Etchart (Torrontes), Goyenechea (Aberdeen Angus Cabernet), Luigi Bosca, Trapiche/Peñaflor, Leoncio Arizu, San Telmo; *Uruguay*: Santa Rosa; *Mexico*: L.A. Cetto; *Brazil*: Forestier.

blended wines from different grapes, regions and vintages with impunity. However, for some observers, the legislation may have been as premature here as it has been elsewhere in the New World.

Aconcagua

One hundred miles north of Santiago, this is great Cabernet country, with old vines that can produce blackcurrant flavours unrivalled elsewhere.

Casablanca

Chile's answer to Carneros in California: a cool, foggy, frost-prone region whose climate is heavily influenced by the ocean. Sauvignon and Chardonnay work brilliantly here, as will Riesling and Gewürztraminer. Merlot and Cabernet have yet to prove themselves here, though those who favour cross-regional blends may use Casablanca reds as components with grapes grown in warmer areas.

New wood: Cellars at Santa Carolina near Santiago, Chile's capital

Maipo

Macul, the region on the edge of Santiago, just above the smog-line, has long proved its worth with the Cousiño Macul reds made here. Now the Paul Bruno estate and a new enterprise launched by Ignacio Recabarren are set to establish definitively that this is still one of Chile's prime sites for red wine. But will that be enough to keep the house-builders at bay? Elsewhere in Maipo, wineries like Santa Rita and Carmen make some of the country's best reds.

Rapel

Rapel is the place to find some of Chile's most intense, slightly cooler-climate reds: crunchy Burgundian Pinot Noirs, black-currant Cabernets and plummy Merlots.

Curico

Curico's cool nights make for tangy whites – from companies like Caliterra – but reds can be made too.

Maule

Even more firmly established as good white-wine territory, thanks to cool breezes at the end of the day which slow the ripening process, this can be the source of impressive – if potentially slightly herbaceous – Cabernet.

Mulchen

The new kid on the block, way down south, beyond the basic region of Bio Bio, this cool region may well prove to be the natural counterpart to Casablanca up north.

ARGENTINA

The fact that this is the fifth largest wine-producing country in the world comes as a surprise to most people. And you can't blame them for their ignorance – after all, until very recently, little Argentinian wine ever left the country. Or not as wine anyway; plenty was shipped in the form of grape concentrate to be diluted, fermented and sold as Japanese or Canadian or even, illegally, European wine.

Conditions are similar to those in Chile, though Argentina lacks the natural protection against the *phylloxera* which is slowly making its way through the vineyards. Most of the vineyards are planted around the small and surprisingly racy city of Mendoza where conditions are as warm as in some of the hottest parts of the Central Valley on the other side of the Andes. The best wines produced here and in the similarly warm region of San Rafael a little further south are red, but increasingly decent whites are now being made nearby in the neighbouring, but higher-altitude, towns of Maipú, Tupungato and Luján.

The technology employed by Argentina's thousand or so producers is often decidedly old-fashioned; most have had little commercial need to modernize their operations, especially since much of the vineyard land is still planted in the basic Criolla grape.

But, thanks to the thirst of North America for inexpensive varietal wines, and an economy that has been restored to good health, Argentina's wine industry is evolving very quickly. At the Catena/Esmeralda *bodega* close to Mendoza, for example, the combined efforts of Paul Hobbs, one of California's best wine-makers, and Pedro Luis Marchevsky, the vineyard manager,

Wired back: Catena's vineyards, Argentina (top)
Wired up: Bodegas Esmeralda, Mendoza

have led to good Chardonnay and some impressive Cabernet, Merlot and Syrah being made.

Peñaflor, the other biggest wine-producer – it boasts the world's largest storage vat – has done similarly well in commercial terms, with its Trapiche wines which are probably Argentina's best-known vinous exports to the US. The Trapiche Chardonnays were among the first to benefit from the careful use of new oak in the late 1980s, and today the company boasts some appealingly woody reds to match.

New plantings are in full swing, though the grape that may be among the most interesting in Argentina could be Bordeaux's reject, the Malbec. Not ideally suited to being used by itself, it can when blended with a dash of Cabernet or Merlot produce some wonderfully spicy flavours. Another Argentinian speciality is the Torrontes, a Muscat-like grape grown in the high-altitude, northern region of Salta. Its wines smell as though they are going to taste as sweet as Asti but are, in fact, drier than many a Californian Chardonnay.

MEXICO

Despite the efforts begun in the sixteenth century by the conquistadors and sustained ever since, this, the country from which the

first vines to be planted in California were imported, is not an ideal place to make wine. Half of Mexico is within the tropics and wholly unsuitable for grape-growing; the rest is divided between areas that are too hot or too dry. To compound the problem, wine-making skills traditionally imported from Spain have also been less than impressive. Until 1982, these handicaps were less onerous than they might have been because wine-lovers had little alternative to the local product whatever its quality; the importation of non-Mexican wine was effectively forbidden. Perhaps unsurprisingly, most Mexicans turned their back on fermented grape juice and took their alcohol in the form of Tequila or beer. In the late 1980s, they drank little more than a tenth as much as their neighbours in the US.

Today, apart from the improving Los Reyes and Château Domecq wines of Casa Pedro Domecq, a subsidiary of the Spanish sherry and brandy producer, made from vines grown on some 600,000 hectares (150,000 acres) of semi-desert area in the Guadaloupe Valley, the best Mexican wines come from the north of Baja California, just south of the US border. Of the producers here, the best is undoubtedly L.A. Cetto, whose Petite Sirah was named Wine of the Year in the International Wine Challenge.

Brazil

The notion of Brazilian wine ought to be familiar to cheapskate US consumers who drink some 12 million bottles of wine bearing the Marcus James label; unfortunately, most of the people who enjoy that undistinguished sweet stuff probably assume that it comes from California. Most of the rest of Brazil's annual production is consumed by Brazilians in the warm conditions of their own country where it is most appreciated in the form of a long, cool, refreshing drink.

Most of the wine-producers are based close to Porto Alegre around the towns of Bento Goncalves and Garibaldi, the latter of which is entered through an arch in the form of a giant concrete barrel. Despite the fact that the climate is far too wet to be ideal for vine-growing, this is where you'll find the Aurora co-operative, Brazil's biggest producer, and the maker of all that Marcus James wine. For quality wine, though, the names to look for are Forestier, de Lantier (a subsidiary of Bacardi-Martini) and Chandon, all of which are making surprisingly good wine. Only the most wickedly mischievous would ask why the latter

company and its fellow Champagne house subsidiaries have continued to sell their Brazilian fizz as "Champanha", while their parent companies in France were so resolute in their efforts to protect the name of their region that even the tiniest European or American soap- or chocolate-maker was threatened with legal action if they made even a passing mention of Champagne when referring to their products.

A far more sensible place to grow grapes is at Palomas on the southern border with Uruguay. Here, in a California-style, high-tech winery, grapes grown in immaculately laid-out, California-style vineyards are regularly and efficiently turned into unmemorable, light, fruity stuff to be drunk in Rio night clubs.

OTHER COUNTRIES OF SOUTH AND CENTRAL AMERICA

Over the years, a number of distinguished visitors, including Professor Denis Boubals, France's leading vineyard expert, have recognized the potential of Uruguay's wine industry and its 20,000 hectares of vines. Until recently, however, that potential remained entirely unrealized; this tiny country's wine equipment was as outdated as the 1940s and 1950s cars which are commonplace on Uruguay's often half-surfaced roads. In the mid-1990s, the industry was taken sufficiently seriously for the OIV – the foremost international organization of wine-producers – to hold its annual assembly here. The Santa Rosa winery is the first to produce international-quality wines, but Calvinor, Juan Carrau/Castel Pujol (who also make wine in Brazil) and Los Cerros San Juan are worth looking out for in Uruguay. Try particularly to get hold of examples of the Tannat that is widely grown here – and compare them with the wines it is used to make in south-west France.

Peru's Tacama winery makes much of the encouragement it claims to have received from visiting French experts – Professor Emile Peynaud apparently described its "Gran Tinto" Cabernet-Malbec as "civilized and full of tenderness" – but the only examples I have tasted seemed "dull and full of oxidation". The days here are warm and dry and the nights are cool; with a little care, decent wine ought to be achievable, especially given the range of French varietals subsequently planted on

Pollo Borracho

Chicken braised with ham, white wine and herbs

*A*lthough the chicken was only introduced into South America by the Spanish conquistadors, it quickly became popular, as is this dish throughout the continent.

SERVES 4

1 onion, minced
3 garlic cloves, peeled and minced
2 tbsp olive or vegetable oil
3 oz/85 g ham, diced
4 chicken breast fillets, skinned
½ tsp cumin
½ tsp dried sage, crumbled
15 fl oz/450 ml dry white wine
10 fl oz/300 ml chicken stock

In a large flameproof casserole, sauté the onion and garlic in the oil until the onion is soft. Add half the ham in a layer, followed by the chicken in one layer, topped by the rest of the ham. Sprinkle with cumin and sage. Add the wine and enough stock to cover the chicken and simmer for 30 minutes or until the chicken is cooked. Remove the chicken and ham to a warm serving dish. Heat the remaining sauce over a moderately high heat, stirring, until it thickens. Pour the sauce over the chicken and serve with rice or warmed pitta bread.

the advice of some of those Gallic visitors.

Venezuela, like India, can make two vintages per year, using a range of French and Italian varieties. The company that performs this feat most successfully is Bodegas Pomar whose French-born wine-maker learned his craft in the somewhat less tropical conditions of Bordeaux. Despite those tropical conditions, Bodegas Verecianas in Colombia makes all sorts of wines, including the hybrid Isabella, the Pinot Noir and Riesling, while Paraguay, Bolivia and Ecuador all try to make wine from *labrusca*. True wine-lovers in all these countries rapidly develop a taste for beer or *pisco*.

AUSTRALIA

OF ALL THE WORLD'S vinous ugly ducklings, few can have achieved a more dramatic metamorphosis than Australia. Back in the 1970s, which of us shouted "Unfair!" when the Monty Python team described Australia's wines as stuff "to lay down … and avoid"? I didn't and I'll bet you didn't either; we were far too busy laughing along with everyone else. A decade later, the laughter had died in a few countries – principally Canada, Scandinavia and the UK – where millions of wine-drinkers had been won over by Australian Chardonnays, Sémillons, Cabernets and, especially, Shirazes, the Aussies' version of the great Syrahs of the Rhône.

Elsewhere, people have been slower to notice the transformation. Robert Parker, the US wine guru, dismisses most of Australia's wines almost out of hand, as does his French counterpart, Michel Bettane. Despite the regular successes of Australian wines in international competitions and the

Green vines, sunburnt grass: Australia has learnt to produce good table wines in hot climates

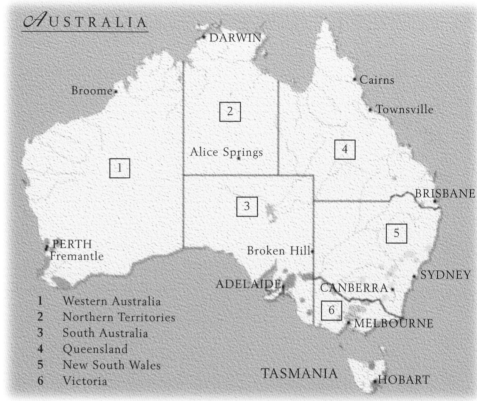

AUSTRALIA

1 Western Australia
2 Northern Territories
3 South Australia
4 Queensland
5 New South Wales
6 Victoria

efforts of the 100 or so Aussie "Flying Wine-makers" who annually show producers throughout Europe, South Africa and South America how to do their jobs, it is a rare French or Californian wine-maker who would acknowledge them to represent any kind of serious challenge. In some ways, it's quite an understandable point of view. For starters, by comparison with those wine industries, Australia produces a laughably small amount of wine. And then there's the fact that the Aussies have been relatively slow to promote their wines. While the world was growing familiar with names such as Mondavi, Stag's Leap and Heitz, few people outside of Australia had so much as even heard of Penfolds, Lindemans or Henschke.

To most outsiders, the Australians were far busier extolling the qualities of their beers. One of the most surprising things about the ever-surprising continent of Australia is the way in which a nation of beer-drinkers has fallen in love with wine. Today the Australians are some of the keenest wine-drinkers in the world, with an annual *per capita* intake of over 20 litres per person – around twice the figure for Britain or the USA. And they don't just drink a lot of the stuff – they take an enormous interest in what it tastes like, how it is made and where it comes from. Books on what most non-Antipodeans would consider to be such obscure Aussie wine regions as the Clare Valley can sell as many copies to a market of 16 million Australians as one on Chablis might to 270 million Americans.

So what was it that turned the Australians on to wine? Travel must have played a part; this is a remarkably well-travelled nation. Europe is liberally scattered with Volkswagen-loads of young Antipodeans eagerly working, eating and drinking their way from one part of the continent to the other, before heading back home with a taste for the good life. Then, of course, there have been the immigrants who have brought with them all kinds of "foreign" flavours that would have been quite unfamiliar to the Anglo-Saxon colonists.

A more mischievous explanation was provided by a cynical journalist who gave the credit to the sexual revolution, which led to young Australian males growing bored with the men-only, beer-swilling ethos of the bars and "hotels" in which they used to do their drinking. Wine was a social drink that you could enjoy with the "barbie" or take down to the beach (in a special, custom-designed cooler pack), or, in the case of two out of every three glasses drunk,

pour at home from a four-litre box with a tap on the side.

None of this would have been possible, however, without the fundamental change that took place in the way wine was made. Even as recently as the early 1980s, Jack Mann, one of the veterans of the Western Australian wine industry, unblushingly told wine writer James Halliday that "unless a wine can be diluted with an equal volume of water, it wasn't worth making in the first place..." Mann's ideal of big, thickly alcoholic red and white wine was shared by most of his contemporaries, and by a great many wine-drinkers overseas. In the days when doctors took a rather different attitude to alcohol, they used to prescribe Guinness to pregnant women and Australian "Burgundy" to anyone who was suffering from anaemia.

As Adam Wynn, one of the modern wine-makers, says: "Thirty years ago, 80 per cent of consumption and production in Australia was of fortified wine. With the exception of Coonawarra, every wine region now existing was then geared to fortified wine. This meant they were in warmer areas, with rich soil, and produced from very, very ripe grapes." In real terms this made for wines that often tasted as though they were fortified even when they weren't. Today, production of those "ports" and "sherries" has dropped to around 10 per cent of the annual production as wine-growers have switched to making lighter wines in the existing regions and steadily gone looking for new, cooler ones.

This is another factor that sets Australia apart. Where the Californians have placed the Napa and Sonoma Valleys on a pretty unassailable pedestal, the Australians are continually discovering wholly new regions in which they hope to produce some of their finest wines. Today's top areas such as Coonawarra, the Piccadilly Hills and Margaret River could, for example, soon face tough competition from recently developed locations with unfamiliar names like Robe, Orange and Tumbarumba.

That word "competition" is crucial to the way the industry has evolved; this is one of the most innately competitive nations in the world, and nowhere is this more true than in wine-making. Every region has an annual show at which hundreds of wines slug it out against each other for medals and trophies. Tastings such as these are held in every wine-making country, but it is the Australians who have elevated wine competitions to a level unknown elsewhere. Interestingly, France, which makes much more wine, has far fewer such events than Australia and none with the national

Stainless steel and temperature control: Large-scale production at Brown Bros

recognition of, say, the Canberra Show. Trophies are worth real money to their winners; a winery whose young red has been awarded the Jimmy Watson Trophy can expect to sell at least a million dollars' worth more wine than it might have done otherwise.

Unlike their counterparts elsewhere, Australia's producers enter almost every wine they make into these competitions, including their most basic bag-in-box reds and whites. And then they allow their top wine-makers to devote as much as six or more weeks per year to vinous jury service. Being asked to judge, though, is an honour. Almost any French producer can be invited to taste at the major competitions in Paris and Mâcon; in Australia, wine "judges" have to undergo a testing apprenticeship that can last several years. I know – I still have the bruises earned from judging in both countries.

Lastly, there has been a welcome Aussie resistance, so far at least, to hype. Of course, there is a growing number of superstar wineries and one or two "gurus" whose advice on what to buy is taken seriously. But, by and large, Australians are as unimpressed by heavily promoted, highly priced "big name" wines as they are by old school ties. What they want is flavour and value for money – which is exactly what most Antipodean wine-makers have provided in increasing quantities, both at home and abroad.

NEW SOUTH WALES

"IF IT WEREN'T for the tourists, the Hunter could almost cease to exist." This bleak prognosis from one of the region's best-known producers was admittedly uttered during a harvest in which the rain almost never stopped. Unfortunately, as he knew all too well, harvests like that are common in both the Lower and Upper Hunter Valleys – as is drought. But if the climate is less than ideal, it's a lot better than the humid weather the first settlers encountered when they planted their vines at Farm Cove soon after dropping anchor in Sydney harbour in 1788.

Almost from the beginning, Australian wine was seen by the authorities as a preferable alternative to rum. Unfortunately, the humidity caused the Sydney vines to succumb to pests and disease, so the shipment to Britain in 1823 was Sydney's vinous swansong. The following year, a 2,000-acre (800-hectare) plot of land in the Hunter Valley was granted to an immigrant engineer called John Busby whose 23-year-old son James had briefly studied vine-growing and wine-making in France. It was James Busby who would not only found the wine industry of Australia, but also, a few years later, that of New Zealand.

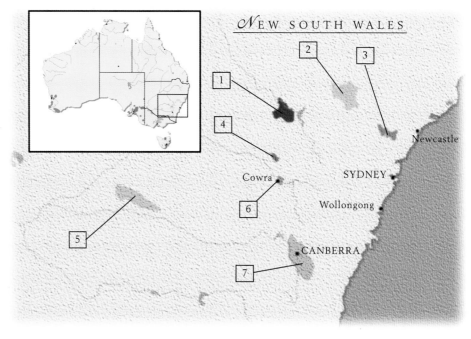

NEW SOUTH WALES

1 Mudgee

2 Upper Hunter Valley

3 Lower Hunter Valley

4 Orange

5 Murrumbidgee Irrigation Area

6 Cowra

7 Canberra

The Lower Hunter

Visitors who today drive along smart tarmac roads, sleep in international-style motels and pay megabucks to go ballooning over the vineyards can hardly imagine the Hunter Valley of as recently as the 1950s and 1960s. It was farming country in which a few big companies made similarly big wines. Much of what they produced was pretty basic fare, but some of the whites made from the Sémillon (described as Hunter Valley Riesling or Chablis) and the Shiraz (usually sold as "Burgundy") by firms like Tyrrells, Lindemans and McWilliams were very impressive in their unashamedly old-fashioned way. They were rarely wines with which a frail man would wish to argue. But, as anyone who has had the chance to taste wines produced in the 1950s by Maurice O'Shea at McWilliams will confirm, they were made to last.

The switch to more "modern" wine-making began with the introduction of Chardonnay and Pinot Noir by the iconoclastic John Wayne-like Murray Tyrrell, and was accelerated by the arrival in the 1960s of young "weekend wine-makers" from Sydney who had discovered wine in Europe and saw no reason why they shouldn't produce some for themselves.

Despite the success of Murray Tyrrell's Pinot Noir in a blind tasting against a set of Burgundies, this is not really Pinot country – unless you like Burgundies made the way they were when Algeria was still a French colony. Similarly, although Lake's Folly and Brokenwood have both produced good Cabernet Sauvignons, these are the idiosyncratic exceptions to an uninspiring regional rule.

No, the three grapes to look for are the classic Sémillon and Shiraz, and Chardonnay, the comfortably installed newcomer. There is a big difference in the way the varieties behave here, though. The Chardonnay is rich and tastily enjoyable, especially with a bit of toasty oak. It rarely improves beyond its third or fourth year. The Sémillon and Shiraz need time to shake off the hard edgy character of their youth. Give them a decade or so, however, and they develop all sorts of complex flavours – and, particularly in the case of the Sémillon, do so best without the benefit of new oak, as the glorious, honeyed, peachy-yet-dry, 1970, unoaked Lindemans Show Sémillon demonstrated when it was uncorked a quarter of a century after the harvest.

The Upper Hunter

In wine terms, the Upper Hunter Valley is a comeback-kid. Wine was made successfully in this hotter, drier region in the late nineteenth century, but there was a dry spell until Penfold's opened a winery in 1960, moving north from the Lower Hunter, made wine for 17 years and gave up. The problem was that they assumed, not unreasonably, that the Shiraz would fare as well here as further south.

The man who proved that assumption wrong was a wealthy businessman called Bob Oatley who bought the Penfold's winery, renamed it Rosemount and, with the help of his wine-maker John Ellis, introduced the world to the unashamedly easy-to-drink white wines that were to make Rosemount's, and ultimately the entire Hunter Valley's, name famous internationally.

Those first 1975 whites were made from the Traminer grape; Rosemount's real crowd-pleasers, the heavily oaked "Show Reserve" and less wooded basic (now Diamond Label) Chardonnays, did not come along until five years later, followed by the more ambitious Roxburgh Vineyard Chardonnay in 1983. Today, the Rosemount engine is driven by two men: Philip Shaw, one of the greatest wine-makers in Australia, even if we have yet to see him make a truly great wine, and Chris Hancock, an unusual blend of wine-maker and brilliant marketer who revels in declaring the Rosemount philosophy: "We want people to *enjoy* our wines. If they don't take them seriously, so be it… ".

Unsurprisingly, this success has led other producers including Len Evans to revise their sceptical views of the Upper Hunter. Among Rosemount's more recent neighbours are Rothbury's Denman Estate and Tyrrells. Even so, the Rosemount crew has no illusions about the potential problems of making wine in the Hunter Valley; a large proportion of its portfolio now consists of inter-regional blends and wines produced in other parts of Australia.

Mudgee

Up in the hills, to the north-west of Sydney, Mudgee takes itself seriously enough to have created its own appellation – Australia's first. There are some good producers here, and some rich reds including the organic Botobolar, but quality and distinctive character both need to improve before most non-Australian wine-drinkers are going to go out of their way to buy a bottle.

Cowra and Corowa

Corowa is fortified wine country where Lindemans once made traditional "port" and "sherry" just across the river and the state boundary from Rutherglen in Victoria. Cowra, by contrast, is a "new" region that is fast gaining a reputation for its cool-climate Chardonnay, thanks in no small measure to the lead taken by Len Evans of Rothbury Winery.

Hats on: Pickers at Rosemount. In the Hunter Valley it's always either hot or raining.

Orange, Hilltops, Barwang, Hastings Valley, Tumbarumba

As the focus shifts away from the Hunter Valley, new regions are being developed in several parts of the state. Cassegrain is the sole supporter of the hot, wet region of the Hastings Valley – where it makes impressive reds and whites. Greater attention though is being devoted to Orange, a source of grapes that traditionally ended up in bottles with Hunter Valley labels. More recently, Reynolds and Rosemount have shown that, despite spring frosts, this is a great place to grow Chardonnay and Cabernet at an altitude of some 900 metres. Hilltops is another cool region to watch (some producers call it Young after the nearest town), and McWilliams' Barwang with deep-red soils and an altitude of 600 metres is yielding top-class Cabernet. For real cool-climate wine-making, though, the name to remember is Tumbarumba. Ian Mackenzie, chief wine-maker of Seppelts, enthuses about the potential of these vineyards for fizz – and then quietly pulls the cork on a stunning experimental non-sparkling Pinot Noir he's made there.

Riverina/Murrumbidgee Irrigation Area (MIA)/ Griffith

Hot and isolated, this is great raisin country and, thanks to excellent irrigation from the Murrumbidgee River, a very easy place to produce huge quantities of wine. In the past, producers here remained true to their Italian roots by making Asti-style wines and vermouths. Recently, Cranswick Smith has done well with inexpensive varietal table wines, while De Bortoli has helped to create a new Australian style with its prizewinning botrytis-affected "Noble One" Sémillon.

The Essentials
NEW SOUTH WALES

Official quality A Geographical Indications system is being worked out; the Mudgee region established its own appellation in 1979, and the Hunter Valley is creating an appellation system of its own. Other notable production areas are Upper Hunter Valley, Lower Hunter Valley, Griffith, Canberra, Cowra, Orange, Tumbarumba, Corowa and the Murrumbidgee Irrigation Area (MIA).
Style Generally warm, soft, ripe wines in all styles, with plenty of richness. The classic Hunter Valley Sémillon is rich and honeyed and frequently tastes oak-aged even when it has had no contact with wood at all. Rieslings and Gewürztraminers are aromatic and show good varietal flavour. Chardonnays are packed full of ripe tropical fruit, often with a good dose of sweet vanilla from ageing in new oak. The famous Hunter Valley Shiraz has a distinctive earthy, peppery character. Cabernet Sauvignon is frequently blended with the Shiraz to produce soft, jammy reds, but on its own the Shiraz produces some of Australia's best wines, all showing vibrant varietal character. Some interesting Verdelhos are made.
Climate The climate is sub-tropical, becoming progressively drier as one heads inland.
Cultivation Sand and clay loams of varying fertility are widespread, with alluvial soils on the valley floors. Vines are grown on low-lying or flat valley sites; the slopes of the Brokenback range and the Great Dividing Range in Mudgee (both up to 500 m) are used.
Grape varieties *Red*: Cabernet Sauvignon, Grenache, Pinot Noir, Shiraz, Pedro Ximénez; *White*: Chardonnay, Chasselas, Colombard, Marsanne, Muscat, Palomino, Riesling, Sauvignon Blanc, Sémillon, Muscadelle, Gewürztraminer, Verdelho.
Production/maturation Modern methods are employed with machine-harvesting, temperature-controlled fermentation in stainless steel and judicious use of new oak for finishing. A number of Chardonnays are barrel-fermented.
Longevity *White*: most are at their best between 2 and 4 years, but top examples will develop for up to 15 years; *Red*: most are best drunk when 3 to 5 years old, but top examples will quite possibly improve over 8 to 12 years.
Vintage guide *Red*: 79, 80, 83, 85, 86, 87, 91, 92, 93, 94, 95; *White*: 86, 87, 91, 92, 93, 94, 95.
My Top 16 *Hunter*: Brokenwood, Simon Whitlam, Lake's Folly, Lindemans, Rosemount, Rothbury, Tyrrells, McWilliams, Mount Arrow, Reynolds, Evans Family, Petersons; *Orange*: Rosemount, Reynolds; *Barwang*: McWilliams; *MIA* de Bortoli, Kingston Estate, Lindemans; *Mudgee*: Huntington Estate, Botobolar.

VICTORIA

*I*N MELBOURNE they say, with some pride, that you can live through four seasons' weather in a day. I did better than that: in the space of an hour in the city's best wine bar, I drank locally produced wines that I'd have sworn had been made in the cool climate of Champagne, moderate Bordeaux and the baking heat of North Africa. Victoria is like a vinous exhibition park, with examples of familiar but unexpected wine styles such as Italy's Barbera and the Rhône's Marsanne, and of frankly eccentric fare such as the sparkling Shirazes of Great Western and the fortified "Tokay" Muscadelles of Rutherglen. South Australia is Big Company country; Victoria's raggle-taggle army of small wineries makes far less wine, but sets off far more fireworks.

THE NORTH-EAST

Rutherglen, Glenrowan and Milawa

If the Australian film industry ever makes a Western, this is the part of the country to which they should bring their cameras. Rutherglen has a main street made for a high-noon shoot-out – and a range of extraordinary "sticky" Liqueur Muscats and Tokays (made from Bordeaux's Muscadelle). Both are – or should be – brilliant, long-aged wines, full of Christmas pudding intensity. The best are made by Mick Morris, but Campbell's and Stanton and Killeen's are good too. Non-fortified wines, apart from some hefty reds, are less exciting, though Chris Pfeiffer and All Saints are both making progress.

Glenrowan is still a one-winery town, but what a winery! Baileys is, like Morris's, a living museum of Australian vinous tradition. Try the Liqueur Muscats; then move on to the Shiraz. It's less beefy than it was, but it would still support a teaspoon. Good Cabernet Sauvignon grapes are also grown in the Koombalah vineyard here. Follow them to the winery and you'll arrive at the Brown Brothers' winery in Milawa. John Brown Sr (a doyen of the industry whose experience rivals that of Robert Mondavi) and his wife head a team of Browns who between them divide the responsibilities of growing, making,

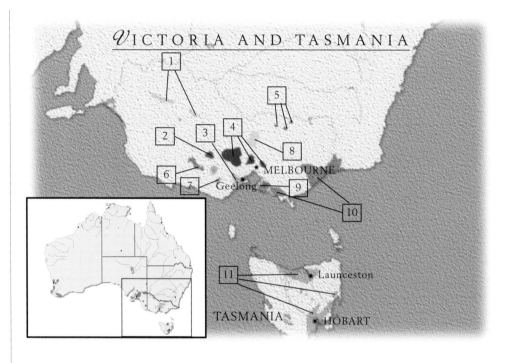

1	Murray Valley	5	North-East	9	Mornington Peninsula
2	Pyrenees	6	Great Western	10	Gippsland
3	Geelong	7	Ballarat	11	Tasmania
4	Yarra Valley	8	Goulburn Valley		

and selling. Brown Brothers produce a wide range of wines, from Liqueur Muscat to lean, dry whites from new, cooler-climate vineyards in the King River Valley and new experimental wines from the frankly chilly Whitlands high in the hills. They have yet to make a really stunning dry red or white, but they produce nothing that is less than good, and wines like the unusual marmaladey Late-Harvest Orange Muscat and Flora have developed a cult following worldwide.

CENTRAL VICTORIA

Great Western, Pyrenees, the Goulburn Valley, Bendigo ... and Giaconda and Delatite

Say "Great Western" to any Australian and he'll think bubbles. Seppelt created an

enviable reputation for their commercial sparkling wines here, including the somewhat variable Salinger. The star of Seppelt's Great Western show, though, is a style made nowhere else in the world: fizzy, slightly off-dry Shiraz that goes by the name of Sparkling Red Burgundy. If the idea appalls you, seek out a 20-year-old bottle and taste it.

The reds here are good too – especially the Shirazes from Mount Langhi-Giran and Best's – while up in the cool foothills of the Pyrenees, Dominique Portet, the son of the former cellarmaster at Château Lafite, makes impressive European-style, long-lived Shiraz, Cabernet Sauvignon and lean fizz from grapes picked over a two-month period in one of the most beautiful vineyards on the planet.

In the warm region of the Goulbourn Valley, Château Tahbilk, the oldest in the state (it was founded in 1860), uses traditional methods to make big, old-fashioned reds which, like the lemony Tahbilk Marsannes, demand patient cellaring.

Bendigo, to the west of Goulburn, is, like Rutherglen, good old gold-rush territory, but today the nuggets to look for are concentrated, often minty, long-lived reds from wineries like Jasper Hill, Passing Clouds and Balgownie.

Finally, there are two more individualists who fit into no specific region. Rick Kinzbrunner's tiny Giaconda winery stands alone, high in the hills near Beechworth. The key wines here are stunning Burgundy-style Chardonnay and Pinot and a Bordeaux-style red. At Delatite, close to Mount Buller, on the other hand, the focus is on concentrated, long-lived wines including a Gewürztraminer with no competitor in Australia or anywhere else.

Murray River/Sunraysia/Mildura

The river water here permits growers to harvest copious amounts of grapes. The Mildura winery never produces table wines that are remotely as good as the ones from its Coonawarra vineyards, or as impressive as the "sherry" and "port" made from ripe Mildura fruit, but they can be undemandingly appealing.

THE SOUTH

The Yarra Valley and Mornington Peninsula

If the traditional Victorian rivalry is between the fortified wines of Rutherglen and Glenrowan, modern Pinot Noir-lovers have the choice of supporting the cool-climate regions of the Yarra Valley or the Mornington Peninsula. The Yarra Valley was first settled by the Swiss who felt at home among its green hills, but vine-growing more or less stopped until the 1960s. The renaissance was led by Dr Bailey Carrodus whose Yarra Yering Dry Red No. 1 is a great Bordeaux-style blend, beaten only by the Shiraz Dry Red No. 2. A growing plethora of star wineries here includes St Hubert's, Yarra Burn Mount Mary (famous for its Pinot Noir), Domaine Chandon (who make some of Australia's best fizz), Tarrawarra (producers of some very complex Char-donnays) and Seville Estate (source of glorious late-harvest sweeties). If the Pinot Noir and Chardonnay (especially Coldstream Hills) have proved themselves here, don't underestimate the Merlots and Cabernets (especially from Yeringberg).

The Yarra Valley has tripled its pro-

duction in recent years and looks set to go on growing, despite the high cost of land. The Mornington Peninsula stands no chance of that kind of expansion – the area is far too close to the city of Melbourne. Indeed it is only just growing out of being a region of part-time wine-makers who play with their

Victorian splendour: Château Tahbilk, a top producer in the Goulbourn Valley

vineyards at the weekends. Among the professionals, Stoniers, Dromana (in a very commercial way) and Hickinbotham have proved that this, too, is great Pinot and Chardonnay country, while T'Gallant has shown what Pinot Gris can do here.

Geelong, Macedon and Gippsland

Stay on the Pinot trail and head west from Melbourne to Geelong where Prince Albert, Bannockburn and Scotchman's Hill make some of Australia's best. Idyll's reds can be good, too. Then head along the coast to the new region of Gippsland to taste Bass Philip's stunning, plummy Pinot and Nicholson River's rich, biscuity Chardonnay. Finally, end your tour in the little-known region of Macedon where the Pinot is used for sparkling wines by producers like Hanging Rock and Cope-Williams.

The Essentials
VICTORIA

What to look for Variety, variety, variety.
Official quality Important Victorian areas of production are: Rutherglen; Glenrowan; Milawa; Goulbourn Valley; Central Victoria; Pyrenees; Yarra Valley; Geelong and Mornington Peninsula; Great Western; Murray River; Macedon, Gippsland.
Style Good-quality whites and reds, some sparkling wines and stunning dessert and fortified wines. Chardonnays are creamy with rich depth of flavour yet also have good acidity and balance. Rieslings show fine varietal character, and there are good examples of Sauvignon Blanc, Sémillon, Gewürztraminer, Chenin Blanc and Marsanne. Cabernet Sauvignons from the more temperate southerly regions exhibit classic blackcurrant and cedar flavours and have great balance. Elsewhere the style is slightly richer. Fine, spicy Shiraz, which generally requires some ageing, is produced, together with small quantities of improving Pinot Noir and Merlot. Glenrowan and Rutherglen produce some luscious and rich fortified Liqueur Muscat and Tokay. These traditional "stickies" are of outstanding quality.
Climate Inland, conditions are hot and continental, but toward the coast the climate is tempered by the maritime influence.
Cultivation The better-quality wines are produced at the cooler, high-altitude sites around 500 m – 1,600 feet – above sea level. Wines of lesser quality are made from vines grown on all types of land. Soils vary widely, from the rich alluvial soils of the Murray Basin to the gravelly soils of the Pyrenees. North-east

Victoria has red loams.
Grape varieties *Red:* Cabernet Franc, Cabernet Sauvignon, Cinsault, Dolcetto, Malbec, Merlot, Pinot Meunier, Pinot Noir, Shiraz; *White:* Chardonnay, Chasselas, Chenin Blanc, Gewürztraminer, Marsanne, Müller-Thurgau, Muscat, Pinot Gris, Riesling, Sauvignon Blanc, Sémillon, Tokay, Viognier.
Production/maturation Modern, high-quality production methods are used, with mechanical harvesting, temperature-controlled fermentation in stainless steel and early bottling common in most districts. The top wines, particularly the reds, are oak-aged. The fortified wines of the North-East are produced using a *solera*-type system.
Longevity *Reds:* The best can age for some 10 to 15 years; *Whites:* Most are excellent upon release but can develop in bottle for up to 8 years.
Vintage guide *Reds:* 85, 86, 88, 90, 91, 92, 96; *Whites:* 90, 91, 92, 93, 94, 96.
Top producers *The North-East:* Bailey's, Brown Brothers, Morris, Chambers, Campbell's, Stanton and Killeen, Pfeiffer, All Saints; *Central and Southern:* Delatite, Giaconda; *Goulburn:* Château Tahbilk, Mitchelton; *Pyrenees:* Taltarni, Dalwhinnie; *Yarra:* Coldstream Hills, Yarra Yering, Tarrawarra, Mount Mary, St Hubert's, Domaine Chandon, Yeringberg, de Bortoli; *Mornington:* Stoniers, T'Gallant, Merrick's; *Bendigo:* Jasper Hill, Passing Clouds, Heathcote, Balgownie; *Great Western:* Best's, Seppelt, Mount Langi Ghiran; *Geelong:* Idyll, Scotchman's Hill, Prince Albert; *Gippsland:* Nicholson River; *Macedon:* Cope-Williams, Hanging Rock, Craiglee.

$\mathcal{S}$OUTH AUSTRALIA

$\mathcal{I}$F AUSTRALIA had to choose just one wine-making state, this would have to be it, for both quality and quantity. That is not to say that the other parts of the country don't make great wines too (the competitive spirit between states is so fierce that my dentist wouldn't allow me to suggest any such thing even if it were true), but nowhere else can combine the capacity to produce around two-thirds of Australia's annual harvest with the ability to make huge quantities of good basic wine, as well as the Antipodes' greatest reds and some of their most impressive whites.

The potential of this state was appreciated as early as 1849, the year in which a horticulturist called George McEwin predicted that "Wine rivalling the most famous growths of the old world will be produced in South Australia as soon as we gain the requisite knowledge and the practical experience necessary to success..." It took just over a century for the wine-makers of South Australia to justify what must have appeared to be an absurdly high-flown prediction.

No one knows who began it all. Walter Duffield, Richard Hamilton and John Reynell are all said to have planted vines near Adelaide in the 1830s, using, in Reynell's case, cuttings from Tasmania, but it was a doctor from Sussex, Christopher Rawson Penfold, who was to found the company which would grow to become the largest in Australia and gain the reputation for consistently making the finest red wines in the continent.

Ironically, given the current medical touchiness about alcohol, Penfold's initial reason for making wine was as a tonic for his patients. South Australia's early success owes much to the efforts of men like Penfold, but it has also to thank the *phylloxera vastatrix* which, though devastating most of the rest of Australia's vines, left this state alone. Which also explains why visitors today have to pass through an anti-*phylloxera* Checkpoint-Charlie when crossing its borders.

THE REGIONS

The Barossa Valley

Although the first vineyards were planted around Adelaide by (non-convict) Britons, the region that would become the most important in the state was more or less founded by 28 families of – to judge by contemporary photographs – spectacularly miserable-looking Lutherans from Silesia in Germany. Today, the Barossa Valley, in which they settled in the 1840s, is still a curious mixture of Australian, British and Germanic, where coachloads of wine-thirsty tourists pour out of the Kaiser Stuhl winery and into the "Olde Englishe Tea Shoppe".

Initially, as elsewhere, the first wines to be made were "sherries" and "ports"; it did not take long, however, for the Germans to use the Riesling to make classy, dry unfortified wine. Despite a few good examples of unfortified reds, the man who taught the region and the rest of Australia a lesson in how to make and, more importantly, blend, red wine was another German, a pint-sized, bow-tied showman known as Wolf Blass. Before Blass, Australia's reds, though often big and tasty, needed to be left to soften before drinking. He it was who, after a spell in Champagne, developed a skill at blending wines from different regions which enabled him to make well-balanced (not too big, not too light) wine that was ready to drink the day it was sold.

Wolf Blass's unashamed preparedness to mix wines from several regions was – and is – completely at odds with the European tradition of making wines in individual vineyards and villages. But he was far from alone. Grange, Australia's most famous – and priciest – red, like most of the other wines made by Penfold's, is also the result of careful blending (see box on page 244).

Another man with German roots whose name will long be remembered in the Barossa is Peter Lehmann, a keen gambler

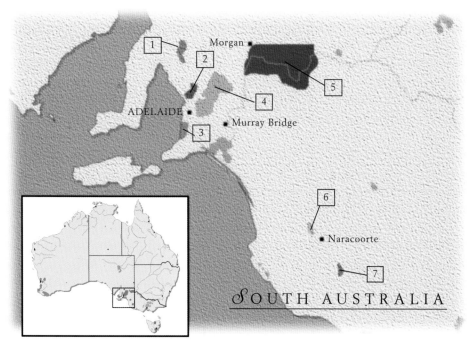

SOUTH AUSTRALIA

1 Clare/Watervale
2 Adelaide Plains
3 Southern Vales-Longhorne Creek
4 Barossa-Eden and Adelaide Hills

5 Riverland
6 Keppoch/Padthaway
7 Coonawarra

Settler country: The Old House at Coriole Winery, McLaren Vale

elsewhere in South Australia. In the plains, heading up the highway north, the fields are full of fruit of almost every kind. Joe Grilli, however, concentrates on grapes, sometimes partially drying them to make wines in the style of traditional Italian *amarones*. His sparkling red is good, too, and his Colombard probably the world's best example of a generally abused variety.

HEADING FOR THE HILLS

Eden Valley, Pewsey Vale, Lenswood

A number of producers have done the same as their counterparts in that other warm wine valley, the Napa in California: they have headed for the hills. In the Eden Valley, Henschke makes what I reckon to be Australia's finest red, the Hill of Grace Shiraz, which owes its depth and complexity of flavour to vines that are 130 years old, and a climate that is not quite so warm as that of the Barossa floor. Climb up to the High Eden Ridge, though, at over 500 metres above sea level, and you'll move right out of Shiraz territory. It was up here that the late David Wynn, the man who planted South Australia's first Chardonnay at Wynns winery in Coonawarra, founded the Mountadam winery with his son, Adam. The wines – especially the Chardonnay – are among the most stylish whites in Australia. Up in Pewsey Vale, Hill Smith and its Yalumba sister company, which make some of Australia's most reliable fizz, are producing similarly stylish Rhine Riesling, particularly from the grapes grown in its Heggies Vineyard, high up in the hills.

At an even higher altitude, however, in one of the buzziest of Australia's "buzz" regions, the Adelaide Hills is the source of a growing range of cool-climate wines. The leader of the pack is Brian Croser, whose Piccadilly Chardonnays have, with those of Leeuwin Estate in Western Australia, become known as the most consistently classy in the continent.

Another name to watch is Lenswood, where Henschke, Geoff Weaver and Tim Knappstein have all planted vines. At first, this seemed set to be great Sauvignon and Riesling territory, but Knappstein's Lenswood Pinot Noir and Henschke's Abbott's Prayer Merlot show that what can be good for the white goose can be just as good for the red gander.

who staked everything to save the Shiraz from being uprooted at a time when no one seemed to want it. Lehmann's guarantee to the growers helped to keep the vines in the ground until the world began to appreciate the special spicy, berryish flavours of Barossa Shiraz. Today, a Shiraz vineyard is in as much danger of being pulled out as the Eiffel Tower has of being demolished. Indeed, the trend today, led by men like Rocky O'Callaghan of Rockford and Bob McLean of St Hallett, is to seek out and buy the fruit from 100-year-old vineyards. As

McLean says, the wines these make are rarely subtle, but they are among the most seductively generous in the world.

Adelaide/Adelaide Plains

Penfold's original Magill vineyard is now surrounded by metropolitan Adelaide, but the winery still makes wine from the fruit grown here as well as from vineyards

Schubert's Masterpiece

OF ALL Australia's very different vinous heroes – men such as Maurice O'Shea in the Hunter Valley; David Wynn, saviour of Coonawarra from sheep farming; Brian Croser, leader of the new wave of wine-making; and, of course, Len Evans in New South Wales – one stands firmly apart. Max Schubert was nothing less than the father of modern red wine-making and sole progenitor of Australia's greatest – and one of the world's very finest – wines.

The Schubert story began in 1931 when, as a 16-year-old blacksmith's son, he joined Penfold's as a messenger boy. After studying chemistry at night school, he caught the attention of members of the Penfold family who encouraged his promotion to assistant wine-maker and, in 1949, sent him to Europe to visit Jerez and the Douro to study the way the fortified wines of those regions were made. His brief stay in Bordeaux on the way home was, ironically, not in the original plan; at the time table wines were of as little interest to Penfold's as they would have been to its competitors. The Bordelais – especially

Christian Cruse – were hospitable and, despite the language barrier, informative. Schubert was fascinated by what he saw, and determined to try his hand at following their example. As a pragmatist, though, he sensibly adapted the recipe to accommodate the ingredients he had to hand. So, instead of Cabernet Sauvignon and Merlot, of which there was little, he used Shiraz, of which there was plenty. Instead of French oak barrels, he bought casks made from American wood.

When it came to wine-making, though, Schubert firmly believed that he was following the French method quite precisely: partially fermenting the red wine on its skins and then drawing the juice off to complete the process in the barrel. The only mystery is why he thought he was emulating the wine-makers of Bordeaux when they invariably finish the fermentation *in the vat*, leaving the wine to draw colour out of the skins.

Given the unambiguous nature of the extensive notes he took on his trip – "Once again

I was surprised to find that the finished wines are placed in new hogsheads at completion or near completion of fermentation" – the only explanation I have come up with is that Schubert just happened to be present in a poor vintage – 1950 – when a Bordeaux château ran out of vat space for grapes which were being picked in haste because of the fear of rain. The cellarmaster may well have ordered the unfinished wine to be transferred directly into the barrels to make way for the next delivery of fruit. All I know is that, while no one has followed this procedure in Bordeaux since 1950, nor is ever likely to do so because it would not suit the grapes picked there even in the ripest years, partially fermenting red wine in new barrels certainly does suit the ripe fruit with which Schubert and all of his successors have had to work. In other words, one of the principal and most attractive characteristics of Grange and a large number of other Australian reds may well have been the result of a misunderstanding…

Coonawarra

There is not a lot to Coonawarra: a couple of "hotels", as pubs are known here, a few shops and a strip of very special, terra rossa soil that runs like a one-mile-wide red carpet for about 10 miles. Australian wine-buffs wax as lyrical about the qualities of this soil as Bordeaux fans do when talking about gravel, and there certainly is something magical about the richness of the blackcurranty-minty fruit that is packed into the Coonawarra Cabernet Sauvignons and Shirazes. But the climate plays a role too; judged by the Californian Winkler system of Heat Units, it is actually comparable to Champagne and Burgundy. Arguments rage over where the boundaries of Coonawarra should be drawn – there are numerous outcrops of Coonawarra-style red soil between here and Padthaway which rightly or wrongly escape the appellation.

Apart from the soil and the climate, Coonawarra benefits from top-quality wine-making, both from local wineries such as Rouge Homme and Wynn's (both of which belong to Penfold's) and by "outsiders" such as BRL Hardy, Mildura and Lindemans (another Penfold's subsidiary).

Padthaway

So far, although some good Coonawarra whites have been made, like the Médoc,

The road from Silesia: The Barossa Valley

with which it likes to be compared, Coonawarra does best with its reds. For classy Chardonnay and Sauvignon Blanc, it is worth heading 40 miles north to Padthaway. Dubbed "poor man's Coonawarra" because it was partly developed in reaction to the rising cost of land and grapes in that area, this region has a small patch of red soil of its own, on which have been grown some very tasty red wine grapes.

Clare/Watervale

If the name puts you in mind of lush, green Irish meadows, think again. The country here is warm, dry and very woody – and about as far removed from the Emerald Isle as it could be. Reds are making a comeback – especially Shiraz – but the famous wines here are Rieslings which seem to thrive as readily on the slatey subsoil here as they do in the rather cooler climate of Germany.

Southern Vales

McLaren Vale, the most famous regional name here, has no shortage of supporters for what is said to be the "European" character of its wines. There is no question that the reds from producers like Château Reynella and Geoff Merrill are leaner than those from, say, the Barossa, but conditions vary enormously from one part of the region to the next. Despite the success of these wines and plentiful local pride, Southern Vales' greatest contribution may be as a top-quality blending component in wines labelled "South Australian".

Riverland

Around a third of Australia's grapes are harvested in this irrigated region. Much of the juice is distilled, but big companies such as Berri-Renmano – now part of BRL Hardy – use high-tech methods to make good, easy-drinking wines.

The Essentials
SOUTH AUSTRALIA

What to look for *Australia's biggest, richest reds – and a growing range of impressive, high-altitude, cool-climate whites.*

Official quality Significant areas: Clare/Watervale; Southern Vales; Riverland; Adelaide Hills; Barossa Valley; Eden Valley; Langhorne Creek; Keppoch/Padthaway; Coonawarra; McLaren Vale; Adelaide; Lenswood.

Style Sauvignons and Sémillons are richly flavoured and Muscats are packed full of grapey fruit. Chardonnays have tended to be rich and buttery but are increasingly being made in a more elegant, balanced style combining rich fruit and good acidity. Of the reds, the best-known are the intensely flavoured, plummy Shirazes and the herbaceous Cabernet Sauvignons which have soft, juicy blackcurrant and stewed-plum fruit flavours. Some top-quality dessert, fortified and sparkling wines are also made, including honeyed – and occasionally botrytized – Rhine Rieslings, together with "ports" and "sherries".

Climate Temperatures range from the very hot continental conditions of the Riverland to the cooler areas of Coonawarra and the Adelaide plains.

Cultivation Soils are varied, but tend to be sand, loam or limestone topsoils over red earth and limestone subsoils.

Grape varieties *Red:* Cabernet Sauvignon, Grenache, Malbec, Merlot, Pinot Noir, Shiraz, Pedro Ximénez; *White:* Chardonnay, Muscat, Rhine Riesling, Sémillon, Sauvignon Blanc, Gewürztraminer, Ugni Blanc.

Production/maturation Mass-production methods are used to produce cheap and well-made basic wines. The producers of premium wines use traditional vinification methods. Oak-ageing is common for these wines.

Longevity Most quality *whites* will develop for 2 to 5 years, and selected examples for up to 20 years; *Reds* improve for 5 to 15 years.

Vintage guide *Reds:* 82, 84, 85, 86, 87, 88, 89, 90, 91, 93, 94, 96; *Whites:* 86, 87, 88, 90, 91, 93, 94, 96.

Top producers *Barossa:* Wolf Blass, Penfold's, Peter Lehmann, Basedows, St Hallett, Rockford, Charles Melton, Krondorf; *Coonawarra:* Katnook, Petaluma, Hill Smith/Yalumba, Wynn's, Rouge Homme, Ravenswood, Hollick, Penley Estate, BRL Hardy; *Adelaide Hills:* Mountadam, Orlando, Shaw and Smith, Henschke, Heggies, Pewsey Vale, Gramps, Jim Barry (the Armagh) Clare, Tim Adams, Petaluma, Leasingham, Pikes, Tim Knappstein, Wakefield/Taylors, Penfold's, BRL Hardy; *Southern Vales:* Hardy's/Château Reynella, Geoff Merrill; *Riverland:* Berri-Renmano.

WESTERN AUSTRALIA,
TASMANIA AND OTHER REGIONS

"*I* KNOW about Australia... I was there a few years ago... The conditions are far too warm to make fine wine." The dismissive Bordeaux château-owner whose experience of Australia consisted of a single mid-summer visit to the Hunter Valley ought to ask his countryman Jean-Claude Rouzaud of Roederer to describe his experiences making Champagne-style fizz in the windy conditions of Tasmania. Or he could ask Gérard Potel of the Domaine de la Pousse d'Or in Burgundy to tell him about the Pinot Noir he has seen growing at Moss Wood, the winery with which he has been associated in the Margaret River in Western Australia. Both of these regions are, in their very different ways, arguably far closer to Europe in the conditions they offer wine-makers than most of their better-known counterparts in the rest of Australia.

WESTERN AUSTRALIA

"Don't forget to take your passport..." It didn't take long for me to understand a South Australian wine-maker's wry response to my comment that I was off to visit his colleagues in Western Australia. If the whole continent seems isolated, this state sometimes appears to have wilfully chosen to cut itself off from the rest of the nation. While Australia as a whole ponders the pros and cons of republicanism, the populace here half-seriously murmurs about secession.

Wine-making began in Western Australia in 1829 at around the same time as it did in Tasmania, a few years before the first vineyards were planted in South Australia or Victoria. For nearly 150 years, although there were vineyards in the late nineteenth century at Mount Barker and Margaret River, almost all of the attention was paid to the wineries of the Swan Valley, where huge amounts of full-bodied red and white were made by men like Jack Mann of Houghton. He firmly believed that all wine should be intense enough to stand diluting with water.

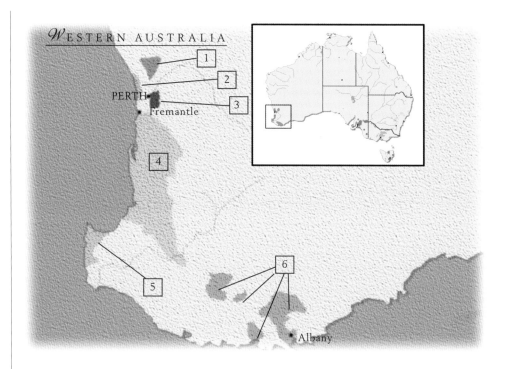

1	Gingin	4	Coastal Plains
2	Wanneroo	5	Margaret River
3	Swan Valley	6	Great Southern Area

Swan Valley

This is the kind of hot, arid country that the Frenchman imagined he'd find throughout the continent; a vast oven, ideally suited to the making of "sherry" and "port" but rather less appropriate for subtler, "modern" table wines. Companies like Evans & Tate and Houghton have managed to produce good wine here, including Australia's best-selling white, a blend known as HWB but more familiar to its fans under its old name of "Houghton's White Burgundy". Even so, most quality-conscious wineries have shifted their focus southward to the cooler areas of Margaret River and Great Southern.

There is one exception that proves the warm Swan rule: a quirky micro-climate called Moondah Brook where a spring provides almost limitless amounts of irrigation water, and a cool breeze is funnelled from the sea through a break in the hills. A range of reds and whites is made

here, but none comes close to competing with the gloriously refreshing, lime-flavoured Verdelho. Otherwise, the Swan wines to look for are Evans & Tate's Gnagara reds and old-fashioned fortifieds like Sandalford's Sandalera.

Margaret River

This cattle-and-sheep-farming, and now world-famous surfing, region saw its first vineyard planted in the late nineteenth century. For around 75 years, however, its potential went largely unexplored; in those days, its (relatively) cooler climate and its wet winters seemed less suitable for wine-making than the well-established Swan Valley. But, in the 1970s, a number of doctors independently followed the advice of an encouraging report published in 1965 and planted vines. Soon, Doctors Cullen, Cullity, Lagan, Pannel, Peterkin and

WESTERN AUSTRALIA, TASMANIA AND OTHER REGIONS

Sheridan had all established their vinous practices and were making wine to rival the best in Australia.

Even today, Margaret River is often mistakenly thought to be cool; in fact its proximity to the sea gives the region what its wine-makers like to call a "Mediterranean" climate: warm enough to ripen the Cabernet Sauvignon with no difficulty whatsoever, but gentle enough to make for some of the classiest, longest-lived Chardonnay and Sauvignon in the country.

The only problems encountered by wine-growers are occasional shortages of rain, vine disease and the unwelcome attention of parrots and kangaroos. In 1978 the region became Australia's first appellation and it still is far more deserving of official recognition than some other regions currently debating the question. Leeuwin Estate's claim to fame – apart from its Californian-style winery, the big-name orchestral concerts held on its lawns, and the fact that its vineyards were originally selected by Robert Mondavi when he was thinking of making wine in Australia – lies in the quality of its Chardonnay. Vasse Felix's success has been with its rich, blackcurrant Cabernet Sauvignon, while Moss Wood, despite its owners' links with Burgundy associates and some early successes with Pinot Noir, now seems to hit the bull's-eye most often with its whites.

Leeuwin's Chardonnay has to fight hard to beat the ones made by Pierro and by Vanya Cullen, one of Australia's most gifted wine-makers who also produces first-class, Bordeaux-blend reds and whites. Cape Mentelle shares its founder, the charismatic David Hoehnen – and now its French owners – with the Cloudy Bay winery in New Zealand. The wines here are as exemplary as they are in Marlborough and include a spice-packed Zinfandel good enough to take on all comers from California. Also worth looking out for are Château Xanadu (for its Sémillon) and, from a little further north, Capel Vale.

Lower Great Southern Area/Mount Barker/ Frankland/Pemberton

A broad and ill-defined area which is still being developed, Lower Great Southern offers a rare chance to buy good wine made in Denmark – a small town almost on the southern tip of the state. Mount Barker is also the region to look for impressive, coolish-climate Rieslings, Pinot Noirs and Chardonnays (the last styles especially from

Shelter from the sun: *Jane Brook winery in the hot Swan Valley*

The Essentials

WESTERN AUSTRALIA, TASMANIA, QUEENSLAND AND THE NORTHERN TERRITORIES

What to look for Cool(er)-climate wines from Margaret River and the southern regions of Western Australia, and decidedly cool-climate wines from Tasmania.

Official quality Margaret River of Western Australia and (heaven knows why) Queensland's Granite Belt have controlled appellations. The Swan Valley, the Southwest Coastal Plain, the Great Southern Area and Mount Barker are important areas in Western Australia. Ballandean is significant while Alice Springs is the only notable region in the Northern Territory.

Style Western Australia, particularly Margaret River, produces some of Australia's finest wines, notably some vibrantly fruity, yet extremely elegant Chardonnay, Sauvignon, Sémillon, Shiraz and Pinot Noir. Queensland produces a wide range of styles from the fruity and delicate "Ballandean Nouveau", a Beaujolais-style wine, to some rich Cabernets and Shirazes and traditional fortified wines. The Northern Territory has very few wineries but those that exist produce Shiraz-Cabernet blends of decent quality.

Climate The climate of Western Australia is very varied. Queensland is hot with moderate rainfall which can cause problems at vintage time. The Northern Territory has a very hot and dry continental climate. Tasmania, with its cooler, windier conditions, produces some rich, elegant Chardonnays and vibrantly fruity Cabernet Sauvignons.

Cultivation Most vineyards in Western Australia

are on flat, coastal plains or river valley basins, although higher-altitude sites are being used in the hotter areas. Soils are rich, free-draining alluvial and clay loams. Queensland and Northern Territory vines are grown at altitude 1600–1900 m (5,240–6,222 ft) to temper the heat. Granite is common in Queensland.

Grape varieties *Red*: Cabernet Franc, Cabernet Sauvignon, Malbec, Merlot, Pinot Noir, Shiraz, Zinfandel; *White:* Chardonnay, Chenin Blanc, Muscat, Riesling, Sémillon, Sauvignon, Verdelho, Traminer.

Production/maturation Modern viticultural and vinification techniques are necessary in most of Western Australia, and in Queensland and the Northern Territory, to combat the problems of heat.

Longevity In Queensland and the Northern Territory most wines are for immediate consumption. *Whites* of Western Australia can develop for 2 to 4 years, the best for some 6-7 years; *Reds* benefit from 3 to 6 years' bottle ageing, with selected examples requiring up to 15 years.

Vintage guide *Red*: 86, 87, 88, 89, 91, 92, 93, 95, 96; *White*: 87, 89, 90, 94, 95, 96.

Top producers *Western Australia:* Alkoomi, Capel Vale, Moss Wood (whites), Evans & Tate, Cape Clairault, Cape Mentelle, Cullens, Houghton, Leeuwin Estate (Art Series Chardonnay), Plantagenet, Goundrey, Wignalls, Pierro, Vasse Felix; *Tasmania:* Pipers Brook, Freycinet, Rochecombe; *Queensland:* Robinsons Family; *Northern Territory*: Château Hornsby.

Wignall's). Local superstar wine-maker John Wade led the way at Plantagenet with some very Rhône-like Shirazes, and is still making impressive wine at Howard Park. Goundrey is the other big-name success story.

TASMANIA

Yes, despite the occasional tendency of Australian cartographers to forget the fact, Tasmania is part of Australia, but it's a very different part. This is either Australia's Oregon, or its Siberia. According to the island's supporters, it has the cool-climate conditions that are essential for lean, long-lived, Champagne-like sparkling wine and Burgundy-style Pinot Noir; for a large number of other Australian wine-makers, it's a chilly wasteland where no one would ever voluntarily choose to grow grapes.

In fact, though, wine-making is no novelty here; vines were growing in Tasmania in the 1830s, some years before they were introduced to South Australia or Victoria. But the first flourish of Tasmanian wine-making did not last long and it was the 1950s before serious attempts were made to try again. The man credited with introducing Tasmania to the world of modern wine-making is Dr Andrew Pirie, one of the Antipodes' first academically trained wine-makers, and a man who disarmingly explains his presence in Tasmania by saying that he was looking for a cheap place to make the kind of expensive wine he had enjoyed in France. In fact, as he discovered, while land is inexpensive here, low yields make wine-making significantly costlier than it might be on the mainland. But he is not complaining – and nor are the people who have bought his wonderful, long-lived Chardonnay (including a Chablis-like unoaked version) and promising Pinot. Jantz, the sparkling wine which was originally produced by a joint venture between Louis Roederer and the Heemskirk winery, Pirie's next-door neighbour, Taltarni's Clover Hill, and the recent investment by Domaine Chandon all indicate Tasmania's potential for fizz.

Despite the success of his wines, Dr Pirie would readily admit that since he and Heemskirk set up shop at Pipers Brook, newer regions have been developed in micro-climates in the south-east and south that are already showing equal and possibly greater potential – especially for red wines. Look out for the excellent, raspberryish Pinot Noir from the tiny Freycinet whose wines sadly rarely leave Australia because of petty opposition by the huge Freixenet sparkling wine producer in Spain, who appear to believe that customers are likely to confuse still, red Pinot from Tasmania with sparkling Cava from Spain.

OTHER WINE-MAKING REGIONS OF AUSTRALIA

Canberra District

Australia's top wine writer James Halliday evocatively described the wine-making of this region as being carried out "on a doll's house scale" at weekends by off-duty civil servants. It's an appealing image; presumably every task is performed slowly and in triplicate.

However they make their wine, though, there's no shortage of customers. In Australia, the inhabitants of big towns like to drink locally produced wine and Canberra is no exception (actually, apart from visiting the excellent National Art Gallery and watching Australian politicians use unparliamentary language, there's precious little else to do).

Until quite recently, though, this area was thought to be too cool to ripen grapes. Now, it has come to be appreciated that the climate is as warm as that of Bordeaux but that there is insufficient rainfall for the needs of the vines. None of the wines is easily obtainable outside the district, nor are they of particularly high quality; the best efforts so far have been achieved by Doonkuna Estate and with red wines made from Bordeaux varieties and lateharvest whites. The vineyards themselves are usually outside the Australian Capital Territory in New South Wales – the reason being that you cannot buy freehold land within the ACT.

Queensland

The Granite Belt, as it is known because of its acidic, decomposed granite soil, is cool, high-altitude, apple-growing country. The grapes that are grown here do not readily lend themselves to the production of stunning wine, though the Robinsons Family tries its best with Shiraz and Chardonnay. Roma, the region that used to be the centre of winemaking here, has shrunk drastically. It is very, very hot.

Cool future: Tasmania's strengths are becoming clear; and they are sparkling wine and Pinot Noir

Northern Territories

The very idea of a wine being made in Alice Springs ought to be the stuff of satire. This is not the kind of country any wine-growing manual would recommend: vines don't really like being asked to perform in the equivalent of a furnace. Denis Hornsby has, however, cleverly overcome the climatic impediments by building an underground winery and a highly sophisticated system of year-round drip irrigation. The grapes – which include Cabernet Sauvignon, Shiraz, Riesling and Sémillon – ripen long before those in most other parts of the country; indeed Hornsby will be able to produce the world's first wine of the new century, from grapes picked within moments of the old one ending. None of the wines is bad, but the light, Beaujolais-style red is the best buy.

Barbeque Marinade

𝒯he "barbie" has become synonymous with Australian cooking. Because food is being cooked at such searing temperatures, it is often useful to marinate it first for an hour or two so that it remains moist and tender.

BASIC MEAT MARINADE

3 tbsp white wine
2 tbsp soy sauce
3 tbsp olive or vegetable oil
2 tbsp Worcestershire sauce
1 tbsp tomato purée
4–5 drops tabasco sauce
1 garlic clove, crushed
½ tsp salt
½ tsp sugar
Freshly ground black pepper to taste

BASIC FISH AND SHELLFISH MARINADE

3 tbsp dry white wine
3 tbsp olive or vegetable oil
2 tbsp lemon juice
1 garlic clove, crushed
1 tsp dried thyme
1 tbsp parsley, minced
½ tsp salt
½ tsp sugar
Freshly ground black pepper to taste

NEW ZEALAND

IF THERE were a prize to be won for late developer of the New World, the wine-makers of New Zealand would carry it off without losing a drop of sweat. That award would end up sharing the mantleshelf with the trophy for fastest learner, too.

A STAR IS BORN

Just look back over the last few decades. At the beginning of the 1980s, a patriotic Kiwi wine-bar owner in London frankly answered a query about the quality of his country's wines: "They're okay, I suppose – just don't get any on your hands". Needless to say, his patriotism stopped short of offering them to his customers. Within five years, however, Montana Sauvignon Blanc from Marlborough in the South Island had been named White Wine of the Year by *Wine Magazine* (of which I was publishing editor) and had developed such a cult following that warehouses were emptied throughout the world.

The commercial success of that affordably priced Montana wine was swiftly followed by the critical plaudits given to the classier, pricier Cloudy Bay Sauvignon produced in the same region. Reckoned by many to be among the finest Sauvignons in the world, this elegantly and evocatively labelled wine soon shared the distinction, along with such illustrious wines as Burgundy's Romanée-Conti, of having to be rationed on its release.

Today, New Zealand – and especially Marlborough – Sauvignon is so well known that it is worth pausing to reflect that the first commercial example of the grape was put on the market as recently as 1981, and that when I visited Cloudy Bay for the first time in 1985, the wine-maker Kevin Judd was still impatiently waiting for the builders to finish constructing his winery.

The influence of what the fans describe as the tangily fresh flavour of these Sauvignons has been felt in countries as diverse as France, Spain, Hungary, and Chile. Even so, some wine-drinkers remain largely immune to their appeal. In North America, for example, where the innately "herbaceous", "leafy" flavours of the variety are unpopular and thus commonly masked in Californian examples by sweetness and/or new oak, New Zealand's wines have been slow to win respect. Robert Parker, a critic who has yet to visit the Antipodes and is similarly dismissive of most Australian wines, attributed New Zealand's reputation almost exclusively to the free trips he believed to have been offered to British critics. Conveniently forgetting the similar number of visits offered by such regions as California, Champagne and Bordeaux, Parker grudgingly conceded that "this country does produce some very fine Sauvignons", but described all except six wineries' efforts to be "often ferociously vegetal and dried out".

French tasters, whose palates are formed by often flavourless, "green" Bordeaux, are not bothered by the "vegetal" character that troubles Parker and his compatriots. What they dislike is the intensity of fruit flavour to be found in these wines. It is true that, compared to a really fine, subtle Sancerre or Pouilly-Fumé, most fruit-salady New Zealand Sauvignons do come across like less than intellectual beach-blondes; on the other hand, really fine, subtle examples of these Loire wines are rare. Far too many are aggressive, over-cropped, over-sulphured – so it is hardly surprising that Sauvignon lovers outside France and the US have taken to the newcomers.

The significant point raised by these differences of tasting opinion is that, in a world that is increasingly full of lookalike wines, New Zealand makes some of the most immediately identifiable reds and whites of all. Some of the character comes from the climate which is generally – but not exclusively – cooler than that of, say, the

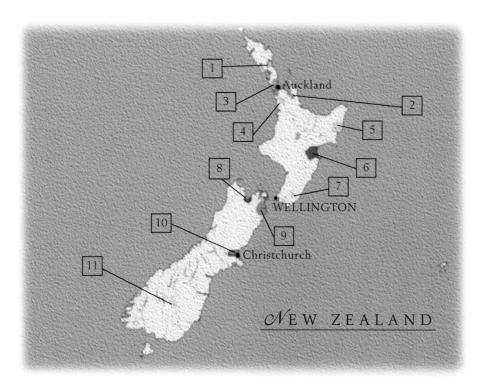

1	Northland	5	Poverty Bay	9	Marlborough
2	Bay of Plenty	6	Hawkes Bay	10	Canterbury
3	Auckland	7	Wellington	11	Otago
4	Waikato	8	Nelson		

Napa or Barossa Valleys. Some comes from fertile soils, and some comes from a young generation of wine-makers who, though often trained in Australia, have increasingly learned that the techniques they use successfully in the warmer regions of that continent often have no place here.

Despite Robert Parker's scepticism, New Zealand has already proved what it can achieve with all sorts of dry and late-harvest white wine. Reds are taking longer to master, but give them a few years and I for one am ready to bet that we'll be including a raft of them in the line-up of the best in the world.

THE BACKGROUND

Even 25 years ago, though, I doubt if anyone in or outside New Zealand could have imagined that its wine-making would attract the international spotlight. In 1946 a Royal Commission on Licensing stated that: "More than 60% of the wine made by the smaller wine-makers is infected with bacterial disorders... A considerable quantity of the wine made in New Zealand would be classified as unfit for human consumption in other wine-producing countries."

Wine-making had begun in New

Zealand 150 years earlier when the "Father of Australian viticulture", James Busby, was made the "British Resident" in New Zealand, planted vines "between the house and the flagstaff" and made a white wine that in 1840 impressed the visiting French explorer Eumont d'Urville as "light ... very sparkling, and delicious to taste".

Busby's career as a wine-maker was, however, curtailed by the ravaging of his vineyards by horses, sheep, cattle and pigs, and by soldiers during local clashes. Although settlers followed his example, it was not long before they realized that they would need to import wine-making expertise. While small groups of French and German wine-growers were persuaded to stay for a while, two shiploads of German vintners who had, as New Zealand author Michael Cooper narrates, "been promised perfect conditions for viticulture by the New Zealand Company, arrived on our shores, contemplated the steep bush-clad hills surrounding Nelson and left for South Australia".

Over the following years several New Zealanders attempted to make a living from wine-making, but only a handful succeeded. Furthermore, in the late nineteenth century, any who might have been tempted to take up vine-growing were deterred by the arrival of powdery mildew in the vineyards, which prevented wine from being made – and a virulent set of temperance societies,

Mountain and plain: Vines growing at Blenheim, in New Zealand's South Island

which sought to prevent it being drunk.

The man who saved New Zealand from full-scale prohibition went by the wonderful name of Romeo Bragato, an Italian-trained wine-maker born in Dalmatian Yugoslavia. Thanks to Bragato, New Zealand's wine industry survived. Thanks to his countrymen, it began to flourish. Because, despite their efforts, it wasn't the early British settlers who really set New Zealand wine-making on its feet, but a group of Dalmatians who had come to tap gum from trees in the far north of the North Island. These men, isolated by racial prejudice, settled, planted vines and opened wine shops for their countrymen.

The peevish Anglo-Saxons, galled by this modest success, opened up yet another avenue of prejudice. As the 1916 Aliens Commission complained, "A great deal of feeling against these men ... is due to many of them being wine-growers, and the belief that Maori women are able to get, through them, intoxicating liquors... Where young and vigorous men, attractive young women free from conventional social restraints, and abundance of intoxicating liquors are found together, debauchery will very certainly result ...."

The Dalmatians, following the exhaustion of the gum trees, began to

concentrate on wine-growing, using expertise learned in Yugoslavia and from Romeo Bragato's book *Viticulture in New Zealand*, and with the assistance of a government research station at Te Kauwhata in the North Island.

During the first two decades of this century, despite the arrival of *phylloxera* (correctly identified by Bragato, whose initial warnings and advice were, needless to say, ignored by the authorities), both the wine-makers and the prohibition lobby strengthened their position. In 1919 the temperance societies appeared to have won a conclusive victory when a national referendum voted for prohibition. Had it not been for a contingency of servicemen returning from the war just in time to swing the ballot, wine-making here might have undergone the same period of hibernation as it did in the USA.

By 1960 there were still fewer than 1,000 acres of vines planted. But, within a few years, a rapid influx of money from outside New Zealand, partly fuelled by the beginnings of the Australian wine boom, encouraged heavy plantation.

Unfortunately, at the time, there was little reason for outsiders to argue with the image of this distant ex-colony as a shared annexe to Australia and Britain with a

climate somewhere between the two.

One visitor who was evidently taken with the idea of New Zealand as a cool place with moderate potential was the German wine and vine expert, Professor Helmut Becker, who advised the New Zealanders to plant a variety he was recommending for such European countries as Germany and England. This grape – the Müller-Thurgau – had the advantage, Becker explained, of ripening early and yielding generous crops of grapes which, with a little "back-blending" (the addition of a little sweet juice), could produce an alternative to cheap German wine.

The New Zealand wine-makers of the 1960s and 1970s saw little reason to argue. After all, the world was not exactly clamouring at the door to buy bottles of New Zealand "port" or "sherry". So, within a decade, the Müller-Thurgau took over the industry.

To say that this was under-exploiting New Zealand's vinous potential is something of an understatement. The arrival of the Müller-Thurgau set New Zealand's wine-making back a decade.

Between 1965 and 1970 the acreage under vines tripled; by 1983 it had risen to 15,000 acres; two years later the country found itself awash with mock-German wine

Now look here: Llamas framed by vines at Gisborne

for which there was something less than a brisk international demand. The glut was solved by a government-funded "vine-pull" scheme which encouraged growers to uproot uneconomical vineyards. Some turned to other forms of farming; others simply replanted the land, using more classic French grape varieties. Today, as an increasing number of sophisticated wine-drinkers have discovered, New Zealand has been transformed from backwater into mainstream.

THE REGIONS

Unlike Australia, where producers routinely blend wines from different areas, New Zealand's producers generally prefer to concentrate on single regions: most notably Hawke's Bay, Marlborough, Martinborough, Kumeu and Gisborne. That is not to say, however, that the larger wineries are loyal to the part of the country in which they are based: most offer ranges of wines representing the way particular grape varieties perform in particular regions.

Given the often uncertain nature of the climate – and the tendency of the North Island and South Island to enjoy quite different conditions – there is a clear argument that a more Australian attitude might sometimes not go amiss. A skilful blend of lean Chardonnay from Marlborough in the South Island and a richer example of this grape from Gisborne in the North Island could produce a stunning wine. So far, of the bigger wineries, Villa Maria remains the only forthright supporter of this kind of wine-making, but I suspect others may follow in its wake.

THE NORTH ISLAND

Professor Becker's impression of New Zealand as a cool-climate, southern hemisphere version of Germany makes little sense to anyone who has spent even a few days on the North Island. Ireland with the volume turned up would be my description of this warm, damp, green, ultra-fertile land. This is the part of the country where the most successful reds have been made – and, until recently, some of the less successful whites. The problem lay partly in that fertile soil: it was too easy to grow large amounts of grapes which never really ripened and were often subject to rot. The answer lay either in finding regions with meaner soil, or in persuading the vines to be less fruitful by a combination of training and pruning that is now known by progressive grape-growers internationally as "canopy management". The father of this technique is Professor

Richard Smart, a visionary who developed it after studying the way vines grow in the best parts of Bordeaux, and now travels the vineyards of the world applying the lessons he learned in New Zealand.

Northland

Northland, the region where wine-making really began in New Zealand, has been largely abandoned, although for two or three years it appeared as though this region might be the source of New Zealand's top red wine. Two lawyer brothers created a California-style mini-estate, grandly called it "The Antipodean", planted Bordeaux-style grape varieties, and presented their first wine "blind" to an audience of London wine experts, who were invited to compare it to a range of Bordeaux first-growths. The experts all spotted the New Zealand wine, but generally acknowledged the potential quality of the challenger. The lawyers hyped the wine for all they were worth, sold every bottle they made for a very high price, had an argument and closed the winery. Today, the winery has been renamed Heron's Flight, but the Cabernet sold under this label is not from the vineyards originally used for The Antipodean.

Auckland

Until about 30 or so years ago the North Island had only two main wine regions: Auckland itself and Hawke's Bay. That number has now risen to five, plus the increasingly successful Waiheke Island, where the Goldwater Estate winery has produced some very impressive Cabernet-Merlot.

Barrels and beef: Ngatarawa winery at Hawke's Bay

While Auckland still boasts an impressive set of wineries such as Matua Valley, Coopers Creek, Selaks and Nobilos, all of which are variously hitting the mark with white wines produced in various parts of the country, the wine-growing region of Kumeu near the city has recently been somewhat overlooked in the rush to areas with starrier reputations. But just taste the white and red wines Michael Brajkovich is making at Kumeu River and the Chardonnay Collards are producing in their Rothesay vineyard, and you'll know that this is once again a region to watch.

At Henderson, 12 miles (20 km) to the west of Auckland, Babich and Delegats are the names to look out for while, to the south of the city, Villa Maria, the country's third-largest winery, regularly produces high-quality wines. Further south still, Te Kauwhata, site of New Zealand's wine-research station, was once thought of as good red-wine country – particularly by the giant Cooks (now Cooks-Corbans) who made Cabernet Sauvignon here. Today, as the wine-making potential of other, less rainy, parts of New Zealand has been discovered, the black grapes have mostly been replaced by white ones. Three wineries that show what can be produced are Morton Estate, de Redcliffe and Rongopai.

From barrel to bottle: Wines at Rongopai winery, in the North Island

Gisborne

Gisborne, out on the east coast, is one of those places whose name rings loud bells with any well-informed wine-drinker. Finding even a well-travelled wine expert who has actually been there, however, is another matter. For starters, while lots of big companies buy Gisborne Chardonnay, often using the name on their labels, only a handful of small estates are actually based in this region. The best-known names are Matawhero, makers of New Zealand's finest Gewürztraminer, and Millton Estate where James Millton has quietly built a reputation for some of the world's most reliable organic white wines, from both the Chardonnay and Chenin Blanc.

Gisborne's creamy Chardonnays deserve their growing reputation, but I cannot help wondering whether this region's greatest contribution to New Zealand wine might not be in blends with some of the more fruit-salady efforts produced in Marlborough.

Hawke's Bay

There are relatively few well-known thoroughfares in the wine world, but two to remember are Gimblett and Church Roads, on which are found some of the best vineyards of the sunny, holiday-resort region of Hawke's Bay. The secret of this region's long-predicted success lies beneath your feet. Look at the gravel of the old river bed, and think claret. Then taste some of the Hawke's Bay Cabernets and Merlots made by wineries like CJ Pask, Brookfields and Ngatarawa. The whites can be top-class too – Montana's Church Road Chardonnay is one of the most reliable in the country, while Te Mata's Elston has long been a benchmark for this style.

It was John Buck of Te Mata who also first demonstrated what could be done with red wine in New Zealand with his Coleraine and Awatea Bordeaux-blends. While others have produced showier wines, these remain fine models for any wine-maker seeking to compete with the best of France.

Wairarapa/Martinborough

Known until recently as Martinborough after the town here, but now more commonly referred to by the regional name of Wairarapa, this wide, flat region has earned an instant reputation for its Burgundy-style reds and whites, but that's not all it can do. The superstar is Larry McKenna of Martinborough Vineyards, whose Pinot Noir and Chardonnay are among the best in the

Antipodes. Palliser is good at these styles, too, but has also done well with Riesling, while Dry River is equally successful with Pinot Gris. Reds, apart from Pinot Noir, have been less impressive, though Ata Rangi has done the seemingly impossible, by making raspberryish Pinot Noir and richly spicy Shiraz, thus producing Burgundy and Rhône-style wine from grapes grown in almost the same vineyard. If only the Burgundians themselves had mastered this trick – just think how much effort they could have saved by not having to ship Syrah for blending up to Beaune in the good old days.

South Island colours: Neudorf winery

THE SOUTH ISLAND

Marlborough

Blenheim airport makes no bones about its isolation in the north of the South Island: a signpost reveals just how many thousands of miles new arrivals are from most of the rest of the planet. But those arrivals have included some of the most distinguished wine-makers and experts in the world, all of whom have been attracted by what seems to be the made-in-heaven marriage of Sauvignon grape, Marlborough gravel and climate.

The union between region and grape was first consummated in 1973 when the large Montana winery bought a dozen or so

farms for a ludicrously low price and bravely planted around 400 hectares (1,000 acres) of vines. At the time, the variety chosen was, almost inevitably, the Müller-Thurgau. Fortunately, though, they experimentally filled a 25-hectare corner with Sauvignon, a grape that was then almost unknown in New Zealand.

The rest, as they say, is history. The vineyard area now covers nearly 20 times Montana's original plantation and land prices are ludicrously high: everyone, from Australians like Rothbury, Hill Smith and Mildara Blass to French Champagne houses like Laurent Perrier and Moët & Chandon, wants a slice of this gooseberry pie.

The only question hanging over the region is what styles of wine it should make. The Sauvignons and fizzes are acknowledged world-class success stories. There have been good Chardonnays – especially from Cloudy Bay – but few with the class of, say, Te Mata's Elston. Marlborough Gewürztraminer and Riesling are both delicious, but generally overlooked by a Chardonnay-obsessed world. As for reds, the jury is still out. Hunters have made some impressive Pinot Noir and Corbans astonished New Zealand tasters with a Cabernet Merlot; even so, it is questionable whether Marlborough's marginal climate will allow these and other producers to hit the bull's-eye as often as they do with their whites.

Close to Marlborough, though, there is another valley where slightly different conditions seem better-suited to red wine. Awatere is the Châteauneuf-du-Pape of New Zealand – not because of the temperature, which is cooler than that of the southern Rhône, but because of the round stones on the terraces that store and reflect the heat of the day. For a taste of what South Island Cabernet can be like at its best, try the ones Vavasour is making here.

Nelson

One of the greatest country-bus rides in the world takes you from Marlborough westward through the folds of the hills to the almost unknown wine region of Nelson. There are five wineries here, but only two that are producing good wine in any quantity. Tim and Judy Finn of Neudorf Vineyards and Hermann and Agnes Seifried of Weingut Seifried and Redwood Valley used ruefully to admit to having something of an inferiority complex. Years of being told by "experts" that their region was too cool, and less ideally suited to wine-growing than

Marlborough or Hawke's Bay, for example, had their effect; wines from Nelson tended to cost less than those of other regions. But talent will out. Neudorf's Pinot Noir and Sémillon (one of the few New Zealand successes with this variety) are among the best in the Antipodes, while Seifried's late-harvest Redwood Valley Rieslings are good enough to teach many a big-name German estate a lesson.

Canterbury

Further south, Canterbury became famous as the cool, dry region in which was situated St Helena, the winery at which, in 1982, a Burgundy-mad wine-maker called Danny Schuster made New Zealand's first world-class Pinot Noir. Less successful subsequent vintages and hotter competition from wineries in other parts of the country have shifted the spotlight of attention away from this southern region, but Canterbury remains a name to watch. Its future may lie less with the Pinot Noir than with the Riesling, a variety in which the German-born Giesen family, who own the region's largest estate, fervently believe. But the Giesens are realists: some of their best wines are made from grapes grown further north in Marlborough.

Central Otago

If Canterbury is cool, Central Otago, the world's southernmost wine region, ought to be positively glacial. But geography is far more complicated than that: where other areas are cooled by sea breezes, this is an area surrounded by land. And, like other such places – Burgundy and the Northern Rhône (its latitudinal counterpart in the northern hemisphere) spring to mind – it enjoys warm summers and cool winters. Pinot Noir has been quite successful in Central Otago, but I suspect the cool nights, which temper the ripening effect of the hot days, will always make this a place to make white wine. And why not?

The Essentials
NEW ZEALAND

What to look for Fresh vibrant whites and improving reds.
Official quality Designated regions are: *North Island:* Bay of Plenty, Fast Cape, Gisborne, Esk Valley, Hawke's Bay, Henderson, Huapa Valley, Ihumatao, Kumeu, Manawatu, Marigatawhiri Valley, Poverty Bay, Riverhead, Te Kauwhata, Tolaga Bay, Tikitiki, Waiheke, Waihou, Waikanae, Waikato, Waimauku, Wairarapa, Wellington; *South Island:* Canterbury, Marlborough, Nelson, Renwick.
Style Wines have crisp, varietal character with plenty of fruit but less heaviness than their Australian counterparts. Chardonnays are rich yet have an elegant freshness too. Sémillons can be rich and tart, or crisp with piercing fruit. Gewürztraminers, when made dry, have excellent spicy character but can also be lusciously sweet when late-picked, as can Rieslings. However, the most famous New Zealand wines are world-beating Sauvignon Blancs, packed full of green flavours – gooseberries, grass, asparagus and nettles – and occasionally oak-aged. Red wines have, until recently, enjoyed less acclaim but as vines grow older the Cabernets and – particularly – Merlots are showing greater depth of clean blackcurrant and plummy fruit, while some Pinot Noirs are showing greater varietal expression. These wines have potential.
Climate In general, a relatively cool maritime climate prevails, although the North Island has more tropical conditions, with higher temperatures and higher rainfall producing greater humidity. This, together with the heavy rains, can cause problems of rot and grape damage during harvest time.
Cultivation Vineyards are planted on a variety of clay and alluvial loams over volcanic subsoils. Drainage is often a problem, so some north-facing slopes have been cultivated on the North Island, although flatter land is used elsewhere.
Grape varieties *Red:* Cabernet Sauvignon, Merlot, Pinot Noir, Pinotage, Pinot Gris; *White:* Chardonnay, Chenin Blanc, Gewürztraminer, Müller-Thurgau, Muscat, Pinot Blanc, Riesling, Sauvignon Blanc, Sylvaner, Sémillon.
Production/maturation Very modern viticultural techniques are used for premium varieties; mechanical harvesting and temperature-controlled fermentation in stainless steel are widely employed. Barrel-fermentation is used to produce top-grade Chardonnays, while new oak is frequently used for maturation.
Longevity While all wines can be drunk immediately, the better-quality *whites* can benefit from 1 to 5 years' ageing. *Reds* can benefit from 3 to 8 years' ageing, although they may last longer in future as the vines become older.
Vintage guide *Red:* 89, 91, 93, 96; *White:* 91, 93, 96 (note that vintage conditions vary widely).
My Top 37 *Auckland/Hastings/Waihiki Island:* Kumeu River, Collards, Babich, Cloudy Bay, Cooks, Corbans, Delegats, Hunters, Matua Valley, Villa Maria, Coopers Creek, de Redcliffe, Goldwater Estate; *Gisborne:* Millton; *Hawke's Bay:* Te Mata, Vidal, Montana Church Road, Mission, Cooks, Ngatarawa, CJ Pask; *Martinborough:* Martinborough, Dry River, Ata Rangi, Palliser; *Marlborough/Awatere:* Montana, Deutz Marlborough Cuvée sparkling, Daniel le Brun, Nautilus, Rothbury Estate, Hunters, Cloudy Bay, Jackson Estate, Allan Scott, Cooks Stoneleigh, Vavasour, Corbans, Merlen; *Nelson:* Weingut Seifried, Neudorf; *Canterbury:* Giesen.
(Note that most medium-to-large producers now make wine in several regions.)

Lamb and Kiwi Fruit Kebab

Lamb and Kiwi Fruit Kebab

Along with dairy produce, lamb is New Zealand's largest export, and nothing could be more appropriate than teaming it with kiwi fruit in a delicious and quick kebab.

Serves 4
3 tbsp olive or vegetable oil
1 tbsp lemon juice
1 garlic clove, peeled and crushed
1 tbsp soy sauce
Freshly ground black pepper
1 lb/500g leg of lamb, boned, trimmed of fat and cut into chunks
6 kiwi fruit, peeled and cut into wedges

In a ceramic or glass bowl, combine 1 tbsp of oil, the lemon juice, garlic, soy sauce and pepper to taste. Add the lamb and marinate for at least an hour. Skewer the lamb and kiwi fruit alternately. Brush with the remaining oil and grill, turning occasionally, for about 8 minutes or until the meat is cooked. Serve with rice and a tomato and onion salad.

SOUTH AFRICA

THE ELECTION of Nelson Mandela as head of state was almost certainly the best thing that could ever have happened to the wine-makers of the Cape – though I doubt that many of them saw it that way at the time. After all, the ruling National Party had, for decades, repaid their votes by featherbedding their industry with a system of quotas and minimum prices. It was thanks to the government that South Africa's annual surplus of grapes – around half the harvest – enjoyed a guaranteed price and found just as guaranteed a home in distilleries where it was converted into industrial alcohol or brandy for export to liqueur producers in countries like France.

Since South Africa's re-admission into world markets, the picture has changed completely. Today, the surplus has virtually disappeared as wine-drinkers in the Netherlands, Britain, Scandinavia and North America, who once fastidiously avoided Cape reds and whites, now queue to sample the efforts of one of the latest passengers on the New-World bandwagon.

Ironically, though, South Africa first climbed on to that wagon long before most of the other New-World countries. In fact, as the proud Boers readily remind outsiders, this is a place where wine has been produced for over 300 years. During the 1960s, before Robert Mondavi had opened the doors of his Napa Valley winery and in the days when most red Australian table wine was indistinguishable from port, South Africa was internationally recognized for the quality of its reds, fortified wines and late-harvest whites.

From the outset, the achingly beautiful region close to Capetown looked an ideal place to grow grapes, with a naturally warm climate tempered by the proximity of the coast, and hills whose slopes cried out to be dressed in vineyards. But, as any wine-maker will tell you, climate and site are only two of a number of essential components that go to make up a wine. Without good soil, grape-growing and wine-making, you might as well have cool, non-stop, wet weather from one end of the season to the other – and South Africa had problems on all three fronts.

The years of isolation did the Cape no good. As the rest of the world's wine industry developed new techniques, South Africa's remained stuck in a conservative groove, brushing fundamental problems under the carpet, and using ordinary grape varieties to make similarly ordinary, old-fashioned wines. Acid soils in much of the flatter land, and vine diseases, said to affect up to 90 per cent of the vineyards, prevented the grapes from ripening fully, and made for harsh, "green" flavours reminiscent of Bordeaux in a cold year. These were, supposedly, softened by ageing in big old casks, but the warmth of the cellars and the state of the wood in those barrels often gave the finished wine a smoky, stewy, cooked character that made South Africa's reds some of the easiest to spot in blind tastings.

Even when attempts were made to join the modern wine-making world, they often went sadly awry. One of the Cape's first shipments of Chardonnay vines proved, for example, to be another, lesser variety. New oak barrels, bought at great expense from cynical French coopers, turned out to have been insufficiently dried and, instead of imparting an attractive, sweet vanilla flavour, merely amplified the green nature of wines made from those unripe grapes.

White wine-making, though generally far more successful, suffered from the influence of the German wine school in Geisenheim, an establishment with which the Cape producers generally had far more contact than they did with its counterparts in California and Australia. The Germans encouraged the South Africans to follow their European quantity-at-the-expense-of-quality lead by increasing production in the vineyards and stripping flavour out of the juice and wines by heavy-handed filtration.

If South Africa's wine-makers were handicapped by their isolation, they also

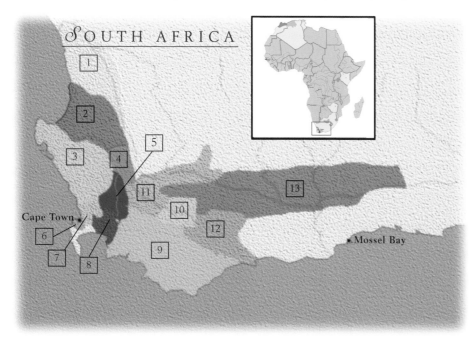

SOUTH AFRICA

1   Olifants River
2   Piquetberg
3   Swartland
4   Tulbagh
5   Paarl
6   Constantia
7   Durbanville
8   Stellenbosch
9   Overberg
10   Robertson
11   Worcester
12   Swellendam
13   Klein Karoo

hobbled themselves by setting up an extraordinary set of constraints. A monolithic organization called the KWV, originally formed for the best of reasons at a time of chronic wine surplus, was allowed to control the entire industry in a way unknown elsewhere in the capitalist world. For example, quotas were established that deterred adventurous wine-makers from exploring new regions and styles. When Tim Hamilton-Russell first began to make what was to become South Africa's first successful Pinot Noir in the now-vaunted region of Walker Bay, he had to sell it under a code name which merely hinted at the identity of the grape from which it was made.

Inevitably, there was a political angle too. The National party relied on the grape-farmers for their votes, so had every reason to allow them, and the co-operatives to which they belonged, to continue to use second-rate grape varieties like the Welsch Riesling to make second-rate wine.

Efforts to promote quality wine were generally misconceived. Large appellation districts such as Stellenbosch and Paarl were established and promoted and a system initiated vaguely mimicking that of France's *Appellation Contrôlée*. On paper, this, like the paper seals introduced to mark quality wines, seemed quite sensible. In practical terms, however, the rules were unnecessarily stricter than those operating in France. In Bordeaux, grapes may legally move around with impunity within the region and within communes; a top-flight château can buy in

Cabernet Sauvignon harvested by any of its neighbours, provided that the land on which they were grown falls within the same *appellation* as its vines. In the Cape, estates were forbidden to bring in wine or grapes from outside their own land. Compare this with the Australian model where such famous estates as Rosemount produce wine across states and Rothbury's Estate appears to extend beneath the sea to reappear in New Zealand. The South African rules – which were finally changed in 1995 – may satisfy the purists; but it is the wine-drinkers who benefit from the more relaxed Antipodean legislations.

Another Gallic tradition that was followed too slavishly in the Cape was the division of labour between wine-making, maturing and bottling. Until very recently, like British upper-class parents despatching their offspring to boarding school, most of the Cape's most prestigious wineries happily handed over responsibility for the ageing and bottling of their wines to the huge Bergkelder. In doing so, they were behaving as the châteaux of Bordeaux used to with their local merchants. Except, that, following the lead of Philippe de Rothschild who decided 50 years ago to bottle every drop of Mouton Rothschild at the château himself, even the humblest Bordeaux producer has since insisted on maturing his own wine.

This review of the background to the industry is essential if one is to appreciate just how traumatic an experience South Africa's wine-makers have undergone in

recent years – and the challenge many of them have faced in adapting to the modern world of wine-making.

Today, the spirit of peaceful revolution is becoming as apparent in the vineyards and wineries as in every other facet of South African life. An army of wine-buyers and investors from other countries has poured through the gates of Cape Town airport while Cape wine-makers have travelled the world learning how things are now being done elsewhere.

The infected vines have been largely cleared from the vineyards and replaced in what has to be the most sophisticated programme of plant husbandry in the world. Previously little-grown varieties – principally Chardonnay and Merlot – have been planted and modern European, Californian and Antipodean wine-making methods introduced.

The first evidence of change came with the improvement in the quality of the Cape's fresh, inexpensive, light, dry and off-dry white wines: Sauvignons, Chardonnays and the Cape's local success story, Chenin Blancs or Steens. Hard on their heels, and even more impressive, were sparkling wines – known here as Méthode Cap Classique – good enough to see off all but the best examples of Champagne, let alone most efforts from other parts of the New World.

The reds, however, and the more serious

whites have taken longer to get right. Too many producers – and their local customers – are so used to unripe-tasting wines that they distrust the richer, more accessible styles produced by some of their more go-ahead neighbours, even when these have been supported by such highly qualified visitors as Paul Pontallier of Château Margaux who is involved with making the wine at the impressive new Plaisir de Merle winery. How, the traditionalists want to know, will the new-wave, ripe-tasting wines age? Like a 1982 claret comes the confident reply, from foreign critics and from local producers, basking in the unfamiliar sensation of international approval. And not, they might have added, in the mean way of 1975 Bordeaux which sometimes seems to have been the Cape producers' preferred model.

The move toward more sensitive wine-making encouraged by Pontallier has brought some surprises. Until recently, foreigners tended to be polite about the wines made from the Pinotage, an odd South African grape with the characteristics of its joint Burgundian and Rhône parentage. Usually, though, they switched their attention from these often muddy-tasting wines to the more conventional appeal of the Cabernet Sauvignon. Today, however, the newer-wave wine-makers are discovering unsuspected potential in the Pinotage which reveals it to be as ideal a grape for fresh, Beaujolais-style wines as for rich, spicy reds to set against the Shirazes of Australia and the wines of the Rhône in France. New styles have been developed too, for the Merlot and Pinot Noir – grape varieties almost unknown in the Cape a decade or so ago

There is still a fair degree of confusion over the direction the wines of the Cape ought to be taking. Some producers reasonably wonder whether the overseas market is not pushing them toward making "big", Australian-style wines, but a growing number are proving that South Africa doesn't have to copy anywhere else – and that they can produce reds and whites with a unique combination of New-World fruit and Old-World subtlety.

THE REGIONS

The future of South Africa's finest wines depends – as in California – on producers shaking off the reverence they have had for over-large and actually quite disparate regions such as Stellenbosch and Paarl, and the realization of the need to promote far smaller areas, the character of which is only now becoming clear. So far, only Walker Bay has been demarcated according to the sort of wines it produced; all the others, including old warhorses like Stellenbosch, were marked out according to already existing administrative boundaries.

COASTAL REGION

Stellenbosch and Paarl

The best-known regions, the first of which owes its name to the quaint Cape Dutch university town, are quite disparate. Temperatures can vary significantly, from North African to Burgundian, depending on the effects of the sea breezes and of the

altitude of the vineyards. The soils are far from homogenous too: some are acidic, others sandy. The best wines will come from hillside vineyards, especially those around the Helderberg mountain, and from valleys like Franschoek where producers like Boschendal, Dieu Donné, l'Ormarins and Clos Cabrière are to be found. For other recommended wineries, see the Essentials box.

Constantia

Tourists to the Cape are well advised to visit the Groot Constantia winery, the oldest in the country, because it is a lovely building. The wines made in this government-owned estate are worth less of a detour; for a decent drink, you would be far better advised to head for Klein Constantia where a delicious replica of the sweet Muscat wine for which this region was once as famous as Sauternes and Tokaj, called Vin de Constance, is now being made. Today Constantia is enjoying a renaissance, thanks to its sea-cooled climate. Buitenverwachting is recommended here as is the recently opened Steenberg.

Olifants River

A hot, productive northerly region where the huge Vredendal co-operative is now proving that it can produce classily labelled, world-class, light, easy-drinking whites with the memorable, if – to non-South Africans – hard-to-pronounce name of Goiya Kgeisje.

Walker Bay/Elgin

The apple-growing region of Elgin has rapidly become one of the most exciting in South Africa – for the whites made by Neil Ellis and by Newald Marais of Nederburg for Paul Cluver, a brain surgeon. Walker Bay, the southernmost vineyard region of the Cape, was pioneered by Tim Hamilton-Russell with Pinot Noir and Chardonnay. His lead was followed by Bouchard Finlayson, a joint venture between Burgundian merchant Paul Bouchard and local wine-maker Peter Finlayson.

Robertson

This is a warm region where lime soil makes for better-balanced wines, and a dynamic co-operative makes highly successful commercial white wines. Look out, too, for Chardonnays made here at de Wetshof.

Swartland/Tulbagh

Warm temperatures and yields kept low by a lack of irrigation make this region ideal for intense, long-lived Pinotage and Shiraz. I shall never forget a tasting of old bottles of Swartland Co-operative Pinotage generously put on by Jan Boland Coetzee which first convinced me of what this grape can do. Allesverloren is also worth watching.

Zimbabwe and Kenya

The economic sanctions of the 1960s forced Zimbabwe into wine-making. The stuff they have made has been a triumph of optimism, effort and ingenuity over climatic adversity. Every year, it rains at almost precisely the time when the grapes are ready to be picked, so rot and dilution are major problems. Nor have the producers been helped by the poor quality of many of the types of grapes and of the soil in which they have been grown. More recent efforts in regions benefiting from rain shadows have been more successful; even so, for outsiders, the wines remain curiosities – as do the small quantities of wine produced by Kenya in its two annual harvests.

NORTH AFRICA

In 1995 an opinion poll was held in France which asked 1,000 consumers to name as many brands of wine as they could recall. The results were not encouraging for anyone claiming that the average Frenchman knows much more about wine than he does about nuclear physics: most were unable to name a single brand. The ones who could, came up with an interesting top four: Château Margaux, Mouton Rothschild, Kriter (an undistinguished French fizz) and ... Sidi Brahim. The familiarity of this Algerian brand is a handy reminder of the relationship which existed between France and North Africa in the 1950s and 1960s before the *pieds noirs* returned home. In fact, if the French take the credit for helping to create the (relatively) modern North African wine industries from the ones whose roots were planted by the Romans, they must also take the blame for largely doing so with such uninspiring grape varieties as the Carignan and Clairette, neither of which will ever produce anything better than pretty basic stuff.

Given the growing influence in Algeria of Islamic fundamentalists, however, and their less-than-sympathetic attitude toward wine, there is little chance of this country modernizing its vineyards. Indeed, as vines die of old age, they are not being replanted. Production will continue to dwindle from the once-huge figures of the nineteenth century, and outsiders will be denied the chance to discover what a little tender loving care might have achieved in the vineyards of the once-famous Côtes de Mascara.

Morocco's vineyards are rapidly shrinking, but wineries like the Domaine de Sahari are bucking the trend by making good Bordeaux-style reds. Elsewhere, Sincomar produces reasonable wines using Rhône varieties, including the memorably named Rabbi Jacob. The wine to drink with the greatest confidence in Tunisia is Muscat which, at its best, can be of world standard.

Still the biggest: The cellars of KWV

The Essentials
AFRICA

What to look for Evolving styles in South Africa.

Official quality South Africa has long had a Wine of Origin system. The regions and sub-regions are: Coastal region: Swartland, Tulbagh, Paarl, Stellenbosch, Constantia, Durbanville, Boberg; Breede River Valley region: Worcester, Robertson, Swellendam; Klein Karoo region; Olijantsriver Region; Overberg; Piketberg; Northern Cape: Lower Orange River, Douglas.

Style North Africa produces all styles of wine, not all attractive to European palates; best are Algerian and Moroccan reds, full-bodied and rustic with a slightly coarse flavour, and Tunisian Muscats which range from the sweet Vin de Muscat de Tunisie to the dry, fragrant Muscat de Kelibia. Grenache-based Moroccan rosé can be pleasant. South Africa's best-sited vineyards should produce great wine, but top-class examples are still rare.
Zimbabwe's attempts to produce wine are hindered by heavy rains during harvest.

Climate North Africa is, of course, hot and dry, as is most of South Africa, though the coast is cooler and wetter.

Cultivation Rich alluvial soils predominate in the flat coastal plains of North Africa, while the cooler hill sites inland have limestone, sand and volcanic soils. South Africa's often acidic soils vary from the sandy gravels of the coastal area to the lime-rich soils inland.

Grape varieties *North Africa:* Alicante Bouschet, Cabernet Franc, Cabernet Sauvignon, Carignan, Cinsault, Clairette, Grenache, Merseguera, Mourvèdre, Morastel, Syrah, Pinot Noir, Ugni Blanc; *South Africa:* Cabernet Sauvignon, Pinotage, Syrah, Sauvignon Blanc, Chenin Blanc, Chardonnay, Muscat d'Alexandre.

Production/maturation In North Africa, a strong French influence persists, notably in grape varieties and appellations. The African climate necessitates strict harvesting control and cool fermentation.

My Top 20 *Algeria:* Cuvée du Président; *South Africa:* Meerlust, Hamilton-Russell, Thelema, Fairview, Plaisir de Merle, Vergelegen, Boschendal, Kanonkop, Simonsig (sparkling), Nederburg (late-harvest), Allesverloren, Mulderbosch, Vriesenhof, Rustenberg, Klein Constantia, Buitenverwachting, Blaauwklippen, Nederburg Auction Wines, Clos Cabrière.

THE OTHER WINES OF THE WORLD

INDIA

*O*NE OF the very nastiest tastings I have ever endured was of an impromptu line-up of Indian wines bought from a busy retailer in the heart of Bombay. The contents of the screwtop bottles were so bad, and so far removed from even the feeblest efforts at wine-making elsewhere, that the best way to treat them was as a kind of satire. My companion at this tasting, however, took a small step toward redeeming India's vinous reputation with the first

Water resources: Vines in Maharashtra, India

offering from his winery, a sparkling wine produced in high-altitude vineyards a day's drive from the city with the help of expertise imported from Champagne.

That fizz, variously labelled as Omar Khayyam and Marquise de Pompadour, was initially made largely from the basic Emerald Riesling, though subsequent bottlings have included Chardonnay. It is perfectly drinkable stuff, provided you catch it young, and the same Indage winery's red and white Riviera wines offer an alternative to poorly cellared European imports. Even so, given the choice, I'd recommend a bottle of locally brewed Elephant beer.

JAPAN

The vineyards of Bordeaux and Burgundy have featured surprisingly rarely in movies – and none has provided as dramatic a setting as one of Japan's did in the final scenes of the Michael Douglas thriller *Black Rain*. Unfortunately, despite the growing Japanese enthusiasm for buying fine wine at international auctions and more basic wine from vending machines, and despite heavy investment, high-tech equipment and expertise and vineyards dotted around all but one of Japan's 47 provinces, the stuff in the bottle is rather less memorable.

Sunhats at Suntory: For grapes and pickers

Wine is no novelty for the Japanese; they have known about it since the twelfth century when the Muscat-like Koshu grape was apparently grown with some success. The problems for Japan's would-be wine-makers are a lack of space and a climate – monsoons, earthquakes, typhoons and worst of all, general humidity – that waterlogs the often over-acidic soil, encourages all kinds of bugs and diseases and dilutes the juice in the grapes.

These conditions are best suited to local grapes, few of which would pass international muster, and hybrids such as the unspectacular Delaware, grown because of their early ripening and resistance to all those diseases. All of which helps to explain why the Japanese import such huge quantities of concentrated grape juice from other countries which they blend with a little local juice, labelling the result as Japanese.

Apart from offering examples of these pseudo-Japanese wines (is there anyone in Tokyo pulling the same stunt with European hi-fi or cameras, I wonder?), whisky giant Suntory tries hard to make French-style wines using traditional French varieties grown in genuinely Japanese soil. Their best wine is probably the Yquem lookalike Château Lion Noble Sémillon, produced from grapes whose bunches are protected from the elements by little paper hats. It costs Yquem-like prices, too and would certainly be a welcome gift to Japanese hosts. Most Japanese wine-lovers would, however, prefer something from overseas – such as a bottle from the (Japanese-owned) Ridge Vineyards in California, Château Lagrange in Bordeaux or Robert Weil in Germany.

CHINA

The sleeping – or more properly waking – giant of the industrial world may well be about to rise from its vinous slumbers. As in Japan, wine once featured as strongly on the cultural agenda as it did in many parts of Europe. Wine was being imported as early as 128 BC and, in the thirteenth century, Marco Polo described the Shangsi province as growing "many excellent vines". Sadly, over the succeeding years, the lines between distilled drink (the Chinese may have invented the process), grape wine and rice wine became quite blurred. When Rémy Martin announced the launch of its Great Wall co-production of wine and rice wine in the 1980, it was the first modern effort at Chinese wine-making to reach the rest of the world.

By 1993, however, China was producing some 500 million bottles: 10 times as much wine as New Zealand and more than other high-profile countries such as Chile, Greece, Austria and Bulgaria. More dramatically, it has a larger area of vineyards than Germany, South Africa and Australia. If you haven't yet come across one of those bottles, don't worry; until now, with the exception of occasional sightings of Dynasty, Great Wall offered as curiosities by wine merchants and Chinese restaurants, most of the wine is light, white and off-dry and – like Chinese computers, cars and washing machines – intended for sale to an increasingly enthusiastic local market. And, like those

cars and washing machines, their production involves a great deal of foreign expertise – in this instance French and Australian.

But, like the Japanese, the Chinese are rapidly (re-)developing their taste for European-style wine. It is chastening to think that, when the 1995 vintage of Bordeaux came onto the market in 1996, large numbers of cases which might once have gone to London or New York were sold to keen wine-drinkers in Hong Kong. When we get to the 2005 vintage, those Hong Kong claret enthusiasts may well have to compete with buyers in Beijing. All of which should help to encourage a new breed of quality Chinese wine-makers.

The Essentials
ASIA

What to look for Memorably off-beat drinking experiences. (Keep a pot of tea or a can or two of lager in reserve, however.)
Official quality You have to be joking.
Style In the Far East plenty of thick, sweet, very unpleasant wine is still produced, but reasonable dry whites are made with French grape varieties under French or Australian supervision in China. The technically well-made Indian Omar Khayyam (*méthode champenoise*) can be a pleasant alternative to Spanish Cava.
Climate Conditions in India are, of course, extremely hot and dry. China's wine-producing areas are generally cool, tempered by the Pacific and Indian oceans. Japan's wine production is at the whim of a climate of extremes with summer typhoons, spring and autumn monsoons and freezing winters, hence the readiness to use imported concentrate.
Cultivation In both China and Japan, the best vineyard sites are on south-facing slopes. China has good alluvial soils; those of Japan are more acidic.
Grape varieties Cabernet Sauvignon, Chardonnay, Ugni Blanc, Pinot Noir, Muscat and Merlot are being introduced. Otherwise *India*: Ariab-e-Shahi, Arka Kanchan and Arka Shyam; *China*: Beichun, Dragon's Eye, Cow's Nipple and Cock's Heart; *Japan*: mostly *labrusca* vines such as Campbell's Early and Delaware and hybrids, together with the native Koshu *vinifera*. Suntory uses Bordeaux varieties.
Production/maturation Increasing use of modern techniques throughout the regions.
Longevity None, though some late-harvest Japanese efforts can last.
Vintages (see above)
My Top 5 *India*: Indage (Omar Khayyam/ Marquise de Pompadour); *China*: Great Wall, Dynasty; *Japan*: Suntory (Château Lion), Château Lumiere.

INDEX

PICTURE CREDITS

The publishers would like to thank the following sources for their kind permission to reproduce the pictures in this book:

AKG London; The Anthony Blake Photolibrary; Michael Busselle's Photolibrary; The J. Allan Cash Photolibrary; Corbis UK Ltd; Greg Evans International; Images Colour Library/Horizon; MC Picture Library/Alan Duns; Robert Joseph; Richard Mayson; Pictor International; Janet Price; Scope/Jean Luc Barde, Charles Bowman, Philip Gould, Jacques Guillard, Michel Guillard, Eugenio Hughes, Sara Matthews, Jean Luc Sayegh, Alain Vivier; Sopexa; Suntory Ltd; Wines of Austria; Wines of South Africa; Zooid Pictures/Richard Philpott.

Special thanks are due to Janet Price.

Every effort has been made to acknowledge correctly and contact the source and/or copyright holder of each picture, and Carlton Books Limited apologises for any unintentional errors or omissions which will be corrected in future editions of this book.